Art and Prudence

ART
AND PRUDENCE

A STUDY IN PRACTICAL PHILOSOPHY

by Mortimer J. Adler

ASSOCIATE PROFESSOR OF THE PHILOSOPHY OF LAW

THE UNIVERSITY OF CHICAGO

1937

LONGMANS, GREEN AND CO.

NEW YORK · TORONTO

TO

H.L.B.

The Prudent Man, on the other hand, as such, judging all things from the angle of morality and in relation to the good of man, is absolutely ignorant of everything pertaining to art. He can no doubt, as he ought, judge the work of art as it affects morality; he has no right to judge it as a work of art.

* * *

In finding fault with a work of art, the Prudent Man, firmly established upon his moral virtue, has the certitude that he is defending against the Artist a sacred good, the good of Man, and he looks upon the Artist as a child or a madman. Perched on his intellectual habit, the Artist is certain of defending a good which is no less sacred, the good of beauty, and looks as though he were crushing the Prudent Man under the weight of Aristotle's maxim: *Vita quae est secundum speculationem est melior quam quae secundum hominem.*

JACQUES MARITAIN,
Art and Scholasticism

By permission of Messrs. Sheed & Ward, Publishers

Preface

In the field of practical philosophy there is always the general problem and the special case. Action is taken in singular situations under particular circumstances. Thinking about action must, therefore, take account of many contingencies, but it must no less rely upon principles of great generality. The clear formulation of the latter is usually supposed to be the province of the philosopher. The man of action is supposed to look to the facts of the case. This separation is unfortunate. There can be no wisdom in action without principles. There can be no determination of action by philosophy without the supplementation of casuistry in the application of principles. Strictly, of course, the practical philosopher is not a casuist. But, recognizing the limitations of reason in practice, he knows that general principles must always submit to the qualifications of casuistry. There is merit, therefore, in considering the general problem and a special case at the same time. The former consists of questions about the applicable principles. The latter raises questions of fact that must be answered before the principles can be applied. On the one hand, discussion of the principles illuminates the particular case. It is understood when it is seen as an instance of a general practical problem. On the other hand, consideration of the special case tests the adequacy of theoretical formulations; more than that, in imposing the obligations of casuistry upon the philosopher it puts him, sympathetically at least, in the position of the man of action. The *rapprochement* of the philosopher and the man of action is certainly a consummation devoutly to be wished. Philosophy is not truly practical unless it can be heeded by practical men. The man of action cannot be wise if he forsake philosophy, mistrusting it as too remote from the perplexities of practice. These two must understand each other if either is to do his work well. Practical wisdom requires not only clarity and correctness in principle, but the fullest appreciation of the intricacies of the particular case.

In this book I have tried to be practically wise about a difficult practical problem. In general it is the problem of the moral and political criticism of the fine arts, occasioned by the conflict in operation of two practical virtues — prudence and art. The special case is made by the current controversy about motion pictures. In different periods different arts have been the focus of such debate. In our time — the last few decades — the primary concern is with the cinema. It is the subject of far more consideration than any of the other fine arts. It has a wider audience, both in terms of gross number and in terms of heterogeneity, than any other. The existence of a tremendous body of opinion about the effects of motion pictures on that audience and about what should be done in the light of these supposed effects, is therefore not surprising. In their substance the opinions current about the movies are not as novel as the movies. They are as old as the problem — of which the cinema merely creates a contemporary instance — and that problem is as old as society. Nor are the principles new which can be used to clarify this field of opinion. The modern mind recoils from the notion that principles which can analyze a contemporary problem may have been discovered before its circumstances arose. Yet everything that can be said clearly about motion pictures was said and well said long before motion pictures existed or were discussed. Nothing has been added in contemporary discussion — except scientific research which, of course, adds nothing in the way of ideas or principles — and much has been lost in the way of insight, clarity and order.

The history of the discussion of poetry and politics, of art and prudence, reveals that the general principles applicable to any instance of the problem of the arts in society were long ago discovered. The classics contain the tradition of European wisdom on this problem, as on every other. The classics are always contemporary because the wisdom they contain is traditional. One way of showing this is to use the classics as if they were a discussion of contemporary problems. In comparison with literature which is contemporary only in the sense of being current, the classics give those who will use them a perspective on present affairs, as well as a richness, simplicity and subtlety not found in thinking that is merely *ad hoc*. In the intellectual sphere, modernism is provincialism. The classics are the remedy for the besetting ill of our times. But, unfortunately, those who have this ill-founded pride in the sufficiency of their own times, have it precisely because they dislike the only medicine which can cure them.

In this, as in almost every other basic philosophical question, practical or speculative, Plato and Aristotle are the primary sources for its dialectical examination. With a few exceptions, the rest is commentary. The chief exceptions, in the case of art and prudence, are two. Christianity adds one dimension to the problem, and we must, therefore, consult such writers as St. Thomas Aquinas and Bishop Bossuet. Democracy adds another dimension, and we must go to two of its exponents who consider the place of the arts — Jean-Jacques Rousseau and John Dewey. At first the basic opposition between Plato and Aristotle seems to be final. As Christian theologians, Bossuet and Aquinas are opposed as Platonist and Aristotelian. As democrats, Rousseau and Dewey are similarly related. But Greek wisdom is not ultimate. It is increased in stature and in depth by Christianity. The opposition between Plato and Aristotle concerning the criticism of the arts is profoundly qualified by the practical theology of St. Thomas. The dialectic almost reaches the moment of synthesis. Because it leans heavily on the moral treatises of the *Summa Theologica* in analyzing the relation of art and prudence to each other and to the other virtues, Chapter 12 is the place in this book where the argument achieves greatest refinement. So far as any resolution is possible of the issues about criticism — whether aesthetic and political criticism are separable, whether technical and moral goodness are independent — it will be found there in principle.

The announcement of an effort to follow an abiding intellectual tradition makes any disclaimer of originality unnecessary.

I have not only used Aristotle and St. Thomas as sources of wisdom, but I have been guided throughout by the commentary of Jacques Maritain, who has employed the same tradition in *Art and Scholasticism*, a book which is for me the best analysis of all the problems of fine art. The scope of that book is much more general than this. I am concerned primarily with one problem and, moreover, with that problem as it occurs in the special case made by the cinema as fine art. The attempt to apply everything that is relevant in the intellectual tradition to this contemporary problem necessarily requires some interpretation and extension of the basic texts I have relied upon. To this extent, and only to this extent, my work has been constructive. I hope it will be understood that I have not cited or quoted these texts as authorities in the sense in which authoritarianism is disreputable in modern times. They are cited as indications of the tradition in which I am working. They are quoted as formulations so clear and precise that it would be rash to try to rephrase them. They are used because of *what* they say and not because of *who* said them. The reader will find much of this material quoted in the notes at the end of the book. These notes are referred to by numbers in brackets in the main body of the text.

The programme of this book required not only an exposition and interpretation of the relevant tradition concerning poetry and politics, but also an analysis of the contemporary discussion of motion pictures. The philosophical task here is the ancient one of clarifying popular opinion. Much of the prevailing discussion proceeds upon the provincial assumption that the problem being discussed is a new one, peculiar to the locale of Europe and America in the twentieth century. As a result it is strikingly unenlightened by reference to the moral, political and aesthetic principles, without which the problem cannot be well analyzed or understood. I have, therefore, tried to explicate the charges which have been made against the movies, as well as to discover what can be said in their defense. This will be found in Part II. Since the principles there employed are traditional, some repetition of Part I is unavoidable ; but I hope that the repetition is justified by a resulting clarification of current polemic. This part is so written, particularly Chapters 6 and 7, that it can be read carefully or hastily according as the reader is more or less interested in the intricacies of the problem.

The most important result of Part II is the separation of different sorts of questions raised by the various claims for and against the cinema. The basic questions of fact are isolated from problems of evaluation and policy. These questions indicate the sort of knowledge needed to solve the practical problem in its present incidence, knowledge not provided by a discussion of the problem in general. At this point consideration of the special case carries us beyond the traditional treatment of the general problem. It is here, also, that the problem of the motion picture is uniquely distinguished. Not only is the cinema exceptional among the arts today in receiving the attention of a papal encyclical; not only is it the one art which is so conscious of its public responsibilities that it seeks "self-discipline at the point of production"; but the cinema is unique, today or any other time, in being the only fine art ever subjected to elaborate scientific research with regard to its moral and social influences.

This scientific research was done for the most part by psychologists and sociologists. It is of the same sort that can be found in the fields of other practical problems, such as crime, urbanization, immigration, etc. Acquaintance with this type of research suggests the need for a critical examination of its methods and findings in order to ascertain the reliability and significance of the answers it gives to questions of fact. In 1932 Professor Jerome Michael and I completed a survey of criminological research. That study grew out of a report made to the Bureau of Social Hygiene, and was subsequently published under the title *Crime, Law and Social Science*. Scientific investigations of the motion picture as a factor in human behavior did not receive special treatment in our survey. Many of them had not yet been completed. As a result of their reading of *Crime, Law and Social Science*, representatives of the motion-picture producers asked me to review for them the recent empirical investigations specifically concerned with the influence of motion pictures on human behavior — to make, in short, a similar analysis of the problems, methods and results of research. Because of the vastness of the materials, the survey of criminological work could not present an examination of each of the investigations in detail. But in reporting on motion-picture research, minute examination was possible, and seemed advisable as a way of making plain some of the characteristics of current work in psychology and social science. I am grateful for permission to use much of the material of my original report in this book, — presented here in a somewhat extended form. This constitutes the substance of Chapters 10 and 11 of Part III. However laborious and distasteful it may prove, a careful reading of these two chapters, in the light of the distinction between knowledge and opinion made in Chapter 9, will enable the reader to form his own judgment on the question whether science has contributed to our understanding of the perennial problem of the arts in society, or supplied us with knowledge which can be used in its solution.

It may be objected, as it has been in certain quarters, that the movies are not an art but an industry and that, therefore, they do not deserve the same kind of consideration which is given to music and poetry. In itself this objection is not worth answering, but the situation it reflects is serious. It reveals a failure to understand the status of the cinema as fine art, particularly on the part of its moral and political critics. The moral and political criticism of an art is usually exaggerated and even distorted by a lack of sensitivity to its problems of workmanship and production, its artistic aims and its technical means. I have, therefore, tried to complete my account of the various parts of criticism by analyzing the relation of the cinema to the other fine arts, by formulating the elements of its technique, and by setting forth the principles by which the cinema can be criticized aesthetically. This will be found in Part IV. It completes the discussion of intrinsic and extrinsic criticism begun in Chapter 12. It also faces the problem of good taste and aesthetic cultivation which is intensified by the popularity of an art.

A word about terminology is necessary. As an analysis grows, verbal usages shift. I have used the word "poetry" in the earlier parts of this book as synonymous with "fiction." Thus used, it includes the motion picture as a species of poetry. Only in the last part have I more narrowly defined the scope of poetry to distinguish it from the cinema. I have used the word "art" narrowly throughout the first eleven chapters, (1) to mean only fine art, and (2) to signify the work of art rather than the technical skill possessed by its maker. It is only in

Chapter 12 that the kinds of art are systematically distinguished and that the word is used in its primary reference to a human virtue and not in its secondary reference to the products of human work. I might add that by "fine art" I mean whatever arts are distinguished from the useful and liberal arts — music, *belles lettres*, painting, sculpture, the dance — and not merely the plastic arts, the works of which reside in buildings unfortunately called museums of art. Until Chapter 9 I have used the words "science" and "philosophy," "knowledge" and "opinion," in their popular meanings. The distinctions made and the definitions given in Chapter 9 make precision of usage possible, and it prevails thereafter. I have been careful throughout to note restrictions or extensions of meaning in the use of words crucial to the analysis. Nevertheless, the reader is obliged to be attentive to the context in which these words are used. Although prudence is not defined until Chapters 8 and 12, the popular sense of the word is so close to its technical meaning that misunderstanding is not likely to ensue from its frequent use in earlier chapters.

Finally, there is the matter of my debt to those who have helped me in this work. My indebtedness to Jacques Maritain is so amply demonstrated by the book itself that I can only add here the pleasure I take in acknowledging it. More than the principles upon which this book rests, I owe to him the understanding of what it means to work in the tradition of the perennial philosophy. I am deeply grateful for the industry and insight with which William Gorman, Carolyn Lewis, and James Martin have assisted me in all stages of research and writing. Their criticisms and suggestions have been the occasion of many dialectical refinements which carry the argument forward. I wish to thank them as well for the gift of friendship without which intellectual collaboration is impossible. This is also my debt to Scott Buchanan, Jerome Michael, Herbert Wechsler, Mark Van Doren and Arthur Rubin, who have read the manuscript and discussed its problems with me. My gratitude is not for this alone but for the many hours of intellectual friendship which have been an inestimable resource. Each of them is associated in my mind with the clarification of one or more of the matters that form the substance of this book. If I make singu-

lar acknowledgment to Scott Buchanan, it is because his work
in philosophy has set for me the standard of courage in the
speculative enterprise.

MORTIMER J. ADLER

Chicago, 1936

Contents

PART I

Poetry and Politics

CHAPTER ONE

Plato

It is a mark of wisdom in Greek political thought that the form and content of education receive primary consideration from those who are concerned with the nature and the welfare of the state. Education is, of course, broadly conceived; it is not limited to the problems of a school system, to the administration of official pedagogues and the curriculum of instruction. Whatever can be taught is educational matter; anything that shapes the body, forms character or gives knowledge or discipline to the mind, is an agency of education, whether or not its human medium is a person having the social status of a teacher, whether or not the environment in which it occurs is a school. Thus Plato, early in the *Republic*, and preliminary to the discussion of how a just state is constituted, turns to the question of the education of the guardians, those to whom the administration of the state will be entrusted. The field of elementary education divides easily into gymnastic for the body and music for the soul. Music includes all the arts whose patrons are the muses, and among these, literature or poetry is distinguished because, employing words, it can express ideas. The issue, therefore, arises for the statesman or him who is planning the perfect city, whether there should be any control of the tales which the poets tell children. Plato asks: "Shall we just carelessly allow children to hear any casual tales which may be devised by casual persons, and to receive into their minds ideas for the most part the very opposite of those which we should wish them to have

3

when they are grown up ?" [1]   It should be noted that what ideas the future guardians *should* have is not here debated, as Plato answers at once that it will be necessary "to establish a censorship of the writers of fiction, and let the censors receive any tale of fiction which is good, and reject the bad." [2]   Mothers and nurses are to tell their children the authorized ones only.

The trouble with the poets who have ever been the great story-tellers of mankind, the great ones such as Homer and Hesiod as well as the lesser ones, is that they tell lies, and unfortunate ones.   It may be the poet's defense that his tale is not a lie if it be understood allegorically ; but, says Plato, "a young person cannot judge what is allegorical and what is literal ; anything that he receives into his mind at that age is likely to become indelible and unalterable ; and therefore, it is important that the tales which the young first hear should be models of virtuous thought." [3]   To tell children the story of how Cronos punished his father Uranus, and how in turn his son retaliated upon him will set them a bad example ; the young are likely to think that in chastising their elders, and particularly their parents, for wrong-doing, they are following the example of the first and greatest among the gods.

It must be remembered that in Greek heroic poetry, the gods and demi-gods were frequently the leading characters.   Lying about the gods is the most serious charge that Plato can bring against the poets.   They do not represent divinity as it truly is. The misrepresentation of divinity is so important that Plato goes further in his censorship ; the old as well as the young should not be permitted to hear the fictions of a changing and changeable God and of God as the source of human misery, the author of both evil and good.   The poet who tells such stories should not be given a chorus, which, translated into the conventions of our day, means that he will be denied the privileges of a public performance in the theatre.

Plato is not opposed to lying in itself.   The intentional lie may be a justifiable political expedient.   But if anyone is to have the privilege of lying, it should be the rulers of the state and not the poets.   Either in dealing with enemies or in ruling their own citizens, the leaders may be allowed to lie for the public good. Plato himself gives us an excellent example of such a necessary

[1] *Republic,* 377 B.   [2] *Republic,* 377 C.   [3] *Republic,* 378 E.

falsehood, a royal lie which aims to keep the members of the various classes of society at rest in their respective positions. Furthermore, the myths which Plato so frequently narrates are admittedly fictions, dangerously misleading unless understood allegorically; only then do they yield the moral point for which they are devised. Are the poets, then, objectionable as liars because they are politically and morally irresponsible, because they tell a story for its own sake and not for the good of the state or the moral maxim to be illustrated? Poetry or story-telling is not in itself bad, but it should be the politician rather than the poet who tells the stories [1]. We shall later find Plato admitting that the poet is a rival of the statesman. One of the offices of government, to use a contemporary title, is the ministry of propaganda and public enlightenment, and the poet filling that office shall be the only poet in the state. But in the early sections of the *Republic*, Plato is interested in the censorship and control of fiction rather than its complete exclusion. He has no hesitation in recommending direct political action in the regulation of the arts, because education is one of the chief concerns of the state, and the arts are among its most effective agencies. He does not fail, however, to recognize some distinction between political and aesthetic standards for judging the arts. What is good according to the former may be bad according to the latter [2]. When we strike out passages from Homer and other poets, we do so, he says, not because they are unpoetical or unattractive to the popular ear, but because, if they are politically or morally objectionable, "the greater the poetical charm of them, the less are they meet for the ears of boys and men." [4]

It must not be thought that Plato criticized the poets only for their misrepresentation of the gods and similar transgressions with respect to matters of religion. There are many today who would dismiss the Platonic attack too lightly if that were its only focus. The poets must be censored not only for fomenting errors in religious belief, but also for engendering laxity of morals among the young. They depict human life and human action in such a way that, though their tales may possibly afford amusement, they do not form the moral virtues and may even corrupt them. "The poets and story-tellers," Plato insists, "are guilty of making the gravest mis-statements when they tell us that

[4] *Republic*, 387 B.

wicked men are often happy, and the good miserable ; and that
injustice is profitable when undetected, but that justice is a man's
own loss and another's gain.   These things we shall forbid them
to utter, and command them to sing and say the opposite." [5]
It is at this point that Plato recognizes an assumption which
underlies his programme of censorship.   If we are to direct the
writer of literature in what he should and should not say about
human life, viewing his stories as a source of moral training, then
we must know the nature of the good man and what are the
aspects and conditions of a good life.[5a]   Failing in this, how
could the statesman regulate the poet ?   This, as we shall see,
is not the only assumption upon which the discussion rests.

Poetry is, of course, only one of the arts ; it is the art of imaginative literature — whether written in prose or verse — the
art of fiction.   And of poetry, the two major kinds are the epic,
in which the poet is the unaided narrator, and the dramatic, in
which the poet tells his story through the actions and speeches
of men upon a stage.   The distinction is important not only
aesthetically but politically, because of the theatre's great popularity with the young and with the masses generally.   The production of dramatic poetry involves pantomime which, aided
by costume and spectacular staging, embodies the poet's imagination in an effective mimicry of nature.   This is what makes
plays so popular with children and with mankind in general.
Either because dramatic poetry is more effective than any other
kind of literature, or because the arts of the stage are more
popular than the other arts, Plato excludes the theatre entirely
from the state which he would rule [2a].   This is the beginning of the long history of censorship, in which dramatic productions have always borne the brunt of the attack.   The same
grounds which made dramatic poetry the primary object of
Plato's concern, leading him to exclude it *entirely*, whereas the
other arts were permitted to exist in the state under supervision,
make the motion picture more than any other art the social and
political problem of our day.   It is not that Plato considers music
and the plastic arts less subject to political supervision.[6]   He

[5] *Republic*, 392 B.   [5a] Vd. *Republic*, 402 C.
[6] Thus, in the case of the plastic arts : "Whenever an erroneous representation
is made of the nature of gods and heroes, — as when a painter paints a portrait
not having the shadow of a likeness to the original." *Republic*, 377 E.

discusses at length the kind of melodies and rhythms that are to be permitted. Music must be directed toward the improvement of the soul. But music and the plastic arts do not as fully represent human life in thought and action as does poetry, whether it be narrative in the form of a novel or of a play. The novel, a modern critic has written, deals fictionally with the conduct of human life; it crosses the path of the moralist at every point. [7] Of the drama, this is even more true, since the conflict of characters in action, without which drama is impossible, is always moral conflict. The difficulty of regulating the drama without regulating it out of existence may be the basis of Plato's discrimination between dramatic poetry and all other arts; to dictate to the poet the moral substance of his play would leave him almost no freedom of creation; it is different from telling the composer of music that it cannot be in the Phrygian mode [3].

Plato concludes the discussion we have here been summarizing by emphasizing the importance of right education for the welfare of the state, and of the control of the arts to effect the right education. Not only must the arts be properly instituted, but in addition, they must not be allowed the privilege of novelties and variations. Any musical innovation, and similarly, any change in poetry from the forms that have been officially authorized, is full of danger to the whole state and ought to be prohibited. It is at this point that Plato seems to recognize the social function of the arts as amusements [4]; but he insists that lawlessness has one of its sources in what at first seems harmless amusement, which if not properly regulated, generates an ever growing spirit of license. "Our youth," he concludes, "should be trained from the first in a stricter system, for if amusements become lawless, and the youths themselves become lawless, they can never grow up into well-conducted and virtuous citizens." [8]

The problem of the arts, and of poetry in particular, is not raised again until the last book of the *Republic*. The discussion that has intervened delineates the structure of a just or well-ordered society. The picture is obviously of the perfect state; it is not an account of earthly cities. It may be an objection to Plato's analysis to say that he has incorrectly analyzed the conditions of an ideally good state; but if that ideal is truly en-

[7] Jacques Maritain, *Art and Scholasticism*, New York, 1930: Note 154.
[8] *Republic*, 425.

visaged, it is no objection to point out that it is only an ideal he is setting before us. He himself points this out, adding that whether such a society now exists or will ever exist is no matter, since the ideal is the standard by which to judge the relative perfection of the cities of men upon earth.

At the opening of the last book, Plato, surveying the elements of the constitution he has devised for a perfect state, says that none of the excellences he has instituted pleases him more than his rule about poetry, his exclusion of the dramatists, the players, and the theatre. Despite what would thus appear to be an attitude well settled on the point, he reopens the question in an attempt to justify further his position. In the first place, the poets and all other artists are imitators. Nature itself is an imitation: its sensible appearances imitate the eternal forms in whose reality physical things participate in order to be what they are, however imperfectly. The artist, imitating nature, imitates an imitation and is thus twice or thrice removed from reality. It is only the philosopher who, seeking knowledge, contemplates basic realities. The poet or painter or sculptor, working by imitation from the models which nature provides, never gets beyond secondary imitations, and is therefore totally unfitted to teach, since to teach must be to impart knowledge and not merely opinion [5]. The common people, unphilosophical and therefore unaware of the distinctions between being and becoming, knowledge and opinion, suffer the illusion that the poets have knowledge of what they write about, and that what they write about is genuinely real. The poets are, however, not only ignorant men; worse than that, they do not seek the truth. From Homer down, they have been copying the images of virtue and have never sought to understand what virtue is; and because they imitate virtue and vice, poets are more dangerous than other artists. The ignorant multitude applauds them, and the philosopher, who should be its preceptor, goes unheard. Here again we see Plato motivated by the sense that the poets are his competitors. Earlier the question was not whether the people should be told stories, but who should tell them, the poet or the statesman. Here the problem is the choice of teachers. It seems that for the most part the people learn from the poets rather than the philosophers. And what they learn from the poets either makes it more difficult or almost impossible for the philosophers to teach them properly. Since in the good state the ruler must be a philosopher, or at least philosophically wise, the poets are a nuisance of which the state would be well rid.

In the second place, the poets arouse human passions, and this is without exception bad. This, says Plato, is the heaviest count in our accusation against the poets, and particularly the dramatists, who are most successful in exciting the emotions. The good man, philosophically trained, may not be misled by the illusions of fiction ; in his case, well founded knowledge will not yield place to opinion and imagination. But even the good man may be harmed by the appeal which poetry makes to his passions, and there are, in fact, few who are not so harmed. "The best of us delight in giving way to sympathy, and are in raptures at the excellence of the poet who stirs our feelings most." [9] Does not this show, Plato asks, the awful power which poetry has of harming even the good man? [10] Furthermore, "poetry feeds and waters the passions instead of drying them up ; she lets them rule, although they ought to be controlled, if men are ever to increase in happiness and virtue." [11]

Plato is thus moved to a conclusion which is more extreme than his earlier one; not only the dramatists, but all writers of fiction, all poets except those who write hymns to the gods or praises of good men, ought to be excluded from the state ; otherwise pleasure and pain, not law and reason, will rule it. Yet at this very point at which Plato is being most drastic in his treatment of the poets, he introduces the most significant qualifications of his entire argument. Addressing the poets whom he is about to exile, he relents by saying that if they will only prove their right to exist in a well ordered state, they will be gladly welcomed. This passage by itself is not easy to interpret. Does it mean that Plato is not convinced by his own analysis — as he would be were it the sort of clear knowledge that dialectic is — that the poets have no place in a well-ordered state ? Or is it only a rhetorical point to mitigate the harshness and the impoliteness of the decree banishing the poets ? The latter interpretation is clearly supported by the fact that Plato asks the question whether the poets can establish their right to participate in the life of a good state, but does not wait for the answer before completely excluding them. Yet the other interpreta-

[9] *Republic*, 605 D.   [10] *Republic*, 605 C.   [11] *Republic*, 606 D.

tion cannot be dismissed; in fact, it is reinforced by Plato's reiteration of a willingness to have the poets defended. "Let them show," he says, "not only that poetry is pleasant, but useful to states and to human life, and we will listen in a kindly spirit; for if this is proved, we shall surely be the gainers, — I mean if there is a use in poetry as well as a delight." [12]

The crucial question is thus neatly put. Plato seems convinced that poetry is bad or, at least, less good than philosophy, as a teacher of men, and that the poet is often a dangerously successful opponent of the statesman and the moralist in governing men by law and in training their characters. Yet, admitting for the first time in a kindly spirit that poetry and the arts are a *delight* to men, he asks whether in addition they are of any *use*. What does "use" here mean? Even if to provide men with pleasure and delight be useful, Plato's question requires that the utility be something other than such joy [6]. From the point of view of the statesman or any other person concerned with the welfare of society, a thing has utility to the extent that it serves some end which should be achieved because it in turn is a means to the welfare ultimately sought. Plato does not answer this question about the political or social utility of poetry and the arts. But though we must wait for Aristotle to answer it, Plato's argument is weakened by his asking it, whatever other merits or defects it may have.

Before we examine the merits and defects of Plato's argument about the poets, we must consider one other Platonic text that is relevant to the issue, namely, the *Laws*. The *Laws* is significant not only because it is a later and more solemn work than the *Republic*, but because it differs from the *Republic* in some of the latter's most radical provisions, such as the abolition of private property, and the destruction of the family as a social institution by communizing women and children. It has been argued against those who have taken the Platonic position about the exclusion of dramatists or the strict censorship of literature, that they do so inconsistently, because they will not also accept what seems to be the extreme communism of the *Republic*. But Plato himself rejected this so-called communism in the *Laws*, while at the same time embracing the position he took in the *Republic* on the poets. In fact, the code of laws he undertakes to prepare

[12] *Republic*, 607 E.

as a guide for human government even more stringently regulates the arts, and as resolutely excludes the dramatic poets.

If the pendulum of political thought swings between the position that the aim of government is to regulate all aspects of our social life by law and official administration, and the position that that government governs best which governs least, Plato's *Laws* marks one extreme point of its orbit.   There is no dictator who reigns in Europe today who has yet been able to put into practice the detail of legal and administrative regulation which Plato advocates and outlines in the *Laws* [7].   There is no apology for the complete restriction or utter abandonment of individual freedom.   Not only must the state determine the canons of art and prescribe their conventions in detail ; even the games of very young children are to be officially outlined and directed, and the prohibition of intoxicating liquors is minutely specific to the extent of determining in what situations what quantities of wine may be drunk.   The only distinction between the policy of the *Laws* and that of contemporary European fascism is not in the policy itself, but in the character of the dictator or law-maker.

Plato held up Egypt and Sparta as models with respect to the political supervision of the arts.   The Egyptians are to be praised for having canonized by law the kind of music which has an intrinsic rightness [8].   Plato goes on to say that if we can detect the intrinsically right in the matter of any art, we should reduce that art to law and system without misgiving, and without yielding to the perpetual human craving for novelty in the arts.   He has not forgotten the point in the *Republic*, that the arts may be a source of delight, and that the pleasure to be derived from them may, in part, rest upon such novelty.   But he does not concur with the popular opinion that the standard by which artists and other providers of entertainment are to be judged, is the amount of pleasure they give.   It is not the pleasure given to every and any person, but that which delights the best men, the properly educated.   He who is to judge the arts and regulate them must take his seat, not to learn from the audience, but to teach them, and to set himself against performers who give an audience pleasure in wrong and improper ways.   Plato is against the prevailing freedom which leaves the merit of amusements to be decided by the majority of the audience.   This practice, he says, has corrupted the poets themselves, "since their standard in composition is the debased taste of their judges, with the result that it is actually the audience who educates *them*, and it has equally corrupted the tastes of the audience." [13] Only in Sparta have the full duties of the statesman as an educator of the people been recognized, and there the arts are as completely regulated as they were in ancient Egypt.

It should be noted that this discussion of the political super-vision of musical and poetical entertainments occurs in the con-text of a discussion of the prohibition and regulation of wine-drinking.[14] The arts as public amusements are like wine; they provide the populace with pleasure. While pleasure is not in itself condemned [9], pleasure cannot be used as the standard by which to measure the political worth of things. The lawgiver must consider only what is morally right, or in other words, he must consult the pleasures of the good man. It should be noted also that Sparta, praised by Plato, was conspicuously deficient in the arts, and particularly in literature. One wonders whether their treatment of the poets, which Plato holds up as a model, was the cause of this deficiency; or, if not, what is the significance of the Spartan example? For if, as Milton says of them, "muse-less and unbookish they were, minding nought but the feats of war," there could have been no problem about poetry in Sparta. "There needed no licensing of books among them, for they disliked all but their own laconic apothegms, and took slight occasion to chase Archolochus out of their city, perhaps for composing in a higher strain than their own soldierly ballads and roundels could reach to; or if it were for his broad verses, they were not therein so cautious, but they were as dissolute in their promiscuous conversing; whence Euripides affirms, in Andromache, that their women were all unchaste." [15]

The *Laws* follows the *Republic* in its essential point of dis-criminating between drama and the arts of the theatre, on the one hand, and music, lyric poetry, the dance, painting, and all other arts, on the other. The latter are to be subjected to close supervision by the Minister of Education, who is at once the official curator of public morals and censor of the arts; but stage productions of dramatic literature are to be prohibited without qualification. The reason Plato gives for this in the

[13] *Laws*, 659. [14] *Laws*, Book II. [15] *Areopagitica*, Cambridge, 1928 : pp. 8–9.

Laws is simple and direct. If the dramatists ask for permission to produce their plays, the ruler or law-maker must answer in the following vein : "Respected visitors, we are ourselves author of a tragedy, and that the finest and the best we know how to make. In fact, our whole polity has been constructed as a dramatisation of a noble and perfect life; that is what *we* hold to be in truth the most real of tragedies. Thus you are poets, and we also are poets in the same style, rival artists and rival actors, and that in the finest of all dramas, one which indeed can be produced only by a code of true laws — or at least that is our faith. So you must not expect that we shall light-heartedly permit you to pitch your booths in our market-square with a troupe of actors whose melodious voices will drown our own, and let you deliver your public tirades before our boys and women and the populace at large — let you address them on the same issues as ourselves, not to the same effect, but commonly, and for the most part, to the very contrary." [16]

This passage echoes the point made in the *Republic* that there is an ancient quarrel between philosophy and poetry. The rivalry between the poet, especially the dramatist, and the statesman, the enmity between the poet and the philosopher, which we have found running throughout the Platonic discussion, and which Plato himself clearly recognizes, can be given many interpretations [10]. The poets are subversive, or at least they arrogate to themselves the privilege of commenting on law and morals and government, and in such a way that their comment is more effective than the frank opposition of political partisans. Did not Shelley boast that "poets are the unacknowledged legislators of the world"? The legislator is a teacher, and to the extent that he teaches by law, he must use the sanction of force. The poet is a rival teacher; he teaches by means of pleasure and persuasion. It is no wonder, then, that the politician fears him and distrusts him. In a state in which free political debate is either not encouraged or not permitted, it would be an inconsistent policy not to silence the poet; if suffered at all, he must speak lines which the rulers, or their ministers of propaganda and public enlightenment, write for him. But even in a state devoted to the political principle of freedom of debate for all public questions, the poet is still feared by those socially-minded

[16] *Laws*, 817.

groups which claim to have the interests of the community at
heart.   He is their rival, and the freedom which they are zealous
to guard for themselves, they are reluctant to grant him.   The
fear of the poet as subversive is, however, not a rational ground
for censoring or exiling him ; although the fact of his being subversive of public morals, law and order, might justify the political remedy.   But this fact cannot be assumed.   It must be
established that imaginative literature, the stage, and the motion
picture, do have the effects upon the populace which their opponents ascribe to them.

The rivalry between the poet and the philosopher has another
significance which is illuminating.   It is the dissonance of great
similarity.   Human wisdom, both speculative and practical, is
expressed alike in the writings of poets and philosophers ; the
poet moves freely in all philosophical realms, in metaphysics and
morals, in theology and politics.   Poetry, said Aristotle, is not
only more philosophical than history, but it satisfies, as philosophy does, the human desire for learning.   It provides both the
matter and the means of contemplation ; the similarity between
poetry and philosophy is in the matter, the difference in the
means.   The enmity between the poet and the philosopher is
thus to be understood ; it is the antagonism between different
techniques for achieving substantially similar ends.   But whereas
Plato felt that such competition was unwholesome in a state
to be governed by philosophers, we shall find that Aristotle
makes the similarity of poetry and philosophy one of the chief
political justifications for the arts of literature.   The common
roots of art and religion in ritual explain the statement that it
is the same impulse which sends a man to church and to theatre.
The common roots of poetry and philosophy in the intellectual
imagination explain their service to the contemplative mind ;
and contemplation is a good which the community should seek
to conserve in any form.   We shall return to this point later
in the Aristotelian analysis of the problem of poetry.

Plato must be protected from his followers, who are many,
eminent, and influential, as well as from his opponents.   His
disciples as frequently misunderstand him as his critics.   This
is particularly true in regard to his doctrine about poetry and
politics.   Here his host of followers includes many who are
not genuinely Platonists, and who unscrupulously cite him as

authority for their own condemnation of poetry, without sharing the intellectual presuppositions which support his position,
without really understanding the position itself. We are, therefore, obligated to make an independent analysis of his doctrine
before turning to its critics, of whom Aristotle is both first and
foremost. In no other way can we determine whether Aristotle understands, as well as disagrees with, Plato. We shall do
this, perhaps too briefly, first by stating the assumptions upon
which his position with respect to poetry rests, and then by
turning the light of other parts of Plato's philosophy upon this
striking point in it.

It is not enough to say that Plato's political philosophy is
directed toward the definition of political ideals. Even if the
Republic is treated as presenting the conception of an ideal
commonwealth, and the *Laws*, the description of the best state
practically achievable, it does not follow that the exclusion of
the poets and the strict censorship of the other arts is entirely
utopian in its significance. Actual societies are to be judged
as having degrees of perfection in proportion as they approximate the ideal. Plato assumes that statesmen or rulers can perform the tasks of government better or worse in proportion as
they are more or less philosophers, men having speculative principles and knowledge, the more speculative the more practical.
He further assumes that it is the state, rather than the home or
any other agency, such as the church, which must undertake
the moral training as well as the intellectual education of its
citizens; and that the arts in their political aspect have *only one*
function, the didactic, directed primarily to forming moral
character, though they may also instruct the mind [6].

These assumptions are somewhat qualified by two points of
unclearness in the discussion. (1) At some places, Plato seems to
be considering the problem of education only with respect to
"the young"; at other places, he views the arts in their possible
effects upon citizens of all ages. We are forced to ask, therefore, whether Plato holds that the state is responsible only for
the moral training of its youth or whether, in extreme paternalism, it treats all its citizens as if they were children to be guided
and guarded. (2) At some places, Plato limits the problem to
the education of the governing classes and ignores what he would
call the artisans and slaves, what we would call the proletariat

and the masses; at other places, he seems to extend his view to the populace as a whole, regardless of these class distinctions. Again we must ask whether he intends his position concerning poetry to be understood in the wider or narrower frame in which the problem of education is considered. Ignoring these difficult questions for the moment, we can summarize his argument as follows: If the indicated assumptions are granted, and if Plato *knows*, first, that the philosopher-statesman is able to direct the moral training of his citizens; second, that the arts will be obstacles in the way of such training unless they are closely supervised by the philosopher-statesman; and third, that the philosopher-statesman is able to direct the arts to good rather than bad results; then in the light of these assumptions and such *knowledge*, Plato is practically wise in recommending strict censorship of most of the arts and the total exclusion of the drama, which Plato singles out for such drastic treatment because the ruler must himself become his people's poet. But are all these assumptions unavoidable, and does Plato have knowledge rather than opinion — in terms of his own clear standards — with respect to the points upon which his conclusion rests?

The Platonic dialogues help to answer these questions, though not fully. Let us concede that Plato knows what virtue is and what the virtues are, that he knows the nature of a good man and the conditions of a good life. So much may be clear philosophical knowledge, and not mere opinion. But does he know how men acquire the virtues or, on the other hand, lose them? Are the virtues taught as geometry is taught? Are they learned by imitation of the examples set by virtuous men? Are they elements of our natural endowment, rather than products of nurture? These questions are part of the more general question: How does one form or corrupt the moral character of others? Unless Plato as a philosopher knows the answer to this question, the statesman who is a philosopher is not likely to be better able than the poet he replaces to alter the souls of men for either good or evil; what either actually succeeds in doing will be as if by chance; certainly the ruler will not be able so to direct the artist or the poet that his work creates the virtues rather than corrupts them. But this question, in general and in all its parts, is one which the Platonic writings most conspicuously leave unanswered; or, what is even more significant, the dialogues reveal many answers to the question, but dictate no clear choice among them. They are so many opinions to be clarified, but not to be accepted as knowledge. Thus, in the *Meno*, it is first assumed that virtue is knowledge, or includes knowledge as an integral part; in which case, it should be teachable as geometry is teachable, but there are no teachers and students of virtue as there are of geometry. Hence it is not merely knowledge, and although it includes knowledge as a part, it includes other parts which differentiate it from geometry and make it unteachable. It is suggested next that the leaders of the state are the teachers of virtue by the examples they set; but it is offered, on the contrary, that virtuous fathers do not produce virtuous sons; hence the proximate example of virtue is insufficient to explain the formation of character. The dialogue ends with the proposition that the virtues are either a gift of nature or of the gods. Whatever this means positively, it means, negatively, that men do not *know* how to proceed in the moral training of others.

The *Protagoras* is a dialogue in which Socrates and Protagoras debate the question whether virtue can be taught. At the end Socrates recognizes the paradox that he has been maintaining that virtue is knowledge, but that it cannot be taught, while Protagoras has been denying that it is knowledge, but insisting that it can be taught. This conclusion is hardly a resolution of the question, and the dialogue as a whole is even less instructive with regard to *how* virtue can be taught or trained. But in the course of it Protagoras makes one long speech that is significant. He says that the fact that Socrates finds no special teachers of virtue in Greece is no more surprising than that he finds no special teachers of Greek in Greece; it does not follow from this that men are not taught and do not learn virtue, any more than that they are not taught and do not learn to speak their native language. Just as, in a sense, every person in the community, and particularly those with whom one is intimately in contact, teaches one how to speak its language, and just as everyone is a student of that language and is learning it on all social occasions, so every citizen is both a teacher and a student of virtue with respect to every other citizen. That is what a city is: it is a community of men who can teach virtue to and learn it from each other. This still does not explain *how* any man teaches or learns virtue. Plato, however, does not agree with

Protagoras. In the *Republic* he defends the sophists against the
charge that they have a corrupting moral influence upon young
men, by saying that the sophists do no more than express current
popular opinions, and that it is, therefore, prevailing public
sentiments which corrupt the youth. It is the public, he says,
which "educates young and old, men and women alike, and
fashions them after their own hearts."[17] So far Plato seems to
agree with Protagoras, but he goes on to insist that the unwel-
come and unpopular task of the philosopher is to counteract the
corrupting effects of public opinion. Only the philosopher can
do this; that is why the philosopher must rule if society is to
improve. But how is he to do it? If by legislation, what force
will laws have if they are contrary to custom and prevailing
opinion? If he must change opinion and custom to give laws
their proper force, he must use persuasion and education rather
than force to achieve this end. But what are the means of persuasion, what are the factors in education, or, in short, how can
the populace be made virtuous? Thus we return to the question which, to the extent that it is not answerable by *knowledge*,
weakens the conclusion that political leaders, whether or not
they are philosophers, should supervise the arts as means of
moral training [11].

It is to Plato that we owe the first clear distinction between
knowledge and opinion. We cannot here discuss it fully, but
the basic point can be made. Knowledge has completeness and
clarity. It is whatever the reason must assent to in terms of
the matter known or in the light of relevant evidence. Opinion
is fragmentary and unclear in the sense that its verbal expression
is more or less ambiguous. What is asserted as opinion involves
willful rather than rational assent. Opinion is prejudice, and
must be analyzed in terms of ignorance and the passions. If
Plato could be asked whether the propositions upon which his
programme of regulation for the arts and his treatment of the
poets rested were knowledge or opinion, he would answer—I
think the dialogues show—opinion. Not only do we not know
how the good in men is created and the evil avoided; he would
admit further that we do not *know* the effects of the arts in
general, and of poetry in particular, upon their audience, young
or old, and of whatever class of men. We do not know, there-

[17] *Republic*, 492 B.

fore, that the arts are impediments to the course of moral training and that the philosopher-statesman, or any other ruler, is able to regulate the arts so as to reduce or eliminate them as impediments. Faced by a practical dilemma, and lacking the relevant knowledge, I doubt whether Plato would recommend that action be taken, even though he seems to do precisely the opposite with respect to the poets. I think he would have agreed with a recent statement of Professor Charles Beard, historian and political scientist, "that the failure to distinguish between knowledge and opinion is responsible for a large part of the tragedy, suffering, insecurity, conflict and poverty in public and private life. If mere personal and class opinions were separated from facts known and established, and were presented in their true guise, a new tone of humility might enter into our public and private discussions."[18] But I do not think Plato would agree with the contemporaries of Professor Beard about the significance of the answers to such difficult questions of fact, which are offered as knowledge in the name of science because they have been obtained by the prevailing methods of empirical research in psychology and the social sciences. We shall return to this point later.[19]

That Plato would admit either ignorance or conflicting opinion on these questions of fact seems to me to be indicated clearly at one place in the *Republic*. Although he has just decided to exclude the dramatists, he challenges them "to prove their right to exist in a well-ordered state."[20] If the question is thus open to dispute — and unless it were, the proof the poets are challenged to make would be impossible — the knowledge which would make the question indisputable does not exist.

Our criticism so far has been in terms of the knowledge which Plato needs and lacks to support his position on the poets. If we turn now to his basic assumptions, we shall see that all of them are not unavoidable and that some of them raise questions which Aristotle answers differently. One of these assumptions is peculiarly useful in providing a transition to Aristotle, because Plato himself has questioned it and Aristotle so clearly answers his question. For the most part, Plato seems to assume that the arts in their political aspect are either good or bad as didactic,

[18] Commencement Address at Union College, as reported in the *New York Times*, June 11, 1935. [19] In Chapter 9. [20] *Republic*. 607 C.

and that there is no other criterion by which to judge their
political merit.   He concedes that they provide pleasure, but
this is not enough to outweigh his opinion that, unregulated, they
fail as instruments of moral instruction.   But, in the context of
his challenge to the poets to prove themselves worthy, he asks
them to show that they are not merely pleasant, but also useful
to the state [6].

Aristotle undertakes the defense of literature, and the other
arts as well, by doing precisely this, by showing the variety
of respects in which they are politically useful.   The superiority of the Aristotelian analysis at this point, as at others, is its
greater detail and balance, its greater analytical fullness.   Basic
questions become more polygonal, and out of their many sides
and angles, the lines of action which solve difficult practical
problems are drawn more temperately, and hence less definitely
[12].   Still, Plato may have the gift of wisdom and insight
which goes directly to the undeniable point.   The issue between
Aristotle and Plato must not be begged here.   It can be properly
reviewed and decided only after Aristotle has been heard.

CHAPTER TWO

Aristotle

THE Aristotelian analysis has no single locus. It is to be found partly in the *Poetics* and partly in the *Ethics* and *Politics*. The *Poetics*, while in large part a treatise on the drama, contains principles for an analysis of the nature of the fine arts. It has many levels of generality; it presents a philosophy of art as well as particular points in the theory of poetry as imaginative literature. We turn to the *Poetics* first because it provides the first step in the complete answer to Plato's question. Of what use is poetry in a well-ordered state? Has it any other function than that of teaching morals, in which it is of questionable value? Plato admitted that poetry was a source of pleasure. But all pleasures are not the same and do not have the same ethical or political value. Aristotle's account of the nature of poetry explains the kind of pleasure and satisfaction it affords. When we have grasped this point, we can go to the *Ethics* and *Politics* to discover the moral value and the political utility of such pleasure and satisfaction.

Poetry is defined as an imitation of human action. To understand this definition one must know what is meant by imitation. Whatever imitation means, it is at once clear that for Aristotle poetry is imaginative narrative; it is fiction. Poetry is generically like history; both are narratives of human action; the specific difference is that history relates what *has* happened, poetry what *may* happen; the one is the narrative of the actual and hence is limited to past particulars, the other is the narrative of the possible, and hence moves in the realm of the universal, unrestricted except by the law of contradiction, and not always even by that. Aristotle is at pains to make clear that the difference between the poet and the historian is not that the former writes in verse and the latter in prose. "The work of Herodotus," he says, "might be put into verse, and it would still be a species of history, with metre no less than without it."[1] It is unfortunate that this confusing identification of poetry with verse is so popular; it was in Aristotle's day; it is in ours. "Even when a treatise in medicine or natural science is brought out in verse, the name of poet is by custom given to the author; and yet Homer and Empedocles have nothing in common but the metre, so that it would be right to call the one poet, the other physicist rather than poet."[2] The poet, like any other artist, is a maker, but he is not a maker of verses but a maker of plots, "since he is a poet because he imitates, and what he imitates are actions. And even if he chances to take an historical subject, he is none the less a poet; for there is no reason why some events that have actually happened should not conform to the law of the probable and the possible, and in virtue of that quality in them, he is their poet or maker."[3]

All art is imitation. The distinction of the arts can only be made in terms of the formal object of their imitation, the medium through which they imitate, and the manner in which they imitate in that medium. Thus, human action, and consequently human passion, is the formal object of the ballet as well as of poetry, but poetry is to be distinguished from the dance because its medium of imitation is language. Within the genus poetry, various species can be distinguished either by reference to subordinate differences in the object of imitation, the kinds of human action, thus tragedy and comedy; or by reference to the manner of imitation, thus epic from dramatic poetry, or what we would call the novel and the play.[3a] In the epic poem or the

---

[1] *Poetics*, 9 1451[b]1–5. [2] *Poetics*, 1 1447[b]16–20. [3] *Poetics*, 9 1451[b]28–32.
[3a] Whenever in the text of this chapter or in the notes appended thereto. genus and species are said of works of art, they are said analogically, and not as they are said of natural things. Similarly in the case of definition, nature or essence, property and accident. By analogy to natural things a work of art can be said to have a nature, or essence, and can be defined; analogically, it is constituted by matter and form; analogically, its properties, flowing from its essence, can be distinguished from its accidents.

novel as a narrative, the poet tells the story, sometimes speaking in his own person, and sometimes in the persons of his characters; in the dramatic narrative or the play, he never speaks in his own person, but presents all his characters as living and moving before us, and it is through their action and speech, aided by the spectacle which is ordered accordingly by the arts of the stage, that their thoughts are revealed, their characters defined, and the plot is unfolded. All the essential elements of narrative which can be found in a novel or epic poem are present in drama, but the drama includes the additional element of spectacle, which all the auxiliary arts of the theatre are engaged to produce.[4]

We must digress briefly at this point to consider the motion picture. Like the ballet, the novel, and the play, it is an imitation of human action. It is most similar to the play because it has the element of spectacle which epic narrative lacks, and because it tells a narrative by means which exclude the author from speaking in his own person. The silent motion picture was, however, closer to the ballet; neither used language as a medium of imitation. The talking motion picture is closer to literature, and more especially to dramatic literature. Yet, as a subsequent aesthetic analysis of the motion picture will demonstrate, the motion picture is a distinct species of poetry, capable of being as clearly differentiated from the stage play as that is differentiated from the novel. The problem requires some subtlety, for an analysis of the arts in terms of their object, medium and manner of imitation shows that these factors combine in various ways to give arts of varying degrees of mixture and purity. This will be seen at once by anyone who will consider the sameness and the difference of the drama and the ballet. For the purposes of the present discussion, it is only necessary to recognize that the motion picture is a kind of poetry, a kind of imaginative literature or fiction; its producer is primarily a maker of plots, though his medium and manner be different from that of the novelist and the playwright.[5]

[4] Vd. *Poetics*, 5, 1449ᵇ15–20 ; 23–24.
[5] Strictly, the name for the genus of which the cinema is a species should not be "poetry," but "narrative" or "fiction." These distinctions are clearly made in Chapter 13 *infra*. In this part of the text, however, "poetry" is used loosely as a synonym for "fiction."

The crucial point, on which Aristotle's *Poetics* is silent, is the nature of imitation itself.[6] It is not surprising, therefore, that the point has been so persistently misunderstood. Many commentators, particularly modern writers, obstinate in their ignorance of the rest of Aristotle's philosophy by which they might have been enlightened, have willfully proceeded to attach meanings to the word which make the Aristotelian analysis patently absurd. Let me illustrate this by taking the most egregious misinterpretation of imitation: that an imitation is a faithful copy, the goodness of which is proportionate to its fidelity in reproducing what is being imitated. It succeeds to the extent that we are deceived and take the imitation for the reality. This is nonsense, as the writers who ascribe this meaning to Aristotle have intelligence enough to appreciate; but, fortunately for Aristotle and unfortunately for these commentators, this is not what Aristotle meant. Imitation does involve likeness to the object imitated; but it also and necessarily involves difference. The copy-notion, which makes imitation an attempt to achieve a maximum of similitude, which makes imitation a counterfeit, a fraud, a deception, misses the essential point of *difference* which makes imitation art. The modern poles of realism and romanticism are extremes of emphasis either upon the similarity to nature involved in imitation, or upon the difference from nature that must be present. The most realistic novel or the most fantastic tale are equally art. Though the misguided intention of the realistic author be to perpetrate a counterfeit of life, the audience is never wholly deceived. They know it is literature and not life. The only confusion they might conceivably suffer is to think they were reading history rather than fiction, and if they did, the author would be condemned when they discovered how his effort at deception had misled them. At the other extreme, the most fantastic fiction would not be intelligible even as fiction, did it not bear the clear marks of similarity to things as they are. We are not here concerned with the ungenuine issue between realism and romanticism, but to see it as ungenuine helps to explain the nature of imitation.

The distinction between form and matter, the universal and the particular, define imitation. The essential elements of simil-

[6] Except for the reference to imitation as instinctive in man and animals, and in man to a greater degree than in other animals. *Poetics*, 4, 1448^{b}5-9.

itude are likeness and difference, likeness with respect to form and difference with respect to matter. Thus, human life and action have certain formal properties, properties which are formal because universal, because common to human action wherever and however it occurs. The individualizing matter of action is to be found in particular men and their motions. Fiction imitates human action by achieving a likeness to its formal properties; but the matter of fiction consists of words and the images aroused by these words. The difference between literature and life, or more generally between art and nature, is in their respective matters; the similarity is formal [13]. Imitation is clear in proportion as a maximum of similarity is combined with a maximum of difference. By this criterion the novel is better than the play which, as produced, involves the bodies and motions of actors upon a stage, including, of course, their audible speech. Nevertheless, it is upon a stage, and however realistic the spectacle, actors are actors and not men, and what they do is part of a plot and not the movement of life. The motion picture achieves a greater distance, a clearer difference, than the stage. Its matter consists of shadows rather than bodies in the round. But we need not here be concerned with the degrees and conditions of imitation in the several arts. It is only important that imitation be properly understood. Though a person who does not grasp the metaphysical distinctions which are involved will understand imitation inadequately, he can at least avoid misunderstanding it by knowing that imitation is not an attempt to counterfeit reality. The remainder of this discussion will assume that this misapprehension has been removed.

The importance of imitation as the essence of art is that art is not nature. The effects of the arts upon men, the emotions they arouse, the lessons they teach if they do, the pleasures they afford, must therefore be different somehow from the effects of nature or reality. To understand this difference we must understand the principle that art imitates nature [14]. It is misunderstood if it is taken too simply. As Aristotle points out, the imitation of nature is an imitation of things (1) as they are, or as better or worse than they are, or (2) as they should be, or (3) as they are said or thought to be by men. This illuminates two points in the Platonic discussion. Plato recognized that works of art were imitations and made this part of his condemnation. The poets, in telling their stories, told lies about both gods and men.   To which Aristotle answers: "If it be objected that the description is not true to fact, the poet may perhaps reply, 'But the objects are as they ought to be,' just as Sophocles said that he drew men as they ought to be, Euripides, as they are. If, however, the representation be of neither kind, the poet may answer: 'This is how men say the thing is.' This applies to tales about the gods." [7]   But there is a further answer to the condemnation of the poets as telling lies.   Their office is not to tell the truth in the same sense that philosophers and scientists do, or should. If the end desired is knowledge of reality, of that which is as it is, philosophy and science are the means.   But Plato seems to be condemning poetry and the arts for failing as a means with respect to an end they are not intended to serve. He has rightly seen that the nature of art is imitation, and his criticism can, therefore, be directly met by showing that it follows from the imitative character of the arts that their proper end is not the same as that of philosophy and science [15].   In Aristotelian terms, if imitation is the formal cause of art, its final cause, its end, must be appropriately determined; or, in other words, the purposes art *can* serve must follow from its nature.

There are those who hold that art has no extrinsic purpose, that art is for art's sake.   There are those who hold that art has only extrinsic purposes and ignore its intrinsic nature, that art is for man's sake, for the sake of morals, or religion, or the state. This is a nineteenth-century issue, between such writers as Pater and Tolstoy, and such promoters as Clive Bell, on the one hand, and Anthony Comstock, on the other.   No Greek would have understood it.   There is no conflict between the nature of a thing and the ends it can serve, no conflict between what we shall call the intrinsic and extrinsic aspects or a work of art; not only no conflict, but there is nothing which must not be considered in both ways.   To be concerned exclusively either with art for art's sake or art for man's sake is inadequate and is likely to lead to error.   The work of art is the end of the artist, that which he seeks to produce.   When it is so considered it raises only aesthetic problems, and the criticism it may receive is intrinsic, technical or aesthetic.   But the work of art is not

[7] *Poetics*, 25, 1460^{b}32–1461^{a}4.

its own end. It is produced in society. It has an audience whom it affects in one way or another; alterations in man and society are its ends. When it is so considered, it raises only moral and social problems, and the criticism it may receive is extrinsic, moral or political. The problem we are discussing, the problem of poetry and politics, arises only when we consider art in relation to its audience, art for man's sake [16].

The extrinsic ends of art are recognized at two places in Aristotle's *Poetics*.[8] First, in the definition of tragedy: "Tragedy is an imitation of an action" . . . which "through pity and fear effects a proper purgation of these emotions."[9] The *proper* purgation of the emotions is not strictly an element in the definition of tragedy; it is a property which necessarily follows from the definition of the nature of tragedy as imitation, as the proper end or activity of any thing follows from its essence [17]. It will be noted that I am here generalizing Aristotle's remark to the universality of the insight which it conveys. The arousal and proper purgation of the emotions is not peculiar to tragedy, though pity and fear may be. It is an end of all kinds of poetry, comic or tragic, novel or play, and of all art, to effect a proper purgation of the emotions. To purge them it must arouse them, and it must do both *properly*, that is, in a manner that is proper to the nature of art as imitation. The concept of purgation is as difficult as the concept of imitation; the text of the *Poetics* is as silent on the nature of purgation, and purgation has consequently been as generally misunderstood as imitation. But the two concepts are closely related, as the nature of art and one of its powers must be. I shall subsequently attempt to clarify the meaning of purgation. For the present, however, we can pro-

---

[8] The word "art" is used here, and throughout this discussion unless otherwise qualified, to name the works produced by the artist and not his disciplined power of making them.

[9] *Poetics*, 6, 1449^{b}22–28. (The only other reference to purgation is in the *Politics*, VIII, 7, 1341^{b}37, 1342^{a}15, at which point Aristotle refers to his treatise on poetry as the place where purgation is more fully discussed. The reference is probably to a lost part of the *Poetics*.) I have quoted from the definition of tragedy only the relevant phrase about the purgation of pity and fear. The following passage should also be noted: "The pleasure which the poet should afford is that which comes from pity and fear through imitation," *Poetics*, 14, 1453^{b}1–12.

ceed without that clarification, using 'purgation' to name one of
the chief effects of art upon its audience and, hence, one of its
extrinsic ends and political values.

Second, in the description of the kind of pleasure which art
affords: Universal, he says, "is the pleasure felt in things imitated. We have evidence of this in the facts of experience.
Objects which in themselves we view with pain, we delight to
contemplate when reproduced with minute fidelity. . . The
cause of this again is, that to learn gives the liveliest pleasure, not
only to philosophers but to men in general, whose capacity, however, for learning is more limited." [10] This passage is richly
significant for all our discussion to follow. The pleasure men
get from art is not the pleasure of the senses as such, although
works of art may give such pleasures also [18]. The pleasure
is the pleasure of learning; it is a cognitive pleasure. Men have
an appetite to know, and the arts, among other things, satisfy
this appetite, and in doing so give pleasure. That works of art
are able to provide this pleasure follows from their nature as
imitations. Being imitations of nature rather than nature itself,
works of art exist to be known, to be contemplated and to give
the pleasure of knowledge and contemplation to those who treat
them as works of art [19]. In other words, the simple fact that
art has an audience means that men are spectators rather than
actors, interested in knowing and contemplating rather than in
doing. This is not to say that only works of art are objects of
knowledge or contemplation; nor is it to say that works of art
are only objects of contemplation, since we know that they can
be produced for money, can be bought and sold, fought over
and destroyed, and even prohibited by the rulers of the state.
It is simply to say that it is appropriate to the nature of works
of art as imitations, that they be objects of contemplation and
give that pleasure which is peculiar to contemplation. Some
men have claimed that they can be spectators of all of life;
others that nothing is so heavy with utility that it cannot also
be viewed contemplatively. This may be true, but it does not
alter the fact that for the most part men find themselves in the
position of spectators only with respect to works of art, or games
and pageants which, like works of art, are imitations rather than
life or nature [20]. We shall return later to this point and to

[10] *Poetics*, 4, 1448b4–15. Vd. *Metaphysics*, I, 980a.

what, from the political point of view, is an even more important point, namely, that all men are not philosophers or scientists,
and yet all men desire to learn and to contemplate. The arts,
it will be seen, yield this pleasure to those "whose capacity for
learning is more limited."

The evidence which supports the statement that men take
pleasure in imitations is overwhelming; it is peculiarly impres-
sive with respect to the kind of imitation that poetry is, the
imitation of action, of human life. The desire for fiction is
present in men at all stages of their development, and in all lo-
calities and epochs. Children cry for stories. Myths are
found wherever man is. Imaginative literature, whether the
oft-told legend or the printed story or the acted play, is
as much a common commodity of life as food and shelter.
It may not be necessary to life as food is, but its omnipresence
argues that it satisfies a universal need. Historical examples may
be added, if further evidence is required: the extraordinary popularity of the Elizabethan theatre as measured by attendance;
the tremendous increase during the 19th century in the circulation of novels, and the growth of circulating libraries when printing costs made it economically possible to satisfy the demand for
fiction; the place of the motion picture in contemporary life,
again as the result of an economic adjustment of the price of the
fiction desired to the power of the multitude to pay. As Mr.
T. S. Eliot, in an essay on Wilkie Collins and Dickens, begins:

"It is to be hoped that some scholarly and philosophic critic of
the present generation may be inspired to write a book on the history
and aesthetic of melodrama. The golden age of melodrama passed,
it is true, before any person living was aware of its existence: in the
very middle of the last century. But there are many living who
are not too young to remember the melodramatic stage before the
cinema replaced it; who have sat entranced, in the front stalls of
local or provincial theatres, before some representation of *East
Lynne*, or *The White Slave*, or *No Mother To Guide Her*; and who
are not too old to have observed with curious interest the replace-
ment of dramatic melodrama by cinematographic melodrama, and
the dissociation of the elements of the old three volume melodramatic
novel into the various types of the modern 300 page novel. Those
who have lived before such terms as 'high-brow fiction,' 'thrillers'
and 'detective fiction' were invented realize that melodrama is perennial and that the craving for it is perennial and must be satisfied. If

we cannot get this satisfaction out of what the publishers present as 'literature' then we will read — with less and less pretence of concealment — what we call 'thrillers'." [11]

The remainder of the essay shows how vague the line is between tragedy and melodrama, and how the elements of melodrama are to be found in some proportion in all fiction. It is fiction for which the craving exists, although the flavor of melodrama may heighten the zest or reach the less sensitive taste.

Plato asked what use poetry might have in a well-ordered state. Aristotle begins to answer this question by showing two human needs which poetry can serve, and universally does serve. Men have emotions. Emotions are aroused either by art or by life itself; if aroused by art — and one of the objections Plato brought against poetry was that it aroused the emotions — they can be properly purged. Men desire to contemplate, to be "spectators of all time and all existence." In a sense all men have the desire to become philosophers, but few can satisfy it. [12] For the many there is poetry, which can exist in all degrees of complexity and subtlety, and can be an object of contemplation for those who do not rise above the level of imagination. Purgation and contemplation can be used to name two values which poetry has for man because it is an imitation of human action. These are extrinsic to the aesthetic values of a poem as a work of art. These are moral values and, as such, are for the statesman to weigh when he considers the place of poetry, and of the arts in general, in society. Plato recognized that music and the drama were *amusements* for the people, but he did not analyze the nature of an amusement. To amuse, as a work of art amuses, is not simply to give pleasure; wine and warmth also give pleasure [21]. A work of art amuses in a way that is peculiar to its nature as an imitation: it amuses by arousing and purging the emotions and by being an object of contemplation, by creating its audience as spectators. These two values are integrally related, since both follow from the imitative nature of art: it is only a spectator whose emotions can be aroused in order to be purged. This analysis can be briefly summarized: viewed intrinsically or aesthetically, all the fine arts are species of the

[11] *Selected Essays, 1917–1932*, New York, 1932: pg. 373.
[12] The philosopher, Plato says, is "the spectator of all time and all existence." *Republic*, 486.

genus *imitation*; viewed extrinsically or politically, all the fine arts are species of the genus *amusement*. There are other species in this genus, such public spectacles as circuses and games, pageants and parades; and we shall later consider their intrinsic nature as imitations. It is enough for the moment to see that the problem of poetry and politics is a special case of the problem of the political values, both positive and negative, of amusements or entertainments of any sort [21a].

It may be objected that we have ignored the arts as agencies of public education. The objection is only partly valid. To the extent that works of art are objects of contemplation and satisfy the desire to learn, they are educative, but this is intellectual education and not moral training. Even this statement must be qualified because the fine arts do not educate the intellect as science and philosophy do. They do not form its speculative virtues. The distinction between intellectual and moral education can be made in terms of their ends: the cultivation of the intellectual virtues, on the one hand, and of the moral virtues, on the other. To the extent that the moral virtues are independent of certain types of speculative knowledge and conversely, a man can be educated in one respect without being educated in the other [22]. We have so far ignored the fine arts as vehicles of moral education because to educate in this way is not a property of fine art; it does not follow from its nature as do the values of purgation and contemplation. If it is objected that the purgation of the passions and aesthetic pleasure contribute toward the conduct of a good life, it should be readily admitted that to this extent the fine arts do their share in helping to make men good, which is the aim of moral education. But this does not mean that as such they are instruments of moral education, any more than they are instruments of speculative instruction because they provide men with objects of contemplation. The arts may in fact cultivate the moral virtues or corrupt them, but if they do so it is an accidental and not a proper consequence of their nature. The extent to which a particular work of art succeeds in purging the emotions it arouses, or the extent to which it wins an aesthetic and not a sensual reception, is a question of fact which cannot be answered by an analysis of the nature of art. In exactly the same way, the extent to which a particular work of art helps to cultivate or to corrupt the moral virtues is a question of fact which cannot be answered analytically. Questions of fact must be separated from analytical questions. Though upon analysis the properties of art appear to be beneficial, the arts may nevertheless be more of a hindrance, may work more harm than good. This is a question of fact, and must be answered as such. Plato either *assumed* the answer to this question or supposed that the question was an analytical one. In the latter case, the crucial difference between him and Aristotle turns on the analysis of the nature of art. No less, perhaps, it depends upon their different conceptions of virtue and the relation of the moral to the intellectual virtues.

Before we turn to the *Ethics* and *Politics* to discover how in the context of an analysis of practical problems Aristotle treats the arts as amusements, there are a number of points made in the *Poetics* which are peculiarly relevant to the political evaluation of poetry as amusement.

Aristotle tries to prevent the misconception that because poetry is an imitation of human action, it must necessarily be "true to life" in one or another silly sense of that phrase. He has distinguished poetry from history in terms of the possible and the actual. But both the possible and the actual can be probable, and those who ask that fiction be "true to life" are asking for a high degree of probability or verisimilitude. We are reminded by the dramatist Agathon, Aristotle points out, that "it is probable that many things should happen contrary to probability." [13] It is because this is often the case in life, that it can be stranger than fiction. But what, then, does it mean to demand that fiction be "true to life"? Although poetry narrates the possible, the poet "should prefer probable impossibilities to improbable possibilities." Although the plot must not be composed of irrational and inconsequential parts, "once the irrational has been introduced, and an air of likelihood given to it, we must accept it in spite of the absurdity. . . The absurdity is veiled by the poetic charm with which the poet invests it." [14] The paradoxical quality of these statements is removed if one remembers that fiction imitates things as they are, as they should be, or as men say or think they are. Thus, the impossible can be "justified by reference to artistic requirements, or

[13] *Poetics*, 18, 1456ª24.   [14] *Poetics*, 24, 1460ª26-1460ᵇ2.

to the higher reality, or to received opinion." [15] We must recognize that the impossible is sometimes ideal, and in this sense
surpasses reality; the irrational is sometimes what is commonly
said to be the case.

This is the full answer to those who, like Plato, accuse the
poet of telling lies, of not being true to life; the charge has been
made repeatedly against novels and plays and movies; those who
make it seldom understand the various senses in which fiction can
be true. Aristotle goes even further, insisting that the element of
the wonderful, even though it be a lie and irrational, is required
in tragedy and the epic, in short, in all fiction.[16] The lie must,
of course, be told skilfully — as Homer has taught all the poets
to do — to "invest it with poetic charm." It is required not because it is a lie or irrational, but because it is wonderful, and
therefore pleasing. That the wonderful is pleasing may be in-
ferred, says Aristotle, from "the fact that every one tells a story
with some addition of his own, knowing that his hearers like
it." [17] He is here making the same point that Mr. T. S. Eliot
makes in the essay in which he insists that melodrama is an essential element of all fiction. The melodramatic is the wonderful;
it is essential because, as Mr. Eliot concludes: "We cannot afford to forget that the first — and not one of the least difficult —
requirements of either prose or verse, is that it should be interesting." [18]

Aristotle reviews the several grounds on which poetry can be
criticized.[19] He distinguishes between criticism of a story in
terms which are essential to its nature as a story, and criticism
in terms of what is utterly accidental, such as that the story is
"not true to fact." We must not criticize fictional narrative for
what it does not pretend to be; technical inaccuracies about
anatomy are wrong in a medical treatise, but not in a story.
"The standard of correctness is not the same in poetry as in politics." He might have added morals. Irrational and depraved
characters in fiction are to be censured only "when there is no
inner necessity for introducing them." The problem here is
one of poetic effect; moral standards are not relevant in the judgment of the intrinsic nature of a poem. The character is good
if it is good consistently in its own type; "even a woman may

[15] *Poetics*, 25, 1461[b]9–15. [16] Vd. *Poetics*, 1460[a]12–19.
[17] *Poetics*, 24, 1460[a]12–25. [18] *Op. cit.*, pg. 382. [19] Vd. *Poetics*, 25.

be good, and also a slave; though a woman may be said to be an inferior being, and a slave quite worthless." Impropriety must be avoided, but this is not moral impropriety, but poetic; thus "there is a type of manly valor; but valor in a woman, or unscrupulous cleverness, is inappropriate." [20] However much one may disagree with Aristotle's particular illustrations in the light of our current prejudices, the principle is clear. We must *separate* the intrinsic and extrinsic criticism of poetry. And the intrinsic criticism of poetry, like moral criticism, is casuistical. "In examining whether what has been said or done by someone in a story is poetically right or not, we must not look merely to the particular act or saying, and ask whether it is poetically good or bad. We must also consider by whom it is said or done, to whom, when, by what means, and for what end." [21]

Fiction in any of its forms can also be criticized extrinsically, from the political and moral points of view. Whether or not it is morally hurtful is one of the criteria listed among the sources of criticism.[22] This one criterion summarizes all of extrinsic criticism. The casuistical question is: does the work of art in question have greater positive or greater negative moral value, does it cause more good or evil? This may be interpreted as the Platonic question, whether the arts cultivate or corrupt the moral virtues. But in the context of the Aristotelian analysis that question must not be asked as though it were an essential function of art to teach. Whether the moral virtues can or cannot be taught, it is not the business of the fine arts to teach them or, as a matter of fact, to teach anything. They are not instruments of instruction, moral or intellectual. This does not mean that men may not learn from literature, in the same way that they learn from life; but then art "teaches" only in the sense in which all experience teaches. Nor does it mean that the arts may not have a bad moral effect because they overexcite the passions or misinform the mind or that they may not have a good moral effect because they purge the passions and give men the pleasure of contemplation. But whatever effect they do have must not be attributed to the arts as essentially didactic. The issue between Plato and Aristotle here with regard to their influence upon the moral virtues turns on *how* the arts are

[20] *Poetics*, 25, 1454ª19–25.   [21] *Poetics*, 25, 1461ª4–9.
[22] *Poetics*, 25, 1461ᵇ22–25.

influential.   If it were the business of the arts to teach morally or
intellectually, they could be easily condemned by an analytic
comparison with obviously better methods of teaching.   This
is the principle of the Platonic condemnation.   If accidentally
they do have a didactic influence which is bad or if accidentally
they do corrupt moral character in some other way, they should
still be condemned but the condemnation must then rest upon
an ascertainment of the facts.   The Aristotelian question is
casuistical.   It looks to the facts of the particular case.

We have already noted that the values of poetry as amusement
are discovered by viewing it in relation to its audience.   In this
connection Aristotle recognizes the levels of capacity in men:
all men enjoy contemplation, but not all men are philosophers.
This observation is of primary importance to a political view of
the arts.   Plato at some places too narrowly conceives the problem of education in terms of one class in society; poetry may be
unnecessary for the select soul who has the gifts for philosophy.
But the statesman must recognize that men are heterogeneous in
their abilities.   Whatever class distinctions he may seek to impose upon society, or whatever class distinctions he may seek
to remove, he must not commit the folly of denying the classes
of men which exist by nature.   That all men are not born equal
in capacity to learn, to contemplate, to think, or to enjoy art,
is a maxim of the *Poetics* as well as of the *Politics*.   The political
function of the artist is to serve his audience, and there are many
levels of audience in human society.   Aesthetically, the poetry
which is for the select few may be better than popular poetry —
the novel, the play, or the motion picture which is for the great
populace.   It *may* be, but is not *necessarily* so.   Politically,
only popular poetry is important; the statesman need not concern himself with the private enjoyments of the few, but he
must consider the public amusements of the multitude.   Aristotle is, therefore, not contemptuous of the poet who seeks to
please the large audience, who tries to hit the popular taste, as
those who are devoted to art for art's sake always are.   He is
at the same time able to praise Agathon, who is skilful in this
respect,[23] and to defend Euripides from censure for introducing
the unhappy ending, even though this was contrary to popular
taste, because it conformed better to the intrinsic nature of

23 *Poetics*, 18, 1456ᵃ18–22.

tragedy.[24]   He discusses the relative merits of epic and tragic poetry, what for us would be the novel and the play.[25]   Here he points out that the epic is, in one sense, better, because it does not use the spectacular effects which tragedies employ to arouse the emotions of low audiences; but, in another sense, the tragedy is better because it can dispense with spectacle and achieve its effects within narrower limitations than the epic. Throughout this discussion he recognizes that "the poet is guided in what he writes by the wishes of his audience."   To deny this would be to deny the political function of art; it must amuse, whether the many or the few.   To assert it is not to confuse the human quality of the audience which is entertained, with the aesthetic quality of the art which performs this function [23].

We are thus prepared for the transition from the *Poetics* to the *Ethics* and *Politics*.   We have seen that one of the ends of poetry, as of all other arts, is to amuse.   But amusement is not an end in itself.   The consideration of the ends which amusement in turn serves as a means now becomes the focal point of our discussion.   The moral and political value of amusement is as a means; what the statesman does about poetry should be determined by the ends he seeks to achieve and the value of poetry as a means thereto.

Aristotle conceives ethics and politics as practical sciences, relatively inexact, uncertain, and correlated with each other as are the private and public aspects of human life [24].   A practical science consists of the leading principles and the relevant knowledge which must be employed in the intelligent solution of problems of action.   It analyzes the problems of conduct and of statesmanship in terms of series of means and ends, and enables deliberation to apply knowledge in the choice of means to a desired end which may, in turn, be desired as a means to a further end.   Men must act in singular and unique situations with respect to contingent things of which they can have only inadequate knowledge.   However certain be the most general principles which guide human conduct, the rules for action in particular types of situations are necessarily inexact because our knowledge is not adequate to make a conclusive determination of the one right way; and even less exact is the reasoning which

[24] *Poetics*, 13, 1453ª24–30.   [25] Vd. *Poetics*, 26.

decides to act one way or another in the particular case. Aristotle is everywhere cognizant that ethical and political theory can issue in practice only through relatively uncertain rules and the ambivalent deliberations of casuistry by which they must be applied. This leads him to the general principle of relativity in ethics and politics; there is one kind of life which is the best that is possible for any man to lead, but there are many different types of men, and appropriate to their natures there is a way of life which is good for them. Similarly, there may be one kind of government which is the best possible state, but according to the character of the men who are the members of a society, and according to a large number of other factors, geographical, economic, and so forth, which vary with time and place, there is a kind of political organization and social order which is good for one society and not for another. Where Plato is concerned primarily with the ideal and considers the actual only as something to measure for its imperfections, Aristotle views the varieties of the actual in human nature and human society in terms of degrees of appropriate perfection. Practical choices must be determined not by the best that is possible absolutely, but by the best that is possible for us in the peculiar situation of our lives, and according to the limitations of our capacities. And the best that is possible for even the best man is not perfection; human happiness cannot be better than human nature. The differences between Plato and Aristotle on particular points must be understood in the light of this fundamental difference in their approach to ethical and political questions [25].

Yet, one must not expect systematic divergence throughout. Like Plato, Aristotle holds that education is the work of the state. It is the statesman's responsibility for the moral training of his citizens, whether by law or by other devices, which unites the treatise on ethics with the one on politics. In the last pages of the *Ethics*, he insists that the formation of the virtuous character cannot be left either to the chance of nature and habit or to the discipline of the home; the authority of a father does not possess enough force or compulsion. "It is best then that the state should undertake the control of these matters," but — and here is Aristotle's principle of the relative good — "if the state altogether neglects it, it would seem to be the duty of every citizen to further the cause of virtue in his own children and friends, or at least to set before himself the purpose of furthering it." [26]   Aristotle admits that it is only in Sparta and a few other states that the legislator seems to have undertaken to control the nurture and pursuits of the citizens.   The reason why it is better for the legislator to control these matters is that he *should* be one who knows the general rules applicable to all people or to people of a particular kind ; if he doesn't, he is no better than the ordinary father who tries to train his children without well-founded precepts or principles.   There is no incompatibility, furthermore, between individualism in education, which recognizes the need to adapt the rules to the circumstances of the particular case, and the advantages to be achieved by having rules to adapt, rules which are scientific in the sense that they are based on general knowledge that is practically applicable.[27]   Thus, while Aristotle does not insist that the training of citizens by the state is *always* preferable to domestic rearing under private and paternal control, he does assert that if laws are properly a means for making men good, the principles of legislation should be learned by those who attempt the task, and the responsibility for moral education belongs properly to the legislator.   We shall find that even this cautious position must suffer further qualification and restriction.

The aim of education is to cultivate the good man, and this must be understood in terms of the cultivation of the body, the formation of moral character, *i.e.*, the acquisition of the virtues, and the instruction of the intellect, *i.e.*, the acquisition of prudence, knowledge and wisdom.   The order of education is indicated by these divisions : we take care of the body for the sake of the soul ; we discipline the non-rational part of the soul, the appetites and the passions, for the sake of the mind.[28]   But whereas we know the techniques of gymnastic and we possess the science of medicine for the proper care of the body, and whereas the only absolute pre-requisite for intellectual education is the intelligence of the student and the knowledge of the teacher, the principles and conditions of moral training cannot be so simply or so easily formulated.   Here Aristotle faces Plato's questions : whether and how the virtues can be taught. He sees at once that there are three sources of virtuous character :

[26] *Ethics*, X, 1180ª30.   [27] *Ethics*, X, 1180ᵇ4–25.   [28] *Politics*, VII, 1134ᵇ6–27.

nature, habit or custom, and reason or intelligence. The gifts of nature, like the gifts of the gods, are beyond human control; reason or intelligence is susceptible of influence by reason or intelligence, but that is not enough to form the right habits because the emotions which must be disciplined seldom submit to reason. They require force and compulsion or, in other words, the rule of law. The philosopher, he says, does from wisdom what other men do from fear of the laws, and most men are not philosophers. It follows, therefore, "that the nurture and pursuits of the young should be regulated by law." [29]

Aristotle knows that young men cannot learn to be good men by studying ethics. For one thing, they do not have enough experience to judge well, to discover or apply the premises of moral reasoning; for another, as a result of their youthful "tendency to follow their emotions, they will not study the subject to any purpose or profit, as its end is not knowledge but action." [30] The *Ethics* is, therefore, not written for young men of unstable character and insufficient knowledge and experience, but for old men, the fathers and the leaders of the state, who still have the problem of using it to train young men. But how? Aristotle recognizes in the *Politics* that laws are not enough, although he does not explicitly define the limitations of law. The only other means is education, and among the instruments of education are the arts. The consideration of education and the role of the arts therein occurs at the end of the *Politics*. This treatise comes to us unfinished; it breaks off abruptly. It is difficult to suppress the suspicion that Aristotle was stopped by questions he could not answer. Let us, however, examine the answers that are given.

Life, says Aristotle, is divided into labor and rest.[31] The politician who composes a body of laws ought, therefore, extend his views to both. The citizens should be fitted for rest and peace, as much as, if not more than, for labor and war. It is to these objects that the education of children ought to tend. The legislator who did not teach his citizens how to rest would be greatly at fault; many social disorders arise from this failure. This points to the utility of the arts in education and in the social life of the state. The great importance of music — and music here includes poetry — is that it prepares men to enjoy

[29] *Ethics*, X, 1179^{b}20–35.   [30] *Ethics*, I, 1095^{a}2–9.   [31] *Politics*, VII, 1333^{a}30–40.

their leisure honorably.[32]   Play or amusement is not an end in itself, but it is a necessary means of relaxation from labor. "Play is more necessary for those who labor than for those who are at rest, for he who labors requires relaxation which play will supply; for as labor is attended with pain and continued exertion, it is necessary that play should be introduced under proper regulations as a medicine; for such an employment of the mind is a relaxation to it, and eases with pleasure."[33]

Relaxation and fun, Aristotle had said in the *Ethics*, are indispensable elements of human life.[34]   They are not the ends of life, but are necessary means; we do not live for amusement but for activity; since we cannot work forever or be always active, we need relaxation.[35]   Amusement is a kind of relaxation.   Relaxation is recreative because it prepares us for more work and activity.   In the *Politics*, Aristotle considers the arts, along with games and sleep and wine, as means of relaxation or recreation.[36]   We have already seen how the nature of the arts as imitative leads to their purgative effect and their satisfaction of the desire to contemplate, thus making men spectators rather than actors.   But whether as a participant in games or watching them, whether as a creator in the arts or as an audience of them, men are at play rather than at work, and are, therefore, relaxed from the cares of life and recreated for its further burdens.   In terms of our problem, we shall consider men primarily in the position of spectators.   Wine and sleep can then be seen to cause recreation differently from the arts and games.   The latter do not require participation; they enable men to become spectators and, as spectators, to be entertained or amused.

Aristotle thus meets Plato's challenge to the poets to show their political utility and their place in a well-ordered state. He does so by recognizing that poetry and the arts do not serve one purpose only, but many;[37] among these purposes, the arts are unquestionably of great positive moral value in one respect: no one doubts, he says, that being sources of amusement, they provide men with relaxation which is indispensable.   But the arts must also be considered in relation to their other ends: the

---

[32] *Politics*, VIII, 1339[b]10-40.   [33] *Politics*, VIII, 1337[b]35-40; also 1337[b]29-35.
[34] *Ethics*, IV, 1128[b]2.   [35] Vd. *Ethics*, X, 1176[b]27-35.
[36] Vd. *Politics*, VIII, 1339[a]11-29.   [37] *Politics*, VIII, 1341[b]35-40.

instruction and the improvement of the soul.   A Platonist might object that although the arts do provide pleasure and amusement, and hence relaxation, the pleasure given is far from harmless, and the bad moral effects overbalance the value of amusement as a means to relaxation.   While not denying the inescapable need for relaxation and rest, he would argue that other means should be sought than those, such as the arts, which have seriously undesirable consequences.

Aristotle faces this objection when he himself asks whether poetry and music tend to be productive of virtue, whether they are of any assistance to prudence in the conduct of life.[38]   On the point of whether the arts tend in any way to improve our manners and our soul, he considers primarily music and poetry because, as he says, these arts are imitations of human life, of its actions and passions.   First of all, he points out that the pleasure which the arts afford is harmless because it is accompanied by purgation; music or poetry "which has the power of purifying the soul affords a harmless pleasure to man."   Such harmless pleasures are conducive to the final end of life.[39]   The objection, that music and poetry are dangerous pleasures because they excite the passions, is thus met.   But on the other point, whether music and poetry improve or degrade manners, whether they are productive of virtue or vice, his answer is not clear. He says that it must be admitted that *in some cases* music has the bad effects which are ascribed to it; but what these bad effects are is not definitely described, nor is it indicated whether the number of cases is large enough to concern the statesman.[40] Can one conclude from Aristotle's silence on this point, that he recognized his ignorance of the matters of fact involved; that he did not know the answer to the question about the effects of poetry or music upon virtue and vice, and that, unlike Plato, he would not assume it or make practical recommendations on the basis of opinion? [41]

The practical recommendations he does make are, therefore,

38 Vd. *Politics*, VIII, 1339ᵃ11–1340ᵇ19.
39 "Those pleasures which are harmless are not only conducive to the final end of life, but serve also as relaxations; and as men are but rarely in the attainment of that final end, they often cease from their labor and apply to amusement, with no further view than to acquire the pleasure attending it." *Politics*, VIII, 1339ᵇ25–30.   40 *Politics*, VIII, 1340ᵇ40–1341ᵃ9.
41 *Ethics*, X, 1179ᵃ16–20 : the facts are decisive in practical affairs.

both few and cautious; they stand in sharp contrast to Plato's complete regulation of the arts, not only for children but for all citizens, and especially to his utter banishment of the dramatists and the theatre from the state. Aristotle limits the political control of the arts to the regulation of them in the education of young children. He says no more, however, than that their governors and preceptors "should take care of what tales and stories it may be proper for them to hear," just as they should supervise the games that children play, the company they keep, and in general, the manner of their life.[42] As for the theatre, Aristotle, far from prohibiting it, only recommends that it be made illegal for young persons to be present "before they are arrived at an age when they are allowed to partake of the pleasures of the table"; indeed, he adds, "a good education will preserve them from all the evils which attend on these things."[43] Aristotle's statement that the young should not be permitted to attend the theatre has often been cited by the Platonic opponents of the stage, but they have seldom, if ever, announced that the statement occurs in the context of a chapter devoted to the care of the child up to the age of seven [26]. The word 'young' has a useful ambiguity for those who quote out of context. It is clear that Aristotle does not have to justify cautious recommendations such as these by definite knowledge of the moral effects of music and poetry; common sense is all that one needs to propose or to concur in the policy of keeping children under the age of seven from the theatre, or in advising their guardians to be careful of the stories they hear.

Thus, Aristotle, agreeing with Plato about the duty of the state in the field of education, seems to disagree sharply about the extent to which he would control the social influence of the arts, particularly music and poetry.[44] He sees that the arts

---

[42] *Politics*, VII, 1336ᵃ22–33.   [43] *Politics*, VII, 1336ᵇ20–24.

[44] This does not mean that Aristotle is unaware that the arts may corrupt the young. We should not permit indecent speeches on the stage, he says; youth should be kept strangers to all that is bad, and especially to things which suggest vice and hate. (*Politics*, 1336ᵇ12, 34.) But in these remarks he is concerned only with the influence of the arts upon the very young. Furthermore, he not only suggests some regulation of the theatre, on the one hand, but also promises to consider how far the liberty of attendance should be permitted to children. The *Politics* is unfinished and this promise is unfulfilled; but it indicates how far Aristotle is from recommending the banishment of

can perform two major functions: (1) they can provide amusement which is a means of relaxation and recreation, and this is a moral and a social good; (2) they may affect public manners and morals in a desirable or an undesirable way. With respect to the first function, it is clear that the arts have great positive value, especially music and poetry. They are enjoyed by the multitude, and the pleasure and excitement this entails is harmless because emotions aroused in men *as spectators* are emotions purged. With respect to the second function, our knowledge is so vague and indefinite that we cannot say whether they have great or little, positive or negative, value. In the light of such knowledge about the actual functions of the arts in society, what would a man having practical wisdom and prudence propose as a course of action? Certainly not what Plato proposed in the case of the dramatists, action too drastic to be practically wise, if prudence requires us to act moderately in the light of knowledge. Aristotle's policy is a better approximation to prudence. Care should be taken about the kinds of music and poetry which are *used* in the education of the young; but the same limitations should not be placed upon the music that is performed for the entertainment of the adult population, or upon the popular theatre, where the aim is to please the audience according to its natural capacities, to entertain and amuse it, to give it recreation. "As the audience is composed of two sorts of people, the free and the well-instructed, the rude, the mean mechanics, and hired servants, and a long collection of the like, there must be some music and some spectacles to please and soothe them; for as their minds are, as it were, perverted from their natural habits, so also is there an unnatural harmony and overcharged music which is to their taste; but what is according to nature gives pleasure to everyone; therefore those who contend upon the theatre should be allowed to use this species of music. But in education, ethic melody and ethic harmony should be used."[45] In short, music and

---

poets because there is a problem about the place of the arts in the moral training of young children. His emphasis seems to be upon the care of the child rather than upon the regulation of the arts. "The Directors of Education should be careful what tales or stories the children hear" (*Politics*, 1336[a]30). He nowhere says that the statesman should determine what stories the poets should write.

[45] *Politics*, VIII, 1342[a]19–31.

poetry are viewed differently according to the different purposes they serve: education or recreation, training the young
or providing pleasure and amusement to the masses in a manner
that is appropriate to their nature [27].

We can now review the issue between Plato and Aristotle.
Aristotle's position depends crucially upon his theory of the
arts, in their political aspect, as amusements. It is this which
enables him to answer Plato's question about the utility of
poetry in a well-ordered state. But the notion of amusement
which is harmless because it is purgative, and good because
it is recreative, in turn depends upon the theory of purgation
and the conception of the spectator as one who is rested by the
pleasure of contemplation from the weariness of practical life.
We must, therefore, see whether the Aristotelian notion of
amusement and all that it involves rests upon a sound psychological foundation.

The genus recreation includes, as we have seen, sleep and
wine as well as amusements; and amusement is itself a genus
which includes athletic games, circuses, and public pageants, as
well as the fine arts. The intrinsic nature of an amusement
is to be an imitation, in which case the fine arts are only one
species of imitation. We shall not attempt here to differentiate
the class of things which includes athletic games and parades,
on the one hand, from the class which includes music, the drama,
and the motion picture, on the other. We are concerned rather
with their generic similarity. In all of them there is the distinction between the participant, whether he be called a performer or a producer or an artist, and the spectator. The
generation of the arts and games out of more primitive social
and religious rituals occurs at the point at which the spectator
is separated from the participant [28]. The nature of the
ritual as imitation is not discerned until the spectator arises;
it is imitation for him because he is a spectator. And because
the imitation allows him to be a spectator of it, he gets rest
from action and work. He enjoys an impractical moment.
But he gets more than simple rest; sleep and also wine as a
soporific yield that. Simple rest is negative, but the enjoyment of the spectator is a positive pleasure; it is not only a relief
from work but it is a relief from dullness and boredom, which
causes greater weariness and restlessness than mere fatigue.

The reason is that imitations amuse by exciting the emotions, the cure for dullness and boredom, and at the same time by purging the soul of them, because the emotions aroused occur in the posture of contemplation and not of action. Life itself is practically exciting, and therefore wearisome, or practically unexciting, and therefore boring. Amusements are impractically exciting, and are therefore neither, but recreate vitality to replace that which has been spent.

I am aided in my analysis of purgation by M. Alain,[46] a contemporary French commentator on the arts and a student of Kant and Aristotle, whose theories converge on this point. I shall try to state this analysis in the language of Aristotle's psychology.

"To purge" in its bluntest sense means "to get rid of." This is its basic medical meaning as well. The body may be purged of its poisons and excesses either naturally, in the course of normal vegetative activity, or it may be necessary to administer artificial purgatives. The artist, in this case, is the doctor. Analogically, the soul may be naturally purged of its passions by action. Each emotion or passion, according to the state it puts the body in, determines a certain uniform class of actions which are usually consequent upon it when that passion can no longer be restrained or controlled, and overflows. In the extreme cases of violent and uncontrolled passion, the purgation may take the form of any action whatsoever; as, for instance, when we are wildly angry, we move vigorously in any direction, we do anything we can so long as we can do it with a certain violence. To complete the analogy: the passions may be artificially purged by being artificially aroused; this is like the purgative administered by the physician which, in some cases, though not all, stimulates the excess which it wishes to relieve. But passions which are artificially aroused, that is, excited by imitations, works of art or games, do not issue forth in the usual patterns of action or with the violence of undirected vigor. Art purges the passions by deceiving them. It arouses them — the mystery of how it does this is the mystery of imitation itself — and then gives them no object with respect to which action can be directed; it seldom arouses them so

[46] Alain (Jacques-Emile Chartier), *Système des Beaux-Arts*, Paris, 1926; *Vingt Leçons sur les Beaux-Arts*, Paris, 1931.

violently that they overflow into indiscriminate violence; if it does, it fails, of course, as purgation.   Because art is imitation, the emotions which it creates in the spectator become part of the spectacle, and are thus understood rather than expended in impulse and activity.   The situations of life which excite emotions make action both possible and necessary; but imitations excite emotions and make action for a time, at least, both impossible and unnecessary.   The soul is thus relieved.   This relief is its catharsis.   And it is intrinsically pleasant, as no purging action ever can be, because action which follows upon passion usually leaves new passions in its wake, as shame follows the explosive actions we commit when angry.   The body walks out of a theatre showing none of the usual effects of passion, but gesticulating pleasantly in the pleasure of its relief from shameful action [29].

The mechanism of artificial purgation follows simply from the nature of imitation as involving likeness and difference. The likeness in the imitation allows participation, and is thus responsible for the excitation which makes what is happening in some fashion happen to oneself.   The difference in the imitation makes for impersonality; or, to put it another way, it allows one to contemplate oneself as an excited spectator of the exciting spectacle, and in this viewing of the soul by itself, understanding is achieved and the emotions are purged.   The soul is both a spectator of the spectacle and a spectator of itself; the reason views the passions as they are aroused by an artificial object, the imitation.   Artificial purgation thus brings order into the soul and cures the disorder which the latent passions always threaten to create.

This disorder occurs when the passions are uncontrollable by reason.   Passions in the disordered soul — passions uncontrolled by reason, not submissive to a prudent will — yield irrational actions as their consequences in the natural effort to purge themselves.   Such actions are in every sense immoral, since the basic, essential trait of all moral action is that it be governed by reason and prudence.   The purgation of the passions through such actions gives the state the problem of crime, the parent the problem of misbehavior in children, and the person who is acting the problem in conscience of his own character, since vices are habits and one becomes vicious by doing vicious things.

Ethically, then, and, of course, politically, the natural purging of disordered passions through the actions which such passions lead to, is clearly undesirable [30].

But no man is perfectly rational, which means that every man has disordered passions to a greater or less degree. Every man needs to learn the discipline of submitting passions to reason. But just as the passions in every man are in varying stages of violence and uncontrol, so the reason of every man is in varying stages of weakness and undevelopment. It is in this situation, in which all men find themselves, that the arts and other imitations perform their valuable political and moral function. It is not the case that man, with no burden of uncontrolled passion, seeks out music or the theatre in order, through the excitation there, to acquire such a burden. If it were, the Platonic objection to the arts as arousing emotions would hold, because it would be both needless and harmful; it would make an ordered soul disordered. But that is not the case; quite the contrary; every man has his burden and he takes it to the theatre or to games — to any imitation which as a spectacle converts him into a spectator — for artificial purging, and thus saves himself from the natural purge of uncommendable actions. The impractical excitation of emotions dissipates them impractically. This is purgation, and it is good, because for the time being — and the medicine must be renewed with a frequency determined by the individual need — threatening disorder has been avoided. It is no objection to the goodness of purgation in itself to say that a person may rely upon it too much instead of making the effort of reason in self-discipline. Medicine taken in overdoses can become a poison or a drug; too much sleep and too much food are also bad [31]. Furthermore, in the matter of acquiring virtue, too much reliance upon the power of reason is a too pious hope. How did Plato and Aristotle answer the question whether virtue can be taught? Aristotle, at one place taking the extreme position that reason is never able to control the emotions, looks to law with its sanctions of force and compulsion.[47] But he knew and we know the ineffectiveness of law. What the laws fail to do negatively by restraints, the arts may be able to do positively by catharsis: that is, aid reason in its unequal struggle with

[47] *Ethics*, X, 1179^{b}30–1180^{a}5.

the passions. That is their basic utility, not in a well-ordered
state, but in a state which strives to be well-ordered.

M. Alain, with great insight and sensitivity, sees the marks
of imitation and the spectacle in many corners of our social
life, and not only in its obvious place among the arts and its
even more obvious locus in the theatre. Such natural events as
public executions, murder trials, fires, mob demonstrations, as
well as such events as parades and pageants which have artistic
direction, are spectacles, and as spectacles are imitations for their
audiences, and effect purgation of the emotions they excite.[48]
Thus, in the public execution, what functions psychologically
for the difference which every imitation must have, is the victim's disconnection from one's self. He is not felt as a human
being to whom something is really happening; one doesn't know
him; one doesn't care much about the consequences of his feelings and actions. Because he is *like* a human being, we suffer
pity and terror; because he is *different* from a human being — a
human being is somebody we know and love — we enjoy those
feelings contemplatively and are, at that terribly low and
ghastly level, purged of them. The murderer on trial or being
hanged is no more a human being than the bull-fighter; and only
slightly more so than the actor in a melodrama. M. Alain is
not ignoring the great range of difference between a murder-
trial or bull-fight and a Greek tragedy. He is merely insisting
upon their common character as spectacles at which the spectator knows himself to be a spectator. The Greek tragedy at
its best is the best sort of spectacle, achieving its perfection by
means of a chorus which offers itself as a sort of model for the
spectator. The emotions of the chorus are aroused and purged,
and the spectacle thus includes the image of a spectator already
purified.

Though this be the case, one art is not *extrinsically* preferable
to another. Whatever works purgation for a given audience
is good as spectacle for that audience. Men are bored with
their animal life, the dullness of its practical turns and issues,
and according to their varying capacities, get the relief of excitement and purgation from different kinds of spectacles, as
well as from those works of art which they enjoy in intimate

[48] On this level, newspapers are literature, i.e., fiction, rather than contemporary history, for most of their readers.

privacy, such as the novel. In all, a certain sublimity is tasted. In all spectacles, in all art, there is something superhuman; in the performance of the juggler, the acrobat, the wrestler, as well as in the tragedy or the symphony. Those who find this sublimity in the boxing match may be judged of poorer quality as men than those who find it in the symphony, by standards of sensitivity and intellectual appreciation; but if those who enjoy the boxing match cannot enjoy the symphony, it is none the less good for them. One might add, as M. Alain does, that if the marvels of the high arts would show themselves as plainly as the blow which floors a man, the crowd would go to the theatre and to music as readily as to the ringside.

M. Alain's mention of the sublimity which men enjoy in spectacles and works of art permits more than a verbal translation from the Aristotelian analysis to that of Freud. I will only briefly indicate it here. Freud discovered the indispensable role which sublimation of the emotions plays in the healthy ordering of the soul. In sublimation, he rediscovered the medical value of catharsis as psychotherapy. Man living in society cannot express all his emotions in their natural directions; he is not able to control them rationally; he must not, for his health's sake, repress them irrationally. The sublimation of them is the prudent alternative; and those who fail to sublimate proportionally to their need become the disordered souls whom society must take care of in one way or another, whether in a prison, in an asylum, or in a psychoanalyst's office. Freud first saw the presence of sublimation in the activity of the artist, as Aristotle saw purgation as an effect of art. Both insights are capable of equally great generalization. Purgation is the effect of any art, of any imitation; similarly, not only the artist achieves the sublimation of his emotions, but the spectator succeeds in this as well. Those who are well acquainted with the Freudian contribution to the analysis of the passions will not only see in greater detail the translation I am here suggesting, but will also observe the way in which the Freudian discoveries complete and corroborate the Aristotelian analysis we have made so far.

The difference between Plato and Aristotle turns on this analysis of purgation. Aristotle would agree with Plato that music and poetry cannot be relied upon as influences which form the moral virtues, but he would also say that this is neither their only nor their primary value to the state. Rather they are amusement and recreation : to provide the relief of purgation for all kinds of men, the joy of contemplation for all kinds of men. Here is the heart of the difference. Plato is not thinking of all kinds of men. Plato is thinking only of men whose souls are already well ordered. In these terms, his attack upon poetry and upon the drama is perfectly sound. A good man is able to restrain and discipline his passions. The arts, and particularly the theatre, excite them unnecessarily. Hence a good man need not and should not go to the theatre. The same point can be made another way. All men desire to contemplate and thus to lift themselves above the animal level of action. For those who have the intellectual power, philosophy is the satisfaction of this desire. Plato, thinking only of philosophers, fails to see that the arts provide this same pleasure to men of more limited capacities. The philosopher can be a spectator of everything and at all times, but the ordinary man needs imitations to convert him into a spectator for the moment. Thus Plato is right. An ordered soul, the soul of a philosopher, would not respond to the arts because he does not need them, either for purgation or for contemplation. Even in the curious way in which emotions are aroused by imitations, his emotions are not aroused and there is thus no catharsis. The intent of the amusement fails with him ; he brings no burden, he seeks no escape from practice, and therefore the experience has no point for him. As M. Alain puts it : being an ordered soul, a good man, he does not become a spectator ; he is one already. Art, then, is not for the good man, the philosopher ; it has no place in a state that is *otherwise* and *already* well-ordered, because it is ruled by a philosopher, and all its citizens are philosophers. It is not enough to say, as Plato does, that the perfect society will occur when philosophers are kings ; philosophers could not rule ordinary men, either by rational persuasion or by force of laws. They could rule only philosophers, but philosophers do not need to be ruled. Plato, therefore, asked an impossible question when he challenged the poets to show their utility in a well-ordered state [32].

But Aristotle understood the question differently. What is the place of the arts in any human society which is trying to achieve *some* degree of peace and order, which lacks it because it is not composed exclusively of good men, and which will never achieve it perfectly for the same reason? Aristotle is thus concerned with the conditions of order in a state where all men are not philosophers, if any are; where most men, if not all, do what they do from fear of the law or from some degree of self-discipline in which the weakness of their reason to cope with the passions is aided by the purgations of amusement. This is a genuinely practical political question; it faces the facts as they are; and, as Aristotle says at the end of the *Ethics*, "it is the facts of life that are the tests of truth in practical matters." [49] It is not only a political matter, but ethical as well. The moral virtues are not the only goods; the practical life is not an end in itself, but for the sake of contemplation, for the sake of freedom from practice. The arts not only help reason in that discipline of the passions which constitutes the moral virtues, but provide the contemplative moment for men who cannot seize it otherwise. This is good in itself.

The basic fact which Aristotle faces is that men are neither by nature good simply nor capable, by means of their imperfect rationality, of more than an analogy to goodness. Art is not for the good man. It is properly the refuge of the people because it is the poor people, alas, who are so susceptible to disorder, so weak in reason. The good man will not go to the theatre or the bull-fight, but everybody else, that is, everybody, will. It can be hoped only that men will go to recreations which are commensurate to their need, the need created by the burden of imperfect rationality which is not the same for all men. There is a hierarchy of the arts, of imitations, which corresponds to the hierarchy of needs. The principle of the series is the degree of complexity in the imitation and the degree of capacity in the spectator: the boxing match and the bull-fight for people with a burden of elementary passions and proportional intelligence; chamber music and the tragedy for people with the burden of more subtle passions, with more refined sensitivity and, again, proportional intelligence.

The popularity of an art as an amusement cannot be taken simply as a measure of the levels of audience in the total popula-

[49] *Ethics*, X, 1179ᵃ16-20.

tion, because the principle of commensurate recreation is generally transgressed.[50]   Men seek amusement from sources which are less complex than is appropriate to their natures, because these are usually so easily available and also because — and this must not be overlooked — even in this respect men are weak. Thus the motion picture, which is clearly the most popular amusement of our day, includes in its audience a vast range of human quality, but it must not be forgotten that it also includes in the imitations it presents an extraordinarily extensive range of complexity in art.   The motion picture offers a hierarchy of recreations commensurate to a hierarchy of needs, though it falls short, perhaps, at either extreme of the series.   In any event, the political and moral problems which the motion picture or any other popular art raises, cannot be considered practically and soundly unless one remembers that a state has every kind of person in it.   For the state, purgation has the same political significance on each level.   Art does what it can for every person in the state according to his needs and talents. The state, therefore, when it understands purgation, will be grateful for even the rudest bit of imitation in it.   Far from readily embracing the *opinion* that the movies cause crime or corrupt morals, the statesman, or whoever has the interests of society at heart, might say : considering their enormous popularity and their surprisingly complex imitations, they *may* be one of our strongest means of prevention, and an aid for the multitude in leading good lives.

This is the sense of Aristotle's answer to Plato.   It does not beg the question whether the arts, particularly such popular ones as the drama and the motion picture, cause disorder in the state, crime and moral laxity.   That is a question of fact which neither Plato nor Aristotle could answer as a matter of knowledge.   Until it is properly answered, only opinions and prejudices can be urged.   There are, however, matters of fact of which we do have knowledge relevant to this practical problem :

[50] Cf. S. H. Butcher, *Aristotle's Theory of Poetry and Fine Art*, 4th Ed., London, 1932 : pp. 211–212. "Each class of audience enjoys a different kind of music and derives from the performance such pleasure as it is capable of. The inferior kind of enjoyment is not to be denied to those who can appreciate only the inferior type of music — better that they should like this music than none at all — but the lower pleasure is not to be taken as the true end of the musical art."

that amusement is a means of relaxation and recreation which is both morally and politically good; that the imperfect rationality of men gives the arts a useful function to perform; that the hierarchy of the arts is responsive to the hierarchy of needs; that human society includes all kinds of men. It was, therefore, not a hollow dialectical victory which Aristotle won over Plato. The dialectical triumph consists in the more adequate analysis of the problem of poetry and politics; but since it is a practical problem, dialectic is not enough, and Aristotle, according to his own principle in such matters, supports his argument by reference to "the facts of life" [33].

The debate between Plato and Aristotle does not, however, solve the problem for two reasons. In the first place, unanswered questions of fact remain to restrain the impetuous. In the second place, although Plato and Aristotle have magnificently outlined the dialectic of the problem — so fully that there is little more to add — subsequent intellectual and social history receives their discussion in new contexts, and the dialectic reflects new lights. It takes new turns. The first of these is Christianity.

CHAPTER THREE

Christianity

THE easiest way to effect a transition from Greek wisdom to Christian doctrine is to notice the essential affinities of Christianity with both the Platonic and the Aristotelian elements in Greek thought. We shall do this, of course, only on points relevant to the problem being considered. But, first, we must recognize alternative ways of viewing the transition itself. If we accept Christianity as a revealed religion, we must accept its teaching as divine wisdom which historically supervenes upon the unaided human wisdom of the Greeks. By divine wisdom here is meant, not God's infinite knowledge, but the wisdom which men are able to receive from God through the medium of sacred sources — knowledge of God and Providence unattainable by the activity of human powers. It is at once obvious that there can be no inconsistency or conflict between the wisdom of revealed truth and the knowledge which men possess as the result of their own efforts, since these efforts are conditioned by a nature which is itself of divine origin. In this acceptation of Christianity, it is both proper and necessary that Christian doctrine should assimilate whatever is true and sound in Greek thought [34]. Scripture, in other words, must be read and interpreted in the light of all human knowledge. If, on the other hand, we do not participate in this faith, Christianity must nevertheless be regarded as a body of teaching which has the unquestionable marks of great human wisdom. The tokens are so clear that there is no reason to be patient or

54

tolerant of those who, lacking faith, commit the brazen folly of dismissing Christianity as totally devoid of wisdom because, in the superiority of their unbelief, they presume to detect superstitions. In this second acceptation, Christian doctrine can be found incompatible with other human knowledge; it is like any other partisan in a dialectical opposition. To write a dialectical account of the Christian position with respect to poetry and politics, we are required, it may be thought, to view Christianity merely as one of many opponents joined in the issue. But this would be to ignore a higher principle of dialectic which demands that we regard Christianity precisely as it offers itself to us, namely, as a revealed religion. Otherwise dialectic is merely polemical and not a technique of understanding.

The affinity with Plato is closer. Platonic insights are nearer to the spirit of Christianity, its heart rather than its mind. From the outset Christian thought found Platonic language miraculously suited to its message. The miracle of this harmony is so astounding that the pagan philosopher becomes, at least prophetically, a Christian [34a]. Christian doctrine struggled long to assimilate Aristotle; perhaps the difficulty made the prize more valuable when it was achieved. At different periods in its long history, Christianity has been partial and emphatic in its devotion to Plato or to Aristotle, but it has seldom lost sight of their duality, and then not for long. Better than saying that Christianity struggled to assimilate Aristotle is to say that, in spirit Platonic, but on many intellectual points informed by Aristotle, Christianity strove to comprehend its own unity. To the extent that it succeeded, a higher point was reached in the dialectic between Plato and Aristotle than they themselves attained.

The affinity with Plato will be seen by those who find implicit in the New Testament that Christ banishes all but Himself as teacher in His Kingdom, as Plato banished all but himself, the philosopher king, from his Republic. As Plato sought to make all men philosophers and objected to the poets as rivals and as obstacles to his attempt — the poets dangerously seductive because they insinuated the spiritual and the rational for the immature, where the immature live, in the sensible world; so Christ lived to make men Christian by imitation of His way of life, itself a miraculous imitation, in this world, of Divinity.

The Church that is founded upon Christ must object to all other imitations, to all other spectacles. The poet is a rival of the priest in Christianity as he is a rival of the philosopher in the Republic [35].

There is also the asceticism which in varying degrees is to be found in Plato and in Christian teaching. The antagonism of the flesh and the spirit is no less in Plato than in St. Paul. As Plato finds no good in the emotions so long as they answer to the senses and motivate the body, and offers, since they exist and cannot be blindly denied, philosophy as the only right way of sublimating them; so St. Paul denounces the passions as bondage to the things of this world, and offers love through faith and hope in Christ as the only path to the Kingdom of God. In neither case are the passions as such denied; in both they must die to be replaced by a spiritual love. The opposition between the emotions and the reason gives way to the more profound opposition between two loves, two opposed directions which can be given all the passions, unified under the concept of desire: the love of this world and the love of God. The arts by their very nature would seem to arouse the emotions in the wrong direction, to foster love for the things of this world. It was inevitable that primitive Christianity should see the matter this way; to see it any other way is more difficult and requires a sophistication that is slowly won against the charge that the original position, in its clarity and simplicity, is avoided only by specious subtlety. Primitive Christianity did not compromise.

It may be objected that Christian asceticism in denouncing the flesh means sex, in considering the passions, stresses carnal concupiscence above all others; whereas, in contrast, the Greek discussion of these problems has no such bias, pity and fear being as frequently named as anger and love. While this is true for Aristotle, it is not so for Plato, and the *rapprochement* of Plato and Christianity is freshly confirmed. The *Symposium* and the *Phaedrus* are valuable evidence on the point. It must not be thought, however, that Plato is exclusively concerned with sexual emotion in his attention to the passions; nor is Christianity, of course; carnal concupiscence is only one of the sins of intemperance. Nevertheless, it is historically true that with Christianity the depravity of sex becomes increasingly the evil which is intended by attacks upon the arts, and particularly the theatre, as inducing moral laxity and corruption. This point must not be dismissed as one of the prejudices of Christianity. The centrality of love among the passions, its protean manifestation in all forms of desire and aversion, is a Christian insight that independently belongs to Plato and to Freud [36]. One is surprised, therefore, to find that Plato, in charging the dramatists with corrupting the youth, did not single out sexual depravity; on the contrary, he seems to be more concerned about fear and anger. One is not surprised, however, to find that in the later centuries of Christianity when the theatre primarily, but literature in other forms as well, was attacked, the charge that it was a cause of immorality and laxity in public manners usually, if not always, meant sexual immorality and laxity in the conventions of sexual behavior. The other major charges which are brought against the arts during the Christian era, blasphemy and sedition, Plato anticipated, the former quite explicitly, the latter by imputation. It is only recently that poetry, in the form of the dime novel and the motion picture, has been accused of causing crime; but this new complaint carries with it less moral indignation than the contemporary form of the traditional Christian attack which expresses itself in terms of decency.

The place at which Christianity diverges from Plato and approaches Aristotle in its basic insight is, curiously enough, in the doctrine of original sin. Plato, in the *Republic* and the *Laws*, certainly tends to ignore the imperfection and the weakness of men; he concedes that men are corruptible — otherwise poetry would be harmless — but he does not acknowledge that they are naturally corrupt [37]. Aristotle's conception of men as rational animals is equally insistent upon their animality and their rationality; he approaches moral and political problems in terms of the inescapable paradox of a being both rational and animal, and in whom the rationality is usually too weak and the animality too strong. It is this very insight, as we have seen, that leads him to take a different view of poetry, and to treat it as a paradoxical good, essentially relative to man's paradoxical and imperfect nature. The Christian doctrine of original sin asserts the same psychological truth, although its theological explanation was not known by Aristotle. To say that men are born corrupt because in bondage to the passions, is to say that men are born with insufficient rational power, its insufficiency being measured by the force of the passions with which it must cope [38].

In this world few men are saints. The problem of the arts in a Christian commonwealth must be understood in the light of this fact. It is only the saint who is the perfect follower of Christ the teacher, as it is only the philosopher who could live in Plato's Republic. But just as Aristotle formulated the political problem in terms of men of different kinds, so Christianity must be concerned, not only with the saints, but with the lives of all. The arts have little value for the philosopher and the saint. They are untouched by the urgency of the needs which the arts fulfill. The question for Christianity, then, is whether the church can minister to the needs that arise from human corruption, whether the priest, unaided by the poet, can save men from themselves, if they are not saints. This opens into the broader problem of the relation between Church and State in making good men of the citizens of a Christian commonwealth: the role of law and secular expedients, including the arts and all other public diversions, on the one hand; the role of the sacraments, ritual, and all other religious observances, on the other. Even if the ideal discipline of the burden of concupiscence is that which *should* be achieved by the parent and the priest who, by the grace of God, makes a sensitive adaptation to the individual soul of the way of Christ, there remains the question: what *should* be the position of the state if, and to the extent that, the ideal fails to be realized?

Relative to our purposes, this must suffice as an introduction to the way in which Christianity alters the problem of poetry and politics [39]. The terms in which the dialectic of Plato and Aristotle will be restated are clear. But before we proceed to the historical account, there are two points in the *Confessions* of St. Augustine which must be noted. The first merely indicates one Christian ground for the rejection of the arts. He regrets the large part that literature played in his early education because, to use Virgil's *Aeneid* as an example, he spent his time weeping for Dido instead of for himself, who had not yet found the way to live.[1] Literature attached his emotions to the

[1] *Confessions*, I, 13.

wrong objects. The second point is profoundly Christian and, for those who will understand it, becomes a comment on the history of the Christian attack upon the arts which we are about to review. St. Augustine recalls that as a child he was frequently rebuked and punished for his devotion to play. He does not deny that excess of play or indulgence in amusements is wrong, but he adds: "Our sole delight was play; and for this we were punished by those who yet themselves were doing the like. But elder folks' idleness is called 'business'; that of boys, being really the same, is punished by these elders; and none commiserates either boys or men."[2] He who condemns play and amusement as wanton idleness should look first to his own occupation to see whether it is really any better than play or idleness, as judged by the highest standard of a Christian life, the standard of saintliness. The distance between saint and sinner is great. Forgetting this, it is easy to pluck the mote out of our neighbor's eye, easy to cast the first stone. Remembering it, we can better follow the changing historical expression of the Christian attitude toward amusements from the early Fathers to St. Thomas Aquinas, not chronologically, but in an order which completes the circle of analysis and finds the most philosophical Christianity no less Christian than its primitive beginning.

The Fathers of the early Church were opposed to the Roman comedies of their time and to the great public spectacles of the Empire, the gladiatorial games and the circuses. Holy Scripture is silent on the point, but as Bishop Bossuet later explained in answer to Father Caffaro, the absence of explicit condemnation of the stage, spectacles, and other public amusements must be understood in terms of their absence from the life of the times.[3] Nevertheless, the passage in St. Matthew 12:36 in which Christ says "every idle word that men shall speak, they shall render an account for it in the day of judgment" is taken, not only by Bossuet, but by the early Fathers, as a generic condemnation for all idle diversions. It is the idleness of amusement which is essential to its sinfulness, although in addition it usually has many accidental features of grossness and vulgarity

[2] *Confessions*, I, 9.
[3] *Maximes et Réflexions sur la Comédie*, Paris, 1694; edition by Eugene Belin, Paris, 1881.

which are disapproved. This point of idleness, which can be interpreted to mean total irrelevance to the duties and practices of a Christian life, is reminiscent of Plato's question about the utility of the poets in a well-ordered state. To the early Fathers, the play-house and the arena seemed entirely lacking in any positive benefits to man and were heavily seductive with the lure of this world, shamelessly obscene, dedicated to the passions, places of dionysiac frenzy rather than of Christian worship. The language of such writers as Tertullian, who devoted an entire treatise to the condemnation of spectacles, is clear and uncompromising, but it is the language of intemperate invective, rather than restrained analysis. I quote from these early writers merely to indicate the temper of Christianity in its formative period.

Thus Tertullian says to the heathens: "We keep off from your public shows because we can't understand the warrant of the original. There's superstition and idolatry in the case. And we dislike the entertainment because we dislike the reason of its institution; besides we have nothing to do with the frenzies of the race track, the lewdness of the play house, or the barbarities of the bear garden." [4] It is no defense of these institutions to say that they give pleasure and delight. What greater pleasure can there be for a Christian, he asks, than to scorn being pleased? And if a Christian cannot wait for the delight that will properly be his, let him make war upon the pagan deities, "batter the principalities and powers, and force the devils to resign. These are the delights, these are the noble entertainments of Christians; and besides the advantage of the quality, they are always at hand and cost us nothing." [5] Clement of Alexandria similarly answers those who hold that "these diversions are taken to unbend the mind and refresh nature a little" by saying that "the spaces between business should not be filled up with such rubbish." [6] St. Cyprian, asking what business a Christian has at such places as these, answers in a more positive vein: "Would a Christian be agreeably refreshed? Let him read the Scriptures. Here the entertainment will suit his character, and be big enough for his quality." It is interesting to note the Platonic language of Lactantius: "A well-worked poem is a powerful piece of im-

[4] *Apology*, XXXVIII, 4-5.   [5] *Of Spectacles*, XXIX.
[6] *The Paedagogue*, III, 11.

posture; it masters the fancy, and hurries it nobody knows whither";[7] "our minds should be quiet and composed, and not overrun with amusements. Besides a habit of pleasure is an ensnaring circumstance. 'Tis apt to make us forget God and grow cool in the offices of virtue."[8]

In similar manner write St. Chrysostom, St. Jerome and St. Augustine. St. Chrysostom makes the point, which has echoed many times since, that it is no defense to say that there are many instances in which the play-house has done no harm. If the virtue of those who say this is impenetrable and out of reach, are all people thus fortified? To go to the theatre, even though you yourself are protected from its hurt, is to condone an institution that has done mischief to many. The weak have miscarried upon your precedent. And he concludes: "Virtuous as you are, I doubt not you would have been much better, had you kept away."[9] There appears to be no ground to justify a Christian in seeking such divertisements. As St. Jerome says: "Some are delighted with the satisfactions of this world, some with the circus, and some with the theatre. But the Psalmist commands every good man to delight himself in the Lord."[10] We must, therefore, as Christians "decline the theatres and all other dangerous diversions which stain the innocence of the soul, and slip into the will through the senses."[11] To those who charged Christianity with attempting to deprive society of amusements, St. Augustine replied: "Their complaint as if the times were less happy since the appearance of Christianity is very unreasonable. Let them read their own philosophers: there they will find those very things censured which they now are so uneasy to part with. This remark must shut up their mouths and convince them of the excellency of our religion. For pray what satisfactions have they lost? None that I know of, excepting some licentious ones, which they abused to the dishonour of their Creator. But it may be the times are bad because the theatres are tumbling almost everywhere — the theatres, those cages of uncleanness, and public schools of debauchery"[12] [40]. Compared to these sentiments of early Christianity, Plato's exclusion of the dramatists was both polite and tentative.

[7] *Divine Institutions*, VI, 21.   [8] *Divine Institutions*, VI, 20.
[9] *Homily to the People of Antioch*.   [10] *On Psalms*, XXXII, 1.
[11] *Commentary on Ezekiel*, VI, 20.   [12] *The Harmony of the Gospels*, I, 33.

The problem of the arts in the life of man is for Christianity chiefly the problem of the theatre and similar places of public amusement, such as the circus and the arena. It must not be supposed that the Christian attack is limited to a period, such as that of the later Roman empire, when the art of the theatre was debased and the popular spectacles were scandalously vulgar and brutal; nor must it be supposed that the attack is to be explained away in terms of the excessive zeal of proselytizing Christianity in its early days. It occurs again and again, the more startling in its essential sameness against the background of political and social differences, changes in the institution of the church, changes in the character of the art that is condemned; thus, the attack upon the Elizabethan dramatists, the onslaught on the Restoration comedy in England and on the French theatre in the same period, the recent movement to reform the motion picture. In every instance, the popularity of the amusement, as well as the improprieties with which it is charged, is a condition of its being attacked. But in the later centuries, the practical objective is seldom the total destruction of the theatre as in early Christianity ; usually the more moderate ends of reform are sought, whether these are to be achieved by a politically imposed censorship or by quickening the conscience of the people to a change of taste which will make the artists follow or lose their audiences. Because of the striking analogy they bear to the contemporary movement to reform the movies, in which the Christian churches are leaders, we shall find it instructive to review the attacks made by the English divine, Jeremy Collier,[13] and the French bishop, Jacques-Benigne Bossuet, both in the 17th century.

The object of Collier's attack was the flourishing comedy of the Restoration period.[14] The popular theme of comedy was *l'amour* ; it made fun of the dullness and sobriety of matrimony by magnifying the sport and cleverness of the adulterer and the rake ; in title, in language, in situation, it transgressed the common decencies, or rather the decencies of the common people

[13] A member of the Church of England, not a Puritan.
[14] For the immediate background of this episode I have depended largely on Mr. Joseph Wood Krutch's *Comedy and Conscience after the Restoration*, New York, 1924 ; for the more remote background, upon J. E. Spingarn's *History of Literary Criticism in the Renaissance*, New York, 1899.

who, in large part Puritan, looked with horror upon the life of the Stuart court and the fashionable set [40a]. Although the Restoration comedy was in a sense popular, we must remember that the audience to which it appealed was highly selected: the gentry and the nobles, the court-followers who exaggerated the gaiety of the Restoration to efface the memory of the sober Puritan commonwealth. The comedy could hardly have been shocking to an audience thus composed; it could not have corrupted their morals if the corrupt morals of this social set were, as it is usually supposed, an importation which Charles brought back from his exile at the French court. The dramatists claimed, in defending themselves, that they had to cater to the taste of their audience; any play which failed to exhibit the *drôlerie* of the engaging but licentious fop failed to succeed in a theatre patronized predominantly by the upper classes, a society of fops and dandies. That the influence upon the theatre of the standards of its patrons, is great, may be seen in the shift which took place with the accession of William and Mary: the inoffensive sentimental comedy, dull in its purity, took the place of the brilliant but bawdy Restoration play, as the sober influence of the house of Orange altered the manners of society. The question of cause and effect must be phrased by the dilemma: does the drama cause the characteristics of the social life of the times, or does it merely reflect the manners, as well as the taste, of those whose attendance and applause support it? Collier's attack upon the stage was, however, not checked by doubts or difficulties concerning the causal nexus. It was an attack upon corruption, in society and in the play-house. It sought to reform both society and the theatre. It did not stop to ask about cause and effect; it was fanatical rather than analytical or inquiring; and since it was easier and less dangerous to attack the stage than the court, the playwrights rather than their patrons, Collier wrote his *Short View of the Immorality and Profaneness of the English Stage.*[15] This diatribe is more famous than is warranted by its effectiveness in bringing about reform; but as the repository of a typical modern discussion of poetry and politics, its fame is justified. It leans upon classical arguments and breathes Christian sentiments, but it has neither the clarity of the one nor the force of the other. We shall find it a source-

15 London, 1688.

book for many of the misleading points and ill-founded contentions that are current today.

Jeremy Collier was not original, even so far as the tradition of English criticism goes. He accepted its prevailing canons. Much of what he said had been anticipated in the discussion of Elizabethan literature and its theatre. Although Elizabeth held a traditional attitude toward the stage, that plays in themselves are not evil, but, on the contrary, entirely justifiable "for honest recreation's sake," Prynne and Gosson, among many others, attacked the play-house and reinforced the efforts of the city council to keep this institution out of the city of London.[16] These pamphleteers established a precedent for Collier, but it is not from them that he acquired the critical dogmas upon which he rested his case. It is rather in Sir Philip Sidney's *Apology for Poetry,* which attempted to answer Gosson and the others who had heaped abuse upon literature and the stage, that we find the sources from which Collier borrowed. Sir Philip's contemporary, Sir Roger Ascham, tutor to the Queen, had denounced the popular romances and tales as immoral, particularly the *Morte d'Arthur* of Mallory, "the whole pleasure of which book standeth in two special points, in open manslaughter and bold baudry."[17] Sidney insisted that it is the business of poetry to teach morals, and that its opponents failed to distinguish between the proper nature of poetry and the abuses of it "which naughty play-makers and stage-keepers have justly made odious." The primary function of imaginative literature is not to amuse but to form the moral character and to guide men to right action, and this is better done by poetry than by philosophy or history. Poetry is better than any other expression of practical wisdom because, arousing the emotions in connection with good ends, it moves men to action; the philosophers, since they scorn delight, must be content to be ineffectual, but poetry, employing delight, "doth draw the mind more effectually than any other art doth." Plato, says Sidney, like St. Paul, did not condemn poetry but the abuse of it. Sidney is the first of a long line of apologists for Plato, including Jowett in our day, who would rather construe Plato's doctrine as not seriously intending

[16] Vd. V. C. Gildersleeve, *Government Regulation of the Elizabethan Drama,* New York, 1908. Also Spingarn, *op. cit.,* Part III, Ch. 2.
[17] *The Scholemaster,* written between 1563 and 1568.

to "expel poetry from human life" than to resist it as such [41].
Sidney holds, as Jowett later said, that Plato is only protesting
against the degeneracy of the poets in his own day "as we might
protest against the want of serious purpose in modern poetry,
against the unseemliness and extravagance of some of our novelists." But shall the abuse of a thing make the right thing
odious? Quite the contrary; by arguing against the abuse,
poetry is the more commended for its proper values. Sidney
thus set the style of defending literature from the attack of
moralists by surrendering literature to them as an instrument of
moral teaching. Thus, Ben Jonson, in his dedication of *Vol-
pone*, a story which would be today on the list of the proscribed,
at least verbally accepts the obligation by admitting that it is
the "office of the comic poet to imitate justice and instruct to
life." And later, Thomas Rymer rules out delight or amusement as an end of poetry; it does delight but only in order to
teach; the best poet is he who has done most to make men
virtuous.[18]

This apology for poetry becomes a dangerous weapon in the
hands of its critics. It disposes of Plato's objection, only by
acknowledging the point that is most questionable, namely, that
poetry has no other political function than that of moral instruction; it fails to understand the nature of poetry as amusement,
and the utility of amusement as recreation [42]. Should it be
shown at any time that the poets are poor as moral teachers, no
plea is left for them. It is in this way that Collier uses the
traditional English theory of poetry against the theatre of his
day. All the poets, however, did not accept that theory. Dryden, in his preface to *The Mock Astrologer*, explicitly repudiates
the obligation of the dramatist to point a moral. The chief end
of comedy, he says, "is divertisement and delight: and that so
much, that it is disputed, I think, by Heinsius, before Horace's
Art of Poetry, whether instruction be any part of its employment. At least I am sure it can be but its secondary end: for
the business of the poet is to make you laugh" [43]. The successful playwrights for the most part concurred in their practice; they earned their living by giving amusement to an
audience; if they agreed to the doctrine of poetry as moral in-

[18] *The Tragedies of the Last Age, Considered and Examined by the Practice
of the Ancients and by the Common Sense of All Ages*, London, 1678.

struction, they did so only verbally and did not let it alter their technique. Even when their agreement is accompanied by honest intentions, it is difficult, as Mr. Krutch points out in the case of Thomas Shadwell, to imagine anyone's moral standards being raised by the plays they wrote.[19]   The degree to which mere amusement is deprecated and deplored is amazingly extreme; the poet ought never acknowledge that his only purpose is to entertain, says Shadwell, for "it makes him of as little use to mankind as a fiddler or dancing master."[20]

This theory of poetry is, however, mainly sponsored by men who are not themselves successful playwrights. Its critical dogmas are well summarized by Mr. Krutch: "1. The fundamental purpose of literature is to teach morality.   2. It is the duty of the tragic, and perhaps the comic poet, to distribute poetic justice.   3. Decorum demands that types be presented in accordance with their typical rather than their occasional characteristics.   4. Obscenity is a fault of taste."[21]   It is upon these dogmas that Jeremy Collier relies in attacking the theatre, rather than upon the Church Fathers from whom he quotes profusely.[22] Thus, Collier's opening passage: "The business of plays is to recommend virtue and discountenance vice; to show the uncertainty of human greatness, the sudden turns of Fate, and the unhappy conclusions of violence and injustice."[23]   He quotes M. Rapin, one of the leading critical writers of his day, as saying that "delight is the end that poetry aims at, but not the principal one. For poetry being an art, ought to be profitable by the quality of its own nature, and by the essential subordination that all arts should have to polity, whose end in general is the public good."[24]   To which Collier adds: "Thus we see how these great masters qualify diversion, and tie it up to provisoes and

---

[19] *Op. cit.*, pp. 20, 41–42, 76–77.

[20] Quoted from his Preface to *The Humorists* by Mr. Krutch, *op. cit.*, p. 42.

[21] *Op. cit.*, p. 71, by permission of The Columbia University Press.

[22] J. W. Krutch, *op. cit.*, 107–108.

[23] *Op. cit.*, 4th edition, London, 1699, p. 1.

[24] *Op. cit.*, p. 157. The quotation is from *Reflections on Aristotle's Treatise of Poesie*, translated by T. Rymer, 1673. Whether Monsieur Rapin is a good Aristotelian or a platonizing one can be judged from the next sentence: "This is the judgment of Aristotle and of Horace his chief interpreter." See also Rapin's *Comparison of Plato and Aristotle*, translated from the French, 1673.

conditions. Indeed, to make delight the main business of comedy is an unreasonable and dangerous principle: it opens the way to all licentiousness and confounds the distinction between mirth and madness. For if diversion is the chief end, it must be had at any price." [25]

What is important for us in this dependence of Collier upon M. Rapin and other critics of the time, is the supposition which then prevailed that their theory of poetry was an expression of the sense of antiquity. It is not surprising to find Plato quoted as an authority, however much distorted; but on the face of it, one is amazed to discover Aristotle cited in complete concurrence [44]. Here, then, in Collier appears a synthesis of Greek and Christian points of view which, upon closer examination, turns out to be a confusion of each in itself and with each other. Collier is so typical of our current discussion of the same problems, in which these confusions are perpetuated, that it is worth our while to examine his critical tenets.

It is held, first, that drama should instruct by showing things as they *should* be, thus setting the standard of morals to be followed. Aristotle can be made the authority for this point only by ignoring the whole of his principle which included the imitation of things as they are or as they are said to be by men. But even if drama did conform to this dictate, an unwarranted assumption is made if it be supposed that by so doing the drama will succeed as moral instruction.

The principle of 'poetic justice' must, in the second place, be observed. Stated briefly, it requires that the good man always be shown triumphant, and the bad man always in ultimate defeat. The patent absurdities and confusions of this doctrine are many, but that has not prevented it from persisting to this day, when the movies are called upon to show that crime does not pay or that virtue is always rewarded with success, in order to teach its audience a moral lesson. No more immoral lesson could be taught. The doctrine of poetic justice is the teaching of Satan and the friends of Job. If there is any basic insight which both Greek and Christian share, it is that virtue is a condition of happiness, and not of material success. The teaching implicit in poetic justice, that one should be good only to succeed in the things of this world, is both immoral and untrue. It is simply

[25] *Op. cit.,* p. 161.

at variance with the facts of life. Even Addison attacked the nonsense of poetic justice by pointing out that "we find good and evil happen alike to all men on this side of the grave." [26] That it pretended to find so iniquitous a doctrine in either Greek or Christian writing, shows how little English poetic theory understood the sources from which it claimed to derive. Plato takes the greatest pains to disprove the sophistical position that justice is thought to be good only because it works in practice, because it is outwardly expedient. In the *Laws*, at the point at which he is outlining what the poets should teach, he insists that the good man should be represented as happy "no matter whether he be great and mighty or small and feeble, rich or poor." [27] Happiness is an inward state of the soul, not external success. Aristotle had insisted upon reversal in fortune as an element of tragedy; the hero who is a good man with some outstanding fault ultimately suffers calamity. But this is not intended as a point in moral instruction; it is essential to the technique of achieving a tragic effect [45]. The error of this doctrine of poetic justice, from either a Greek or a Christian point of view, is exceeded only by the stupidity of the supposition that an audience who witnessed a play poetically just in plot, would be morally improved or fortified in virtue. It was pointed out by some in Collier's day, as again more recently in the case of the movies, that the ultimate disposition of poetic justice would not prevent depravities incidental to the plot from influencing an audience to imitate the malice which seemed to succeed for part of the time at least, and to be otherwise attractive.

The exposition of the errors upon which his programme to reform the drama was based would not entirely dismiss Collier, even if analysis had weight with him. It could only challenge his simple assumptions about the way in which the drama might be made a better vehicle of moral instruction. It would not question his assumption that the drama should be such a vehicle and only that, nor would it make him doubt that the drama un-purified was, as a matter of fact, a source of moral corruption. He was a practical man and fanatically devoted to getting something done. Like others of his kind, before and after, he saw the problem narrowly. He may have pretended to be interested in purifying the stage, but his deeper interest was to

[26] *Spectator, #40.*   [27] *Laws, 660.*

destroy it.   He was against all imaginative literature, seeing only
evil in it and no good.   He had no hesitancy in dismissing
Shakespeare as smutty.[28]   His lack of sensibility is clearly evidenced by the list of plays he cited as atrocious and by the items
in them he singled out for rebuke.[29]   His lack of taste and dis-
cernment indicates that he was competent only to express prejudice and not criticism; and, as Mr. Krutch points out, these
examples of his prejudices "show that no possible stage could
really have pleased him, for he was able to find blasphemy and
obscenity in the most innocent phrases."[30]   What is important
for us to observe is the way in which he is able to quote Plato and
Aristotle, as well as the Fathers of the Church, to his purpose.[31]
It is no protection against the rhetorical effectiveness of such
marshalling of authorities, to replace the citations in their contexts and to discover that when properly understood they are
inconsistent with or irrelevant to his point.   Collier is a terrifying example of what can happen in the modern period of the
European tradition when that tradition becomes intellectually
attenuated.   In his discussion of the place of poetry in human
life Collier represents himself as an heir of Greek and Christian
antiquity, but he is so far removed from the sources to which
he piously appeals, that one can find in him neither the Greek
understanding of the many sides of the political problem which
poetry raises nor the Christian conception of a life apart from
the things of this world and its seductive ornaments, such as
poetry.

The discussion which follows Collier is intellectually on the
same plane, but at least it has the virtue of seeing the problem
more broadly.   Nothing new is added in the way of basic doctrine, although the bulk of books and pamphlets which Collier
stimulated is tremendous.[32]   In this literature of attack and
defense there is everywhere discernible the effort to regain the

[28] Collier, *op. cit.*, p. 50.   [29] J. W. Krutch, *op. cit.*, p. 111 ff.

[30] J. W. Krutch, *op. cit.*, p. 120, by permission of The Columbia University
Press.

[31] Collier's subtitle was: "Together with the Sense of Antiquity Upon this
Argument."   The authorities are classified as heathen philosophers and Chris-
tian Fathers; in the former group Plato, Xenophon, Aristotle, Tully, Tacitus,
Plutarch; in the latter group, Tertullian, Minutius Felix, St. Cyprian, St.
Chrysostom, St. Jerome, and St. Augustine.

[32] J. W. Krutch, *op. cit.*, pg. 264 ff.

wisdom of the ancients, but eighteenth-century efforts in this direction seem to be necessarily attended by the misquotation and misunderstanding of Plato and Aristotle, and a specious use of Scriptural texts as well. The questions which this controversy tried to resolve were chiefly two: (1) Is the theatre a permissible institution? (2) Should it teach morality, or has it any other social function by which it can be justified? Let us examine the answers briefly.

It was generally admitted that there had been abuses of the stage which justified rebuke and reform. The middle classes who were involved in the Societies for the Reformation of Manners which had recently been organized, naturally approved of Collier's attack upon an art that had transgressed the conventions by which they lived. For the most part, this approval was moderate; it looked to an elimination of what had been offensive. But the more extreme question of the defensibility of any stage at all, of the justification of secular literature in the Christian life, was raised by such writers as the Prince de Conti, William Law and Arthur Bedford. Bedford's book was the most extreme. Its contents are indicated by its title: *The Evil and Danger of Stage-Plays: Showing their Natural Tendency to destroy religion and introduce a general corruption of manners; in almost two thousand instances, taken from the plays of the two last years, against all the methods lately used for their reformation.* Bedford was able to find evil everywhere. In a later book he could list 1400 texts of Scripture which had either been ridiculed or exposed by the stage, or were at least opposite to its present practices.[33] The Prince de Conti was more genuinely devout but no less uncompromisingly extreme in his opposition. "A Christian," he wrote, "having renounced the world, its pomp and pleasure, cannot seek pleasure for itself, nor diversion for the sake of diversion."[34] Diversion that is not necessary is sinful, and the stage is not necessary. William Law, like the Prince de Conti, echoed the ascetic denials of the patristic church. The choice was not between good plays and bad plays. Law had no interest in reform, since it was not genuinely possible.

[33] *The Evil and Mischief of Stage Playing: a sermon preached in the City of London,* 1730.
[34] Quoted by J. W. Krutch, *op. cit.,* p. 133, from *Traité de la Comédie,* published in English in 1711.

Any imaginative representation of this sinful world — and this must include all poetry, all imaginative literature, as well as the stage — is necessarily sinful. The stage is thus sinful "not as things that may only be the occasion of sin, but such as are in their own nature grossly sinful" ; "to talk of the lawfulness and the unlawfulness of the stage is fully as absurd, as contrary to the plain nature of things, as to talk of the unlawfulness and mischief of the service of the church." [35] His argument is clear : the theatre represents the world and is necessarily worldly ; worldliness is anti-Christian ; therefore the theatre is anti-Christian. It is clear, but not unanswerable. We shall find that an answer can be given which is thoroughly consonant with the spirit of Christianity, even though it modifies somewhat the rigorous asceticism of the early Fathers.

The answer is only in part and not well given by the immediate opponents of Collier and his following. Dryden and Congreve, among the dramatists who had been scourged, contented themselves with defending particular passages against excesses of misinterpretation ; but to show that Collier had exaggerated the obscenity and vulgarity which did exist, or had found corruption where none was, fails to meet the attack except obliquely. Nor was it sufficient to show, as did Father Caffaro, whom Motteux quoted in his preface to *Beauty in Distress*, that the Bible does not specifically condemn plays, since it can always be argued that it does so implicitly. If plays teach immorality, they must be utterly condemned by any Christian, and even if they teach morality, they are bad relatively, because Holy Scripture and the Church are better, divinely ordained means to the same end. "That which God hath appointed sufficient means to accomplish, it is unlawful for men to appoint other means to accomplish." [36] John Dennis met the attack directly by dissociating Christianity from undue asceticism and by insisting on the usefulness of the stage and other public diversions.[37] Dennis admitted that the contemporary abuses were so great that there was need for amending them. He was willing to praise Collier for the service he may have rendered to reform, but he fought him as a fanatical

---

[35] *The Absolute Unlawfulness of the Stage-Entertainment fully demonstrated*, London, 1726. [36] *The Stage Condemned*, London, 1720.
[37] *The Usefulness of the Stage to the Happiness of Mankind, to Government and to Religion*, London, 1698.

enemy of the theatre *in toto*. The theatre is directly useful to the state, and to morality and religion as well. It is a public diversion, in fact the best possible public diversion, and amusement is necessary for the contentment and recreation of the people and, consequently, for the safety of the state. Dennis thus strikes an Aristotelian note which the eighteenth-century opponents of the stage, like Plato and the Fathers of the early Church, had ignored. But he does not fully realize the strength of his position. Although he argues that pleasure is not in itself an evil, that human happiness in this world is not inconsistent with Christian morality, that the drama does not unduly stimulate the passions but, arousing them, also chastises them, he fails to analyze the moral utility of this chastisement which is purgation, he fails to distinguish the pleasures of contemplation from other pleasures, he fails to consider the duality of the political and the Christian life and the problem that is consequent thereon: the domain of Church and State in the affairs of man.

Dennis' argument is the best of its kind at the time. It is repeated in substance in an anonymous tract which increases its rhetorical effectiveness by the citation of authorities.[38] The author attempts to show that the charges against the stage are based not on the natural effects of drama itself, but on abuses that are accidental in particular plays. Even St. Chrysostom read Aristophanes, and St. Paul read Epimenides and Menander; they found good where Collier, Ridpath, and their ilk could find only smut. The pulpit and the stage co-operate in teaching morality: the pulpit states the rule, the stage gives the example. Here the anonymous author too readily accepts the obligation of the arts in moral instruction. But he does not rest with this, making the further points that the drama effects purgation of the passions, a good end which the drama serves better than any other means; and that harmless recreation is necessary for human life. The doctrine of the Gospels does not intend to make people unsocial or to deny harmless pleasure; and he quotes St.

[38] *The Stage Acquitted, Being a Full Answer to Mr. Collier and Other Enemies of the Drama: With a Vindication of King Charles the Martyr, and the Clergy of the Church of England, From the Abuses of a Scurrilous Book called 'The Stage Condemned,'* London, 1699.

Thomas to the effect that it is the part of a wise man to unbend his mind sometimes by diverting words and actions.

Father Caffaro had also cited the authority of Thomas Aquinas on the point that play-going is a lawful diversion.[39]   The issue between Plato and Aristotle is thus insinuated within the ranks of Christianity.   None of the English writers in the seventeenth or eighteenth century fully realized the dimensions of this controversy.   The arguments of Dennis and his anonymous colleague about the political and religious utility of the arts, particularly literature and the theatre, were not answered.   But the authority of St. Thomas supporting the position that the drama is neither essentially immoral nor useless, was a challenge that the Christian world could not ignore.   It aroused a more learned man than any of the English publicists, the French Bishop Bossuet, who was a preceptor to the Dauphin, son of Louis XIV. Bossuet sought to unite the Platonic and the Christian positions against what thus appeared to be an intellectual rift in Christianity itself.   But before we turn to his famous *Maximes et Réflexions sur la Comédie*, published in 1694, we must complete our account of the Collier controversy by noting its sequel in the eighteenth century.

The sequel in fact was the rise of the purified sentimental comedy, in which virtue always led to success, and in which the respectability of middle-class merchants was extolled.   How much the change was due to the effectiveness of Collier and his allies and how much it was due to the social shift which occurred with the accession of William and Mary, the rise to importance of the mercantile bourgeoisie, and the efforts of the various societies for the reformation of public manners, is difficult to judge ; but it would be an obvious fallacy to attribute the

[39] *Lettre d'un théologien illustre par sa qualité et par son mérite, consulté par l'auteur pour savoir si la comédie peut-être permise ou doit être absolument defendure*, prefixed to the *Oeuvres Dramatiques du Boursault*, Paris, 1694. This letter was also prefixed by Mr. Motteux to *Beauty in Distress*, London, 1698, with the note that this discourse of the lawfulness and unlawfulness of plays, by the learned Father Caffaro, Divinity Professor at Paris, had been sent to him by a divine of the Church of England.   According to Mr. Krutch, Caffaro had retracted his opinions concerning the theatre in 1694, the same year in which Bishop Bossuet prefixed an answer to his letter in the *Maximes et Réflexions*.

alterations entirely to Collier.[40] The middle classes had other
reasons than Collier gave for objecting to the courtly drama of
the last years of the Stuart régime. It was too glittering; it
represented life as more romantic than it actually was, and thus
tended to undermine the sober industry which was essential to
the prosperity of trade. When these working middle classes
became the patrons of the theatre, the drama was responsive to
the tastes and prejudices of its new audience. Plays which
would have failed miserably twenty years before became successful pieces. We are not here concerned with the character
of this change from the point of view of literary criticism; we
are concerned primarily with the fact that the drama continued
to be a popular form of public amusement, despite the extremists
who could find no justification for it whatsoever; and that the
change away from the obscene and the vulgar was accompanied
by a similar change in the standards of the dominant social class.
Whether this was a shift in fundamental morals or only in superficial manners is a question we shall return to later. Whether
the society of England under William and Mary is judged morally less corrupt than under the later Stuarts certainly depends
upon which social class one tends to identify with the society
as a whole. In any case, Defoe's appeal to the audience of the
drama to reform the theatre by reforming its own taste, by
making its attendance a mark of approval or disapproval which
the dramatists must feel, seems to have been answered. Yet the
personnel of the audience had altered, and with it the criteria of
impropriety. Steele's theory that the audience regarded dramatic characters as models to be imitated — a point that has recently been revived in connection with motion pictures — and
hence, that the drama must show its audience only examples of
good men and right actions, is not only in itself questionable, but
must be balanced by the point that the theatre, and literature in
general, is only a mirror reflecting the already-existing manners
and morals of its time.

What is most instructive from our point of view is that the
attack upon the theatre and literature which had begun long
before Collier in the diatribes of Prynne and Gosson and the
censures of Ascham, which had been intensified by the fanatical
zeal and rhetorical power of Collier into a great public con-

[40] Cf. J. W. Krutch, *op. cit.*, Ch. VII; 239; 247–248.

troversy, resulting in the increased use of the legal expedients of censorship, continued in slightly different channels in the subsequent century and down to our own day. William, shortly after coming to the throne, issued orders to the Master of the Revels with respect to the censorship of plays, using Collier's words. In the successive reigns of Queen Anne and George I there were various attempts to strengthen the censorship, culminating in the Licensing Act of 1737; these were not always motivated solely by moral considerations; sedition and treason must also be expunged. Nevertheless, such bills were usually introduced as moral measures to prevent the theatres of London from continuing to corrupt the youth and encourage vice. But though the stage was censored and the character of the drama had manifestly changed, the reformers were not satisfied, and the charges which they made were substantially the same as had been brought at an earlier period. The attack shifted from the stage to the novel. Addison in *The Spectator* looked askance at the fiction of Smollett and Fielding; *Tom Jones* and *Tristram Shandy* were accused of improprieties and of being corrupting influences. Fielding was not thus to be deterred by the censors of *The Spectator*; he answered more definitely than Dryden and Congreve had answered Collier. He clearly pointed out the superficiality of the sentimental comedy which had developed according to Steele's adaptation of the theory of poetic justice. Virtue is not taught by making it appear successful in the last act.[41]

Thus the times change, the occasions of and the participants in the controversy are different, but the arguments *pro* and *con* remain the same. Three centuries of English discussion of the problem of poetry and politics exhibit the multiple repetition of the same opinions [46], usually unsupported by evidence and never clarified by sound analysis, against a background of social movements for the reform of public morals and amusements, on the one hand, and the persistent demonstration of the utility

[41] *Tom Jones*, VIII, 1; see also, V, 1. In the episode of the puppet show (XII, 5), the Master says: "I remember when I first took to the business, there was a great deal of low stuff that did very well to make folks laugh, but was never calculated to improve the morals of young people, which certainly ought to be principally aimed at in every puppet show." Tom answers that the removal of Punch and his merry wife Joan has spoiled the show.

of diversions by popular participation, on the other. The controversy about motion pictures today reiterates the same opinions against the same background. Mr. Krutch's study of Collier, his precursors and followers, provides an abundance of opinions, well tested only in their endurance, for contemporary publicists and reformers who would either attack or defend the movies. If one seeks refinement of analysis or some advance beyond the positions of the ancients, one cannot learn anything from the close study of this perpetual debate. On the contrary, we are impelled to return to the texts of Plato and Aristotle to discover the genuine issues which have been muddled or lost in the modern polemic. We must also be impressed by the irony of each successive generation threatening the utter corruption of society unless its literature is immediately reformed. The prediction is always based upon the same objections to the depravity of the theatre or the novel, and unless society is in each epoch either equally or increasingly corrupt, the threat must lose its sting for those who review such predictions in the light of the facts. This is not an argument against those who hold that both society and literature are corrupt, but against those who do not hesitate to blame the corruption of the former upon the depravity of the latter. It also raises the question whether art and literature can be better than the human nature they are intended to amuse.

This last question returns us to the problem of Christianity's attitude toward amusements and diversions of all sorts. Collier and those who joined with him give poor expressions of the Christian point of view ; like so many Anthony Comstocks, with greater or less scholarship, they represent religion and morality in a way that tends to discredit their cause. We must avoid the counter error of scoffing at or dismissing Christianity because of its Colliers and its Comstocks.[42] It is just as fallacious to refute a doctrine in terms of its unsound expositors as to insist upon the essential evil of the arts because some of them have been abused. We must look to the best statements of the Christian position if we are fairly to understand its attitude toward the arts as amusements. Only then shall we be able to decide whether the ad-

[42] Vd. Horace Kallen, *Indecency and the Seven Arts*, New York, 1930 ; Morris Ernst and William Seagle, *To the Pure*, New York, 1928.

vent of Christianity alters the case as Plato and Aristotle left it, whether the place of diverting imitations in a Christian commonwealth is or is not the same as in a Greek state.

Bishop Bossuet's *Maximes et Réflexions sur la Comédie* is not limited to a consideration of the contemporary French theatre of the seventeenth century. It is more generally a Christian Platonic discussion of dramatic literature and theatrical spectacles, and an answer to the Father Caffaro who had cited St. Thomas Aquinas in defense of plays as lawful amusements. The controversy between Bossuet and Aquinas, although the latter is four centuries earlier, can thus be dialectically reconstructed as the argument between Plato and Aristotle reset in a Christian frame.

Bossuet takes the extreme Platonic position [47]. The theatre excites dangerous passions; it would cease to attract an audience unless it did; therefore it should not be reformed but exterminated. It cannot be denied that it is the design of the dramatist to stir the emotions; this is apparent from the nature of his work and the circumstance of its production upon a stage. Bossuet is equally certain that it cannot be denied that the passions are bad, and should not be aroused under any circumstances. The passions lead naturally to sin. Dramatic amusements are, therefore, essentially sinful.[43] He points out that among so many serious invectives of the early Fathers against the theatre, one never finds that they chose the expedient of reforming it. They knew too well that it would be "vain to try to reduce the drama against its nature, to the severe rules of virtue."[44] Moreover, "to charm the senses is a bad way to introduce virtuous sentiments, even if it were possible." It may have been possible for the pagans, whose "virtue was imperfect, gross, worldly, superficial," to insinuate it by the theatre, but the "theatre has neither the authority nor the dignity nor the efficacy to inspire virtues befitting Christians."[45] Therefore, it must be rejected entirely.

Bossuet notes the passage in Aristotle's *Politics* in which it is recommended that children under seven be not permitted to attend the theatre. He remarks: "I do not know why he was not willing to extend further this precaution. Youth, and even

[43] *Op. cit.,* (ed. 1881), pp. 25–37. [44] *Op. cit.,* p. 96. [45] *Op. cit.,* p. 102.

infancy, remain for a long time with men; or rather, they are never entirely outgrown." [46] He is fully cognizant of other points in Aristotle's analysis. To the defense that poetry not only arouses the emotions, but also purges them and thus does man a moral service, he replies: "Let us leave to Aristotle this mysterious manner of purifying the passions which neither he nor his interpreters have known how to explain with good reasons." [47] It is important to observe here that the theory of purgation is dismissed not as incorrect, but as unintelligible. To the objection that amusements are useful and good because they serve the ends of relaxing and recreating the human spirit, he simply replies that there are less elaborate, more modest, more simple, less dangerous, modes of relaxation for a Christian than the theatre and, it goes without saying, similar arts and spectacles. [48] Plato's discrimination of the refined from the gross forms of enjoyment should be followed. Yet even ancient tragedy, although better and more serious than ours, was condemned by the principles of that philosopher. [49]

He meets Father Caffaro's point that Scripture is silent on the theatre by explaining the generic condemnation that is implied in Christ's proscription of "idle words." "It is to read the Fathers of the Church too negligently," he says, "to think that they blame in the spectacles of their day only the idolatry and the manifest shamelessness. It is to be deaf to the truth not to feel that their reasons carry further. They blame in the plays and in the theatre the inutility, the prodigious dissipation, the trouble and commotion of the mind little befitting a Christian, whose heart should be a sanctuary of peace; they blame there the excitation of the passions, the vanity, the great ornaments which they classify as the pomps which we have abjured by baptism, the desire to see and to be seen, the unhappy meeting of eyes which seek each other, the too great occupation with vain things, the bursts of laughter or the tumults of passions which make one forget the presence of God. . . Who would dare say that he is at the theatre for the love of God or to please God? . . . If one wishes to penetrate to the principles of their morals, what severe condemnation will not one read there of the spirit which leads one to spectacles?" [50] The *least* evil that the

---

[46] *Op. cit.*, p. 57.   [47] *Op. cit.*, p. 57.   [48] *Op. cit.*, p. 52.   [49] *Op. cit.*, p. 54.
[50] *Op. cit.*, pp. 48–49.

Fathers find in the drama is its inutility, which puts it in the class of "idle words" spoken of by Christ.[51]

Father Caffaro had argued that in confession he never found the theatre to be a cause of sin. Bossuet charges Caffaro with naïveté in supposing that the only evils which men suffer are those which they feel and confess. One must not believe men on the subject of their evils and dangers, because "their corruption, the error of their wounded imaginations, their *amour-propre*" prevent a clear view of the state of one's soul.[52] Caffaro had said that thousands of people of eminent virtue and delicate conscience approve of comedy and attend it without trouble. Bossuet answers that these people forget the words of St. Paul: "Wherefore he that thinketh himself to stand, let him take heed lest he fall." "These people forget that even if they are so strong that they have nothing to fear for themselves, they should fear the scandal they give to others, and the harm they do to others by participating in something which may be evil for them."[53] Caffaro had pointed out that "one cannot take a step, read a book, enter a church, live in the world, without meeting a thousand things capable of exciting the passions." Bossuet answers: "Without doubt, his conclusion is good; everything is full of danger; one must then increase the number. . . All the objects which present themselves to our eyes can excite our passions; then one should prepare objects exquisitely and with great care in order to excite them and to render them more agreeable by disguising them."[54] It should be noted that neither Caffaro nor Bossuet distinguish the manner in which natural things excite our passions, with the consequence of relief through natural action, from the way in which imitations excite our passions artificially and artificially relieve them to effect purgation. Yet Bossuet seems to be touching on this point when he observes that art makes the emotions it arouses "more agreeable by disguising them."

Finally, Father Caffaro had called the laws to his help. If comedy, or the theatre in general, were so bad, it would not be tolerated by a Christian commonwealth, but there are, nevertheless, no laws to this effect. He forgets, says Bossuet, that St. Thomas, whom Caffaro quotes on his side, distinguished between the spheres of Church and State, and in the light of this distinc-

[51] *Op. cit.,* p. 84. [52] *Op. cit.,* p. 43. [53] *Op. cit.,* p. 44. [54] *Op. cit.,* p. 45.

tion held that human laws, those which are made and enforced by the State, are not intended "to repress all evils, but only those which attack society." [55]   This should not prevent the Church, in the light of Divine Law, from condemning institutions which, whether or not they are socially undesirable, jeopardize the Christian life.   Moreover, if the State is not aware of public perils, it is the duty of the Church to instruct it and guide it.

Nevertheless, the authority of St. Thomas on the lawfulness of amusements which are neither good nor evil in themselves, cannot be disregarded.   Bossuet attempts to interpret the texts in the writings of Aquinas which bear upon the point, in such a way as to diminish their discrepancy from what he holds to be his own, the patristic, the right, Christian position.   He insists that the theatre is intrinsically injurious because it excites the passions, and this excludes it from the class of innocent arts.   It would be absurd to say, and St. Thomas would not agree, "that it is not injurious to excite the most dangerous passions, or that they are not excited by the delectable representation of them" which is made upon the stage.   "Such absurdities could be most easily disproved by the words of the Saint himself." [56]   Yet after he has finished commenting on the relevant articles in St. Thomas, Bossuet is forced to concede the discrepancy.   He frankly says : "After having purged the doctrine of St. Thomas from the excess with which he has been charged" by Caffaro, "it must be admitted finally, with the respect due to so great a man, that he seems a bit removed, I will not say from the basic sentiments, but rather from the expressions of the ancient Fathers on the subject of divertisements." [57]   The discrepancy is greater than Bishop Bossuet was willing to admit.   We shall find in the writings of St. Thomas the rift which can occur in Christianity because of the difference between Plato and Aristotle.

On one important point St. Thomas differs from both Plato and Aristotle.   In Greek political theory there is no limitation upon the state with respect to the education of its citizens.   Both Plato and Aristotle argue the superiority of uniform public control of education and moral training to the vagaries of the domestic system in which these matters are left to the judgment of parents and private tutors.   Education is the province of the

---

[55] Op. cit., p. 46.   Cf. Aquinas, *Summa Theologica*, I–II, Q. 96, A. 2.
[56] *Op. cit.*, p. 69.   [57] *Op. cit.*, p. 84.

legislators; the aim of law is to make men good.   It follows that
the regulation of the arts as an important element in education
is within the proper sphere of human law.   That Aquinas takes
a different view of these matters is thoroughly intelligible in
terms of the distinction between the things that are Caesar's and
the things that are God's.   Aquinas asks whether it is properly
the aim of human law to make men good, and answers in the
affirmative, but with a significant qualification: human law seeks
to make men good relative to the constitution of a particular
state, but it cannot make men good absolutely in all respects.[58]
The reason is to be found in his answer to the question whether
it is proper for human law to command all virtues and to prohibit all vices: human law should be limited to the regulation
of those aspects of conduct which are predominantly social rather
than private, which are directed toward the common good rather
than to the intrinsic goodness of the soul, or, as we would say, it
should be concerned only with matters that are affected with the
public interest.[59]   St. Thomas is not taking the nineteenth century position that that government governs best which governs
least, but he is insisting upon the line, usually difficult to determine in particular cases, between moral problems which are
political and for the legislator, and those which are intrinsic,
which involve man in relation to God rather than to other men,
and hence are theological and for the church [48].

The problem of poetry and the arts is thus a dual one: to the
extent that amusements are affected with the public interest,
there is one set of questions which are for the State to consider;
to the extent that poetry and the arts provide diversions which
the soul either should enjoy or avoid in its career toward ultimate salvation, there is another set of questions which are for the
Church to consider.   The theologian cannot be unconcerned
with the first set of questions, because men must live in society,
and the welfare of the state is itself an essential condition of the
goodness of human life in this world [49].   Difficult issues may
arise in which there is an *apparent* conflict between temporal
happiness and eternal salvation.   Such conflicts will always be
only apparent.   Nevertheless, in the casuistical resolution of
such difficulties, it would be just as ill-advised for the Church to

[58] *Summa Theologica*, I–II, Q. 92, A. 1.
[59] *Summa Theologica*, I–II, Q. 96, AA. 2, 3.

ignore the political calculation of the value of means to the
common good as for the State to ignore the ecclesiastical estimate
of the conditions of beatitude.   There is in St. Thomas's discussion of any political problem, a delicate balance of mundane and
spiritual interests — arising from the insight that the spirit dwells
in this world and must therefore reckon with it — which is
achieved by few other Christian thinkers, and less frequently in
modern times than in the middle ages.   The Collier controversy,
the writings of Bossuet, and their analogues in the nineteenth
and twentieth centuries, exhibit the exponents of Christianity as
other-worldly to a degree that is characteristic of the Fathers of
the early Church but not of the theologians of the thirteenth
century.

Art is a fundamental necessity in the human state.   "No man
can live without pleasure.   Therefore, a man deprived of the
pleasures of the spirit goes over to the pleasures of the flesh." [60]
To understand this we need only return to the Aristotelian
analysis which Aquinas is here following.   The pleasure which
men get in their enjoyment of imitations, the arts and other
spectacles, is the pleasure of the spectator, the joy of contemplation.   It would be manifest error to suppose that because the
arts are appreciated through the senses, the pleasure which they
yield is sensual; as it would be error to hold that because all
knowledge depends upon the activity of the senses, the universal
truths of science and philosophy are sensitive apprehensions.[61]
The senses are means which the spirit employs in the contemplative enjoyment of art, just as they are means which the intellect acknowledges in its acquisition of general truths.   The
failure to distinguish the kinds of pleasure and the kinds of
knowledge is a peculiarly modern confusion which, in its unintelligible view of the relation of body and spirit, tends to make
sense the only cognitive or evaluative organ of the soul.

St. Thomas' conception of beauty further explains the kind of
pleasure which the arts yield.   Beautiful things are those "the
mere apprehension of which gives pleasure"; [62] they are those

---

[60] Maritain's phrasing (Art and Scholasticism, New York, 1930 : p. 80) of the
passage in Summa Theologica, II–II, Q. 35, A. 4, ad. 2.   The Saint says this
according to the Philosopher.   Cf. Ethics, VIII, 5, 6 ; X, 6.
[61] Vd.   Note 18, p. 597, infra.
[62] Summa Theologica, I–II, Q. 27, A. 1, ad. 3 : "ita quod bonum dicatur id quod

things "which please upon being seen." [63]   As a commentator on these passages points out, Aquinas is here fully cognizant of the dual nature of man, sensitive and rational ; he acknowledges the work of the senses in presenting the object without ignoring the work of the intellect in fully apprehending it.[64]   Both sense and intellect are cognitive faculties.   The pleasure of the beautiful is a cognitive pleasure ; "beauty refers to the force of knowledge." We desire to know ; we get pleasure from the satisfaction of any appetite ; we call those things beautiful which satisfy our intellectual desire to apprehend them [50].   This pleasure should be distinguished from the bodily pleasures which are merely sensual ; it is properly called joy or delight, and it is in this sense that we speak of our enjoyment of works of art, of all imitations as spectacles of which we are spectators.[65]

Cognitive pleasure is, of course, relative to the nature of the individual person, and is according to the degree of intelligence and capacity for contemplation.   As Aristotle had said that all men desire to learn, but that the pleasure which some derive from philosophy, others "whose capacity is more limited" get from the arts ; so Aquinas' conception of beauty makes it relative to the nature of those who judge of it.   Taste will vary with the faculties of the individual ; what is beautiful to one may be ugly to another.   This does not make beauty entirely subjective, which is another modern fallacy that Aquinas could not possibly commit.   Beauty is in the object according to the perfection of its being, the proportion of its parts ; and in a metaphysical sense, all things which are, are beautiful.[66]   But beauty is in the subject

---

simpliciter complacet appetitui, pulchrum autem dicatur *id cujus ipsa apprehensio placet.*"   Also note : "Sed ad rationem pulchri pertinet quod in ejus aspectu seu cognitione quietetur appetitus."

[63] *Summa Theologica*, I, Q. 5, A. 4, ad. 1 : "Pulchrum autem respicit vim cognoscitivam : pulchra enim dicuntur *quae visa placent ;* unde pulchrum in debite proportione consistit, quia sensus delectatur in rebus debite proportionatis, sicut in sibi similibus ; nam et sensus ratio quaedam est ; et omnis virtus cognoscitiva."

[64] L. Callahan, *A Theory of Aesthetic According to the Principles of St. Thomas Aquinas*, Washington, 1927 : p. 36 ff.   Cf. Maritain, *op. cit.*, Note 56.

[65] *Summa Theologica*, I–II, Q. 31, AA. 3, 4.

[66] *Summa Theologica*, I, Q. 39, A. 8 : "Nam ad pulchritudinem tria requiruntur ; primo quidem *integritas* sive perfectio, quae enim diminuta sunt, hoc ipso turpia sunt ; et debita *proportio*, sive consonantia ; et iterum *claritas.*" (Beauty includes three conditions, *integrity* or perfection, since those things

according to his capacity to receive, to apprehend the proportions of the thing. There is no inconsistency between the objective ground of beauty and its relativity to the subject in casuistical judgments of taste. That the order in things, which is their intrinsic beauty, must be proportioned to the powers of human intelligence if they are to be judged beautiful because they give pleasure on being seen, is the basis for the principle of commensurate enjoyment which conceives a hierarchy of arts or imitations proportional to a hierarchy of degrees of intelligence and sensitivity in men [51].

The pleasure which men get from art is the first step away from the lusts of the flesh and toward the yearning of the spirit. As Jacques Maritain points out in a commentary on this passage in Aquinas,[67] "Art teaches men the pleasures of the spirit"; "it prepares the human race for contemplation (the contemplation of the Saints), the spiritual joy of which surpasses every other joy and seems to be the end of all human activities. For what useful purpose do servile work and trade serve, except to provide the body with the necessaries of life so that it may be in a state fit for contemplation? What is the use of the moral virtues and prudence if not to procure that tranquillity of the passions and interior peace which contemplation needs? To what end the whole government of civil life, if not to assure the exterior peace necessary to contemplation?"[68] Art is, therefore, not only a fundamental necessity in the human state because no man can live without pleasure; it provides a better kind of pleasure and one which, in the infinite gradation of things, is a step in the direction of the greatest good. Furthermore, it not only is good in itself as a source of contemplative joy but, through its purgative efficacy, is itself a means, co-operating with the moral virtues and civil government, to assure both interior tranquillity and exterior peace. It must not be thought that we are here praising only the highest art, that which the most sensitive and refined souls can enjoy. In the hierarchy of commensurate re-

---

which are impaired are by that very fact ugly; due *proportion* or harmony; and lastly, brightness or *clarity*.) This indicates the metaphysical character of beauty as a transcendental term. Cf. Maritain, *op. cit.*, Note 63b.
[67] *Summa Theologica*, II–II, Q. 35, A. 4, ad. 2.
[68] Maritain, *op. cit.*, p. 80, by permission of Messrs. Sheed and Ward, Publishers. Cf. *Summa Contra Gentiles*, III, 37.

creations, as Alain points out, art serves the same purposes for all levels of human nature. Maritain constructs a scale which descends "from the beauty of Scripture and Liturgy to the beauty of the mystic writers, and then to art in the proper sense of the term: the spiritual fullness of mediaeval art, the national harmony of Greek and classic art, the pathetic harmony of Shakespearean art." [69] But this hierarchy of the arts arranged in terms of their specific value in civilizing men, in terms of their degree of spirituality, goes much further because men are much less able than Maritain here acknowledges: it reaches down to the popular arts, the current theatre, the music which reaches great audiences, the motion picture, as well as to the prize-ring and the bull-fight.

So much then for the primary merit of the arts in human life, the pleasure which they directly afford. Aquinas also considers them, in their political aspect, as sources of relaxation and rest. Considering the virtue of games, which without violence to the essential meaning of the text can be made generic for all arts viewed extrinsically as amusements, Aquinas writes: "Just as man needs bodily rest for the body's refreshment, because he cannot always be at work, since his power is finite and equal to a certain fixed amount of labor, so too it is with his soul, whose power is also finite and equal to a fixed amount of work. Consequently, when he goes beyond his measure in a certain work, he is oppressed and becomes weary, and all the more since when the soul works the body is at work likewise, in so far as the intellective soul employs forces that operate through the bodily organs . . . whether the operations with which it is occupied be those of the practical or the speculative reason. Yet this weariness is greater if the soul be occupied with the work of contemplation. . . In either case, however, one man is more wearied than another, according as he is more intensely occupied with works of reason. Now just as weariness of body is dispelled by resting the body, so weariness of the soul must needs be remedied by resting the soul: and the soul's rest is pleasure, as stated above. Consequently, the remedy of weariness of soul must needs consist in the application of some pleasure, by slackening the tension of the reason's study. . . This is in agreement with the statement of the Philosopher (*Ethics*, IV, 8) that *in the inter-*

69 *Op. cit.*, p. 81, by permission of Messrs. Sheed and Ward, Publishers.

course of human life there is a kind of rest that is associated with games: and consequently, it is sometimes necessary to make use of such things." [70]

This view of games, and hence of all imitations which are play for the participant and spectacles for the onlooker and which in either case relax the spirit through enjoyment, meets Bossuet's condemnation of the arts and, consequently, games as generically "idle words" or idle deeds which have no moral utility. Arts and games are useful by reason of their nature as recreations, and recreation is indispensable [52]. Yet Bossuet had insisted that if one must relax the human spirit, there are more or less dangerous modes of relaxation, and that this is the ground of preferring one kind to another. His point cannot be denied, but one must ask what knowledge of the effects of the arts he has by which to judge of their perils; and one must also remember that the modes of relaxation must be proportional to degrees of need and ability in the gradations of human nature. As St. Thomas points out, in this matter of recreation, there are three points which require caution. The first and chief is that the pleasure in question should not be sought in things that are otherwise indecent or injurious. This is the caution which Bossuet urges, but the principle must be applied casuistically; so far as injury is concerned, we require knowledge of the effects of the particular game or art to make the application. The second thing to be observed is that one's balance of mind should not be altogether lost; not only is there proper moderation in this matter of recreation, but whatever recreations we indulge in should be consistent with good behavior, should reflect an upright mind. In the third place, he says, "we must be careful, as in all other human actions, to conform ourselves to persons, time and place, and take due account of other circumstances, so that our fun befit the hour and the man." [71]

In answering a subsequent question, whether there can be sin in the excess of play, Aquinas speaks directly to the point of

[70] *Summa Theologica*, II–II, Q. 168, A. 2. Cf. on the virtue *eutrapelia* which is the proper or moderate use of games, I–II, Q. 60, A. 5; II–II, Q. 160, A. 2. Cf. also *Summa Contra Gentiles*, III, 25.

[71] *Loc. cit.*, fn. 70 *supra*. Aquinas concludes the passage thus: "Now these things are divided according to the rule of reason; and a habit that operates according to reason is a virtue. Therefore there can be a virtue about games." Note ad. 2, ad. 3.

Bossuet's objection, the theatre, and particularly comedy [53]. Recreation, it has been pointed out, is necessary for the intercourse of human life. "Now whatever is useful to human intercourse may have a lawful employment ascribed to it. Wherefore the occupation of play-actors, the object of which is to cheer the heart of man, is not unlawful in itself; nor are they in a state of sin provided that their playing be moderated, namely, that they use no unlawful words or deeds in order to amuse, and that they do not introduce play into undue matters and seasons. . . Wherefore those who maintain them (play-actors) in moderation do not sin but act justly, by rewarding them for their services. On the other hand, if a man spends too much on such persons, or maintains those comedians who practise unlawful mirth, he sins as encouraging them in their sin." [72] It is also vicious, however, he indicates in the next article,[73] to go to the other extreme of refusing "pleasure to others" and of "hindering their enjoyment" [54].

The basic principle which Aquinas enunciates in discussing the art of the dress-maker, summarizes the whole problem of the arts in human society from the point of view both of the Church and of the State.[74] An art is, in the first place, not sinful in itself if its products may be employed by man either for a good or for an evil use. This applies to all the arts, useful and fine. A fine art may be used for evil if it is primarily a source of sensual pleasure rather than of contemplative delight, and only then if it incites disorder among the passions. If art arouses the passions by its sensuous appeal, it does so in the guise of nature rather than of art, and the excitement being natural, will not be subject to catharsis. Art which is received as imitation and as spectacle cannot be sensual; it can only be enjoyed in being witnessed, and if emotions are aroused, they are also purged. What is properly in itself fine art is neither moral nor immoral; but fine art in relation to man is moral or immoral according to its consequences in human life, its use for good or for evil. Now it is obvious that the arts which provide amusement and recreation for large numbers of people have a utility which is good; it would be clearer to say that *as* providing amusement they are

[72] *Summa Theologica*, II–II, Q. 168, A. 3, ad. 3.
[73] *Summa Theologica*, II–II, Q. 168, A. 4 : "Whether there is a sin in lack of mirth." [74] *Summa Theologica*, II–II, Q. 169, A. 2.

good because they are means to good ends: (1) spiritual pleasure rather than sensual; (2) the rest of relaxation and recreation [55]. But the same arts may also be bad to the extent that they can be put to evil use: as sources of sensual pleasure, and as stimuli to conduct which may be sinful and, if it becomes habitual, vicious. This requires the second part of the Thomistic principle: "In the case of an art that produces things which for the most part some people put to an evil use, although such arts are not unlawful in themselves, nevertheless, according to the teaching of Plato, they should be extirpated from the State by the governing authority." [75]

The two parts of this principle must be interpreted in conjunction. By doing so we shall be able to avoid, as Aquinas does, the error of Platonism, while at the same time finding a part of wisdom in Plato. The nature of practical problems requires us to calculate both the good and bad consequences of anything connected with our actions. It would be folly to act in terms of less desirable ends if, in doing so, we ignore a greater good. Here is the heart of the difficulty in the political problem of the arts as amusements. We know their good results if we know the extent to which the populace enjoys them, and through this enjoyment suffers purgation and gets rest and recreation. But to know their bad results is more difficult; the evidences are not as apparent and must be sought by research, partly because the bad results do not follow from the nature of these amusements as art, but from features which are accidental to their nature, and partly because the causal nexus is more difficult to determine. In any case, the statesman or person concerned with the public welfare, must approach the problem quantitatively. The use of such words as "some" and "for the most part" are admonitions to this effect. The Church considers sins without any regard to the number of persons or the frequency of the acts. But the State, by the principle that human laws are not intended to repress all evils, but only those which substantially affect society, must look to the extent of matters which it judges to be undesirable, in order to weigh

[75] *Summa Theologica*, II–II, Q. 169, A. 2, ad. 4. Maritain adds: "Fortunately for the rights of man, our fine states have no Prince, and the workers in the service of idolatry and lechery, of dressmaking and literature, are not troubled by Plato" (*op. cit.*, p. 75).

the desirability of political action. It is for this reason, perhaps, that Maritain translates the passage which states the second part of the principle, as follows: those products of art which "are put *in the majority of cases* to an evil use" call for the intervention of the State. Even this is not sufficiently precise. It is not only the number of cases, but the quantity of evil and its gravity under particular circumstances, which must enter into the calculation.

In short, the rulers of a Christian commonwealth are not called upon, because it is Christian, to condemn the arts and other amusements, unless it is clear in the case of a particular art that it is intrinsically evil. Otherwise, the arts may be used for either good or evil. Only in the light of such knowledge as we may have or may discover concerning their utilities and their undesirable consequences, and in terms of a balance which we then can strike between the extent to which they are advantageous to the State and the extent to which they are disadvantageous, can we act reasonably to exterminate or supervise or censor one or another art in the particular case. The extermination of an art is drastic treatment, and will usually be warranted only in the case of useful arts, the products of which are intrinsically evil, such as, for instance, the making of drugs which are poisonous and have no medicinal value whatsoever, or the production of pornographic pictures. In all other cases, regulation and supervision are the remedies by which the State can preserve and increase the utility of an art and at the same time diminish, and perhaps eliminate, its disadvantages and undesirable consequences. This is the principle which justifies censorship of the arts, whatever the *modus operandi* by which the censorship is accomplished — by law and by officials, or by public sentiment and unofficial groups. The aim of censorship is good, whether or not it is well or ill advised in its actual practices, and whether or not censorship itself is less desirable, because of its own social consequences, than the evils it seeks to remedy. The principles which Aquinas thus formulates for the direction of the State with respect to the arts as a factor of social life, apply also to the policy the Church must take, either as a part of the State in its political status as a social institution, or as separate from the State in the division of secular and spiritual powers. Not only are religious communicants also citizens, but even in those ethical considerations which do not involve social and political ends, it is necessary to weigh the positive values of an art, which is not evil in itself, against its negative values. Ecclesiastical rule, no less than civil law, cannot be applied without casuistry ; ecclesiastical practice, like political action, must proceed by deliberation which involves judgments based upon knowledge of relevant factors and circumstances, leading to the calculation of good and evil.

The ancient issue between Plato and Aristotle is thus reconstructed in the wider terms of Christianity, which adds the problem of the relation of Church and State. Aquinas provides a Christian answer to Bossuet as Aristotle gave a Greek answer to Plato. The point of superiority in either case is the same : it is based in part upon a sounder view of the nature of practical problems, sounder because essentially more pragmatic ; and in part upon an analysis which locates the utility of the arts as well as their possible perils. The superiority is apparent at once in the way in which the problem is stated. As Maritain reformulates the problem in Thomistic fashion, the basic issue is between art and prudence.[76] In one respect, by reason of its speculative character, art is independent of prudence; but in another respect, in which art is viewed not in itself, but in relation to man, prudence must govern art. The prudent man, who judges all things from the angles of morality and politics, judges the work of art only in terms of its consequences and not in terms of itself. Aesthetic and political criticism are independent of each other ; but art is nevertheless properly subject to the extrinsic considerations of morality and politics and religion. These considerations require prudence. The control of art in the interests of man can be as unfortunate as its utter freedom. "Prudence was sacrificed to Art at the time of the Italian Renaissance, in a civilization solely inclined to the *virtu* of the Humanists" and "Art was sacrificed to Prudence in the nineteenth century, in 'right thinking' circles inclined solely to Respectability." The prince or the people can rule wisely over works of art only to the extent that the rule considers both the ends of prudence and the ends of art. "Wisdom, being endowed with the outlook of God and ranging over Action and Making alike, alone can completely reconcile Art and Pru-

[76] Maritain, *op. cit.*, Ch. 9 on Art and Morality, especially section 6.

dence." [77]   In its narrower field, prudence requires knowledge. Neither prince nor people can rule the arts prudently without knowing both the advantages and the disadvantages they yield to man.   It may be questioned, therefore, whether Plato's king, though a philosopher, had the wisdom to reconcile art and prudence, or the knowledge whereby to regulate the arts prudently.

Plato is right only upon the supposition of ideal human government — perfect ruler and perfect subjects — and this is equivalent to the denial of the need for government of any sort or, for that matter, the need for art of any sort.   Bossuet similarly is right upon equally impossible conditions.   He is considering a Christian commonwealth in which all men are ideally Christians. Thus, both Plato and Bossuet deny the problem rather than solve it.   Neither understands art as amusement in terms of purgation and recreation, because neither formulates a problem to which such understanding is relevant.   Art and government are not for saints or for philosophers, for souls already well-ordered, but for the people.   The necessity of the one is the same as the necessity for the other.   Thus the conflict of art and prudence arises.   Both the State and the Church must consider every kind of person, not only philosophers and saints.   Civil and ecclesiastical rule must be adapted to the character of its subjects, just as the arts must be proportional to their spectators.   Seeing the problem as Bossuet does not, Aquinas is able to see it in terms of the State as well as in terms of the Church, and to correlate these two aspects of it.   There is no conflict between the Christian ideal of the saint and the recognition that most men are not saints, but corrupt, and therefore lead worldly lives under civil government.   The peace and harmony of the State, the public good which the arts can serve in their purgative and recreational functions, is indispensable as an external condition of the religious life itself.

One final comment must be added.   The spirit of Christianity which one finds in St. Augustine and St. Thomas Aquinas is not morally self-righteous.   It may aspire to, but it does not pretend to speak from the position of, saintliness.   This pretension has too often caused the spiritual blindness of Christian reformers, like Collier or even like Bossuet.   They have not

[77] *Op. cit.*, p. 86.

understood human problems in terms of human corruption — corruption not corruptibility. They have not acknowledged that the best man who is not a saint is a poor thing. The range in the gradation of the qualities of men or of the arts which they enjoy, can be viewed either by human eyes or, by religious feeling, through the eyes of God. In the first view, the difference between the extremes appears immense, and one is in danger of committing the sin of pride, becoming a moral prig or an aesthetic high-brow, failing to understand the popular appreciation of poor art, condemning the mass of men, and utterly missing and misconceiving the tragic difficulty of human practical problems. In the second view, the separation between the extremes is slight, and one can be sorry only for not being a saint, or sorrier still for not even wishing to be one [56]. Out of such sorrow, which is the heart of Christian feeling, one can approach all human problems with a compassion that makes them genuine as well as intelligible. Since they arise because man is weak, they can be understood only by taking the position of the weakest man.

It is not in the spirit of Savonarola that the arts must be scourged and expunged, but in the spirit of St. Thomas who, at the end of his life and in religious ecstasy, could say of his own *Summa Theologica* — incomparably magnificent as a production of human art — "It seems to me rubbish." [78] It is through such manifestations of Christian vision that one can appreciate, though in a feeble way, the Franciscan impulse to make a huge conflagration of all the classics of the western world, with Hollywood film as tinder.

[78] Maritain, *op. cit.*, p. 117.

CHAPTER FOUR

Democracy

DEMOCRACY, as John Dewey has said, is a mode of human association and not merely a kind of government. In the deepest sense, all contemporary European societies are democratic, whether their government is republican and legislation is representative, as in England, France and the United States, or whether it is totalitarian, and the rule is by a dictator or by a single party, as in Germany, Italy and Russia. In the narrower Greek meaning of the word, a democracy was a state in which the people ruled themselves directly ; the small populations of Greek city-states did not require representative government. The Roman Republic was a democracy of a different sort, in which different social classes had different political status, and were represented in the control of affairs by different legislative assemblies. According to our modern conception, democracy did not exist in the ancient world at all, partly because of the distinctions between citizen and slave and those involved in the political hierarchy of social classes, and partly because of the physical conditions of society itself. It is the second of these reasons which I wish to consider first, since it will enable us to understand the sense in which even Russia, Italy and Germany today are democratic.

As the result of mechanical inventions which are the fruits of modern investigative science, modern societies are conditioned by the tremendous mobility of their people and by what, in one sense, is almost a maximum of communication. The so-

called industrial revolution which altered the economic techniques of modern life also changed, of course, its social structure
— created cities, increased populations — but not without the
co-operating influence of the means of transportation and the
avenues of communication which make it necessary for any
government, whether autocratic, oligarchical or representative,
to reach the people in great masses in order to rule them.   The
importance of the ministry of propaganda in Italy and Germany
indicates the democratic aspect of these societies.   Whether
or not the people actually wield political power, the physical
conditions of modern society create a kind of popular sovereignty and universal suffrage which no political organization
can efface or dare to ignore.   Another indication of the basic
change produced by the printing press, the telephone, the radio,
the motion picture, and the means of transportation, is the existence in all contemporary states of popular education in some
form.   The difference between Germany, Russia, and Italy, on
the one hand, and England, France, and the United States, on
the other, is not the former's attempt to eliminate or reduce the
fundamental democratic institution of popular education, but
rather that they attempt to control it in a different way and
for different ends.   The relation between education and political propaganda is closer in Russia than in the United States, but
it is not altogether absent in the United States, since no kind of
government can afford to leave its education entirely free [57].
The education of its citizens in a certain way is indispensable to
its self-preservation.

The physical conditions of society in modern times, with their
consequent alterations of economic organization and process,
are also in part responsible for a shift in class distinctions that is
essential to democracy.   One does not have to be a communist
to recognize that the economic basis of social classes has gradually
replaced all other methods of distinction [58].   It may be politically important in Germany, Italy, and Russia, whether one is
a member of *the* party, or whether one is a member of *the* race;
nevertheless, there is no political hierarchy of social classes as
in republican Rome, and with the exception of Germany, there
are no slaves or disenfranchised persons.   Wage slaves are not
politically but socially in a different position from their economic
masters.   This can best be understood in terms of the democratic

principles which were enunciated in the eighteenth century, the notions of equality, liberty, and fraternity. The basic concept of equality certainly did not involve the denial of the natural inequalities of men; to suppose that it did, is the worst misunderstanding of the maxim that all men are born equal. It must be interpreted to mean that all men should be *treated* equally, and in the light of their natural inequalities, the equal treatment of unequals must be proportional. What the communists call wage slavery is consistent with democracy insofar as it depends upon an equality of economic opportunity which is proportional to the abilities of different men. Communism itself calls for an economic equality which is proportional, not absolute [59]. Similarly, the institutions of popular education and universal suffrage do not give *equal* amounts of education or political power to all men, but there is an equality in the proportion between what is given and what can be received. Popular education, which cannot ignore the range of abilities in the human materials it works upon, but works with these materials accordingly, is the prototype of all democratic institutions and expresses the essence of democratic society.

I am not trying to minimize the differences between Germany, Russia and Italy, on the one hand, and England, France and the United States, on the other. I am merely trying to understand what is common to all contemporary European societies because they exist in a modern world which imposes the same conditions upon them. The issues between fascism and communism, or between fascism and republicanism, are based upon differences in economic and governmental policy, but all shades of policy must face the same economic problems and must take account of the same social factors: the size of populations, the concentration in cities, the mobility of people, and the nature of the community which results from maximized communication. Democracy as, following John Dewey, I am using the term, describes the nature of modern society and not any particular economic or governmental policy. The word can be used more specifically, of course, to name peculiarly republican or liberal institutions,[1] in which case the United States is democratic, Italy

[1] Professor Dewey in recent writings uses the word "liberalism" as a synonym for "democracy" in its narrower meaning. Vd. *Liberalism and Social Action,* New York, 1936.

is not, and Russia hopes to be when its period of revolution is over and the accomplishment of widespread education makes it possible.[2]   I am not using the term in its more generic sense in order to obfuscate a great many important issues in the contemporary world, but because it is only in this more generic sense in which democracy prevails in modern civilization that the problem of the arts takes on new meaning.   Just as the advent of Christianity requires a fresh examination of the Greek discussion of poetry and politics as that becomes translated into Christian terms, so the occurrence of a new kind of community of men — a product of machinery that the ancient world did not possess — calls for a similar extension of the discussion.

Christianity had to overcome looking upon all the secular arts with disfavor; it had a primitive antipathy to worldliness, to the pleasures of a worldly life; and the arts, particularly those of literature and the theatre, were inextricably caught in the meshes of this world.   But democracy is initially and essentially predisposed to favor the arts.   The arts are means of communication; they succeed as instruments of popular education where more formal procedures fail; most particularly the arts of literature, which use the printing press for wide dissemination, and the arts of the theatre, which bring about the congregation of people.   It is not difficult to see why the invention of the motion picture, which has multiplied theatres many times, should have created an art that has become one of the sinews of the democratic community.[3]   Art is important to democracy in proportion as it is popular.   From the democratic point of view, the arts are essentially good because they are involved in the texture of society; it is only secondarily that the question of their moral influence is raised.   It may be necessary to control or direct them, but democracy, unlike Christianity, never even raises the question of whether the arts are permissible, whether they have any place in society at all.   This explains why, in the nineteenth and twentieth centuries, the attacks upon the theatre, for instance, seldom, if ever, go to the Platonic or primitive Christian extreme of asking for its abolition.   Censorship is

[2] As this is written, Russia is instituting a system of parliamentary government with some measure of popular representation.

[3] The invention of the radio is equally, if not more, important; but so far at least the radio is primarily an instrument of communication and not the medium of a new art.

proposed, but not extermination.   The Christian commonwealth
has become a democracy.   The difference that this makes in the
approach to the problem of the arts is clear.   Christianity, viewing the arts with suspicion, is able in the case of St. Thomas to
make an apology for them in terms of their social utility.   Democracy, viewing the arts as fundamentally useful to society,
apologizes for having to censor or control them for the sake
of morals.   The merger of Christianity and democracy is possible because, when fully expressed, the two points of view can
be matched, but the emphasis is different.

Democracy, like Christianity, has its primitive moment [60]
and its full expression; it also has its Platonists and its Aristotelians.   It would be erroneous to suppose that all thinkers
who have been exponents of democratic principles and institutions are in complete concurrence.   Certainly that is not the
case with respect to the arts.   Jean Jacques Rousseau, a father
of the French Revolution, is in this sense a father of primitive
democracy; he enunciated some of its leading principles, but
he did not fully comprehend its nature or clearly see its problems.
John Dewey is also a democrat but, within the frame of a common doctrine, he differs from Rousseau enormously.   It will
be instructive to treat the positions which Rousseau and Dewey
take in regard to the arts, as Platonic and Aristotelian, although
Rousseau is a sentimental Platonist and Dewey only analogically
an Aristotelian.   The translation of the ancient issue into its
modern democratic phase can thus be most effectively accomplished.

Rousseau was provoked to an extended statement concerning
the place of the theatre in the state by an article in the great
French *Encyclopedia* in which D'Alembert had recommended
to the people of Geneva that they institute a theatre of comedy.
Rousseau was reading Plato's *Republic* at the time.   With the
aid of Plato's principles, to which he declared his indebtedness
in an appendix of material culled from the *Republic* and the
Laws, he proposed to inform his beloved city of the insidious-
ness of D'Alembert's suggestion.   The points which Rousseau
makes in this *Letter to D'Alembert* [4] are restricted to the theatre,
but it must be remembered that in one of his earliest works [5]

[4] *Lettre à M. D'Alembert sur les Spectacles*, 1758 ; ed. Hachette, Paris, 1916.
[5] *A Discourse on the Moral Effects of the Arts and Sciences*. The *Discourse*

Rousseau had attacked all the arts, and the sciences as well, for causing the corruption of society and human manners [61]. The arts and sciences have produced a cultivated society which is vastly inferior to the natural state of mankind. Culture is for Rousseau opposed to Nature. It is artificial. And since Nature is the standard of goodness, the arts which are responsible for culture are bad. Man is good naturally; it is only by his institutions, his arts and sciences, that he is made bad. This was Jean Jacques' great insight on the road to Vincennes when he learned of the prize for which he wrote this early essay. It is violently extreme: devotion to the arts leads to luxury which saps the military and the moral virtues; every useless citizen is a pernicious man, and even the best scientific men and artists are useless; sovereigns who are wise will banish the deadly art of printing which perpetuates the extravagances of these useless men. These extremities are supported by an elaborate historical *post hoc ergo propter hoc*, which consists of the recital of the downfall of the great nations of the past at some time *after* their highest accomplishment in the arts and sciences. Rousseau later admitted that this first discourse, although it expressed a vision to which he attributes all his greatness, was wanting in logic and order, was feeblest in reasoning of all his writings. But his *Letter* on comedy, which expresses the same insight, is Rousseau's favorite among his works, because "produced without effort, at the first inspiration, and in the most lucid moments of my life." [6] Voltaire's comment on the *Letter* is more significant for our analysis. He asked: "Has Jean Jacques turned a father of the church?"

Rousseau's exposition of democracy is to be found in his *Discourse on Inequality* [7] and his *Social Contract*. [8] They abound in confusions and inconsistencies. One wishes that his self-proclaimed discipleship to Plato had resulted in some analytical skill. Were he more rigorously a Platonist, he could not have been so inconsistently a democrat. Thus, we find the concepts of popular sovereignty and popular education basic to his political theory. Man is free in a state of nature. He can only

---

won the prize at the Academy of Dijon in 1750, answering the question proposed: Has the Restoration of the Arts and Sciences Had a Purifying Effect upon Morals?

[6] John Morley, *Rousseau*, London, 1873.   [7] 1755.   [8] 1762.

be free in society, which is the artificial result of a social contract, if the rule to which he submits is his own rule; hence the paradox of each citizen being at once both ruler and subject, and each contributing to the rule of all by the expression of his will in political action [62]. But popular sovereignty will produce a good government of human affairs only if the people are educated to this task, share common interests and participate in the community as a whole in the same way that each participates in the life of his own family. The widest possible education of the citizens, and their closest integration through communication, are the indispensable conditions of the democratic state in which men can be subjects without ceasing to be equal and free. Yet when one looks further into the source of the constitution of such a state and into the origin of its body of laws, one discovers the hand of the Lawgiver, who is neither a citizen nor a governor, who, quite apart from actual affairs but with complete wisdom in such matters, constructs the state and dictates its laws because he does not trust the uneducated will of the people. Rousseau cannot wait for the fruits of popular education to make the people able to rule. The mystery of the Lawgiver whose interference entirely nullifies the democratic process, is solved when it is recognized that the Lawgiver is Rousseau himself.[9] Rousseau is dreaming of himself as the philosopher-king of Plato's Republic, and is not bothered at all by the fantastic inconsistency of his position in a democratic society. It is this inconsistency which explains the further inconsistency that Rousseau, who should favor the theatre as a medium of communication and education, wishes to exclude it from the democratic city of Geneva. It does not explain the violence of his animosity or the extraordinary view of human nature which is expressed in the *Letter to D'Alembert;* that can be accounted for only in terms of the intricacies of his disordered soul.

In brief, his position is that the moral effect of the stage can never be salutary in itself though it may easily be extremely

[9] Vd. *Social Contract,* II, 7, Cf. Maritain, *Three Reformers,* New York, 1932 : pp. 138–139. "But what then is this extraordinary and extra-cosmic lawgiver ? We have not far to seek. It is Jean-Jacques himself — Jean-Jacques who, quite meaning to be the perfect Adam who completes his paternal work by education and political guidance, finds comfort for bringing children into the world for the Foundling Hospital in becoming Emile's tutor and the lawgiver of the Republic."

pernicious, and that the habit of frequenting the theatre, the taste for imitating the style of the actors, the cost in money, the waste in time, apart from the morality of the matter represented, are bad in themselves absolutely.   As John Morley points out, the *Letter* is essentially a supplement to the first *Discourse*, an application of its principles to a practical case, and while it deals only with the theatre, it is part of Rousseau's general protest against philosophers, poets, men of letters, artists, and all their works.

Dramatic spectacles are amusements and only amusements. But who needs amusements?   Only men who are ill-employed, men who are restless in conscience, men who are idle, men who have lost the taste for simple and natural pleasures, seek out such amusements.   Discipline of the will, which is essential in moral-ity, cannot be achieved by the theatre.   Those whom it attracts it can only amuse, for they come to the theatre only because they are avoiding or are without duties in life.   The principal aim of the theatre is to give pleasure and not to be useful; it does this by exciting the passions, and this is never good.   Rousseau denies purgation [63].   "Must we become temperate and wise," he asks, "by first being furious and mad?"[10]   He concludes: "Whether one deduces from the nature of spectacles in general the best forms of which they are capable, or whether one ex-amines all that the lights of a century and an enlightened people have done for the perfection of our drama, I believe that I can conclude from these divers considerations that the moral effect of the spectacle and the plays can never possibly be good or salutary in itself, since, to count only their advantages, one finds there no sort of real use without disadvantages which surpass them.   But, in consequence of its very inutility, the theatre which can do nothing toward correcting morals, can do a great deal toward altering them.   In favoring all of our penchants, it gives a new ascendancy to those which already dominate us; the continual emotions we feel there enervate us, weaken us, make us more incapable than ever of resisting our passions; and the sterile interest we have in virtue only serves to throw a sop to our self-love without constraining us to put it into practice."[11]

To the objection that the theatre is a lesser evil which prevents other and greater evils, Rousseau answers in effect that this means

[10] *Op. cit.*, p. 31.   [11] *Op. cit.*, p. 89.

that the theatre is good only for corrupt men and a corrupting influence upon good men. Thus, even if Rousseau understood the nature of purgation, he would deny its utility because good men do not need purgation, and bad men cannot profit by it. He takes the position that the theatre can do people no harm only if they are so bad to begin with that nothing worse can happen to them. But men are not naturally corrupt; they are only corruptible, and the arts are one of the chief sources of their corruption.

It should be noted that Rousseau does not deny the place of recreation and amusements in the state, particularly in democratic states. It is precisely in republics, he says, that the public spectacle has its origin. The representation of things before the people as a whole has always been one of the bonds of their union and a support of liberty. Great public celebrations must produce the atmosphere of one great family. The democratic note is here apparent. But the recreations should be natural rather than artificial; they should be spectacles or fêtes which express the social interest, reviews of the soldiery, the reproduction of national antiquities, and so forth.

It is not worth our while to criticize Rousseau's analysis in detail. Most of the points he makes have already been fully refuted in the discussion that has gone before. It is clear that he does not understand the nature of the arts as imitations in the genus of spectacles, nor their function as objects of contemplation and sources of recreation; he cannot, therefore, see their moral and political utility. He sees no value in contemplation, but only in action, and yet inconsistently with that he holds any arousal of the emotions, which are the springs of action, to be bad. The theatre cannot improve the moral character because that must consist in the discipline of the will; the attitude of the spectator in the theatre is incompatible with the exercise of the will, and hence, it cannot be there disciplined. But by the same argument, the theatre cannot cause vice which like virtue is habitual and must result from a will trained in the wrong direction. The argument is worse than self-contradictory, for it is based upon an impossible separation of the will from the faculty of moral judgment. But what is the worst error in Rousseau's attack, the error which explains his violent antipathy to all the arts as sources of human corruption, is his conception of man as a natural saint,[12] a creature naturally perfect except for his corruptibility. Man is pure and good until he is defiled by the institutions of human society and culture, by the arts of civilization. The argument is simple. If man is in his original nature good, and if man is everywhere found corrupt under the influence of society and civilization, in which the arts are leading factors, the conclusion follows that civilization and its arts have corrupted man. The conclusion can be avoided simply by questioning the first premise, as anyone must who recognizes the paradox of rational animality or who understands the doctrine of original sin. Rousseau is as heretical a Christian as he is a muddled Platonist. He deserves our consideration, as Collier did, only as a bad example. It is just as possible for great exponents of democracy to violate its principles in considering the arts, as for reformers in the name of Christianity to be less Christian than they should.

Though a century earlier than Rousseau, John Milton is a better democrat as well as a better Christian. His famous tract, the *Areopagitica*,[13] written against a proposal to license the printing press, is uncompromising in its opposition to any censorship of literature. The principles upon which it is based are both democratic and Christian ; the fusion of the two makes his position different from that of St. Thomas. Milton insists upon man's individual responsibility for his moral welfare. He goes much further than Aquinas in limiting the field of political action to matters of eminently public concern. He is against paternalism, either in church or state, and whether it be benevolent and wise or not. His individualism is as extreme, on the one hand, as is Plato's regulation of every aspect of human activity in the *Laws*, on the other. We have not found this note of individualism in either ancient or mediæval thought; it is a peculiarly modern note and one of the expressions of the democratic temper.

It is man's lot in this world to have knowledge of both good and evil. The knowledge of good is involved and interwoven with the knowledge of evil. The Apostle said : "To the pure, all things are pure." Milton adds : "Not only meats and drinks, but all kind of knowledge, whether good or evil : the knowledge

[12] Vd. Maritain, *Three Reformers*, New York, 1932 : pp. 93–164 devoted to *Rousseau or Nature's Saint*. [13] London, 1644.

cannot defile, nor consequently the books, if the will and conscience be not defiled." [14]   God does not captivate man under a perpetual childhood of prescription.   Man has the gifts of reason and prudence ; these are the implements with which his character must be formed, working upon the materials of good and evil which grow in this world together.   This is the benefit that may be had of books promiscuously read : they provide a survey of vice as well as virtue.   The scanning of error is necessary to the confirmation of truth ; so a survey of vice to the constituting of human virtue [64].   "This is that doom which Adam fell into of knowing good and evil ; that is to say, of knowing good by evil.   As therefore the state of man now is ; what wisdom can there be to choose, what continence to forbear, without the knowledge of evil ?   He that can apprehend and consider vice with all her baits and seeming pleasure, and yet abstain, and yet distinguish, and yet prefer that which is truly better, he is the true wayfaring Christian.   I cannot praise a fugitive and cloistered virtue unexercised and unbreathed, that never sallies out and seeks her adversary, but slinks out of the race where that immortal garland is to be run for, not without dust and heat. Assuredly we bring not innocence into the world, we bring impurity much rather ; that which purifies us is trial, and trial is by what is contrary.   That virtue therefore which is but a youngling in the contemplation of evil, and knows not the utmost that vice promises to her followers, and rejects it, is but a blank virtue, not a pure ; her whiteness is but an excremental whiteness." [15]

The consequence is clear.   If good men can be harmed by what they read, then how shall we trust the licensers or censors "unless we can confer upon them, or they assume to themselves, above all others in the land, the grace of infallibility and uncorruptedness ?" [16]   If, on the other hand, a wise man cannot be harmed, able like a good refiner, to "gather gold out of the drossiest volume" and if "a fool will be a fool with the best book, yea, or without a book ; there is no reason that we should deprive a wise man of any advantage to his wisdom, while we seek to restrain from a fool that which being restrained will be no hindrance to his folly." [17]

[14] *Op. cit.,* ed. by Sir Richard Jebb, Cambridge, 1918 : pp. 17–18.
[15] *Op. cit.,* p. 20.   [16] *Op. cit.,* p. 24.   [17] *Op. cit.,* p. 24.

It is, therefore, to be expected that Milton will read the patristic injunctions against the theatre and pagan literature differently from Bossuet; that he will defend the poets against Plato. Milton delights to point out how many of the Fathers of the Church read the Greek poets, and that Plato commended the reading of Aristophanes, the loosest of them all, to his royal scholar, Dionysius of Syracuse. He dwells upon the exclusion of the philosophers from Rome by Cato the Censor as if it were an ironical counterpoint to Plato's expulsion of the poets. That Plato himself transgressed his own rules, being much addicted to reading Homer, Sophron, Aristophanes, and the tragic poets, can only be accounted for by the fact that Plato did not live in the perfect state of his own imagining. He knew, says Milton, that his licensing of poems "had reference and dependence to many other provisoes there set down in his fancied republic, which in this world could have no place; and so neither he himself nor any magistrate or city ever imitated that course which, taken apart from those other collateral injunctions, must needs be vain and fruitless."[18] Milton thinks to reduce the Platonic position to an absurdity by suggesting that if we license printing to rectify morals, "we must regulate all recreations and pastimes, all that is delightful to man."[19] He proceeds in sarcasm to enumerate all the regulations that would then have to be imposed: upon songs and dancing, upon games and festivities, upon drinking and personal adornment, upon domestic conversation, and the consort of the sexes. Yet in all this he goes not one bit further than Plato actually went in the prescriptions of the *Laws*. The argument *per impossible* thus loses some of its force, but the polarity of Milton and Plato, as sounding the antiphonal notes of modern democracy and ancient politics, is clear.

It must not be thought, however, that Milton entirely neglects the political problem in the excess of his individualism. He wishes merely to be pragmatic about practical problems in an Aristotelian fashion. Wine, woman and song will be and must be parts of human life; "how they shall be least hurtful, how least enticing, herein consists the grave and governing wisdom of the state"; it must ordain wisely "in this world of evil, in the midst whereof God hath placed us unavoidably."[20] Milton is thoroughly consistent in praising Plato for his positive institu-

[18] *Op. cit.,* p. 26.   [19] *Op. cit.,* p. 26.   [20] *Op. cit.,* pp. 27–28.

tions, for what he calls the "unconstraining laws of virtuous education." [21] If these provisions include restrictions upon the recreations of children and supervision of the poetry they shall be given, he cannot object because it is only against regulations which regard all men as in a perpetual childhood that he is protesting. "If every action which is good or evil in man at ripe years were to be under pittance, and prescription, and compulsion, what were virtue but a name, what praise could be then due to well doing, what grammercy to be sober, just or continent. Many there be that complain of divine Providence for suffering Adam to transgress. Foolish tongues! when God gave him reason, he gave him freedom to choose, for reason is but choosing; he had been else a mere artificial Adam, such an Adam as he is in the motions." [22] Yet even in the tutelage of the young, or those who while chronologically adult are still immature, Milton would be cautious in choosing means for the cultivation of virtue, chary of using prohibitions and restraints. He has considered the ancient question whether virtue can be taught and knows at least that it is by some co-operation of nature and reason and habit that character is formed. If habit plays some part, it cannot be blind habit, but guided by rational choice. Reason must be given alternatives, and even though in the case of children it needs instruction, it cannot be exercised in a world from which all dilemmas have been banished by laws which seek to create a purified and perfect environment. God created the passions within us and pleasures around us that these rightly tempered may be the very ingredients of virtue. "This justifies the high providence of God who, though he command us temperance, justice, continence, yet pours out before us even to profuseness all desirable things, and gives us minds that can wander beyond all limit of satiety. Why should we then affect a rigour contrary to the manner of God and of nature, by abridging or scanting those means which books freely permitted are, both to the trial of virtue, and the exercise of truth?" [23] Since the matter of both vice and virtue are the same, to expel the occasions for the one is to expel the conditions of the other, so far as the rational formation of right habits is concerned.

The *Areopagitica* is an argument, not merely against the extremities of Plato and Rousseau in excluding the poets or pro-

[21] *Op. cit.*, p. 28.   [22] *Op. cit.*, p. 28.   [23] *Op. cit.*, p. 29.

hibiting the theatre, but even against censorship or supervision
in any form. It ultimately rests upon a profound skepticism
concerning any attempt or proposal by one man to form moral
virtues in another. Who can be protected from corruption by
a licensing of books or a censorship of plays? And if the aim
be to make men good, who has the wisdom and knowledge to be
a censor or a licenser? Milton made plain the paradox of
censorship, so plain that it has never been avoidable in all subsequent discussions of the problem [65]. Rousseau had failed
to see that if men are corruptible, they must be imperfect in
nature. Milton sees that the imperfection of human nature, its
intrinsic corruption, is the seat of its further corruptibility. But
if all men are corruptible, what is the distinction among them
which enables some to examine into matters without harm which,
if exposed to others, would corrupt them? Who are to be
protected: children, women, the poor, the illiterate, classes
which in one sense or another are considered incompetent or
under-privileged? But even if we knew that one kind of man
was more corruptible than another, and even if we knew that
one influence was more contagious to his weakness than another,
we could not make him less corruptible by censorship, or give
him strength that he does not have, to accomplish virtue.
Milton is not facing the wider political problem of the effects
of poetry and other arts upon human conduct. *If* it could be
shown that they are causes of criminality, of laxity in public
manners, or other types of subversive behavior, he would not
object to political action taken for the preservation of the commonwealth. He is more narrowly attacking censorship as a
political expedient only if its professed aim is to achieve the
moral improvement of those who are supposedly protected by it.
Milton is clear that it can never do this. He is, furthermore,
clear that no form of literature can ever be by itself the essential
cause of either virtue or vice. Literature can only provide the
matter, as does the rest of life, upon which the powers of the
human soul must work for good or evil. Literature and kindred
arts, therefore, perform an indispensable service of public education which is hindered, for the most part without any demonstrable profit, by censorship and control.

Finally, we must turn to John Dewey for the most recent and

the fullest exposition of the democratic evaluation of the arts. Dewey, as I have already suggested, does not treat democracy as a political theory; it is rather a state of affairs which exists to be described. Like any other existing organization of human affairs, its values are implicit in its being, its ideals are to be evoked from its actual practices. Dewey is normative in his discussion of democracy only to the extent that he is able to find in its nature the criteria by which to judge what is more or less appropriate to the fulfillment of that nature, but he would insist that the discovery of the nature of democracy is not made by a dialectical examination of political concepts or principles, but by an investigation of the democratic order, which is the modern order, in society. Democracy has happened as a product of many historical forces. Since we are living in its day, we had better learn how to live well under its reign, which means through conformity to its nature. When Dewey attempts to go further and say that we are fortunate in being alive today in a democratic society, that democracy is *better* than the social order of the ancient or mediæval world, then his judgment must be supported by norms which history does not provide. The values which are intrinsic to democracy cannot be used to judge the merits of other kinds of society which do not generate those values. Dewey would certainly wish to avoid the ethnocentricity of such a judgment. To insist, as he sometimes does, upon the superiority of democracy to all other forms of society, particularly those of the ancient world, Dewey must appeal to the nature of man and find therein the criteria by which one type of social organization can be judged *absolutely* better than another. Whether this can be done, and whether, if it is possible, the superiority of democracy can be demonstrated, are questions we need not answer here. For our purposes, it is important only to understand that the evaluation which Professor Dewey makes of the arts in a democracy is determined by the nature of democracy as Professor Dewey finds it existing and not necessarily as he wishes it to be. To be a democrat in his sense, is primarily to be a person who is responsive to the conditions of contemporary life, and only secondarily to be a person with a programme and a policy. Aware of these conditions, one evaluates what goes on in terms of them, and plans action accordingly. It is in this sense that John Dewey speaks as a democrat about the arts in *Democracy and Education*.[24]

Education must be understood much more broadly than as a process of intellectual instruction which is carried on by teachers in schools, and a process of moral training under the influence of particular individuals who are associated with such institutions as the home, the church and the school. Education is what happens to an individual as the result of the impact on him of his total environment, physical and social. Any social relation which is vitally shared, Dewey says, is educative to those who participate in it. Since democracy is "a mode of associated living, of conjoint, communicated experience,"[25] education in this broadest sense is essential to its nature. Democracy intends, because of what it is, to make as numerous as possible the points of shared common interests within each of its groups and to see to it that there is as wide and as free an interaction as possible between each of its groups. Each group, that is to say, must be aware so far as is possible, of the attitudes, standards, activities and manners of all other groups. How is this interpenetration of groups to be achieved? By increasing the scope of vitally shared experience. There must be some way of appreciating the activities of the other groups, in the activities and standards of which one does not participate. All mediums of representation are means to this democratic end. Education must include all the various mediums of representation; in fact, education is the process which enables an individual to participate most fully in society. It follows that democracy and education are two aspects of the same situation; democracy exists only to the extent that education, in the sense defined, succeeds, since democracy is the situation in which each individual participates as fully as possible in the life of society as a whole. While it is true that all societies, which are communities, depend upon the communication of their members, democracy is distinguished as a community by the degree to which communication is achieved. Individuals do not compose a social group merely because they all work for a common end; they must all be cognizant of that common end and be interested in it. It is in this sense that social life is identical with communication and dependent primarily upon education.

24 The Macmillan Company, Publishers, New York, 1926.   25 *Op. cit.,* p. 101.

The arts are educative because they are primary means of communication; they are modes of social representation which enable the individual to share imaginatively in activities and interests in which he does not participate [66]. Dewey has gone so far as to say that the arts are the prime instruments of education, since they are best suited to represent, by appealing to the imagination, the whole dimension of unparticipated activities which are nevertheless appropriable. And among the arts, those of literature, because they use language and because their object of imitation — Dewey would say representation — is human activity itself, are the most important instruments of communication. It follows also that any particular art is socially important to the degree that it is a vehicle of communication, and this is measured by its gross popularity and by the variety of different groups in society which are able by means of it to enjoy a vicarious participation in the life of society as a whole. The motion picture and the presentations of the radio are thus democracy's arts. They are almost the perfect image of democracy itself. They are creatures of the same factors of mechanical invention which have produced democracy, and they are most perfectly adapted to its needs by reason of the size and character of the population they are able to reach. A democrat would as soon ask the value of democracy itself as question the value of the arts which the camera and the radio have brought into existence [67].

"Every expansive era in the history of mankind has coincided with the operation of factors which have tended to eliminate distance between peoples and classes previously hemmed off from one another."[26] Democracy is the culmination of this tendency. The democratically organized society is characterized by two traits: "(1) A more numerous and more varied group of shared common interests which leads to a greater reliance upon the recognition of mutual interests as a factor in social control; (2) a freer interaction between social groups and a consequent flexibility of social habits by continuous readjustment through meeting the new situations produced by varied intercourse."[27] Ancient societies, typically non-democratic from

[26] *Op. cit.,* p. 100, by permission of The Macmillan Company, Publishers.
[27] *Op. cit.,* p. 100, by permission of The Macmillan Company, Publishers. Cf. *The Public and Its Problems,* New York, 1927: Ch. 3 and 5.

Dewey's point of view, are characterized by sharp social stratifications and barriers to communication and intercourse, and by static customs which tend to preserve themselves from change. The criteria by which Dewey is able to criticize the political and educational ideals of Plato and Aristotle are thus made clear, but it is also clear that these criteria are democratic standards, the rightness of which has been assumed.

Dewey appreciates that the devotion of democracy to education is not its distinguishing mark. Plato and Aristotle, as the exponents of a non-democratic society, are concerned, no less than he is, with the problems of education. The difference lies in the character and aims of education which are imposed by the nature of different societies. It is superficial to explain democracy's interest in education in terms of popular suffrage which cannot be successful unless those who elect and who obey their governors are educated. There is a deeper explanation. Democracy is more than a form of government; it is the kind of society which arises as social stratifications disappear. "A society marked off into classes need be specially attentive only to the education of its ruling elements." [28] A society which is mobile in its parts requires that education fit each individual to move anywhere in its domain. Again it becomes apparent that the arts are indispensable to education of this sort, and are serviceable in proportion as they achieve the widest range of communication. Since they are representative, that is, since they are imitative, they are not sufficient by themselves; they must be supplemented by direct participation, which the various forms of play and occupation provide; but they are indispensable, since they supply the materials of imagination which must be drawn upon in play and work. "They are not the exclusive agencies of social appreciation in the most general sense of that word, but they are the chief agencies of an intensified, enhanced appreciation. As such, they are not only intrinsically and directly enjoyable, but they serve a purpose beyond themselves. . . They are not the luxuries of education, but emphatic expressions of what makes any education worth while." [29]

The arts have one further basic value, and in recognizing this value, Dewey and Aristotle are in perfect agreement. "No

[28] *Op. cit.*, p. 102, by permission of The Macmillan Company, Publishers.
[29] *Op. cit.*, p. 279, by permission of The Macmillan Company, Publishers.

demand of human nature is more urgent or less to be escaped than that for recreation. The idea that the need can be suppressed is absolutely fallacious, and the Puritanic tradition which disallows the need has entailed an enormous crop of evils. If education does not afford opportunity for wholesome recreation, and train capacity for seeking and finding it, the suppressed instincts find all sorts of illicit outlets. Education has no more serious responsibility than making adequate provision for recreative leisure, not only for the sake of immediate health, but still more for the sake of its lasting effect upon habits of mind. Art is again the answer to this demand." [30] Moreover, in a democratic society, leisure is the common property of all, not the privilege of the few. That the arts be popular, and not the possession of special classes, becomes necessary. To be universally enjoyed, to be able to provide amusement and recreation for all men, the arts must be commensurate with the range of human abilities which, even in a democracy, are not everywhere the same [68]. Again, it can be seen that the motion-picture camera and the radio have implemented arts which more nearly meet the needs of democracy, both as recreational and as socially educative, than the other arts of literature depending on the printing press.

The agreement between Dewey and Aristotle is extraordinary in the light of Dewey's failure to realize it. By his own standards, Dewey is right in treating Greek society and its values as non-democratic. He is further right in reading the *Republic* and the *Laws* as political treatises in which democracy is certainly not envisaged as the best form of society. Plato's educational policy, and his disposition of the arts in education, are not in accordance with democratic principles. And Dewey, praising Plato for his profound sense of the function of education in discovering and developing personal capacities, excuses him for "not being able to work out a solution of the problem whose terms he saw so clearly, because the society in which the theory was propounded was so undemocratic"; [31] he could not do

[30] *Op. cit.*, p. 241, by permission of The Macmillan Company, Publishers.
[31] *Op. cit.*, p. 104, by permission of The Macmillan Company, Publishers. Dewey also says, in this chapter, that although Plato's educational philosophy was revolutionary, it was none the less in bondage to static ideals. The breakdown of his philosophy is made apparent for Dewey in the fact that he

otherwise. Whether or not Plato needs this kind of apology, Dewey correctly recognizes an ideal opponent in him. Had Plato the opportunity of being his contemporary, and of studying the kind of society which the forces of history have produced, there seems good reason to believe that he still would have been Dewey's opponent and dispraised democracy as far from the ideal state. But the case of Aristotle is different, and this Dewey fails to see.[32] Aristotle may agree with Plato that there is one form of human society which is the best absolutely, although the *Politics* is not finally clear on this point; yet at the same time it is the basic principle of his political theory that there are many forms of society and government, each of which can be good relative to the conditions and circumstances of a particular people at a particular time and place. He would not necessarily have agreed with Dewey — had the opportunity been his to survey the conditions which have produced democracy — that the democratic organization is the best of all forms of human society; but he would certainly have recognized its appropriateness to the conditions of life in Europe and America from the eighteenth century on. He would have insisted, as pragmatically as Dewey, that the government of human affairs in the present era must take account of its historical conditions. Although, lacking any knowledge of such conditions by the historical accident of his birth, he did not see the value of the arts as communicative, and hence as democratizing agencies, Aristotle nevertheless recognized their value as amusements, as means of recreation and the enjoyment of leisure; he recognized their imitative or representative nature, which enabled them to

---

could not trust to gradual improvements in education to bring about a better society which would then improve education and so on indefinitely. Plato's great error was that he divided society into a limited number of classes, not recognizing that each individual constituted his own class!

[32] In the chapter on Labor and Leisure, Dewey criticizes the Aristotelian philosophy as arising from, and being relative to, a particular society. In this context he charges Aristotle with maintaining the distinction between those who are and those who are not capable of leading the life of reason, as a permanent division in human society, to which two different types of education must be adapted. The problem of education in a democratic society, Dewey says, is to do away with this dualism and to construct a course of studies which makes thought a guide of free practice for all, and which makes leisure a reward for accepting responsibility for service, rather than a state of exemption from it.

provide vicarious experience; and, most extraordinary of all, he recognized that the arts are able to perform essentially the same function for every type of man in the community, whereas philosophy and science, because of the special demands they make upon the abilities of the individual, can serve the same end only for the few.

Aristotle and Dewey alike are primarily concerned with the arts in their political or social function, and are thus to be distinguished from Plato, whose primary consideration of the arts was with regard to the formation of the moral virtues. Yet Aristotle, more nearly than Dewey, meets the typical Platonic objection to the arts in terms of his theory of purgation, a theory, by the way, which can be perfectly translated into the language of contemporary behavioristic psychology, and thus be made congenial to the pragmatic philosophy. If it is a mark of the pragmatic temper to find all values, moral and political, in utilities, in the adaptation of means to desirable ends, then Aristotle's justification of the arts by reference to their purgative and recreational utilities makes him a perfect pragmatist — as any prudent man would be in solving practical problems! It is thus thoroughly fair to view Dewey as an Aristotelian who, living in a democratic society, sees a further justification of art as a medium of communication, and hence of social education,[33] a utility and a value that is relative to the nature of democracy. If Dewey makes the error of supposing that this value is intrinsically superior to any other, we can apologize for him as he did for Plato: his philosophy is propounded in a society which is so democratic that he could not think otherwise. He is a poor Aristotelian to the extent that he does not apply the principle of political relativity to democracy and himself.

Despite this error, if he commits it, Dewey as an Aristotelian analyst of democracy makes one thing perfectly clear for us. We are living in a democratic state, both with respect to the broader meaning of democracy as a social structure, and its narrower meaning as a type of government and political policy. The contemporary problem of the arts must, therefore, be stated

[33] Strictly speaking, these are not two separate values. The arts are socially educative *as* sources of communication. To the three Aristotelian utilities — contemplative pleasure, purgation and recreation — Dewey then adds this one further value of communication *or* social education.

in democratic terms, just as it must be stated in Christian terms. In the sense in which we have seen Aquinas and Dewey as Aristotelians, we can therefore state that problem — which in its most insistent current appearance concerns the motion picture — in Aristotelian terms. Thus, we shall have the most adequate analysis of the issue, which will take account of its Christian and democratic elements as well as meet the persistent Platonic objections which, naturally enough, are found in Christianity and which even occur, paradoxically, in the democratic Rousseau. Whatever the negative values of the arts in general, whatever the charges brought against the motion picture, Dewey has made clear, in the light of Aristotelian principles, that the arts, and particularly the motion picture, have an undeniable and tremendous positive value for democracy. They are not an evil to be suffered because unfortunately inevitable, or because of some minor good. They are intrinsically and primarily good, and the problem which they raise must be formulated in terms of those accidental effects which, in the opinion of some, are undesirable. One cannot live in a democracy and deny popular education, though one may regret it — which is like regretting the time and place of one's birth. It would be wiser to recognize the faults of popular education and seek to increase its essentially democratic goodness. The case of the arts is the same. One cannot live in a democracy and despise the popular arts. Here, too, one may wish the impossible and dream of living at a time when the arts were not lowered to the people. But the only genuinely practical problem which is raised is one of discovering the undesirable consequences of the popular arts and then seeking, if possible, to improve them, not in the spirit of rendering them less evil, but rather hoping to make them greater goods.

PART II

The Motion Picture as
Popular Poetry

CHAPTER FIVE

Historical Transformations

WE are living in a world which seems to be choosing between Christianity and paganism or atheism, and between the kind of government which is appropriate to a democratic order of society, and dominations which make a mockery of it. It is in such a world that the perennial problem of poetry and politics has become the problem of the motion picture in society. To some extent the radio and the press raise similar problems; but the movies are more fitly the heir to this ancient and traditional political question. There is a fundamental conflict in man's life between art and prudence. Of all the arts, poetry — that is, imaginative literature of any sort — has been most insistently at the center of this conflict, primarily because it is an imitation of human actions and passions and is, therefore, heavily freighted with moral significance, but also because it employs the medium of language which is the medium of ideas. In ancient times music received considerable attention, yet the difference in Plato's treatment of music and poetry signifies that the latter more ominously challenged prudence. In the long history of the discussion of these matters, the plastic arts are seldom mentioned, and music is not honored in modern times by the consideration of statesmen [69]. But poetry has always been and still remains the problem child of the muses. Of the various forms of poetry, the dramatic narrative presented as a spectacle in the theatre has always been the first and foremost object of the parental concern of society for the welfare, not of the arts, but of itself. In more recent times the novel has attracted some attention, but the history of the controversy about poetry reveals the predominant and overwhelming emphasis upon the theatre and its arts. For the same reason that poetry has ever seemed more menacing than music or painting or sculpture, the drama has magnified the menace of poetry. Whether it be comedy or tragedy, moral problems are its matter. The auxiliary arts of the theatre provide a spectacular presentation which intensifies the narrative and makes it more effective in arousing the emotions. The theatre is a place of congregation, and the audience is thus a social group in which individuals must participate publicly in order to become spectators, whereas the audience of the novel consists of separate persons in their privacy.

That the movies rightfully inherit the onus of the problem is clear. The motion-picture theatre is the theatre of democracy, and the motion picture is its most popular poetry. The theatre as a place for dramatic spectacles, the so-called legitimate stage, has become progressively unimportant; it is confined to the very large cities and, for the most part, it is found only in the great metropolis of any country. It reaches a small part of the total population and, compared to the movies, it reaches only a small part of the citizens of the great cities. This does not mean that the drama, as a form of literature, is in any way altered in aesthetic status; it means only that the rise of the motion picture in the last half century has so completely dwarfed the stage by its tremendous popularity that the stage has necessarily yielded its position as the most menacing of the arts to the movies [69a].

The art of the motion picture is not the art of the drama. Both have generically the same object of imitation. In this sense, the drama, the motion picture, and the novel, are all species of the same general art of fiction, which is the primary determination of poetry as imaginative narrative. But each is specifically different in terms of its medium and manner of imitation. We shall return to these points in the last part of this book, in which the aesthetic nature of the motion picture is analyzed.[1] Here it is necessary only to understand the sense in which the movies are the most popular form of poetry, and at the same time to avoid the error of identifying them with the drama because of the accidental circumstance that they also employ the theatre as a

[1] Vd. Chapter 13, *infra*.

place for the social gathering of their audience. Though this circumstance is accidental to the aesthetic character of the motion picture and does not make it any less independent of the drama, any less essentially different, nevertheless, the fact that movies are seen in theatres — in tremendous theatres by great crowds, in theatres which are themselves spectacles, in theatres abounding both in large cities and in small towns, and which are open day and night to a continual flux of people — is not accidental to the cinema's inheritance of the drama's title to first place among the arts as a social problem. The title not only passes, but the crown of popularity is much heavier with thorns as well as with laurels. Along with the devoted patronage of the masses, the movies have reached the floors of national parliaments where their merits and deficiencies have been debated, though not always in a manner which Plato would have thought statesmanlike or wise; they have frequently engaged the attention of the League of Nations as an international problem; at all times they are on the agenda of local and community governments due to the agitation of unofficial social groups and organizations. If the stage never had such popularity, neither did it have such troubles. The movies have the distinction of being the only officially censored art in a country such as ours, which is by tradition and principle opposed to censorship. Even though official censorship is not national, but limited to six states, the movies are self-censored, abiding by a self-imposed code of regulations which have regard for the moral and social responsibilities of the screen.[2] In their case, the aesthetic highbrows and snobs have not risen to declaim about the inalienable right of the arts to be free from interference; only professional liberals have recited the traditional formulae in their defense,[3] but the position of the professional liberals about censorship is too much an expression of an appetite for liberty, not tempered by those considerations of prudence which show that control and supervision of the arts is sometimes a justifiable political expedient. The passion for liberty, though equal and opposite to the pas-

[2] *A Code to Govern the Making of Motion and Talking Pictures*, adopted March 31, 1930 by the Association of Motion Picture Producers, Inc. and the Motion Picture Producers and Distributors of America, Inc.
[3] Vd. H. M. Kallen, *Indecency and the Seven Arts*, New York, 1930; M. Ernst and W. Seagle, *To the Pure*, New York, 1928.

sion for censorship, does not contribute to the analysis of a difficult political problem. It is a factor in political action, not a
term in political controversy and analysis.

In proportion to their extraordinary popularity, motion pictures have aroused, during their relatively short career, contemporary Platonists of all sorts, churchmen who are Platonists
as well as Christians, politicians who are Platonists as well as
democrats, parents who are almost always Platonists about their
own children. The Platonic position about the arts, about
drama, about the movies, cannot be answered by aesthetes who
talk about art for art's sake, or by liberals who worship liberty
as if it were the only good or even a good in itself. It is met,
in sound controversy, only by Aristotelians. The issue about
the movies must be understood, whether or not it is practically
solved, in terms of Aquinas against Bossuet, Dewey against Rousseau. We have surveyed the great moments and turns in this
dialectic about art and prudence in order now to be able to
analyze the contemporary controversy in such a way that we
can at least formulate an intelligible practical problem; in order
to reduce a huge field of ill-expressed and rhetorically exaggerated opinion to the few, simple, clear points which can be made;
in order to discover what knowledge we have that justifies action
and what knowledge we need to act more intelligently and hence
more prudently.

The history of political action is, however, not the same as
the history of the dialectic which is involved in political theory
and discussion. They run in parallel but often unrelated
grooves. What Plato and Aristotle say *should* be done is one
thing, what Greek tyrants do or Greek demagogues propose is
another. Collier's attack remains the same, but English policy
toward the theatre changes when William and Mary replace the
Stuarts on the throne. The contemporary problem of the
movies is a practical one; one sort of action or another is taken
and resisted, proposed and opposed. While the history of the
relevant dialectic illuminates that problem and helps us to formulate it intelligibly, a brief history of past political action is
needed in order to see current issues in full perspective and with
all the light that analogies can throw upon them. In such a history we must regard not merely the manner and extent of
political interference with the arts, but also the surrounding

social and cultural circumstances which condition the status of an art in a society at a given time. The drama and the theatre are, of course, the primary focus of this history.[4]

In the ancient world, the drama was censored in various ways and with varying degrees of severity.[5] In different Greek states, the attitude toward, and the employment of, censorship differed; Sparta, at one extreme, is supposed to have resorted to the Platonic expedient of complete exclusion of the theatre; Athens, at the other, not only endured, but cultivated the institution of the stage and its arts. Yet even in Athens, the office of the choragus performed censorial duties, since it had the power to grant or refuse the economic subsidy, in the way of a chorus, which the dramatist needed in order to produce his play. It must be remembered, however, that such official interference was usually, if not always, based on two points: the blasphemous or atheistical character of the writing; its libellous or seditious content. There is no clear evidence that the choragus exercised the kind of censorship which Plato wished to create through his Curator of Public Morals. The drama was not supervised for its influence upon the behavior of its audience. Although we are left somewhat in doubt by the suppression of a play by Aristophanes and the punishment of Euripides, it is reasonably clear that blasphemy and libel, particularly if against the officers of the state, and therefore seditious, were the chief grounds of political action against the dramatist, and not obscenity or the corruption of public manners. But again it must be remembered that the audience of the drama was highly selected; women, slaves and children did not attend the Greek theatre. Although the drama was a popular art in the Greek cities in which it flourished, reaching, in a sense, the whole population of *citizens*, that population was only a part of the total mass of people who constituted the society, and who had to be governed. The citizens formed an aristocracy, whether or not the government to which they submitted was aristocratic in the sense in which this is understood in Greek political theory. The Greek situa-

[4] The historical account here given makes no claims of adequacy. It is a brief review of some historical episodes which have a bearing on the case of the motion picture.

[5] Vd. G. H. Putnam, *Authors and Their Public in Ancient Times*, New York, 1923; J. B. Bury, *History of the Freedom of Thought*, New York, 1913.

tion nicely exemplifies the difference between the problem of the
arts in an aristocratic and in a democratic society. Popular
poetry and popular theatre are not the same thing in these different social orders; the significance of the status of popularity
changes. Finally, it must be remembered that the Greek censorship of the stage was no different from its censorship of blasphemy and sedition in purely intellectual work; thus, Anax-
agoras was exiled for blasphemy; the books of Protagoras were
commanded by the Areopagus to be burned, because a discourse
began with the confession that he did not know whether there
were gods or not; and Socrates was condemned to death for
corrupting the youth of Athens, not morally so much as intellectually, by the skeptical procedure which his judges could not
distinguish from atheism.

Rome, like Greece, was an aristocratic social order under the
Republic as well as under the Empire; but in its attitude toward
the arts and in its devotion to the military virtues it was more
like Sparta than Athens. It did not cultivate the arts originally;
it conquered them and then nourished them in captivity as it did
other symbols of conquest. The office of the censor was a
Roman institution long before the Hellenistic period, but in that
period the Romans became concerned with the supervision of
the arts and sciences of the Greek world which had come within
their dominion. The censor was in part an official census-
taker and in part a custodian of public morals and manners. It
was his duty to prosecute individuals who behaved in ways unbecoming a Roman citizen, or who in any way endangered the
moral and material welfare of the state. It is an expected consequence of his traditional powers that the censor should have
interfered with the arts, and particularly with the theatre, but
curiously enough there is little historical evidence that he often
did so. There is the familiar story of how Cato the Censor
banished the Greek philosophers and teachers from Rome, but
this, from its very notoriety, appears to be the exception rather
than the rule. It is true that the aedile who had the duty of
securing plays for public performance, was a public official, and
to this extent may have exercised a political control over the
drama, but the end which such control served was chiefly the
suppression of sedition. It certainly was not motivated primarily
by the considerations which Plato and Aristotle had raised with

respect to music and poetry in their political treatises. It is true also that under later Roman law an actor had a degraded political status.   Actors lived in Rome as foreigners rather than citizens, which means that they were not included in the censor's list of individuals for whose moral respectability account had to be given.   But there is little evidence that this discrimination against the actor's profession diminished the popularity of the theatre as an amusement for the upper classes, or in any way restricted the art of the dramatist.   Libel was, of course, prosecuted, but the dramatist can hardly be said to be restricted as an artist because he is not free to libel whom he pleases.   It should be noted that under the Empire there was some distinction between the amusements of the multitude — the gladiatorial shows, the circus, the races — and the entertainment of the upper classes in the theatre.   This indicates the limited sense in which the drama can be considered a popular art in this period and in a society which was not democratic.   Even after the emperors became Christian, and Christianity was at least nominally the the state religion, the situation did not change considerably so far as the theatre was concerned, although the range and matter of blasphemy and sedition necessarily altered.   That the Fathers of the early church so violently and excessively attacked later Roman comedy indicates that it must have been officially tolerated as popular entertainment, even though the Theodosian Code incorporates the earlier deprivation of citizenship for those who are actors.

The situation in the ancient world is thus clear on at least two points.   In the first place, though the arts, and particularly dramatic spectacles, were popular in the limited sense appropriate to an aristocratic order of society, they were not popular in our modern democratic sense: they did not reach the great masses of the population.   The problem of protecting the state, its peace and order and security, from whatever subversive effects can be attributed to the arts, is necessarily different when the arts belong primarily, if not exclusively, to the ruling classes. And in the second place, the subversive effects which are attributed to the arts are in consequence different: the emphasis is upon offenses against religion — blasphemy and heresy; and upon offenses against private and public peace — libel and sedition.   There is little or no concern about the effects of the arts upon manners or as corrupters of moral character; there is slight consideration of obscenity and indecency. The indecency of dramatic spectacles could hardly be condemned if the practices of the ruling classes during the later Empire set the standard in such matters.

It is difficult to continue this history through the Middle Ages. The secular arts play such a relatively unimportant part in human life and society that there is little occasion for their supervision to become a practical problem for either the state or the church. An art must achieve a certain degree of popularity before the question whether its effects are inimical to public safety can arise. Since the great masses of people were illiterate, and since the circulation of books and the acquaintance with any art except those which the Church employed for religious purposes was extremely limited, official administration was accordingly concerned with the suitability of pagan literature for those who could read, and with the detection and elimination of heretical doctrine. In so far as there was any censorship during the middle ages, it was directed not at poetry or imaginative literature, but primarily at intellectual literature; if pagan poetry was considered, it was viewed in its intellectual or doctrinal, and not its imaginative, dimension.[6] This accounts, as Bossuet pointed out, for the absence of any explicit condemnation of the theatre by St. Thomas; but the significance of this omission does not require the interpretation which Bossuet tried to impose upon it, namely, that had the theatre been a popular art in the thirteenth century, St. Thomas would have called for its extermination.

We must turn to the Renaissance and the beginning of modern times, therefore, to observe the characteristically different modern problem at its inception. The invention of printing is among the earliest and deepest roots of the democratic order, and just as the art of the printer is in part responsible for changing the structure of society, so it is responsible for giving both the church and the state a new form of an old problem. Printing soon made literature more generally available, and encouraged the use of the vulgar languages so that more people could read what was written. Under such circumstances, it was natural that

[6] Cf. J. E. Spingarn, *Literary Criticism in the Renaissance*, New York, 1899: pp. 4–7.

the translation of the Bible, and its publication for popular consumption, became an extraordinarily difficult problem for the church. The beginning of the various *Indices* of prohibited and expurgated books, compiled both by Catholic and Protestant authorities, occurs in this early period of the printing press. It is not that literature suddenly became more heretical or blasphemous or immoral in any sense, but rather that there was suddenly a new public for literature, which accounts for these expedients of censorship and control. Those to whom the difficult tasks of censorship and expurgation were entrusted, were certainly not in danger of any sort of corruption from the sources which they had to examine and either purify or condemn ; such men were representatives of an entire class in society who had always been able to read, and for whom literature was available in classical tongues. They were the protectors, not the protected. It was the new public which the printing press created, the public which gave a different meaning to the popularity of literature, that had to be protected from whatever baneful influences lurk in literature, intellectual or moral. Though the scope of the matter to be censored increased somewhat, the emphases were still on heresy and blasphemy, so far as the church was concerned, and upon libel and sedition, so far as the state was concerned. It was only later that obscenity and indecency became important at all, and gradually came to the front as the popularity of imaginative literature increased and it became a source of pleasure and a form of entertainment for many people. Even then, the legal language which proscribed "obscene libel" indicated the traditional roots of the prohibition.

The objection to obscenity and indecency is not new in the Renaissance. It is an expression of the Christian understanding of the moral iniquity of excesses and transgressions of the flesh, and the recognition of carnal concupiscence as foremost among the passions which corrupt the soul. Christianity's profound insight into the essential corruption of fallen human nature requires it to hold, as a consequence, that it is essentially corruptible or, in other words, that it is extremely difficult for men to live well, to avoid the lure of the senses and the evils of the flesh. It was in these terms that the writers of the patristic church condemned the theatre. It is in these terms that the obscenity of literature, which is its seductive power to aid the dominion of the flesh over the spirit, is always condemned by the church as well as by the state in Christian countries. It is not important, as the liberals who protest against all prohibition of obscenity so blindly insist, that particular determinations of what is obscene change from time to time;[7] so do particular determinations of what is just. Justice is no less the goodness of laws which are its particular determinations, than obscenity is, from the Christian point of view, an intrinsic evil in literature, however it is described in the particular case. To question the evil of obscenity is either to deny basic Christian values or to doubt that obscene literature has any *great* effect upon the human soul. The latter may be a question of fact to be investigated; but the former is not a question of fact, but a moral principle in which Plato and Aristotle concurred with Christianity. The censorship of literature should, of course, be guided by the answer to the question of fact involved, as well as by this principle, unless obscenity is offensive *per se*, regardless of its effects. This is, of course, the Christian position, and one which must be considered by any state whose citizens are entirely, or in large part, Christians.

While the objection to obscenity was not new in the Renaissance, it was the popularity which literature then achieved, because of the range given it by printing, that required various types of censorship, such as the political and ecclesiastical expedients in Christian countries for eliminating or reducing offensive indecency, and the harmful effects it was either known or supposed to have. This phase of the general problem of the arts increased in importance as the middle and lower classes rose to literacy, and as the perfection of machinery surmounted the economic obstacles to a wider and wider circulation of books. One can almost say that its importance is directly proportional to the degree to which society is democratized by the external conditions of its existence. The inventions of the radio and the motion-picture camera are the latest stages in this concomitant development of democratic society and the problem of censorship.

One observation must be made before we proceed. The problem of censorship in the ancient world or in early modern times, as it actually appears in the record of actions taken or proposals

[7] Vd. Ernst and Seagle, *op. cit.*: Chapters 8, 9, 10.

made, whether by state or church, never attains the clarity or fullness of analysis which it is given in the writings of Plato and Aristotle. For them, it was not an isolated question of repressing blasphemy and heresy, libel and sedition, or even obscenity. It could only be understood in terms of the larger problem of the arts in the state. Censorship is only a means to an end, and only one means among many. The first question, therefore, is about the desirability of the end to be achieved, and this in turn raises many other questions about the values which the arts realize, and the effects they have upon their audiences. The actual record shows only that men have thought blasphemy and heresy, libel and sedition and obscenity, undesirable; and that they have made various laws and adopted various expedients to avoid them. The more general consideration of the influence of the arts upon moral character and behavior, and an analysis of their social and political values, both positive and negative, seldom, if ever, appear in the record of actual practice up to this point in our history. It is interesting that the main points in the theoretical discussion of this practical problem, as old as Plato and Aristotle, do not become factors which actual practice considers, until the attack upon the theatre in the seventeenth and eighteenth centuries, and even then only incompletely and indecisively; it is really only in connection with the contemporary issue about motion pictures that the deliberations of practice fully reflect the theoretical analysis, though the reflection is often vague and confused. We turn, therefore, to the situation of the drama in modern times, as a necessary introduction to the more recent situation in which the movies are involved.

The chief difference between the theatre in the ancient world and in modern democratic society is the character and extent of its popularity. Just as in ancient times the drama arose out of the conditions and materials of religious ritual and mythology in Greece,[8] so in the modern world the drama has its origins in the ritual and legends of Christianity, but it finally achieves a more complete separation than did the theatre in Greece. Before classical models were copied and the theatre became a secular institution, there was the Passion Play and the allegory of Everyman. It has recently been shown that the cycle of Arthurian romances was similarly rooted in both Christian and

[8] Vd. F. H. Cornford, *The Origin of Attic Comedy*, London, 1914.

pagan religious materials.[9]   The tales of Chaucer are imaginative literature further removed from religious sources, more
clearly differentiated and secularized; yet they clearly bear the
mark of such origins.   With the development of the Elizabethan
theatre, and the dramatic writing of Shakespeare and Jonson,
Marlowe, Chapman, Middleton and Heywood, the separation is
almost fully achieved.

The Elizabethan stage, furthermore, made literature popular
in a way that, at its time, exceeded the power of the printing
press.   Of the many thousands who witnessed plays, only a
small proportion were able to read, had books been available to
them as cheaply as the theatre.   The attack upon the theatre by
many reformers led by Prynne and Gosson,[10] its exclusion from
the city of London proper, its patronage by Elizabeth if not by
the scholars and the *literati* of her court, were all a natural and
instructive consequence of the new popularity of the drama and
the character of its audience.   As Professor Ashley Thorndike
points out in his account of *Shakespeare's Theatre*,[11] this was the
first time in the history of modern Europe that literature found
its support in the people, rather than in the patronage of the
great.   Whatever be the comparison of this popular drama with
the glories of Athens, it must be remembered that it was achieved
in a heterogeneous democracy — a democratic society though it
was still governed monarchically — and under conditions which
tended to confuse artistic ideals with the demands of the populace.   The democratization of literature was already producing
its mixed effects.   Here at the beginning of the democratic era,
the theatre achieved the status of a popular art which, as Professor
Thorndike says, "has not been equalled since, in the patronage of
the drama until the present success of the motion pictures.   In
its ability to interest all classes in the population and to afford
unfailing amusement at a low price, — standing room in the pit
could be had for a penny, and an additional penny or two secured
a seat in the galleries, — the Elizabethan theatre has no rival except
the movies; like them, it had novelty in its favor, and for twenty
years or more after the first professional playhouses, London

---

[9] Vd. J. L. Weston, *From Ritual to Romance*, Cambridge, 1920.
[10] Spingarn, *op. cit.*: pp. 265 ff.
[11] The Macmillan Company, Publishers, New York, 1916.

went theatre mad." [12]   The analogy between the Elizabethan theatre and the movies is most strikingly evoked by the facts of attendance.   "There were five or six theatres giving daily performances in a city of a hundred thousand inhabitants.   There were thirty thousand or more spectators at the plays within a week, which is proportionally almost as great as the current attendance at the movies in this country and abroad.   Furthermore, when it is remembered that a large part of the population disapproved of the theatre, and that women of respectability were not frequent patrons of the public playhouses, this attendance is hard to account for.   There has been no such patronage of the drama since then until the present success of the movies." [13]

The analogy that is here uncovered is worth a slight digression about the character of the Elizabethan audience and the attitude of those who criticized the theatre, its playwrights and its people. The position which Elizabeth took against those who attacked the theatre, demanding its repression and, in some cases, its extermination, is the first sign of the modern consideration of the political problem which extremely popular arts raise in a democracy.

The audience was representative of various elements in the population of London.   It included "the military man and the military hanger-on; the young man about town, foolish or less foolish; the fille de joie; the good grocer and his wife; the noisy apprentices who applaud all the mechanical devices; the animated clothes-props and tobacco-drinkers; a sprinkling of gallants, scholars, wits, country bumpkins, and the average steadygoing hard-working citizen." [14]   It was an audience which had the scantiest background of culture; it even lacked the miscellaneous information which is necessary for a sophisticated response.   But, as Mr. Thorndike suggests, "too sharp a distinction should not be drawn between the taste of the nobles and the groundlings.   The young lords of Elizabeth's court were

[12] *Op. cit.*, p. 407, by permission of The Macmillan Company, Publishers.
[13] *Op. cit.*, p. 407, by permission of The Macmillan Company, Publishers.
[14] M. St. Clair Byrne, *Shakespeare's Audience* in a collection of essays on *Shakespeare and the Theatre* by members of the Shakespeare Association, London, 1927: p. 215, by permission of the Shakespeare Association and the Oxford University Press.

not distinguished by their learning; they were probably not much superior to the apprentices in their liking for obscene jokes and bad puns." [15]   It is no wonder that a scholar and humanist like Sir Philip Sidney looked with disapproval upon this professional stage and its public, both ignorant of the traditions of classical drama.

The other public entertainments against which the theatre competed were both less literary and more brutal.   Public executions were popular spectacles; the bear-baiting and cock-fighting shows drew crowds in the immediate vicinity of the theatres; there were puppet shows and circuses in which acrobats, animals and monsters were exhibited.   The theatre was no more or less expensive than these alternative amusements.   That it succeeded so extraordinarily in this competition indicates that it satisfied a craving which the other spectacles could not, the desire for story.   The theatre provided food for the imagination as well as the kind of excitement which could be had at the cock and bear fights.   It was the only cheap medium for the dispensation of fiction; there were no magazines, no novels, and few cheap books.   The people who attended the theatre came, not as visitors to a museum in devotion to high art, but with a child-like desire to hear stories told, and a fresh, unsophisticated responsiveness to anything which played upon their imaginations. As St. Clair Byrne has pointed out, "if we judge from the whole mass of dramatic fare submitted to it, the exciting stories, the medley of incidents, the abundance of displays of physical skill, the general atmosphere of alarums and excursions, the audience went to the theatre primarily to please and amuse itself.   If a parallel is illuminating, the audience was, psychologically speaking, an amalgam of the *Bulldog Drummond* and the musical-comedy or variety audiences of today.   It received its pleasure from a good story, from having its emotions thoroughly aroused; from having its senses appealed to by music, dancing, noise and spectacle; from being deliciously thrilled by exciting events and crises; and finally from observing, — as the *Bulldog Drummond* audience does today, — the spectacle of behavior on the part of the characters which would arouse in it not any 'obstinate questionings' but a continuous and sympathetic moral assent." [16]   In

[15] *Op. cit.*, p. 411, by permission of The Macmillan Company, Publishers.
[16] *Op. cit.*, pp. 206-207, by permission of the Shakespeare Association and the Oxford University Press.

short, the audience was not interested in the type of problem play which the Ibsens, Shaws, and Galsworthys think elevate the drama above the level of mere entertainment to one of intellectual provocation.   The leading dramatic critics in this tradition have a way of looking down upon this Elizabethan audience, seeking the delights of entertainment in the theatre rather than the intricacies of mooted social questions.[17]

There seems to be no question that the character of this audience had a definite effect upon Shakespeare and the other dramatists who wrote to please their patrons, the public.   It is well to remember that the authors were not artists in the above-and-beyond-money sense of this word; they were *playwrights*, makers of plays for popular consumption, and their rewards were liberal, not only in applause, but money.   Writing for the theatre and producing plays was a lucrative profession.   The records show that huge profits were made by all who were involved, the writer, the actor, the organizer.[18]   Shakespeare retired one of the richest, self-made men of his day.   The distinction between the amateur literary man, who wrote scholarly classical copies for private performances at the University or the Court, and the professional playwright, who wrote for the public and the profits it yielded, was clear.   The great *entrepreneur* of his day, Henslowe, was quick to recognize what marketable commodities plays were, and hired writers to make them just as he employed tailors to make costumes.   Young men from the Universities who saw an opportunity to make a living at this business, soon replaced the literary drudges and the Grub Street hacks.   The level of the productions was raised, but the impetus which profit gave to the whole affair still remained and required that authors please their audience no matter what else they did to manifest their talents in an ancient art.   Dramatists had been supported by civic subsidies in Athens, or rewarded by the patronage of the court in Rome, but the Elizabethan period is probably the first in which writers had the double role of artist and merchant, competing in a free market for both plaudits

17 See, for example, William Archer, *The Old Drama and the New*, Boston, 1923. Compare Gilbert Seldes, *The Seven Lively Arts*, New York, 1924 : pp. 27-38, 309-330.
18 Lamborn and Harrison, *Shakespeare, the Man and His Stage*, Oxford, 1923 : pp. 94, 97, 104-105.

and profits. Thus, at the beginning of modern times, when the literary arts became popular amusements in a democratic society, the literary artist also became a figure in commerce. Those who deplore such commercialism may either look back to the kind of patronage given artists in aristocratic societies of the past, or look forward to the utopian communism in which artists will be supported without competing in the market-place which our capitalistic economy imposes upon them. It is not only the democratic order, but a competitive economy which is the modern note that first appears in the case of the Elizabethan theatre. Whether one prefers aristocracy to democracy, or communism to capitalism, the new status of the arts in the kind of society, both social and economic, which begins after the Renaissance, is clearly indicated. Other arts, music and painting, may continue for centuries to enjoy the anomalous freedom of private patronage by the wealthy, but the theatre from the outset, probably because of the difference in its internal economy and the requirement of an audience, became a public enterprise at once commercial and artistic.

There are those who, without being communists, regret this situation, and fail to check their despair by remembering that art is never wholly free, but merely changes its masters.[19] Being sentimental aristocrats, they suppose that art supported economically by the upper classes — though these be upper only through hereditary patents of nobility or the self-made accumulation of wealth — is necessarily better as art than that which, in order to thrive, must please the vulgar public, large in numbers and therefore low in taste. In Shakespeare's day, the scholars and the 'University wits' were contemptuous of the popular plays, mainly because they committed the fallacy of supposing that to be popular was necessarily to be bad. They made contemptuous references to Shakespeare because of the popular favor he had won. But as the stage became more and more a democratic and a profitable institution, even the high-brows were lured into trying their hand at winning the same rewards. This type of criticism does not cease, however. In recent years, a poet-laureate of England wrote in a superior fashion of the in-

[19] Thus, John Drinkwater, *Art and Popularity* in *The Gentle Art of Theatre-Going*, London, 1927.

fluence of Shakespeare's audience upon his plays.[20] Robert Bridges bemoaned the vulgarity and the bad taste that is to be found in the plays. Poor Shakespeare! Having to please an audience with whom Robert Bridges can have so little sympathy, he could not aim at maintaining all parts of his work on a high artistic level. *Othello*, for instance, exasperates the poet-laureate because it is so obviously calculated to give pleasurable excitement to an audience, for the sake of gratifying which Shakespeare played false the high artistic ideals Bridges insists upon attributing to him. Nor does the parallel between the Elizabethan theatre and the contemporary movie stop here in this contempt which both evoke from the high-brows because they cater to a vulgar audience for profit.[21] Bridges, almost in the spirit of Collier, who dismissed Shakespeare as smutty, and with the intentions of Thomas Bowdler, who expurgated Shakespeare's plays so that the volume of them could lie safely on the respectable Victorian family table, suggests that Shakespeare should not be put into the hands of the young without the warning that "the foolish things in his plays were written to please the foolish, the filthy for the filthy, and the brutal for the brutal."[22] We must not degrade ourselves or our children to the level of Shakespeare's audience — which is, of course, the same as any popular audience today — or "learn contamination from those wretched beings who can never be forgiven their share in preventing the greatest poet and dramatist of the world from being the best artist."[23]

But Professor Thorndike takes a different view of the matter in his *Shakespeare's Theatre*, a view which not only seems more intelligently cognizant of the levels of commensurate recreation which must be made explicit in a democracy, but which also finds no reason for regret in this situation, since the arts are not harmed by it. "Shakespeare and his contemporaries," he writes, "may be deemed fortunate in having an audience essentially popular."[24] We can see what Sir Philip Sidney failed to see: that

[20] Robert Bridges, *The Influence of the Audience on Shakespeare's Dramas* in his *Collected Essays*, V. I, London, 1927.
[21] Cf. The chapter on "Shakespeare and the Cinema" in Allardyce Nicoll's *Film and Theatre*, New York, 1936. [22] *Op. cit.*, p. 28. [23] *Op. cit.*, p. 29.
[24] *Op. cit.*, p. 430, by permission of The Macmillan Company, Publishers.

a popular form of entertainment can produce great literature. The Elizabethan audience should not be "extravagantly praised for its quick-wittedness and appreciation of poetry,"[25] or extravagantly blamed "for forcing its vulgarity on the plays of Shakespeare."[25]   Nevertheless, its general effect on Shakespeare and his colleagues, whether for good or bad, is unmistakable. "If the audience must share in the censure for some of the lapses and excesses that result from the playwright's effort to please their taste, it must also receive some share of the credit for the breadth and multiplicity of life which is to be found in the plays and which his audience welcomed. . . Intimate and constant in its intercourse with the theatre, this audience impressed its demands upon the dramatists, but at the same time it showed a quick and generous receptivity for whatever experiment or innovation the playwright might attempt."[26]   The vitality of this great period of English drama reflects the vitality of its audience.   The stage suffered when this audience itself died of a surfeit of the plays which had been created to satisfy its amazing appetite.

In the light of the fact that the theatre had become important in the daily life of Englishmen, in the country at large but particularly in London, we can understand the agitation for its control and the quarrel between the city magistrates and the Queen and her Privy Council.[27]   The municipal government which was under Puritan domination had succeeded in forcing the theatre outside the city limits and into the less respectable purlieus inhabited by the stews and the bear gardens, where *Midsummer Night's Dream* competed with the attractions of houses of ill-fame and *Hamlet* contended with Blind Hunks, a famous bear, for the patronage of the crowd.   The Privy Council, representing the views of the Queen, took the attitude that plays are not in themselves evil but, on the contrary, are entirely justifiable "for honest recreation's sake."   The Court yielded to the City to the extent that it permitted various restrictions upon attendance at the theatre to be enacted, but the record indicates that these enactments were seldom enforced.   When the Lord

---

[25] *Op. cit.,* p. 429, by permission of The Macmillan Company, Publishers.
[26] *Op. cit.,* p. 430, by permission of The Macmillan Company, Publishers.
[27] For the following account of this subject I am indebted to V. C. Gildersleeve, *Government Regulation of the Elizabethan Drama,* New York, 1908.

Mayor of London protested against the laxity which the Crown smiled at, he was answered that the immense public demand for plays was so acute that public opinion itself tended to prevent the enforcement of the municipal restrictions.   The reformers could not succeed primarily because the plays received the enthusiastic approval of a large body of the citizens, and not merely because of the opposition of the Court.   They had ultimately to be satisfied with keeping the public play-houses outside of the city limits and with preventing performances on Sunday, although they attained even this latter end only with great difficulty.   It must be remembered, of course, that the City's opposition to the theatre was only in part based on moral and religious grounds; in larger part, perhaps, it arose from the dangers to public health and peace which the congregation of large crowds threatened in the way of rioting, fire, and spread of the plague.   Even the moral objections were not directed entirely against the content of the plays which may have influenced the audience, but against the demoralizing environment of the playhouse itself, and the evil associations it helped to form.   It did not seem to occur to the city that it had itself forced the theatre into dangerous proximity with houses of prostitution and low dives of all sorts.   So far as objection was taken to the indecency and immorality of the plays, it seems to have been based upon the intrinsic evil of dramatic representations as "sinful, heathenish, lewd, ungodly spectacles and most pernicious corruptions; condemned in all ages as intolerable mischiefs to churches, to republics, to the manners, minds and souls of men."   The language here is admittedly borrowed by Prynne from the invectives of the Fathers of Christianity.[28]   But we must not be misled by such writers as Prynne into thinking that he represented either public opinion or the views of the official censors.   It is clear that the censor sought to repress anything which touched on current political and religious questions; he struck out blasphemy, sedition, and libel, and was not concerned with decency and obscenity in our contemporary sense.[29]

While the Elizabethan theatre is in many respects the closest parallel to the motion picture, as a form of art achieving great

[28] It is taken from the title page of *Histrio-Mastix*, London, 1633. Vd. Note 70, *infra*.
[29] Vd. Fowell and Palmer, *Censorship in England*, London, 1913 : pp. 1–125.

popularity as a public recreation and gaining, through that popularity, the emoluments of commercial success, there are many differences in the political problems which each create that must be accounted for in terms of the social and economic changes of the intervening centuries. All of the notes of a democratic and commercial society are sounded by a survey of the Elizabethan drama in the life of its times, but that kind of society is then just at its beginning. We must follow the history of its rapid growth through to its present complicated development in order to discover all the factors in the contemporary situation.

This history is so well known to everybody, it has become so much the legend which we tell ourselves and our children about how we came to be what we are, that its main points need only be mentioned here. The industrial revolution occurs; the middle classes rise to greater and greater prominence and exert increasing influence upon public policies and social standards; the position of the tradesman and the merchant changes and captains of industry wear the badge of wealth that glitters as attractively as the insignia of government, the military or the church; the perfection of the printing press and new methods of production and distribution make the newspaper a widely consumed commodity and create cheap magazines, inexpensive books and circulating libraries; the means of transportation become available to larger and larger numbers; the separation of the country and the city, the provinces and the capital, diminishes; cities grow in size as population generally increases and become places of tremendous concentration of cheap industrial labor, of persons whose roots are in the factory or the office rather than in the land or a home upon the land; the gradual improvement of machinery, the formation of labor unions for collective bargaining, the increasing legislative control of industry in so far as it is affected with the public interest, results in the progressive reduction of the hours of labor and the greater leisure of the inhabitants of large cities and smaller industrial towns; there is a definite tendency toward the adoption of the political forms appropriate to the social order which these changes have brought about: government becomes increasingly representative and republican, the goal of universal suffrage is gradually attained and, whether actual power is concentrated oligarchically in the

hands of the magnates and the industrialists, political power expresses itself through votes and elections; the techniques of
propaganda and persuasion become almost indispensable in moving large masses of the electorate who must be reached by the
various avenues of communication, which themselves augment
the solidarity of the masses or of the parties into which they
divide; popular education keeps pace with the increase of political suffrage, the spread of communication, and the augmented
use of propaganda; education not only becomes popular in the
sense that larger numbers pass through public-school systems, but
also in the sense of a rising level of minimum educational achievement; colleges and universities cease to be places devoted merely
to the preservation of scholarship, or for the education of a
leisure class, for the training of government officials and the
literacy of the clergy; individuals of any social or economic
class by birth are able through the opportunities which occur,
and the advantages of education, to move freely into any quarter
of society, changing their status and their mode of life. This
is, in brief, the moving picture we have learned to see of the
changes which happened progressively from the sixteenth to the
twentieth centuries. It is, of course, the democratic story of
the development of democratic society, the capitalistic story of
the fruitions of an industrial economy. A recent report of the
social trends in the United States during a brief period, presents
in miniature a chart of just such changes which have been going
on for a long time; their directions are supposed to be clearly
marked. Communists may tell the story of these centuries differently, in terms of the class struggle, the trend of which is
toward the dictatorship of the proletariat and the abolition of
private capital with its profit system: but the trend is no less in
the direction of an increasing democratization of society, even as
the communist sees the process. Recent developments in Italy
and Germany may be interpreted by some to mean that the
trend in governmental policy, at least, is away from democratic
forms, but even in these countries the fruits of industry, the
benefits of science and invention, with their consequences in
the fields of mobility, communication, education, and in the
social organization of life, are not hidden from view by what
seems to the democrat an anomalous political atavism.

I shall not attempt to prophesy the future from the trends

which this history seems to reveal. That is a perilous undertaking in which Marxists, Spenglerians, fascists, and even occasional democrats, somehow feel competent to engage, sometimes upon the curious principle that current political and social problems must be solved today in conformity with a destiny that seems inherent in the nature of things. Those of us who lack such gifts of prophecy or faith in the predictability of history, must content ourselves with the solution of contemporary practical problems in terms of the existing conditions and circumstances of practice. This history is not recited, therefore, to divine a destiny which, learned, will tell us what we *should* do, because of necessity we *cannot* do otherwise. It is rather to enable us to recognize the emergence of those factors which have given the problem of the motion picture aspects peculiar to it alone, which differentiate it from similar issues about the arts, and particularly the theatre, in all other ages, and which distinguish it even from the problem of the Elizabethan stage, which is most analogous to it in basic features.

The most significant single factor which emerges in the course of this history is the changed character of censorship, its source, its medium, and the objects upon which it focuses. At the time of Elizabeth, the attack upon the theatre was led by a church and religious party. For the most part, the large population which attended the theatre and was, therefore, the interested party, did not get involved in the quarrel between the religious opponents of the theatre and the Court which defended and cherished it. Yet both argued for the good of the people, the former to save the masses from an iniquity and corruption which they were obviously not apprehensive of, the latter to preserve for them a form of entertainment and recreation which they obviously desired and enjoyed. Moreover, the final control of censorship, the final guaranty of the existence of the theatre, was in royal hands, in the power of a prince rather than of the people. It was natural for censorship under such circumstances to be directed primarily against politically seditious and subversive influences. At the close of the seventeenth and the opening of the eighteenth centuries, we find the rise of societies for the reform of public manners.[30] These unofficial organizations,

[30] Vd. J. W. Krutch, *Comedy and Conscience After the Restoration*, New York, 1924 : pp. 159-164, 190-191.

under clerical leadership, but enlisting a large middle-class following, became involved in the attack upon the stage during the
period of the Collier controversy.   Such organizations not only
became sources of propaganda for reformist doctrines, but ex-
erted political influence upon legislation concerning the theatre ;
they could effectively represent popular sentiment as demanding
the reform of abuses.[31]   More than that : the theatre being dependent upon public patronage for its economic support, such
social groups, organized to criticize the drama, were able to
threaten the theatre with what amounts to boycott, an instrument of control many times more powerful than official censorship. The professional literary critic became an important
figure during the Restoration period when the drama was under
attack ; he could not help but take account of moral as well as
aesthetic considerations in his comments on the current play,
and these soon became confused for him.   It was not long before
the various societies for the reformation of public manners engaged in literary criticism themselves and multiplied the confusions.   Thus, as the arts, and particularly the theatre, come to
enjoy the new kind of popularity which democracy affords, they
are also subject to a new kind of censorship and criticism which
is equally a creature of the democratic order.

   Official censorship does not, of course, cease.   The office of
the Master of the Revels,[32] which licenses all plays produced in
London, has a long and unbroken history.   But, under the influence of organized social groups which grow in importance
with the increasing eminence of the middle class, the object of
official censorship changes from a primary concern with blasphemy and treason to a predominant interest in obscenity, indecency, and, more generally, in the power of the arts to corrupt
and demoralize public manners and private life.   In an age when
the Church ruled supreme, heresy and blasphemy were the focus
of censorship ; in an age of absolute monarchs, sedition and
treason became central ; in the age of democracy and the dominance of the middle classes, morality, and particularly sexual
morality, are the matters chiefly considered.   The last shift is
only partly intelligible in terms of the conservatism of the middle
classes and their interest in preserving established manners.   The

[31] Vd. Fowell and Palmer, *op. cit.* : pp. 125–184.
[32] Later the office of the Lord Chamberlain.

objection to obscenity and indecency is to be found both in the Greek world and even more emphatically in the Christian tradition. Sexual morality and sexual taboos are not a product of eighteenth and nineteenth century European civilization. What is new in these centuries, however, is the popular concern with these matters and the development of agencies to express popular sentiments of taste and criticism which are more effective than official censorship upon the character of any art that thrives on popularity.[32a]

One example of the force of popular censorship in the nineteenth century will suffice.[33] The three-volume novel of Dickens and Thackeray, Bulwer and George Eliot, achieved great popularity through the medium of the circulating library. The publisher did not sell directly to the public, but to these libraries; he was, therefore, dependent for his sales upon the purchasing power of these institutions. The libraries could make or break a book so far as popular success was concerned for the author, or financial success for the publisher. Under these circumstances, the libraries became an unofficial bureau of censorship, interpreting the current standards of propriety, and forcing authors to conform thereto. Whether the circulating libraries rightly interpreted the Victorian sentiments about indecency and obscenity, whether these unofficial censors were motivated by anything more than opinions about what had injurious effects upon public morals, whether they understood the full complexity of the problem of art and prudence, they were able by economic measures to impose an effective censorship upon nineteenth-century literature, which few writers or publishers could resist. It is not the merits of such procedures which we are here considering, but the fact that they came into existence. What the circulating libraries did in supervising the production of the nineteenth-century novel may have been for better or worse so far as the ultimate moral and social effects go; but that they were able to do what they did indicates the power of these new forms of popular control of the arts. As we shall see, the motion picture has had to submit much more to such popular agencies

[32a] Vd. Fowell and Palmer, op. cit.: pp. 300–323; and Ernst and Lorentz, Censored, the Private Life of the Movie, New York, 1930.   [33] For this, see Ernst and Seagle, To the Pure, New York, 1928: Ch. V.

of censorship and control than to the interference of official boards of review.

There is one other concomitant of the changing character of censorship. Milton, objecting to a law which proposed to license the press and subject all books to examination before publication, did not argue that books which were blasphemous, libelous or seditious should escape prosecution as inimical to public safety and order. The distinction he made was between a censorship over literature before publication and the punishment of offenders against law and order after the offense had been committed by the act of publication. This distinction reflects the general social interest in freedom of speech which leads us to interfere with it in advance only when the results of its abuse are too dangerous for us to tolerate. It does not rest on a distinction between libel and sedition, on the one hand, and obscenity and indecency, on the other, but rather on the degree of social utility attached to freedom for various kinds of utterances and the degree of danger which attends abuse in different types of cases. Nevertheless, in the matter of obscenity and indecency, interference before the fact has more frequently been advocated than in the case of blasphemy and sedition. Although officially it has not taken this course except in the supervision by the Lord Chamberlain over dramatic productions in the City of London, and more recently by official state boards of motion-picture censorship in this country, that must not lead us to overlook the fact that the popular forms of censorship, such as that exercised by the circulating libraries in England in the last century, have usually proceeded in that way. It is in this sense that the motion picture is the most censored of all the arts, much more than literature or the stage. The popular insistence upon censorship before production has forced the producer of motion pictures to censor himself. He has had to become an interpreter of public standards in drafting the code which governs motion-picture production,[34] just as the circulating libraries took this task upon themselves. He has had to establish an association of producers who submit the whole enterprise of the motion picture to the rigorous supervision of self-government.

[34] The production code referred to in footnote 2 *supra*.

We must turn, finally, to another factor which has become more and more important. There has been an increasing amount of leisure for all classes in society and, at the same time, an increasing concentration of the population in large cities. Under these twin circumstances, the need for amusement and recreation becomes a more and more insistent demand which must be properly satisfied in the social economy. At one time it was thought that the efficiency of labor was impaired by indulgence in pastimes, as in liquor; the worker's sober virtues were undermined by such profligacies. This has much to do with various prohibition movements in the last few centuries. But later it was recognized that the efficiency of labor depended upon rest and relaxation from it. An industrial economy began to see some positive value in harmless amusements and sought to encourage them rather than repress them. And those who took a broader view of social and political problems were able to appreciate the truth that man cannot live without pleasure, without recreation and rest, and that unless he is provided with better forms of pleasure and relaxation, he will seek or invent worse ones. The stage was defended as saving men from the obviously more harmful debaucheries of the saloon and the brothel. Thus, in 1857, the pastor of All Souls Church in New York, the Rev. Henry W. Bellows, argued that the lack of wholesome pleasure produced vice.[35] Amusement, he said, is not merely defensible; the want of it is a calamity and an injury to the sober and solid interests of society; it is an aid to industry. The theatre is not only compatible with Christian sobriety, but the most complete and interesting of all amusements. The primary goodness of the stage, he insisted, does not depend upon its moral teaching or influences. Its end is amusement and not instruction, and it serves the community best when it most effectively entertains the population and affords them recreation which in itself cannot be considered vicious.

Bellows' defense of the stage in the middle of the last century is cited here merely as an index of a changing attitude in the Protestant clergy toward amusement. A century earlier, both in this country and in England, Puritan asceticism prevailed; amusement was confused with license, and the sober interests of an industrial society had to be protected from excesses of indul-

[35] *The Relation of Public Amusements to Public Morality*, New York, 1857.

gence in pleasure. Unfortunately, any indulgence was thought to be excessive. Bellows pointed out the natural consequence: the first hundred years of Puritanism in New England were marked by ascetic public manners and the prevalence of vices almost unheard of in the present, less strict society. The change that Bellows himself marks is not entirely due to a recognition of this consequence. It had come to be realized that the 'sober interests of an industrial society' were better served by amusements which could be publicly recognized; their denial seemed to increase the surreptitious and more vicious recreations. Aristotle and St. Thomas had clearly recognized these alternatives and had emphasized the prime political and also moral utility of the arts as amusements; but they could not have foreseen how great would be the need for recreation in a society in which the wheels of industry must constantly be kept turning [71]. Not only private happiness and public order, but economic prosperity was at stake. The industrial revolution achieved self-consciousness in the nineteenth century and was soon to discover that even the arts could serve its ends.

What Bellows said about the theatre in the middle of the last century has often been repeated about the movies. The Rev. J. J. Phelan, investigating the motion pictures as a phase of commercialized amusement in Toledo,[36] clearly saw the advantages of cheap entertainment for the workers of an industrial city. The movie theatre had counteracted the influence of the brothel, the saloon, the dance hall and other questionable forms of amusement; moreover, it had promoted family unity by family attendance. Recreation and amusement are as necessary as food and raiment, and unless better forms are not only provided but made more attractive than worse forms, the latter will increase their dominion necessarily. The investigators of "Middletown" offer corroborating evidence of the effect of the motion picture upon the level of recreation in what is supposed to be a typical American industrial city.[37] As early in the history of the motion pictures as 1914, Frederick C. Howe, as Chairman of the National Board of Censorship, had echoed Bellows' argument, pointing out that whatever could be said for the social

[36] *Motion Pictures as a Phase of Commercialized Amusement in Toledo, Ohio*, Toledo, 1919.
[37] R. and H. Lynd, *Middletown*, New York, 1929: pp. 265-269.

utility of the theatre was many times magnified by the role the motion picture played. It was not limited to New York or a few large cities; it served both rural and urban populations; being cheap entertainment, it was economically available to extraordinarily large numbers; it was, in short, democracy's theatre.[38]

We are now prepared to see the peculiar intensity of the political problem which the movies raise. They not only create the contemporary instance of the conflict between art and prudence in human life; they are not only the obvious heir to the moral and social questions which the arts of literature have always provoked; but, being democracy's theatre and the most popular form of amusement in an industrial society, they have inherited the problems of the theatre, as well as its recognized values, to a degree many times magnified by the conditions under which they exist and operate. The Elizabethan theatre, their nearest analogue, existed under much simpler conditions: society was just turning democratic and had not yet become industrialized, although commerce had begun to change the status and the occupations of men. Furthermore, the audience of the Elizabethan theatre, however large proportionally to the population of London, was limited to the capital city of the nation, and consisted mainly of adults. Finally, the forces of censorship and criticism were still well under the control of princely power and had not become the widely exercised prerogative of the people.

Consider the movies in comparison and it will be seen that the acuteness of the problems they raise is due not only to their enormously greater gross popularity, but also to the mixed character of their audience. They reach, first of all, an international audience; then an audience which is both urban and rural, and so far as it is urban, both in the capital city and the great metropolis as well as in the small provincial town; and finally, an audience which is at once composed both of adults and children of almost all ages.[39] Add to this that the internal economy of their production and distribution requires that the movies, much more than any other form of art, even the theatre, reach this

[38] 107 Outlook 412–16 (June 20, 1914).
[39] See the discussion of this point in the code governing the production of motion pictures, quoted in Note 76 *infra*.

tremendous audience continually, and please them with the satisfactions of amusement and recreation. In a society in which profits are the recognized rewards of private enterprise, the movies need not apologize, any more than the Elizabethan theatre, for being a commercialized art which earns money by pleasing its patrons; the only difference is the economic complexity of the motion-picture enterprise and the amount of money it must earn in order to exist, a difference which is a significant condition of the character of the art. Add to this that in the development of the democratic order, the functions of censorship — the moral and social criticism of art which arises from a concern for the welfare of the state and the virtue of its citizens — have been taken over by unofficial groups in society organized for this and kindred purposes, so that the movies must not only please their patrons as the Elizabethan theatre did, but also please the organized groups which have become the unofficial custodians of public manners and the common good. Moral and social standards are explicitly set by the organized sentiment of the community, and the movies must be responsive to the direct force of such sentiment as well as the indirect effects of the political pressure which critical groups can powerfully exert. The motion picture cannot succeed commercially merely by satisfying the masses who seek amusement in it, since the masses are to a considerable extent moved by the better organized groups in the community which approve or disapprove of the movies on other grounds than their entertainment and recreational values. Finally, add that the motion picture is peculiarly adapted to all the conditions of the society in which it occurs, that it is an art which almost perfectly reflects the needs of an industrial democracy for communication and social education, in Dewey's sense of these terms, as well as for effective recreation, and it will be seen that the problem of the movies is amazingly difficult, both for those who try to produce them either for the sake of art or profit, and for those who, seeking the common good and the increase of human happiness, are forced to weigh the balance of their clear positive values and great utility against whatever injurious effects they claim to find and wish to eliminate by reform.

The movies happened accidentally. They are the result of a series of mechanical inventions and of a variety of economic opportunities which alert *entrepreneurs* seized. But these accidents of their origin are at the same time essential conditions of modern society. The invention of the printing press was similarly an accident, and similarly an essential factor in the beginning of modern times. Through the accident of invention, literature became popular and a public problem to an extent it had not been before. The case of the motion picture differs only by the rapidity of the social change in which it is involved. Within much less than a half century, and long before it had matured as an art, the motion picture became one of the leading problems of its day.

CHAPTER SIX

The Contemporary Issue

WE have now surveyed the historical conditions which make the movies the problem that they are. History is able to throw light on the nature of a contemporary problem by placing it in a tradition which separates its essential features from the circumstances of its particular occurrence. By showing a current problem to be a traditional one — one that seems to occur in some form or other in every society — it enables us to extract from the dialectic which that problem has occasioned, an analysis that is applicable to it in its present form. We have already examined in their historical settings the arguments of Plato and Aristotle, Bossuet and Aquinas, Rousseau and Dewey. The significance of this dialectic about art and prudence, about poetry in the state, is universal. It transcends the historical order in which it occurs. It applies to the contemporary issue about motion pictures. The only supplementation that is needed here is a brief commentary on the issue as it is currently formulated.

The question is not, as Plato might have framed it, whether movies should be allowed. The policy of absolute prohibition was last proposed with regard to the theatre in England and France in the seventeenth and eighteenth centuries. More recently the practical issue has been formulated, not in terms of exclusion, but rather in terms of some kind of supervision or control. The proposal of any type of supervision or control of the production, distribution and exhibition of motion pictures raises a series of questions : (1) What are the ends which the proposed control aims to serve? (2) What other alternative measures might be taken to achieve the same ends? (3) Of the various means to a given end, which is positively most efficient in accomplishing it and negatively least objectionable in its other consequences? (4) Is the given end, for which one or another means is proposed, desirable in itself or as a means to some further end, and does its positive value if achieved outweigh the negative values that may be incident to achieving it? Those who propose action of any sort must do so because they think some good will be accomplished by it or, what is the same thing, some evil will be remedied. It follows, therefore, that persons urging action must claim to know that an existing state of affairs is bad in some sense and that it can be improved. We need not ask, for the moment, whether they actually have such knowledge or whether they are proceeding upon opinions that have as yet no foundation in ascertainable fact. The point here is that they *claim* to know that there is something bad, wrong, undesirable about motion pictures at the present time, and that such deficiencies can be remedied or such evils eliminated. In addition, they must *claim* to know that the course of action they propose will be efficient in improving the situation and will ultimately yield advantages that outweigh any disadvantages which may attach to the means employed or to the end sought. If all men agreed to their claims, there would, of course, be no practical problem. The existence of a practical problem about the movies must mean that just such claims are denied.

The controversy can be summarized by a statement of the various charges which have been made against motion pictures, and of the defenses made in their favor. Such a summary will give us a picture of the positive and negative values, moral and social, which are *claimed* for the movies, and will enable us to ask the further question about each of these claims, whether it is based upon knowledge or opinion regarding the relevant facts. It should be noted at once that two sorts of questions must be separated. Failure to separate them leads to confusion. What are the facts of the matter is one question. What value should be placed upon the ascertainable facts is another. They are answered by different methods: the former by experience and investigation; the latter in the light of principles and standards which, though ultimately resting on experience, are not directly the products of investigation. It is profoundly important to make the distinction. Agreement about matters of fact may be accompanied by different moral or political judgments about the values involved, because of an ultimate disagreement about the standards or principles upon which such judgments are based.

The charges that are made against the movies have a number of sources. In part they are made by legislators and other officials of the state, *either* as a result of their own direct consideration of the movies as an art and a popular amusement, or as an industry and a phase of commerce which is so greatly affected with the public interest that it warrants official regulation of some sort; *or* as a result of the pressure which legislators and other officers of the state feel from unofficial organizations and groups in the community who have the moral and social interests of their fellow citizens at heart. In the latter case as in the former, the consideration of the matter is usually with a view to official regulation since the consideration is by officials. In larger part the charges against the movies are made by the unofficial organizations and groups in the community which we have mentioned, societies affiliated with particular churches, organizations of parents and teachers, women's clubs, groups organized for the specific purpose of studying the problem of the movies, committees of social hygienists and the like, or by unaffiliated individuals who as moralists, reformers, publicists or cranks, raise their voices for the public weal or the private good of man. In either case, such groups or individuals make whatever charges they do with a view either to influencing the course of official action through pressure upon legislatures, local magistrates, police or other public agencies, or to influencing public sentiment in such a way that a large number of people will be moved to threaten the movies with an unofficial instrument of correction — economic boycott, though it is seldom called by that name or explicitly recognized as such. The aim of threatened boycott is, of course, the self-regulation of the movies as opposed to externally imposed official regulation. The movies, since they can exist only by wide popular patronage, are extremely sensitive to such threats. Finally, there are the aesthetes, always unorganized and seldom if ever making their charges with a view to official or unofficial public action.[1]

[1] The aesthetes are more fully considered in Chapter 15 *infra*.

They do not seek to have laws passed to elevate the movies to what they hold to be a higher level of art. They seldom contemplate influencing popular sentiment to demand such elevation in some way, although they might. They are usually content to express themselves and turn away with resignation or contempt.

A number of preliminary statements must be made. In the first place, the literature — perhaps it were better called the printed matter — on this subject is overwhelming. Its vastness is only exceeded by the countless reiterations of the same point again and again in language that is distinguished by its rhetorical vehemence rather than its analytical clarity. We must eliminate the rhetoric, avoid the repetitions, and reduce the available materials to their lowest terms. This will make it impossible to give an impression of the extent to which sentiment is aroused on a given point but for analytical purposes it is the point and not the number of adherents which counts. Nor is it important for the most part to name the particular authority or source of the charge, although in some cases the source may have a significance which justifies indicating it.

In the second place, many of the charges are made against particular movies or consist of the citation of harms supposed to have been done in singular cases. To the extent that these are unique, we shall, of course, ignore them as of little consequence; to the extent that they are merely particular instances of general points they will be covered by the summary of those points.

Finally, it must be remembered that although the movies as an art and a kind of amusement have had an extremely short career, they have nevertheless changed much in character, in type and quality, in content and technique, during the brief period of their existence. It is interesting to observe, therefore, that for the most part the same charges are made in 1910 and 1915 as in 1925 and 1930. This fact is extremely difficult to interpret. Does it mean that the objections are to the movies essentially rather than to accidental features which have changed from time to time? Does it mean that the objections are to features which are accidental and therefore are still susceptible to alteration, although such changes have not yet occurred? Does it mean that the critics are expressing inherited prejudices which are only given up slowly because of the general stasis of public opinion and that they are not well enough acquainted with the actual phenomena to be entitled to speak? This is not true of all charges; some have either been withdrawn in the course of time as the movies have changed in character, or have been repeated with much less frequency and insistence.[2]

The charges which are made on moral and social grounds can be set forth in the following manner:

I. Some motion pictures are immoral ; that is,
   A. Some are offensive or shocking to moral sensibilities;
   B. Some violate moral principles; by failing, for example, to show that immorality does not succeed;
   C. Some are obscene.
II. Motion pictures influence the behavior of the adult population, and this influence is bad because
   A. It tends to corrupt public manners; and
   B. It tends to form vicious habits in individuals and thus corrupts moral character.
III. Motion pictures are one of the causes of adult criminality.
IV. Motion pictures have a number of bad effects on children:
   A. They are injurious to health;
   B. They corrupt the moral character of the child during its formative years by causing vicious habits and inculcating moral standards and attitudes which do not conform to those prevailing in the adult community;
   C. They interfere with the processes of intellectual education, and are a source of false notions and unfounded opinions;
   D. They are one of the causes of juvenile delinquency and misconduct.

These charges are not at all points as definite and clear as the

[2] Since 1931–32, the improvement in motion pictures has been generally noted and widely acclaimed. Reviewing the work of the Legion of Decency, Pope Pius recently said : "It is an exceedingly great comfort to us to note the outstanding success of the crusade. Because of your vigilance and because of the pressure which has been brought to bear by public opinion, the motion picture has shown improvement from the moral standpoint : crime and vice are portrayed less frequently ; sin no longer is so openly approved and acclaimed ; false ideals of life no longer are presented in so flagrant a manner to the impressionable minds of youth" (*Vigilanti Cura*, issued July 2, 1936).

reasons which Plato gave for excluding the dramatists from the state and for supervising the poetry that would be permitted; nor as clear as the indictment made by primitive Christianity. Yet the tenor of these charges is essentially similar to Platonic and Christian criticism. Though they are less clear in some respects, they are more elaborate and specific in others. Our first task, therefore, is to understand as clearly and as precisely as possible what is involved in each element of the current complaints about the movies. We shall examine them in the order indicated. But, first, it should be noted that the effects of movies on children is here separated from their effects on the adult population. Plato in his consideration of the role which poetry and music play in education, both moral and intellectual, thought primarily if not exclusively of the young. The same is true of Aristotle. Christianity, on the other hand, in objecting to the theatre, did so without making this discrimination. The contemporary situation is different, partly due to the fact that for the first time in history, children and adults share in the enjoyment of the same art, go to the same theatre for amusement. But the problem of the influence of an art and a kind of amusement upon children is, nevertheless, clearly different from the problem of the influence upon adults. The distinction between the child and the adult is, therefore, important to make, and even more important to understand. It is not simply a matter of chronological age. We shall return to this point later.

Since our task is primarily to understand these charges rather than to criticize them, I propose to analyze them by trying to define the terms in which they are stated, to discover the principles upon which they depend, and to separate the various questions which they raise. And, for the sake of brevity and perspicuity, I propose to do this by reducing the whole matter to an outline. Otherwise, the very complexity of the attempt to clarify so many indefinite and opaque opinions might defeat its purpose. Wherever possible I shall try to make the relevant intellectual tradition throw light on this contemporary discussion, which is unclear and vague because it is almost without tradition of any sort, ancient or modern. If lengthy digressions are necessary for background or interpretation, I shall indicate them as such and subordinate them to the main points of the

outline, in the hope that anyone will be able to use the outline
to get as general or as specific an analysis as he desires.

I. INTERPRETATION OF THE CHARGE THAT *SOME* MOTION PICTURES ARE
IMMORAL.

   A. The word "immoral" must not be understood here in the
same sense in which it is said that some men are immoral.

     1. Strictly, only men are moral beings, only men can be
immoral.

     2. The word is, therefore, being used analogically. A
work of art can be called moral or immoral only in
relation to the morality of men, as food is called
healthy or unhealthy only in relation to the health of
men. (This explains why those who insist upon considering art for art's sake can never understand questions about the morality of art. It is only when art
is not considered for its own sake that it comes within
the field of morals.)

     3. If a work of art can be spoken of as immoral only in
its relation to man, the nature of this relation must be
further determined.

        a. It is either the way in which the work of art influ-
ences human acts, or some other type of relation.

        b. If the only relation of art to man is of the first sort,
then this first charge cannot be distinguished
from the second charge, which is to follow.

        c. Therefore, if this first charge is to be distinguished,
the immorality here spoken of must be inter-
preted as referring to the content of motion pictures, *apart from their influence on human
behavior:*

           (1) Either as that content is offensive to moral
sensibilities;

           (2) Or as that content violates moral principles;

           (3) Or as that content betrays the immorality of
the artist. (We need not consider this
point here. It is discussed later.)

   B. A work of art may be called immoral because it offends the
moral sensibilities of its audience in a manner analogous
to the way in which ugliness offends our aesthetic sensibilities, or even in the way in which unpleasant and painful objects offend our sense-organs.

     1. But there is a difference between a sense-organ and the

moral sense. The former is biologically determined. The latter is constituted, in part, by accepted moral standards.

    a. The moral standards involved are usually those expressed in terms of the prevailing conventions of decency and propriety in public manners. (Thus, for example, not so very long ago the picture of women smoking or standing at a bar was offensive to any audience which accepted the prevailing *mores* in regard to such matters.)

    b. It does not matter that the standards are local, that they have not always been the same nor always will be, that they are not now the same in all countries.

        (1) Manners are necessarily conventional, but they are not merely or arbitrarily conventional. They are conventional determinations of more general moral considerations which formulate the principles of right and wrong conduct.

        (2) The manners which we adopt at any time, the prevailing *mores*, are thus particular determinations of morality, just as human laws are particular determinations of justice.[3]

        (3) Transgressions of the *mores* are, therefore, offensive to our moral sensibilities.

2. There is no question that that which is offensive in this way is undesirable.

    a. That which offends us is unpleasant and we obviously avoid the offensive.

    b. We do not willingly submit to the offensive in the field of our moral sensibilities, any more than we seek out ugliness or expose ourselves to unpleasant odors.

3. But there is the question: To whom are particular works of art offensive in this way? There are two possibilities: they are offensive (1) either to the audience which they entertain, or (2) to others.

    a. But the first is impossible over a long period of time, unless the offense is so slight as to be negligible. Thus, if the movies were gravely offensive to their audience, they would soon lose it.

[3] Cf. St. Thomas Aquinas, *Summa Theologica*, I–II, Q. 95, AA. 2, 4.

       An art cannot succeed as a popular amusement and at the same time be seriously offensive to its public.

b.   The second alternative, then, must be the case ; that is, individuals or groups in society who are not the regular patrons of an art must be offended by it and protest either because they, too, would enjoy the art were its offensiveness lessened or eliminated ; or because they maintain that the part of the public which does not seem to be offended, *should* be offended.

Digression :

Although the basic principles of morality are everywhere the same, the *mores* or conventions not only are not the same at different times and places, but are not even the same in the same country at a given time.   One of the chief differences between what are called primitive societies and what are called civilized ones is that in the former there is a much greater uniformity in the *mores* at a given time.   In modern societies particularly we find the phenomenon of conflicting *mores* due to the presence of different social groups having different standards and manners.   This fact makes the charge that the movies are offensive to moral sensibilities extremely difficult to interpret.   The question is whose, and further, whether there is any clear ground for choosing among alternative and conflicting conventions.

The charge of immorality, thus interpreted, is an old one.   Plato made it against certain passages in Greek literature which offended his moral sensibilities and those which he thought *ought* to prevail in the population of an ideal state.   Whether they actually did prevail in Greek society is a point of history.   If they did not, the passages in question could hardly have been offensive to the audience which enjoyed that literature.   The early Christian attack upon pagan literature, and upon the theatre especially, is partly this : these arts are offensive to a good Christian in so far as they present transgressions of Christian values and manners.   But Christian manners are no less conventional than other manners.[3a]   They have changed from time to time, although essentially always remaining expressions of Christian morality, since as conventions they are determinations of the principles of that morality.   What Christians find offensive has, therefore, changed in the course of centuries.   The pros and cons

[3a] In his recent encyclical, Pope Pius recognized this difficulty : "circumstances, usages and forms vary from country to country ; so it does not seem practical to have a single list for all the world."

of the Collier controversy in the seventeenth century are thus to be understood. The Restoration comedy was not offensive to the moral sensibilities of the particular audience which enjoyed it, though the fact that it existed and was enjoyed by the gentry and the court gave offense to the moral sensibilities of a large class in the population, the Puritans. When this class became politically dominant and when, after the accession of William and Mary, its *mores* reigned, the theatre which could only succeed by pleasing its audience could no longer afford to give offense to the people who had become its patrons.

It is clear, then, that an art is never greatly offensive to the moral sensibilities of its persistent patrons. The extent of the patronage, the degree of popularity of an art, is thus some measure of prevailing manners. It is able to indicate the conventions and standards of the majority, or of a large group, in a society in which there are conflicting codes. Moreover, it indicates the relativity of these conventions to place and time. The plays of Shakespeare can contain parts that are offensive to the moral sensibilities of Robert Bridges and persons like him, although they were not similarly offensive to the thousands upon thousands of their Elizabethan audience [72].

The first interpretation of the charge that some movies are immoral requires no further discussion. If it be said further that the movies are not offensive to a large portion of the population because they have degraded the moral sensibilities of their audience, then we pass to another consideration, namely, the influence of the movies upon human behavior and consequently upon manners and standards generally. This matter will be examined later; it is part of the second charge. It is not relevant here because we are considering whether the movies are offensive and to whom, and not why they are *not* offensive to the audience which enjoys them [73].

> C. A work of art may be called immoral because it violates moral principles. It can violate moral principles only if it be somehow construed as *asserting* their contraries. Thus, if a narrative be construed as asserting that men achieve happiness by vicious deeds or that men seek evil knowingly rather than good, it is immoral *as so construed.* (We need not stop here to discuss the necessity of the qualifying phrase "as so construed," beyond saying that works of art do not of themselves *assert* anything.) The charge that some movies are immoral can be interpreted in this sense.[4]

[4] A fuller discussion of the intrinsic morality of works of art, in relation to aesthetic goodness, will be found in Chapters 12 and 15 *infra.*

1. They are said, for example, to violate the canon of poetic justice as that has been traditionally formulated in English literary criticism.
   a. The doctrine of poetic justice says that vice and crime should always be rewarded by obvious failure and punishment, and virtue and lawfulness should always be as obviously rewarded by success in some clearly recognized form, which usually means external prosperity and contentment.
   b. It does not require that narratives confine themselves only to good men and good deeds.
2. But as we have seen,[5] this doctrine is a confusion of moral and aesthetic principles and is intrinsically pernicious.
   a. This does not mean that criminals should not be punished by the state or that those who are known to be vicious should not be despised, or perhaps pitied, for their weakness.
   b. But to try to teach a moral lesson by showing virtue always outwardly triumphant and vice always ending in the gutter or on the gallows is to distort the truth and pervert the moral lesson. History is full of contrary examples of vice prospering in all the external circumstances of life.
3. It may be objected nevertheless that the application of the principle of poetic justice to the movies is justified, even though it is intrinsically unsound.
   a. On the ground that unless the story abides by the canon of poetic justice, the influence upon the behavior and character of the movie audience is harmful.
   b. But this raises a question of fact: Is it the case that, despite the abundant evidence which history and life itself provide to the contrary, the outward triumph of virtue and the punishment of vice must be shown in motion pictures in order to help men, for morally pernicious reasons, to lead morally good lives? (Since the reasons are wrong, only the appearance of virtue can be thus achieved.)

---

[5] See Note 45 *infra*.

Digression:

It should be mentioned as a relevant fact that for the most part the movies have followed the principle of poetic justice, not only because it has been thought that that is the way to teach a moral lesson [74], but also because that is the way stories must be told to achieve their proper poetic effects.   Despite the fact that almost all movies are so written and produced, their critics have many times insisted that the right ending does not prevent the movie from having insidious effects because of incidental elements in the plot.   This raises an obvious question of fact about whether such is the case. In any event, the point raised nullifies the demand for poetic justice as a device for inculcating morals which, superficially formed for wrong reasons, must ultimately be worse than no morals at all.

- D.   There is one further interpretation of the charge that some movies are immoral, namely, that they are obscene.   We must ask whether this interpretation of the charge adds anything to the two preceding interpretations.
    1.   We must first attempt to define obscenity.   Obscenity is usually a transgression of the *mores* with respect to sex, although it may also involve other matters connected with the exposure of the body, the customs governing the performance of certain bodily functions, the use of language of a certain sort, and so forth.
        a.   It would thus appear that obscenity is the same as indecency and is objectionable to persons who are outraged by it.
        b.   The standards by which obscenity is judged are conventional and local, just as all other standards of decency and propriety are.   But that they are conventional makes no difference to the point. It does not lessen the shock of outrage which some people are made to suffer.
        c.   So far the charge that some movies are obscene adds nothing to the charge that they offend moral sensibilities.   But additional grounds may be offered for the objection to obscenity, particularly sexual obscenity.
            (1)   It is not merely that some persons are outraged by such indecent manifestations.
            (2)   Those who criticize an art for indulging in sexual obscenities have grounds for doing

so, even though the large popular audience of that art may not be in any way shocked or offended.

2. The first of these reasons is the same as that which underlies the objection to pornography. It is the moral condemnation of sensuality as such.

   a. As St. Thomas said, man cannot live without pleasure; and unless he is provided higher pleasures, he will seek lower ones. The distinction which St. Thomas has in mind here is between sensual pleasures and the intellectual pleasures of contemplation.

   b. The pleasure which is appropriate to a work of art is, of course, the latter. Any sensual pleasure which a work of art may give is thoroughly accidental to its nature.

   c. But if a work is intentionally obscene, it aims to give sensual pleasure to its audience, and to this extent is not a work of art but a piece of pornography.

      (1) It may be that not all members of an audience will be responsive to the obscenity, but this makes no difference to the point of criticism if, according to prevailing standards of sexual morality, it is highly probable that the obscenity of the artist will gratify the desire for pornography and the lust for sensual pleasure in a large number of people.

      (2) Nor does it make any difference whether the obscenity is or is not intentional, if the words, acts or spectacles in question are, by the customs of the community, such that they will probably be received as obscene.

Digression:

There are some liberals who are never able to understand the objection to sexual obscenity or pornography in any terms. This can only be because they do not accept Christian standards of sexual behavior or, for that matter, any other code which predominates in their own society. They would be unwilling to admit the distinction between higher and lower pleasures, which is Greek as well as Christian and, curiously enough for modern hedonists, Epicurean as well as Stoic. They sometimes recognize the justification of laws which prohibit and punish pornography, but hide in ostrich fashion behind a distinction impossible to make between the obscene and the pornographic. They treat the question of obscenity and pornography as if it were a curiously Christian foible, utterly forgetting or ignoring that sexual taboos are both more complicated and more rigid among primitive peoples and that the punishment of their transgression in life or in art is universal. It is not necessary to deal with them further. In the same sense that society is justified in legally prohibiting pornography, the precise nature of which must be determined according to the standards held at the given time and place, so it is justified in protesting against sexual obscenity in motion pictures and in advocating censorship or other means to prevent it. In their code of self-regulation the motion picture producers have fully recognized the objection to obscenity [75].

Consider the wisdom of Maritain's position in contrast : "There are, says St. Paul, some things which must not be so much as mentioned among you. Yet he immediately mentions them himself. What does that mean ? Nothing by *its kind alone* is a forbidden nutriment for art, like unclean animals to the Hebrews. From this point of view art can mention them all, as St. Paul mentions avarice and lechery. But on condition that, in the particular case and *in relation to the people* it is aiming at and with whom it comes in contact, the work does not soil the mind and the heart. From this point of view if there are certain things which the artist is not strong enough or pure enough to mention without conniving with evil, he has no right to mention them." [6] And Maritain adds in a note : "In practice, printing and modern methods of vulgarization, by confusing different publics more and more in one shapeless mass, run the risk of making a problem already singularly difficult well-nigh impossible." [7]

> d. Thus understood, the charge that some movies are obscene raises two questions of fact.
>> (1) Are the standards by which the obscenity of any particular movie is judged standards which the community generally accepts, such as the standards of Christianity and of contemporary American life ?
>> (2) What proportion of motion pictures are obscene, and to what extent is any particular

[6] *Art and Scholasticism*, Messrs. Sheed and Ward, Publishers, London, 1930 : pp. 117–118, by permission.
[7] *Ibid.*, Note 185, by permission of Messrs. Sheed and Ward, Publishers. See also Note 154.

       motion picture obscene, as judged by such standards?

3. The second reason for the objection to obscenity is that such matter tends to arouse the passion of lust in any of its myriad forms.

    a. Mere sensuality or sensual pleasure is distinguished from the passion of lust in that the latter is a movement of the appetite. It is a natural consequence of sensuality. In other words, the second reason adds to the first an objection to obscenity on the ground that it stimulates desires and initiates types of behavior which are condemnable.

    b. It is no answer to this objection to say that if art arouses such passions, it also purges them; because an art may arouse the passions so excessively that it fails to effect a sufficient catharsis, in which case man's burden of concupiscence is made heavier rather than lighter.

      (1) Whatever in a work of art arouses lust or concupiscence to such an extent that the correlative purgation is inadequate is obscene.

      (2) It must be admitted, however, that to whatever extent a work of art arouses and purges lust, it is not only not obscene in this sense, but serves a positively good end which ancient psychology called catharsis and modern psychology calls sublimation.

    c. Understood in this way, the second objection to obscenity raises a question of fact about the influence of motion pictures upon human behavior, upon the desires and actions of men.

      (1) If some movies are objectionably obscene only to the extent that they fail adequately to purge the lust which they excessively arouse, the question of fact can be answered only if the unpurged passion has some determinable effect upon behavior or character.

      (2) Furthermore, since the unpurged passion may cause action of a sort which either conforms to or transgresses the sexual *mores* of the community, the determination of

obscenity rests upon this additional question of fact.

(3) These questions of fact indicate that, on the second meaning of obscenity, the charge we are here considering reduces to the charge that some movies influence human character or conduct in ways that are undesirable. That is the second major charge presently to be considered.

Digression:

This charge is the ancient Christian objection to the theatre as essentially obscene: it intensifies the carnal concupiscence which is a heavy burden of potential sin in man's corrupt nature. The objection has been many times repeated, notably by Prynne and Collier, by Bossuet and Rousseau. It is much emphasized in the recurrent disapproval of the movies by the churches.

II. INTERPRETATION OF THE CHARGE THAT THE MOTION PICTURES IN- FLUENCE THE BEHAVIOR OF ADULTS AND THAT THIS INFLUENCE IS BAD BECAUSE (a) IT TENDS TO CORRUPT PUBLIC MANNERS AND (b) IT TENDS TO CORRUPT THE MORAL CHARACTER OF INDIVID- UALS.

   A. It is, first, necessary to understand the relation of public manners to moral character.

      1. Habit is the root of both public custom and private character.

         a. The public manners of a community are those customary forms of conduct which are maintained by habits of social behavior in the individuals of that community. The moral character of these individuals is also constituted, in part, by the same habits.

         b. Moral virtues and vices are habits of voluntary conduct, concerned with action and passion (with behavior and emotion).

           (1) These habits may be regarded as constituting the moral character of the individual in himself;

           (2) Or they may be regarded as constituting his moral character in relation to other men.

           (3) This is one distinction between justice and the other moral virtues. Justice, consid-

ered generally, comprises all the moral virtues when they are regarded as relating man to man in the community.

(a) Thus, a good man is one who is properly directed to his final end by the rectification of his appetite resulting from the moral virtues;

(b) And a just man is a man who is good socially, a man who is not only properly directed to his own end, but to the common good of the society in which he lives, and hence to the good of other men.

(c) Anything which tended to make a man unjust would also tend to corrupt his moral character, and conversely.

(4) Justice must also be considered in relation to law and custom. Laws and customs, in so far as they are ordained to the common good, are expressions of political justice. In part, they are determinations of what is naturally just, that is, they are determinations of justice as the sum of all the moral virtues socially regarded. In part, however, they are conventional regulations which are justified as providing order and rule in society.

(a) The just man is, therefore, not only one who is morally virtuous but also one who is law-abiding and who in his social behavior conforms to the established customs of the community.

(b) It must be remembered that laws are only one expression of the types of conduct which are desirable for the common good. The unlegalized customs of a society are equally, if not more profoundly, an expression of the regulation of individual behavior in the interests of society.

(c) No law or custom is merely conventional; as such, it would be utterly arbitrary and an expression of tyrannical force rather than of justice.

On the other hand, every law or custom is conventional to the extent that what is just, what serves the common good, must be determined in a particular society according to its nature and circumstances.

2. Although the basic conditions of human society are everywhere the same, different societies composed of different types of men living under different physical conditions are specially conditioned by these circumstances. The principles underlying human law or social custom are common to all bodies of law and custom. (These principles are the *ius gentium*, deductions from natural law.) Particular bodies of law and custom are conventional determinations of these principles, appropriate to the particular circumstances of a particular society at a given time.

3. Essential human nature is everywhere the same, but men differ in many accidents of body and soul. The moral virtues which constitute individual character are thus, in a sense, conventional determinations of the moral principles common to the virtues, determinations made by individual reason appropriate to the accidental traits of the individual.

4. Moral principles are not, in any case, relative because what is good character in one individual is not the same as what is good character in another, but relative to the peculiarities of his capacities and circumstances. Nor are the principles of law and custom, which aim at the common good, relative because the determination of these principles in particular laws and customs are relative to the conditions of the particular society.

5. *To summarize:* the principles which underlie private character and public behavior are ultimately the same. They are traditionally distinguished as moral and political according to the way in which they are regarded: either with respect to the individual in himself or with respect to the individual in society. Ethics and politics are thus analytically separated, but actually no separation can be made. The conditions of a good life for the individual and of good order in society must ultimately be the

same, since men are social animals and society is composed of men.

Digression:

The difference between law and custom must be understood in terms of their sources, their manner of promulgation, and their sanctions. The difference is such that laws may be made to reinforce or to change customs, and customs, either as they are or as they change, may support or abrogate laws. Ignoring for the purposes of this analysis, the distinction between law and custom, we can see that public manners are patterns of social behavior which conform to rules of law or to established customs. Crime is only one kind of anti-social behavior. Any behavior which does not conform to established customs is anti-social in essentially the same sense. It must be remembered, furthermore, that habit — and habit is always a state of the individual — is the basis of both law and custom. The force of law is not primarily its official sanctions, but the effect of these sanctions in forming habits of behavior in individuals. The force of custom is also the force of the habits which a community of men commonly share. It follows, therefore, that the moral character of individuals will be correlative to the laws and customs of their society, and conversely. The underlying habits must be the same. This explains a point previously made, that the moral sensibilities of individuals are correlative to the social standards and conventions of the community in which they live.

B. There can be no question that anti-social conduct is undesirable from the point of view of society.

    1. Breaches of public law are thus condemned by society as crimes, and society tries to prevent such conduct in one way or another.

    2. Breaches of custom are similarly reprehensible. As St. Augustine said: "Those offenses which are contrary to the customs of men, are to be avoided according to the customs generally prevailing; so that a thing agreed upon and confirmed by the custom or law of any city or nation may not be violated at the lawless pleasure of any, whether citizen or foreigner." [8]

    3. Men who act anti-socially, whether criminally or contrary to the customs generally prevailing, are in the same sense morally vicious.

[8] *Confessions*, III, 8.

Digression :

Conformity to prevailing customs would thus appear to be no different from conformity to law, both with respect to the social values involved and with respect to the moral character of the individual. But there is a difference which is extremely important in modern societies, though not so much the case in primitive societies. The body of law which regulates the social order of a community is one at any given time. It may have internal conflicts and inconsistencies, but it is not, as a whole, in conflict with other bodies of law governing that community. Furthermore, the administration of a body of law takes account of the difficulties which arise from such internal conflicts. But there is not a single body of customs prevailing exclusively in the community at any time. There are, in a society such as ours, different sets of conventions which regulate the manners of different social groups within the whole community. Some of these differences may be negligible ; but others may constitute seriously conflicting *mores*. This is not to say that there are no conventions or customs common to our society as a whole. There may be many which are universally shared by the habits of men in all social groups, apart from those which the laws enforce. But it is to say that there can be, and usually are, some customs which are shared only by the habits of men in a particular social group, and which conflict with the conventions of other social groups. We raised this same point before in connection with obscenity and that which outrages moral sensibilities. One part of the population, persistent in their attendance at movies, can hardly be seriously offended by them, while another part of the population, whose moral sensibilities would be shocked if it attended, charges the movies with obscenity. This difference between the moral sensibilities of the audience and of the reformers of motion pictures indicates that there are in the community divergent and, perhaps, inconsistent standards and conventions. It does not indicate, of course, on which side moral rectitude lies.

C. In the light of the foregoing analysis, the charge that the movies influence the behavior of the adult population in a way which tends to corrupt or degrade public manners, can be interpreted to mean that the habits of behavior which movies form in their audience are either (1) contrary to customs which prevail generally, i.e., in the whole community, or (2) contrary to customs which prevail partially, i.e., in one or more of its divers social groups.

1. In the first of these alternatives, there is no question of evaluation, because if the movies influence men to act anti-socially in this sense, they are condemnable in the same way as if they influenced men to act criminally. (It should be noted that we are here distinguishing between law and custom, in order to separate the charge that the movies cause violations of public manners from the charge that they cause criminality. The latter will presently be considered.)

2. In the second of these alternatives, there is a difficult question of evaluation because of the conflict of customs. It becomes necessary to evaluate the custom, the violation of which is attributed to the movies, in order to evaluate the influence of the movies supposed to be responsible for that violation.

Digression:

To make this clear, let us suppose that the influence of the movies on behavior forms habits in a large number of individuals, and that these habits then constitute a set of public manners for the group to which these individuals belong. Let us further suppose that these manners are divergent from and in conflict with the conventions of one or more groups in the population. The criticism of the movies can be based, then, only on the supposition that the conventions which obtain within the social group in which the criticism arises are, in some sense, superior or preferable to the manners which the part of the population under the influence of the movies have adopted. But what are the criteria of such superiority or preference? Since we are dealing with customs and manners, it must be recognized that we are not facing here a conflict of basic moral principles, but rather a conflict of different conventional determinations of such principles. We have already seen that many different conventional determinations of the same principles are possible. The superiority of one determination to another must be based on its appropriateness for a given group or upon the interests of society as a whole. If the first criterion is employed, it cannot be said that the conventions which one group adopts are not appropriate for it because another group has different conventions. It is only if the second criterion is employed that the relativity of special conventions to particular groups can be transcended, and the manners of one group can be criticized as undesirable from the point of view of the common good. Such criticism of convention is, of course, always possible.   It is exactly the same as the criticism which can be made of proposed laws, namely, that however much they may be to the interest of a particular group in society, they will not be as productive of the common good as some alternative legal regulation. The popular debate of what customs should prevail in society is thus the same as the legislative debate of what laws should be made or changed.

Such issues are extremely difficult to resolve.   Both sides can appeal to the same common principles and yet differ reasonably in their judgment of the relative adaptability of different laws or different customs to serve the end which is commonly acknowledged.   That men, seeking the same end, can frequently disagree about the expediency and hence the desirability of different means, arises from the very nature of human practical problems.   Men do not have sufficient or adequate knowledge by which they can prudently determine the one right way to act in most cases.   The problem is not always equally difficult.   Sometimes knowledge makes one solution clearly preferable to any other.   When this is not the case, however, equally prudent men seeking the same end can disagree about the means to be chosen.   Since the disagreement is reasonable, one solution cannot be more reasonable than another.

The charge that the movies corrupt public manners must, therefore, view the conflict of *mores* attributed to the influence of the movies, in terms of the common good of society as a whole.   The choice between conflicting conventions may be an easy one, so that it can be clearly shown to all reasonable men that one rather than another sort of public behavior is more desirable.   If, then, it can be shown that the movies cause the less desirable kind of behavior, they can be justifiably criticized in the same way that they can be condemned for causing criminal behavior.   But if the choice between the conflicting conventions is a difficult one, and if it cannot be clearly shown to all reasonable men that the kind of behavior in question is more or less desirable, then the justification of the criticism is itself a debatable point, and no further question need be raised about whether the movies do in fact cause the behavior being criticized.

D.   We can now enumerate the various questions of fact raised by the moral criticism of the movies in this charge.
  1.   Do the movies influence the social behavior of their adult audience in any ascertainable way?
  2.   If the answer to the first question is affirmative, then we may ask: Are the habits of social behavior which the movies cause contrary to customs which prevail in the community as a whole?   (If the answer to

this question is affirmative, no further question of evaluation is raised because behavior which transgresses such customs is anti-social and undesirable in the same way that criminal behavior is.)

3. If the answer to the first question is affirmative, and the answer to the second question is negative, one further question can be asked : Do the habits of social behavior which the movies cause constitute in whole or part a new set of manners which conflict with conventions prevailing in one or more social groups, but not in society as a whole?   (If the answer to this question is affirmative, a difficult problem of evaluation remains, as we have already seen.)

E. We have so far considered this second charge with respect to the first of its two clauses, namely, the corruption of public manners. Its second clause maintained that the movies corrupt the moral character of individuals by forming vicious habits.

1. It is not necessary, however, to undertake a separate analysis of this second part of the charge. The analysis is the same as in the case of the first part because :

a. The standards of good moral character are the same as the standards of good social conduct.

b. The same basic principles are involved. Where before we considered habits as they are shared by many individuals and as such constitutive of customs, here we consider habits as parts of the individual character. In either case they are determinations of the same principles.

2. The questions which are raised here are also the same as before.

a. Do the movies influence the behavior of their adult audience in any ascertainable way?

b. If so, does the resulting behavior form habits contrary to the standards of moral character generally accepted by all men?

c. Or, if so, does the resulting behavior form habits contrary to standards accepted only by some particular social group?

d. As in the preceding analysis, the distinction between the second and third question is important because it is only the latter which raises further questions of evaluation. In the former there is no further problem, because if the movies are the cause of vicious habits they are certainly condemnable. (A vice is a habit of action or passion contrary to reason. What is contrary to reason may differ with the circumstances of action and the nature of the agent; but that habits are vicious if contrary to reason is a principle of moral conduct which is generally accepted by all reasonable men.)

Digression:

It has been said that the movies corrupt adult character by presenting patterns of vicious behavior which get imitated. This echoes an ancient complaint against the drama which, since it must deal with the materials of virtue and vice, necessarily presents the actions and passions of bad men as well as good. One of the conditions of the imitability of what the drama or the motion picture contains is the 'realism' of the imitation which the art achieves. In other words, the drama or motion picture is itself an imitation of human action. The imitation of nature by art makes it possible for men, whose natural actions have thus been imitated, to 'imitate' this imitation, in the copy-sense of imitating. But copying is more or less possible according to the degree of realistic fidelity which the artistic imitation achieves. In this connection, the movies are charged with influencing behavior because, being terribly realistic as imitations, they are highly imitable or copy-able. On the other hand, the movies are accused of being so 'untrue to life,' so wildly romantic and even fantastic as imitations, that they offer their audience types of conduct, values and standards, which cannot be copied or adopted and are therefore 'misleading ideals.' These two accusations are obviously inconsistent if they are meant to apply to all movies. What may be meant, however, is that the movies which are copy-able are bad morally, whereas those which are uncopyable are bad because misleading and hence are sources of discontent or frustration.

This is, of course, a minor point, since it makes little difference whether, if the movies do in fact corrupt character, they do so through being copied, through setting up false ideals, through exciting the passions, or through any other way.

III. INTERPRETATION OF THE CHARGE THAT THE MOVIES ARE ONE OF THE CAUSES OF ADULT CRIMINALITY.

    A. This charge requires little further interpretation because the analysis of the preceding charge, for the most part, explains it.

1. Criminality covers the field of anti-social behavior which is prohibited by law.
2. As we have seen, there are other types of anti-social behavior, involving the transgression of prevailing customs, but the transgression of law is the clearest manifestation of such behavior because there can be no irresolvable argument about what are the laws, as there can be dispute about whether a given custom is accepted by the community as a whole or is merely the convention of one of its constituent groups.

B. This charge raises no question of evaluation, except perhaps about the justice of the laws being violated.
C. It raises one question of fact: Are the movies one of the causes of adult criminal behavior?

Digression:

That question of fact is difficult. The causes of crime are many and co-operative. Almost any aspect of the social environment or any factor in the development of human character may be found to be one of the contributing causes of crime in a particular case. It is not a sufficient answer to the question, therefore, to find merely that in *some* cases, movies are in *some* way connected with criminal behavior. If this charge is to have any practical significance, we must know more than this. We must know something about the aetiology of crime in general, and we must definitely know something about the role of the movies in that aetiology, that is, we must know the way in which the movies as one factor enter into the general causal nexus. We cannot merely cite a few cases of a supposed influence. If cases are cited, they must be adequately analyzed; if numbers are used, they must be treated with statistical sophistication. The general problem of the aetiology of human behavior is discussed later.[9] It is not necessary to say more here.

IV. INTERPRETATION OF THE CHARGE THAT THE MOVIES HAVE A NUMBER OF EFFECTS UPON CHILDREN — PHYSICAL, MORAL AND INTELLECTUAL — WHICH ARE BAD.

A. It is necessary to analyze this charge with respect to each of these spheres of influence separately. To the extent that the distinction between adult and child makes no difference to the point under consideration, the analysis of the first three charges will enable us to cover many points briefly here.

[9] In Chapter 9 *infra*.

B. *Physical effects:* such things as eye-strain, excessive fatigue,
   nervous irritability, impairment of sleep, and the physiological conditions of neurotic disorder. Two sorts of
   questions are raised by this aspect of the charge:

   1. Questions of fact about the precise nature and extent
       of the various physiological effects upon children of
       attendance at the movies. Further questions may
       be raised concerning the correlation of the extent of
       these effects and the amount of attendance, etc.
   2. If the foregoing questions can be answered definitely,
       then questions of evaluation may be raised; that is,
       are the effects ascertained injurious, or to what extent
       are they injurious, as determined by medical or
       physiological standards of normal health in children?

Digression:

Thus, for example, it must be shown first that the movies do or do
not cause eye-strain under certain conditions; and if they do, it
must be considered whether this eye-strain is greater than that
caused by normal reading, whether it is injurious to an extent that
is undesirable; and similarly in the case of such matters as fatigue,
sleep, etc. The play of children or their school-work may also
interfere with sleep and produce fatigue. We must inquire, therefore, about the comparable effect of the movies and whether, in any
case, the effect is negligible or sufficiently injurious to warrant attention from those who have the care of juvenile health.

The point about neurotic disorder is slightly different from these
others. It is claimed, for instance, that movies excite children's
fears so violently that morbid anxieties and phobias of a relatively
permanent character result. Even if this claim has some basis in
fact, psychological analysis and investigation have shown how many,
how various, how unpredictable and hence how uncontrollable are
the causes of abnormal fear in children. We must ask, therefore,
whether there is any reason to suppose that fewer children would
suffer panic, and the more or less lasting consequences of fright, if
there were no movies at all. There is always the story which
Chesterton tells of the little girl "who had an insomnia of insane
terror entirely arising from the lyric of *Little Bo-Peep*, because as a
psychoanalyst later discovered, the word 'bleating' had some obscure
connection in her mind with the word 'bleeding.'" As he points
out, nobody could possibly provide against that sort of mistake, yet
this is precisely what preventive and prophetic science seeks to do,

trying to calculate the incalculable in order to surround the child with a totally aseptic environment.[10]

  C. *Moral effects:* it is charged that the movies influence the immature so that, to an extent which is not negligible, they become morally depraved and criminally delinquent during their youth and come to manhood with deformed moral characters. Analysis is required fully to understand this charge.

   1. It must mean, first, that during the period when their habits of action and passion are being formed, children under the influence of motion pictures are being habituated in wrong directions — wrong because contrary to the laws and other generally prevailing customs, wrong because contrary to reason, or wrong because contrary to customs or standards which are accepted in one or another social group.

   2. It must mean, second, that the movies cause children and youth to act in ways which are criminally delinquent or otherwise anti-social.

Digression:

If either of these counts can be sustained, the movies can be properly charged with corrupting the youth in the Platonic sense of that accusation. Wrong habits are vices. Delinquency like criminality is merely one manifestation of vicious character. Since the standards by which we judge and the attitudes we take, arise from our habits of action and passion, vicious habits are the source of standards and attitudes which are not socially approved. Any further meaning of the charge, such as that the movies give children standards and attitudes which are not those of the adult society into which they will grow, is implicitly contained in the notions of virtue and vice.

The charge that some movies are obscene, which we have already considered in relation to their adult audience, may be repeated here. The movies can offend the moral sensibilities of children only to the extent that they have already adopted the moral standards upon which such sensibilities are founded. Otherwise they will not find shocking whatever it is that outrages some portions of the adult population. If they are seriously shocked it can only be because

[10] *Fear of the Film*, in a volume of essays entitled *Fancies versus Fads*, New York, 1923.

their moral sensibilities are firmly defined, and then no harm is done. When children are as mature as this, they are adults whatever their actual age may be. If, on the other meaning of obscene, the movies are charged with arousing the passion of lust in children to an extent that influences their subsequent behavior, then this influence has already been included in the claim that the movies cause depravity and delinquency, in which sexual misbehavior may be a large element.

3. This charge raises the same series of questions which we have already distinguished and ordered in the case of the second major charge.

 a. It must first be shown as a matter of fact that the movies do influence the behavior of children and youth; and the extent and nature of this influence must be ascertained.

 b. If that can be done, then it is necessary to show that the acts, the habits, the attitudes which result, are morally and socially undesirable.

  (1) If law, common custom or basic moral principles are transgressed, the problem of evaluation is easy.

  (2) But if the behavior which is under consideration is condemned as subversive of the conventions and standards peculiar to a particular social group, rather than common to the whole society or shared by all reasonable men, then the charge that the movies demoralize youth by causing such behavior must be further supported by showing that the manners and standards which result from their influence are inferior morally and socially to those which obtain in the particular group from which the disapproval comes. This may be an easy or a difficult task, as we have already seen.

D. *Intellectual effects:* it is charged that the movies are a distracting influence which interferes with children's application to school-work, that they are sources of misinformation, that they foster habits of intellectual passivity rather than activity, that they are too readily substituted for other and more difficult occupations, such as reading or listening to music, etc.

1. Each of these subordinate points raises an obvious

question of fact. Thus, do the movies interfere with a child's application to school-work and to what extent in relation to the frequency of attendance? Are the movies a source of misinformation and to what extent? And so forth.

2. In each case, if affirmative answers can be given, further questions of evaluation may have to be answered, such as, is the amount of interference with school-work, or the amount of misinformation, detrimental to the child's education. In answering these questions, it may be necessary to consider the positive educational influence of the movies. To the extent that the motion-picture programme includes news reels, travel pictures, nature studies and similar materials, in addition to narrative, it has many points of integration with the school curriculum and may be educationally beneficial in the same way that supplementary reading is. In other words, the problem of evaluation here depends upon the balance of educational advantages and disadvantages afforded by the movies.

3. In the case of the last part of the charge, that the movies attract children away from other intellectual occupations, such as reading, it must be shown, if this is the case, that it is undesirable.

Digression:

One further comment must be made in regard to the charge that the movies are a source of misinformation and distorted notions of reality. The educators who say this are obsessed by a naïve realism which leads them to suppose that the sole aim of education is to bring the child into contact with the 'realities' of the contemporary world. They understand 'reality' in some absurdly simply and confused sense. They advocate an early introduction of courses in social science. Such courses should become the framework of the curriculum, and everything else, literature, history, and even mathematics and the natural sciences must be fitted into it. Apart from the distortions of subject-matter which such an organization of studies produces; apart from the increasing loss of imaginative stimulation and aesthetic cultivation which results from the degradation of literature, as handmaiden to sociology, providing at best case-materials and indices of social change; apart from the magnification of history and particularly current events, although such studies can contribute nothing more than a bulk of information, gross and unanalyzed — there is the wholly uncritical supposition that history, current events and social studies are purely factual, that they are solid information totally free from local prejudice and propaganda, from ideas or constructions of the imagination. It is unfortunately true that the intellectual content in such studies is slight and that their imaginative flights are crippled by a naïve adherence to the facts and nothing but the facts. But it is just as unfortunately true that there is as much untruth, as much distortion and unreality, in the history and social science which is taught as in the fairy stories and highly fanciful fiction which children will always read and love unless they are corrupted by schools into becoming social scientists at an early age. The proponents of this type of education are unable to understand that poetry is more philosophical than history, that fairy tales are more philosophical than social science. Should they ever get this insight, they would probably be even more insistent upon the elimination of literature or would further debase it as a source of 'factual materials,' because they would be unable to overcome the prejudices of an ultra-scientific era against philosophy.

Plato's concern with poetry occurs in the context of his consideration of an educational programme. He seems to be making the same point that we have just criticized in contemporary educational theory. The poets must be supervised to the end that they do not inculcate false opinions, that they be prevented from telling lies about the gods or human nature. Education must be directed toward the fullest knowledge of reality and toward achieving the clearest distinction between knowledge and opinion. One might hazard the guess that Plato would be even less happy about the teaching of history and social science than he was about the poets. Such influence is more insidiously an obstacle to the proper course of education because it is even more deceitful than poetry. It is better able to fool the immature mind by its counterfeit of knowledge and its presentation of appearance as reality. How much more Plato would find contemporary psychologists and social scientists telling lies about the gods and human nature and weaving them into the very texture of education, than the Greek dramatists whom he criticized!

Furthermore, the materials of history and social science lack the imaginative dimension of poetry which is indispensable in the early stages of education. It will be remembered that Plato himself was addicted to story-telling, to the concoction of myths, not only as means by which the statesman can persuade common men about things they cannot understand, but also because the road to intellectual insight is through the imagination for most men and for all children. Imaginative literature is, therefore, the substance of primary education and the first step toward science or philosophy. Plato excluded the poets from the state on grounds which today would call for the exclusion of social science from the curriculum. But he did not eliminate poetry from education. On the contrary, poetry is an instrument which the teacher must use and Plato is only insisting that philosophers rather than professional poets should write or at least select the stories which children should hear. The contemporary exponent of social science may answer that his insistence is the same. He, too, may agree that stories must be told, only asking that he be permitted to write them. I can say to this only that I share the doubt Plato would probably have, whether social scientists can tell better and more instructive stories than the movies or other forms of popular fiction. There was a rivalry in Greece between poets and philosophers; there is a rivalry today between the novel, the movie, fiction in general, and social science. If I understand *Democracy and Education*, John Dewey is there saying that the arts, and particularly literature, are essential instruments of social education and communication. Literature and social studies are two ways of achieving this same end. There may be some difference of opinion about which is the more effective.

The analysis of the moral and social criticism of motion pictures, which we have just concluded, failed to emphasize sufficiently the basic distinction between the influence of the movies on the mature and on the immature. Correction for that inadequacy must, therefore, now be made. It will throw further light on the significance of some of the charges.

The distinction between the mature and the immature can be made in a number of ways. The least satisfactory of these, because the most superficial, is by reference to chronological age. The best for our purposes is in terms of moral stability and instability. The mature person is one whose moral character is formed, for better or for worse. He is stable because moral character is constituted by habits, whether they be virtues or vices, and it is part of the essence of habit that it be a disposition difficult to change.[11] Habits are relatively permanent modes of operation; it takes many similar acts to establish them, and many contrary acts to destroy them. All moralists, from Aristotle to John Dewey, who have recognized that character is constituted by habits voluntarily formed and voluntarily exercised, are able to distinguish between the morally mature and immature in

[11] Cf. St. Thomas Aquinas, *Summa Theologica*, I–II, Q. 49, A. 2, ad. 3.

terms of stability. The moral problem for the young is the formation of good habits; for the mature it is rather the problem of maintaining good habits by exercising them through activity in accordance with them, or of removing bad habits by the performance of contrary acts. What makes the immature much more susceptible to moral training — their lack of habit and hence of stable character — also makes them much more susceptible to the movement of momentary passions and all other influences productive of vice. It is because youth can be so readily formed in either direction that the period of immaturity is the crucial one in the moral life.

It is generally acknowledged that there are often great discrepancies between age and actual maturity. The chronological age which differentiates the mature from the immature differs both by law and custom in different societies and at different times; but the essential meaning of maturity is not changed. It is indifferent that in modern times the age of maturity has been advanced almost a decade, that what in the ancient world and in most primitive societies would be considered a man is among us only a youth in his formative years. It is indifferent furthermore that there may be some proportion of persons, achieving any chronological age that marks the state of manhood from childhood and youth, who are not adults because not mature essentially. Every population has its feeble-minded, its moral and social imbeciles, whether the cause of their persistent and perhaps incorrigible immaturity be lack of intelligence or neurotic disorder. Whatever their age, they are children and the problem of the influence of motion pictures on them is the same as that of its effects upon children. For the most part, however, those who are chronologically regarded as adults are also morally and socially mature. If that were not the case, there could be no such things as generally prevailing customs or generally accepted standards, since these depend upon fixed habits shared by the greater part of the population.

This conception of an adult as a person of stable character throws critical light upon the charge that the movies influence the adult population. The persons who come within the scope of such influence must already be men of virtuous or vicious character, men who habitually behave socially or anti-socially. We need not inquire here into the conditions under which they have matured. It may be that the movies are in part responsible for the vicious and the criminal among them, being one of the causes which operated in the formation of their characters. But that is not the point in question. Rather it is whether the movies or any other art can exert a significant influence upon the character or behavior of mature men. As Aristotle says, it requires great force, almost brutality in fact, to change habits once they are formed. The difficulty of reforming adult criminals or of corrupting genuinely virtuous men bears witness to this fact. Let us take extreme cases to make the point clear. A perfectly virtuous man could certainly not be harmed by any influence in his environment. A thoroughly vicious man would be as impervious. But the incorruptible and the incorrigible, it may be said, are only ideal cases set up for the sake of analysis. Adults can change their habits, and the change may be either for better or worse. Nevertheless, the virtuous man is one in whom, for the most part, the discipline of reason is strong and in whom the existence of the moral virtues furthers the exercise of prudence in the formation of new habits. Thus, a virtuous man is one who is corruptible only by relatively extraordinary forces or circumstances. If the movies can be charged with corrupting such men, it must follow that the same kind of men who bring the charge are capable of being corrupted by the movies. This charge would be of such gravity, if it could be upheld, that it would call now, as at the time of the early Christian Fathers and later Bossuet and Rousseau, for the complete elimination of an art so dangerous. The charge against the movies is seldom, if ever, made in this vein. It is not that everyone in the adult population is seriously endangered by them, but only that some are — those whom the critics and the reformers properly seek to protect. Those endangered must be adults only chronologically; they must be men whose moral characters are not so much bad as weak and unstable, in whom the discipline of reason is slight, and who are such mixtures of virtue and vice that, forming new habits, they are as likely or more likely to become worse rather than better because prudence in them is not equal to the task of governing a disordered soul. The movies, it might be claimed, are among the factors which increase this disorder, which hinder rather than aid prudence, which further subject the individual to the bondage of his vices and lead him to form new ones. But this analysis reduces the charge that the movies corrupt adults to the charge that they influence only those among the adult population who are not really adults because not morally stable. The important question of fact, then, is how large a part of the general population this involves.

Whatever the potency of the arts to influence the immature, it is certainly questionable whether the movies or any other art is potent enough to affect a stable and disciplined soul. In short, there would seem to be a reasonable presumption against the proposition that the arts are able to corrupt mature persons. But by the same principles it must follow that there is a reasonable presumption in favor of the proposition that the arts are able to corrupt children and youth because of their instability and susceptibility to influence. Even though the arts be only one among many influences, and a weak one at that, children may be affected where adults could not be. The charge that motion pictures influence the behavior of children, make them depraved and corrupt, cause them to become delinquent and anti-social, is therefore a much more serious criticism than any of the charges which concern adults. Whatever the evidence may be in answer to the various questions of fact that are raised, this charge is supported by an initial presumption in its favor. The facts may strengthen or nullify the presumption, but we would be imprudent if we did not consider the charge seriously, whereas one might with some reason be much less concerned about all the other criticisms.

It is well to remember here that Plato attacked the poets on this score, charging them with the corruption of youth. It was the effect of poetry on the developing moral character, its deficiencies and, what is worse, its injurious consequences, which Plato made the basis for his policies of rigorous censorship and supervision. He was much less concerned about the effects of poetry on the mature. We do not find him accusing the poets of having caused adult criminality, or having degraded the moral standards of the adult population. Such things may, of course, result when a generation which has been demoralized during its youth, comes of age. But the primary danger, because the source of all others, was the effect of poetry on the habits and attitudes of the young. So today, the most serious of all the charges that are made against the movies has to do with their moral effects upon children and youth. The largest part of the critical and polemical literature bears on this point. The emphasis is obviously right. If the present adult population had come to moral maturity with characters well formed, it is difficult to see how the movies or any other influence could undermine their moral strength. The crux of the whole problem is certainly in the moral training of the young. In facing this problem we must not forget, of course, that the arts are only one among many other factors at work. It may be that society itself fails through its agencies of law, the church, the school and the home to produce relatively virtuous men, men relatively immune to the corrupting influences which always abound in the human environment [76].

The practical problem is made peculiarly difficult by the fact that the movies as art and entertainment are shared by the mature and immature and seem to be equally popular with both. Any attempt to control or supervise the production of motion pictures must take this fact into account [77]. The movies are a major source of recreation and artistic satisfaction in an industrial democracy, as well as a means of communication or social education, in Dewey's sense. Their positive values for the tremendous adult audience which they reach cannot prudently be ignored in an effort to make them entirely suitable and harmless for children, if they are not now suitable and harmless. No other popular art or public amusement has ever faced the practical problem of having to please and entertain both the mature and the immature, at the same time being morally obligated to both. The censorship of movies, whether officially directed or self-imposed, may therefore not be the most expedient means to this end, because it may have grave disadvantages with respect to the movies as adult entertainment. It may be more prudent to regulate the attendance of children, to prohibit their witnessing certain types of films if it can be established that such types are definitely injurious, or to attempt to produce movies which are known, not supposed, to be more suitable for the juvenile audiences [78].

The peculiar practical difficulties which the movies face because they are for both adults and children should not be underestimated. Plato considered poetry almost entirely in terms of its juvenile audience and as part of the educational process.

Bossuet considered the stage almost entirely in terms of its adult audience and as a kind of public amusement. Aristotle in his political consideration of the arts distinguished sharply between their role as entertainment in adult life and their place in early education. Furthermore, Plato did not hesitate to make the task of rearing children in all of its aspects the business of the state. The Greeks were not jealous of their "personal liberties," or considerate of an individualism they would have regarded as license rather than liberty. Similarly, Bossuet, living in an absolute monarchy, could call upon the state for the thoroughly paternalistic protection of all its citizens against the theatre. Some European nations, today returning to monarchical forms and denying the claims of individualism in the corporate state, may not hesitate to follow the Platonic principle of subjecting every aspect of private life to public control. But where the democratic forms still exist in government, and where social life is in the democratic order, moral problems are still distinguished as public and private, and moral training is as much, if not more, the province of the home and the church, as of the public school and the state. St. Thomas, William Whewell and John Dewey are, therefore, better guides in this practical problem, *as it exists for us,* than Plato or Bossuet. Both Aquinas and Whewell insisted upon the distinction between the spheres of state and church in the matter of morals and the training of the young. Whewell went even further in recognizing that the home may have the ultimate responsibility, although under the direction of the church [79]. Dewey sees political, religious and domestic agencies as sharing in the task of moral and social education. It cannot be shirked by any or appropriated by one to the exclusion of the others.

The problem of the movies in a democracy is, therefore, the most complicated instance of the problem of poetry and politics, of the conflict between art and prudence. Not the least part of its complication is the conjunction of adults and children in the audience. *If* the movies are found to be to some extent a bad influence on children and youth, the question of what should be done is not only for the state, but for the church and for the home. The best practical policy may not be the regulation of the movies but greater care and wisdom in the rearing of children. If children are harmed, it must be because they *can*

be harmed. That they *can be* may be due to the failure of
church and home to give them the moral strength to assimilate
any experience which may befall them either in life or in art.
On the other hand, it may be necessary to remove obstacles to
the effective training of children. This is the reason for concern about the arts.

To whatever extent some form of paternalism is unavoidable
because in some sense all men are children of the state and of the
church, it is nevertheless wise to distinguish between the protection of the mature and the care of the immature. All members of the community are not children in the same sense. The
problem of the cinema with respect to children must, therefore,
always be distinguished from the problem it raises with respect
to adults. If children — and moral imbeciles and morons who
have attained the age of manhood — are susceptible to influences
because immature, we must remember that others who are mature, are for that reason not similarly susceptible. To make laws
for the entire community as if everyone needed the same regulation which children and the irresponsible deserve, would be
no less folly than to treat the movies, which belong to both
children and adults, without regard for their differences. Because in the past no art has been so shared, the history of the
discussion of poetry and politics fails to illuminate what is the
most difficult point in the problem of the movies. To repair
this inadequacy and to get further light, I propose one final
historical digression : a brief account of literature designed specifically for children and of the criticism of such literature in modern
times.[12]

Except to make one comment, I shall pass over the popular
mediæval tales, compiled in the *Gesta Romanorum* and the *Bes-
tiaries,* as fables and stories for grown-up children, for ignorant
or half-instructed folk who might get a childish pleasure from
the fanciful narratives without catching the moral points concealed within the tracery of elaborate allegory. The surface of
these stories is earthy and fleshy ; they deal primarily with love
in its carnal manifestations. The mediæval church permitted
such fiction in the hands of simple folk, perhaps because those

[12] For this material I have depended largely on the exhaustive study made by
F. J. Harvey Darton : *Children's Books in England : Five Centuries of Social
Life,* Cambridge, 1932.

who could read were sufficiently protected by monastic sur-
roundings, perhaps because they relied upon the allegory to
translate base passion into the love of the Church for Christ.
However the matter stood during the Middle Ages, when books
were few and the children who were taught to read were usually
also dedicated to a clerical life, it is worth noting that the themes
of these mediæval tales have reappeared in later fairy stories and
romances for children.

In 1544 we find Hugh Rhodes in his *Book of Nurture* — its
purpose was to "teche vertew and connynge" — telling parents
to "take heed your children speak no words of villainy, nor show
them much familiarity, and see that they use honest sports and
games.   Mark well what vice they are specially inclined to, and
break it betimes.   Take them often with you to hear God's
word preached, and then enquire of them what they heard, and
use them to read in the Bible and other godly books, but especially keep them from reading of feigned fables, vain fantasies
and wanton stories, and songs of love, which bring much mischief to youth." [13]   At about the same time Roger Ascham, the
humane and tolerant master of Queen Elizabeth, had written:
"In our forefathers' time, when Papistry, as a standing pool, covered and overflowed all England, few books were read in our
tongue, saving certain books of chivalry, as they said, for pastime
and pleasure, which, as some said, were made in monasteries by
idle monks or wanton canons: as one, for example, *Morte
Arthure*: the whole pleasure of which book standeth in two
special points, in open manslaughter and bold bawdry. . .   Yet I
know when God's Bible was banished from the court, and *Morte
Arthure* received into the Prince's chamber.   What toys the
daily reading of such books may work in the will of a young
gentleman or a young maid, that liveth wealthily and idly, wise
men can judge and honest men do pity." [14]

Such criticisms indicate that romances, such as the tales of the
Round Table, were read by the privileged adolescents of Tudor
England.   The existence of the Books of Courtesy, written at
the same time by the exponents of good breeding, show, however,
the same opposition which Ascham expresses to the idea that
the young should read anything like what we should call fiction,
even juvenile fiction, had it existed.   Such opposition became

[13] Harvey Darton, *op. cit.*, p. 45.   [14] *Ibid.*, p. 45.

clamorously triumphant under the Puritans, who later echoed the sentiments of Rhodes and Ascham. During the Puritan régime, books were written for children, but they were as a rule "conceived and executed with so strong a didactic and religious bias that they seem not to be 'children's books' at all. Yet the authors meant them to fulfill that end, to give children pleasure and to make them happy." [15]   It is in the same spirit of starting children early on the difficult road to salvation that John Bunyan and his contemporaries attempted to write children's books.   A century later, Isaac Watts composed works for children to the same end, although he softened the threat of hell-fire somewhat.   The same purpose is apparent in all early American books for children.   It is even implicit in such "moral tales" as those written in the last century by the Lambs and by Charles Kingsley.   Children's books which aim merely to please and to excite, which offer romance and fantasy, adventure and the marvellous, because such things entertain the imagination, without any ulterior point of moral or religious instruction, were not approved until late in modern times when fairy tales, adventure stories and books that followed the invention of *Alice in Wonderland*, finally won favor in the last century.

Fairy tales and nursery rhymes — in a sense the heart of juvenile literature — came into their own despite neglect and deliberate persecution.   They were at first contemptuously dismissed as the imbecilities of the peasantry.   They were frowned upon by the moralists of the seventeenth century and the theorists of Rousseau's school.   Lord Chesterfield sought to deter his son from reading trivial stories for amusement, declaring himself against the old romances and against the new — fashionable fairy tales of Perrault, the rhymes of Mother Goose.   Rousseau violently objected to the fables of La Fontaine because the child is not saved by the moral in the epilogue but misled by it [80]. The culmination of the attack on fairy tales came at the beginning of the nineteenth century with Mrs. Trimmer, who founded a magazine, *The Guardian of Education*, the main object of which was "to contribute to the preservation of the young and innocent from the dangers which threaten them in the form of infantile and juvenile literature." [16]   Such stories as those of Cinderella and Robinson Crusoe must be banished from the

[15] *Ibid.,* p. 53.   [16] *Ibid.,* p. 264.

hands of the young. One of Mrs. Trimmer's correspondents wrote of *Cinderella* that "it paints some of the worst passions that can enter into the human breast, and of which little children should, if possible, be totally ignorant, such as envy, jealousy, a dislike of mothers-in-law and half-sisters, vanity, a love of dress, etc." *Robinson Crusoe* might lead to "an early taste for a rambling life and a desire of adventures." [17]

The fear and dislike of fairy tales, as Mr. Darton points out, "is not dependent to a great extent on the feeling of any one period. It is a habit of mind which has often been dominant without much basis in contemporary circumstances. It appears as recently as 1929 when Teachers' College of Columbia University decided that Titania's Kingdom was ridiculous, that fairy stories were useless and must be banished utterly from the nurseries of an intelligent democracy to be replaced by science" [18] —probably in the form of current events.

Nevertheless, paradoxical as it may seem, the Victorian era was one of amazing productivity in the field of children's literature. Magic and fancy were no longer rebuked and nonsense was free to work its charms. Children were permitted to dwell on mediæval romances, such as the Arthurian legends, without being surrendered to the Devil. Fables and fairy tales were recommended even though they were not history or plain recitals of fact. Yarns of adventure multiplied, and the dime novel and two-penny thriller contained both the best and the worst of their substance. The stories of James Fenimore Cooper and Robert Louis Stevenson became models which the dime novels copied. The nineteenth century in England and America may have been strict and sober in other fields, but its children were allowed to seek fun and excitement in fiction without being told that they were silly or not facing hard reality.

The sale of dime novels and other cheap fiction by the millions was such an astonishing event in the middle of the last century, that they naturally attracted the usual attack and defense.[19] On the one hand, judges, teachers, clergymen, Sunday school superintendents and even police chiefs began to denounce dime novels. The dime novel afforded an easy explanation of juvenile crime,

---

[17] *Ibid.*, pp. 96–97.   [18] *Op. cit.*, p. 99.
[19] An account of this episode is given by Edmund Pearson, *Dime Novels,* Boston, 1929.

and it held this place in criminology until it was supplanted by the newspaper and then by the motion picture. During the trial of Jesse Pomeroy, a youthful murderer, in 1874, it was suggested that he had been prompted to his offenses by "cheap literature of the dime novel type," but unfortunately Pomeroy insisted that he had never read a dime novel or even the newspaper report of a murder case.[20]   On the other hand, the staid *North American Review* published in 1864 a critical review of the popular dime novels, in which they were found "unobjectionable morally, whatever fault be found with their literary style and composition. They do not even obscurely pander to vice or excite the passions." [21]   So it went back and forth for many years during which children devoured thrillers by the thousands. The nineteenth century adventure stories and romances provide a nice parallel to the movies as fiction for children. They were widely popular; children were generally permitted to read them, as they are taken by their parents to the movies today, even though their popularity and character provoked similar attacks by those who feared for the morals and sobriety of the rising generation.

One other parallel to the movies as children's entertainment is to be found in the Punch and Judy shows.[22]   It is peculiarly instructive because one of the points of criticism of the movies is their making vice seem attractive to the juvenile mind. Think, then, of all the ruined sensibilities which must have followed in the wake of the Punch and Judy shows. Mr. Punch may well be the most uncompromising rogue in all literature; and the children of all countries have in great numbers widely applauded his villainies. Punch's entire character lies in a vigorous insistence that no one shall disburb the peace he enjoys in his strutting hilarity. He wields a huge stick and is never so happy as in making vicious attack with it. He will with impunity hurl his baby off the stage to an applauded death if the baby, as it always does, insists upon crying and thus annoying him. If his wife Judy, as she always does, dare complain of his treatment of their child, he will hurl her after the child. The murderer of his wife and child naturally has no qualms with others. One of his most sensational triumphs is his success in hanging the man

---

[20] Pearson, *op. cit.*, p. 93.   [21] Pearson, *op. cit.*, p. 91.
[22] Vd. George Cruikshank, *Punch and Judy*, London, 1828.

who was to be his hangman. His final victory — striking in that it is a complete denial of poetic justice — is his destruction of the Devil himself who comes to take him away to the Hell which is his just desert. The effort was made, but with no lasting success, to make poetic justice reign by letting the Devil carry off Punch at the end. The crowd would not have it. His admirers rejoiced too much in the utter villainy of Mr. Punch, totally unmarred by any reversals of fortune or inner qualms. We are naturally led to ask what effects such shows had in the course of centuries upon the countless children who gleefully witnessed them again and again, devoted with unqualified sympathy to the character of Mr. Punch.

This brief history of children's literature and entertainment may help to prevent us from forgetting what appealed to the imaginations of the young prior to the movies. The taste of children for adventure and mystery, for thrillers of all sorts, has not been cultivated by the movies, although it may be satisfied by them. Similarly, the delight children take today in Mickey Mouse, Silly Symphonies, and other animated cartoons is the joy they have always found in fanciful stories of the animal kingdom, in fairy tales and nursery rhymes. The study of children's preferences for different types of motion-picture entertainment has become statistically elaborate in this era of scientific method, but the charts and tables reveal nothing that any intelligent parent or teacher did not know about juvenile tastes long before the movies came. I am not saying that the persistent critics of children's literature, of the thrillers and the fairy tales, have been demonstrated to be in error. I am only insisting upon the great similarity in the themes which have appealed to children for many centuries and which, occurring in the movies, have made them popular with children. It is not surprising, therefore, to find great similarity in the positions taken today by those who criticize the movies as juvenile entertainment and those which have been taken for the last five centuries. This fact of similarity does not answer the criticisms — though it may raise a doubt that any generation is better or worse than any other — but it does make absurd the attitude which laments the popularity of the movies because children are "deserting the gentle books that held their elders spellbound." [23]

[23] Charles Hanson Towne in an article on *Juveniles and the Movies* in The

To be horrified that children go to the movies instead of reading *Tom Sawyer* and *Huckleberry Finn*, for instance, is simply to forget the horror with which respectable people viewed such books in the day of their popularity.   The games which children played before they went to the movies, cops and robbers in its myriad forms, playing house and playing doctor; the romantic dramatizations in which the characters of *Little Women* indulged; the fears which children suffered reading *Pilgrim's Progress* and other moralistic tales which threaten hell fire, or reading *Treasure Island* and *The Last of the Mohicans*, in which blood-thirsty pirates and scalping Indians abound — these also must not be forgotten when the perils of our movie-made children are painted vividly in the foreground of the present, without perspective, without the honest balance which an equally vivid recollection of the past would give.[24]

But those who charge the movies with corrupting the youth of our day may, nevertheless, dismiss such memories as irrelevant for two reasons.   In the first place, the sins of the past cannot be justified in perpetuity.   Let us save our children even though the generation to which we belong and those of our forefathers were not saved.   The hope that the world can be made a better place is one of the mainsprings of moral criticism and the reforms which it proposes.   That there are always children who can still be saved is its perennial source, its strongest foundation. In the second place, the comparison between the movies and all other forms of juvenile entertainment fails in a number of important respects.   The popularity of the motion picture exceeds the hold which any of its predecessors had upon children and youth; the greater their thralldom, the greater their danger. And the movies, it is said, are so much more realistic as art than fairy stories and Punch and Judy shows, that they possess the child, seduce him into copying what he views as if it were life itself instead of merely imitation, produce excitements which cannot be purged because the art has so successfully counter-

Bookman, New York, January, 1919.   He was answered by Rupert Hughes: *Viewing with Alarm* in The Bookman, May, 1919.   Mr. Towne had said: "The child of today knows more than is good for it.   Murder and arson are its daily food."   Mr. Hughes added: that has been said of every generation; the young always know too much.

[24] Vd. Charles G. Muller, *Are Today's Children Different?* in Scribner's Magazine, New York, November, 1935.

feited reality, excitements which, therefore, necessarily flow into behavior. Whether a movie is more or less realistic to a child's fancy than puppets or illustrated stories, over which in other days he wept and trembled, whether the movies can be at once criticized for being too realistic and too fantastic, the point in issue is clear. The charge that movies corrupt youth depends upon the ascertainment of the facts about their influence upon children's behavior and attitudes. Do they in fact stimulate mimicry? Do they in fact excite excessively and without the purgation which is the proper ministry of art, whenever it is received as art and not reality? Is the conduct to which they lead, if any, morally and socially undesirable? It is only by knowing the answers to such questions that we can judge the merits of this charge. The examination of the evidence must be postponed until later.

CHAPTER SEVEN

The Contemporary Issue

(continued)

To complete the analysis of the contemporary form which the traditional problem of poetry and politics has taken, it is necessary now to consider the positive values of the cinema as popular poetry in a democracy. This can be done very briefly, since these values have been indicated and discussed in the chapters devoted to the historical development of the controversy between Aristotle and Plato.

But, first, we must understand the relation between the unfavorable criticisms we have just analyzed and the things which can be said in favor of the movies. The relation is not one of affirmation and denial. Those criticisms are not here to be denied. In so far as they are intelligible complaints, they enumerate the possibilities of intrinsic evil or of harmful influence. The extent to which these possibilities are actual can be known only when the various questions of fact and evaluation that the charges raise, are definitely answered. Those who deny the charges must do so by an appeal to the relevant facts, if they can be ascertained. Those who make them must support them in the same way. The points which can be made in favor of the movies must, therefore, not be construed as answers to the charges. Rather they, in turn, enumerate the possibilities of moral worth and social advantage which can be attributed to motion pictures in the political consideration of them as art and as popular amusement. The relation is, thus, an opposition of negative and positive values. This opposition involves no contradictions. To say that the movies can confer certain benefits on the people they serve is not to deny that they may also have objectionable features and undesirable consequences.

The nature of this opposition has been fully indicated by the history of the problem, in which the Platonic emphasis is upon the negative values and the Aristotelian answer turns our attention to the positive values. The Aristotelian answer constitutes a criticism of the Platonic position, not by denying the points it makes, but by challenging its incompleteness, its one-sidedness. Our historical survey of this dialectic has not indicated, however, the way in which the political problem of the arts must be formulated as a practical issue. The prudent man who judges an art morally and politically and who may be considering the advisability of one or another practical programme, such as extermination or regulation, must weigh the balance of positive and negative values. What judgments are to be made, what actions to be taken, if any, are thus to be determined. But since the opposition of these values involves no contradiction, the prudent man cannot deliberate about the arts without taking counsel concerning each of the values. He must consult the facts. As we have seen, the charges merely *claim* that there are negative values. In every case, the claim indicates no more than a possibility to be substantiated. Similarly, the defense of the arts *claims* that there are positive values. Here, too, substantiation of some sort is needed. When it is said that it is for the prudent man to weigh the balance of positive and negative values, the process of weighing must be understood as a determination of the substance of the opposing claims in the light of the facts. A prudent man does not judge or act in terms of mere possibilities.

The claims which can be made for the positive values of the cinema raise questions of fact. The motion pictures will have these values only if, and to the extent that, they are properly received as art. But whether or not they are so received is an accident which depends upon many factors extrinsic to their nature. The positive values are, therefore, only possibilities to be substantiated by the facts about the way in which movies are received. The questions of fact are raised differently, but once raised they are of the same sort as the questions of fact involved in the charges. Both the good and the evil that art may do depend upon extrinsic factors. Because accidental in this way, the effects of art are contingent. Because contingent, inquiry of some sort is required to support all claims, favorable and unfavorable. The inquiry may consist in nothing more than taking counsel from common opinion, or it may involve scientific research. If the actual effects were not contingent, the positive values of art in human life could be philosophically demonstrated. There would be no need either to move in the field of opinion or to have recourse to special investigation [81].

One further point remains before we proceed to the analysis of the positive values which can be claimed for the cinema. In making this analysis we must rely, for the most part, upon the traditional discussion of poetry and politics. The contemporary literature about the movies abounds with the reiteration of attack and defense, but the defenses which are made consist largely of denials of fact. The opponents in the contemporary controversy confront each other by giving opposite answers to the questions of fact involved in the charges. We are not concerned here with the relative validity of their answers. For the most part, it is an opposition of opinions, asserted on either side with a violence that is proportional to suppressed uncertainty. Yet here and there in the literature one can find an Aristotelian insight about the moral and political benefits which the arts confer, applied to the movies. The insight is, however, seldom clearly expressed. Ignorance of the intellectual tradition which might illuminate the contemporary problem is greater on the part of those who have tried to speak favorably of the cinema than is the case with their opponents. In part this may be due to the exigencies of the current polemic which require that the facts claimed by the charges be challenged. In part, it may be due to a failure to understand the cinema as an art in the genus of fiction, with the result that the traditional defense of poetry is not thought to be available in the case of the movies. Whatever the reason, the inadequacy of one side in the contemporary discussion does not prevent us from employing the relevant tradition to supply the lack. The defense of poetry by those who have explicitly undertaken it — witness Sidney, Dryden, Shelley! — has never been adequate or competent. Poetry is badly defended by poets because they are usually too much Platonists at heart. The defense is better found in passages from Aristotle,

Aquinas and Dewey, in the context of a larger political consideration of the arts. We shall present this defense here briefly by stating the claims regarding the positive values of art as these apply to the motion picture. They can be enumerated as follows:

I. Motion pictures are effective as popular entertainment.
   A. As such, they provide men with the pleasure of contemplation;
   B. As such, they provide men with rest and recreation.
II. Motion pictures provide emotional relief through effecting a purgation of the emotions they excite.
III. Motion pictures are effective as an instrument of communication (or social education) in a democracy.

It should be noted at once that there is no defense of the movies as "teaching morals," the kind of defense so frequently made in the modern tradition which could think of no other use that poetry might have in addition to delight.[1] To say that art is not essentially a means of moral training is not to say that art has no moral value. To whatever extent the arts provide contemplative pleasure or recreation or purgation, they are involved in the moral life as means to the end of good character and right activity; but this does not mean that they are involved as instruments of instruction. Virtue in human character may be an accidental result of the ministry of the arts, just as the arts may be an accidental circumstance in the surrender to vice. The arts do not *teach* virtue or vice, even though they may be praised for aiding in the attainment of virtue, or damned for abetting propensities for vice and crime. Nor is it inconsistent with the third of the positive values enumerated to say that the arts should not be defended as didactic. We have already seen that what Dewey means by social education is the same as communication, the sharing of common experiences.[2] If education be understood in this very broad sense, and not merely as the formation of habits, moral or intellectual, then it can be said that the arts are educative essentially. What is being denied here is that it follows properly from their nature to be educative in the sense of habit-forming.

[1] Vd. Chapter 3 *supra*.   [2] Vd. Chapter 4 *supra*.

It should also be noted that, in enumerating these defenses, we have not distinguished between the mature and the immature in the movie audience. This can be provisionally explained by saying that these various positive values *seem* to apply to both children and adults; both seek amusement, both can suffer excitement and purgation, both need social education. But it may be objected that this is only apparent, that, as a matter of fact, these values have different significance for the mature and the immature, and may be operative to a greater or lesser extent for the two groups. We shall return to this objection after concluding the analysis which must now be made. Here, as before, I propose to reduce the whole matter to an outline, summarizing briefly points which have already been sufficiently discussed in other parts of the text, and subordinating explanatory comments as digressions.

I. INTERPRETATION OF THE CLAIM THAT MOTION PICTURES AS POPULAR ENTERTAINMENT PROVIDE THEIR AUDIENCE WITH CONTEMPLATIVE PLEASURE, REST AND RECREATION.

    A. There is no question of fact about whether they amuse the multitude. The facts of attendance are clear. That between forty and sixty million persons pay for admission to movies every week in this country, and between twenty and thirty millions in Great Britain, is indisputable evidence both of the gross popularity of the movies as amusement, and also of the range of human quality, the levels and sections of the population, which the audience includes.

    B. Entertainment is not a good in itself. It is good only as a means. The moral and political value of an art as entertainment, therefore, depends upon the ends it serves. These are the positive values of entertainment: (1) the type of pleasure it affords in contrast to other pleasures; and (2) the rest it gives and hence the recreation for more work or activity of any sort.

        1. THE TYPES OF PLEASURE.

            a. As St. Thomas said, following Aristotle, men cannot live without pleasure, and "a man deprived of the pleasures of the spirit goes over to the pleasures of the flesh."

            b. These two sorts of pleasure can be formally distinguished in terms of the operations of sense and intellect. The pleasures of the flesh are sensual; the pleasures of the spirit involve intellectual activity. The latter are superior because they are distinctively human pleasures, whereas the former are shared by men and brutes alike.

(1)   The pleasure we have called the pleasure of contemplation is an intellectual pleasure. It is the delight of knowing something in a manner that is not possible by the senses alone.

(2)   It is the pleasure which, as Aristotle says, all men take in learning. Learning may, of course, be of many different kinds, and there may be subordinate distinctions in pleasure accordingly.

c.   The arts, as imitations, are objects to be known in themselves and in relation to what they imitate. It is appropriate to their nature as imitations that men take intellectual pleasure in knowing them. (It should be remembered here that works of art are primarily objects to be known and not means of knowing something else.[3])

(1)   All men desire to learn, but all men are not equally gifted with the talents for knowing. All men are not philosophers or scientists for whom anything can be an object of knowledge.

(2)   Men of more limited capacities, men who are for the most part engaged in toil or practise, get the delight of knowing in good part from what presents itself to them for such enjoyment.

(3)   Works of art, being imitations, make men spectators. As spectators men are, for a short time, free from practice and toil, free for such contemplation as is within their power.

(4)   High art, in the sense of the subtle and refined, is not for most men any more than philosophy and science are. It is for the aesthetically sophisticated, the *connoisseurs*.

(a)   But great art need not be high art in this limited sense, as Elizabethan drama and its popular audience attest.

[3] Vd. Note 19 *infra*.

(b) The range of complexity in artistic imitation is great enough to give the same kind of pleasure to every kind of man, proportional to his nature.

(5) The merit of motion pictures as art is that they are imitations which almost every member of the community is able to appreciate and enjoy in due proportion. They not only provide enjoyment, but a range of enjoyment which is commensurate with the kinds of men, according to their powers.

d. No question of evaluation is raised by the claim that motion pictures provide men with intellectual pleasure, because as we have seen such pleasure is demonstrably better in itself than sensual pleasure and is also a good insofar as it saves men from seeking lower pleasures.

e. But a question of fact is raised because it is possible for a work of art not to be properly received. It may, therefore, be a source of sensual pleasure rather than an object which we delight to know.

(1) Works of art appeal *to* the mind, but *through* the senses. Because the senses are necessarily the medium through which we know the work as an individual thing, it is possible for men to convert the instrumentality into an end, getting pleasure from the activity of the senses as if that activity were for its own sake.

(2) The question of fact is, therefore, to what extent motion pictures are properly received by their huge audience, to what extent they are debased as sensual provocations.

(a) It should be noted here that this question of fact is the same as the one raised by the charge that movies are immoral because sources of sensual pleasure.[4]

(b) The determination of the fact in question will depend, in part, upon knowledge about the way in which the cinema is received by its audience and, in part, on knowledge about the content of motion pictures which makes it more or less probable that they will be received one

[4] Vd. Chapter 6 *supra*.

way or another by different groups in
the audience.

Digression:

The moral value of the proper enjoyment of art is clear. Since
pleasure of some sort is indispensable, a man is better or worse according to the things in which he takes pleasure. He is better
according as his aesthetic cultivation is better. But if, because of
limited powers, he cannot enjoy the more subtle and refined arts, he
is still better off for enjoying any art than if he must seek pleasure
in sensuality and brutal indulgences. He is the more a man, and less
an animal. The judgment of value here is based upon the profoundest ethical principle : that to be a good man is to be good as a man,
to be as human as possible, to approximate as nearly as possible the
paradoxically difficult essence of a creature both rational and animal.
One good the movies may do is to enable men to be good in this
sense. As long ago as 1916, when motion pictures were so much less
developed and refined than they are today, Professor Münsterberg
of Harvard recognized the mission they had to perform in the community. They could achieve the aesthetic cultivation of men who
did not read novels, go to the theatre or visit museums. They could
win new members into the ranks of spectatorship and aesthetic pleasure. He wrote : "No art reaches a larger audience daily, no aesthetic influence finds spectators in a more receptive frame of mind.
On the other hand, no training demands a more persistent and plan-
ful arousing of the mind than the aesthetic training, and never is
progress more difficult than when the teacher adjusts himself to the
mere liking of the pupils. The country today would be without
any symphony concerts or operas if it had only received what the
audience believed at the moment they liked best. The aesthetically
commonplace will always triumph over the significant unless systematic efforts are made to reinforce works of true beauty. The
moving picture audience could only by slow steps be brought from
the tasteless and vulgar eccentricities of the first period to the best
plays of today, and the best plays of today can be nothing but the
beginning of a great upward movement which we can hope for in
the photoplay. Hardly any teaching can mean more for our community than the teaching of beauty where it reaches the masses." [5]
His prophetic accuracy now justifies him for dismissing the shal-
low critics who, in their prejudice against 'canned drama' and the
machine-made theatre, did not recognize that all arts employ material

[5] Hugo Münsterberg, *The Photoplay*, D. Appleton-Century Company, Inc.,
Publishers, New York, 1916 : pp. 228–229, by permission.

techniques. They could not foresee, as he did, "the ways which the new art of the photoplay will open." [6]   They did not understand how the principle of commensurate enjoyment in the field of art enables individuals to mount the gradations of complexity if the arts provide these levels, and therefore they did not wish, as he did, "to make the art of the film a medium for an original creative expression of our time, and to mold by it the aesthetic instincts of millions." [7]   For anyone who compares the motion picture of today with what Münsterberg could have seen, there can be no question that the level of popular enjoyment has been raised by an art increasingly complex in its technical achievements.

2.   REST AND RECREATION.
  a. The arts are good as recreations or sources of rest and refreshment, as well as enjoyments or sources of spiritual pleasure.
  b. Their service as recreational is closely related to the kind of pleasure they afford.
    (1) Recreation is rest from work done and a renewal of vitality for more work. It is rest from either intellectual activity, whether speculative or practical, or from bodily labor. For most people it is from the latter.
    (2) To be a spectator is to be free from activity. The spectator is activated, rather than active through self-initiative.
      (a) The passivity of the spectator is in part emotional and in part intellectual : the passions are aroused, the imagination is stirred, the intellect is informed.
      (b) But the spectator is not entirely passive. To the extent that contemplation is an effort to satisfy the desire to know, it is an active process of learning.
      (c) Nevertheless, contemplation as learning is freedom from practical activity, from doing and making of all sorts, on the one hand ; and as aesthetic contemplation — the kind of learning involved in knowing works of art — it is freedom from more intense and difficult speculative activities, on the other.

[6] *Ibid.*, p. 232.   [7] *Ibid.*, p. 232.

(d) This is the value which Schopenhauer saw in the aesthetic moment. It was for him as complete a denial of the will to live as is possible for man while alive. In contemplation man transcends action of an animal sort. The arts which amuse men, and in doing so make them spectators and contemplative, rest men from work. It may be thought that this can be true only in the case of practical work or bodily labor, since philosophy and science, as intellectual work, are contemplative. But philosophy and science as contemplative are so much more active than aesthetic contemplation that the arts provide rest from intellectual work as well.

c. Recreation must be commensurate with the needs of men as well as proportional to their powers.

(1) The arts amuse and rest only if they neither bore nor tire. They must strike a mean, for each man, between too little and too much excitement, so far as the passions are concerned; and with respect to the intellect, a mean between insufficient complexity to interest and too much complexity to satisfy.

(a) If a drama, for instance, leaves a man wholly passive — his passions unexcited and his intellect unengaged — he is bored.

(b) If, on the other hand, a drama overexcites his passions or engages his intellect without satisfying its desire to know — leaving him exasperated and bewildered — he is fatigued.

(c) This indicates that purgation, on the one hand, and the proportionality of the object to the cognitive power of the spectator, on the other, are essential complements to the emotional excitement and the intellectual interest of a work of art. If they are lacking, the work of art fails as entertainment because it tires rather than refreshes.

(2) What different men need in the way of recreation will, therefore, be different.

   (a) The power of a work of art to give rest and recreation depends upon the factors of excitement and purgation, intellectual stimulation and satisfaction, and this cannot be the same for all men since their powers, both emotional and intellectual, differ in many degrees.

   (b) What bores one man may delight and give recreation to another; what delights and rests one man may tire and frustrate another.

   (c) The conditions under which a particular work gives pleasure to a particular man are exactly the same as those under which it gives him rest and recreation.

   (d) Because the arts cover a vast range of complexity in imitation and vary between wide limits in the grossness or subtlety of the emotions they excite, every kind of man can get pleasure and rest from some kind of art.

   (e) The same work of art may have within itself many levels of complexity and so be able to delight and give recreation to many different kinds of men.

  d. It follows, from the foregoing analysis, that the claim for the movies that they provide rest and recreation raises no question of fact; as the fact is clear that many men, and men of all sorts, get pleasure from motion pictures, so is it clear that they get rest and recreation.

Digression:

There may be some whom movies bore and others whom movies tire, either all of the time or some of the time. But such men for whom the movies are for the most part either too simple or too difficult, too gross or too refined, obviously do not constitute the millions of weekly patrons who persistently seek pleasure and recreation in motion pictures. The audience of the movies is not only large, but regular. Its patrons are devoted, not casual. And since it is beyond question that men will not submit to being bored or fatigued when what they pay for is pleasure and relaxation, there can be no question that the movies fulfill this function for many men.

> e. But a question of evaluation remains. Rest is not a good in itself ; it is good only as a means to further activity. The man who rests more than he needs is slothful ; unnecessary recreation is a vicious indulgence. The virtue of *eutrapelia* is moderation with respect to mirth and play. Rest and recreation in the proper amount, meeting needs, are good. But it may be asked about the movies whether they tempt men to seek more recreation than they need and thus become a condition of vicious indulgence, of sloth, idleness or undue relaxation. This is a difficult question to answer, since the facts upon which the judgment must depend are so difficult to ascertain.

Digression :

Rest is good as a means to what is intrinsically good, namely, activity, speculative or practical. As Aristotle says, it is because we cannot work forever that we need relaxation. Human happiness consists in activity. "It would be paradoxical to hold that the end of human life is amusement, and that we should toil and suffer all our life for the sake of amusing ourselves." [8] Rather we amuse ourselves in order to refresh ourselves from labor and prepare ourselves for work. Rest is thus not final. Its proper function is better stated in terms of re-creation than relaxation. Relaxation is its negative aspect : freedom from activity, rest *from* work done. Re-creation is its positive aspect : freedom from weariness, rest *for* work to be done. As sleep is the appropriate rest from bodily labors, so amusements are the appropriate rest from the labors of the soul, whether practical or speculative. And, as in the case of anything else which is good only as a means, a proper proportion must be maintained between excess and defect. Too much sleep is as bad as too little, since sleep is not for its own sake but for the sake of work. Similarly, over-indulgence in amusements, which may lead to the error of treating amusement as an end in itself, is as bad as a misguided avoidance of them. Furthermore, what is the right proportion in such matters must be determined prudently by the individual man according to his nature and circumstances. Some men working more may need less rest, and others working less may need more. The general principle that

[8] *Nichomachean Ethics*, X, 6.

recreation is morally good because a means to activity is not altered by casuistical misapplication of the principle by particular men who may be imprudent in this matter.

Recreation is not only a moral good for each man, but a social good for the political community since the prosperity and welfare of a society depend upon the labors of its members. Furthermore, as in the case of pleasures, if socially harmless recreations are not provided, men overworked and in need of relaxation, will seek rest in recreations that are socially harmful in their consequences, as well, perhaps, as morally bad intrinsically. This problem is acute in an industrial, urbanized society in which most men are overworked in practical employments and, living in cities, have limited opportunities for natural enjoyments and relaxation. This may be one reason among others why the arts flourish in cities, particularly such popular arts of entertainment as the motion picture.

II. Interpretation of the claim that the movies purge the emotions which they must arouse in order to amuse, and in doing so relieve the persistent burden of the passions.

A. The analysis can be briefly made, because of prior discussion.[9]

1. Works of art do not excite emotions *only* for the sake of purging them. If they failed to excite, they would be dull and boring, and would fail to entertain.

2. But unless they purged the passions as well as aroused them, they would tire rather than rest. Nothing is so fatiguing as unrelieved emotional tension.

3. Both the arousal and the purgation of emotions are, therefore, necessary to the success of the arts in their function as entertainment and recreation.

4. To the extent that the arts effect the catharsis of the emotions they excite, they do not increase but rather diminish the burden of the passions which man must master in order to live well. (Bossuet asked why arouse the emotions in order to purge them. What is gained that would not be achieved if men were freed from the passions entirely? Nothing, it is true; but the impossibility of such angelic freedom for a rational *animal* is what gives purgation its moral point.)

[9] Vd. Chapter 2 *supra.*

Digression:

The moral virtues, in which man must be habituated in order to live well humanly, result from the discipline which reason imposes upon the passions, the motions of the sensitive appetite. Discipline is not destruction, however. Man does not cease to be an animal when the animal part of his nature is thus rationally controlled. The passions, though moderated by prudence and transmuted into virtues, persist to be excited in all the circumstances of life. Reason must at all times support the habits it may have succeeded in forming, and may at any time be defeated in its unequal struggle with the passions. That reason is in most men inadequate to its moral task, the existence of laws in all human societies clearly indicates. Laws rule men by force and through fear. They would be unnecessary if most men did through reason what they now do through fear of the law. The same conditions which necessitate the regulation of social life by law, give value to whatever purgation of emotion the arts are able to achieve. Purgation temporarily relieves the burden of ever-present passion, and thus aids reason in its office of discipline and control. Ever susceptible to being naturally aroused, the passions are for the moment dissipated by being artificially excited and artificially expended; more than that, they are assimilated by being understood and are thus made more susceptible to rational control. Purgation is thus a sublimation of the passions and man is saved from the disrupting force they have when they issue in the natural channels of conduct. The good of purgation is at once moral and social, two aspects of the same thing: *moral* in that reason is aided in its unceasing effort to maintain the virtuous habits it has formed; *social* in that behavior which might transgress these habits, and be criminal or anti-social, is prevented. Purgation cannot make a vicious man good, but it can help a virtuous man to remain good, and may even diminish the propensities of vice for undesirable action.

B. It follows from the foregoing that this claim for the movies raises no question of evaluation. To the extent that they effect purgation they are morally and socially good.

C. But purgation to be effective depends on two things.

    1. What is offered as art must be received as art, must be taken as imitation and not as nature, if the emotions are to be artificially aroused. Unless they are so aroused, they are not subject to sublimation or catharsis through the ministry of art.

    2. There must be a proportion between the power of the work of art to excite and its power to dissipate the

passions. Not only must art not fail to excite at the peril of being dull or boring, but it must not overexcite at the peril of being tiring and, worse, of increasing the burden of passions.

3. Art fails as art, in short, if it arouses more emotion than it can purge.

D. A question of fact is thus raised : Are motion pictures effective in purging the emotions they arouse ?

1. They may fail because their audience, in whole or part, improperly receives them ; or they may fail because of intrinsic defects as art [82].

2. The first alternative raises the further question of fact : whether motion pictures are equally effective in purgation for all their audience, for most, for children as well as adults. It may be that they are too realistic for the children in their audience or the large number of adults who, being aesthetically uncultivated, mistake like children the imitation for reality.

3. The second alternative raises a question that is involved in the charges against the content of motion pictures : are they too violent in the way they stir the feelings, too lurid and sensational, thus provoking a storm of passions that no art could dispel.

4. In either case, the main question of fact remains the same. In either case, if the answer is negative, moral damage is being done and social harm may ensue.

Digression :

Whether or not the movies are effective in purgation depends upon their essential goodness as art and upon their proportionality to the audience they reach. A work is bad as art in relation to a given audience if it is not received by them as imitation, if it passes as a counterfeit for reality ; in fact, it is not art at all for them. The failure may be due either to the art or to the audience ; to the former, if the producer of the art has sought to achieve the counterfeit ; to the latter, if their receptivities are so untrained as to permit the deception. Considering the audience of the movies and the temptation toward excessive realism in their medium of imitation, it would not be surprising if the movies failed as art for some part of their audience.

A work of art is also bad unless it strikes a mean between too much and too little excitement, employing devices which are either too gross or too subtle. Again considering the range of human quality in their audience and their task of entertaining so many kinds of men, it would not be surprising if the movies failed in this respect, tending in the direction of overstimulation in order certainly to avoid dullness and boredom. It is clear only that, for most people, they do not excite *too little*. The attendance indicates this. But whether they excite too much, beyond the efficacy of purgation, is a difficult question of fact. We not only do not know the answer, but it is even difficult to determine how we could ever learn the answer. Let us suppose, for instance, that the movies are not effectively purgative because they excite excessively. The excess emotion may or may not lead to observable results in behavior. Let us even suppose that behavior must be influenced by such overstimulation. Such behavior may not be socially undesirable or morally vicious. In the case of the virtuous man, the discipline of his character may enable him to assimilate this excess or to direct it into proper channels of action ; whereas the undisciplined man may be incited to vicious conduct. But what proportion of the mature in the audience is relatively virtuous and what proportion is relatively vicious, and to what extent? In the case of the immature, such overstimulation, particularly if accompanied by the failure of the movies to be received as imitation, may result in imprudent conduct and hinder the formation of virtuous habits. The contingencies are such that we cannot say that the movies fail to purge the emotions they arouse if we discover that they have evil consequences in conduct ; nor can we say that they are effective in purgation if we find the opposite to be the case.

In short, if the movies do not effectively purge, it does not follow that their influence upon character and conduct is necessarily bad. All that can be said is that to whatever extent the movies sublimate the passions of their audience, in large or small part, they perform a ministry appropriate to their nature as art and they have a positive moral and social value. This cannot be denied by those who charge the movies with one or another sort of evil influence. Nothing is added to such charges by *supposing* that the movies do not discharge this ministry for the most part ; since, granting the supposition, it is still necessary to ascertain the facts about the effect of the movies upon the characters and conduct of their audience. Ineffective purgation may help to explain the evil influence of the movies, if any, but assuming it cannot establish the facts which are in question. Even if we *knew* that their purgation was ineffective for the most part — which is obviously impossible to know — the basic questions of fact upon which the charges rest would still remain to be answered.

III.   Interpretation of the claim that the movies serve the ends of democratic society by increasing the communication of its members [83].

A.   Here, too, the analysis can be briefly made because of prior discussion.[10]

    1.   Even in a democracy individuals cannot help living under limitations : within the confines of particular social groups, restricted by occupation or profession, having greater or less actual mobility but in any case sectionalized by residence or business.

    2.   There is, furthermore, the limitation of great finitude in human experience : the types of social experience in which a person actually participates are few and unvaried compared to their number and variety in the whole of social life.

    3.   Democracy depends upon communication. A community is democratic to the extent that its members are able to share in the whole range of social activity — if not through actual participation, then at least through imagination and vicarious experience.

    4.   The arts as imitative or representative are sources of vicarious experience.

       (a)   They educate socially through the imagination, as actual participation educates through doing itself.

       (b)   Thus, the arts counteract the inevitable individual limitations upon the range of participation in social activities, which tend to defeat democracy by isolating individuals, reducing their communication and narrowing their sympathies.

    5.   The arts, therefore, have greater social utility in a democracy than in any other kind of society. They are as essential to it as popular education ; the more popular they are, the better, just as the more extensive education is, the better. Motion pictures as the most popular art in our society have this utility to an enormous degree. So far, at least, no question of fact appears to be raised.

---

[10] Vd. Chapter 4 *supra.*

{

Digression:

In a sense, the popular arts are a more effective means of social education than the schools in which the curriculum has gradually been adapted to serve democratic ends. In one respect, the schools can be superior. By employing the project method, they may be able to create situations in which the child performs the actual operations of social life; but even here their range is limited and imagination must supervene in order to give the model experiences their full significance. Verbal instruction about the practices and techniques of man in society must be resorted to whenever the child cannot be trained through doing. They can be made effective as experience only if given life by the imagination.

The arts, enriching the imagination and providing vicarious experience which can be directly appreciated, are almost indispensable in social education, both for children in schools and for the adult population. Of the arts, those of fiction serve best because of what they represent; their proper object of imitation is all of human life. Of the arts of fiction, the movies are at once the most popular and the most vivid representation of contemporary society. Their vividness, which is held to be responsible in part for the power they have over children, makes them exceptionally useful as an educational instrument.

B. This claim for the movies raises a question of fact when it is objected that they give a false and distorted picture of contemporary society.

    1. We have already met this question of fact in the discussion of the charge that the movies are educationally detrimental to the extent that they falsify and distort in their representation of life.

    2. Upon the answer to this question of fact, the final determination of the utility of motion pictures in increasing communication or social education must, of course, rest.

        a. But it should be reiterated here that art need not be true to life in a simple realistic sense in order to avoid falsehood and distortion. Every type of representation has a flaw of untruth which is peculiar to its nature, the teaching of current events in the schools as much as the movies, although the distortions are necessarily different in the two cases.

        b. Furthermore, the different distortions of the various educational media compensate for each other. The claim being considered is not that the motion picture is the *only* agency of communication or social education, but that it is one among many, and an extremely important one which, although it has its own peculiar bias, helps to counteract the distortions of schools, newspapers, the radio and other media of representation.

C. No question of evaluation is raised. Communication is unquestionably a good for democratic society; it is a good, though perhaps to a lesser degree, for any kind of society, since in essence human society is a *community* of men.

1. Democracy differs from other societies in that it seeks a maximum of communication to insure all of its members a maximum of mobility and participation.

2. Communication in any society depends upon a common mythology and common rituals or customary practices.

   (a) Although there are many differences among human societies, simple and complex, primitive and civilized, there is, nevertheless, much that is everywhere and at all times the same in mythology and ritual.

   (b) These common elements are the surest indication of the constancy of human nature and the sameness of human life under all the conditions and circumstances which the accidents of time and place impose upon it.

Digression:

In the legends of all peoples, common forms are easily discoverable and detected in common matter. These mythopoeic elements provide the form and matter of all poetry which may disguise its basic substance by elaborate invention, but can never do more than work variations, however subtle, on the basis of simple themes. When they are heavily embroidered and subtly varied by poetic skill, deliberately seeking to hide their nakedness, these themes may not be detected by most men. The clever artist succeeds in his purpose if he gives the impression of great novelty, and hence great distance from the common mythology. But such poetry is not for the masses; its artistry selects a cultivated audience. The stories which all men are able to appreciate, which can be significant for them as vicarious experience because within the reach of their imaginations, have the basic mythology nearer to the surface. They are good stories and widely appreciated just because they are old stories and neither subtle nor novel. That their common mythopoeic elements can be easily recognized establishes the widest communication of men because the mythology of any community formalizes the experiences which all men share.

The movies easily betray the mythopoeic elements out of which they are composed. The covering of contemporary and local material which they add does not hide the mythology upon which they are based. This not only explains their extraordinary popular appeal, which crosses national borders and even the boundary between east and west, but enhances their power to consolidate the community of men. Tolstoy demanded of all art that it serve the end of human brotherhood. He was requiring it to be, like ritual and mythology, fundamentally religious. The brotherhood of man is the ideal limit of communication. The demands of democracy are essentially the same, although they seem to be restricted to the area of a particular society. What serves the ends of communication within a particular society must be rooted in common human mythology and ritual, as well as be representative of its peculiar features. Because their roots are so plainly visible, the movies are much more effective than other forms of narration which, being more sophisticated in their artistry, can only succeed in telling their story to a smaller audience.

This concludes our analysis of the claims which can be made for motion pictures. Many of the questions of fact raised by this defense of poetry are the same as those involved in the charges previously examined. The knowledge that is needed in the one case is of the same sort as in the other. Our need for knowledge is practical. We shall understand this better if we attempt to formulate, as precisely as possible, the nature of the practical problem. But, first, one point remains to be made.

The point that the positive values are not the same for both the mature and the immature must be considered. There is no question that the movies entertain children as well as adults, but it may be asked whether the needs which justify entertainment morally and politically are the same in both cases. To the extent that the period of immaturity is a period of play rather than of work, children do not need the recreational services of art. To the extent that it is a period of study, of intellectual activity, the

need may exist. Movies may give rest to students as well as
to their teachers. But, then, it may be said that during a period
of study, the delight of learning is sufficiently provided by the
sources of instruction. Art cannot be justified as giving *students*
the pleasure which others derive as spectators. One may wonder, however, how many children are genuinely students. It
may be that the same proportion exists for the immature and
the mature between those who get pleasure in knowing through
the arts and those who achieve it otherwise.

As for the value of purgation, it is difficult to estimate the
difference for children and adults. On the one hand, the immature are more excitable. The instability which characterizes
immaturity is in part due to the responsiveness of the passions
to all sorts of stimuli, the intensity and volatility of the emotions.
That immaturity is the period when moral training is most necessary, when the discipline of the passions is most required, is
thus also the reason why the immature could profit from purgation and the clarification which ensues. But, on the other hand,
though the need be as great, if not greater, the efficacy of the
arts to produce catharsis may be less because children are less
able properly to receive works of art as imitations. A certain
amount of sophistication is required on the part of the spectator
for a spectacle to draw the emotion it arouses into itself as something to be witnessed and understood rather than indulged.
What has recently been called psychic distance — which is only
another name for the condition of a proper reception of art —
is very short in children, and is frequently entirely lacking. It
may be thought, therefore, that the arts, particularly so vivid
and exciting an art as the cinema, are much more likely to fail
in their purgative function for children. Failing in this, but
not failing to excite, the movies may increase rather than reduce
the emotionality which makes the rearing of the young so
difficult. This change has been made, and the facts must be
ascertained.

Finally, with regard to the value of communication or social
education, there is less difference between the mature and the
immature than in the previous cases. The child must be socialized in order to become a man. As we have seen, the process
of socialization requires many co-operating factors, not the least
among which are the arts. Because the child is more impres-

sionable — more educable as well as more corruptible — the movies may be more effective in this function for them than for adults. If this is the case, the responsibility of motion pictures to the children they are developing into members of the community is, of course, greater than to the adults whose communication they may increase.

Though the comparative estimate is difficult to make in the case of each of these three positive values, it would appear in general that these values are clearer and less questionable for the mature than the immature. As in the case of the negative values indicated by the charges, there was a presumption that they were of greater moment for the immature than the mature, so here there is the reverse presumption. This can be simply summarized as follows: our common sense and common knowledge raise the presumption that the balance of positive and negative values weighs more heavily on the positive side in the case of adults, and more heavily on the negative side in the case of the immature. A presumption is not evidence. It is what men proceed upon when evidence is lacking. And presumptions may be rebutted or supported when evidence is obtained, when the relevant facts are learned. In the long history of the problem of poetry and politics, the practical judgments which have been made have, for the most part, rested on presumptions. It is only in the current instance of the problem, made by the movies as popular poetry, that there has been an effort, as we shall see, to get evidence. It is in this respect that the problem of the motion picture differs radically from kindred problems in other times.

CHAPTER EIGHT

The Need for Knowledge

PRACTICAL problems are concerned with action. The distinction in universes of discourse between the practical and the speculative is thus made. In the speculative order, the operations of knowing or judging are for their own sake. In the practical sphere, knowledge is ordered to the ends of action. Practical judgments involve the will as well as the intellect. Knowledge enters the practical order to the extent that the will is moved by the intellect. The will is intellectual appetite. It is desire determined by intelligible goods. But the intellect is also moved by the will. Knowledge is itself an intelligible good and with respect to knowledge as an end, the will moves the intellect in its speculative operations. Knowledge is also good as a means; it can be used in determining operations which are not cognitive. With respect to knowledge as a means, the will moves the intellect in its practical operations. Thus, the relation between the intellect as practical and the will as intellectual is seen in the reciprocity of the intellect and will: the will moving the intellect to know for the sake of action, on the one hand, and the intellect as possessing knowledge moving the will to command action, on the other. The will is a moved mover. It is moved by knowledge. As moved, it moves man to action of various sorts by its power to command the operations of all other powers of the soul [84].

The word "action" has an ambiguity that must be clarified for the sake of this discussion. Any operation is an action. The

operations of knowing are actions; they are acts of the senses or
the intellect. So the operations of desiring, of intending and
choosing, are actions; they are acts of the will. These operations
are intrinsic. They are changes in the soul itself. Nothing
outside is altered in any way by a man's knowledge or volition,
unless the knowledge or volition leads to further operations of
an extrinsic sort. Extrinsic operations are those which involve
motions of the body in relation to other things which may in
consequence be altered in one way or another. Doing and
making — we need not pause here to distinguish between them
— are operations of this sort. In both doing and making, man
changes other things. The motions of his body are causally
involved in the motions of other bodies. This holds for the
operations of the teacher and the physician as well as for the
engineer and the plumber. The word "action" is popularly
used, in its narrower significance, to refer to all sorts of extrinsic
operation, both doing and making. It is sometimes used more
narrowly to refer to doing exclusively. Since we shall not
here distinguish between doing and making, we shall use the
word "action," unless otherwise qualified, to name extrinsic
operation of any sort, and we shall use the word "operation,"
unless otherwise qualified, to name both external actions and
intrinsic operations.[1] According to this usage, to say that practical problems are concerned with action means that they are
concerned with doing and making. The broader meaning
should not be forgotten, however, in which practical problems
are concerned with any activity, intrinsic or extrinsic, that is
subject to the will.

It is necessary to make two further distinctions [85]. First,
the acts of the will are distinguished as interior or exterior according as they are determinations of the will itself or according
as they are operations of other powers commanded and used by
the will. Thus, the actions which we will to do or not to do
are exterior acts of the will. Second, the interior acts of the

---

[1] In Chapter 12 *infra*, the distinction of doing and making is more fully discussed. It will there be seen that "action" and "doing" are sometimes used
synonymously, as are "production" and "making." Furthermore, action or
doing is identified with intrinsic operation, production or making with extrinsic operation. But until these usages are discussed and clarified, we shall
employ the word "action" as it is popularly used.

will are distinguished according as they regard ends or means. Whatever we desire we desire either for its own sake or for the sake of something else. In the order of means and ends, only the final end is desired for its own sake absolutely and everything else is desired as a means to it. But there are many levels in the practical order. There are goods which can be desired for their own sake as well as for the sake of something further; such, for instance, are the moral and intellectual virtues. There are things which are not at all intrinsically desirable, but are good only as means; such, for instance, are all external goods, the objects of consumable wealth and the means of producing it. Thus are distinguished absolute ends, mere means, and terms which are intermediate, serving as both means and ends relatively. In dividing the interior acts of the will according as they regard ends or means, it is necessary to keep in mind that a given end may be either absolute or relative and that what is willed as an end in one relation may be willed as a means in another. With regard to ends, the acts of the will are simple volition, or the desire of that end as a good, and intention, or the desire of whatever means are available thereto [86]. With regard to means, the acts of the will are choice and consent, or the selection of and adherence to one among alternative means, and use, or the employment of that means through commanded operations [87]. The objects of choice, consent and use are always *as such* means, whether they be external goods or intrinsic operations or actions. The final end is always the object of volition and intention, though other goods, intermediate terms regarded as relative ends, can also be objects of volition and intention.

Actions are always objects of choice and use. They are always means; they always refer to some further good. Practical problems, as concerned with action, are therefore always concerned with means. Furthermore, actions are always particular. They are extrinsic operations occurring at a particular time and place and made singular by unique circumstances and an individual object. The particularity of actions is, as we shall see, very important in the understanding of practical problems.

But, first, it is necessary to understand that practical problems depend upon the freedom of the will. If the will were not free to choose among alternative means, to use this or that operation for the sake of some end, there would be no practical problems for men. When it is said that there are no practical problems about ends, what is meant is that the will is not free in the determination of its final end, that which the will *must* desire because it is moved essentially by whatever is most completely good. The will is free with respect to all relative goods, some of which may be both ends and means; but even here practical problems arise only when these relative goods are regarded as means to be chosen or used and not as ends desired or intended. That practical problems depend upon the freedom of the will is readily seen by reflection on the meaning of a problem. A problem is a question to be answered. It is speculative if the question is answered by the affirmation or denial of a proposition. It is practical if the question is answered by an operation or, in the narrower sense, by an action. If the intellect were bound to give one and only one answer to a speculative question — and to some extent this is the case — not only would the intellect not be free in this operation, but the question would not strictly be a problem. So if the will were determined to make one and only one choice, it would not be free, and the formulation of alternatives would be the statement of a specious practical problem [88].

The freedom of the will can be regarded either in itself or as dependent in a certain way upon the intellect which determines it. In itself the will is always free to act or not to act. In this respect, the will is even free with respect to the final end, the absolute good. It is free not to desire the good because it is free not to desire anything [89]. If it acts, however, it is not free in this way; it must desire what is conceived to be good. Here the will depends upon the intellect, since the intellect and not the will is the power by which we conceive. So far as anything is conceived by the intellect as absolutely good — whether rightly or wrongly makes no difference to the point being considered — the will is absolutely determined to desire it if it desire anything. The will is, thus, not free with respect to whatever moves it as a final end. But so far as the intellect conceives anything as relatively good, it conceives that thing in relation to other goods, all of which are means to the final end. Here the will is determined by the intellect to a number

of different objects.   Here the will may or may not be free.
If these objects are intrinsically good, are ends as well as means;
if they are determined to be indispensable means to the final
end as certain conclusions follow inevitably from self-evident
principles; if, in short, the will in willing its final end *must*
intend these means as ordained to it, the will is not free.   But
if the goods are relatively good only as means; if they are not
determined to be indispensable, as propositions are sometimes
not necessary but only contingent; if, in short, the will in willing
its final end, or whatever is ordained thereto, may or may not
intend these means, the will is free to choose among them or to
choose none of them.   Thus, a man who properly conceives
his happiness is not free to avoid the virtues, or to choose one
cardinal virtue rather than another since all are necessarily ordained to his well-being; but such a man is free to perform
this or that particular action as a means to forming the virtues
or, in a particular case, to choose not to act at all [90].

Because actions are particular our knowledge with regard to
them, their objects and circumstances, is always inadequate.
The propositions which our intellects can form about particular
actions are always contingent and not necessary.   Hence, as
possessing only inadequate knowledge about the matter of
action, the intellect as moving the will does so indeterminately;
it is not a total lack of determination but a lack of absolute
determination.   To the extent that the intellect is indeterminate
in this way, the will, as moved by the intellect, is free [91].   In
other words, there is a freedom of choice because there are
genuine alternatives—action or inaction, one action rather than
another.   All of this can be briefly summarized as follows.   In
itself, the will is always free; thus a man who denies a self-evident
truth by which his intellect would be bound if it were not
moved contrary to its nature by the will, is said to do so willfully.
As depending on the intellect, the will is not always free.   In
so far as it is moved by the intellect it is free only to the extent
that the intellect itself is relatively indeterminate because its
knowledge is inadequate concerning contingent things.   From
this it follows that in the field of extrinsic operation which
comprises particular actions, the will is always free.   Such actions are always mere means.   They are exterior acts of the
will which, in itself, chooses, consents and uses with regard to

them. Thus it is seen how practical problems concerning particular actions as means depend upon the freedom of the will
in choice, consent and use.

Finally, we must consider the difference between the alternatives of action and inaction and alternatives of different courses
of action. We are not now thinking of the operation of the
will itself — whether it wills at all or whether it wills this or
that — but rather of the will as directed toward objects through
exterior operations, because to will inaction is itself an act of
the will. The distinction formally is between the opposition
of positive and negative, on the one hand, and the opposition
of contraries, on the other. The first is obviously more general
than the second, since contraries are always related as species
in a given genus. In speculative matters, the attribution of one
or the other of a pair of contrary qualities to a thing presupposes
that the thing is generically qualified in a certain way. What
lacks size, is neither large nor small. So in practical matters,
the consideration of alternative courses of action presupposes
that a generic type of action which includes these alternatives
as species, is desirable. If inaction were preferable, there would
be no further practical question about contrary courses of
action. The practical problem involving a choice between action and inaction is, therefore, always prior to that involving the
choice between alternative actions. If the prior problem is
solved, the other problem still remains, of course. It is not
enough to decide upon action in general. Men do not act in
general. A particular action must, therefore, be chosen. In
some cases, however, it is enough to decide not to act. That
decision by itself can solve a practical problem, as the decision
to act cannot, since the latter requires the further choice among
alternative courses. The choice of inaction rather than action
is as much the choice of a means to an end, as the choice of
action in general and of some course of action in particular.

Though the will is free in the solution of practical problems,
it can use this freedom well or poorly. According to the way
in which men use their freedom in practical matters, we speak
of them as practically wise or unwise, as circumspect or incon-
siderate, as deliberate or hasty, as men of sound judgment or as
prejudiced and capricious. These distinctions among men are
related to the virtue of prudence and the virtues annexed to it.

Prudence, like all other virtues, is a habit. It is distinguished from the moral virtues by being an intellectual habit, and it is distinguished from the other intellectual virtues by being a habit of the practical rather than the speculative intellect [92]. Art and prudence are the two virtues of the intellect as practical, as concerned with operations, both intrinsic and extrinsic. We shall later more fully consider the difference between these two practical virtues, and their intricate relationship.[2] But for our present purposes it is enough to show how prudence is a condition of the good activity of the will in facing practical problems.

Prudence is at once a habit of the intellect and the will, of the intellect as practical and the appetite as intellectual. On the side of the intellect, prudence is the habit of using knowledge for practical purposes. On the side of the will, prudence is the habit of commanding action in the light of knowledge [93]. This can best be seen in terms of the analysis of the act of choice. The act of choice should be preceded by counsel, which is any sort of inquiry seeking knowledge relevant to the alternatives the will faces [94]. The prudent man is one who habitually takes counsel before choosing, who habitually chooses in the light of counsel and who habitually commands exterior operations in accordance with the choice the will makes in its interior act [95]. Thus, prudence is a virtue because it is the habit of rightly exercising the power of free choice. This does not mean that the choice itself is right, that the action decided upon is necessarily better than some other. It means only that the action was itself rightly chosen. In all matters in which the will is free, the will can make errors of choice because its freedom depends on the inadequacy of knowledge. But to make an error because knowledge is inadequate is one thing, and to make an error because the act of choice is not preceded by inquiry, by deliberation and careful judgment in the light of whatever knowledge is available, is another. Practical errors of the latter sort are much more serious morally because they are due to imprudence. In short, the extent to which man needs prudence for his moral welfare is the extent to which he has freedom of choice. Both are based upon the same condition: the *need* for prudence depends upon the inadequacy of our knowledge about particulars which, in turn, renders the will free in so far as it is moved

[2] Vd. Chapter 12 *infra*.

by the intellect. And just as our freedom of choice is concerned with means, so is prudence concerned with means rather than ends [96]. Here arises the distinction between perfect and imperfect prudence. The latter considers only the means to a given end without any evaluation of that end; so a thief or a business man can be prudent in the determination of his actions. But perfect prudence is directed to man's fullest well-being, and not merely to the success of a particular action [97]. Therefore, it requires that any means chosen be ordained to man's final end. It is not enough that it is the best alternative among many to a proximate end, which may or may not be so ordained. This, as we shall later see, makes prudence dependent upon the moral virtues which confer rectitude upon the will in all its acts, the volition and intention of ends as well as the choice and use of means [98].

One more distinction must be made: between private prudence, directed to the well-being of the individual, and political prudence, directed toward the common good, the well-being of men as members of the community [99]. The distinction is important here because the problem of the arts, as we have been considering it, is a political problem. It is a practical problem because it raises questions of action with respect to which we are free. It is a political problem because it regards the good of other men, not only ourselves, and the welfare of the community. As practical and political, it is clearly a problem of means and not of ends. The ends we have in view in considering the arts in relation to man are unquestionable goods: the virtues of individual men and the peace and order of society. The history of the attack upon and the defense of the arts makes this clear. The practical problem which has been raised in every period has always been framed in terms of the alternatives of action. If a prudent choice were made, there would be no further question of the justification of the choice because the end served by such a choice is clearly good. Here, then, is the problem which political prudence must face when the arts are attacked or defended as being detrimental or conducive to moral and social goods: it must direct the will in its decision — with respect to the arts — between action or inaction, or between different sorts of action.

In the long history of this practical problem, inaction has

been proposed by those who think that the arts better serve human welfare if left alone; and action has been advocated by others who think that the arts cannot be left alone if human welfare is to be served.   On the side of action, the major alternatives have been total extirpation, as in the case of Plato's banishment of the dramatists, and regulation or control, as in the case of Plato's supervision of music or Aristotle's exclusion of the very young from the theatre.   Extirpation requires no further analysis: it is a simple, drastic and perfectly plain expedient. Not so with regulation: there are many types of censorship and supervision of the arts, many ways in which regulation can be achieved.   The series of questions for the prudent man are, therefore, as follows: (1) Shall the arts be left alone or shall some action be taken?   (2) If the latter, shall the action be extirpation or control?   (3) If the latter, what specific type of regulation or supervision is most expedient?   Since the basic division in the types of action is between extirpation and control, the practical problem must be reformulated whenever either of these two general policies is excluded or ignored for one reason or another.   Thus, for Bossuet and Rousseau the primary issue, was between extirpation and inaction; they did not consider the possibility of regulation.   And for us today, the primary issue is between inaction and some type of regulation.   Only after this is decided need we consider the further problem of alternative forms of regulation as more or less politically expedient.

When I say that this is the problem for us today I am merely reporting the practical proposals which have been made recently in regard to the arts, novels, plays, motion pictures.   I am not saying how the problem *should* be considered.   Thus, in the case of the movies, no one has suggested that they be totally prohibited.   The most drastic proposal which has been made is total regulation, namely, that the state control the production and distribution of motion pictures.   The nationalization of the theatre as a form of public amusement and as an important agency of propaganda is not inconsistent with the governmental policy of Germany, Italy and Russia, however shocking it may seem to Americans and Englishmen.   Short of this, various types of control have been suggested: (1) censorship or supervision by (a) official boards, (b) committees of social scientists who will try to direct the motion pictures into channels of 'scientifically' approved influence, (c) unofficial social groups or institutes which will operate in an advisory capacity to producers, (d) the producers of motion pictures themselves, in the manner of their self-imposed code.   (2) Economic boycott of motion pictures has seldom been explicitly proposed, but various social groups have indicated programmes of action which threaten curtailment of patronage.   It has also been suggested (3) that movies be marked for adults only or for children and adults, and that attendance be regulated accordingly by law; or (4) that special programmes for children be instituted and that juvenile attendance be restricted to programmes especially prepared for them.

Even though extirpation is not part of the contemporary practical problem, it would be well to consider it briefly. St. Thomas stated the principle which should guide the prudent man in considering the alternatives of leaving an art alone or totally excluding it from the state. If the art in question, he said, is not intrinsically evil, it is permissible; if permissible, the further question is about its influence. If the art is for the most part put to an evil use, that is, if its influence upon man and society is for the most part bad, extirpation may be prudent even though drastic as a means to the end which justifies it. If the prudent man were faced by the alternative of regulation or extirpation with respect to such an art, he would have to answer the further question: is there any good influence of this art, which can be saved or augmented? If this can be answered affirmatively, it will still be necessary to decide whether some type of control can eliminate the evil as well as conserve the good. The evil might so preponderate and be so difficult to eliminate by any type of supervision, that extirpation would remain the only expedient action in the situation. This analysis of the problem indicates another type of consideration for the prudent man to weigh. He must not only assess the positive and negative values of the art, but he must also weigh the positive and negative results of the action to be taken. Thus, in the case of extirpation, its positive value is its total elimination of the evil of the art to which it applies. Its negative value is its equally complete elimination of whatever good is served by that art along with the evil. The chief practical ground of preference for control instead of extirpation is that the former is able to conserve and perhaps even increase the good while at the same time eliminating or reducing the evil.

If we turn now to the other set of basic alternatives, inaction or some type of control, the practical problem must be formulated somewhat differently. Here obviously the art being considered is neither intrinsically evil nor even so obviously and excessively detrimental to human well-being that extirpation is the only remedy. Rather, the problem arises in this way for the prudent man when the art can be charged with having negative values and be defended as having positive values and when the balance of these opposing values does not preponderate clearly on one side or the other. In this situation, the prudent man would obviously choose to leave the art alone if any sort of action would markedly diminish the good without proportionally lessening the evil. Action rather than inaction could only be prudently desirable if it promised a favorable balance of benefit, that is, if the prudent man felt assured that by some type of regulation he could minimize the unfortunate influences of the art without impairing or destroying its contribution to human welfare. The questions which a prudent man must answer, therefore, to solve this practical issue are as follows: (1) Is the given plan of action expedient in the sense that it will accomplish the end desired, namely, the reduction or elimination of undesirable consequences? (2) Is the plan expedient in the sense that it will not at the same time defeat other ends, by impairing or destroying, for instance, the moral and social benefits of the art being considered? (3) Is the plan expedient in the sense that it does not have other undesirable consequences, political or economic, even though it would be profitable to pursue with regard to the balance of positive and negative values to be derived from the art in question? We can make these three questions concrete by rephrasing them in terms of the problem of the motion picture. Thus: (1) Is the given type of regulation proposed able to remedy the defects with which the movies are charged? This must be asked about censorship or state control or any form of positive action. (2) Is a given type of regulation, such, for instance, as seeks to improve movies for children, likely to make the cinema dull and unattractive as entertainment for adults? (3) Does the plan, such as any form of official censorship or state control, have other objectionable features — for example, the undue increase of bureaucracy?

One further general point must be raised. Any plan of action with respect to the arts is proposed as a means to the end of better morals and a better society. But it is obvious that the influence of the arts depends upon many extrinsic factors, the way in which they are received by men, and hence the nature of particular men and a variety of circumstances. It may be possible, therefore, to achieve the same end — the alteration of the effects of art upon men and society — by changing one or more of these extrinsic conditions under which art operates as an influence, instead of changing the character of the art itself. Thus, in the case of children supposed to be corrupted by the movies, it is possible that if they were better disciplined by such agencies as the home, the church and the school, if their habits were otherwise and already well formed, the influence of the movies would be different without any modification of the movies. In considering action with respect to the influence of the arts it is necessary, therefore, for the prudent man to remember that the good he has in view may be achieved in many ways, only some of which attempt to alter the influence by altering the arts.

We have so far only formulated the political problem of the arts as a prudent man would consider it practically. After envisaging the alternatives in this way, he would take counsel as a precondition of deliberation, judgment and command. As we have already seen, counsel is the search for, the memory or the acquirement of, all relevant knowledge. Without such knowledge there can be no process of deliberation which weighs evidence favoring a course of action against unfavorable evidence. Without deliberation, it is unlikely that a sound judgment can be made in a difficult problem. In comparison, how easy it is to be imprudent, hasty and rash, to make free will capriciously willful, to act in terms of prejudice or passion! Habituated otherwise, the prudent man faces the practical problem by suspending judgment until he can assess the available knowledge. We can indicate his process here by stating the schedule of questions which the problem of the arts evokes for him. Since the problem arises practically because a particular art has been, or can be, attacked and has been, or can be, defended, there is

a whole series of questions involved in the positive and negative
values which are thus claimed. As we have fully seen, each
positive or negative value may raise, not one, but a number of
questions of fact and evaluation. They can all be reduced to
the form: (1) does the art have the specific influence or character which is claimed? and (2) is that influence or character
good or bad, as judged by clear moral and political principles
and generally accepted standards? These two sorts of questions must never be confused, for they are not answerable in the
same way. It may be easy in some instances to establish the
influence and yet not know whether it is good or bad; in other
cases, it may be easy to evaluate the influence if it exists, but
difficult to determine whether it exists. And these two questions
must not be confused with a third question about the positive
and negative values of any course of action that is proposed.
We have already analyzed this question into its component
parts. Even though we know that there is an influence and
that it is bad, we may not know what to do about it. In short,
since the problem of the arts is practical in so far as action
is considered, and action with respect to the arts views them
in relation to men, the prudent man recognizes the need for
knowledge about the arts in relation to men, on the one hand,
and about the efficacy of any sort of action with respect to
this relation, on the other.

Is such knowledge available? To what extent? Of what
sort is it? The difficulty of these questions lies in the ambiguity
of the crucial word "knowledge." Our discussion has many
times suggested that there is a distinction between knowledge
and opinion, a distinction between adequate and inadequate
knowledge, a distinction between presumptions and probabilities
based upon definite evidence. The word "opinion" is equally
ambiguous. There are all sorts of opinions: those which men
commonly accept, those which experts in a given field commonly
accept, those about which there is opposition either among
ordinary men or among experts. Furthermore, the claim of
knowledge must be distinguished from the actual possession of
it. What is no better than opinion is often advanced as if it
were knowledge, what is only probable is often asserted as true,
and what is at best slightly probable is often given an exaggerated
weight.

However these difficulties are settled, the prudent man is aided by a number of definite criteria in seeking counsel and in the process of deliberation. He knows, first, that *mere possibilities* should be given no weight in practical decisions. An enumeration of possibilities, if no more than that, can only indicate intellectual problems to be solved. Prudent action is never guided by questions *alone*. He knows, second, that discrimination must be made between conflicting opinions and opinions which are generally shared, and that preference should be given to the latter. They represent fairly dependable probabilities and upon these action may be taken, however inadequate they are as knowledge. For many practical problems nothing better is available than such presumptions. He knows, third, that if counsel has nothing to offer except conflicting opinions, the task of being prudent is almost insuperably difficult because the decision between action and inaction is just as much a choice of means, as the decision in favor of one plan rather than another. If a practical problem exists, it cannot be perpetually avoided therefore, though solution may be postponed. Among the reasons for postponement is the hope that the future will provide knowledge to resolve the conflict. Wherever conflicting opinions exist, particularly if this is the case for a long time, there is little hope that the conflict will resolve itself into general agreement one way or the other. The only hope, therefore, is that investigation of some sort may gather evidence to throw the weight of probability on one side. This, finally, the prudent man knows: that knowledge which results from careful investigation, though inadequate and merely probable, is better than opinion, whether commonly shared or conflicting. Evidential probabilities — probabilities for which definite evidence can be cited — are better than presumptive probabilities — probabilities the evidence for which cannot be definitely assembled [100].

In the light of these criteria how would a prudent man face the practical problem raised about motion pictures by contemporary controversy? If he took counsel from the history of the perennial dispute about the arts in the state, he would find two things: (1) that the possibilities *pro* and *con* had been analyzed by Plato and Aristotle, to be repeated many times thereafter and seldom expanded: (2) that these possibilities raised questions of fact, eliciting, for the most part, unsettled or conflicting opinions. In different periods of the history of this problem, the weight of opinion has shifted from one side to another, at times even having enough presumptive strength to move prudent men to definite action. But such shifts have never been entirely on one side or lasting on either side. The way in which the problem has been reopened again and again, the way in which opposite policies have been advocated for opposite reasons, would make the advice of history inconclusive for the prudent man concerned with the problem in its latest form.

If — history being equivocal in counsel — the prudent man sought help from the contemporary controversy itself, his situation would seem equally hopeless. We have reviewed the criticism and defense of the movies as an enumeration of positive and negative values. But these are the same possibilities the ancients knew, and the numerous questions raised by them are the same. If the prudent man looked for answers to these questions in the controversial literature of the day, he would find, as always in the past, a few presumptions and, for the most part, unsettled and conflicting opinions. He might, therefore, be rightly cautious and circumspect, seeking postponement until more or better knowledge was available.

It is at this point that a new element enters. There are many today who would object to this description of the situation. They would say that knowledge is available for the prudent man, that scientific research, careful, systematic investigation, has discovered evidence of a sort which takes the problem out of the realm of conflicting opinions. Let the prudent man turn to science for help and he will get it. This is not the first time during the modern period that the scientist has offered himself as a source of counsel for the prudent man facing perplexing practical problems. But it is the first time in the history of poetry and politics that questions of fact about the arts in relation to man have been subjected to scientific inquiry. It is singularly appropriate that motion pictures, the latest and most modern of the arts, should be the first to become a matter of investigation by methods which are the chief exploit of modern times, — the procedures of empirical research.

To see the problem through it will be necessary, therefore,

in the next part of this book, to examine what is currently offered
as knowledge based on scientific evidence, as well as to survey
the field of opinion whose conflicts have occasioned such research.   Plato and Aristotle, Bossuet and Aquinas, were they
alive today, would not, could not ignore or dismiss the contemporary scientist.   But they would certainly have asked the
credentials of much that is currently regarded as science.   They
would have brought an analysis of knowledge and opinion to
bear upon the claims of science, particularly the social sciences
and empirical psychology.   Out of regard for the virtue of
prudence, for the sake of all the intellectual virtues, we cannot
do otherwise or less.   However great is the need of the prudent
man for knowledge, today — when devotion to "science" is so
often uncritical — his need for a clear distinction between knowledge and opinion is greater.

PART III

Science and Prudence,
Prudence and Art

CHAPTER NINE

Knowledge and Opinion

Much of the difficulty which attends any distinction between knowledge and opinion arises from the limitations of language. There is no satisfactory word to name that which is divided into knowledge and opinion. If the word "knowledge" itself be used, then the distinction must be made between opinion and scientific knowledge or science. But the word "science" has, in modern times at least, many ambiguities. According to modern usage, it is necessary not only to distinguish science from opinion, but science from philosophy. Any decision to use words one way rather than another is, of course, arbitrary, particularly if divergent usages are well established. But for the sake of analysis, the obligation to make this decision cannot be avoided. That the choice among verbal usages is arbitrary is not of itself unfortunate. What is unfortunate is that the distinctions, for which the words have been chosen, are often dismissed as if they were arbitrary or "merely verbal." This error must be scrupulously avoided. A distinction is not a matter of words, though words must be used to name the things distinguished. The distinction between two kinds of human cognition remains the same whether the words used to name the kinds be "knowledge" and "belief," or "science" and "opinion." For the time being I shall use the words "knowledge" and "opinion" to divide the field of cognition. I say for the time being because as the analysis proceeds it will be necessary to qualify these words or to use other words in order to express more refined and subordinate distinctions.

231

Words make difficulties for analysis not only because they are ambiguous and insufficient but because they operate in a rhetorical dimension in which they arouse emotions as well as in the logical dimension in which they embody terms. The word "opinion" is derogatory. The word "knowledge" is, in contrast, eulogistic. We dismiss what others advance as knowledge by calling it opinion. Those who are most obstinate in their opinions seldom acknowledge them as such, but claim that they are knowledge. There is nothing wrong in the use of words to praise or deprecate, if the evaluation is based upon sound analysis. Knowledge *is* better than opinion. Men should be praised for being steadfast in their knowledge, and condemned for obstinacy about opinions. Such evaluations can be based upon a distinction between knowledge and opinion that warrants their being made. Unfortunately, however, men frequently object to a distinction when it leads to evaluations which they dislike. Thus, historians are likely to dissent if the distinction between knowledge and opinion leads to the classification of historical cognitions as a species of opinion. They are really not objecting to the distinction, but to the dispraise of history which comes from calling it opinion rather than knowledge. If the distinction had been made by using Alpha and Beta to name two types of cognition, they would not have objected to the conclusion that history is a sort of Beta, even though it was further said that Alpha is a better, a higher or a nobler sort of cognition. It is the word "opinion" which displeases them because of its rhetorical connotations. It is unfortunate that they should be offended where no offense was intended; but it is more unfortunate that their displeasure should provoke them to deny a distinction which, had the words been different, they would have readily acknowledged.

There are difficulties of another order, due to the fact that different criteria have been employed to distinguish the kinds of cognition. Distinctions have been made on the part of the object cognized, or in terms of the content of the cognition — *what* is apprehended of *that which* is apprehended — or on the part of the subject who cognizes, in terms of the faculties of cognition or the manner of their operation. In the history of the discussion, different words are used when the distinction is based on different criteria. Here, again, we must not permit verbal usages to obscure analytical points. Though there is a multiplicity of distinctions, they are not without relation and order. Our task, therefore, is first to enumerate the distinctions according as they are made by different criteria, noting the linguistic peculiarities of each, and then to correlate and order the distinctions, adopting, if possible, some uniform language for expressing all of them. It may not be possible to solve the linguistic aspect of this problem to the equal satisfaction of all readers, because certain words may have such currency or force for them that they cannot or will not submit to the verbal impositions which this analysis requires.

There is one prior point, raised by the question whether any distinction in kind can be made in the field of human cognition. It has been contended that there are only differences in degree. It is further held that, by comparison with what is genuinely knowledge, man has nothing better than opinions, graded in excellence by degrees of completeness and clarity. God has knowledge. Human opinion can be called "knowledge" only analogically. It is more or less *like* knowledge in proportion as it possesses certain traits, especially completeness and clarity, the perfections of immediacy and intelligibility. This position is sometimes attributed to Plato, though there are many indications in the dialogues — in the *Meno*, the *Republic*, the *Thaeatetus* and the *Timaeus* — that science is to be distinguished from right opinion, the truths of mathematics from the probabilities of physics, knowledge from belief. In any event, there is a sound point involved and an erroneous consequence. The sound point, theologically understood, is the inadequacy of human cognition at its best. As in the case of any other predicate which is said both of God and creatures, the attribution of knowledge to God and man must be analogical. In the sense in which there is divine knowledge, in which God knows all things at once and perfectly through His own essence, man does not have knowledge at all. Even in the beatific vision, though it surpasses all natural knowledge which man is able to achieve by his own unaided powers, man does not know God as God knows Himself. But it does not follow from this point that no distinction in kind can be made within the field of human cognition itself. Even though all human cognition be inadequate by comparison with the Divine, we can distinguish between what is for man adequate and inadequate knowledge, or knowledge and opinion. In proceeding now to examine these distinctions, it is important to remember the theological point, first, because it induces a proper humility and skepticism befitting human imperfection, and second, because opinion is peculiar to man whereas there is an analogy between what is knowledge for man and for God. No distinction between knowledge and opinion in the field of human cognition is sound unless it reflects this analogy [101].

1. *The object of cognition as a criterion.* Here we have the distinction between the eternal and the temporal. If the realm of being be identified with the eternal and the realm of becoming with the temporal, then knowledge is correlative with being and opinion with becoming. But this Platonic distinction between knowledge and opinion is based upon a faulty analysis of the relation of sense and intellect in cognition. It would follow that mathematics is knowledge because it treats of ideas, i.e., eternal objects, whereas physics, concerned with the changing world of material things, is at best opinion, a likely story. Although the words "knowledge" and "opinion" can be used in this way, it is analytically better to use "wisdom" as the name for knowledge of the Eternal, and "science"[1] as the name for knowledge of the realm of changing things. This makes the point that it is possible to have *knowledge* with respect to both realms. Only God is eternal. Wisdom is knowledge of God. This properly identifies wisdom with sacred theology or with that part of metaphysics which is natural theology.

2. *The content of cognition as a criterion.* Here a number of distinctions can be made according as there are a number of ways of discriminating what is apprehended of the same object. Excluding wisdom for the time being, the object of human cognition is the physical world. Physical things are at once individuals and particular instances of kinds. It is possible to apprehend them, therefore, in their singularity or in their universality. This gives rise to a distinction between two sorts of cognition: one, expressed in general or universal propositions about the relation of classes or kinds of things, the other, expressed in singular propositions about particular things or individuals. The former has sometimes been called knowledge,

---

[1] The word "science" is here used without distinction between the philosophical and the experimental or empirical orders.

and the latter opinion.   But further analysis questions the tenability of this distinction.   In the first place, the type of cognition is determined not only by the universality or singularity of the subject term, but by the type of universal term which occurs as predicate and consequently by the relation of predication. Thus, we have the distinction between essential and accidental predications and between necessary and contingent general propositions.   To identify knowledge with apprehensions of the general sort and opinion with apprehensions of the singular sort, would be to ignore the more refined distinction between necessary and contingent generalizations.   Nor are all singular propositions of the same sort, though all are contingent.   The distinction between knowledge and opinion cannot, therefore, be perfectly correlated with the distinction between the general and the singular, or between the necessary and the contingent. Just as in the case of the first criterion, the distinction that is here indicated is better expressed in other words : the generality of cognition distinguishes philosophy and science from history, which is concerned with changing things in their particularity.

But if we consider only general propositions, the modal distinction between necessity and contingency succeeds in differentiating knowledge from opinion.   The modality of cognition is determined, as we have seen, not by that which is apprehended but by *what* is apprehended of *that which* is apprehended.   If the predicate in a general proposition be a genus or a specific difference or a property, if the proposition states, in short, either the essence of the thing or what follows from the essence, the proposition is necessary.   The linguistic marks of necessity are such words as "all" or "must" in the verbal expression of the proposition.   If the predicate is an accident, that is, a trait which is neither part of the essence nor follows from it, the proposition is contingent, and this is indicated in the verbal expression by such words as "some" or "may."   The opposite of a necessary proposition is impossible.   The opposite of what must be the case cannot be the case.   But the opposite of a contingent proposition is possible.   If something may be the case, it may also not be the case.   The distinction in modality is formal. It depends on an analysis of predication in the light of an analysis of terms according to the predicaments and predicables.   And it provides a tenable distinction between knowledge and opinion so far as general propositions are concerned, a distinction in kind and not in degree. But it can be extended to the case of singular propositions, as subsequent discriminations will show.

3. *The subjective conditions of cognition as criteria.* The distinction just made above is logical. It regards the proposition in itself as possible knowledge or opinion. The proposition is actual knowledge or opinion only when it is asserted in some way by a mind. We turn, here, to psychological criteria, distinguishing between knowledge and opinion by reference to the way in which the mind operates cognitively. The act of knowing is, in short, different from the act of opining.

There are three cognitive acts: (1) the apprehension of terms, either by sense-perception or intellectual abstraction, (2) judgment, which is the assertion of propositions formed by the composition or division of terms, and (3) reasoning or inference, which is the drawing of conclusions from premises. We shall ignore the first of these because single terms are neither true nor false. The basic distinction in terms as singular or universal, according as they are apprehended by sense or intellect, does not provide a distinction between knowledge and opinion. But the second and third acts indicate an important difference. Whatever is asserted by the mind is asserted either immediately or mediately. Some assertions are possible without any prior assertions because the truth of what is asserted is apparent to the mind through its understanding of the terms of the proposition asserted. Such propositions are called self-evident, axiomatic, propositions *per se nota,* propositions known through themselves. Some propositions can be asserted only as the conclusions of reasoning, that is, only as the result of the prior assertion of other propositions as premises. Such propositions are called theorems or demonstrated propositions.

Immediate propositions may be either general or singular, according as they are intellectual or sensitive intuitions.[2] The proposition which formulates my immediate sensitive experience is indemonstrable. There can be no actual separation between the formulation of such propositions and their assertion as true. The immediacy, the self-evidence, of such perceptual judgments makes them knowledge, even though the propositions are modally contingent and even though they are, as knowledge, about

[2] Vd. *Nichomachean Ethics,* VI, 11, 1143ª35–1143ᵇ8.

things in their particularity.   For the same reason, the general propositions which are intuitive inductions from experience are knowledge.   Intuitive apprehensions, whether sensitive or intellectual, are most like Divine knowledge, the knowledge of vision.   If the first principles, the indemonstrable premises, in the field of human cognition are not knowledge, then nothing else deserves to be so called.   If it be granted that they are knowledge, the question remains whether anything else is.   In a recent essay, Mr. A. E. Taylor distinguishes all else as belief or opinion, reserving the word "knowledge" to name only immediate apprehensions.[3]   For him any judgment properly based on premises, the result of a process of reasoning or inference, is belief ; and if the same judgment is made without proper grounds, it is opinion.   But I prefer to follow the ancient tradition which admits the conclusions of demonstration to the status of knowledge as well as the principles thereof, the primary inductions. In the Aristotelian analysis, two intellectual virtues are distinguished : (1) understanding (intuitive reason), or the habit of first principles and (2) science or the habit of demonstrated conclusions.[4]   Both are habits of knowledge.   Opinion must be sought elsewhere.

Not all demonstrable propositions can be fully or adequately demonstrated.   The criterion of adequacy in demonstration is that the conclusions are supported by self-evident propositions. Only when the grounds of an assertion are immediate truths, first principles, can the proposition be spoken of as demonstrated in a strict sense.   If each of the premises in turn is a demonstrable proposition which must in turn be demonstrated, there is an indefinite regressus.   The conclusions of such quasi-demonstration — demonstration only in form — must be as unsupported as their premises.   It is proper to call conclusions which are adequately demonstrated knowledge because they rest upon knowledge.   But where demonstration is inadequate, where any premise that is chosen is itself in need of demonstration, the conclusions are not knowledge because they do not rest upon knowledge.   We are thus led to another clear distinction between knowledge and opinion.   That is knowledge which either is asserted immediately or, if mediately, is asserted

[3] *Knowing and Believing* in *Philosophical Studies*, London, 1934.
[4] Cf. *Nichomachean Ethics*, VI, 3, 6.

as the result of strict demonstration. That is opinion which is asserted without demonstration though demonstrable or which is asserted as the result of inadequate demonstration, i.e., supported by premises requiring demonstration. Knowledge and opinion are thus seen to be synonyms for what has been called adequate and inadequate knowledge. In the Aristotelian tradition, this distinction is made in terms of scientific and dialectical syllogisms: the premises of scientific syllogisms are either self-evident truths or rest thereon; the premises of dialectical syllogisms are probabilities which are assumed for extrinsic reasons. Whatever reasons can be given for assuming them do not constitute their demonstration.

This can be clarified by a brief discussion of truth and probability. I am here concerned only with what has been called subjective or logical probability to distinguish it from objective or statistical probability. The latter is not the value of a proposition; it is the measurement of the value of observed frequencies. Such measurements can be stated in propositions which themselves are true. By probability is here meant a mode of assertion, a judgment of doubt or uncertainty. Similarly, truth viewed subjectively is a mode of assertion, a judgment of certainty. A probable proposition is one which is provable or demonstrable but which, nevertheless, can never be adequately proved because if its premises were ever true propositions it would cease to be probable, and unless its premises are true propositions, either self-evident or resting on first principles, there must be an indefinite regressus of probable propositions. The regressus is stopped, in any instance of quasi-demonstration or dialectical proof, only by the assumption of premises. The basic paradox of probability is thus revealed: by its nature, a probable proposition is one which should not be asserted except in the light of evidence, and yet in order to assert a probable proposition properly we must assume one or more other probable propositions, which means that we must assert them improperly, without adequate evidence. Regardless of how much evidence is offered in what looks like the proof of a probable proposition, the paradox remains because what are taken as the first principles of such proof must always include probable propositions which are not proved. In his analysis of dialectical syllogisms, Aristotle describes the propositions which are acceptable premises as opinions which are shared by most men or opinions which are shared by most experts in a given field [102]. The measure of their probability is thus an extrinsic sign; it is not determined by evidence which, in a strictly logical sense, is probative.

That any proposition which can be asserted as true, whether immediately or mediately, is knowledge, whereas any proposition which can be asserted only as probable is opinion, connects this distinction with the one previously made in terms of modality. Necessary propositions cannot be asserted as probable, if they are asserted in a manner proper to their mode. I shall indicate presently what I mean by proper and improper assertion. The case of contingent proposition is complicated by the fact that both singular and general propositions are contingent, whereas only general propositions are necessary. Contingent general propositions cannot be asserted as true. To be asserted properly, they must be assumed as probable in the light of certain extrinsic marks or proved to be probable in dialectical syllogisms. This follows from the fact that no contingent general proposition is self-evidently true or adequately demonstrable. But singular propositions, though contingent, can be immediate; as such they can properly be asserted as true. As mediated they, like contingent general propositions, can be asserted only as probable. In the field of human cognition, knowledge consists of all those necessary general propositions and immediate singular propositions which are asserted as true, and opinion of all those contingent general propositions and demonstrable singular propositions which are asserted as probable.

The distinction now to be made between proper and improper assertion throws further light on knowledge and opinion. Assertion is proper if the modality of the judgment is appropriate to the modality and character of the proposition asserted. Thus, a man may assert a mathematical truth not because he understands the demonstration of it but because he relies on the authority of the great mathematician who enunciated it. The mathematician can properly assert the proposition because he can assert it as true and this is appropriate to the nature of mathematical theorems; but those who rely upon his authority can only assert what is true as probable because the grounds of their assertion are not the proper ones. This is one type of improper assertion: it occurs whenever men assert propositions on the

authority of others in a manner different from the way in which
the authorities themselves assert the *same* propositions.   There
is another type of improper assertion that occurs only in the case
of demonstrable propositions, whether necessary or contingent.
(I shall ignore the improper assertion of immediate propositions,
which raises only the moral problem of prevarication.)   If a
proposition which can be demonstrated is asserted without such
demonstration, as well as without reliance upon authority, the
assertion is improper.   The familiar name for such improper
assertion is assumption.   This analysis enables us to extend the
meaning of opinion somewhat.   All assumptions, whether the
propositions asserted are assumed as true or probable, are opinion
rather than knowledge.[4a]   It follows, of course, that whatever
rests upon assumptions is opinion.   Any proposition, furthermore, which is asserted on the authority of another is opinion
rather than knowledge, regardless of whether that proposition
is knowledge or opinion for the authority himself.   In other
words, what is called the opinion of the expert may not be an
opinion for him, because the proposition he enunciates may be
held by him as self-evidently true or adequately demonstrated;
but it is opinion for those who hold it on no other grounds than
his authority as an expert.

   This leads to a final distinction between knowledge and opinion in terms of the manner in which the intellect assents to whatever is proposed to it.   What we have distinguished as proper
assertion is purely intellectual assent, that is, the intellect is
moved by its own principles or nature to the assertion as true of
whatever is self-evident to it or is adequately demonstrated for
it.   It is not free to do otherwise, if it consider what is thus proposed, though it is always free not to consider the matter at all.
But in the case of contingent demonstrable propositions, the
intellect is free to affirm or deny, even when demonstration is

[4a] What in Chapter 8 we referred to as a presumption is related to the general notion of assumption as a special case.   A presumption is a highly
probable proposition, which is assumed rather than proved, and the authority
for which is usually, if not always, fairly stable and widely prevalent common
opinion.   Cf. *Republic*, 533 C, D.   The reason why Plato treats mathematics
as a mean between dialectic, which is truly science, and opinion, is that
mathematical demonstrations rest on what he calls "hypotheses", i.e., assumptions.   Dialectic is science because principles are the foundation of its discourse.

offered because such demonstration must be inadequate and the intellect is free to accept or reject the premises which have been assumed. In this condition of freedom, the intellect if moved at all must be moved by the will. The assertion of opinions is voluntary in a sense in which knowledge is not. There is always a choice between opposite opinions, because opinions are contingent propositions whose opposites are possible. The choice may be well-advised if the will takes counsel from sound authorities or consults whatever inadequate evidence is available, or it may be ill-advised, rash and impetuous. Thus we distinguish between a man of sound opinion and a man of prejudice. But it is opinion in either case and voluntary, though we usually speak only of prejudices as willful, because of their violence and obstinacy.

St. Thomas summarizes this distinction between knowledge and opinion in a passage devoted to the definition of faith as a mean between them: "The intellect assents to a thing in two ways. First, through being moved to assent by its very object which is known either by itself (as in the case of first principles, which are held by the habit of understanding) or through something else already known (as in the case of conclusions which are held by the habit of science). Secondly, the intellect assents to something, not through being sufficiently moved to this assent by its proper object, but through an act of choice, whereby it turns voluntarily to one side rather than to the other: and if this be accompanied by doubt and fear of the opposite side, there will be opinion, while, if there be certainty and no fear of the other side, there will be faith." [5] This explains the characteristic marks of opinion: that it is wavering, unsettled, and subject to opposition or conflict [103]. The ideal of knowledge involves contrary traits: men expect permanence in knowledge and general agreement among all who are competent to make proper judgments in the case. Even so depraved a skeptic as David Hume granted mathematics the status of knowledge because in addition to the certainty of its propositions, its truths had stability above the contingencies of experience and commanded the assent of all who were competent to judge of them. Whatever we hold as knowledge we hold as stable and certain truth about which there can be no disagreement among men

[5] *Summa Theologica*, II–II, Q. 1, A. 4.

whose intelligence has been properly instructed. But the field of human opinion is one in which we are prepared to shift sides from time to time, in which we overcome the natural tendency of doubt to suspended judgment only by an exercise of will, and in which we are always prepared for the irresolvable opposition of conflicting positions.

The foregoing analysis of knowledge and opinion can now be summarized by showing the relation between the various ways in which the distinction has been made. The distinction between necessity and contingency is basic to all the rest, but it is not sufficient in the case of singular propositions, all of which are contingent. Here it was necessary to distinguish between immediate and demonstrable propositions. These two distinctions enabled us to understand the difference between what we can properly assert as true, either immediately or through adequate demonstration, and what we can assert only as probable, by inadequate demonstration, by assumption or some other improper mode of assertion. Knowledge is adequate cognition: self-evident truths and the truths of demonstration. Opinion is inadequate cognition: probabilities, assumed in one way or another or resting on assumptions. Because the opposite of the contingent is possible, because all subjective probabilities are relatively indeterminate and have probable contraries, because the intellect is not determined to one side rather than another in the field of opinion, and assumption or opinionative assertion must, therefore, ultimately depend on an act of the will, opinion is shifting, unstable and subject to conflict whereas knowledge has permanence above the fluctuations of controversy. One further distinguishing trait of opinion follows: the assent of the intellect to truth is without passion; but because they are voluntary, shifts in opinion often reflect the movement of the passions. Opinions thus prompted are held stubbornly and defended violently. The obdurate vehemence of opinionative assertion compensates for uncertainty and poorly conceals a fear of opposition.

The distinction between knowledge and opinion is not invalidated because what is thought to be knowledge is discovered to be error [104]. The discovery of error does not transgress the line between knowledge and opinion, since error is falsity and the assertion of a proposition as false requires that we assert its contradictory as true. We can, therefore, correct wrong claims of knowledge only by making other claims of the same sort. Nor is the distinction obscured by the fact that what some men hold as opinion others hold as knowledge, and conversely. If the distinction were not clear, the difference between them on this point would vanish. The distinction between knowledge and opinion is itself a matter of knowledge, though disputes about what shall be regarded as knowledge or opinion are frequently carried on as if it were a matter of opinion. Knowledge never becomes opinion or opinion knowledge, but in the history of a particular man or of mankind in general, learning produces the transformations which constitute the progress from opinion to knowledge. There is also the equally important advance which comes from the unmasking of opinion pretending to be knowledge.

Within the field of opinion, a number of subordinate distinctions can be made. In the first place, an opinion may be capable of some demonstration. The assumptions upon which it rests may be explicitly indicated to support it and to furnish some estimate of its probability. Such opinions may be asserted either in the light of such support or nakedly, lacking even the inadequate demonstration that is possible. The latter type of opinionative assertion bears the outer marks of opinion more plainly; the former *looks more like* knowledge. We shall refer to this difference by the words "supported" and "unsupported" opinion. The former is much less frequent than the latter. The verdict of the jury in a judicial trial is a good example of explicitly supported opinion. It provides a standard by which to measure the degree of support given to opinions in extra-judicial controversies. In the second place, the dialectical premises, or assumed opinions, may be distinguished according to their source. They either lack extrinsic authority entirely, in which case they can be spoken of as "personal opinions," or their authority is the relatively stable concurrence of most men, in which case they can be spoken of as "common opinions," or their source is the explicit testimony of experts, in which case they can be spoken of as "expert opinions." These distinctions involve differences of degree, and it is always a matter of opinion whether an opinion is of one sort rather than another. Men can disagree about what is the prevailing common opinion in a given respect and there can be conflicts, therefore, between contrary opinions for which this authority is cited. Experts can disagree: the issue may be with regard to what is the prevailing opinion among experts, or if what the experts hold is not for them a matter of knowledge, the issue may be a difference of personal opinion among them. The personal opinion of an expert is better than the personal opinion of an ordinary man by reason of his special qualification to form the opinion in the light of his experience.[6] Expert and common opinion may conflict, and personal opinion may conflict with both.

Though these oppositions are often difficult to resolve, though the line dividing these different types of opinion is difficult to draw, the distinctions are, nevertheless, indispensable. There are no other standards by which to adjudicate disputes in the field of opinion. In any controversy, the ultimate appeal must be to what is regarded as common or expert opinion. The more we are satisfied that an opinion has long endured and received wide popular consent, the higher must be our estimate of its probability; so, too, in the case of expert opinion, the estimate is determined by the degree of stability and concurrence. Where there is a division of experts, where there seems to be common opinion on either side, where common and expert opinion conflict, there will be an approach to equiprobability in opposite assumptions. Nor must it be forgotten that anyone can hold resolutely to his personal opinion despite the contrary indications of extrinsic authority. It is not generally prudent to do so, however. The prudent man is one who, in the field of opinion, looks on both sides and seeks every indication whereby to make as sound an estimate of competing probabilities as possible. If common opinion is relatively clear, or if the authority of experts in a given matter is not impugned by their own polemic, he will be swayed by such weight whatever his own prior inclinations may have been. In other situations, his own personal opinion may be the deciding factor in the balance of opposing positions. If action is urgent and inescapable, it may be necessary for him to rely upon what is the lowest and weak-

[6] A man may be regarded as an expert either because he possesses knowledge, philosophical or scientific, or because he is a practical man of much experience in affairs of a certain sort. In the latter case, his personal unsupported opinion has greater dignity than that of other men.

est grade of opinion. Common and expert opinion have a certain dignity which personal, inexpert opinion always lacks. When we speak of "mere opinion" or when we use the word "opinion" without qualification in a derogatory sense, it is to personal and unsupported opinion that we usually refer.

Our analysis of knowledge and opinion would now be complete, if it were not for the fact that there is a problem about the meaning of "science" in the modern world. I say in the modern world because in the ancient and mediaeval tradition there is no distinction between philosophy and science, and also because in modern times so many different types of cognition are called "science" and treated as if they were knowledge rather than opinion. It is necessary, therefore, first to examine the distinction between philosophy and science, and second to determine whether what is currently regarded as science is knowledge or opinion or something which, sharing in the traits of both, is a mean between them.

The distinction cannot be made satisfactorily in terms of subject-matter for, as we shall see, philosophy and science share, in part, the same subject-matter. To the extent that metaphysics as natural theology deals with eternal things, philosophy and science diverge in subject-matter, but as concerned with the physical world, the realm of corporeal things, their object of knowledge is the same, though they may apprehend it at different levels of abstraction. Nor can the distinction be made primarily in terms of the type of proposition which it is the aim of philosophical discourse and scientific research to establish. Both seek to apprehend things in their generality and are thus distinguished from history by the same criterion. A closer examination of the general propositions which constitute philosophy and science reveals a subtle difference: the propositions of philosophy are genuinely necessary, whereas the propositions of science are intrinsically contingent. The significance of this difference cannot be understood until philosophy and science are otherwise distinguished. That must be accomplished in terms of method. What characterizes everything that is called science in the modern world is a distinctive type of procedure: investigation or research, whether or not it be experimental in the strictest meaning of that term.

To say that science is investigative whereas philosophy is not must not be construed to mean that only science is observational. All human cognition depends upon sense-perception. There are no truths to which the intellect assents, no probabilities which men assume, that do not rest ultimately upon the experience the senses provide. Except in the case of those sensitive intuitions which grasp pure immediacy without articulation or intelligibility, the process of cognition always requires the operation of both sense and intellect. If we speak of all the intellectual operations — the acts of abstraction, judgment and reasoning — as reflection, and of all the sensitive operations — the acts of sensation, discrimination and imagination — as observation, we can say that both science and philosophy involve observation and reflection. Neither is purely one or the other. Both are inductive and deductive; both are analytic and synthetic; both acknowledge that what is true must agree with experience. The difference lies in the kind of experience from which the basic inductions are made. Men cannot live without observing. The senses are active whenever we are awake. In no sense of the word can the observation which accompanies the normal routine of daily living be called investigation. Investigation is a special process of observation: it is observation which seeks to solve a problem and it usually, though not always, requires special operations designed to make that observable which is not ordinarily so. I do not mean that only scientists investigate. But there is no science without investigation, and scientific investigation, unlike that performed by ordinary men, employs techniques and instruments which create a new realm of experience. What the scientist observes as a result of investigative operations does not fall within the normal experience of ordinary men. The data of science thus constitute a realm of special experience which is distinguished from the realm of common experience shared by all men because they live in the same world and have senses which normally operate in the same way.

Philosophy rests upon common experience, arising therefrom by reflection. The metaphysician and the mathematician do not *need* any more experience than that which is possessed by the least experienced of men. Their reflective process would be unhampered if they were confined to a small room for most of their lives. Science, on the other hand, rests on special experience: its reflective process depends upon the data discovered by investigation. For science, restriction of observational inquiry must result in stagnancy. It is inconceivable that a chemist or a geologist could long carry on his work in a small room without any apparatus and without any opportunities for investigation. That investigation is the distinguishing mark of science is clear from the history of its development in modern times : the progress of science has been occasioned by the invention of new techniques of observation, new methods of inquiry, with consequent accretions of new data and extensions of special experience. Even in the sciences which apply mathematics, as mechanics and electricity, advances ultimately depend upon experimental work. Investigation is required to determine the choice between alternative mathematical formulations. In the early centuries of the scientific development, the scientist distinguished himself by the name of *experimental* philosopher. By the addition of that qualification, he ceased to be a philosopher. There are no experimental metaphysicians; there are no mathematicians who observe investigatively in order to proceed with their work. Even those who dismiss metaphysics because it is not "scientific" acknowledge in doing so the distinctive method of the metaphysician. Their error is in supposing that knowledge is not possible without investigation. If they admit that mathematics is knowledge, the possibility is at once established. They need only to be instructed in the subject-matter of metaphysics to see that it has the same status [104a].

A number of consequences follow from this distinction between philosophy and science. (1) There can be no conflict between philosophy and science if each is properly conducted, because if a question cannot be answered by a given method, nothing learned by that method can refute answers achieved by whatever method is appropriate. Thus, if mathematical questions cannot be answered by the method of science, answers achieved by the non-investigative method of mathematics cannot be refuted by investigation. (2) Philosophy is independent of science in the sense that no advance in science can alter a single philosophical truth. Though the work of science extends the realm of what is experienceable by man, the addition of special to common experience cannot alter the latter, and upon the latter the truths of philosophy rest. (3) Philosophy should rule science. The distinction between science and philosophy is itself a philosophical distinction, as the distinction between knowledge and opinion is. Neither are the result of investigation. It follows, therefore, that the philosopher can set the proper limits to scientific inquiry and can judge the accomplishments of scientific work. The scientist *as a scientist* has no criteria for judging philosophy. (4) There is progress, or at least growth and change in science, as there is not in philosophy. The basis of philosophy does not change. Common experience is always and everywhere the same, as man and the world are. Progress in philosophy can only be achieved through an increasing perfection of analysis. What is thus perfected is not discarded. Philosophy is, therefore, traditional and conservative. But the basis of science changes continually as new data are gained by scientific research. The advances which science makes are radical. Old formulations are discarded for the sake of new ones that better fit the evidence; one induction replaces another as the data suggest more refined generalizations. The continuity of science is in its method and aim and not in its doctrine.

It is this last point which enables us to see the way in which science is, in one respect, like knowledge, and in another like opinion. Philosophy is either knowledge or nothing. Those who treat it as if it were opinion might just as well deny its existence. The propositions of philosophy are either self-evident truths or truths demonstrated therefrom. It is further clear that a necessary proposition must be a truth of this sort. It is incompatible with the nature of necessary propositions that they be subject to investigation. In the strict sense in which we have defined knowledge, philosophy is knowledge and science is not. Scientific propositions are intrinsically contingent: there is no scientific proposition the opposite of which is impossible. This can be understood in terms of the fact that scientific method is suited only to the study of accidents and their correlations. But the contingent propositions of science are not established as probable in the sense in which opinions are asserted with relatively indeterminate probability. The basic inductions of science, upon which everything else rests, are asserted as true *pro tem*. They are true generalizations from the data available at the time. It is this relativity to the data on hand which best reveals their contingent truth [105]. When in the course of investigation more data are assembled, a new generalization may have to be made which will have the same contingent truth relative to this new data that the superseded induction had with respect to the prior evidence. The contingency of scientific truth is generally recognized by scientists themselves. The scientific spirit is tentative, open-minded, prepared for a future forever lacking in finality.

"Scientific knowledge" — I shall use this phrase since there is no word to name what is strictly neither knowledge nor opinion — is like knowledge in that its propositions, as established by the state of the evidence, are asserted as true and are asserted by intellectual assent in the light of the evidence and not by an act of will moving the intellect to one side or another. The scientist acknowledges one aspect of the ideal of knowledge, namely, that all competent minds must agree to what is scientifically established, but he must disavow the other aspect of that ideal, namely, that what is scientifically established be regarded as the final and permanent truth. Science, like philosophy, differs from opinion in that the scientist looks upon disagreement as a condition which can always be remedied by an examination of the evidence. But unlike philosophy, science is like opinion in that the scientist looks upon instability and fluctuation as a condition which is intrinsic to the nature of scientific achievement. Contingency and the susceptibility to radical change is a mark which science and opinion have in common. Involuntariness and the resolution of all disagreements by the appeal to evidence in the light of accepted intellectual standards is a mark which science and knowledge have in common. St. Thomas conceived faith as a mean between knowledge and opinion. The paradoxical character of science can be similarly understood. To the extent that it is like knowledge, science is better than opinion, though both are inferior to philosophy. Science has been idolized in modern times because in our era it has accomplished what formerly philosophy did for men in lifting them up above the field of opinion. The praise of science is just, wherever it is based upon the recognition of this accomplishment. Unfortunately it is too often accompanied by dispraise or scorn for philosophy because in the modern world the superiority of philosophy, both theoretically and practically, is so seldom recognized. Though modern man has won great mastery and control over the physical world through the applications of physical and biological science, all of which testifies to the greater usefulness of science than opinion, he forgets that this power which science confers is a mastery of means and that philosophical analysis is needed to determine the ends which they should serve. As philosophy is superior to science in the speculative order because it is knowledge of first principles, so it is better in the practical order where it is concerned with the ultimate good of man. It is not enough to know how to make useful things. It is necessary to know under what conditions their use is justified, by reference to final ends.

The consideration of knowledge and opinion in relation to human affairs brings us to a sharp distinction among the sciences: between the physical and biological sciences, on the one hand, and psychology and the social sciences, on the other. The history of the natural sciences has been a history of success in the achievement of scientific knowledge. The same cannot be said for empirical psychology or the social sciences. It is necessary to inquire here whether this is entirely due to their immaturity or whether they face intrinsic obstacles to scientific accomplishment which they can never overcome.

A number of preliminary points must be made. In the first place, we must recognize that the natural sciences are not all of the same sort: they differ *inter se* not only in subject-matter but in method. Some are experimental, and some are not, such as astronomy and anatomy. Some involve the application of mathematical principles to natural phenomena, such as mechanics and electricity, and some do not, as qualitative chemistry and physiology. Some employ statistical techniques. Some are purely taxonomic, such as zoology, whereas others are aetiological, such as genetics. In the case of those natural sciences which are applied mathematics, there is a kind of imperfect aetiology consisting of functional statements of covariation, although in the experimental operations of these sciences a genuine aetiology is necessarily involved. In the second place, it must be noted that in so far as the natural sciences have physical as opposed to mathematical principles and develop a genuine causal analysis instead of functional formulae, they depend on a branch of philosophy which was anciently called "physics" but must now be named "philosophy of nature" in order to distinguish it from the investigative sciences dealing with particular kinds of bodies and particular types of change.   In the third place, of all the subject-matters psychology is the only one which is common to both philosophy and science.[6a]   As a body of philosophical knowledge, psychology stands to all the biological sciences as philosophical physics stands to all the natural sciences: it is concerned with the principles of vital phenomena.   But in the analysis of living things, philosophical psychology distinguishes man from all other animals as having a rational soul, the activity of which cannot be fully explained in terms of the acts of a body. Being the study of man as essentially different from all other living things, psychology is a very special branch of philosophy.   The history of scientific psychology, as an investigative study of man, reflects this peculiar status of its subject-matter: it has never been able to decide whether it belongs with the natural sciences or whether it is separate.   Finally, it is necessary to take account of the way in which subject-matter names are currently used. Psychology names the study of animal as well as human behavior. Sociology, anthropology, economics and what is called "political science" study human behavior as much as does psychology. Human behavior is not the only subject-matter, however, which is included under these rubrics.   Thus, psychometrics is a branch of scientific psychology dealing with the application of mathematics to the measurement of human abilities; mathematical economics is similarly an application of mathematics to the measurement of economic phenomena; anthropology includes linguistics, comparative human anatomy and comparative ethnology, and so forth.   In order to avoid verbal confusions, I shall speak of the study of human behavior and disregard whether the study is carried on by men who call themselves psychologists, sociologists or anthropologists.   The problem we now turn to

[6a] Psychology is the only knowledge, having as its object a particular kind of substance and a particular kind of change, which can be purely philosophical, i.e. constituted without investigation. In the case of all other particular branches of physics, investigation is necessary. The exception is due to the fact that man is at once the subject and object of knowing in psychology. The reflexivity of the intellect in knowing itself and related powers of the soul dispenses with the need for empirical research, the need but not the possibility. Hence man can be investigated scientifically as well as known philosophically.

can, therefore, be formulated by the question: Is a science of human behavior possible in the same sense in which the natural sciences now exist?

The answer to the question is negative. The reason is that human behavior is a unique type of change. It is voluntary. Among corporeal creatures only man has free will, because only man is rational. By free will I do not mean the pleasant fiction that men act *as if* they had freedom even though their actions are as fully determined by natural causes as the motions of a stone. I mean that human behavior cannot be reduced to natural causes, that in human behavior reason is the first cause, and that the operation of the will as rational appetite is uncaused except by God. Only Divine Providence is compatible with the freedom of the will.[7] To assert what is usually called a thorough-going natural determinism is to deny that man is genuinely different from the rest of corporeal nature. If human motions were caused in the same way as all other natural motions, man would not act freely.

Man's animal motions are not human behavior. These can be studied by the physiologist in the same way as all other biological phenomena. What is essentially *human* behavior consists of all those actions which are voluntary and being voluntary are moral, susceptible to the distinction of good and evil [106]. The range of voluntary conduct is determined by power of the will to control action. Thus, the activity of the vegetative part of man is not voluntary because not subject to the will. But the passions are capable of being commanded by the will [107]. The movement of the passions, even when contrary to reason, is voluntary in this sense. The distinction between good and evil in human acts turns on the relation of the act to reason. What is vicious and evil is due to the insubordination of the passions, on the one hand, and the failure of reason, on the other, but vice is voluntary in the same sense that virtue is. Both are within the power of the will though in the case of vice the will's freedom is not properly exercised. In short, that man has free will is due to the fact that he is rational, that, having intellect as well as senses, he has both intellectual and sensitive appetites. But that the intellect is the principle of freedom does

[7] Vd. Chapter 8 *supra*. Cf. St. Thomas Aquinas, *Summa Theologica*, I–II, Q. 9, A. 6; Q. 10, A. 4.

not mean that the will is always moved by the intellect. It can be moved by the passions. The passions do not cause involuntariness, though the voluntary conduct they cause may be good or evil according as it conforms to or transgresses the rule of action which reason would dictate.

The ancient question about the causes of virtue and vice can be answered by a psychological analysis of the relation of reason to the passions. The virtues and vices which constitute moral character are habits formed by voluntary acts. What makes an act good or evil in itself, or a cause of virtue or vice in relation to the habit it tends to form, can be stated by reference to the role which reason plays, but what makes a man act rightly or wrongly cannot be stated because the moral act is voluntary. In other words, the psychological analysis of moral behavior indicates the role of reason as a cause but cannot give the cause of reason's operations [108]. In the psychological order reason is a first cause, an uncaused cause. This explains the limitations of ethics which both Plato and Aristotle so fully recognized. No analysis of the causes of virtue and vice can answer the question of how to teach virtue. For one man to be able to make another virtuous, by teaching or any other process of influence, it would be necessary for him to know more than the causes of virtue ; it would be necessary for him to be able to cause these causes, one of which is reason, the principle of human freedom and as such indeterminable by any exterior influence [109]. As St. Thomas points out, the circumstances of any voluntary act are accidents of it. No set of circumstances can determine the act in one way rather than another. This can be generalized by the statement that every exterior factor in the moral life is accidental, excepting the will of God. Under exactly the same circumstances, having the same virtues or vices, two men may still act differently because neither the outer circumstances nor the moral character which has been formed by prior voluntary acts can abolish freedom [110]. The virtues and vices are not only habits freely formed ; they are habits freely exercised or transgressed. Moral behavior is, therefore, essentially contingent and relatively unpredictable. The formation of moral character is in the realm of freedom.

The impossibility of knowledge about the causes of human behavior is clear. To know that human behavior is voluntary is to know that there are no necessary causal propositions about it. As an object of cognition, human behavior must be in the field of opinion. This does not mean that human behavior is absolutely unpredictable. It means only that at best there are highly probable propositions about what men can be expected to do under certain circumstances and in the light of their characters. These highly probable propositions are, for the most part, matters of common opinion. They have long been the possession of men who have been guided by them in their dealings with other men. These probabilities are of two sorts : (1) those about the behavior of men whose habits or characters are fairly plain and (2) those about the influence of extrinsic factors which constitute the circumstances of voluntary action. The latter are less probable than the former. The very nature of habit entails the probability of conduct of a definite sort. There is nothing in the nature of any outer circumstance, or of any set of circumstances, which indicates the probable direction which behavior will take under the circumstances in question. This can be learned, if at all, only from much experience. In other words, there is much more difference of opinion about the conditions under which moral character is formed in one way or another, than about the way in which men of definite character will act.

In the light of the foregoing analysis, all of the empirical researches which try to constitute a science of human behavior can be distinguished from the natural sciences. While the propositions of the latter are essentially contingent, they are nevertheless established by the data of research as contingently true. The possibility of scientific knowledge of this sort about natural phenomena is based upon the fact that natural changes are involuntary, are determined entirely by the natures of the changing things. In the case of human behavior, which is voluntary change, the indeterminacy of the phenomena makes scientific truth impossible.[7a] There can be a "science" of human

---

[7a] The indeterminacy here spoken of is genuinely constitutive. The indeterminacy in nature, about which contemporary physicists get so 'philosophical', is not ontological contingency. Unavoidable ignorance of determinations is improperly converted into a description of nature. The Heisenberg principle of indeterminacy is only a recognition of uncertainty in knowledge, due to its own intrinsic limitations. It is false to infer freedom in the phenomena with respect to which science fails ; it is a fallacious conversion

behavior because human behavior can be investigated and generalizations can be made from the results of such research.   But
this science is much more like opinion than natural science : its
conclusions can never be better than probable.   While there is
little doubt that science is better than opinion about natural
phenomena, it is often questionable whether scientific conclusions about human behavior are better, because more probable,
than what has long been held as a matter of common opinion.
The aim of scientific work in this field is obviously to improve
upon opinion.   Its success must be judged accordingly.   For
the most part, the empirical psychologists and social scientists
who have investigated human behavior have devoted themselves
to the problem of the influence of external factors upon conduct
and the formation of character.   The need for research here is
indicated by the unsettled state of opinion about such matters.
The need is much less in the case of the problem of habit as a
source of behavior.   But in either case, scientific work is significant and valuable only if its conclusions are better than the
prevailing opinions.   To be better, the scientific work must
establish probabilities where none are clear or must decide between the opposing probabilities of conflicting opinions.   It is
not sufficient that scientific conclusions be speciously technical
statements of what is already widely assumed, or documentations
of the obvious.   Thus, little of what has been accomplished by
research in the field of criminology has improved upon the state
of common and expert opinion — the "unscientific" opinion of
men experienced in dealing with criminals.   At best, research
has been confirmatory of our doubt about any factor or set of
factors as causative of crime.[8]

   In the light of speculative standards, the attempt of scientific
investigation in the field of human behavior should always be
praised, even when its achievements are of no practical significance.   To be practically significant, science must definitely
alter the state of existing opinion ; but even when it fails to do
this, the same probability is better held as a matter of scientific

of the true proposition that where there is freedom, a true science of the
phenomena is impossible.
[8] Vd. S. Glueck, *On the Causes of Crime* in the American Mercury for
August, 1933 ; and also J. Michael and M. J. Adler, *Crime Law and Social
Science*, New York, 1932.

knowledge than as a matter of opinion. The intellectual process is better. The probability is made to rest upon definite evidence, and it can be changed by further accretions of data. But by the same speculative standards, we must distinguish between what is good and bad as scientific work. The intrinsic weakness of the study of human behavior *as science* is further complicated by the methodological incompetence of most of the attempts which have been made. Empirical psychology and the social sciences are not only inferior to the natural sciences with regard to the status of their best conclusions, but in their short career they have again and again transgressed or ignored the simplest canons of scientific procedure. What is held as a matter of common or expert opinion is thus often intellectually more respectable than the pretensions of scientific research to conclusions which are no more probable and which are either not supported by the evidence or supported by evidence of questionable accuracy and validity.

I am aware that the opinion current among most scientific students of human behavior is that man is not essentially different from other animals, that human behavior is no different from all other naturally determined motions in the physical world, and that, therefore, there is no distinction in kind between natural science and the science of human behavior. It is an opinion which adequate philosophical analysis would remove. But I am also aware that in the same quarters, philosophy is not regarded as knowledge and philosophical demonstrations are dismissed as dialectical trickery [111]. I shall be content, therefore, to state the contradiction which contemporary investigators must face if, on the one hand, they deny the uniqueness of human behavior as voluntary and if, on the other, they suppose that the fruits of their scientific research can be useful in solving practical problems. The point here is not that scientific work in this field cannot improve upon opinion. The prudent man may indeed be aided in his deliberations by taking counsel from the empirical psychologist and social scientist wherever the latter have added to or altered the prevailing opinions. The possible utility of a science of human behavior in the solution of practical problems must be conceded, but this very point entails the further admission that human behavior is voluntary, since otherwise practical problems would not exist for man.[9]   The paradox can be stated by the following dilemma : *either* human behavior is not voluntary, in which case there is no distinction between the sciences of nature and of man, but in which case also there are no practical problems that science of any sort can be used to solve ; *or* there are practical problems for the solution of which men seek the aid of scientific research, in which case human behavior must be voluntary and the sciences of man and nature are radically distinct.   To make this clear, the case of criminological research can again be used.   The practical utility of scientific knowledge about criminal behavior must be in the help it gives legislators, administrators and social workers of various sorts.   These men are attempting to solve the practical problem of crime prevention or reduction.   If they were not free to choose between one policy and another, between one course of action and another, they could not in any sense be said to be trying to solve a practical problem.   But if they have free choice in the matter of what to do about criminals, so have other men free choice about whether to obey the law or transgress it. For the same reason that crime can be a practical problem for men, criminology is different from the natural sciences.

Another consequence follows from the relation of empirical psychology and the social sciences to practical problems.   In the ancient and mediæval tradition, the problems of human behavior were considered primarily as practical rather than speculative.   These problems fell to ethics and politics as branches of practical philosophy.   That they were denied the status of speculative philosophy — the status of metaphysics, mathematics and physics or what we have called the philosophy of nature — indicates the ancient perception that *knowledge* of the causes of human behavior is impossible.   Ethics and politics have speculative content, derived from metaphysics and philosophical psychology primarily ; from the former with respect to the analysis of the good, from the latter with respect to the analysis of human nature and its potentialities for perfection.   This knowledge as it occurs in ethics and politics is ordered to the ends of a good life and good society.   It determines the nature of these ends. But though ends are in the practical order as first principles are

[9] Vd. Chapter 8 *supra*.

in the speculative order, they are never sufficient for the solution of practical problems which require a prudent choice of means in particular cases of action.   All the knowledge which speculative philosophy can offer is not enough.   The prudent man must take cognizance of a wide variety of particular circumstances and the many contingent conditions of human behavior. For this reason ethics and politics are said to be inexact.   Their practical utility depends upon the kind of cognition we have called opinion : probable generalizations and apprehensions of particular matters of fact.   The existence of scientific research about human behavior and social change does not alter the essential inexactitude of ethics and politics as practical disciplines.   It merely enlarges the sources of counsel for the prudent man. Such scientific research, to be useful practically, must be subordinated to the principles of ethics and politics, as means are subordinate to ends.   When empirical psychology and social science are regarded as practical they cannot avoid the normative character which follows from this subordination.

In trying to be like the natural sciences, the investigative study of human behavior has sought to suppress its intimate affiliation with such normative disciplines as ethics and politics. It has tried to be purely objective or descriptive in the sense in which these words mean an avoidance of all questions of value and all criteria of moral judgment.   And rightly so, because according to the modern conception of science, a science cannot be normative or practical.   But the *human* behavior which is scientifically studied is necessarily moral or political behavior. It is, therefore, much more difficult for the scientific student of such phenomena to be entirely objective, to avoid evaluations, to see the utility of his conclusions without making moral or political judgments which can be properly made only in the light of principles that are not scientific.   The literature of empirical psychology and social science reveals how frequently the scientist speaks in the capacity of a moralist rather than an investigator.   There would be no harm in this if the transition from science to practical philosophy were explicitly acknowledged, if the scientist were willing to support his judgments by an appeal to basic principles.   But the social scientist wishes to have his cake and eat it too.   He wants all of his utterances to be received as if they were the conclusions of research and yet he is unwilling or perhaps unable to forego a kind of comment which must appeal to principles beyond the domain of science. To the extent that he tries to conceal this duplicity from himself as well as from his audience, the confusion of social science with moral philosophy is an insidious affair.   It is made more insidious by the fact that many social scientists who do not hesitate to moralize surreptitiously are explicit in their denial of the principles of morality, insisting that there are only *mores* or arbitrary conventions which social scientists can investigate objectively.

Empirical psychology and social science, in so far as they attempt to investigate human behavior, would better achieve the status of science if they recognized their limitations, in the speculative order, and their subordination to ethics and politics, in the practical order.   In the former respect, they might do better work if they were not misguided by false pretensions to the same kind of knowledge which is possible for the natural sciences, if they were content to establish by careful and reliable methods probable generalizations that were superior to existing opinion.   In the latter respect, they might do more useful work through being more attentive to the needs of the prudent man and they could at least avoid the taint of unprincipled moralizing. In both respects, the fundamental inconsistencies which we have noted would be eliminated.

The problem of the moral and social effects of the motion picture is a practical one.   It belongs to ethics and politics.   That is the traditional locus of the problem of the arts in relation to man.   That it is incapable of being solved alone by the empirical sciences of human behavior can be readily shown by analyzing the problem into its three major questions: (1) What are the effects or influences of the motion pictures on moral character and conduct?   (2) If there are any effects, to what extent are they good, bad or indifferent?   (3) If there are bad effects, what should be done about it?   The last two questions clearly require ethical and political principles as the norms of judgment. Only the first is strictly a question of fact.   It can be answered either by opinion, common, expert or personal, or by the probabilities of scientific research.   It can never be a matter of knowledge, nor can the answer ever be given by the type of contingent truth that the natural sciences afford. The fine arts are among the accidental circumstances, the external factors, of the moral life [111a].

It is only recently that scientific research has been attempted in the field of this practical problem. There were scattered and inadequate studies made during the years between 1920 and 1930, but as late as 1928 a writer paused in his consideration of the movies to emphasize that "nobody has yet enquired, on scientific lines, what effect is produced by films on the mind of the world."[10]   In 1930 the International Institute of Educational Cinematography proposed a world-wide inquiry because of its conviction, after a thorough review of the materials available, that there was no scientific evidence pointing definitely to any conclusions about the influence of the cinema.[11]   And in 1933, the nationally instituted research which culminated in the report on *Recent Social Trends* contained a chapter on the motion picture which was silent about the effects of the movies upon social habits because nothing could be reported as known until the matter had been investigated scientifically.[12]   In the same year a "series of twelve studies of the influence of motion pictures upon children and youth" were published by "the Committee on Educational Research of the Payne Fund at the request of the National Committee for the Study of the Social Values in Motion Pictures," which then became organized as the Motion Picture Research Council.   "The studies were designed to secure authoritative data which would make possible a more complete evaluation of motion pictures and their social potentialities."[13] The Motion Picture Research Council had invited university psychologists, sociologists and educators as early as 1928 to confer about the problem of discovering by scientific methods just what effect motion pictures have upon children, a subject "upon which many conflicting opinions and few substantial facts were in existence."[14]   While these Payne Fund researches were

[10] E. Betts, *Heraclitus, or the Future of the Films*, London, 1928 : p. 42.
[11] International Review of Educational Cinematography, March, 1930 (Vol. II, pp. 241–252, 329).
[12] *Recent Social Trends*, New York, 1933 : Vol. I, p. 209 ff. ; Vol. II, p. 790 ff.
[13] These quotations are from an announcement on the back of the title-page of the published Payne Fund studies.
[14] From the Chairman's Preface (p. vi) to the series of twelve Payne Fund studies in *Motion Pictures and Youth : A Summary* by W. W. Charters,

not the first or only investigations of the influence of motion pictures on character and conduct, they constitute today the bulk of our scientific knowledge about the movies. If they achieved their aim of resolving conflicting opinions by probabilities resting on scientific evidence and of increasing the number of "substantial facts" the prudent man would indeed be greatly indebted to empirical psychology and social science. But that is precisely the question which remains to be answered and to which we shall devote the next two chapters. Is the prudent man better off today as the result of scientific efforts than he was in the time of Plato or St. Thomas, Bossuet or Rousseau? Has science altered the state of opinion about the influence of the arts, in the particular case of the motion picture?

The critical task that lies before us is necessarily a tedious and painful one. In order to judge the merit, both speculative and practical, of the scientific work we must survey the field of opinion as well as the science which tries to supplement it. There is no way of making an adequate appraisal of the worth and significance of such materials without a detailed application of the criteria of criticism. Much of the material will be found unworthy of such careful and minute examination. In good conscience much of it could be completely dismissed upon superficial examination as unreliable and insignificant. But the readiness of the public and the leaders of opinion to accept whatever professors tell them is the case, in the high name of science, requires that the criticism be made relentlessly complete [112]. At the risk of being repetitious and of making points that will seem generally obvious, the showing must be made in every detail and in all respects.

It will facilitate our inquiry to summarize here the critical criteria we shall apply to what is offered as science. (1) We must determine whether the scientific conclusions are better than, or alter in any significant way, the prevailing opinions, particularly common and expert opinions. We shall use the phrase "expert opinion" narrowly to mean, not the testimony of a scientist reporting the conclusions of research, but the unsupported personal opinion of a practical man who speaks from his special

New York, 1933. This Preface can be found also in other Payne Fund volumes.

experience.[15]   (2) We must detect the confusion of scientific
conclusions with moral judgments, particularly if the latter are
insinuated or surreptitious. We must everywhere separate the
probabilities the scientists have discovered from evaluations and
determinations of policy which they *as scientists* are not competent to make.   The separation of questions is a basic principle of
criticism which must be applied to much of the research work
because the questions are so frequently confused by the investigators themselves.   (3) We must determine the relevance of
any conclusions which are validly founded on reliable data, to
the practical problem that stimulated the research.   (4) Finally,
we must determine whether what is offered as a scientific conclusion is supported by the evidence that is presented.   This type
of criticism is much more necessary in the fields of empirical
psychology and social science than in the case of the natural
sciences, because the investigators themselves are so frequently
uncritical, and the procedure of their research is so often a
travesty on scientific method. Here a number of subordinate
criteria will be employed: (a) Are the basic data reliable in
terms of the method by which and the conditions under which
they were obtained?   There is also an external mark of reliability,
namely, the consistency of one set of data with other sets similarly obtained.   (b) Are the data significant?   Can they be generalized unambiguously?   Do they justify an induction, statistically or otherwise?   If no findings of general significance are
unambiguously supported by the data, they must be interpreted
as only descriptive of some set of particulars.   As such they are
merely current history and not the findings of science in any
sense of that word.   (c) We must be particularly careful to
guard against loose and ambiguous interpretations of data, expressed in the form "this *may* be the case," unless there is a
definite indication that it is more probable than not that it *is* the
case.   Wherever conclusions are so expressed, we must recognize
that the data are to that extent inconclusive, particularly if contradictory conclusions of the may-be variety are possible in the
light of the same data.   The detection of conclusions so expressed will discover the extent to which what is offered as

---

[15] What Aristotle calls "the man of experience" is peculiarly competent in the
field of practical problems. In fact, the man of experience is superior to the
man of science who lacks experience. Vd. *Metaphysics*, I, 981[a]14–[b]9.

science is no better than opinion, and more dangerous because the name of science is invoked.   (d) We must note inconsistencies and contradictions among the conclusions of different researches or in different parts of the same research.   This will indicate how much more like opinion are the scientific findings in the field of human behavior than are those of the natural sciences.

The performance of this critical survey will also be made easier for both reader and writer if the plan of the discussion is here stated.   There are three principles for classifying all of the available materials: (1) whether they deal with adults or children, (2) whether they deal with the movies as a cause of crime and delinquency, or with all other influences of the movies upon men and society, (3) whether they are offered as the expressions of opinion, common, expert or personal, or are offered as the findings of scientific research.   We shall, therefore, organize the survey in the following manner.   In the next chapter, we shall examine the materials relevant to all questions about the influence of the movies on adults, first with respect to crime and then with respect to all other effects, in each case summarizing the field of opinion first and then proceeding to the results of research.   In the chapter following that, we shall do the same for the material relevant to all questions about the influence of the movies on children and youth.   While the Payne Fund studies are primarily devoted to the problem of motion pictures and youth, they do to some extent include the adult population within the scope of their investigations, especially with regard to crime. Certain transgressions of this plan may, therefore, be unavoidable in order not to repeat the criticism of the same work under two different heads.   They will be indicated wherever, from necessity, they occur.

CHAPTER TEN

Attempts at Scientific Research:
The Mature

WE shall divide this survey into two parts: (1) the question whether motion pictures are a cause of crime, and (2) the question whether motion pictures have any other influences on moral character and social conduct. In each case we shall first report the prevailing opinions answering these questions affirmatively and negatively, and then proceed to an examination of the attempts at scientific research to improve the state of opinion.

1. WHETHER MOTION PICTURES ARE A CAUSE OF CRIME?
   (a) *Affirmative opinion.*
In 1921, Mr. P. W. Wilson in an article on *The Crime Wave and the Movies* expressed his opinion that the crime wave *may* be the result of the films.[1] He gave as the reason for this opinion that the movies portray crime enticingly, and this *may* increase its appeal for children and alien adults. He cited the comparative crime rates of England and the United States, and at least recognized the point that since the same movies which appear in America entertain large audiences in England, it is surprising to find no corresponding crime wave in England. Without giving any reasons whatsoever, Mr. Wilson dismissed the negative force of this point.

In 1928, Mr. Roger Babson wrote an open letter to his clients, in which he claimed that statistical studies of the increase of

[1] Current Opinion, March, 1921 : pp. 320–323.

crime in the United States, and for that matter throughout the world, forced him to form the opinion that the movies were chiefly responsible for this condition.[2]   He said: "Prohibition cannot be the cause because the disregard for law is world-wide; immigration cannot be the cause because the homicide rate has increased in the years during which the rate of immigration has diminished; movies are a world-wide influence and have made an unfavorable impression on me, through my own observation in pictures and what the manager of the Wellesley Theatre has told me of his difficulty in getting good pictures.   Therefore, the movies are the basic cause of the crime wave of today."

In 1934, at the opening session of the Attorney General's Conference on Crime, the Hon. Henry L. Stimson, former Secretary of State, expressed his opinion that the movies and the sensational press had made us sentimental about crime to an hysterical degree and were thus largely responsible for the breakdown of our system of justice.   It should be noted in passing, first, that the representatives of the press forcefully challenged Mr. Stimson's opinion, and second, that at no point during the course of the subsequent meetings did any of the experts who addressed the Conference corroborate Mr. Stimson's charge.[3]

The opinions of Mr. Wilson, Mr. Babson and Mr. Stimson are their personal convictions.   They do not have the status of experts in the field of criminal statistics or criminology.   The answers which Mr. Babson elicited from experts indicate how little right he had to pretend to being a student of criminal statistics.   As examples of expert opinion, the following are offered.   In 1921, Professor Poffenberger of the Psychology Department of Columbia University expressed the opinion that the movies *may* be an important cause of crime, particularly among mentally deficient adults and children because they are so highly suggestible.   "One who knows the mechanism of suggestion would expect the prevalence of crime, especially when advertised, to breed more crime." [4]   He offered no supporting evidence of any sort.   In 1935 Dr. Amos Osborne Squire, Chief

[2] Reported in the International Review of Educational Cinematography, Sept., 1929 : pp. 303-314.
[3] Vd. *Proceedings of the Attorney General's Conference on Crime*, Washington, 1934 ; especially pp. 82-139.
[4] Scientific Monthly, April, 1921 : pp. 336-339.

Physician at Sing Sing Prison, New York, in a public address expressed his conviction that motion pictures depicting crime have contributed in a measure to crime through creating a disregard for life and limb and through the public's familiarity with murder on the screen.[5]   He also thought that newspapers could help by refraining from giving too much space to murder trials and crime news generally.   Opinions of this sort, both personal and expert, have been answered by personal and expert opinions to the contrary.

(b)   *Negative opinion.*

Mr. Babson was answered by the statistician for the Prudential Life Insurance Company who is an expert in homicide rates.[6] Dr. Hoffman found a distinct negative correlation between the proportion of the two sexes in the average motion-picture audience and the proportion of the two sexes arrested for various crimes.   He found that there was no significant relationship between the motion-picture theatre seating capacity of the various states and the number of commitments to penal institutions, the population in the penal institutions, and the populations in the asylums for the insane in those states; in fact he found a greater percentage of crime in the South and in rural sections where motion-picture theatres are fewest.   Hoffman, furthermore, cited Dr. Thorstin Sellin's study of crime rates in Europe from 1900 to 1923.   Mr. Babson had mentioned an increase of crime in Europe concomitantly with the growing popularity of the movies, but Dr. Sellin found that maximum crime rate in this period was reached between 1903 and 1907.   We need not be concerned here with Dr. Hoffman's own opinion as to the major causes of homicide, since we wish only to indicate the dubious character of any opinion which claims to be based upon crime rates.   Dr. Sellin in an address before the Attorney General's Conference pointed out how undependable such rates are because of the way in which they are currently determined.   He said:

[5] Reported in the Altoona (Pa.) Mirror, Feb. 20, 1935.
[6] Reported in the International Review of Educational Cinematography, Sept., 1929: pp. 303–314.   In an open letter, Dr. Hoffman said: "Mr. Babson has used my homicide statistics to develop the idea that the motion picture is the primary cause of the increase in homicides in this country during recent years.   I myself have made no such statement and nothing contained in my figures could be construed to justify such a conclusion."

"Even when the records of any given agency are excellent, they may be so different in character from those of a similar agency in the same state that comparative analysis of the consolidation of statistical data may be impossible."[7]   Nevertheless, the tremendous disparity between the crime rates of England and the United States is such that their significance cannot be completely dismissed in terms of the difficulties of comparing the data.   The newspapers, as well as the movies, have been accused of responsibility for the increase of crime in this country.   Mr. Grove Patterson, as President of the American Society of Newspaper Editors, pointed out to the Washington Conference that the English newspapers of great circulation print as large, and in some cases, a larger volume of crime news than similar American newspapers, yet in England there is much less crime, particularly murder.[8]   It must similarly be remembered that England and the United States have substantially the same motion-picture entertainment.   The negative case of England is thus often cited to support the opinion that the prevalence of movies dealing with crime or the publication of crime news in newspapers is not a significant cause of crime.

Balancing the expert opinion of Dr. Squire, we find its opposite in a statement made by Dr. George W. Kirchwey, formerly Dean of the Columbia Law School, then Warden of Sing Sing Prison, and later head of the Department of Criminology of the New York School of Social Work.   In a recent public address, he said: "In my ten years' experience in dealing with the criminal, I have never heard of an authentic case of any person who committed a crime because of the influence of a motion picture. Insofar as motion pictures have any direct effect they do not encourage crime, they discourage it.   In the motion picture the criminal is never triumphant.   The films tell the same moral over and over again—'You can't get away with it.   You can't get away with it.'"[9]   We must remember here Professor Poffenberger's point that the moral ending of a lurid tale may not

[7] *Proceedings of the Attorney General's Conference on Crime*, Washington, 1934: p. 382.
[8] *Proceedings of the Attorney General's Conference on Crime*, Washington, 1934: pp. 82–86.
[9] Quoted by Carl E. Milliken in an open letter to Roger W. Babson, May, 1929. Cf. Dean Kirchwey's statement at a recent crime conference, particularly in reference to the attempts at scientific research (*Proceedings of*

efface the excitement of criminal scenes which may have a permanent effect upon the highly suggestible minds of the mentally deficient.   To which Dr. Kirchwey can be found replying: "I don't see any way in which the world can be made safe for morons."

In Judge Albert Hellwig, Head of the Provincial Tribunal of Potsdam, we have another expert partially corroborating the opinion of Dr. Kirchwey.   In an article on *The Cinematograph and Crime*, he had, first of all, the good sense to recognize the intrinsic difficulty of determining any of the causes of crime.[10] His experience on the bench convinced him, furthermore, that the importance of the cinema in crime causation is greatly exaggerated.   Since criminals are not reliable reporters of their own motives, their statements to the police in which they may happen to mention the movies as an influence, are hardly dependable. Judge Hellwig did not deny that the movies may be in some sense and to some extent a cause of crime, particularly in their influence upon individuals who are psychopathic or have already developed criminal propensities.   Rather he insisted upon suspending judgment until research has succeeded, if it ever can, in establishing the causal connection.   He said that his experience on the bench over a period of years during which slot-machines, bicycles, dime novels, automobiles, newspapers and movies have successively been in vogue as a leading cause of crime, made him skeptical of rashly expressed opinions on such matters.

Nevertheless, experts do express opinions of this sort in either direction, accusing or praising the movies.   Thus, Mr. Joseph Fishman, formerly United States Inspector of Prisons, wrote in 1933 that films of crime and the underworld not only do not cause crime, but rather "to these films belongs entirely the credit for the public understanding of, and revulsion against, gang rule today.[11]   And further to balance the opinion of Professor Poffenberger, we find Dr. A. A. Brill saying from his experience as a psychiatrist that "motion pictures do not hurt anybody or

the Governor's Conference on Crime, the Criminal and Society, Albany, 1935 : pp. 316–317).
[10] International Review of Educational Cinematography, August, 1930 : pp. 253–266.
[11] *More Delusions about Crime* in Harper's Monthly Magazine, July, 1933 : pp. 239–249.

anything.   The defective, who is a criminal, will commit a crime without any suggestion from motion pictures.   If anything, the films are helping to combat crime.   The average person with criminal tendencies views an underworld picture almost with a sense of participation.   It provides him with an outlet for those tendencies.   He takes a vicarious thrill in living with the film criminal and goes away from the theatre satisfied." [12]

In 1935, Dr. Raymond Moley, Professor of Public Law in Columbia University and for many years involved in the work of crime commissions and crime surveys, expressed his expert opinion in an address directed to the problem "Do the Movies Teach Crime?" [13]   He first pointed out that "there is a very, very great difference of opinion, even among the so-called experts on the subject, as to the effect of motion pictures on crime." In the light of his own reading of the technical literature on the subject, he questioned "whether modern psychology has discovered an adequate and accurate formula to justify specific determination of what is the motive power that lies behind crime and anti-social conduct."   He concluded that "in any balance sheet on the subject the overwhelming evidence is present that there are more factors in the motion picture situation that tend to the repression and elimination of crime than to the other side."

All of this so far is the expression of personal opinion, expert or otherwise.   But the use of questionnaires has succeeded in eliciting and gathering the opinions of many ordinary observers and in this way indicating the consensus and direction of common opinion.   Common opinion seems to move in opposite directions.   On the one hand, Mr. Babson reported that of a group of public-school principals from whom he solicited replies to the question of what was the chief influence upon character and conduct, 70% answered "the movies," rather than church, school or home.   On the other hand, of 109 answers to a similar questionnaire sent out by a psychologist, 70 voted for the home and 37 for the school.   It is certainly difficult to say what such returns indicate.   Of greater significance is the report of the Indian Cinematograph Committee in 1928.   They questioned the police officials of the Indian Government in the light of a statement by the London *Times* that there was "definite proof

[12] Reported in the New York Morning Telegraph, April 14, 1931.
[13] Delivered before the Motion Picture Club of New York, March 11, 1935.

that the abduction by natives of an officer's wife was suggested by a serial film in which scenes of violence occurred." They sought in vain for any evidence to this effect. "The responsible police authorities of the Northwest Frontier Province, the province no doubt alluded to, laughed the tale to scorn. In fact every responsible police officer in every province assured us that in their judgment the cinema had had no effect whatever on crime or its methods. A person with criminal propensities might, they admitted, occasionally get an idea from a film, but given those propensities, his natural abilities or observations would be much more likely to be a source of action. There is little doubt that sometimes prisoners untruthfully plead the influence of the cinema as an extenuating circumstance, in this country as in others, and this makes a good headline for the sensational press. A Bombay trade witness actually showed us a headline in a local paper attributing a crime to cinema influence, although the body of the report contained nothing whatever to justify such an attribution." [14] Whether or not the police evidence is, as the Committee holds, conclusive on the point that the movies are not a cause of crime, the evidence does express a consensus of what in this case is expert opinion of a sort. Furthermore, the observation which the Committee makes about the unreliability of statements by prisoners about the influence of the movies on their criminal careers is worth noting because, as we shall presently see, a great deal of the so-called scientific evidence which Professors Blumer and Hauser have collected is of this kind. The naïveté of social scientists in accepting and accrediting the tales of criminals contrasts sharply with the more critical judgment of men of experience.

The foregoing is a fair sample of the field of opinion about the movies and crime, by no means exhaustive but certainly typical. Opinions bearing on the influence of the movies with respect to juvenile delinquency have been omitted. They will be reported in the next chapter. It should be said here, however, that those who charge the movies with being a cause of crime tend to emphasize their effects upon juvenile behavior, on the assumption that the delinquents of today are the criminals of tomorrow.

[14] *Report of the Indian Cinematograph Committee*, Madras, 1928 : p. 113. Cf. P. F. Cressey, *The Influence of the Motion Picture on Students in India* in the American Journal of Sociology, Nov., 1935, pp. 341-350.

This summary of opinion calls for little comment. There are conflicting opinions on all points. Taking the opinions at their face value, a balance is struck. Those which are negative are no better than those which are affirmative. But some of the negative opinions indicate a skeptical temper which is justified by the best analytical insights into the problem of the causes of crime: first, that we do not know the causes of crime, and second, that no single environmental factor, nor any combination of them, can be the *sufficient* cause of criminal behavior since such behavior is for the most part voluntary and involves the conflict of reason and appetite. On exactly the same grounds, it can be denied that poverty is a sufficient cause of crime, or slums, alcohol, drugs, newspapers, prisons, etc. Aspects of particular environments may constitute the conditions under which particular individuals behave criminally, but it must always be remembered that other individuals under the same conditions do not act criminally. Even if it were admitted that scenes of criminal activity in the movies, or sensational reports of actual crimes in the press, instructed individuals with criminal propensities in the manner or techniques of crime, it could hardly be said that these factors caused their criminal propensities or their ultimate choice to commit crimes rather than obey the law.

Those opinions which rest upon supposed correlations between attendance at movies and crime rates not only fail completely to understand the aetiological problem, but are thoroughly uncritical in their use of crime rates and in their interpretation of statistical correlations of this sort. The negative correlations which Dr. Hoffman found must not be interpreted as showing definitely that the movies are not a cause of crime. The importance of the negative correlation in this country, the significance of England as a negative case, is primarily a showing that crime rates cannot be significantly used. Dr. Sellin's analysis of the inadequacy and incomparability of existing crime rates makes critical points which hold against all the "statistical arguments," both *pro* and *con*.

But it may be said in the case of the movies that scientific research has lifted us above the level of conflicting opinions, and that the prudent man has been given sufficient knowledge upon which to act. Let us, therefore, examine the findings of science with regard to the movies and crime. Because the study, made by Professors Blumer and Hauser, of the Department of Sociology of the University of Chicago,[15] includes both crime and delinquency, it will be necessary for us to transgress our scheme of discussion and consider both adults and children at this point.

(c) *Scientific research.*

The problem which Blumer and Hauser set for themselves was : to determine (1) the role of motion pictures in the lives of delinquents and criminals of both sexes, (2) the effects of motion pictures on the inmates of correctional schools, reformatories and penitentiaries, (3) the effects of crime pictures on non-delinquent boys and girls. The data they gathered consist of autobiographies, some of them written under the guidance of the investigators, and answers to questionnaires. In the opening chapter, they state the numerical extent of their materials in the following manner. In connection with the first problem, they obtained 110 questionnaires, 258 brief essay documents and 40 motion-picture life histories from about 300 young criminals between 16 and 24 years of age ; they obtained autobiographies from 55 ex-convicts, many of them on parole, and most of them between the ages of 25 and 30 ; they obtained 252 schedules, 118 brief essays and 50 life histories from about 300 girls and young women delinquents, ranging from 12 to 28 years of age ; they obtained life histories from 20 girls in a truant and behavior-problem school, between 10 and 15 years of age ; they obtained stenographic interviews with 42 delinquent boys from 13 to 15 years of age and from 18 delinquent girls from 14 to 17 years of age ; they obtained questionnaires and essays from 184 school boys and 146 school girls in a high-rate delinquency area, from 181 boys and 208 girls in a medium-rate delinquency area, and from 75 boys and 81 girls in a low-rate delinquency area, all in the city of Chicago ; they obtained similar materials from 139 boys in a truant school and from 90 delinquent and non-delinquent boys in a high-rate delinquency area in Chicago. I have not stated all the details, nor shall I report the enumeration of the materials gathered in connection with the other two problems. I have bothered to make the foregoing enumerations from the opening chapter of this book because they tend to give the

[15] *Movies, Delinquency and Crime,* The Macmillan Company, Publishers, New York, 1933.

reader an impression of a vast amount of data. It is surprising therefore to see this statement in the last chapter of *Movies, Delinquency and Crime*: "Our sample of autobiographical and interview materials was unavoidably less extensive than originally intended."[16]   And relegated to a footnote we find: "Ninety motion picture life history documents from boys in a high-rate delinquency area, 40 from male inmates of a state reformatory, 20 from female inmates of a truant and behavior-problem school, and 55 from ex-convicts were obtained. These, together with 42 stenographic interviews with delinquent boys and 18 with delinquent girls; 258 brief essays from male convicts and 118 from female inmates comprised all our personal account material. Some of these were too incomplete to be of much value."[17]   The confession of this footnote in a concluding chapter is an interesting commentary on the scientific method of stating the *intentions* of one's research in the opening chapter.

Let us now consider the reliability and significance of the data in the light of the methods used to obtain the raw materials. The authors frankly tell us that they did not use "more sophisticated and refined techniques of research" because in their opinion they were not suited "for the exploratory work which our study required."[18]   It should be remembered later that they describe their research as exploratory. Exploration, as I understand its meaning in scientific research, is an initial effort in a field of phenomena to determine the formulation of problems for further research. It will be surprising therefore to find Blumer and Hauser reporting definite conclusions as the result of exploratory research. But these investigators go even further in their confession of inadequacy. I quote in full: "A word of caution should be given about the significance of the statistical data present in this report. These statistical data are based on questionnaire tabulations and must be interpreted with great care. *They should not be taken as definitely proved measurements of different forms of motion-picture influences but rather as rough approximations suggestive of a likely extent of such influences.*" (The italics are by Blumer and Hauser, but I

---

[16] P. 197, by permission of The Macmillan Company, Publishers.
[17] *Op. cit.*, p. 197, footnote, by permission of The Macmillan Company, Publishers.
[18] *Op. cit.*, p. 2, by permission of The Macmillan Company, Publishers.

should like to double the underlining of such words as "definitely proved," "rough approximation," "suggestive," "likely extent.") "As opposed to the life-history data, the questionnaire responses are in the nature of *opinion* and *judgment* and are subject to the uncertainty and instability which attends such kinds of response." (Here the italics are mine.) "We have sought to guard against this uncertainty by presenting tabulated results usually only where our autobiographical materials show clearly the existence and nature of a given type of motion picture influence. Even here, however, they may convey a false sense of accuracy, so the reader is again reminded to regard them merely as distributions of replies roughly suggestive of the extent of different kinds of motion-picture influences. Finally, it is perhaps necessary to caution the reader to guard against interpreting these percentages as applicable to the general population and to remind him that they apply only to the population types sampled." [19] No clearer confession of the statistical worthlessness of data could possibly be made. One wonders, therefore, why scientists should present such utterly meaningless tabulations and insignificant percentage figures, particularly since they seem to be aware of the dangers of misinterpretation and the "false sense of accuracy" that is likely to result. The "statistical lie" may be pardonable as a rhetorical device; but it should be avoided by scientists who certainly must know that their preliminary cautions will not guard against the illicit rhetorical effect of figures presented in the body of the text.

The authors are right. Their materials have no statistical significance whatsoever. We shall, therefore, ignore the numbers which they nevertheless continue to cite, and examine the raw materials to see if they permit any definite interpretation. But, first, we must consider the reliability of the materials. Can they be taken on their face value? Blumer and Hauser admit that questionnaire responses are in the nature of opinions. As used in this research, the questionnaire is a device for collecting the *opinions* of criminals and delinquents on the subject of what influenced their anti-social behavior. Since questions are asked about the movies, it is natural for opinions to be expressed on this point, both affirmative and negative; whether or not subjects questioned would have any opinion about the influence of the

[19] *Op. cit.*, pp. 9–10, by permission of The Macmillan Company, Publishers.

movies were they not so interrogated, is difficult to say. The questionnaire method, employed in the manner of Blumer and Hauser, is notoriously unreliable, even in the circles of social science. Professor Blumer himself admits, in reporting another piece of research in which he eschewed the questionnaire method, that questionnaires are unreliable because they solicit arbitrary answers.[20] In another one of the Payne Fund studies, we find Renshaw, Miller and Marquis completely dismissing this method. Their problem was simpler than Blumer's and Hauser's. They were trying to find out the effect of movies on children's sleep, but they concluded after "considerable time interviewing children, that very little reliable evidence as to the influence of movies can be obtained from this procedure."[21] How much less reliable, then, are answers to questions about the influence of the movies on prior conduct. Carry this one step further to the point that the persons interrogated by questionnaires were mainly criminals and delinquents. Is the moral character of a delinquent or criminal such that one would naturally expect honest and dependable answers to questions, particularly if the questions can elicit only vague opinions?

Blumer and Hauser consider their autobiographical materials, their so-called motion-picture life-histories, more reliable. They say, in conclusion, that "although for purposes of investigation reliance on accounts of personal experience is, in general, a controversial matter, it seems quite clear that the objection is not of great import as regards this investigation."[22] The reason they give is that they took precautions of the following sort: they gained the confidence of their subjects, they stressed the impartial

[20] *Movies and Conduct*, New York, 1933: p. 8. This is not the only or greatest defect of the questionnaire. The reliability of answers depends upon the veracity of the interrogated; but even supposing absolute veracity, the answers are unsupported personal opinions, the probability of which cannot be satisfactorily evaluated. The questionnaire merely collects *opinions*. The data it yields can be interpreted as representing the facts about opinions held by those questioned, but not as representing the facts which the opinions themselves claim to be about. This criticism applies not only to the questionnaire, but to all other social science techniques for eliciting opinions, such as the personal interview, the getting of autobiographical documents, whether guided or unguided by questions, etc.
[21] *Children's Sleep*, New York, 1935: pp. 146–147.
[22] *Movies, Delinquency and Crime*, p. 197, by permission of The Macmillan Company, Publishers.

character of the study, they called for concrete experiences in which movies were involved. But they are certainly naïve in supposing that such precautions avoid the unreliability which is intrinsic to materials of the sort they collected. They tell us, for instance, that "the informants were asked to avoid general statements and conjectures. Expressions of judgment or opinion were not accepted as valid data to show the influence of motion pictures." [23]   But if answers to direct questions about the influence of the movies are expressions of opinion, why are statements of the same sort made in the course of an autobiography any less opinion or conjecture? In a large part of the material quoted, we find statements of the sort "I *think* the movies. . . ." Such statements, Blumer and Hauser assure us, are introduced "into the text only when it is of interest to see what are *opinions* and *judgments* of delinquents and criminals." [24] This interest is, of course, irrelevant to the purposes of the research. Even where the autobiography contains statements which are phrased like statements of fact, taking the form, "The movies led me astray," the utterance is, of course, no less an expression of an opinion. Individuals do not *know* the causes of their own behavior. Any person of ordinary common sense realizes how conjectural must be any account of the influences which have operated to give his life the course it took. Yet these social scientists are willing to credit the life-stories of delinquents and criminals as revealing, by their own say-so, the major influences which lead them into their anti-social activities. Their naïveté goes even further. They point to the internal consistency of the story that is told as an index of its reliability, as if this tests anything but a mastery of the art of story-telling. They say: "We were especially fortunate in receiving the autobiographical material in the institutional situation. . . The inmate with time on his hands and the monotony of the routine to endure, frequently welcomed the opportunity to fill the schedule forms and write his motion picture experiences." [25]   Yes, and welcomed the opportunity to tell a good story in which the inmate is able to find some extenuation for his faults by placing the blame on forces outside himself, whose pawn he was. The movies are an excellent scapegoat and excuse. The report of the

[23] *Op. cit.*, pp. 7–8.   [24] *Op. cit.*, p. 8.
[25] *Op. cit.*, p. 6, by permission of The Macmillan Company, Publishers.

Indian Cinematograph Committee for this reason completely disregarded stories of this sort told by prisoners. They are not only too unreliable as opinion but too obviously motivated as rationalization.

Naïveté is not the only blemish on the method of this Payne Fund study. Many of the autobiographies were elicited by a schedule of guidance questions, given to the informant to direct him to specific topics and "concrete experiences." A large number of these questions are so patently leading questions that naïveté, no matter how enormous, cannot excuse them. I cite the following as examples: "Please write a page or two telling what you think is responsible for your getting into trouble. How important do you think the movies were in getting you into trouble?" [26] If the second question were not added, how many of these story-tellers would have thought about the movies? "Write about an experience in which the movies (a) tempted you to engage in crime or (b) caused you to imagine yourself being a bold gangster or burglar, or (c) led you to pull a job. (Give the name of the picture, or who was in it, what was it about, and what you did after you saw it.)" [27] Or, "Describe your feelings when you see crime pictures. Do you think such pictures are true to life? Do they give you new ideas on how to pull jobs and fool the police? Does the punishment given to criminals in such movies help to keep you away from pulling another job?" [28] And both of the following two directions are equally bad as leads, even though they are opposite in the effects of their suggestion: on the one hand, "tell if the movies you see here help you in any way to keep out of trouble after you get out"; and on the other, "tell if the movies you see here make you feel bitter toward society, make you feel that you have not had a square deal." [29] What is amazing about a procedure of this sort is the lack of psychological insight on the part of the investigators using it. If the way in which the movies are supposed to cause crime is by working upon the highly suggestible minds of persons of weak character and criminal propensities, how can anyone who makes this supposition fail to

[26] *Op. cit.*, p. 210, by permission of The Macmillan Company, Publishers.
[27] *Op. cit.*, p. 221, by permission of The Macmillan Company, Publishers.
[28] *Op. cit.*, p. 229, by permission of The Macmillan Company, Publishers.
[29] *Op. cit.*, pp. 218–219.

make the further supposition that the way in which such questions elicit answers is through similar processes of suggestion? If, instead of getting motion-picture life-histories, these investigators had been trying to study the effect of automobiles, the home, the church, the school, or anything else, upon criminal careers, and had constructed similar guidance sheets for the writing of autobiographies, they would certainly have obtained the same kind of results, equally unreliable, of course, as scientific data.

Blumer and Hauser offer one further check upon the reliability of their materials. They say: "There was no occasion for and no evidence of willful and conscious fabrication. As one indication of this, attention might be called to the fact that *the major portion of our material is negative in showing any influence on the delinquent or criminal behavior* of informants." [30]   (Italics mine.) In the first place, the fact that for the most part negative results were obtained is in no way an indication of the reliability of the results. That the investigators think so suggests the interpretation that they were aware that they asked leading questions, and hence they hoped that the getting of predominantly negative results would convince someone that their transgression of scientific method did not vitiate their data. But what is much worse, in the second place, is the statement they make two pages later: "Space limitation prevents the presentation of documents showing no motion picture influence. For purposes of maintaining perspective as well as for purposes of information, statistical data showing what proportion of the population acknowledge being affected by certain types of motion picture influences are included wherever possible." [31]   They have warned the reader that their statistical tabulations and percentage figures are untrustworthy as well as insignificant. And yet in their report of the raw materials, they give only the positive evidence. Even though the negative evidence is as intrinsically unreliable as the positive, what possible justification can there be for presenting the latter in a huge mass, and excluding the former entirely? In what sense could space limitations prevent the authors from presenting samplings of the negative and positive materials in their proper proportions, the negative in much larger bulk than the positive? If by the investigators' own statement the reader

[30] *Op. cit.*, p. 7, by permission of The Macmillan Company, Publishers.
[31] *Op. cit.*, p. 9, by permission of The Macmillan Company, Publishers.

learns that their data *seem to show* that the movies had very little influence on criminal and delinquent behavior, why is the reader taken through page after page of case histories that *seem to show* the opposite? [113] These questions are embarrassing. Instead of answering them, let us turn now to the findings and conclusions as Blumer and Hauser state them, remembering throughout that the conclusions are based upon data that are statistically insignificant and intrinsically unreliable, at best a record of mere opinions. In surveying their conclusions, we shall note the series of restrictions they impose upon their findings, until finally they are left with no definite conclusion at all.

They admit that motion-picture experiences are never the sole factor. "It is scarcely conceivable," they say, "that any instance of criminal behavior could be traced to a single factor."[32] Finding only 10% of 368 male criminals reporting that motion pictures had *some* direct effect on their criminal careers, they suggest that the motion picture is more influential indirectly. But they find a much larger proportion of criminals reporting no indirect influence than the proportion of those who reported some. They interpret this finding as follows: "One cannot declare with certainty that phantasy or daydreaming of this sort" (occasioned by witnessing motion pictures) "induces one to crime. Yet it is not unreasonable to *presume* that it *may*, and *perhaps* does. The belief by some criminals that their criminal phantasies have something to do with their careers *suggests* the *likelihood* of a similar relation in the case of others, even though it may not be consciously observed by them."[33] (Italics mine.) This indicates that when Blumer and Hauser are not satisfied with what their biographical materials report, they feel entitled to read between the lines. They conclude: "The fact that the number of delinquents and criminals who speak of having imagined themselves in criminal roles exceeds those who feel that the movies have had something to do with their criminal acts suggests, in the light of our discussion, an indirect and undetected effect of the movies in their cases."[34] This is typical of their reasoning in other places. The fact that some individuals *feel* certain causal relationships between the

[32] *Op. cit.*, p. 35.
[33] *Op. cit.*, p. 62, by permission of The Macmillan Company, Publishers.
[34] *Op. cit.*, p. 63, by permission of The Macmillan Company, Publishers.

movies and their criminal careers, *suggests* that it *may* exist in
the cases of those who do not have the feeling. At the end of
the chapter dealing with the indirect influences they say : "While
this indirect connection is not proved conclusively, we have
sought to show through the use of our materials that the presumption of such a connection is large." [35]   To make this point
clear they then summarize their findings numerically in percentage figures which are viciously misleading as well as totally
insignificant in the absence of satisfactory control groups which
might show similar percentages for non-criminal and non-
delinquent individuals. We are asked to accept the likelihood
of this presumption because "there are always a *few* delinquents
and criminals who can trace in their own experience a connection between such influences and their own crime. What presents itself as a conscious connection to some, *may* exist as an
unconscious connection in the experience of others." [36]   (Italics
mine.) *And may not!*

All through these pages in which case histories are reported,
figures cited, and similar may-or-may-not conclusions drawn,
there is no recognition on the part of the investigators that they
are proceeding without control groups.[37]   For all they know, if
non-delinquents and non-criminals were made to write their
autobiographies under the same type of guidance, they *might*
find exactly the same kind of items reported as having been im-
pressive in or memorable from the motion pictures they had
seen. One would then be entitled to presume that there *may* be
an unconscious connection in their lives between motion pictures
and law-abiding behavior, or perhaps the opposite — *maybe* they
were law-abiding in spite of motion pictures. We shall later
report, in connection with juveniles, evidence of this sort obtained from control groups of boy and girl scouts, showing that

[35] *Op. cit.*, p. 70.
[36] *Op. cit.*, p. 72, by permission of The Macmillan Company, Publishers.
[37] The one exception consists of biographical documents obtained from 203
young high-school boys and 255 young high-school girls. This is the material
used by Professor Blumer in his other study, *Movies and Conduct*. It is
presented in the present volume entirely in Chapters VII and VIII, and is
inadequate as control data for the percentages offered in earlier chapters.
In so far as it shows anything at all, it suggests that differences in the documents reflect gross differences in environmental background.

for the most part boy and girl scouts react to the movies as do boy and girl delinquents.

Considering the admitted worthlessness of their statistical data and the admitted unreliability of questionnaire responses, how are Blumer and Hauser able to conclude the chapter on female delinquents with the statement: "It seems clear from the statistical data and from the autobiographical accounts" (although most of the evidence in this chapter was obtained by questionnaires) "that motion pictures are of importance, both directly and indirectly, in contributing to female delinquency."[38]   On the other hand, although the materials they present are statistically no better or worse, no more or less reliable, they are able to conclude the chapter on the deterrent and reformative influences of motion pictures with such statements as: "The materials which we have presented in this chapter make it clear that the deterrent influence of motion pictures on crime is not definite or consistent"[39] and "Here it suffices to call attention to the inconsistent and indecisive character of motion pictures as an agency of deterring observers from engaging in delinquency or crime."[40]   But the evidence is no more indefinite, inconsistent and indecisive here than in the preceding chapters which concluded with relatively definite statements about the rightness of presuming an effect of the movies in causing crime.   The evidence throughout the book is on the same level, and at any point Blumer and Hauser could conclude either way in their delightfully tentative and suggestive manner.   It is interesting, therefore, that they go in one direction when the question is whether the movies cause crime and in the opposite direction when the question is whether the movies prevent crime.

Blumer and Hauser solicited opinions from the heads of 122 penal and correctional institutions.   Of these, 48% maintained that the ordinary run of movies are *likely* to lead *some* to lives of delinquency and crime; 25% felt that they were not likely to; 27% expressed no opinion.   They find it interesting to quote *only* from the answers of those who expressed an affirmative belief; and then add: "We are making no evaluation of the judgments of these prison wardens or heads of correctional institu-

[38] *Movies, Delinquency and Crime*, p. 112, by permission of The Macmillan Company, Publishers.   [39] *Op. cit.*, p. 133.   [40] *Op. cit.*, p. 134.

tions." [41]   They find, in another chapter, that individuals are differently influenced by the movies according to the differences in many other of the environmental conditions of their lives. But they do not see any significance in this fact, that delinquent children may be affected by movies differently from nondelinquent children, which might require qualification of their other findings.

Finally, we come to the summary conclusions of the study. "It seems clear that the motion pictures were a factor of importance in the delinquent or criminal careers of about 10% of the male and 25% of the female offenders studied." [42]   "On the other hand, movies may redirect the behavior of delinquents and criminals along socially acceptable lines and make them hesitant about, and sometimes deter them from the commission of offenses." [43]   These two conclusions, it should be noted, are the same as the conflicting opinions which prevail in the community, without the benefit of scientific research.   Since the percentages are unreliable, scientific research adds nothing but rhetorical force to the opinions which ordinary men hold.   "It is evident," the scientists are at last able to say, "that motion pictures *may* exert influences in diametrically opposite directions. . .   They *may* direct the behavior of persons along socially acceptable lines or they *may* lead, *as has been indicated*, to misconduct. They *may* be, therefore, an agency of social value or of social harm.   As the former they raise no issue, as the latter they raise problems of social control." [44]   (Italics mine.)   But they do not raise a practical problem for social control so long as we can only say "may."   This elaborate and costly piece of scientific research does not in the least lift us above the level of conflicting opinions.   The position of the prudent man remains unchanged.

As I have said before, research of this sort does not warrant the amount of critical attention I have given it [114].   It could be dismissed in terms of the authors' direct or implied admissions of the inadequacy of their method, the unreliability of their raw materials and the insignificance of their numerical data.   But there are good reasons for exhibiting this piece of research in

[41] *Op. cit.*, p. 148.   [42] *Op. cit.*, p. 198.   [43] *Op. cit.*, p. 199.
[44] *Op. cit.*, pp. 201–202, by permission of The Macmillan Company, Publishers.

such a way that all of its defects are plain to anyone. For one thing, the work of Blumer and Hauser has been cited by laymen who are bent upon reform, as a *scientific* demonstration that the movies are a cause of crime.[45] For another, this type of work is considered creditable by some social scientists.[46]

The time devoted to this piece of work is justified because it is one of the Payne Fund studies and is typical of some, *although not all*, of the other contributions to this elaborate research project. Professor W. W. Charters, Director of the Bureau of Educational Research of Ohio State University, and Chairman of the Committee on Educational Research of the Payne Fund speaks for the research project as a whole. It is interesting therefore to note his comments on the Blumer and Hauser report. He refers at a number of places to the massive and significant data they assembled.[47] He says, as if it were a valid and unambiguous conclusion, that "crime pictures have a pronounced effect upon delinquents."[48] He plays up the learning of specific techniques of crime, and adds: "To be sure, the delinquent might have learned these techniques without the movies. We had delinquency before commercial motion pictures were invented. But crime movies are handy, and it is easy to learn from them if one is

---

[45] As Professor Moley said, in the paper already cited (fn. 13 *supra*), this pseudo-scientific research "should be very carefully examined before those leaders of opinion who do the talking in the world accept it as authentically scientific. The value of the conclusions made on the basis of such research as a guide to the ordering of the world is proportionate to the common sense and the disinterestedness of the individual who makes the study." Consider, for example, the fact that Mr. Henry James Forman addressed the Governor's Conference on Crime, held at Albany in 1935 and made much of the massive scientific work of the Payne Fund studies as a cause for alarm. Vd. *Proceedings of the Governor's Conference on Crime, the Criminal and Society*, Albany, 1935 : pp. 306–312.

[46] Vd. a review of ten Payne Fund studies by Professor Kimball Young in the American Journal of Sociology, Sept., 1935, pp. 249–255 ; and also one by Professor Sidney Pressey in the Educational Research Bulletin, April, 1936, pp. 111–114, 122.

[47] *Motion Pictures and Youth : A Summary*, The Macmillan Company, Publishers, New York, 1933 : p. 5. Here he refers to a study by Cressey and Thrasher, *Boys, Movies and City Streets*, which has not yet been published. Elsewhere (pp. 10, 12–13), he cites the findings of this unpublished research. Forman also includes the Cressey and Thrasher study in his popular summary. [48] *Op. cit.*, p. 54.

interested in delinquent behavior. One's education in crime advances more rapidly by means of crime pictures." [49] He plays up the more lurid case-studies of sexual delinquency. He nowhere mentions that the greater part of the biographical materials constituted a massive negative finding, showing no influence of the movies on crime and delinquency.[50] He makes no criticism of the methods of this research; he does not indicate the extent to which the materials are unreliable; he does not report the authors' own confession of the statistical insignificance of their numerical data; he says only: "Granted that reports from delinquents are *not completely reliable*, the fact still remains that enough of them can quote chapter and verse to show that crime and sex pictures are at least an aggravating influence in their conduct." [51] (Italics mine.) Worst of all—since Charters has undertaken to summarize all the Payne Fund studies—is his failure to cite the findings of other research which are inconsistent with the report on *Movies, Delinquency and Crime*, particularly the finding by Blumer himself in *Movies and Conduct* that for the most part the influence of the movies is of extraordinarily slight duration.[52] This, and May and Shuttleworth's finding that for the most part there is little difference between the social conduct and attitudes of movie fans and the social conduct and attitudes of others,[53] would seem to qualify the significance of even the few cases in which Blumer and Hauser found criminals and delinquents reporting that they *believed* that the movies influenced them in their behavior.

It may be that Professor Charters can be criticized only for having the same remarkably low standards of scientific work which prevail throughout our university schools of education, psychology and social-science departments. Thus, we find Professor Kimball Young, of the Department of Psychology in the University of Wisconsin, referring to these Payne Fund studies as constituting "one of the finest pieces of research done in studying the problems of personality and conduct that have been pro-

---

[49] *Op. cit.*, p. 54, by permission of The Macmillan Company, Publishers.
[50] "The major portion of our materials is negative in showing any influence of motion pictures on the delinquent or criminal behavior of informants" (Blumer and Hauser, *Movies, Delinquency and Crime*, p. 7).
[51] *Op. cit.*, pp. 54–55.   [52] Discussed in Chap. 11 *infra*.
[53] Discussed in Chap. 11 *infra*.

duced in this country. It is a real contribution to the study of moral problems today." [54]   The rigor of Professor Young's standards can be tested by the kind of examination we have made of Blumer and Hauser's work and which we shall make of all the others.   Professor Young goes on to say: "The writers of these monographs are all very cautious in their conclusions and their interpretations.   They are all aware that the movies are but one of the many influences playing upon children and adults, and most of the writers are aware also that it is difficult to say what precise influence on conduct, ideas and attitudes the movies have, when we come down to concrete cases.   What does a particular movie do to particular children?   Not one of the studies can answer that question because we do not know."   It is amazing that Professor Young thinks so well of research which does not answer such questions definitely.   But what is even more amazing, particularly in the light it throws upon the Payne Fund project, is that Professor Charters does not share the estimate which so sympathetic a colleague as Professor Young makes of Henry J. Forman's book *Our Movie Made Children*.[55]   Professor Young said: "Unfortunately for science and also for the ultimate good effect of these and like studies upon improvements of the movies, the reformers who sponsored this research were not satisfied with these cautious and milder reports.   They evidently wanted to shock the American people into a realization of the seriousness of the movies in relation to American children. They therefore turned these reports over to a free-lance writer named Henry James Forman, who dressed them up in rather sensational terms in a book called 'Our Movie Made Children.' This book was published in May, 1933, some months before any of the separate monographs or reports of the research were made available.   It seems to me that this publication, by an apparently prejudiced writer, had the effect of giving a totally false impression to the American public regarding the findings of the research

[54] In an address before the Wisconsin Federation of Women's Clubs at Madison, October 10, 1934.   This sentiment is echoed with slight *pianissimo* in his later review of the Payne Fund series (*loc cit.*, fn. 46 *supra*).   Professor Pressey in his review of the series (*loc. cit.*, fn. 46 *supra*) says: "The total investigation would seem the outstanding example to date of the application of methods from the experimental sciences to a large social problem — a milestone in the progress toward a real social science."

[55] The Macmillan Company, Publishers, New York, 1933.

workers. It was distinctly unfair to them and distinctly misleading to the American people. I think it was a rather serious
mistake to give the public such a biased view of the movies based
upon alleged scientific works, when the monographs do not
actually support the treatment in this popularized account." [56]
Professor Young substantiates his charge by citing a number of
the worst distortions and misrepresentations in Forman's book,
showing the way in which Forman omits the contradictory
evidence and reports tentative and ambiguous findings as if they
were definite and clear.

What then does Professor Charters, the responsible head of
the Payne Fund research, say of Forman's journalistic efforts?
I quote from his Introduction to *Our Movie Made Children*:
"To Mr. Forman was entrusted the task of preparing a popular
summary, and I was charged with the responsibility of attesting
the accuracy of the scientific findings as set forth in this book. I
have examined Mr. Forman's manuscript. He shows a thorough
grasp of the facts in the complicated materials presented in the
nearly three thousand pages which constitute the report of the
twelve studies. His interpretation of the studies, however, his

---

[56] Professor Kimball Young again felt it his duty to attack the Forman book
in his review of the Payne Fund series (*loc. cit.*, fn. 46 *supra*). There he
said : "When we turn from these carefully conducted studies and their
cautious interpretations to the sensationalism of Forman's summary and reinter-
pretation, we are struck by the sharp contrasts in tone, in emphasis, and in the
special pleading of the author, who was asked to make this summary for
popular consumption. In fact, the contrast of his discussion with that in the
original monographs at many critical points is so great and the apparent public
acceptance of his book as an authoritative review of the original findings is
so evident that we have here a good case of the psychology of myth-making
itself. His volume is in fact a form of propaganda evidently stimulated by
those supporters of the original research project who felt that motion pictures
constitute a serious menace to public and private morals. The upshot of the
matter is that Forman has tended to select only those features of the reports
which give grounds for a mass movement to reform the movies. . . Whereas
most of the writers of these monographs have been careful not to claim too
much for their findings, the author of this popular account of their results
has done them personally and the fields of psychology, education and sociology
a genuine disservice. And we are now witnessing, partly as a result of this
sort of misinterpretation or partial interpretation, a wave of sentiment against
the movies which is likely to prove a boomerang when all the factors making
for change in conduct are better known and understood by the man on the
street" (pp. 254–255). This quotation and the one in the text are by permission
of Professor Young.

selection of illustrative material, his literary style, his dramatic and emphatic presentation are of necessity entirely his own." [57] Why does not Professor Charters, who must have been acquainted with the details of the research, detect what Professor Young sees so readily, that the Forman book is a journalistic exaggeration, in which scientific work — however poor in itself — "has been twisted and misinterpreted"? [58] Does not Professor Charters know what Professor Young does not hesitate to divulge, that many of the research workers themselves "feel firmly that they have been let down by such a book because of the creation of false ideas as to the nature of the work"? [59] Whatever be the answers to these questions, one thing is clear. Professor Charters does not object to Mr. Forman's "interpretation" of the studies, his "selection" of the materials, and his dramatic "emphases." His own summary is not free from these defects. [60] As I have shown in the case of Blumer and Hauser's work, and as I will show subsequently in the case of the other researches, such interpretation, selection and emphasis are not only thoroughly unjustified by the actual data, but are a clear manifestation of bias and prejudice unbecoming scientists and university professors unless social scientists are unwilling to impose upon themselves higher standards than those of sensational journalism [114a]. Professor Charters feels that he is justified by scientific research in referring to the commercial movies as "an unsavory mess." [61] The critical examination of this research not only shows him to be unjustified, but when the particular studies are reviewed critically, and the Charters summary and Forman popularization are included as parts of the Payne Fund report, these words become a boomerang. Our universities have an even

---

[57] Pp. vii–viii, by permission of The Macmillan Company, Publishers.

[58] Vd. *Our Movie Made Children*, pp. 197, 212, 232, 241, or better, all of Chapters 11–14, for examples of such distortion of the Blumer and Hauser study, as well as of others. [59] *Loc. cit.*, fn. 54 *supra*.

[60] Even though he is willing to praise the Payne Fund studies as "an excellent contribution to sociology and social psychology," Professor Kimball Young's review of the series is much more critical, careful, and impartial than Professor Charters' official Summary. The two should be closely compared. It should be noted, for instance, that Young definitely discriminates between the character of Blumer's work and that of other studies employing more precise methods. It should also be noted that Young nowhere in his review refers to the Charters' Summary.

[61] *Op. cit.*, p. 55.

greater responsibility than the movies to see that an unsavory mess is not perpetrated in the name of science and scholarship and for the sake of the public welfare [115].

2. WHETHER THE MOTION PICTURES HAVE CERTAIN OTHER EFFECTS?

We are here concerned with the charge that the movies corrupt character and demoralize public manners. Upon analysis, this charge was found to depend upon the following questions of fact and evaluation: [62] Do the movies influence adult conduct in definitely ascertainable ways? If so, are the resulting habits of social behavior in conflict with conventions which prevail throughout society or in particular social groups? If the movies are to any extent responsible for a change in moral standards and public manners, is the change for better or for worse? This last question requires that an evaluative judgment be made in terms of moral and political principles. It need not and should not be raised until it has been shown that the movies are in some degree responsible for an ascertainable change. We shall first survey the opinions which are in any way relevant to these questions, and then turn to the scientific investigations which try to answer them.

(a) *Affirmative opinion.*

In 1921, Mr. Arthur Weigall in an article on *The Influence of the Kinematograph upon National Life* [63] observed that standards of conduct change rapidly. With every generation they are different; what shocked one is commonplace to another. The films can do much, he said, to alter standards. The English should, therefore, be on their guard against American productions. They may influence English manners. He pointed out, for instance, that some American films reveal a failure to understand English habits of fair-play. This is typical of many similarly expressed convictions that the movies do influence standards and manners. Thus, in the same year, William Allen White is reported as saying that the movies influence the masses to an extent not equalled by the churches, schools and all similar institu-

[62] Vd. Chapter 6 *supra.*
[63] Nineteenth Century and After, April, 1921 : pp. 661–672.

tions. In 1925, Mr. C. K. Allen, in an article on *Movies and Morals*, did not hesitate to express the opinion that the movies subtly corrupt moral standards.[64] And in 1931, Mrs. Ambrose Diehl, Chairman of the Cinema Committee of the National Council of American Women, wrote that the movies endangered morals and culture by exaggerating sex, by confusing religious ideals and ethical standards, by weakening support for established institutions, by extolling excesses, by glorifying the material goal and standard for life.[65] In 1926, Canon William Sheafe Chase, Superintendent of the International Reform Federation, was reported as saying: The unregulated motion-picture screen "has ridiculed marriage and holiness of pure sex relations, the sacredness of the home and obedience to father and mother. It has advocated theft, gambling and disrespect for law. It has justified divorce, free love and violation of the Volstead Act, and of all laws."[66] In this period books were published with such titles as "The Devil's Camera: The Menace of a Film Ridden World";[67] churchmen and editors of religious papers, women's clubs and reform associations were heard on all sides calling for some regulation of the abuses which morals and culture, society and civilization were suffering under the influence of the movies. The tone of this attack is only slightly less expressive of violent alarm and slightly less vituperative than Gossen's attack upon the Elizabethan stage or Collier's onslaught on the Restoration comedy. This mass of opinion is so unanalytical and so unclear that it is impossible to tell whether the main objection is to sexual obscenity as offensive to the moral sensibilities of the audience or to the influence of the movies upon human behavior, and consequently upon customs and standards. If the former, the only question is whether those who complained spoke for themselves or for the audience; if the latter, it must be noted that no evidence of any kind was ever given to support the charge and that those who made it were in no sense qualified to speak as expert observers, or even as reporting common opinion.

Throughout these opinions about the movies as corrupting

---

[64] Quarterly Review, October, 1925 : pp. 313–330.
[65] International Review of Educational Cinematography, Dec., 1931 : pp. 1126 ff.
[66] Quoted by W. M. Seabury, *The Public and the Motion Picture Industry*, New York, 1926 : p. 157.
[67] By R. G. Burnet and E. D. Martell, London, 1932.

morals, the emphasis was upon the conventions of sexual behavior.   Crime, disrespect for law and other conventions, the goals of material success as opposed to spiritual welfare, received some attention, but the predominant complaint was that there was too much sex in the movies and that the way in which the movies treated sex and love had a bad effect.

(b)   *Negative opinion.*

In 1930, Dr. Kolsch, State Councillor of the Bavarian Government, is reported as saying: "We are at the present time convinced that films are for the most part an indispensable factor in the common weal.   I am of the opinion that if our century had not witnessed the triumphal application and spread of the cinematograph, and if technical skill had not attained to the heights to which American industry has carried it, the giddy and formidable routine of our modern life would have ended by stunting human emotions and would have so strained the nervous system of mankind that we might actually fear that, sooner or later, a sort of explosion would ensue, of such violence as actually to threaten the stability of society." [68]   This is a sample of opinion running to the opposite extreme.   It is only by implication an answer to the question whether the movies corrupt character and demoralize society.   In this connection, it has no greater weight as opinion than the affirmative opinions previously examined. Similar negative opinion is to be found in *The Film in National Life*, the report of an enquiry conducted in England by the Commission on Educational and Cultural Films, published in 1932.

In 1926, Mr. Aldous Huxley had deplored the effect of western films upon eastern audiences, and in 1927 the British Parliament in considering the problem of motion pictures throughout the Empire heard similar charges that India was being demoralized and that respect for western manners was being jeopardized. The Indian Cinematograph Committee's Report, published in 1928, answered these charges.   It expressed a consensus of common opinion about the effects of motion pictures upon adult Indian audiences.   It recognized, in the first place, that the cinema is primarily an instrument of recreation, distinguished from all others by its degree of popularity.   It denied, in the second

[68] International Review of Educational Cinematography, Jan., 1930 : p. 51.

place, that the supposed moral and social dangers existed to any
great extent or were serious.   "In the forefront of our report,"
the Committee wrote, "we desire to place our unanimous conviction that the general effect of Western films in India is not
evil, but, on the whole, is good." [69]   It should be remembered
that the Report is not the opinion of the Committee but is their
digest of the prevailing common opinion which they solicited by
means of questionnaires, or obtained by the direct interrogation
of witnesses.   They received 320 replies; they examined 353
witnesses.   They asked specific questions about the influence of
films upon morals and manners.   This Indian Report has something of the character of social-science research, but it does not
pretend to be more than a survey of opinion for the sake of giving the practical man some guidance.   It affords a striking contrast to similar American surveys of opinion which are published
as scientific research, and with which we shall presently deal.
The most important criticism of the films, in the opinion of the
Committee, was the charge of their demoralizing effect.   "When
we began our inquiry, some of us at least were inclined to consider that this criticism was well founded.   We found, however,
that it had almost invariably been expressed in general terms.
We accordingly set ourselves the task of trying to obtain from
witnesses definite instances of objectionable films, and of the
type of subject and scene which they considered objectionable.
We were surprised at our lack of success.   Many witnesses pred-
icated that the cinema was a demoralizing influence, but when
examined had to admit that they very seldom visited cinemas for
the very reason that they believed them harmful, inartistic or
boring.   Their logic is obviously vitiated by a *petitio princi-
pii*." [70]   After they discarded a large mass of ill-informed general
criticism, the Committee found "a considerable body of sober
opinion, both European and Indian, that the cinema unduly emphasizes the lower side of life and the cruder passions of mankind, and must therefore tend to lower morality and inflame the
passions." [71]   But when those who held such an opinion were
further questioned, and other aspects of the survey were completed, the Committee found it necessary to state that "we are
without exception satisfied that the overwhelming majority of
films certified for public exhibition in no way tend to demoralize

[69] *Op. cit.,* p. 2.   [70] *Op. cit.,* pp. 109–110.   [71] *Op. cit.,* p. 110.

the Indian public, or to bring Western civilization into contempt." [72]

One of the chief critical values of this Indian Report is the way in which its Committee uncovered the lack of information upon the part of those who made bold, broad charges. In 1926, the British Social Hygiene Council had sent a delegation to India to investigate the motion-picture situation. The opening paragraph of the Delegation's memorandum contained this striking pronouncement: "In every province and state visited by the Delegation, the evil influence of the cinema was cited by educationists and the representative citizens as one of the major factors in lowering the standard of sex conduct, and thereby tending to increase the dissemination of disease." [73] The Committee tried to discover the educationists or representative citizens who had expressed such views. All the witnesses they interrogated returned distinctly negative evidence. The British Social Hygiene Council was given an opportunity to support these charges, but declined to do so. The Committee was, therefore, forced to conclude as follows: "Frankly we cannot accept such *ex cathedra* statements, which are unsupported by evidence tendered to us by the makers or discovered by us in a lengthy and careful enquiry. Not only can we not accept them, but it appears obvious to us that they were made without any attempt at serious enquiry, and partly, at least, as a result of a pre-existing obsession. We greatly regret that such an institution as the Social Hygiene Council should, from whatever motives, have lent its authority to support statements which one witness, not without some justice, described as preposterous." [74]

This throws a great deal of light on the state of opinion in this field. If we have nothing better than opinion to go by, at least we should examine the information and experience, the prejudices and affiliations, of those who hold the opinion. The Indian Cinematograph Committee made a systematic effort in this direction. No analogous investigation has been made in this country by an official body. On the other hand, our social scientists have undertaken the task of giving us scientific knowledge about such matters, to save us from the currents of opinion. Let us see to what extent they have succeeded.

[72] *Op. cit.*, p. 111.   [73] *Op. cit.*, p. 116.   [74] *Op. cit.*, p. 117.

(c) *Scientific research.*

There are only a few investigations of the relation of motion pictures to moral standards and social conventions. Two of these were published in 1926 and in the Annals of the American Academy ; one by Professor H. B. Stephens, of the University of Tennessee, on *The Relation of the Motion Picture to Changing Moral Standards;* one by Professor Donald Young, of the University of Pennsylvania, on *Social Standards and the Moving Picture.* The third is one of the Payne Fund studies; it deals with *Motion Pictures and Standards of Morality* and is by Professor Charles C. Peters of the Department of Education of Pennsylvania State College.

To the question whether the motion picture is in any way responsible for changes in moral standards, Professor Stephens replies that "no competent observer will deny that certain changes in moral standards in the United States are to some extent linked up with moving picture exploitation." [75] He declines to say how important a factor the movie is or whether the changes occurring help or hinder social progress, however this is defined. But what is the evidence for his statement about the unanimity of competent observers, and what grounds does he give for thinking this supposedly unanimous opinion correct?   The only evidence cited is a few motion pictures the content of which Professor Stephens describes. In the *opinion* of Professor Stephens, the movies cited contain *bad* elements, and it seems to him an indisputable *fact* that they must have bad effects.   "Will anyone deny," he asks in one place, "that making questionable conduct attractive adds to its dangers?" [76]   And with respect to a story of Apache love, he asks: "Is it inconceivable that such vivid picturizations of sadistic, lustful abandon should stimulate young people to act anti-socially?" [77]   The level of such scientific work is hardly any better than the formulation of opinions by the British Social Hygiene Council.

Professor Young's article is of the same sort. He begins by criticizing the reformers for holding opinions about the motion pictures which either are not based upon sufficient evidence or rest upon evidence procured by unscientific means. What then is Professor Young's scientific evidence? It consists (1) of an examination of the titles of motion pictures, and (2) of the judg-

[75] *Loc. cit.,* p. 151. [76] *Loc. cit.,* p. 152. [77] *Loc. cit.,* p. 153.

ments about motion pictures reported by "trained observers,"
such as a group of 22 ministers who viewed 134 different films
and a Committee of the General Federation of Women's Clubs
who viewed 1765 films. What is the significance of the finding that the ministers judged 65 movies good, 31 bad, and 38
indifferent? Or that the representatives of the Women's Clubs
found 21% bad, 20% good, and 59% indifferent? Is this
evidence from which it can be concluded by scientific inference
that the movies do influence human conduct, and that the influence is socially undesirable? Professor Young seems to have no
hesitation in drawing this conclusion, because he has no hesitation in *assuming* that what is shown on the moving-picture
screen will have a character-molding influence on those who see
it. But this assumption begs the whole question to be investigated. Even if the assumption be granted — and unquestionably
it should not be — it would not follow that the "trained observers" cited by Professor Young were right in their judgments of
good and bad or that, even if they were right, the so-called bad
movies necessarily have a bad effect on character or conduct.
The data upon which Professor Young relies consist of nothing
but opinions, but in his concern to tell us how to improve the
movies and society he is not bothered by such inadequacies.
What we need are movies which will teach true social values,
and these must be scientifically determined. One gathers that
the State should take over the production of motion pictures,
and perform this task under the advice of a group of social
scientists.[78] This is a terrifying indication of the contemporary
mania for what is eulogized as science to replace common sense
and prudence in the conduct of public affairs. If the work of
Professor Stephens and Young is currently accepted as scientific
in any sense, and if it is by their methods that social standards
and public policy should be determined, the menace of social
science is obviously much worse than the movies could ever hope
to be.

Professor Peters' study has, on the surface at least, a much
greater claim to be regarded as scientific.[79] It does not *seem* to
be merely a collection of opinions and evaluative judgments.

[78] This proposal is made more explicitly in an earlier paper, *Motion Pictures:
A Study in Social Legislation*, Philadelphia, 1922.
[79] *Motion Pictures and Standards of Morality*, New York, 1933.

Professor Peters constructed an elaborate rating scale by which
to measure deviations from the currently accepted norms of social conduct and moral standards.   The statistical operations by
which this scale was constructed, and the further statistical operations involved in the use of it to measure described samples of
conduct, on the one hand, and scenes from motion pictures, on
the other, are of great technical subtlety.   Professor Peters used
the most highly prized techniques of contemporary educational
measurement, techniques which have made education scientific
in this country.   He frankly tells us of the difficulties he encountered and had to surmount in employing these devices; he
makes explicit the various assumptions without which his statistical procedures would be illegitimate, such, for instance, as the
assumption of a normal distribution of judgments of approval
and disapproval.   His work is open to inspection at every point
in procedure and method.   Whether or not it is at all points
above technical reproach, it is nevertheless a monument of labor
in the use of calculating machines and statistical formulae.   I
shall not bother to raise technical objections to his methods.
For the purposes of this analysis, I am willing to grant the reliability of his statistical data.   It is the interpretations which he
makes of these data that must be critically examined and, before
that, the basic assumptions which underlie the interpretations.

The problem which Professor Peters set himself was a measurement of the degree of divergence of motion pictures from
prevailing moral standards.   It should be noted at once that Professor Peters is not investigating the influence of motion pictures
upon prevailing standards and manners, yet we shall find him
making interpretations in that direction which are both illicit in
terms of his own data and inconsistent with his own assumptions.
Our first inquiry, however, must be into Professor Peters' notions
about morality.   Since this is to be an *objective* study, employing scientific methods of measurement instead of *a priori* principles, the traditional philosophical analysis of changing moral
standards as conventional determinations of universally accepted
principles must be disregarded.   Instead we find Professor Peters
turning to the *folkways* and the *mores* and, in general, to the
ideology of that great imaginative writer on human society, the
late Professor William Graham Sumner.[80]   The folkways are

[80] Vd. Chapter 1 on "Morality and the Mores."

the established social practices of any human group. When the folkways are explicitly recognized as means to the end of the social welfare, they become mores. The mores, as Professor Sumner said, are the social rituals in which we all participate, unconsciously, or consciously if we are philosophers trying to find the ethical generalizations as to societal welfare which are implicit in the prevailing customs. In either case, the mores are primarily the traditional customs of a social group which are supported by various kinds of sanctions. It is natural for the mores to differ from group to group, and from time to time ; and in the complicated structure of European society it is natural for one society to include subordinate social groups with conflicting mores. Only the mores which are supported by the sanctions of law, or in some cases created by law, are the explicitly recognized common customs of the society as a whole, although, of course, there may be many others. So far no serious objection can be taken to this description of human social life. But the next step which Professor Peters takes, and which defines not only the basic attitude of his book but also what he calls "the outlook of his age," [81] is a challenge to the fundamental truth of moral science as a branch of philosophy. Professor Peters says : "Now society's moral code is simply its system of mores. Morality is conformity to the mores ; immorality consists in failure to conform. There is, therefore, a difference between morality and fundamental rightness, if this latter means such conduct as an omniscient judge would prescribe as the 'best' way. Morality is always limited by the knowledge and the experience of the group. There is no certainty that what is 'moral' in this generation will continue to be so in the next generation. Perhaps it should not be. For morality should change as conditions change — a thing it stubbornly resists doing. Folkways are at their best when they continue changing so as to keep best adjusted to the changing situations with which they must cope, and morality is at its best when it lends sanctions to the most 'fit' folkways." [82]

In other words, there is no standard of right and wrong except conformity to the prevailing customs or mores. Only

[81] *Op. cit.*, p. 5.
[82] *Op. cit.*, p. 4, by permission of The Macmillan Company, Publishers.

God can judge the fundamental rightness of human actions. Human reason cannot distinguish between one set of mores as better or worse than another. What is morally good here and today may be morally bad elsewhere or tomorrow. One wonders, therefore, how Professor Peters is able to say that morality, that is, the mores, *should* change as conditions change, assuming, of course, that the use of the word "should" indicates a distinction between better and worse. One wonders how Professor Peters can talk about the folkways at their "best," and the goodness of morality being achieved when it lends sanctions to the "most fit" folkways. Either these are moral and political principles which are above the folkways and mores, unchanging with time, place, and particular societies, or they are just an expression of the mores of the particular European society to which Professor Peters belongs. As such they can have no status as principles by which to judge the mores of other societies. Professor Peters would then be violating what he would gladly recognize as his own ethnocentric predicament. But he seems to make the more radical choice; that is, of denying that there are any standards whatsoever which have a validity above the shifting mores. For he says: "It is our purpose in this study to learn whether motion pictures conflict with morality, as morality stands in our society. We are concerned to know whether the acts depicted in commercial motion pictures conform with the mores of our society. Or, if they deviate, we wish to learn at what points, in what direction, how frequently and how far. *This is evidently a very different thing from asking whether the movies are 'right' or 'wrong,' 'good' or 'bad.' This latter question the author, at least, is incompetent to answer because he is too much imbued with the outlook of his age.* Very few persons are competent to answer it, though many think they are. But we can set the whole problem of evaluating motion pictures in relation to morality in better perspective when we have before us detailed factual evidence as to where and how the movies deviate from present moral standards. Seeing just where these deviations lie and how great they are, we can then think on a factual basis about the question as to whether these deviations are *toward better* or *toward worse.* Perhaps we may even wish to lay these factual findings before a jury of far-visioned 'philosophers' and ask their verdict as to whether these tendencies seem to point *upward or downward*." [83]   (Italics mine, but the sarcasm of putting the word "philosophers" in quotes is Professor Peters'.)

It is clear, at once, that Professor Peters will be unable to remain consistent with the point of view he is trying to adopt. The question, whether the deviations are toward better or worse, are upward or downward, is meaningless on his assumption that morality is conformity to the mores.   Any deviation, in either direction, is immoral and "bad" in the only sense in which Professor Peters should be able to use the word.   He is not only inconsistent in his introductory chapter, but throughout the rest of the book this inconsistency arises again and again to vitiate the "objectivity" of his method and to confuse his "scientific conclusions" with "moral judgments" he has no right to make. The confusion and the inconsistency are unavoidable because the position which Professor Peters is vainly trying to take is an impossible one, is as obviously self-contradictory as any extreme skepticism.   It is not a new position, even though it is expressed in the language of Sumner and is the "outlook of this age," at least the outlook of American sociologists.   It is as ancient as the Greek sophists who tried to teach that all moral principles were merely formulations of the prevailing customs.   There are no standards of right and wrong, good or bad, they tried to say ; morality has no rational basis, it is entirely conventional and has only the sanctions of force which attach to such conventions. Plato completely refuted the sophists on this point, showing that their denial of morality, or their assertion that moral standards were absolutely arbitrary and conventional, amounted to a denial of man's rationality which is everywhere the same because human nature is everywhere the same.   To deny human reason and to hold that all propositions and judgments are merely expressions of opinion is impossible for anyone who is sensitive to the self-contradictions involved.   Aristotle went further and rescued the sophists from the error of their extremism, saving the truth that they perceived.   Moral and political principles, which are constituted by human knowledge in the practical order, are too general to govern action in particular societies under the particular circumstances of their time and place.   Men must make

[83] *Op. cit.*, pp. 4–5, by permission of The Macmillan Company, Publishers.

prudent determinations of these principles in order to apply them casuistically in particular cases. Such determinations are conventional in the sense that they are adapted to local conditions, but they are at the same time rational in the sense that they are made by prudence in the light of reason. Thus all human laws are in part conventional as particular determinations and in part natural as determinations made by reason. What is natural in all bodies of law is common to them; what is conventional about them differs from society to society and from time to time. Exactly the same analysis must be made of all other mores or customs not enforced as laws. They are in part natural and in part conventional. There are, therefore, moral and political principles in terms of which reason is able to criticize laws as just and unjust, human actions as right and wrong, social customs as better or worse. In another sense, however, one custom may not be better or worse than another; if alternative customs are viewed as determinations of right principles, it may be indifferent which convention is adopted.

In terms of Platonic and Aristotelian analysis, Professor Peters could formulate his problem intelligibly and consistently. He is enquiring, first, whether the movies deviate from the prevailing conventions of our society. Second, he should ask whether the deviations are merely in the direction of other conventions which are neither better nor worse as determinations of the basic principles of morality, than those conventions which now prevail. Third, there is the possibility, to be discovered by applying universal principles, that the deviations can be morally criticized as worse rather than better because in the direction of conventions which would be clearly less desirable than the accepted ones. These last two questions, however, cannot be answered by the so-called "objective methods" of scientific measurement to which Professor Peters so rigidly adheres. Professor Peters would have to become a philosopher, would have to recognize abiding moral principles above the shifting mores, and would have to evaluate the shifting mores by exercising prudence in the light of principles. This by his own confession and by the evidence of his work he is neither willing nor competent to do. He prefers to remain a sophist in the worst sense of that word, the sense in which to be sophistical is to be utterly insensitive to inconsistencies and self-contradictions, and which permits one to try to impose one's own poorly disguised moral judgments on others while at the same time holding that all moral judgments are only matters of opinion, except one's own.

The paradox of Professor Peters trying, on his assumptions and by his method, to improve the movies for the greater good of society is only part of the picture. It is not a pleasant spectacle. Sophistry unaware of itself never is. As we have already seen,[84] this paradox is the inevitable consequence of the revolt of the social sciences from moral philosophy while, at the same time, they continue to deal with moral problems. The attempt to equate the mores with morality is merely one expression of the rebellious anti-moral teaching of contemporary sociology and anthropology; the denial of rational, voluntary conduct is another. But the other part of the picture, the other side of the paradox, is even less attractive. There always have been sophists; they are perennially refuted only to arise again because they are untouched by any refutation which is *merely logical*. But the failure of a great tradition to sustain its intellectual posture is disheartening. That is what we find in the contemporary situation: Christianity facing the current instance of the traditional problem of the arts in society is unembarrassed to cite researches that rest upon assumptions utterly opposed to its most fundamental truths [116] — not only Christian churchmen, but moralists and reformers whose principles must ultimately be philosophical and who should therefore abominate sophists, even in the guise of social scientists. When Christianity loses its active dislike of heresy, it loses its dignity as a revealed religion and becomes no better than one among many warring creeds, as it was in the Hellenistic period. When philosophy ceases to be opposed to sophistry, it ceases to be. Yet in their preoccupation with what is *comparatively* a minor practical problem, contemporary churchmen, moralists and reformers have found heretics congenial and have tolerated sophists. I am not trying to invigorate a conflict between religion and science or philosophy and science. It is peculiarly a modern error to suppose that science as science can possibly conflict with either philosophy or religion. But when investigative science, natural or social, goes beyond its limited domain and becomes dogmatically anti-

84 Vd. Chapter 9 *supra*.

religious or anti-philosophical, this excess must be corrected
for the sake of maintaining the proper order and harmony of the
truths of religion, philosophy and science. It is necessary in order
to preserve the integrity of science itself. If contemporary
Christianity and contemporary reformers do not see that this
is their most important task, more important speculatively and
practically than the problem of the conflict between art and
prudence, then the great intellectual tradition of western Europe
is near its end.

It is certainly clear that Plato and Aristotle, St. Augustine and
St. Thomas and Bishop Bossuet, and even Jeremy Collier and
Rousseau, would deny the assumptions which underlie Professor
Peters' research as, excepting Rousseau perhaps, they would
root out the inconsistencies and sophistry which necessarily
follow. If we have attained their understanding of the problem of poetry and politics, we can see that they would find
Peters' statement of that problem thoroughly unintelligible.
Many Christians and Platonists of our day obviously do not
understand their own tradition, yet in their concern about the
movies, in the charges they make, they are certainly in the tradition of Platonism and Christianity. That morality is only conformity to the mores, which are products of irrational habit and
feeling and have no justification in absolute principles, is contrary to the revealed moral truths of Christianity and the
profoundest insights of natural wisdom. If the truths of Christianity and the truths of Greek philosophy, which gave rational
articulation to Christian doctrine, are to be defended against the
contemporary liberals who scoff at Greek wisdom and Christian
teaching as if they were outlived prejudices, to be dismissed as
the rationalization of outmoded mores, how much more important it is to defend philosophy and Christianity from sociologists
and educators like Dr. Peters. He, for instance, is the author of
a popular textbook of educational sociology. He is a teacher of
teachers. I do not know whether the movies through influences
more or less indirect corrupt youth and demoralize society, but I
do know, without the aid of research, that the profoundly anti-
moral and anti-Christian teaching of Professor Peters and all
others of his kind does corrupt youth and demoralize society to
whatever extent it is successful. Unfortunately even on this last
point there is little room for doubt. The sophistical teachings

of social science are terribly successful, if we can judge by the prevalence of the point of view which Dr. Peters shares with most of his colleagues in social science, and by the inroads of anti-intellectualism among the students and professors of our colleges and universities, and now increasingly even in our high schools. The corruption of students who have been indoctrinated by social science is plain to any teacher of philosophy. It permeates the entire scene of study, of scholarship and research. Its marks are evident in current legal teaching and research : law students smile at the mention of justice. It is no less evident in the humanities where aesthetics and criticism have been reduced to empirical psychology and the expression of unprincipled opinions. It is even manifest in the natural scientist's skepticism about morals. Such intellectual corruption is also moral, since the speculative and practical are aspects of the same truth. If the society in which we live is not already demoralized by the progressive corruption in our universities during the last half century, it will happen unless the tide is turned. No art, no matter how bad, could be so directly evil an influence as the kind of thinking and, consequently, teaching which Dr. Peters represents.

Let us, for the moment, forget Dr. Peters' assumptions and examine the method and findings of his research. He devised a method for measuring degrees of deviation from the mores, by having 187 individuals, comprising students and members of the faculty and their wives in his own institution, socially élite young women of New York and Baltimore, factory boys in Bridgeville, Pennsylvania, and factory girls in York, Pennsylvania, place brief verbally described bits of social conduct in three piles, according as they approved, disapproved or found such behavior indifferent or neutral. The items were classified in four categories according to the type of situation and conduct involved. As the result of statistical operations, he developed four scales in which each item was placed a measured distance above or below the indifferent point. He then had thirteen groups, each supposedly representing a different selection from the population in terms of age, race, locality, occupation, sex, etc., make similar ratings of the items in these scales. The purpose of this was primarily to test the reliability and consistency of the scales, although it also showed something about the uniformity of the

groups which Dr. Peters chose.   If he had made selections from
the population in terms of differences in moral character, if he
had sampled the radical and conservative elements in the community for instance, he might have discovered less uniformity in
his groups, and also less reliability and consistency in his scales.

He wanted to know more than the judgments of approval and
disapproval which such groups make.   In order to find out how
these approvals and disapprovals compared with the actual practices prevailing in the groups making such judgments, he asked
the members of some of the groups to make a second rating, this
time to mark the described conduct according as the majority of
their social group would do the same thing under similar circumstances or not.   After these various ratings had been made, Dr.
Peters had a small committee of judges rate particular scenes in
motion pictures, falling in one or another of the four categories,
according to the rating numbers for similar conduct on the scales.
It should be noted that the judges in this part of the work were
not the same individuals who were involved in the construction
and testing of the original scales.   Who they were we are not
told.   These judges were supposed to make a relatively simple
comparison of motion picture conduct with the rated specimens
on the scales.   The number assigned by them to a movie scene
was thus interpreted as a measure of the deviation of that scene
from the established mores; the pluses and minuses affixed to
these numbers indicated whether the deviation was in the direction of approved or disapproved conduct.   Again, Dr. Peters
tested these judgments for their statistical reliability and consistency and, satisfied with the soundness of his method and his data,
he was able to determine by the judgments of his committee what
he thought to be the degree and direction of deviations in motion pictures from the standards of morality.   One hundred and
forty-two feature films provided the primary materials upon
which these judgments were made.   There is no indication of
how these films were selected and whether or not their number
and character constitute a fair sampling of motion pictures.   It
is curious that an investigator who was so attentive to statistical
problems of reliability should have missed this point.

Before we examine the findings, a number of criticisms must
be made of Professor Peters' method on other than statistical
grounds.   In the first place, the samples of conduct which con-

stituted the rating scales are, for the most part, morally indifferent. What is described are customs which are the conventional determinations of moral principles, remote from these principles and for the most part neither better nor worse than each other as conventions. I am making this judgment as a person acquainted with the nature of moral principles and the criteria involved in the choice among conventions. It is no wonder that Professor Peters complains about the more intellectual among his respondents, whose replies were spoiled for his purposes because they tried to think before judging.[85] After reading the various samples which Professor Peters makes available in an appendix,[86] it is perfectly apparent that no intelligent person could possibly make a rational judgment of approval or disapproval with respect to most of them. As readily could one judge whether it would be better to regulate traffic according to the left or to the right side of the road. But Professor Peters tells us that he did not want rational judgments at all; according to him such judgments are not rational anyway, but idly speculative and rationalistic. What he wanted was emotional and impulsive expressions of approval and disapproval. Granted that he was fortunate enough in not having too many intellectually competent persons in his groups, persons who could not agree that morality was nothing but conformity to the mores, what is the significance of these emotional, impulsive and by definition non-rational approvals and disapprovals. Dr. Peters tells us that they are reliable indices of the mores; since the mores are supported by feeling, feeling is sensitive to deviations; anything which is other than the accepted practices that have become emotionally congenial is shocking, and the shock is registered in these expressions of approval and disapproval. But what, then, do approval and disapproval mean? Is not that which is rightly disapproved bad, and that which is rightly approved good? And must we not ask whether an evaluative judgment is right or wrong? Not on Dr. Peters' assumption that the only scientific meaning of good is conformity and the only scientific meaning of bad is deviation. To ask for judgments of approval and disapproval is, therefore, inconsistent with his own false assumptions.

Let us ignore this inconsistency for the moment. Since Dr.

[85] *Op. cit.*, pp. 44-45. [86] *Op. cit.*, Appendix A.

Peters did ask for judgments of approval and disapproval, the point I am making is that the materials he submitted for such judgment could not be intelligently so judged. If one examines the samples of conduct under the four heads — female aggressiveness in love-making, kissing and caressing, democratic attitudes and practices, and the treatment of children by parents — one finds that they are, for the most part, indifferent as conventional determinations of conduct. Thus, for instance, what is the moral problem involved in female aggressiveness in love-making, or in kissing and caressing? Ancient moral principles inform us that sexual intemperance and excess of sensuality are vicious. Christianity prohibits fornication and adultery. But whether or not women should be aggressive in courtship by one technique or another, whether the natural acts of kissing and caressing should be performed one way or another, is a matter of convention, *morally indifferent unless fundamental principles and rules are transgressed.*[87] Such conventions differ in different societies and at different times, and individuals may be called upon to say whether a given instance of such conduct does or does not conform to, or how closely it approximates, the prevailing convention — supposing there is one and not many. But if individuals approve and disapprove, they can do so intelligently only by applying moral principles to the conventions themselves. That the materials judged were for the most part conventional and indifferent and that the judgments were not supposed to be intelligent but expressions of passion and appetite, likes and dislikes, indicate the utter meaninglessness of Professor Peters' scales, except as statistical surveys of current unreasonable likes and dislikes. It should be noted in passing that of the four scales, the two on sexual behavior contain the least material capable of moral judgment. This is significant because it is his findings by the use of these scales, which color Professor Peters' conclusions and permit him to do a little moralizing on his own account.

In still another way, the procedure of this research violates the theory of the mores upon which it is based. The mores at any given time are the actual practices and customs of a society or a social group. If Professor Peters was interested in studying

[87] Cf. St. Thomas's moral discriminations of right and wrong sexual behavior in the Treatise on Temperance, *Summa Theologica* : II–II, QQ. 151–154.

the deviation of motion-picture conduct from the mores, his primary comparison should have been between some report of actual practices and a description of the content of motion pictures in the categories of such practices. If this were done well — and it is doubtful whether reliable descriptions and comparisons of this sort can be made — Professor Peters might have been able to discover whether the movies as fiction imitate human actions as they are, as they are said to be, or as they should be. As a matter of fact, he did try to do something of this sort by asking individuals to say whether the majority of the members of their social group actually did behave in a manner described. He nowhere doubts the accuracy and reliability of their reports. To suppose ordinary observers able to make such reports is to suppose that social scientists as observers of the mores have no special claims to competence. Whether or not that be the case, and whether or not the data on this point are reliable enough to be even worth considering, the finding is significant. For the most part, the mores, that is, the actual practices of the community were reported as being less admirable than those which the individuals representing a given social group approved. This indicates the anomalous character of the rating scales based on approvals and disapprovals. It indicates completely that the scales are in no sense expressions of standards which are moral *because in conformity to* the mores. Since the judgments were not made intelligently and in the light of moral principles, the scales cannot be taken as indices of rational moral standards. At best, they express what people in a community *feel* conduct should be. It is natural to find that they feel it should be better than it is, even though no reasons can be given for their feelings and no meaning can be given to *better* as applied to conventions that are morally indifferent.

In analyzing Professor Peters' findings to see whether any of his interpretations of the data are tenable, we must therefore keep the following points in mind. First, that whether the movies deviate from the mores must be judged in terms of a comparison of the movies with actual practices and not with ratings of approval and disapproval. Second, that popular reports of what the actual practices are in any community are untrustworthy, particularly if made in terms of so rough an estimate as what the majority do or do not do. Third, that in the light of such crude data, it is impossible to tell whether on any given point of conduct there is only one existing convention or many practices, and whether there are conflicting practices existing side by side in the same society. It is, therefore, impossible to say in any case what it is the movies deviate from. Finally, it is perfectly clear that the rating of movie scenes in terms of Professor Peters' scales, however accurately made, does not reveal any relationship between the movies and moral standards in any sense in which moral standards can be conceived, not even Professor Peters' own sense of conformity to the mores. The only interpretation that can be made of such ratings is to say whether the movies imitate actions as they are or as people *feel* they should be.

The findings are as follows. With respect to female aggressiveness in love-making, movie scenes are not as people feel they should be, that is, they receive ratings of disapproval. But, Professor Peters informs us, "so also does conduct as reported by our respondents" fall below the approval level "and to just about the same degree." [88] In other words, in this category the movies imitate human actions as they are, if the report of existing practices is reliable. It is interesting to detect Professor Peters trying to avoid this unavoidable interpretation of his data by defining the mores as "*approved* customs." [89] Only by such double definition, which violates his own assumptions, can he reach the conclusion that the movies fall below the prevailing "moral standards" in the matter of female amorous conduct. He saves himself from absurdity only by adding the comment that some people claim that art should imitate action as it should be, whereas others claim that it should imitate action as it is. He does not see, however, that there is no genuine issue between these two claims, nor does he realize that even if the movie scenes corresponded for the most part to the approved samples, they would not be imitating action as it should be in terms of rationally formulated moral principles, but only action as people *feel* without reason that it should be.

With respect to kissing and caressing, conduct in the movies "almost precisely parallels life, from the standpoint of both approvals and practices." [90] At one end, the movies are a little

[88] *Op. cit.*, p. 94.   [89] *Op. cit.*, p. 96.   [90] *Op. cit.*, p. 107.

"better" than practice according to the rating scales; at the other, they are a little "worse." Again it should be noted that Professor Peters feels called upon to ask "whether art is on a satisfactory basis when it merely parallels life, or whether it should have as one of its functions to set for us patterns of our better selves?" [91] Leaving aside for the moment the problem of the functions of art, what can Professor Peters mean by "our better selves"?

With respect to what Dr. Peters calls democratic practices, such things as treatment of employes and subordinates, and social, occupational or racial discriminations, conduct in the movies is clearly better than current practices as these are reported. Some people, says Dr. Peters, would disapprove of the movies for this reason, thinking that "movies tend to make the rank and file of common people dissatisfied with their station in life, less disposed to respect their 'betters' and less reverent toward the wealthy and elite"; [92] whereas others would praise the movies for stressing what they think is an ideal of human conduct.

With respect to the treatment of children by parents, conduct in the movies is even more clearly superior to actual practices according to the rating scales. Now by his own assumptions, Dr. Peters should condemn the movies in the fields of sexual behavior, since in the first two measurements the movies deviate from the mores and hence are immoral, while in the last two the movies conform to the mores and hence are moral.[92a] Instead, however, we find him suddenly recollecting his other prejudices and asking: "In which direction are deviations toward *better*, when they are toward the plus end of our scales or toward the minus end?" [93] This suggests that there may be a way of condemning the movies no matter what one finds. If they deviate at all, they are bad; if they deviate toward the disapproved end they are also bad; perhaps, even if they deviate toward the approved end, they are bad; and maybe if they do not deviate at all, they are bad because they should deviate toward the ap-

[91] *Op. cit.,* p. 107.   [92] *Op. cit.,* p. 117.
[92a] Here the mores are taken as indicated not by the actual practices, but by the ratings of approval. If the actual practices were taken as the mores, the relation of the first two to the last two measurements would be reversed.
[93] *Op. cit.,* p. 128.

proved end. This last point is suggested by another question which Dr. Peters asks: "How far above 'practice' must 'art' stand before it is fulfilling its ideal as art and its functions in social control?" [94] Previously he had left the question open as to whether art should imitate actions as they are or as they should be. He now seems to have decided that point by reasons not given, except the obvious one that the decision provides another way for condemning the movies.

An impartial review of Professor Peters' data shows how limited and relatively insignificant his findings are. All that his elaborate and costly research discovered is that in some respects the movies imitate action as it is and, in other respects, action as some people feel it should be. But in every case, they imitate action as some people feel it should not be. In other words, he always found both approval and disapproval of the kinds of conduct which the movies display. Furthermore, in every case, Dr. Peters reports the feeling on the part of some that the movies are bad because they imitate action as it is and the feeling on the part of others that the movies are bad because they imitate action as some people feel it should be. This, after all, is nothing but a statement of current conflicting opinions about the movies. Scientific research has added nothing, particularly when it is remembered that the report by ordinary observers of what the customary practices are is untested for accuracy and reliability and that the judgments of approval and disapproval were not rationally made, nor could they be so made about the kind of materials submitted for judgment.

Not only are Professor Peters' findings no better than ordinary conflicting opinions, but in addition they are not even relevant to the question whether the movies corrupt moral character and demoralize social conduct. He tries to make them relevant by stating as the hypothesis of his research that the movies affect morality by presenting patterns of conduct which are imitated to some extent by their audience. He cites studies made by Blumer, Thurstone, and Mitchell to support this hypothesis of influence through imitation, even though the data of their studies do not make such a conclusion more probable than its opposite.[95] His next step is even worse. He cites the physiological re-

94 *Op. cit.*, p. 128.   95 *Op. cit.*, p. 66.

searches of Pavlov on positive and negative conditioning as a basis for the guess that people will tend to imitate action by characters they consider attractive and resist imitating action by characters they consider unattractive.[96] He could just as easily have guessed that people will imitate action they approve of and resist imitating action they disapprove of. In terms of his own assumptions and guesses, the answer to his problem is clear. He asks: "*If* the patterns of conduct exemplified in motion pictures tend to get imitated, how will their acceptance affect the mores?"[97] (Italics mine.) According to his findings, patterns of conduct in the movies are either the same as those in actual practice or better. In the first alternative, imitation would have no effect whatsoever either because the patterns already exist in the prevailing customs or because, to the extent that the conduct in the movies is disapproved, it will not tend to be imitated. In the second alternative, imitation must improve the mores, if the plus end of the rating scale is interpreted as indicating what is morally better, the ideals of "our better selves." On the other hand, since people seem to recognize that they do not behave as well as they feel they should, it is doubtful whether the movies can seduce them into behaving better than they do. All of this guessing is, of course, based upon the big *if* in the original question, and the far-fetched analogy of moral conduct to positive and negative conditioning in physiological action. All that can be said definitely is that Professor Peters' data do not afford any conclusions whatsoever about the influence of the movies upon the mores, or upon character and conduct. Nevertheless, if he is going to do any guessing about this matter, all of his own assumptions and data indicate that he should be of the *opinion* that the movies are a great influence for good, unless he suddenly recollects his original prejudices and decides that he is not competent to say whether any change in the mores is for better or for worse.

It is surprising, therefore, to find, not that he forgets his doctrinaire position about the equation of mores and morality but that he talks about ways and means for improving the movies to aid morality and augment the social welfare. He does this by turning philosopher and uttering weighty pronouncements about the social function of art, which seem to say that good art must

[96] *Op. cit.*, p. 67.   [97] *Op. cit.*, p. 68.

never conflict with the mores at any point.[98]   It is difficult to
determine whether this means that literature, for instance, should
imitate actions as they are (the mores in practice) or as they
should be (the mores as represented by feelings of approval).
Professor Peters might profit by a reading of Aristotle's *Poetics*
on the various objects of imitation in fiction.   He might then
understand that it is properly within the range of poetry to imitate actions as they are, worse than they are, better than they are,
as they should be and as people say they are or should be.   By
his own canons, Professor Peters must wish to improve Homer
and Virgil, Shakespeare and Molière, as well as the movies.   But
I misrepresent him if I suggest that he is really approaching the
problems of the nature and functions of art as a philosopher, as
an aesthetician or a moralist.   No questions can be answered
except by empirical research.   To discover whether the movies
can perform a meritorious social function, we do not consider
the nature of art and discover its contemplative, recreational and
purgative values.   We need a scientific analysis to tell us what
are "the fundamental services wanted by men and women from
art throughout the ages, of the factors and their combination
that have been present in successful art, and of the rise of social
changes which might react upon the sorts of recreations and
informations people are likely to need.[99]   Not only would scientific research of the kind Professor Peters practises be totally
unable to answer these questions, but intelligent men already
know the answers.

There are two reasons for Professor Peters' failure to understand the limited significance of his own data, in terms of which
he could not possibly argue that the movies need to be improved
in their social effects.   His data do not show this need; if anything, they show the contrary.   The first is his amazing faith
in scientific method as a way of creating heaven on earth.   His
zeal to do more and more research of the kind this book contains
fathers in him the opinion that the movies should be improved.
It is his belief "that a few good social science research men could
render as important service in improving motion picture production as research in agriculture has rendered to scientific farm-

[98] Vd. his Chapter on "Relation of the Morality to the Success of a Motion
Picture," especially pp. 137-142.
[99] *Op. cit.*, p. 155, by permission of The Macmillan Company, Publishers.

ing or research in physics to the improvement of the radio and refrigeration" ; [100] this could be done by a small group of research workers "at an expense of not exceeding a hundred thousand dollars a year." [101]   Dr. Peters lists a number of projects which occur to him at random and which are only a few of the infinite possibilities for research about the movies.   It is clear at once that they would be just about as significant and serviceable as the investigation we are here reviewing.   It is also clear that the wheels of the already much-overgrown industry of social science research would thus be kept turning.

The second reason is the kind of bias which we found in Blumer and Hauser's report and which is present, though a little better concealed, in the work of Peters.   I refer, for instance, to the way in which he suggests criteria by which the movies can be condemned regardless of what relationship they are found to have to the mores or to approval-disapproval ratings.   The way in which Professor Charters reports Peters' findings in his general summary further confirms this suspicion.[102]   Charters gives slightly disproportionate prominence to the case of female aggressiveness in love-making, the only one in which conduct in the movies is not as most of Peters' informants feel it should be. He completely concurs in Peters' reduction of morality to conformity with the mores and does not recognize the deceptions which arise from the double definition of the mores as existing practices and as approved types of conduct.   Furthermore we find in Forman's book, which Professor Charters says shows a thorough grasp of the facts in the Payne Fund researches, not only the same tendency to play up the one case of female aggressiveness, but the explicit statement that "Peters *finds* generally against the movies with respect to mores." [103]   (Italics mine.) If one could not expect Professor Charters to see through the inconsistencies in Peters' method and assumptions, to appreciate how insignificant his findings are, or to realize that if they are significant at all they are favorable to the movies ; at least one could hope that he would not have permitted so obvious a misstatement of fact.

[100] *Op. cit.,* p. 155, by permission of The Macmillan Company, Publishers.
[101] *Op. cit.,* p. 165.   [102] *Op. cit.,* pp. 55–59.
[103] *Op. cit.,* p. 139 ; see also pp. 39, 134, 226.

This concludes our review of the field of opinion and scientific research about the effects of motion pictures upon the adult members of their audience.   The questions of fact raised by the charges against the movies that they cause crime, that they corrupt morals and manners, are no better answered by science than by opinion, and opinions are in conflict on all points.   The position of the prudent man remains unchanged.

CHAPTER ELEVEN

Attempts at Scientific Research:
The Immature

WE shall divide this survey into two parts: (1) the question whether motion pictures are a cause of juvenile delinquency; and (2) the question whether motion pictures have any other effects on the moral character and social conduct of the immature. In each case we shall first report the prevailing opinions answering these questions affirmatively and negatively, and then proceed to an examination of the attempts of scientific research to improve the state of opinion.

1. WHETHER MOTION PICTURES ARE A CAUSE OF DELINQUENCY.

    (a) *Affirmative opinion.*

As early as 1910, Mr. William Inglis in an article in *Harper's Weekly* which praised the recently established National Board of Censorship, cited the opinion that the beginnings of crime were developed in the unescorted attendance of children at the movies.[1] No evidence of any sort was offered in support. It is interesting to note that the National Board in those days censored as objectionable, scenes showing crime for crime's sake, or details of pocket-picking and burglary. On the other hand, thrilling scenes which in their opinion were not incitements to crime were allowed, such, for instance, as a gang of counterfeiters at work, or the smothering of Desdemona by Othello.

[1] *Morals and the Moving Pictures*, in Harper's Weekly, July 30, 1910: pp. 12–13.

The incidence of specific censorship can be taken as an index of opinion.

In 1919, the Rev. Dr. J. J. Phelan surveyed motion pictures as a phase of commercialized amusement in Toledo.[2] Among other social dangers, he gave prominence to the causation of delinquency. He reported juvenile-court officials as holding the opinion that two-thirds of the girls arraigned for immorality owe their misfortune to movie influences directly. He also cited particular cases of the following sort: one boy who shot a revolver at his playmate's feet said that he had seen it done in the movies; another held up a street car on a bet with a chum after seeing the stunt in the movies. He reported the testimony of probation officers in seven large cities that at least 70% of the delinquents whom they examined derived their ideas about life from the movies. The Rev. Dr. Phelan offered no critical estimate of the reliability or significance of the opinions he assembled. Taking them on their face value, he unhesitatingly recommended national censorship and rigid enforcement of laws about the attendance of minors.

In 1921 Mr. Rowland C. Sheldon wrote an article on *Moving Pictures, Books and Child Crime* in which he reported that children told him that movies gave them ideas about stealing and shooting. Mr. Sheldon was General Secretary for the Big Brother Movement. The article was written after a visit with some boys in a reformatory. It was published in The Bookman and its chief recommendation was that children be compelled to read books instead of seeing movies.[3] Reading gives them time to think and form judgments, but the movies go too fast. Mr. Sheldon asked: "What is happening to the reasoning power of our children?" If he had pursued this question a little further, he might have had some insight about the causes of delinquency which would have placed a different interpretation upon the stories which boys in reformatories tell.

We have already quoted the opinion of Professor Poffenberger that the movies may be a cause of juvenile delinquency through the processes of suggestion.[4] The child, like the mental defective, is supposed to be highly suggestible. At about the same time that his article appeared in the Scientific Monthly, Dr. S. B.

[2] *Motion Pictures as a Phase of Commercialized Amusement in Toledo, Ohio*, Toledo, 1919.   [3] May, 1921: p. 242 ff.   [4] Vd. Chapter 10 *supra*, fn. 4.

Heckman, a child psychologist on the staff of the College of the City of New York is quoted to the same effect by several writers in popular journals.[5]   As in the case of Professor Poffenberger's opinion, Dr. Heckman's statements were not accompanied by any evidence.   They are to be taken as the opinion of an expert. We have also already quoted an article by Mr. C. K. Allen in the Quarterly Review for 1925.[6]   Mr. Allen mentioned the famous Leopold and Loeb case.   He admitted that they were not shown to have been influenced by the movies; nevertheless in his opinion their trial indicated that they lived in just such a world of fantasy as the movies instil.   In England, he said, there have been two cases of brutal murder committed by men behaving like movie heroes.   He cited the authority of Cyril Burt's book on *The Young Delinquent* to support his opinion that the movies may exercise a great influence on youthful minds; but he also added that Dr. Burt cautions against overemphasizing the faculty of imitativeness.   The expert opinion of Dr. Burt thus appears to be somewhat in conflict with that of Professor Poffenberger and Dr. Heckman.   This conflict will be shown more fully as we proceed.

In 1930 the International Review of Educational Cinematography[7] considered the question of the primary causes of juvenile crime and delinquency.   In this connection statistics from Belgian Children's Tribunals were published.   The figures are difficult to interpret.   On the one hand, it was reported that 70% to 80% of the cases are attributable to bad home conditions; on the other hand, we find that for 80% of the boys and 46% of the girls dancing clubs are a cause, for 31.5% of the boys and 61.3% of the girls, alcoholism is a cause, for 39.6% of the boys and 77.5% of the girls, the cinema is a cause.   It is nowhere stated how the causal relationship was determined.

Since 1925, and probably earlier, magistrates and judges have included in their *obiter dicta* statements about the movies as a cause of delinquency and crime.   Such opinions can hardly be classified as expert, even though handed down by the learned men of the bench.   Thus in 1925 Judge Martin of Kings County, New York, sentencing seven youths for crimes of vio-

[5] Current Opinion, April, 1922 : pp. 505–507 ; and Forum, April, 1923 : pp. 1404–1414.   [6] Vd. Chapter 10 *supra*, fn. 64.   [7] Vd. pp. 467–468 of Vol. II,

lence, blamed the movies for teaching them crime.[8]   Society, he
said, and not the culprit, is responsible.   Society through the
movies teaches children to act and think like criminals.   And in
1935, Judge Panken of the Children's Court in New York and
Judge Charles A. Walsh of Providence similarly accused the
movies in *ex cathedra* statements from the bench or in public
addresses.[9]   One suspects that such opinions are formed in the
light of the excuses which children give for their misdemeanors.
As the Indian Cinematograph Report pointed out, it is natural
for culprits, young or old, to blame anything they can to ex-
tenuate their misconduct.   The movies are particularly easy to
blame.   When in 1935 three boys, all thirteen or younger,
robbed and killed, a shocked public jumped to easy conclusions,
led by a police official who expressed the suspicion that the
movies had something to do with their depravity.[10]   One commentator pointed out, however, that these children went to
movies which "foster in the childish breast the desire to be a
G-man rather than a Dillinger." [11]   Another remembered that
there always have been bad boys, even before the days of motion
pictures.[12]   But public sentiment is, nevertheless, readily formed
by the suspicion, which police officials and magistrates express
on such occasions, that maybe the movies have something to do
with it.   Such suspicions soon become a point of official doctrine.
Thus, when in 1935 Mr. Sanford Bates, Director of the United
States Bureau of Prisons, writes an article[13] about the young
criminal, his enumeration of the causes of delinquency is nothing
more than a reflection of popular and semi-expert opinion.   He
mentions the "new freedom," the automobile, the radio and the
movies.   All of these have at one time or another in recent years
been repeatedly blamed for what bad boys do, by pulpit and
press, by police and judge.   The same opinion can become im-
pressive through repetition and cross-quotation; the resulting

[8] Reported in the New York Times, Jan. 22, 1925 : p. 8.
[9] Reported in the Albany (N. Y.) Knickerbocker-Press, June 30, 1935 ; and in
the Providence (R. I.) Bulletin, June 28, 1935.
[10] New York Sun, June 18, 1935 : p. 20.
[11] New York Post, June 20, 1935 : p. 11.
[12] New York World-Telegram, June 18, 1935 : p. 18.
[13] *The Young Criminal: A Sharp Challenge*, in the New York Times Magazine, August 4, 1935 : p. 8.

impression is that there is a great mass of public opinion on the point. It is clear from this brief survey how the opinion that the movies are responsible for juvenile crime and delinquency gradually becomes part of the widely but uncritically accepted notions of the day.

(b) *Negative opinion.*

In 1909 Mr. John Collier, then Secretary of the National Board of Censorship, delivered an address on the motion pictures before the Child Conference for Research and Welfare.[14] He said that when he first began to come in contact with truants and delinquents, he was impelled to blame the movies after listening to truant boys acknowledge "the soft impeachment of motion pictures." But, he went on to say, "older heads on the committee reminded me that truants had existed long before motion pictures caught their roving eye. So did juvenile delinquency, I may add, and when I read in the newspapers that a boy has robbed, hurled stones or run away from home 'because he saw it in the motion pictures,' I am inclined to wait for the evidence." [15]

In 1926, Professor Joseph L. Holmes, then of the Department of Psychology of Columbia University, conducted a study of *Crime and the Press* [16] in the course of which he attempted to determine whether the movies incite to crime. He sent a questionnaire to law-enforcement officers asking for their opinions on the matter. Of the 111 replies which he received, 29 were affirmative, 57 were negative, and 25 irrelevant; of the 29 affirmative answers, only 7 attempted to cite any cases. Professor Holmes considered the fact that many newspapers, either in editorial comment or in the way they play up the news, have tried to suggest that lurid fiction and movies are a major factor in crime, and suggested that the obvious reason for this was a desire to shift the blame which in recent years they themselves have attracted. In 1927 a New York newspaper reported the case of a boy slayer as an instance of murder incited by a motion picture.[17] Dr. Holmes interviewed the boy, and the same news-

---

[14] *Proceedings of the Child Conference for Research and Welfare*, New York, 1910 : pp. 108–118. [15] *Ibid.*, p. 110.
[16] Journal of the American Institute of Criminal Law and Criminology, Vol. XX, pp. 6–59, 246–293. [17] New York Telegram, Feb. 8, 1927.

paper published his comments: "Michael has been quoted in the newspapers as having stated that he got the idea from moving pictures, and again as having gotten the idea from newspapers. This phase of the case particularly interested me because for many months past I have been engaged in the investigation of just this problem. Refraining from leading questions, as I suspected the newsgatherers did not, I let the boy tell his story; then checking up on him by questioning I found that he was able to name but a few pictures that he had seen within the last several weeks and those only the most wholesome." It may be objected, of course, that the boy's memory of recent films he had seen is insufficient evidence on the point.

Dr. Holmes' study, while it is no more reliable as scientific research than the Blumer and Hauser investigation we have already criticized, led him to an opposite conclusion from theirs. Although the conclusions of scientific research in this field are no better than what prevails as conflicting popular opinion, it is instructive to note that there is as much conflict in so-called expert opinion. The conclusion which Holmes reached should be compared with that of Blumer and Hauser. "I am convinced," he said, "that the people who claim the movies are demoralizing this generation cannot back up their vague generalizations with facts. I believe my studies in this field have proved the actual unimportance of the films as producers of young delinquents. . . The movies provide an outlet for the romantic imagination rather than jeopardizing our emotional stability. . . All the evidence points to the innocence of the motion picture as a stimulator of youthful depravity." [18] This is just as extreme in one direction as the contrary opinion is in the other.

The following can also be cited as expert opinion. Drs. Healy and Bronner, in their textbook on *Delinquents and Criminals* [19] say: "It has been our regular practice to make inquiry concerning the indulgence in and effect of such amusements as moving pictures. Starting with ideas somewhat to the contrary, we have been surprised to find that moving picture shows seem to have very little effect in the production of delinquent tendencies; we could discover no reason to attribute more than 1% of the cases to this cause." [20] Dr. Phyllis Blanchard in her book

18 Reported in the New York Herald-Tribune, April 28, 1929.
19 New York, 1926. 20 *Op. cit.*, p. 181.

The Child and Society [21] writes: "In five years of daily contact with more than a thousand problem children in different parts of the country, the author is unable to recall more than five cases in which the motion picture was intimately related to the causation of conduct disorders. . . Although scientific studies do not corroborate the belief that movies are very prominently concerned in the production of juvenile delinquency, it is easy to see why this idea is popular. Mankind is always glad to find a scapegoat upon which it can project its sins. It is much less painful to accept the opinion that the motion pictures, together with other new economic and social forces, are the causes of unruly conduct in children than to face the fact that the failure of family life is in large measure the most responsible agent." [22] Dr. Cyril Burt, Professor of Education in the University of London, in his book on *The Young Delinquent* [23] says: "It is alleged in the first place that what is called 'his faculty of imitativeness' renders the child peculiarly prone to copy whatever he witnesses upon the screen. . . But how far, in point of fact, are children influenced in this way? On sifting the evidence adduced by those who express these fears, it is plain that both their inferences and their psychological assumptions are by no means free from fallacy. Nor are their facts better founded. They have between them hardly one well-attested instance from their own first-hand knowledge, hardly a single analyzed case to put forward in proof." [24]

The conflict of opinions can be similarly indicated by quoting from officials who disagree with the officials we have already cited in the affirmative. Thus Judge Camille Kelley of the Juvenile Court of Memphis says: "I have questioned many, many parents about the influence of pictures on their wayward children, and on the whole the amount of juvenile delinquency resulting is so small as to be negligible. It used to be the fashion to blame youthful crime on dime novels. Now the pictures get the blame." [25] Mr. Joseph Fishman, formerly United States

[21] Longmans, Green & Co., Publishers, New York, 1928.
[22] *Op. cit.*, pp. 202–203.
[23] D. Appleton-Century Company, Inc., London, 1927.
[24] *Op. cit.*, pp. 137–143, by permission of D. Appleton-Century Company, Inc. Vd. case histories on p. 298 ff.
[25] Reported in the Detroit (Mich.) News, May 29, 1934.

Inspector of Prisons, writes: "In a remarkable experience with boys, continuous during the past thirty-three years, Frederick C. Helbing, Superintendent of the House of Refuge for Boys at Randall's Island, New York, has not found a single instance in which a boy's delinquency was traceable directly or indirectly to the movies."[26]   Dr. George W. Kirchwey, formerly warden of Sing Sing Prison, New York, says: "It is the home, not the school and still less the motion picture that is the character forming agency. . .   It is ludicrous to think that human nature is so susceptible that it can be molded by sporadic experience in the motion picture theatres.   Character is formed by a tougher process."[27]   And Sir Herbert Samuel, then Home Secretary of Great Britain, said in the House of Commons in 1932: "There are some who think that the cinema is another factor contributing in that direction (crime) especially among the young, but there is much division of opinion as to that.   My very expert and experienced advisers at the Home Office are of the opinion that on the whole the cinema conduces more to the prevention of crime than to its commission. . .   In general, the Home Office opinion is that if the cinemas had never existed, there would probably be more crime than there is, rather than less, although at the same time we are far from saying that it is not necessary to raise the standard of the films that are produced.   No one suggests that they are by any means free from objection in many cases at the present time."[28]

The balance of affirmative and negative opinion is clear.   The negative side of the case is no better *as opinion* than the affirmative.   Neither the weight of opinion nor the evidence which has been alluded to in these various statements would permit a rational mind to form a decisive judgment.   Two differences should be observed here in comparing the affirmative and the negative statements.   In the first place, the affirmative opinion has, for various reasons, become the expression of a much more widespread popular prejudice than the negative.   Perhaps, those who hold the affirmative point of view are better propagandists;

[26] Harper's Monthly Magazine, July, 1933: p. 244.
[27] Reported in the Boston American, Feb. 14, 1934. Cf. his remarks before a recent crime conference, as reported in the *Proceedings of the Governor's Conference on Crime, the Criminal and Society*, Albany, 1935: pp. 316–317.
[28] Cited in *The Cinema for the Young*, a memorandum submitted in 1935 by the British Home Office to the League of Nations Committee on Child Welfare.

perhaps, that point of view is in general more congenial with the
other prejudices of most men or, as Dr. Blanchard pointed out,
because it provides them with a scapegoat for their sins.   It cannot be that there is either a greater weight of affirmative opinion
or that those who express it are more respected in the community
as experts.   There is one other possible explanation.   It is a
common fallacy to exaggerate the significance of a few cases.
The powers of induction are too readily exercised by most men,
lacking the intellectual discipline requisite for validity in generalization.   They hear about a few cases, or even a single case, in
which a boy criminal refers to the movies in connection with
his crime and lo! they have an unqualified causal generalization
which they assert as if it were highly probable or even true.   It
is thus that most parents draw conclusions about all or most children from the peculiarities of their own.   Furthermore, as Dr.
Horace Kallen pointed out in an address in 1928 on *The Censor,
the Psychologist and the Motion Picture*,[29] "that a boy, having
seen such and such a movie, runs away to crack safes or fight
Indians is news; that millions of other boys, having seen the
same movie, do not, is not news."   To whatever extent public
opinion is formed by the news the papers print, an obvious distortion occurs, and a common error in induction.   People learn
about the single case "of a girl fallen because she had read a novel,
of a boy turned thief by contagion from a movie" and the generalizations they leap to are, as Dr. Kallen says, "sheer superstition and rationalization.   How many people are there who are
afraid of starting anything on Friday or getting involved with
the number 13?   They cite cases of misfortune following the
13th at the table or an adventure begun on Friday.   Such cases
stick out.   Such cases make a deep impression.   But the endless
millions of cases in which the sequence accrued without misfortune, or as likely as not with good fortune, are not so much
as thought of."[30]   Add to this the unreliability of the original
information about the single case.   Most of these newspaper
reports, or the single cases cited by judges or policemen, ultimately reduce to nothing more than stories told by children.
Certainly the child's word is not to be taken as clear evidence of

[29] Reprinted in *Indecency and the Seven Arts*, Liveright Publishing Corporation, New York, 1930 : pp. 50-51.
[30] *Ibid.*, pp. 32-33, by permission of the Liveright Publishing Corporation.

what caused his misbehavior or criminal conduct, nor is it even to be trusted as a vague reference to a likely factor in his conduct. As Dr. Frank Astor, Field Director of the National Child Welfare Association, recently said, "Children have an almost remarkable capacity for saying what they believe adults want them to say. They have heard adults put a taboo on certain films and immediately think that there is something wrong with them. On being brought before a judge for committing some crime they begin searching for an excuse. The motion picture provides just that and the child blandly declares that 'I saw it in the movies'" [31] [117].

In the second place, opinion is better to the extent that it is an expression of skepticism about any causal explanation of this sort in general, or about the influence of the movies in particular. The affirmative opinion is necessarily not skeptical; it asserts that the movies cause delinquency and crime or are one of the causes. The negative opinion also fails to be skeptical when, not satisfied with merely questioning the validity of the affirmative assertion, it asserts that the movies prevent crime. The negative opinion is not better as founded on the evidence of cases; it is only better in proportion as it is skeptical [118].

This is the state of opinion. It is not necessary to add here a third section on scientific investigations of the influence of the movies on juvenile misbehavior. We have already discussed the study made by Dr. Holmes and seen that it is only a collection of opinions. There are two other studies of totally indeterminate value because of the way in which they are reported; one by Dr. Peyser which claims to find not a single case out of 714 instances of juvenile delinquency which can be traced to the influence of the movies; [32] the other by Margaret Leonard which makes a similar claim based upon the examination of 42 girls from sub-adequate families. [33] Even if the reliability of the data

[31] Reported in the New York Herald-Tribune, Jan. 12, 1933.
[32] Reported by Joseph F. Fishman in Harper's Monthly Magazine, July, 1933: p. 244.
[33] *Study of the Motion Picture as a Factor in the Life of 42 Girls from Sub-adequate Families*, in Social Science Monographs, Jan. 15, 1931: pp. 27-33. Cf. M. V. Seagoe, *The Child's Reaction to the Movies*, in the Journal of Juvenile Research, 1931, Vol. XV: pp. 169-180; and C. Thomas, *A Comparison of the Interests of Delinquent and Non-Delinquent Boys*, in the same journal, 1932, Vol. XVI: pp. 310-318.

could be examined, such findings have no generalized significance whatsoever. There is also a finding by Mrs. Alice Miller Mitchell.[34] She obtained responses to questionnaires from 10,-052 Chicago children, including boy and girl scouts, boy and girl delinquents, a much larger number of cases than that covered by any other investigation in this field. She reports that "there were not many of the juvenile delinquents utilized for this study who 'blamed the movies.' Some looked upon them as havens of refuge from temptation, but most of these children were interested in the movies as movies and as 'the best entertainment in the world.'"[35] She cites a few cases in which delinquents felt "that their conflict with the law had been because of some contact with the movies."[36] But she also recognizes that such evidence is neither entirely trustworthy nor sufficient. She concludes: "The findings of this study show that the delinquent child's contact with the movie far exceeds that of other children. His active interest in it is apparently a protest against the bareness and drabness of his own life. . . The delinquent child's extensive contact with the movies may or may not be due to the fact that he is a delinquent and because of the things back of his delinquency. Whether or not the movie enters into his delinquency is a subject for further research and is out of the realm of this study."[37]

It may be thought that Blumer and Hauser did this further research. But their evidence, in its general character and the proportion of positive findings, is no different from Mrs. Mitchell's, and much less extensive in terms of the total number of cases. No further discussion of their research is needed here. We have already sufficiently demonstrated the unreliability and insignificance of their data.[38] The only conclusions which they would have any right to draw — although they frequently exceed this limit explicitly or by insinuation — are no better than the conflicting opinions already prevailing popularly and among experts.[39] Their conclusions, it should be remembered, were

[34] *Children and Movies*, The University of Chicago Press, Chicago, 1929.
[35] *Op. cit.*, p. 135, by permission of The University of Chicago Press.
[36] *Op. cit.*, pp. 135–142.
[37] *Op. cit.*, p. 143, by permission of The University of Chicago Press.
[38] Vd. Chapter 10 *supra*.
[39] The danger which results from Blumer and Hauser's failure to be critical can be seen in the popularizations of their work which lack even the tentative-

all of the following sort: "It is evident that the motion pictures may exert influences in diametrically opposite directions. . . The movies *may* help to dispose or lead persons to delinquency and crime, or they *may* fortify conventional behavior." [40] (Italics mine.)

2. WHETHER MOTION PICTURES HAVE OTHER EFFECTS.

It is charged that the movies have a number of effects upon children and youth in addition to causing delinquency and crime.[41] These can be classified as physical, intellectual and moral. It is the last which is most frequently stressed. The charge that the movies corrupt moral character and demoralize manners rests, in the case of the immature, upon the same kind of questions of fact that it does in the case of adults. The only difference is that here the movies must be considered in relation to the other influences, such as home, school and church, which play upon moral character during its formative period. In surveying the field of affirmative and negative opinion answering these questions, we shall not separate the three spheres of influence. In the case of the scientific researches, however, the separation is made necessary because different investigations have properly limited themselves to one or another topic.

(a) *Affirmative opinion.*

In 1909, the *Proceedings of the Child Conference for Research and Welfare* published a report by Mr. E. H. Chandler on how much children attend the theatre, the quality of the entertainment they choose and its effect upon them.[42] This early inquiry set the style for all those that were to follow, even those done by university scientists as research projects. The charge that the movies corrupt youth is usually supported by these three steps: (1) the frequency of attendance, (2) the content of mo-

---

ness and ambiguity of their conclusions. We have already noted this in Forman's book. Another instance is an article by Mr. J. Rorty in Parent's Magazine (July, August, 1933) which purports to be a popularized summary of the facts found by the Payne Fund studies and thus to tell parents "how the movies harm children." Mr. Rorty asserts that the movies — specifically sex and gangster pictures — *definitely* influence a *considerable* number of children toward careers of delinquency and crime.

40 *Op. cit.*, p. 201.   41 The analysis of these charges is in Chapter 6, *supra.*
42 Pp. 55–59.

tion pictures and juvenile preferences, (3) the effects upon youthful character and conduct. It is usually the first two of these three items about which more or less definite evidence is obtained; the third is often developed conjecturally out of knowledge about the first two. Whether the inferences that are made in such a procedure are justified is one of the most important critical questions we must consider. Mr. Chandler's evidence on any of these points was slight; his report consisted largely of opinions. Thus, from scattered testimonies he surmised that nearly all children from 10 to 14 years of age attend movies occasionally and that not less than 10% of them go as often as once a week. He then reports the opinion of a director of boys' clubs that "theatregoing makes the boys crave excitement and unable to apply themselves to a serious task. The results of the late hours are laziness and dullness in school, loss of interest in work, leading to slow promotion, dropping out of school at fourteen and a small paying job for the rest of their lives." [43] Another sample of opinion was that of the head of an industrial school who felt that "lowered moral standards and the desire for excitement" were "caused by the incessant theatregoing." [44] Chandler further cited the fact that a group of girls in a settlement, when giving amateur representations of what they had seen at shows, chose elopements, burglaries, and tragic scenes. He obviously forgot the types of romantic and tragic scenes which the girls of *Little Women* played long before the movies.

In 1920 the Judiciary Committee of the City Council of Chicago appointed a commission to make a thorough study of the motion-picture problem. [45] Reliable representatives of the motion picture interests had reported that 2,500,000 persons attended the movies every week in Chicago. "It is evident, therefore, that this most popular form of entertainment must be having a tremendous influence on the rising generation." [46] Ignoring the *non sequitur*, let us examine the opinions about the matter which Professor Burgess of the University of Chicago collected by means of a questionnaire sent to all the teachers in about 125

[43] *Loc. cit.*, p. 57.   [44] *Loc. cit.*, p. 57.
[45] *Report of the Motion Picture Commission*, Chicago, 1920.
[46] This statement is in a preface to a questionnaire sent to Chicago school teachers; *op. cit.*, pp. 131–133.

Chicago schools. The teachers were asked to answer questions about the average attendance of their pupils at movie theatres, the effect of the movies on their school work and mental development, the views of life children acquire from the movies, the moral effects, the effect of the movies on the children's respect for parents, teachers and all lawful authority, the physical effects, and children's preferences. Professor Burgess' report includes a citation of newspaper comments and the direct testimony of persons in child welfare work, as well as the tabulated answers to the questionnaire. Burgess summarized these tables as showing the following facts: the movies interfere with school work; their moral effect is bad; the view of life and life's duties is false and distorted; sex and vampire films appeal to children; respect for authority is lessened; children seven years old and older are precocious about sex; there is a noticeable disregard for marriage ties and a bad effect on modesty and purity; children disregard the home and are dissatisfied with it; there are harmful physical effects, such as eye-strain, nervousness, decreased vitality; in general, the effect on the rising generation is bad. It should be remembered that these alleged facts are based upon the opinions of teachers and that the tables show a clear difference of opinion among them. Thus, in the matter of the effect of movies upon school work, 96 said that they interfered, 37 said that they accelerated mental development and improved general information, 41 said that they had no effect or that they did have educational value, 91 said that they retarded mental development or that the mental powers of children were affected by them; in the matter of moral effect, 51 said it was generally bad, 33 said there was none; 16 said disrespect for law was promoted; and so on. The predominant opinion of these teachers, however, was unfavorable toward the movies: 137 said that their effect upon the rising generation was bad, 200 said that they had harmful physical effects, 182 said they had bad effects upon home life. One hundred and eighty-three of the teachers, therefore, favored the creation of a Board of Censorship; they also suggested special performances for children and the exclusion of children from evening performances.

The Report of the Commission also includes the opinion of Dr. D. P. MacMillan, child psychologist of the Board of Education, called as an expert witness: that the motion pictures are the most important factor in minor school-misconduct cases. But Dr. MacMillan also cited the finding of Miss Curtis, in the light of data collected from 25 cities, that there was no correlation between time spent at movies and progress in school work. The Report also contained the opinion of church workers that a 65% decrease in the attendance of school children at churches is due to the movies.

In 1921 Mr. Ellis P. Oberholtzer, then Secretary of the Pennsylvania State Board of Censors, wrote an article on *What are the Movies Making Our Children*.[47]   Among other things, he said with respect to the then popular serial films and slapstick comedy: "The psychological effect of such exhilaration of the ganglia of the young may be left to those who know the subject scientifically. A layman can merely conclude that a given amount of crime and violence, unrelieved by any lesson in virtue, administered to a brain in a formative state, each day or week, is not without grave influence."[48]   Here we see the inference about the influence of movies being made from some knowledge about the fact that children frequently attend and the fact that the films they see are exciting.

In 1923 Mr. Joseph Roy Geiger, then at the University of Chicago, wrote an article on *The Effect of the Motion Picture on the Mind and Morals of the Young*.[49]   The article contains no evidence of any sort, not even the testimony of collected opinions. It presents Mr. Geiger's own opinions. He considered, first, the positive values usually assigned to the movies as amusement and as educational. But the movies are not good as amusement, he held, because they do not encourage the child's activity or self-expression; rather they require the child to be a passive spectator. This is an interesting misconception of the nature of amusement. Further, they are not wholesome because of their physical effects, the eye-strain, the poor ventilation, and so forth. Time spent at movies would be better spent outdoors. The movies overstimulate the imagination, yet, despite the implied admission here that the movies do stimulate the child's imagination, Mr. Geiger asserts that they have little educational value, again because they fail to provide for creative expression. At this point can be discerned a typical misreading of the doctrine

[47] World's Work, Jan., 1921 : pp. 249–263.   [48] *Loc. cit.*, p. 259.
[49] International Journal of Ethics, Oct., 1923 : pp. 69–83.

of John Dewey's *Democracy and Education* in which the primary emphasis is upon the educational value of art as a medium of vicarious experience and social communication. Having dismissed the positive values that have been claimed for the movies, Mr. Geiger then turns to their evils. He assumes that children necessarily imitate behavior which they observe and employs this assumption to attribute to the movies the precocity of young people in sexual matters. The moral breakdown can be seen everywhere: in immodest clothes, indecent dancing, promiscuous drinking parties, midnight joy rides. These, he says, are an expression of the spirit of the times, a spirit of immodesty and irreverence and lawlessness generated, in part at least, by the unparalleled assault which, for a decade or more, has been made through the motion picture on society's most valuable assets, its innocence and youth. Mr. Geiger seems to forget that the times he speaks of are the post-war years and the early era of prohibition evasion. He also seems to forget that *if* the movies are so effective in demoralizing youth, the church, the school and the home must be relatively ineffective in forming their character positively. By looking into the moral breakdown of other generations—the gay nineties, for instance, when there were no movies—he might have gained not only historical perspective about such matters, but a greater reluctance to point definitely to causes. Finally, he charges the movies with operating upon the suggestibility of the young to make them accept false ideas uncritically. What are these obviously false ideas? The movies are not realistic enough, that is, they do not represent the social reality as Mr. Geiger sees it. They set up false standards of value, about money, luxury, leisure, beauty, clothes, pleasure, popularity. They teach techniques of anti-social and criminal conduct. In the light of Professor Peters' finding about the relation between conduct in the movies and the prevailing social practices, one is led to wonder whether Mr. Geiger knows what the prevailing ideas are about such things as money, luxury, leisure, etc., which the movies are supposed to misrepresent. The attention I have given to Mr. Geiger's personal opinions is out of deference to the scholarly International Journal of Ethics in which his article was published.

Mr. Geiger's article is typical of similar opinions expressed by others during the same period. Thus, Mrs. Charles E. Merriam

assumed that the movies were an evil influence on morals and
health of children, making them emotionally unstable and nervous.[50]   Hence the duty of the schools should be to keep children away from the movies and to prevent the movies from
becoming a community center.   Among other things she proposed that teachers watch for the coming of bad films and assign
more homework to keep their pupils busy.   Mr. Carleton Kemp
Allen, in an article we have already noted, pointed to the unreality of the films, the improbability of their stories, as the
source of their evil influence upon the minds of the young.[51]
Like Mr. Geiger he seems to have been uninformed about the
history of children's literature, its fanciful and romantic character.   Moreover, neither of these writers understand the poetic
principle that fiction need not aim to imitate life as it is, that improbability as measured by the failure to give a facsimile is not
the important criterion but rather the intrinsic probability which
the art of the story-teller can give even to impossible events.
Mr. Allen, like Mr. Geiger, bewails the vulgar display of riches
which holds up the dollar as the only standard of success and
happiness, and like Mr. Geiger he does not ask about the extent
to which wealth is the prevailing measure of achievement in our
society.

In the course of years, with the mechanical improvements in
motion-picture production and projection and the alteration in
the character of motion-picture theatres, the opinion is less frequently expressed that the movies have dangerous physical effects
upon the health of the child, causing eye-strain or lack of vitality,
supposedly due to poor ventilation.   The concern about the
child's health has recently taken other forms.   Thus, the emotional agitation which children suffer under the influence of the
movies, their frights and nightmares, is supposed to be responsible
for neurosis and milder emotional instability.   As a neurologist,
Dr. Victor Ruette expressed an opinion of this sort in the International Review of Educational Cinematography in 1933.[52]
Juvenile attendance at movies in the evening is supposed to have

[50] *Solving the Motion Picture Problem*, in the Journal of the National Education Association, May, 1924 : pp. 167–168.
[51] Quarterly Review, Oct., 1925 : pp. 313–330.
[52] *The Cinema—An Educational or Demoralizing Agent* (I. R. E. C., Vol. V,
pp. 277–282). Cf. the opinion of Dr. Frederick Peterson, cited by H. J. Forman in *Our Movie Made Children* on p. 103.

effects upon the soundness of their sleep, and consequently upon their health. These two matters, the emotional excitement caused by movies and their effect upon children's sleep, have been scientifically investigated as part of the Payne Fund project. We shall, therefore, return to the consideration of them later.

(b) *Negative opinion.*

It is interesting to observe two things about the negative opinion concerning the effects of the movies upon children: first, that the volume of such opinion is slight compared to the mass of opinion, which can be found in all sorts of journals and periodicals, expressed by teachers, reformers and others, holding that the movies are demoralizing youth, injuring their health, etc.; second, that the negative opinion has been expressed only recently, whereas the affirmative opinion can be found from the early days of the motion picture onward. Thus, in 1932 St. John Ervine wrote an article about *The Cinema and the Child*, in which he said that the evil effects of the cinema have been over-stressed.[53] In so far as films have done any harm, the responsibility lies with those who were in authority over the young and were indiscriminating in allowing them to see harmful pictures. The harm done by what adults call indecent pictures is less than is usually supposed; children are bored by them and cannot follow the plots. Nevertheless, he concludes with the statement that although the influence of the cinema is a matter of conjecture, "the conjecture cannot be made without fear."[54] Investigation of the problem is necessary to support or unfound the opinions which educators, too ready to condemn, have easily formed. At about the same time, Mrs. Sidonie M. Gruenberg, Director of the Child Study Association of America, said in her book *Your Child Today and Tomorrow*:[55] "The moving picture shows, which supply so many of the children with their chief opportunity to learn life, have been on the whole fairly wholesome; and the movement to improve the films further will probably leave these sources of instruction safe, from a moral point of view, so far as concerns the knowledge of life that the adolescent gets. The only real danger from the movies and the

---

[53] Fortnightly Review, #137, p. 426 ff.   [54] *Loc. cit.*, p. 443.
[55] J. B. Lippincott Company, Philadelphia, 1928.   Cf. the opinion of Dr. Soper, reported in *The Film in National Life*, London, 1932: p. 74.

theatres is likely to be the cultivation of the habit of passive entertainment." [56]

The negative opinion is, thus, not only slight but it is qualified by residual concern about the possible evil in the influence of motion pictures on youth. While the dangers that may lie in juvenile attendance are not denied, the point has been frequently made that the major responsibility for the avoidance of these dangers rests with the parents. Not only are the home, the school and the church the obvious positive factors in forming the child's moral character and giving him the strength to meet any of the influences in his environment, but parents have the additional responsibility of intelligently supervising their child's interest in movies, as they would guide his reading and his play.

The strongest expression of negative opinion is to be found in the report made in 1932 by the Education Committee of the London County Council and in a similar report made by the Edinburgh Cinema Enquiry in 1933. Both deal with the problem of the influence of the film on school children and adolescents; both are the result of very extensive surveys made by the use of questionnaires. The method of these surveys is like that of some of the Payne Fund studies. The London investigation covered 21,280 children in 29 schools distributed over various districts of the metropolitan area; the Edinburgh investigation collated answers from 2,580 boys and girls in public institutions between the ages of 9 and 18. Unlike the Payne Fund studies, the English investigations make no pretense at being scientific. They represent attempts by practical men to learn something about the relevant facts. They offer statistical summaries of their data but do not try to draw "scientific conclusions" from them; in the light of such evidence, they do no more than formulate what is acknowledged as an opinion. This evidence, by the way, is neither more nor less reliable than similar data collected by means of questionnaires and interviews in the Payne Fund studies.

We shall examine the London report on *School Children and the Cinema* first. [57] With respect to frequency of attendance, the report says: "Taking children of all ages, and neglecting for the moment any distinctions between boys and girls, we find

[56] *Op. cit.*, p. 181, by permission of J. B. Lippincott Company.
[57] London, 1932.

that nearly 9% of all children attending school from the age of
three upwards go to the cinema twice a week, and 30% go once
a week. Another 48% go at irregular intervals, and about
13½% do not go at all." [58] There is very little difference for
different age groups; thus for the ages 11–14, 40.9% attend
once or twice a week, for the ages 8–10, 41.1%, for the ages
5–7, 36.5% and for the ages under 5, 30.0%. By far the commonest time for visiting the cinema is Saturday afternoon." [59]
Attendance is not confined to neighborhood cinemas. Regarding juvenile preferences it was found that infants and young
children prefer animated cartoons of the Mickey Mouse variety;
the comic film is extremely popular at all ages. "For the rest,
after allowance has been made for the personal factor in the
inquiry, it remains true that the order of preference for the
classes of films differs not only according to sex but to some
extent according to district. It is not possible therefore to set
out with complete accuracy any generalized order of preference.
It is possible, however, to give some reliable information of the
probable truth." [60] Cowboy films are popular at all ages, but
more so with boys than girls, with younger than older children;
war films are very popular with boys and definitely unpopular
with girls; "mystery," "detective" and "crook" films are high
in the order of popularity for boys, and much less so for girls;
topical films, nature films, travel and animal films are usually
ranked very low; "romance" or "love stories" are definitely
disliked by boys, but they are frequently placed high in the
order of preference by girls between the ages of 11 and 14.
"One experienced investigator makes the remark that children's
taste 'is not formed by what it is fed on, but that innate longings
determine taste, and some of these are soon satisfied,' and he
notes that as the age of the children rises the interest in Mickey
Mouse, cowboy films and war films diminishes while interest in
the 'mystery' film increases." [61]

I now quote what the Chief Inspector of Schools holds to be
well established points about the effects of attendance at the
cinema. First, "all the inspectors who mention it, and in this
they are supported by most of the evidence of teachers, are convinced that the morally questionable element in films (i.e. that
reserved for adults) is ignored by children of school age. The

[58] *Op. cit.*, p. 2,   [59] *Op. cit.*, p. 3,   [60] *Op. cit.*, p. 4.   [61] *Op. cit.*, p. 4.

element which the adult would most deprecate to be put before children does, in fact, bore them. That it may do harm in particular cases is not denied, but there appears to be no widespread mischief. It does not follow that this would be equally true had the inquiry included young people, say, of fifteen to eighteen years old." Second, "the younger children for a time imitate in their play what they have seen on the films. . . But these external evidences of film influence are usually fugitive, and at least are confined to play." Third, "though film influence seems not to affect conduct outside of play, and the worst delinquent in a school is sometimes a child who never goes to the pictures, nevertheless some children absorb film knowledge which seems to be kept in a mental department used in school only when an appropriate stimulus is applied." Fourth, "the one distinct evil that is mentioned with such frequency by inspectors and teachers, and with such specific examples as to leave little doubt of its existence, is that children are often frightened at the films, and that the fear remains with them and causes dreams. . . There can be little question therefore that war pictures, gruesome and terrible details from which are undoubtedly remembered, often no doubt subconsciously, by the children, and the 'mystery' plays with terrifying incidents have undesirable and possibly permanent effects upon children. . . Apart from this single point, the inquiry brought out no other point upon which there was definite evidence of harm. In spite of the strong opinions of some able and devoted head teachers to the contrary, the preponderance of evidence is that the actual effect of the pictures on the children is not substantially harmful. For instance, though specific inquiry was made, instances of children having stolen in order to get money to go to the films are negligible in number. Nor is there any evidence of imitative misconduct on the part of these school children." Fifth, "there is little doubt that, as a means of enlarging the child's experience (not by any means always in an undesirable way) and of giving clear cut knowledge of certain kinds, the cinema is an effective instrument." [62] On the other hand, there are the opinions "of a smaller number of witnesses who state that children do not recollect what they see in the pictures and that, therefore, if the harm done is negligible, the use of films as a positive instrument in

[62] *Op. cit.*, pp. 4-5.

education has little to be said for it.   But the evidence in these cases is that the children can seldom repeat consecutively the story of a film seen some weeks before." [63]

On the question of physical effects, "it is impossible to say much without a more extended inquiry conducted by medically qualified people.   There is a good deal of evidence that children are tired after evening performances, attendance at which for children, however, always seems to terminate at 8:30 or 9 P.M. . .   The present evidence on the point of health is not sufficient to justify even a common sense lay conclusion, still less a 'scientific' one." [64]

The Report concludes with an expression of opinion by the Chief Inspector.   This opinion has been cited favorably in the memorandum submitted by the British Delegate to the League of Nations, and also by the Commission on Educational and Cultural Films in Great Britain in the monograph on *The Film in National Life*.   I quote it in full: "My general impression, after reading a fairly large mass of evidence carefully, is that there is no need for serious alarm.   Boys do imitate the dashing or the desperate film hero and girls do worship him or pine to be 'her.' But is there anything new about this?   The film is no worse than the old time 'blood,' universally read by the boys only a few years ago.   What man of fifty has not been a pirate in his youth?   These children at least seldom see anything on the film in which virtue and right are not merely ultimately, but immediately triumphant; that is, at the end of twenty minutes. Evil, on the films, never pays.   The crook is always frustrated, and the amateur, if not the professional, detective is always successful.   It is quite evident that the children expect this to happen; and that the vindication of the virtuous, the oppressed or the sorely tempted satisfies their elementary ideas of justice.   I think it very likely that the war films, 'Journey's End,' 'The Victor of Verdun' and the like, which, I understand, do purport to show the violence and cruelties of war, do more real mischief by frightening the children through their realistic detail than all the 'romances' or 'crook' films which children (or most of them) know to be false to life." [65]

I turn now to the report of *The Edinburgh Cinema Enquiry*.[66] Taking children from the age of 9 upward, it was found that

[63] *Op. cit.*, p. 5.   [64] *Op. cit.*, p. 6.   [65] *Op. cit.*, p. 6.   [66] Edinburgh, 1933.

69% attend the cinema at least once a week; of these 19% attend at least twice a week, and 13% attend at least once a month. Boys are more frequent attenders than girls. Children in the poorer districts attend more frequently than those in the better-off districts. These figures are slightly larger than those obtained in the London inquiry, and are in turn smaller than the figure for the much smaller town of Dundee where it was found that 80% of the children went at least once a week; [67] or for Galashiels where the proportion going as frequently as this was 75%. In the matter of preferences, the Edinburgh results confirm the London finding. With boys, war pictures, cowboy, gangster, mystery, sea and detective films are the most popular; comics, nature, song pictures, animated cartoons and child characters are less popular but not objected to; and films of love, society life and tragedies were clearly disliked. With girls, it is the war pictures, gangster films and tragedies which are disliked, while child-character stories, cowboy films, comics, animated cartoons, song pictures and detective films are popular; the girls' preferences are fairly divided on mystery thrillers and love stories. These preferences are analytically summarized in the statement: "The kinds of pictures popular among boys are those showing swift action, bold decisions, and personal bravery. . . Those which display the primary emotions — love, jealousy and even hate — are disliked. . . In the class most favored by the girls are the pictures giving light amusement and those pleasing to their artistic sense. . . The pictures disliked are those showing violence, fierceness and ruthless disregard of justice. The girls, for instance, see war in one aspect, the boys in another. Regarding pictures displaying emotion, some of the younger girls want to see love pictures. The older girls from the better districts will have none of them, but the poorer senior girls give love pictures a high place." [68]

A questionnaire was given to young people of adolescent ages, belonging to various juvenile organizations, such as the Scouts and Guides. Two hundred and fifty returns were received, 139 from boys and 111 from girls. After surveying the answers on points of criticism and enjoyment, the Committee concluded that "pictures are providing materials for interesting discussion and the exercise of the young people's faculties. At the worst,

[67] Vd. *Report on Cinemas and Youth*, Dundee, 1932. [68] *Op. cit.*, pp. 16-18.

as Dr. Johnson said about smoking, it is preserving their minds from total vacuity." [69]   The children were also questioned about the influence of the movies upon their conduct.   The replies were disappointing, many children failing to answer.   The Committee observed that the children "do not seem to know what ultimately causes" their actions.   "Altogether this question seemed too difficult and has elicited no definite information." [70]   This is an extremely significant point.   American investigators, such as Professor Blumer, seem to have no difficulty in eliciting great masses of information on this matter of the causes of conduct.   Can it be that American children know more about such matters than their Scotch sisters and brothers?   Or is it because Professor Blumer asked very specific and what were, perhaps, leading questions?

The Committee also distributed a questionnaire to the parents of school children, receiving about 900 replies.   They were asked, among other things, whether attendance at the cinema made their children nervous, sleepless and more difficult to control.   "More than 90% replied No to all three questions; less than 2% replied Yes to all three." [71]   This clear consensus of opinion should be noted because of its marked variance from the stated and implied conclusions of the Payne Fund studies which we shall presently examine.   To the question, "Do you consider the Cinema has a good or bad effect on your child?" a great many gave no definite answer or said it depended on the pictures, and so on.   Such answers are classified as doubtful.   In the case of parents whose children attended most frequently, between 50% and 60% said the influence was good, 30% to 40% were doubtful, and about 10% thought the effects were bad.

Teachers were interrogated, because as the Committee said, the opinions of the teachers is of only slightly less value than the opinions of parents, and of great value on the question of the influence of the cinema on the child's mental development and school work.   In contrast to the report of a similar Chicago Commission made by Professor Burgess in 1920, the attitude of this Edinburgh Committee with respect to the judgments of teachers is exceptionally critical.   They say: we must bear in mind that "the teachers are indicating their professional point of view.   It is not of itself a complete condemnation of the cinema

[69] *Op. cit.*, p. 32.   [70] *Op. cit.*, p. 32.   [71] *Op. cit.*, p. 35.

to say that it interferes, even seriously, with school work; neither would any teacher so declare, any more than he would seek to prevent a pupil's pursuit of a hobby on the ground that it was hindering some school study." [72] We are further cautioned that "the answers are all given as opinions, formed as the result of experience and accumulated impressions, and not on definite experimental evidence." [73] To the question whether children suffer from frequent attendance at the pictures with regard to lack of concentration, 68.8% said Yes and 22% said No, the remainder having no judgment; with regard to restlessness, 67.5% said Yes, and 21% said No. To the question whether school work suffers or gains from children's attendance at the pictures, 55.4% said that it suffers, and 26.8% said that it gains, 17.8% being non-committal. The reasons given for the suffering included such points as neglect of home-work, loss of rest and sleep — contrary to the opinions of the parents — greater difficulty in interesting the children in their school work, and the fact that children read less. The reasons given for the gain are the extension of knowledge, the acquisition of new ideas and a wider outlook generally. To the question whether children acquire false ideas of life from the pictures, 61.2% said Yes and 21.4% said No; the grounds given were that much of the life depicted was abnormal, that extremes of wealth and poverty are unduly prominent, that too great prominence is given to crooks and gangsters, and that "too many of the ideas are peculiarly American." To the question whether frequent attendance at the pictures tends to destroy the child's originality and creative impulse, 45% said No and 37.4% said Yes. The Committee concludes this part of its inquiry in the following language: "At the risk of making generalizations which may be regarded as too sweeping, we venture to sum up the teachers' view on the effect of attendance at the cinema on the children's education in its threefold aspect, physical, mental and moral. Physically, the effect is bad; mentally it is good; morally, it is bad." [74] The generalization may be too sweeping in the light of the actual percentage figures; at any rate, it disagrees with the opinions of the parents and of the London school inspectors.

The results of these two English inquiries, as summarized by the opinions of the reporting Committees, plainly disagree with

[72] *Op. cit.,* p. 40.   [73] *Op. cit.,* p. 40.   [74] *Op. cit.,* p. 48.

what seems to be prevailing American popular beliefs as well as with the "convictions" of scientists and other investigators. There is much to wonder about in this. Do American investigators find, and the American public believe, what their prejudices lead them to expect, whereas the English find according to opposite pre-convictions? And if so, why are the prejudices so different? Has the fact that the problem of crime and delinquency in England is much less grave than in this country, anything to do with the fact that the Chief Inspector of Schools in London says that there is no need for alarm, while in America there is general and persistent agitation about the movies by reformers and others? Can it be that in England the influence of the home, the church and the school—not to mention the homogeneity and firmness of the national morale—is so strong a positive influence in the formation of the moral character of the young, that there is both less actual demoralization and less fear of corruption from the movies? It is necessary here to remember that the character of the motion pictures presented in Great Britain is, for the most part, the same as in this country. These perplexing questions are related to the further question raised by the comparative crime and delinquency rates for the two countries. Is there any explanation except the profoundly discouraging one that the moral and social fibre of the British is distinctly superior, that we have more crime and disorder—just as we are more given to the continual agitations of reform—because, fundamentally, we do not want to live well socially and morally as much as they do? Whatever answers be given to these questions, the consensus of English opinion about the problem of the movies must not be forgotten, nor must the detailed findings of these two reports be overlooked, when we come to examine the Payne Fund studies on similar points. Whatever significance be attributed to the clear discrepancy between English and American opinion or "science," the fact of inconsistency must be reckoned with.

Because its method and field of inquiry are very similar, we turn from the British reports to consider Mrs. Alice M. Mitchell's study of 10,000 school children in Chicago, made on a grant from the Wieboldt Foundation in 1929.[75] Her findings consist of nothing more than the statistical summaries of replies received

[75] *Op. cit.*, in fn. 34 *supra.*

from the school children to quizzes she gave them. These summaries represent the distribution of children's opinions about a number of points, such as frequency and time of attendance, manner of choice of movies, movie preferences, and so forth. In such matters, the opinion of children can be treated as fairly reliable; these are simple questions compared to ones about the influence of the movies upon conduct. We have already discussed the results of Mrs. Mitchell's attempt to discover whether the movies are "blamed" by delinquents for their misbehavior. Here we shall merely report her summaries. In the light of these data, she has formed an opinion about the problem of the movies which will be worth considering *as such*. It should be noted that Mrs. Mitchell does not offer this opinion as a scientific conclusion.

The 10,000 children Mrs. Mitchell interrogated comprise three groups: public-school pupils, boy and girl scouts, boy and girl delinquents in correctional institutions. There is, of course, some overlapping in this classification, since all scouts are school children; but the figures are assembled in such a way that the responses of the scouts and the delinquents are separated from those of school children who are neither. Of the 10,000 children only 1.7% reported that they did not go to the movies at all; 90.6% go to the movies at regular intervals, varying from seven times a week to once a month;[75a] 64.1% of the entire group attend as often as once or twice a week. Boys go more frequently than girls; boy scouts go less frequently than boy delinquents; while 69.4% of the scouts go as frequently as once or twice a week and only 48.9% of the delinquent boys go that frequently, 27.2% of the delinquents go three or four times a week compared to 6.9% of the scouts, and 20.4% of the delinquents go five times a week as compared to .4% of the scouts. We have already quoted Mrs. Mitchell's comment on this difference in frequency of attendance.

As for time of attendance, 43.2% of the total group go to the movies in the evening exclusively, 25.4% go both afternoon and

---

[75a] Rather "90.6 *say* that they go." For the sake of brevity, I shall omit such qualifying words as "say" and "report," in summarizing Mrs. Mitchell's and other surveys of children's opinions. But it must not be forgotten that it is opinions, and not the facts the opinions are about, which these investigations survey.

evening, and 29.2% go only in the afternoon.   The juvenile delinquents go more frequently in the evenings than other groups; in the light of the other factors which condition the lives of delinquent children, particularly the lack of adult or parental supervision, this finding is to be expected.   Yet most boys, whether delinquent or not, attend the movies unaccompanied by their parents; 80.8% in the case of delinquents, 72.5% in the case of boy scouts and a slightly higher percentage in the case of high-school and grade-school boys.   The situation is slightly different with girls; 75.3% of delinquent girls are unaccompanied by their parents, whereas this holds for only 53.8% of girl scouts; the percentage is again slightly higher for grade-school and high-school girls.   For the most part, the way in which children attend the movies, alone, with friends or with parents, is the same for boy scouts and boy delinquents, girl scouts and girl delinquents.

Mrs. Mitchell investigated the manner in which children select the movies they see.   Of the entire group, only 1.6% of the children have their movies selected for them by their parents. The rest choose their own by various methods, and there is no clear-cut difference here between the several sub-groups.   Movies are picked according to posters in the lobby, newspaper reports, titles, favorite actors, recommendations by friends.   In only one instance is there a clear difference: only 4.6% of the girl scouts are guided by posters in the lobby whereas 23.9% of girl delinquents choose in this way.   As Mrs. Mitchell says, "girls inclined toward delinquency are more often on the streets and loiter about theatre entrances more freely than do girls who have some definite organized interest in their lives, as have the Girl Scouts." [76]   The obvious differences in their other conditions of life also account for the fact that the delinquent children more frequently attend the big theatres downtown in the business district whereas the scouts and public-school children more frequently attend the smaller neighborhood houses.   The same can be said for the finding that the boy scouts and school boys prefer football to the movies, whereas the delinquent boys prefer the movies; on the other hand, even the delinquent boys prefer baseball to the movies; only the delinquent girls prefer the movies to baseball.   It is natural that the scouts prefer hiking to the

[76] *Op. cit.,* p. 60.

movies, whereas the delinquents have the opposite preference, but so also do school children, boys and girls, who are not scouts. All groups prefer to go to parties rather than to the movies, the delinquents a little more so than the other children. 65.6% of the entire group would rather go auto-riding than go to the movies; here there is hardly any difference between the various sub-groups. The majority of the 10,000 children prefer the movies to reading books; it is not surprising to find that only the girl scouts and the high-school girls prefer books and that delinquent children care less about reading than other children. As Mrs. Mitchell observes, "delinquents are usually from families in which books are not part of the necessary equipment." [77]

Mrs. Mitchell classified movies according to the following types: adventure, comedy, education, historical, mystery, romance, sport, tragedy, war, western. She found that "western, adventure, comedy and mystery are the most popular types of movies with the boys, and romance, comedy and western are the most popular with girls." [78] What is most instructive here is the finding that "the sub-groups, — the scout group, the delinquent group and the public-school non-scout group, — show few characteristic variations compared to one another." [79] Thus, the only outstanding difference between delinquent boys and boy scouts is that the former's preference for western films is much more marked. There is, however, a slightly greater difference in the tastes of girl scouts and delinquent girls. Whereas the majority of girl scouts prefer comedy, the delinquent girls like romances and westerns better than any other; romances are very unpopular with girl scouts, which is certainly not surprising any more than their great popularity with delinquent girls, particularly in the light of the finding that in the case of high-school girls who are neither scouts nor delinquents, romances are also most popular. Slightly more than 10% of all the children reported no choice, saying that they liked them all.

I think it will be generally admitted that most of these findings by Mrs. Mitchell do little more than state numerically what any intelligent person would have expected [119]. In only a few instances are the numbers genuinely instructive, *if reliable*. Although it is widely known that children attend movies without

[77] *Op. cit.,* p. 92.   [78] *Op. cit.,* p. 105.   [79] *Op. cit.,* p. 107.

their parents, the extent to which this is the case is somewhat surprising. Although anyone who knows anything about boys and girls — and hence knows the difference between children who are and who are not scouts — could have predicted that girls would like romances better than mysteries, that girl scouts would not like romances as much as other girls, that scouts would prefer hiking to movies while other children would not, it might not have been the common opinion that the preferences of delinquent children would be about the same as those of non-delinquents, or that the manner in which delinquents choose and go to the movies is, for the most part, the same as that of the non-delinquents.

These findings are instructive in another way. They indicate that the movies cannot be used to explain why some children *become* delinquent and others do not. A boy scout likes and learns a great deal from crime and gangster pictures and remains a boy scout, while a delinquent boy having the same preferences and enjoying the same stories remains a difficult and misbehaving child. The same can be said for high-school girls and delinquent girls who share a common devotion to stories of love and romance. This challenges the sociologist's attempt to state the causes of behavior exclusively in terms of environmental influences. I am not limiting the point to the influence of the movies. The same can be said even for poverty, slums and broken homes, with respect to which sociologists claim to find a difference between the environments of delinquent and non-delinquent children. I would go further than Professor May, who said in the light of his investigation of the social conduct and attitudes of children who frequently attend movies: "It is certainly true that bad boys attend the movies, but whether they are bad because they attend the movies or whether they attend the movies because they are bad, or *whether movie attendance and badness are in any way related is a question we have not pretended to answer.* It is equally obvious that good boys attend the movies, and one has exactly the same argument whether goodness is the result or the cause of movie attendance, or whether it is entirely dissociated from it." [80] (Italics mine. Professor Blumer and others, however, do *pretend* to answer such questions.) To

[80] In a letter to the Christian Science Monitor, Jan. 3, 1933.

Professor May's caution must be added a more fundamental point of criticism. The sufficient causes of virtue and vice cannot be found anywhere in the environment.[81] No scientific investigation of the sort done by sociologists will ever be able to answer these questions. Nor will the empirical psychologists, who explicitly or implicitly deny the role of reason and its conflict with the passions in voluntary behavior, ever be able to tell us by their kind of research why some boys are good and others bad. The moral character is formed by some combination of the factors of nature, nurture and reason. The way in which they combine is inscrutable to observation of any sort. Intelligent parents, exercising their good intentions with the greatest care, have always succeeded in rearing *some* children well and have always failed in the training of others, and always will. And some children have become good men and exemplary citizens in spite of, rather than because of, the lack of training and all other adverse circumstances of their youth. There is fundamental human wisdom in the reflection that there but for the grace of God go I.

In summarizing what has been surveyed so far, it must be said that conflicting opinions are not as evenly balanced in regard to children, as in the case of the effects of motion pictures upon adults. Whatever be the ultimate validity of the position, the weight of opinion indicates a general concern about the physical, intellectual and moral effects of the movies on children. This may be no more than an expression of the great burden of responsibility which every age feels it has with regard to the rising generation. Men have always been fearful about what is happening to children, long before there were movies and with respect to many other things than art and literature. "Save our children" is a perennial cry, a cry of distress arising largely from the feelings of incompetence and ignorance that most intelligent adults have when they face the problem of training the young. The answer may be the one which Chesterton gives: save the parents first. "This cry of 'save the children' has in it the hateful implication that it is impossible to save the fathers. . . Unless you can save the fathers you cannot save the children." And we cannot save the fathers unless we can save ourselves. "It is vain to save children; for they cannot remain children. By

[81] Vd. analysis of this problem in Chapter 9 *supra*.

hypothesis, we are teaching them to be men; and how can it be so simple to teach an ideal manhood to others if it is so vain and hopeless to find one for ourselves." [82]   This is, of course, a counsel of despair to those who are already in distress.   The more hopeful answer is the kind which Plato gave.   Primarily concerned about the effect of certain kinds of poetry on the young, he proposed that something be done about it by supervising the literature that is given to children.   Perhaps his answer was more ironical than hopeful for, as we have seen, he confessed ignorance as to whether and how virtue can be taught.

This is an age when prudent men — and parents may be among them — turn to science rather than philosophy for help in facing the perennial problem of the rising generation.   In the particular phase of the problem which involves the movies, sociologists and psychologists have made their kind of effort to be of help. It might be wrong to say that they have *tried* to confirm the general fear that the movies may not be altogether good for children; but they have at least tried to obtain relevant knowledge and to resolve the oppositions of opinion.   We turn now, therefore, to the scientific studies of the Payne Fund.

(c)   *Scientific research.*

My interest in the remaining Payne Fund studies is twofold: first, as investigations which may or may not provide useful scientific knowledge, and second, quite apart from the problem of the movies, as examples of empirical research about human behavior.   In both these respects they deserve careful and detailed criticism.

Let us first examine Professor Charters' statement of the plan of the studies.[83]   It may be safely assumed, he tells us, that a child's behavior is influenced by what he knows, his attitudes, his emotions and by the state of his health.   The assumption can be granted only if its inadequacy is clearly admitted.   It is this assumption which guided the formulation of the research project.   *If* the general influence of motion pictures on children can be ascertained, and *if* their content is known, and *if* the frequency of juvenile attendance is known, *then* the total influence

---

[82] *What's Wrong with the World,* New York, 1910: pp. 248–249.
[83] In *Motion Pictures and Youth: A Summary,* The Macmillan Company, Publishers.

of the pictures can be determined as a product of these three factors.[84]   There are a number of slippery points in this conditional statement.   In the first place, are the three factors to be combined independent of each other and independently ascertainable?   If not, a product of them is obviously illicit.   In the second place, the general influence must either be ascertained independently of the factors of content and frequency or, if not, then reason must be given for inferring the influence that movies have upon children from knowledge of their content and frequency of attendance.   It does not obviously follow that, *if* in somebody's judgment movies are *bad* in some sense, and *if* children frequently see such movies, *then* the influence upon them will be bad, *unless* the badness of a movie is defined in terms of its known bad influences, in which case the whole question to be investigated is begged.   Worse than that, the question whether the movies are a bad influence will be illicitly answered by a viciously circular argument.   Examine this statement made by Professor Charters: "If motion pictures have any influence upon children, *if the pictures are good* and if the attendance is optimally spaced, we can *assume* that the influence upon behavior will be beneficial.   If motion pictures have no influence it will not matter from that point of view whether children go to the movies or not nor what they see when they go.   If however any influence is discovered, *if the pictures are bad*, and if children attend the theatre, we may reasonably *assume* that the influence upon conduct will be harmful." [85]   (Italics mine.) Notice first that someone must judge whether pictures are good or bad.   This must either be a moral or an aesthetic judgment. If it were an aesthetic judgment, it would be irrelevant because it does not follow at all that art which is technically good by aesthetic criteria has a good effect upon human behavior.   But if it is a moral judgment, it means that the work of art judged to be good is so judged because its effects upon character and conduct are beneficial.   Hence to judge a work of art on moral grounds, we must first know the influence of the work upon men.   It follows, therefore, that there is a vicious duplication in Professor Charters' formulation of the problem: there are not two independent questions here, whether the movies have a good or bad

84 *Op. cit.*, p. 5.
85 *Op. cit.*, p. 5, by permission of The Macmillan Company, Publishers.

influence, and whether the movies, in terms of their content, are good or bad. The only way in which the second can be answered is in terms of answers to the first. Furthermore, an empirical scientist cannot by his techniques of investigation answer the first question.[86] He should recognize that he is limited to discovering, if he can, what the effects of anything are on human behavior. If the effects of the movies can be scientifically determined, then a moralist or a philosopher, a person who is able to apply the principles of morality to make casuistical judgments, must say whether the movies are a beneficial or a harmful influence. By their own assumptions or by the limitations which their methods impose upon them, judgments of this sort cannot be made by men writing as empirical scientists.

Professor Charters seems to recognize this when he says "it is important to know that pictures do or do not exhibit potency without respect to goodness or badness." [87] Unfortunately, he himself surreptitiously transgresses this insight, and some of his collaborators, notably Professor Blumer and Dr. Dale, violate it even more outrageously. We shall find that Professor Charters permits himself to draw conclusions about influence from Dale's summary description of the content of movies and the frequency figures, although such data have no significance for the question of influence unless influence has already been independently shown.[88] Furthermore, we shall see that Dr. Dale does not confine himself to *mere* description.[89] He confuses description with moral evaluations that he cannot properly make without already knowing the influence of motion pictures and without explicitly stating the moral principles that underlie his judgments. Furthermore, we shall find that Professor Blumer's investigation is directed by the double question: What are the bad effects of motion pictures on conduct? This should be two questions: (1) What are the effects, and (2) Are the effects, if any, good or bad? Professor Blumer, like Dr. Dale, is obviously competent to answer only the first of these two questions; but

[86] It should be noted, furthermore, that Charters agrees with Peters' equation of morality and the mores, and hence with his denial of independent principles of moral judgment. Vd. Charters, *op. cit.*, p. 55.

[87] *Op. cit.*, pp. 5–6.   [88] *Op. cit.*, pp. 47, 55.

[89] Dr. Edgar Dale was at the time of this work a Research Associate in the Bureau of Educational Research at Ohio State University.

the illicit double question permits him to confuse the two separate problems and to give his conclusions an apparent status
they cannot possibly really have.   The point I am here making
can be emphatically repeated in this way : the only questions
which these investigators should answer are about the frequency
of attendance and about influence, and the latter must be answered independently of the former.   Dr. Dale's study of content can have no significance until it is determined that pictures
having a specific type of content have a specific type of effect.
This Professor Charters seems to realize ; he places it last among
the studies which he summarizes.   But Dr. Dale does not seem
to realize this point in his report on the content of motion pictures.   I shall, therefore, consider this study in its own terms
and, hence, in a different order.

(a)   We must first briefly examine Dr. Dale's investigation
of the frequency of juvenile attendance.[90]   His method was
twofold : (1) he gave a questionnaire to 55,000 school children
in 50 different Ohio communities and several communities in
Iowa ; (2) he stationed observers near ticket-takers who noted
the proportion of the audience which was composed of persons
under the age of seven, from seven to thirteen, from fourteen to
twenty, and twenty-one and over.   Only the population of the
city of Columbus was investigated by this last method.   Let us
not question the reliability of data obtained by either of these
methods, any more than we did similar data in the case of the
British surveys and Mrs. Mitchell's investigation.   Dr. Dale's
findings add very little to what we have learned from these other
studies.   In the city of Columbus, 2.8% of the audience was
under seven, 11.8% was between seven and thirteen, 22.1% was
between fourteen and twenty, and 83.3% was twenty-one and
over.   By means of the questionnaire, he discovered that 53%
of the children between the 4th and 12th school grades attend at
least once a week ; 22% reported that they never go to movies.
Boys go more frequently than girls.   Approximately one-third
of the attendance is in the afternoon and two-thirds is in the
evening.   Children are most frequently accompanied by their
friends, and least frequently accompanied by their parents.   As

[90] *Children's Attendance at Motion Pictures*, New York, 1935.

Dale himself points out, after reviewing 18 similar prior investigations made between 1914 and 1931, his findings do no more than corroborate the results of all the other studies on the point of frequency; that his average figures are slightly lower is to be explained by the fact that his investigation was made during the depression.[91]   On other points, such as time of attendance, locality of attendance, companionship, sex and age differences, his findings are substantially like those of Mrs. Mitchell.[92]   One wonders whether it was necessary to repeat the prior research unless it can be maintained that the statistical reliability of 55,000 cases is appreciably greater than that of 10,000.

But Dr. Dale does enrich his report with opinionative evaluations of a sort that cannot be found in the British surveys or that of Mrs. Mitchell.   Thus, in the chapter in which he finds that children are very infrequently accompanied by their parents, he observes that this is unfortunate because we can assume that the presence of older relatives might lessen the more harmful effects of motion pictures; he does not add "if any."   He expresses his own opinion that "literally hundreds of times one notes there (in the movies) a portrayal of character and depiction of conduct which give *totally erroneous* notions of an event as it actually occurs in *real life* or as it might occur in an *ideal situation*."[93]   (Italics mine.)   This opinion could not possibly have been formed in the light of or with respect for Professor Peters' findings.   In the context of reporting the usual time of attendance, he says: "There is no implication here that the evening hours should not be used for such attendance.   But it is a *fact* that evening attendance demands great self reliance on the part of children and youth.   Finally, evening attendance, especially on school nights, *may* interfere with school work.   We present no evidence to show that motion picture attendance does so interfere."[94]   (Italics mine.)   Finally, we note Dr. Dale's general interpretation of the significance of any findings about attendance.   He says that in order to attribute any aspect of human character or conduct to the influence of the movies we must find

91 Vd. Table 10, *op. cit.*, pp. 42–43; also p. 44.
92 He criticizes (*op. cit.*, pp. 65–67) the data on the age composition of the movie audience, reported by Holmes in his study, *Crime and the Press*, cited earlier (vd. fn. 16 *supra*).   93 *Op. cit.*, p. 27.   94 *Op. cit.*, p. 47.

that that element *"always has motion-picture attendance and no other variable as a constant antecedent."* [95] (Italics mine.) I quote this merely to ask whether, as we proceed, we shall find this canon of inference adhered to.

(b) I turn next to Dr. Dale's companion study on *The Content of Motion Pictures.*[96] This is supposed to be an "objective" classification of the major themes of motion-picture stories, and a statistical distribution of motion pictures according to these categories. In his concluding chapter Dr. Dale admits that he has "no special insight into the fundamental generalizations that can be logically drawn from these data."[97] Nevertheless, he feels that he has "a certain obligation to indicate what they mean to him, however fallible that judgment may be"[98] and — since by his own confession his judgment is not a generalization which he is able to make *logically* — however prejudiced. Furthermore, at the very beginning he warned us that "this study does not deal with the effects of motion pictures on children and youth except by inference. A study of content deals only with possible effects."[99] Instead, however, of leaving his data to be interpreted "in the light of other investigations dealing with the actual reactions of children and youth to varying motion picture content,"[100] he is reluctant to shirk the responsibility of giving us his own judgment of the facts discovered. He acknowledges that these judgments are *inferences* from the data, and that other people may draw different inferences.[101] He must be using words loosely. An inference is a logically drawn conclusion. Dr. Dale, having the modesty to disclaim any insight into conclusions so drawn, should have carried it a step further and referred to his judgments as his personal opinions, with which, of course, the opinions of others may differ. As we shall see, these opinions are almost all evaluative; they are judgments of aes-

[95] *Op. cit.,* p. 8. Reporting his findings, Dale says the "fact of universal exposure is proved. Proof of the effect of the exposure is left to other contributors in this series of volumes" (p. 5).
[96] The Macmillan Company, Publishers, New York, 1935.
[97] *Op. cit.,* p. 224.   [98] *Op. cit.,* p. 224.   [99] *Op. cit.,* p. 8.   [100] *Op. cit.,* p. 8.
[101] *Op. cit.,* p. 9.   He adds: "However, it is the writer's belief that the inferences which he draws from the data are the one's best justified by the facts presented."   Cf. the statement cited in fn. 97 *supra.*

thetic and moral worth.   If these judgments of value are offered as extrinsic criticism of the movies, *i.e.*, in terms of their effects, they are not founded on any data Dale collected.   If they are offered as intrinsic criticism, they are irrelevant to the purpose of this study and the whole Payne Fund project as scientific research about the effects of the movies.   In either case, it is necessary to test Dr. Dale's competence to make such judgments by examining his "philosophical principles" in these fields.   I shall first report his "objective findings" and then proceed to the opinions of all sorts which are scattered throughout the book.

The method employed was threefold.   (1) It consisted in the classification of 500 films produced in the years 1920, 1925 and 1930 according to their major themes.   Here the classification was made in terms of verbal synopses of "what competent observers say has occurred on the motion-picture screen."   One wonders at once about the reliability of such materials as accurate representations of the nature of motion pictures in their fullness. These written accounts primarily told the plot.   Would not such accounts distort a motion picture as much as they would a long novel or a play?   Dr. Dale appreciates the inadequacy of data of classification based on such materials and therefore tried by his second and third methods to compensate for it.[102]   (2) One hundred and fifteen films, 45 released in 1929, 46 in 1930 and 24 in 1931 were actually viewed in theatres and specific features of their content, as well as their major theme, were reported by observers who had "read a review before attending the theatre . . . recorded pertinent comments at the theatre and wrote the complete report immediately after viewing the film."[103] Here the problem is one of sampling.   Are these 115 films, distributed as they are over three years, fair samplings of the 500 films which are produced every year?   Dr. Dale attempts to justify his random samplings as fair by showing that the proportions in which various themes occur in these 115 pictures are about the same as the proportions in the 500 films of 1930 examined in the first part of the study.   But the correctness of this test depends upon the accuracy and validity of the prior classification of films according to brief written synopses of their plots. (3) Forty of these 115 films were analyzed in much greater de-

[102] *Op. cit.*, pp. 2–3.   [103] *Op. cit.*, p. 10.

tail, after being viewed under conditions which permitted the taking of stenographic notes. The dialogue script of the picture was read before the picture was seen.

The findings are as follows. In the fifteen hundred pictures the descriptions of which were classified, three themes were found to predominate in all three years. Thus, in 1930 29.6% dealt with the theme of love, 15.0% with sex, and 27.4% with crime. The figures are approximately the same for 1920 and 1925. The distinction between the closely related themes of love and sex is a moral one; sex is the theme of any story which emphasizes extra-marital bonds, involves adultery, seduction or illegitimate children, plays up "sex situations" or borders on sexual impropriety as do "bedroom farces"; love on the other hand is the theme of any story which involves "love against a background of thrills, suspense, melodrama," includes courtship, flirtations or marital difficulties, deals with historical romances, is an operetta having colorful scenes and songs, or portrays character in which a love interest is present though not dominant.[104] In the light of this, what does Dr. Dale's finding amount to? It is not surprising that the 500 pictures for each of the three years show the predominance of these three themes. One could take similarly written synopses of Greek tragedies and comedies, of Elizabethan drama and Restoration comedy, of all the novels written in any ten year period, and, defining the categories of love, sex and crime as Dr. Dale does, find the same if not a greater predominance of these three themes. The remaining seven themes, mystery, war, children, history, exploration-travel-animal, comedy, social propaganda, simply never were and are not now the major themes of fiction of any sort. That 72% of the motion pictures produced in 1930 deal with love, sex and crime is, therefore, hardly surprising; it would be amazing if that were not the case. The substance of poetry in all its forms is the moral behavior of men. The major moral conflicts which men face in life and in literature revolve around the relation between the sexes and the relation between the individual and the society in which he lives. A significant analysis of the character of a body of literature, such as Greek tragedy, Elizabethan drama, the Victorian novel or contemporary motion pictures, would not be concerned with the predominance of themes classified in

[104] Vd. table of classifications, pp. 15–16.

this manner, but would look to the manner in which these traditional themes are developed. Dr. Dale's assignment of a given picture to a given category is based upon flat and brief descriptions of plot. This could hardly indicate the way in which the theme was treated, as anyone familiar with brief synopses of Shakespeare's plays well knows.

What is Dr. Dale's opinion about this extraordinary finding that the major themes of motion pictures are the same themes which predominate in all literature and in any age? He does not doubt that this shows how great is the need for careful parental supervision in the selection of motion pictures.[105] The fact that two-fifths of the pictures deal with crime and sex indicates to him that "a purpose of the movies is to deal with life problems and their solution."[106] It seems more obvious that the purpose is to tell a good story; crime and sex have always provided the material for good stories. He asks: "Are there not other problems which might well be handled on the screen? Would not the motion picture be a good one in which to present government, commerce and industry? Are there no social problems other than those of crime and sex which could lend themselves to dramatic treatment?"[107] It should be noted that Dr. Dale has omitted love which is the first in importance of the three major themes. If, in addition he considered war, mystery and comedy, which are the next three in frequency, he would have named six themes which almost exhaust the possibilities of literary material. In other words, motion pictures are not unusual in their thematic emphases. Dr. Dale might amuse himself by trying to think of a large number of novels or plays dealing predominantly with government, industry and commerce.

The study of the selected 115 pictures is supposed to supply the inadequacies in the flat classification of the 1500 movies according to synopses. In this study, not merely a simple version of plot but the detailed manner of treatment is considered. Forty of the 115 pictures were closely studied. I shall attempt briefly to summarize Dr. Dale's findings by this method. Thus, in the matter of locale and setting, he reports that over half the pictures are set in the United States, and above one-fifth are entirely foreign; metropolitan settings predominated, and of

105 *Op. cit.*, p. 21.   106 *Op. cit.*, p. 22.
107 *Op. cit.*, p. 22, by permission of The Macmillan Company, Publishers.

these New York City is the frequent specific locale; of the interiors shown, bedrooms and living rooms came first, and then offices; of all the residences shown, 69% were the dwellings of the wealthy, 25% moderate homes, and only 4% the hovels of the poor. In the matter of the characters, Dale reports that for the most part the leading characters are in their twenties; the female characters are younger than the male characters; male villains are older than male heroes. In economic status, slightly less than half the characters are in moderate circumstances, 37% are wealthy, and 12% are poor; more than half the characters are not shown as having any occupation, although it must be remembered that 50% of the women are married; of definite occupations, commercial comes first and illegal, second. In the matter of the clothing worn by characters, Dale says it is difficult to draw conclusions, even from the data based on the close examination of 40 pictures; he does tell us however that informal and occupational clothing was seen in almost all pictures, intimate clothing in three-fourths of the pictures, formal clothing in a little less than three-fourths, and recreational clothing in over one-half. In the matter of romantic meetings and love-making, the report based on 40 pictures classifies the types of love-making as intense, moderate and friendly, and finds that moderate love-making is shown in 78% of the pictures, while friendly and intense love-making are seen in 73% and 70% of the pictures respectively. Eight techniques of love-making are shown, of which the kiss and the embrace — in the movies as in life — are commonest. Love-making occurs most frequently in the living-room, more than twice as frequently as in the bedroom. The proposal of marriage occurs in only 5% of the scenes of love-making. In the matter of sex, marriage and romantic love, the study of 115 pictures showed that winning another's love is the most common individual goal of the leading characters, whereas illicit love ranked sixth, and was most frequently the goal of villains. In 40 pictures, three-fourths of the leading characters were unmarried at the beginning of the story and marriages occur in approximately one-fourth of the pictures. In the matter of crime, 97 out of 115 pictures showed 449 crimes attempted or committed. Villains are responsible for almost one-half of the violent deaths attempted or committed. Eight techniques of murder are seen, and fifty-seven types of crime. In 40 pictures, about one-fourth of the criminals are not punished, and in more than one-fourth the punishment which does occur is more or less accidental. In the matter of vulgarity, the report, based upon the study of 40 pictures by three adults who were asked to select incidents they *considered* vulgar, says that one or more vulgar incident is shown in 65% of these movies; thirteen types of vulgarity were observed, the most frequent being "hinted improper sex relationships." In the matter of recreations, the study of 40 pictures showed that in 85% of them the leading characters indulge in 28 kinds of indoor recreations, in 50% of them 15 types of outdoor recreation, and in 50% of them 16 types of miscellaneous recreations. In 87.5% of 40 pictures, tobacco is used, the hero doing the major part of the smoking, and the heroine smoking more than either the villain or the villainess. Liquor appears in three-fourths of 115 pictures; the drinking of intoxicants in about two-thirds of these; intoxication occurs in 43%. Finally, in the matter of the goals sought by the leading characters — goals being classified as sought by the individual for himself, or for a small group of intimates, or for society and humanity at large — 97% of 115 pictures show 27 types of goals of the first sort, 83% show 18 types of goals of the second sort, and 33% show 10 types of goals of the third sort; 65% of all goals are of the first sort, 26% of the second, and 9% of the third. Of the first sort, the three most commonly seen are "winning another's love, marriage for love, professional and vocational success"; of the second sort, "happiness of loved ones, happiness of friends, protection of friend"; of the third sort, "performance of duty, welfare of country, and apprehension of criminal."

What does all of this mean? If it be remembered that over 70% of motion pictures deal with the themes of love, sex and crime, the more detailed findings are hardly surprising. But it should also be remembered that the 115 pictures studied closely may not be a fair sampling of the production, and that there is no indication whatsoever that the 40 pictures selected from these 115 have been tested in any way for fairness of sampling.[108] Furthermore, the competence of the observers is not clear, par-

---

[108] "It must be remembered that this includes only about one tenth of the annual production of motion pictures and may not represent an adequate sampling" (*Op. cit.*, p. 169).

ticularly in the case of the three who were called upon to express their opinions about "vulgarity." Is their judgment in this instance more than merely their personal opinion? [109] Waiving for the moment further questions about the reliability of the data, we can discover what the significance of these findings is *supposed to be* by noting Dr. Dale's running commentary on the materials he reports. Dr. Dale is thus revealed to us, not only as a scientist, but as a moralist and aesthetician.

Thus, in the matter of settings he says that the effect upon the immature, or even the mature, is not easily determined, but he nevertheless goes on to add: "The conclusion seems *inescapable*, however, that not infrequently envy and dissatisfaction are *likely* to follow the consistent and extravagant display of wealth in motion pictures." [110] (Italics mine.) He notes, furthermore, that the preoccupation with characters drawn from the more favored social groups, especially the ultra-wealthy, may be justified by the principle that movies thus give the majority of their audience, persons of meager income, a "release from actuality." But "this view of the function of the drama is one with which the writer (Dr. Dale) is not in accord." [111] Citing Mr. H. G. Wells as his authority, he seems to suggest that it would be better if the movies were to tell stories about "the problems of land tenancy, the changing mores of agricultural communities, the fading of pioneer psychology and so on. Science, transportation, common labor, get short shrift at the hands of the movie makers." [112] It nowhere occurs to him that if he were to take

---

[109] "Any study of vulgarity is hazardous. What is vulgarity? . . . We have attempted to meet this dilemma in two ways. First of all we are using as one of our standards of inclusion of *possible* vulgarity those activities which a group of selected individuals characterize as such. Therefore, no inclusions of vulgarity are here made which are not so considered by at least three individuals. . . Some of these statements of vulgarity will seem exceedingly tame to some of our readers. No charge of harmfulness is made by the writer. He does not say that any or all of them should be omitted from the pictures. For some of them the exclusion or inclusion is primarily one of convention. It may be considered vulgar today and inoffensive tomorrow. . . In other words, the writer does not set down here his personal standards for exclusion and inclusion, because his personal standards may reflect only a minority opinion. He does, however, present the evidence and prefers to let the readers decide what they consider good and bad taste" (*Op. cit.*, pp. 154–155, by permission of The Macmillan Company, Publishers).
[110] *Op. cit.*, p. 40.   [111] *Op. cit.*, p. 49.   [112] *Op. cit.*, pp. 53–54.

the bulk of literature belonging to all ages and peoples, he would find that the leading characters come from what he calls the socially favored classes, kings and princes, the nobility, the land-owners, the wealthy bourgeoisie, and so forth.[113] He does not grasp the poetic principle which requires this selection; nor does he understand that if one of the democratic functions of art is to provide vicarious experience, literature must imitate a section of social life that its audience, for the most part, does not actually experience.

In the matter of race prejudice, Dr. Dale exhibits a curious twist of thinking. He admits that the movies may produce a favorable attitude toward a given race, such as the negro. He does not make sufficiently clear, however, that the formation of such attitudes is precisely what Professor Thurstone in another Payne Fund study found. Nevertheless, he says, the negro, for instance, may object to the way in which the movies depict his race even though the result is favorable; in the light of which he concludes that the movies, by failing to emphasize the better members of a race, "*may* set up harmful prejudice." [114]   (Italics mine.) The researches of Professor Thurstone and Professor May should have been fully cited on this point.[115]

As one might have expected, Dr. Dale's comments on love-making and on sex in general, are richest. "Have the movies improved," he asks, "on the old fairy tale pattern of love and romance? Love at first sight persists and the unusual surrounds the circumstances of meeting. This is not much better than the old fairy tale. It would undoubtedly take a great deal of skill to present dramatically the average love affair. It has been done in literature. It could be done in the movie. Would not such a presentation be desirable? Would it not enrich and en-hance the experience of youth?" [116]   Dr. Dale does not seem to realize, on the one hand, that *Romeo and Juliet*, which is cer-

[113] They are not "intrepid workers, such as Koch, Pasteur, Grenfell, Steinmetz and others, who through their scientific investigations have profoundly modi-fied the world in which we live" (*Op. cit.*, p. 54).

[114] *Op. cit.*, pp. 61, 63.

[115] Dale's study was published in 1935. Those of Thurstone and May were published in 1933. Dale had every opportunity to take full account of their findings in the interpretation of his data. He does so only at a few points; thus, see pp. 124–125.

[116] *Op. cit.*, p. 101, by permission of The Macmillan Company, Publishers.

tainly one of the greatest love stories, contains all the elements which he disdains as parts of "the fairy tale pattern"; and on the other hand, he does not seem to be aware that the type of fiction he is praising is that found in the realistic novel of recent times, the stories of Zola, D. H. Lawrence, Dreiser, Hemingway and others. These are the stories which pretend to be about the "average love affair." The extremities of realism often make them sordid and vulgar to an extent that the movies seldom achieve. Only a sociologist would so easily dismiss the genuinely romantic as fairy-tale and prefer literature which imitates life as the sociologist thinks it is "on the average." But the canons of aesthetics cannot be thus dictated; nor, as a matter of fact, is it clear that realism would not be more harmful to youth than romance.

The chapter on "sex, marriage and romantic love" opens with a series of questions to be considered, first among which is "What role *should* the movies play in setting up desirable standards in the field of sex, marriage and love?"[117] Needless to say, Dr. Dale cannot answer this question. It is certainly not a question which the scientific collection of data is able by itself to answer. If Dr. Dale subscribes to Professor Peters' point of view about the equation of the mores and morality, the words "should" and "desirable" become almost meaningless, if not treacherously ambiguous, in any use he can make of them. But the tone of the entire chapter insinuates, at least, that Dale does have an answer to the question, namely, that the movies do not fulfill the role they *should*, they do not set up the standards which Dale thinks are *desirable*, even though he cannot have forgotten Professor Peters' findings. He gives one-sentence synopses of about a dozen pictures to suggest the way in which the movies treat this theme.[118] Similar synopses could be made of the plays of Shakespeare or the novels of Thackeray, with the same effect. With respect to the many problems of marriage, he tells us in the light of his review of 40 pictures that the motion-picture treatment does not touch these problems as they are faced by the average man. "If the major function of the drama," he adds, "is to clarify the thinking of the individuals who view it, then motion pictures as judged by this sampling have been grossly

117 *Op. cit.*, p. 103.   118 *Op. cit.*, p. 110.

inadequate in fulfilling their function." [119]   That the major function of the drama is to clarify thinking is a highly questionable proposition in aesthetics unless the clarification is that which
is produced by the purgation of emotions.   This, however, is
not what Dr. Dale means.   Considering that the "unreality" of
movie problems may provide escapes, he adds: "Frequent excursions into the field of unreality may unfit one wholly or in
part to face the problems that still remain unsolved when one
leaves the motion-picture theatre." [120]   In other words, the function of the drama is to solve life's problems for its audience.
Finally, holding that it is socially desirable to present "accurate,
appropriate and artistic sex pictures," [121] he points out that the
only questions are about their number and their manner of treatment.   But what is an accurate or an appropriate sex picture?
And who shall say whether one out of seven is too many?   Mr.
Dale's standards of adequacy are clear.   The movies are inadequate, inaccurate and inappropriate, unless they present sex or
married life "realistically," which means for him true to the
average as the sociologist would determine it.

I pass rapidly over Dr. Dale's discussion of crime in the movies
because, as we have already seen, there is no scientific evidence
whatsoever that the movies are a cause of crime.   But a number
of comments which he makes should be noted.   On the one
hand, he points out that two-thirds of the leading criminal characters are classified by adults as unattractive; whether or not
children would so classify them is open to question.   On the
other hand, he suggests that unless parents train their children to
make a proper evaluation of criminal behavior, "there is some
reason to believe that the attractive qualities of a number of the
leading characters *may* give children inaccurate data concerning
crime and criminals." [122]   But Dale has already said that the interpretation of his data on this point is difficult to determine; and
further that "common sense tells us that criminals are neither
wholly good nor wholly bad.   We cannot, therefore, expect the

[119] *Op. cit.*, p. 118.   [120] *Op. cit.*, pp. 118–119.   [121] *Op. cit.*, p. 120.
[122] *Op. cit.*, p. 130. He fails to note here that Thurstone's research showed
that some crime movies develop unfavorable attitudes toward crime.   In
general Dale fails to consider the bearing of Thurstone's findings, and also
those of May and Shuttleworth, on his survey of the contents of motion
pictures.

motion picture to show characters in a light other than that in which we know that they truly exist." [123]   In his conclusion to this chapter, Dale again attempts to suggest what the movies *should* do in their treatment of crime.   They should inspire their audience "with an ambition to develop a society more immune to its ravages.   Such a motion picture drama might develop zest, energy and enthusiasm for the improvement of the social order. It might picture the better promise of the society in which we may sometime live.   It would portray the causes and cures from crime realistically but with appropriate emphasis." [124]

Dr. Dale's aesthetic principles seem to reduce to this single one : that the function of art is to teach about life in the manner of sociologists.   He recognizes that there may be some who will object to his point of view "and insist that it is not the function of the screen to educate the public in regard to crime" [125] — or anything else, in Dr. Dale's meaning of education.   "Instead, they will say that violent emotion expressed on the screen represents a catharsis, a purging of the emotions, an escape from life, that it has no meaning at all in terms of the general improvement of society." [126]   I offer this as an indication of Dr. Dale's competence in aesthetics.   The confusion of catharsis with "escape from life," the failure to understand the moral and social value of purgation the aim of which is, of course, not to preach social improvements, are only part of his error ; in addition, he refers to the theory of purgation, identified with the "escape-motif," as offering "a very low conception of the function of recreation in an industrial civilization."   It is a conception of the movies "as a national aspirin."   He concludes : "A strong case, therefore, can be made for the present type of crime pictures as a dangerous kind of opium." [127]

Dr. Dale's interpretation of his data on the goals sought by leading characters is of a similar sort.   In the first place, he does not hesitate to assume that "large portions of our population will seek goals shown on the motion picture screen as commendable." [128]   This is Dale's own opinion about the way in

[123] *Op. cit.*, p. 129, by permission of The Macmillan Company, Publishers.
[124] *Op. cit.*, p. 151, by permission of The Macmillan Company, Publishers.
[125] *Op. cit.*, p. 151.
[126] *Op. cit.*, p. 151, by permission of The Macmillan Company, Publishers.
[127] *Op. cit.*, pp. 151–152.   [128] *Op. cit.*, p. 176.

which the movies influence behavior; it is in no sense based upon his data.   He goes to the data already convinced that when persons "meet situations in life which are analogous to those they have seen on the screen, we may expect that, other things being equal, they will accept the solution offered in the motion picture." [129]   Not only is this not necessarily so in the light of either common sense or scientific knowledge, but Dale seems to have forgotten that he has already blamed the movies for dealing so infrequently with problems of the sort that occur in life. If this is the way the screen influences behavior, its influence must be very slight, but the *if* remains.   He complains that success in love is predominantly the end of human striving in the movies, as if it were not so in life as well; he complains that the movies do not criticize the pecuniary motive, although he at the same time admits that this motive is one of the "strong drives of our current civilization"; [130] while he recognizes that the way in which the motive of revenge is presented in the movies reflects mass sentiment on this matter, he seems to ignore a similar relationship between the movies and the mores in the case of the desire for wealth and material success.   He complains, finally, that only 9% of 115 pictures showed individuals seeking what he calls "social goals" and observes that even in these cases "certain of these goals labeled as social are probably inimical to the best interests of society." [131]   He would like the movies to tell more stories about the kind of ambitions which animated such men as Lister and Pasteur, Thomas Aquinas and Jesus Christ, Plato and Aristotle, Grenfell and Edison, Washington and Lincoln. He wants, it seems, a different kind of success story.   This indicates the standards by which Dr. Dale is judging the art of fiction.   The motion pictures which he selects as examples of "something to think about" further indicate that he belongs to that recent school of dramatic criticism which asks for problem plays, such movies as "All Quiet on the Western Front," "Broken Lullaby," "Street Scene," and "Our Daily Bread."   He would like to see such novels as *Red Bread* and *The American Tragedy* filmed.   In short, Dr. Dale proceeds as if his prejudices in favor of realism and the social-problem in fiction were indisputable canons of aesthetic excellence.   In this discussion he seems to forget that there is no evidence that fiction of the sort he praises

129 *Op. cit.*, p. 176.   130 *Op. cit.*, p. 180.   131 *Op. cit.*, p. 185.

would have a better or a worse effect, if any, upon the mature and the immature in the audience.   Yet he reiterates his assumption, his *opinion*, that "we can expect that the goals which are sought by the leading characters will also be sought by large proportions of our population"; [132] not because the movies reflect the already existing standards, but because the movies impose their standards upon the people.   While it must be admitted that certain of the individual and personal goals shown in the movies are — or at least it seems so to Dr. Dale — eminently desirable ones, it is evident to him "that undue emphasis on individual or personal goals is at variance with the views that we are trying to develop in the schools, homes and churches." [133]   This is so evident to him, that he wonders if public funds should not be appropriated to guarantee the production of what he thinks are socially desirable motion pictures, in case such pictures fail to meet with popular approval and hence not be profitable for commercial producers.   Dr. Dale obviously does not know the difference between art and propaganda; nor has he considered the grave dangers that lie in the policy which such countries as Russia, Italy and Germany have taken in employing the cinema and the drama as vehicles of propaganda.

This discussion is indicative of the superficial and unfounded character of Dale's consideration of aesthetic, moral and political questions.   His lack of hesitation in expressing his opinions is equal to his lack of careful analysis, his lack of relevant knowledge.   To illustrate this, I cannot refrain from quoting the concluding paragraph of this section: "Surely if the motion picture has a social purpose, and if it has a social vision, those who are responsible for it cannot be content to have it merely reflect current weakness in our social environment.   We ought to expect the motion picture to show a better way of living than the average which we find outside the theatre.   There is so much that is commonplace in life outside the theatre, there are so many commonplace motives, so many commonplace activities, so much commonplace thinking, that it seems unfortunate to have a motion picture merely reflect current life.   We need to see the screen portraying more of the type of social goals which ought to be characteristic of a decent civilization.   We need more often to catch a glimpse of the immortality of great charac-

132 *Op. cit.*, p. 186.   133 *Op. cit.*, p. 187.

ters who have sacrificed opportunities for personal aggrandizement in order that the larger community may have a fuller measure of life." [134]   No comment is needed to point the illustration; but in addition to the shallowness and essential error of the aesthetics in this passage, there is an obvious inconsistency.   Dr. Dale has previously accused the movies of not frequently enough reflecting life as it is, of not being realistic, of not giving a good sociological account of things.   Here he complains that they do no more than "merely reflect current life."   Like Professor Peters, Dr. Dale is able to shift his ground and be critical of the movies for inconsistent reasons.   Their essential difficulty is that neither of them understands the nature of art as imitation or the variety of objects that can be imitated.   Whether the movies imitate life as it is or as it should be or as some people think it is or should be, they are bad because they do not imitate life *as Dr. Dale or Professor Peters thinks it should be.*

I turn finally to Dr. Dale's concluding summary.   I wish to emphasize the definiteness of his conclusions from data which are totally incapable of supporting them.   The most that can be said for his study is that it is a more or less reliable survey of the detailed content of what may or may not be a fair sampling of motion pictures.   How then is he able to say that "we have seen that the motion picture errs not only in what it includes and excludes, but also in an over- and under-emphasis of certain elements"? [135]   Obviously only by dogmatically assuming highly questionable propositions about the proper function of the arts, and by presuming, as well, to suppose that if the movies were as he might wish them to be, their social influence would necessarily be better, even though what their social influence is as they are now constituted is the question we do not know how to answer. How is he able to say: "We need films for children and youth. They have been the *innocent victims* of escape movies made for tired, jaded adults"? [136]   (Italics mine.)   He may be right in concurring in the generally prevalent opinion that it would be desirable to have more movies specifically made for the juvenile audience, but this opinion does not follow as a scientific conclu-

---

[134] *Op. cit.,* p. 188, by permission of The Macmillan Company, Publishers.
[135] *Op. cit.,* p. 228.   Dale offers a "balance sheet for motion picture content" (p. 229) which indicates how he would correct the situation.   It should be inspected.   [136] *Op. cit.,* p. 229.

sion from his data.   He admits that "the motion picture should
always play a significant role as an instrument of diversion," [137]
and then, of all things, says that we need further psychological
and physiological research to explain the nature of recreation.
Perhaps social problems in the movies would more effectively
give us recreation than "meaningless escape drama," that is, all
movies which do not formulate and solve current social problems as Dr. Dale sees them.   And at the end he again suggests
that we should look forward to the time when the movies are not
under the domination of commercial interests, forgetting entirely
that the Elizabethan theatre was a thriving industry and that
novels have always been published for profits.   The commercial
producers, like the Elizabethan dramatists and stage men, have
succeeded in satisfying popular tastes to an enormous and profitable extent.   But the primary purpose of an art is not to give
pleasure and enjoyment, recreation and purgation.   "Our major
present need is not for escape literature or drama.   Instead, we
need in the arts a vigorous handling of social realities.   We need
sensitive poets, dramatists, scenarists, men with artistic integrity
who can view the current scene with clarity and insight and
present us their findings in gripping, dramatic form." [138]   It is
hardly consistent with Dr. Dale's scientific integrity for him to
lay down the conditions of artistic integrity.   The one thing
that artistic integrity would require is the avoidance of sociology.   Dale writes as if poets should be observers, doing his type
of research and reporting his type of findings in "gripping, dramatic form." [139]

   Professor Charters' summary of this study by Dale is uncritical.
It fails to point out the possibility of a sampling error.   It fails
sufficiently to separate the bare data from the tone of Dale's
opinions about his findings.   It fails to note the inconsistency
between Dale's assumption that the movies should teach moral
lessons and Peters' denial of moral standards apart from the
mores, with which Charters declares himself in agreement.   It is
clear that Dr. Dale's work shows nothing at all about the influence of the movies upon the character or conduct of adults or

[137] *Op. cit.*, p. 225.
[138] *Op. cit.*, p. 230, by permission of The Macmillan Company, Publishers.
[139] Dr. Dale is also the author of *How to Appreciate Motion Pictures*, New
York, 1935.   This work is discussed in Part IV *infra*.

children.   How then can Professor Charters say that "from all
these data collected about the content of motion pictures the
conclusion is inevitable that from the point of view of children's
welfare the commercial movies are an unsavory mess"? [140]   He
could only say this if, for example, the findings of Blumer and
Hauser supported the conclusion that crime movies are a cause
of juvenile delinquency and crime.[140a]   Perhaps, his basis is the
study made by Blumer alone on *Movies and Conduct*.   But unless the findings of this latter investigation are better substantiated
than those of *Movies, Delinquency and Crime*, Professor Charters is without any ground for his assertion that the content of
the movies shows that they are harmful to children or to adults.
We shall presently show that *Movies and Conduct* is, if anything,
even less reliable in its materials and less conclusive and unambiguous in its findings than the study made by Blumer and
Hauser.   But before we do that, we must consider a number of
other investigations which, like these two by Dale, are not concerned directly with the effects of the movies upon the social
conduct or attitudes of children.

(c)   *Getting Ideas from the Movies*,[141] by Perry W. Holaday
of the Indianapolis Public Schools and Dr. George D. Stoddard,
Director of the Child Welfare Research Station at the State
University of Iowa, stands first of all in sharp contrast to all the
other Payne Fund studies which we have so far reviewed.   Like
the reports of Professors May and Thurstone later to be discussed, it shows how empirical research can be well done and
done within the restricted sphere of a problem that is answerable by appropriate methods of investigation.   There are nowhere in this book any conclusions which are not firmly based
on the data, and the report of the findings is never mingled or
confused with the opinions and evaluative judgments of the investigators.[142]   Whatever be Holaday and Stoddard's prejudices,

[140] *Op. cit.*, p. 55.

[140a] How can he say of the fact that one out of four are crime pictures, that
"this is a rather sorry layout for the children to see when they go to the
movies" (p. 51). Thurstone's research showed that *some* crime pictures
developed attitudes unfavorable toward crime. The gross number of them is,
therefore, not significant.

[141] The Macmillan Company, Publishers, New York, 1933.

[142] "No reports of findings are given unless these findings are still present

their scientific report neither contains them explicitly nor insinuates them by the none too subtle innuendo we have detected
in other Payne Fund books. The work of Holaday and Stoddard, like that of May and Thurstone, makes even clearer by
contrast what is already plain enough in the other studies — their
confusion of science and morals, their presentation of unsupported opinions as if they were conclusions, their bias and
prejudice.

Holaday and Stoddard attempted to measure two effects of
motion pictures on the memories of children: (1) the retention
of the stories told by the movies, and of the various details of
information which are incidental to the telling of a story; (2)
the changes in the quantity and character of what is remembered
in the course of time. To do this, they employed approximately
3,000 children in the second, third, fifth, sixth, ninth and tenth
grades, and 200 superior adults. All were given a number of
tests about the content of 17 motion pictures to which they were
sent. In each age group, the observers were equated for age,
intelligence and reading ability.[143] The tests were carefully
constructed and adapted to the ages and intelligences of the subjects. Sufficient effort was made to validate the objectivity and
to insure the reliability of the tests themselves. The techniques
employed in this investigation are those which have been most
skilfully perfected in modern experimental studies of memory,
techniques of which the psychological laboratory can justly be
most proud. Furthermore, the investigators attempted to show
that the 17 motion pictures used in this experiment were a fair
sampling or cross section of the totality of movies produced during the years of the investigation. Finally, they were extremely
cautious in their interpretation of the data, recognizing wherever necessary the difficulties arising from their techniques and
the consequent possible unreliabilities in their data.

In their preliminary work, they found that the correlation
was high between the scores on the tests of general retentiveness
and scores on the tests for memory of specific details, but that
there was a low correlation between both sorts of memory tests

---

after a careful statistical analysis has been made, and the data proved to
be statistically significant" (p. 37).

[143] It is not clear that the methods of equating the various groups were
adequate. See pp. 10–13.

and chronological age, mental age or educational age. "The ability to remember the salient facts of a motion picture is a trait somewhat related to mental ability, reading ability, and general ability to learn, but the relationship is not strong."[144] In their main research, they found that the retention of specific information from motion pictures is high. "The retention of second-third grade and older children was 59 per cent or more of that of superior adults. Retention over a period of a month and a half averaged 90 per cent of the amount retained the day after the picture for the three groups of school children, and 82 per cent for the adults. On many of the items the retention of a younger group was higher than that of one or more older groups."[145] Holaday and Stoddard also tried to discover what kinds of items children remembered best. They found that such things as bootlegging, business and drinking were not remembered well, "nor were items with little emotional appeal nor items occurring in unfamiliar and interesting settings which would attract attention away from the action occurring at the time."[146] This is related to their finding that children remember, better and longer, items which are directly related to the plot or major action than incidental items. The specific items children remember best are in scenes of action, particularly those of sport and crime, scenes which occur in a familiar type of background, such as home or school. This finding corroborates the London report that children do not observe and remember the same items in movies which impress adults. A child notices and retains chiefly what is already somewhat familiar to him.[147] Furthermore, this finding is significant for any difference that may be discovered in the effects of the movies on delinquent and

[144] *Op. cit.,* p. 35, by permission of The Macmillan Company, Publishers.
[145] *Op. cit.,* p. 65, by permission of The Macmillan Company, Publishers.
[146] *Op. cit.,* p. 66, by permission of The Macmillan Company, Publishers. Cf. p. 79.
[147] "When total tests are considered, each age-group has higher retention than each younger age-group, but it is a different kind of retention. A young child has not the sense of values of an older child or an adult, and he seizes upon some inconsequential detail which has been ignored by the adults. Conversely, young children do not adequately comprehend the plot of a picture and do not grasp or do not remember certain important portions which register automatically with adults and older children" (*Op. cit.,* p. 44, by permission of The Macmillan Company, Publishers).

non-delinquent children. Coming to the movies with different backgrounds, different things will be familiar and hence observed and remembered; this difference *may* be related to differences in conduct.

The educational significance of this research can be briefly summarized. Many pictures made solely for entertainment are found to have genuine value in the fields of English, history and geography.[148] "Pictures contribute a considerable amount to our scientific information, but much of this contribution is fallacious and, therefore, worse than useless."[149] In this connection, it is important to note that "general information presented incorrectly by the pictures is frequently accepted as valid unless the incongruity is quite apparent."[150] Holaday and Stoddard conclude that "motion pictures appear to have more of a possible contribution to visual education than was previously suspected."[151] In the narrower meaning of education as the formal process of academic instruction, the movies have a positive educational value despite the fact that in many fields incorrect information is imparted and imbibed. It was found that younger children are less bothered by inconsistencies and inaccuracies in information than older ones. The fact that children are misinformed as well as informed by the movies must be considered in the light of this, as well as in relation to all other sources of misinformation which even schools are not able to avoid in the education of young children. The elementary history books are also filled with misstatements and distortions of fact which the child must correct in the course of his further education. Considering that the movies are not primarily a vehicle of academic instruction, their defects in this regard are a less serious charge against them than the criticism that must be made of almost all elementary textbooks, even those which are used in scientific courses at the college level. Whether or not misinformation is avoidable, either in the movies or in elementary textbooks, is a difficult educational question; but certainly the movies seeking to tell a story and thereby to entertain have less reason than the writers of textbooks to be accurate, particularly

[148] *Op. cit.*, p. 75.   [149] *Op. cit.*, p. 74.   [150] *Op. cit.*, p. 78.
[151] *Op. cit.*, p. 75. Note also : "The general information of children and adults is increased to a considerable extent by correctly shown information from motion pictures" (p. 77).

if inaccuracy fits better into the texture of the plot. As Aristotle said, even an impossibility is justified in poetry if it is made probable.[152] "A probable impossibility is to be preferred to a thing improbable and yet possible." It must be added that it is probable that a thing may happen contrary to probability. Even absurdities and irrationalities are proper in poetry if they "are veiled by the poetic charm with which the poet invests" them. It is through failing to understand the criteria by which errors and lies in poetry must be judged that Holaday and Stoddard make their chief mistake. They tell us that "by reliability of information" in a movie, they mean "the probability that a certain action or situation as shown by the movies will in real life have the same outcome a large majority of the times."[153] Reliability of information is not the same as the validity of information about specific historical, geographical or scientific facts, which is tested by the generally established knowledge in these fields. I have no criticism of their finding that much information in motion pictures is invalid, but I do insist that their definition of reliability transgresses the best canons of what is proper to the technique of poetry as an art of fiction.[154] As Aristotle said, a story must not be judged as if it were a treatise. If the poet "has represented a horse as throwing out both of his legs at once, or introduced technical inaccuracies in medicine, for example, or in any other art, the error is not essential to poetry."[155] This is the answer to all—from Plato to the social scientists and psychologists of our day—who accuse the poet or story teller of telling lies.

Professor Charters in summarizing this piece of research relates it to the work of Blumer and Thrasher.[156] He points out that Blumer and Thrasher did not employ the careful methods of Holaday and Stoddard, but "it may be reasonably assumed that the acquisition of facts in these specific areas described by Blumer and Thrasher proceeds with the same effectiveness as in the areas studied by Holaday and Stoddard."[157] That this may not be reasonably assumed is shown by the latter's finding that

---

[152] Vd. *Poetics*, Ch. 25.   [153] *Op. cit.*, p. 60.

[154] Moreover, unless it can be determined that what is "unreliable" in their sense of the word has bad effects on character and conduct, this criterion is irrelevant in research directed toward extrinsic criticism.

[155] *Poetics*, Ch. 25.   [156] Charters' *Summary* : p. 10.   [157] *Op. cit.*, pp. 10–11.

children learn and remember best what is already most familiar to them. Are we asked to assume that love-techniques for instance are familiar to children or even to most young adolescents? Furthermore, in putting the various separate researches together, Charters should have noted the effect of Holaday and Stoddard's work upon Dale's study of content. Holaday and Stoddard found that children remember both longer and better the general plot of a picture than such items as clothing, settings and locale, etc. "Action was best remembered when it concerned activities such as sports, general action, crime and fighting." [158] Must this not qualify the significance of Dale's survey of the content of pictures with regard to such matters as clothing, setting and locale, and the range of details and activities involved in scenes of love and sex? The opinion of the Chief Inspector of Schools in London that what *may* be the morally questionable element in films is ignored by children of school age is supported by Holaday and Stoddard's data. But Charters does not make this point when, in reviewing Dale's work, he emphasizes the preponderance of the themes of sex and love. His defense may be that here he is not thinking of younger children but of adolescents. We shall subsequently see whether this defense is justified, since it is based on Blumer's second study.

But first we must examine two other Payne Fund studies, one made by Dysinger and Ruckmick, of the Department of Psychology in the State University of Iowa, on the emotional responses of children to the motion-picture situation, and one by Renshaw, Miller and Marquis on the effect of the movies upon children's sleep. Neither of these studies is directly concerned with the causes of juvenile behavior. That is Blumer's problem. Yet their findings may contribute to that problem. Emotional stimulation is certainly one of the factors of conduct; loss of sleep, with resultant fatigue and irritability, may also be a determinant. The study of the influence of the movies upon children's emotions is more closely related to Blumer's investigation, and it is preferable, therefore, to reserve it until after we have considered the one on children's sleep.

(d) The investigation made by Dr. Samuel Renshaw, Professor of Experimental Psychology at Ohio State University,

[158] Holaday and Stoddard, *op. cit.*, p. 79.

and his two assistants, Mr. Vernon L. Miller and Miss Dorothy
P. Marquis, both of whom were sometime Payne Fund Research
Fellows, is the most pretentious of all these researches in its
"scientific technique," its concepts and interpretations.[159] The
problems of sleep and fatigue are primarily physiological. The
nature of normal sleep, the range and character of divergences
from the normal, the causes of different kinds and degrees of
sleep, and the effects of these differences upon fatigue, recuperation and health in general, are as yet matters upon which physi-
ologists do not agree. This piece of research depends upon the
assumption that the amount of motility during sleep is a measurable index of the quality of sleep. Yet, as the authors admit
after surveying the literature of the subject, "the situation in
1932 seems to be that there is a wide variety of theories based
on almost every conceivable set of physiological and psychological hypotheses."[160] The assumption that motility is an index
of quality of sleep is only one of these hypotheses, formulated
by one of these theories. An hypothesis is a problem to be
solved by further research. It is highly questionable, therefore,
whether the present state of knowledge about sleep in the science
of physiology warrants the kind of research done by Renshaw,
Miller and Marquis. It is not as if their effort were to solve the
problem of motility as a measure of sleep. They proceed as if
that problem were solved to answer the further question of the
effects of movies upon children's sleep by means of measurements of motility. They thus convert an hypothesis into an
accepted theory and in many places state as knowledge what is
a problem for further investigation. They are unable, however,
to conceal the extent of our ignorance in the field of their investigation. The way in which they are forced to adopt conflicting theories and to make ill-founded interpretations in order
to obtain conclusions from their data indicates, better than an
explicit statement could, how slight is the established knowledge
which can be used to direct such research.

The authors seem to depend greatly upon the work of Dr.
Jacobson[161] on progressive relaxation. The interpretation which
they make of Jacobson's work is that "muscular hypertension in
however small an amount is detrimental to the best, most re-

159 *Children's Sleep*, The Macmillan Company, Publishers, New York, 1933.
160 *Op. cit.*, p. 16.   161 *Progressive Relaxation*, Chicago, 1929.

cuperative sleep." [162] In other words, *good* sleep is a process
of progressive relaxation of the skeletal muscles. Muscular
hypertension is incompatible with relaxation. Therefore, *if*
motility during sleep can be used as a measure of such hypertension or absence of relaxation, it can be used as an index of the
goodness or recuperative efficacy of the sleep. It would seem
to follow from this line of argument that variations in the direction of increased motility can be used to measure degrees of disturbance in sleep. But at this point the authors introduce the
notion of the normal as a mean between extremes of hypertension
and hypotension. "The limiting case of hypotension, or relaxation, would be a complete cessation of all bodily functions, *i.e.*,
death. The limiting case, similarly, of hypertension would be
the extreme tonic contraction, seen in exophthalmic goiter,
eclampsia, etc., which leads to coma and death." [163] Too much
relaxation, it would seem, is as bad — as contrary to health — as
too little. But certainly there is some play here on the word
"relaxation." Jacobson does not confuse relaxation with muscular flaccidity. This is what the authors appear to be doing
in identifying hypotension with relaxation. Furthermore, they
are now required to define good or healthful sleep in terms of
some range of values which are neither too much nor too little
relaxation. They know, of course, that such a range of values
has never been determined. They must know also that the concept of normality is a treacherously ambiguous one to use in
connection with such a process as sleep. Is "normal sleep"
ideally healthful sleep in which relaxation has progressed just
far enough? If so, we must have some physiological criteria
for determining the proper amount of relaxation. Neither
Jacobson's work nor any other research has made this determination. Or is "normal sleep" a statistically established mean between extremes, a mean which may or may not coincide with
the ideal mean between too much and too little muscular tension?

The authors proceed without even considering these questions.
They implicitly make the extraordinary assumption that just as
variations in the direction of increased motility can be used to
measure disturbance of sleep, because this increased motility is an
index of hypertension, so variations in the direction of decreased
motility can also be used to measure disturbance of sleep, because

[162] *Op. cit.,* p. 21.   [163] *Op. cit.,* p. 22.

this decreased motility is an index of hypotension.[164] But such variations in opposite directions must be variations from a normal degree of motility. *If* muscular hypertension, in however small an amount, is detrimental to the best, most recuperative sleep, and if muscular hypotension is similarly assumed to be detrimental to the recuperative quality of sleep, then ideal sleep must be that in which there is a proper amount of motility. The experimental procedure of Renshaw, Miller and Marquis therefore depends upon the determination of a normal motility from which any variation in the direction of increase or decrease can be taken as an indicator of diminished recuperative efficacy. Since the concept of normality here involved is that of an ideally healthy sleep and not that of a statistically average sleep, the determination cannot be made until we have much more physiological knowledge about the nature of sleep and relaxation.[165] We certainly do not know enough about fatigue and recuperation to determine the normal range of muscular tension during healthy sleep. Measurements of motility cannot possibly do this for us, since those measurements do no more than describe the amount of skeletal movement during sleep. It is questionable, in the first place, whether such amounts of movement indicate degrees of hypertension and hypotension of the skeletal muscles; and in the second place, we do not know the physiological null point between hypertension and hypotension.

One thing is clear. The authors of this study go beyond the generally accepted knowledge and opinion in the field of their problem. Previous studies have considered movement during sleep as some indication of failure of relaxation, but Renshaw, Miller and Marquis introduce the notion that absence of movement or decreased motility must also be considered as a sign of defective sleep. No theoretical justification for this position is given other than the principle that an extreme of hypotension is as antagonistic to life and health as an extreme of hypertension. This is hardly sufficient to support the procedure of measuring

[164] Vd. *op. cit.*, pp. 22, 24, 102. The authors do not think this is an assumption, but neither are they sure that it is scientifically established knowledge: they speak of being able to indicate "some reasons for believing that changes in motility *in either direction* indicate increased fatigue" (p. 152). See also No. 10, p. 183.

[165] Note the authors' comments on statistical procedure in work of this sort: pp. 22–23.

"increases" and "decreases" in motility to determine the approximation of sleep to an ideal of recuperative efficacy. Furthermore, the literature on the subject of sleep shows, as the authors admit, that the pattern of sleep is fundamentally habitual and therefore individual. We cannot talk about normal sleep as we talk about normal temperature or normal vision. According to differences in temperament, general bodily constitution, particularly with respect to nervous and endocrine factors, and according to the biographical accidents which have conditioned the formation of sleeping habits, different individuals sleep in characteristically different ways. We commonly recognize these differences when we speak of heavy and light sleepers, quiet and restless sleepers. But we do not yet know the significance of these individual differences; we do not know whether an habitually restless sleeper sleeps "better" when he sleeps quietly on a particular occasion, or whether an habitually quiet sleeper sleeps "poorly" if he sleeps restlessly; we do not know whether an excess of fatigue or not being tired enough is the cause of such variations from habitual manner of sleeping. Movement during sleep is certainly only one of the factors describing the general physiological state of sleep; and it must be considered in relation to the individualized character of the pattern of sleep for different individuals.

These facts present difficulties which Renshaw, Miller and Marquis seem to recognize. They tell us that "no statistical answer in terms of the standard deviation or other such measure could possibly give answer to the question as to how much motility, hypernormal or hyponormal, is bad for or good for a child. It happens that this is one of those cases in which the statistics of variables does not wholly apply. In fact many misleading constructions can be placed upon the figures we shall present, if one is not ever mindful of the fallacies and artificialities which may grow out of the logic of this form of mathematics. . . However, it is necessary to present *some* figures to indicate the *trends*, or rough generalizations that may be drawn with safety from a study of a representative sampling of individuals. This we shall attempt to do. We shall also attempt to indicate those portions of the data which in our best judgment are suitable for statistical summarization, in distinction to those which we hold to be interpretable only in terms of ex-

perienced judgment.   The real question becomes then a matter
of the analysis of individual cases." [166]   This statement is not
entirely clear; nor is it a sufficient acknowledgment of the
difficulties that surround this attempt to discover whether the
movies have a bad effect upon children's sleep by measurements
of motility.   We shall find that these authors grow even less
cautious as they proceed, in the course of their report, to present
a large quantity of statistical data and to draw conclusions
therefrom.

The procedure of the experiment is briefly described as follows.   171 children, boys and girls, between the ages of 6 and
18, were used as subjects.   The children were all residents of
the home maintained by the Ohio State Bureau of Juvenile
Research at Columbus.   This Bureau does not maintain a cus-
todial institution, but one devoted to the observation and study
of children who present behavior problems of various sorts.
"Children are brought to the institution on reference from
juvenile or probate courts; or are voluntarily brought in by
parents seeking advice; legal guardians, private parties seeking
to adopt a child, or by various child-caring agencies; or are
referred for diagnosis by other divisions of the State Department
of Public Welfare." [167]   The question naturally arises whether
the children used as subjects in this experiment can be considered
a fair sampling of the children living at home in the average
community.   The investigators point out that the children they
used were normal physiologically, even though they may have
been slightly abnormal from the point of view of their behavior
or other conditions of their life.   Only children who were in
good health were used as subjects.   Since the experiment was
primarily a physiological one, the psychological factors that
differentiate problem children from others are not considered as
relevant to the fairness of this sampling.   Whether the assumption is justified, that such psychological factors as emotional instability have no bearing on the process of sleep and the conditions influencing it, can only be answered by the use of control
groups.   The experimenters did not attempt to make this more
careful test of the fairness of their sampling.

It is not necessary to describe the apparatus which was at-

[166] *Op. cit.*, pp. 22–23, by permission of The Macmillan Company, Publishers.
[167] *Op. cit.*, p. 28, by permission of The Macmillan Company, Publishers.

tached to the beds in order to measure the occurrence of movement during sleep. The mechanical aspects of the experiment were carefully checked and continually supervised. It is sufficient to know that the apparatus recorded movement in bed in such a way that the number of separate movements could be determined, and the serial order of active and quiet phases could be described. The experimenters used the minute as their unit of time. If movement or activity occurred in any portion of any minute, it was counted as an active minute. The experimenters employed these data to determine the mean number of active minutes in each hour of the total stay in bed, and also the length and distribution of the quiet periods. In a period of two years, a number of experiments were performed; in the first of these ten boys were used as subjects; in the remaining eight, ten boys and ten girls were used. In these various experiments, the sleep of the individual child was analyzed for normal nights, for nights of movie-going, for nights following movie-going, or for nights in which special circumstances other than movie-going occurred. Thus, in the first experiment, there were 19 normal nights, 5 consecutive movie nights, and 5 post-movie nights; in the fifth, there were 35 normal nights followed by 5 movie and 10 post-movie nights; and so forth. Each experiment used a different group of children.

The first problem was, obviously, to establish the normal pattern of sleep for each individual child. By the normal pattern of sleep is meant the pattern of sleep on the nights called normal because they did not involve attendance at the movies or any other special circumstances. The pattern of sleep was described by the mean number of active minutes in each hour between nine and five. The mean number of active minutes per hour was obtained for individual nights, for five night periods, for series of odd and even nights, and so forth. The mean number of active minutes per hour was also obtained for each of the successive hours in any given night. It was discovered that from ten to fifteen nights is sufficient to establish a stable norm. It was discovered that the motility curve has certain general characteristics: the greatest motility is in the period immediately following going to bed; it then gradually decreases to a minimum, during a period of from about fifteen minutes to an hour and a half; from that point there is a gradual hourly

increase throughout the night until the time of awakening.   It
was discovered that temperature and relative humidity are not
important factors in influencing hourly motility; that significant
changes in the motility pattern are not occasioned by variations
in daily activity, environmental noises, diet, etc.; that sex differences in motility patterns are not significant before the age
of ten and one half years, but are marked thereafter; that in
general motility varies inversely with age, the younger children
sleeping more quietly than the older ones.   The investigators
found significant seasonal variations in the motility pattern and
therefore took account of this factor in their further work.   But
most important of all are their findings, first, that there are
significant individual differences among children of both sexes
and all ages from six to eighteen; and second, that "there is
justification for the belief that the *least motile* and *most recuperative* sleep is indulged in during the first half of the stay in bed." [168]
(Italics mine.)   I stress these findings because the first indicates
that the influence of motion pictures upon sleep must be studied
in relation to the established "normal motility pattern" for the
individual child, and because the second *seems* to imply the
proposition that a minimum of motility is desirable as achieving
a maximum of recuperative efficacy.   One would expect, therefore, that if after going to the movies, a child was found to sleep
more quietly, to have fewer active minutes per hour, it would
be concluded that the child had benefited from attendance at
the movies, the benefit being in the direction of more recuperative sleep.   Whether or not the authors are justified in their
assumption that the amount of motility measures the goodness
of sleep, they certainly seem to be saying at this point only that
variations in the direction of greater motility are undesirable.
We shall find them contradicting themselves on this point in
reporting their findings about variations in the motility of sleep
after attendance at the movies.

In order to study the influence of motion pictures, it was first
necessary to eliminate the contributory influence of an excursion
from the institution.   Twenty children were taken for a two
hour automobile ride through the city and suburbs of Columbus.
It was found that "eighteen of the twenty children slept a little
more quietly following the trip than was their normal." [169]   The

[168] *Op. cit.,* p. 93.   [169] *Op. cit.,* p. 97.

experimenters also report that for the group of ten boys, there is an increase of only 1.7 active minutes per hour for the entire night; for the girls, an increase of .1 active minutes. They therefore concluded that what they called the "holiday effect" is not an important factor in the total change in sleep pattern resulting from leaving the institution to see a movie.[170]   It should be noted that the measurement of holiday effect was made for a single night.

The change in the motility pattern on movie nights is therefore to be interpreted as a consequence of the witnessing of motion pictures. The results are thus reported: "Approximately 60.5 per cent of the ninety four children on whom we have movie data show increased motility, whereas 39.4 per cent show a decrease. Of the 60 per cent showing increases, 45.5 per cent show increases of 10 per cent or less, 26.3 per cent show 11 to 20 per cent; 14.1 per cent show 21 to 30 per cent; 12.3 per cent show 31 to 40 per cent; and less than 1 per cent show more than 40 per cent. Of the thirty seven children who show decreases, it is interesting to note that 67.5 per cent show 10 per cent or less decrease; 21.3 per cent show 11 to 20 per cent decrease; while only 10.8 per cent show decreases in excess of 20 per cent. . . In other words, only 12.8 per cent of all children show more than 10 per cent quieting after the movies, whereas 33 per cent of all the children show more than 10 per cent increase."[171]   Although they have previously made the point that quieter sleep is more recuperative, they now suggest that "both decreased and increased motility following movies are equally significant."[172]   Their reasons will be given later, but it must be seen at once that such an interpretation presupposes that the normal sleep curves are physiologically the optimal sleep curves. "Normal," as the experimenters use this word, does not mean the physiological ideal, but merely the average sleep patterns obtained from what the experimenters have called the normal nights, nights on which the children did not go to the movies. There is no evidence or even physiological theory to support the assumption that the amount of motility which oc-

[170] *Op. cit.*, p. 98.
[171] *Op. cit.*, pp. 99–102, by permission of The Macmillan Company, Publishers.
[172] *Op. cit.*, p. 102.

curs on these nights is a measure of ideally good sleep, from which a deviation in either direction is necessarily bad.

They also found that "the changes in motility are greatest in the forepart of the night, that is at the time when sleep is at its maximum,"[173] i.e., in their own terms, when sleep is usually quietest. They tell us, furthermore, that "recuperative sleep lost during the night following a motion picture brings the child to a new day incompletely recovered from fatigue."[174] There is no evidence whatsoever to support this statement; nor is there any clear physiological knowledge of the relation between fatigue and various motility patterns of sleep. They found that "children below about ten years of age show relatively less influence from the movies than do older children. The younger children frequently exhibit decreases in motility."[175] This finding parallels the finding that the sleep of older children is "normally" more active than that of younger ones. In interpreting the amount of increased motility, they compare the increase due to the movies with what they call the normal amount of increase resulting from the average growth changes occurring between the ages of 8 and 15. It is about half this amount. The significance of this comparison is unexplained, and there is no other standard by which the gross size of the change is to be interpreted. They repeatedly warn us that group averaging is "a poor representation of the true situation," and yet their major findings are expressed in terms of group averages. Anyone who inspects the detailed tables and graphs is left with a much less definite impression of significant change in either direction as a result of movie influence. If, as they insist, "movie influence is a highly individual affair," it may be asked whether they have not over-emphasized the extreme cases in the way in which they presented their data. Furthermore, summarizing the various tables may give a false impression of the results; thus, in their sixth experiment, they found no change whatsoever in the average motility records for ten boys, and a decrease of only .3 in the case of ten girls. The statistical average is, of course, no more significant here than in the other tables in which larger changes are found.

The final conclusion of the chapter devoted to the experi-

[173] *Op. cit.,* pp. 153–154. [174] *Op. cit.,* p. 154. [175] *Op. cit.,* p. 154.

mental study of movie influence on sleep is extraordinary, indeed, and deserves quotation in full. "The movie influence is not limited to changes in motility during sleep. The extent to which the total impression effect from a film may be reintegrated later, to influence the course of subsequent thought or conduct, is not revealed by our technique. We can conclude, however, from our results that seeing *some* films does induce a disturbance of relaxed, recuperative sleep in children to a degree which, if indulged with sufficient frequency, can be regarded as detrimental to normal health and growth." (No evidence has been presented to support this statement.) "For certain highly sensitive or weak and unstable children the best hygienic policy would be to recommend very infrequent attendance at carefully selected films. On the other hand, certain films may have an instructive or cathartic and sedative effect that is good. We do not believe that any sweeping generalization can be made about the 'type' of film, or the 'type' of child most likely to be influenced, excepting, of course, the abnormals. There is a distinct need for careful, intensive study on individual children's reactions to movies, observed over a longer period of time than we have had at our disposal." [175a] It is difficult to understand how any policy to govern juvenile attendance at movies can be formulated in the light of this confession of ignorance. The only definite conclusion seems to be that *some* films disturb relaxed or recuperative sleep in children — here, too, they should have added *some* — to a degree which, if indulged with sufficient frequency, *may* be detrimental to health. The present study certainly does not tell us what frequency of indulgence would make the degree of disturbance detrimental; nor is it clear from the evidences of physiology what is the effect upon health of the kind of disturbance of sleep measured by motility records.

What is even more extraordinary is the way in which Renshaw, Miller and Marquis are able to find any effect from the movies — a decrease in motility as well as an increase — to be detrimental to health. They tell us that "the final and ultimate interpretation of increases and decreases in motility can be made only after more intensive research studies have been carried out. . . Our facilities have not enabled us to do more than present the results of our studies of the problem given above and

[175a] *Op. cit.*, by permission of The Macmillan Company, Publishers.

to indicate, in the next chapter, some reasons for believing that changes in motility *in either direction* indicate increased fatigue."[176] In other words, if a child sleeps more quietly than usual or more actively than usual, it is because he is more tired. But this statement is concerned with the cause of changes in the sleep pattern, and not with the effects of those changes. Even if it be granted that either an increased or a decreased motility indicates increased fatigue at the time of retiring, it does not follow that there is increased fatigue at the time of awakening. Yet this is the type of inference which the experimenters try to make, and attempt to support by their study of what they call experimental insomnia. Children were deprived of one third of their normal ration of sleep. It was found that "all children show significant reductions in mean hourly motility as a result of a loss of a third of the usual night's sleep over a period of three to five nights."[177] It is interesting to observe that whereas the movies produce changes in motility in either direction, the deprivation of sleep produces only decreases in motility. This does not seem to prevent the investigators from saying that "fifty per cent of the boys show *half as much or more change from the normal in motility* after seeing *all* types of movies as they show following loss of the first third of the night from enforced waking."[178] It seems clear to them that the motility changes produced by the movies, whether an increase or a decrease, indicate sleep impairment of the same sort that is caused by sleep deprivation, although the latter results only in decrease of motility. They present no evidence to show what effect loss of sleep has upon the health of the child; but even if there is sufficient physiological knowledge of the effects of persistent loss of sleep to warrant the conclusion that frequent loss of sleep in amounts equivalent to one third of the normal ration, is detrimental to the health of children, it does not follow that the effects of the movies upon sleep, as indicated by the motility records, can be identified with the loss of sleep or with the effects of loss of sleep. These investigators continually forget that motility is only *one* measure of sleep and that we are still generally ignorant of its significance in relation to the efficacy of sleep to dissipate fatigue. There is no evidence that if children sleep more

176 *Op. cit.*, p. 152, by permission of The Macmillan Company, Publishers.
177 *Op. cit.*, p. 184.   178 *Op. cit.*, p. 185.

quietly or more actively than usual, they arise in the morning more tired than usual. There is certainly no evidence which connects changes in the motility pattern of sleep with the general health of the child. The fact that deprivation of sleep to the extent of one-third of the normal time does *seem* to have some effects upon the disposition and health of a child cannot be made the basis for an inference to the effect of the disturbance of sleep by the movies on the disposition and health of the child, even though there is *some* similarity in the motility records in the two cases. In the first place, the investigators ignore the fact that there is greater dissimilarity; in the second place, even if there were perfect similarity in the motility records, an inference of this sort would not be justified. Pulse-rate is one measure of physiological state. Exercise and certain drugs both change the pulse rate. Can one argue, therefore, that the effect of exercise upon health is the same as the effect of certain drugs?

The relatively slight significance of this study is obscured by a mass of assumptions, theoretically questionable interpretations, and unwarranted inferences. There is the assumption that the statistically obtained average sleep pattern is also physiologically the ideal or optimal sleep pattern; the assumption that motility changes have clear physiological significance with respect to the dissipation of fatigue and general health; the assumption, on the one hand, that good recuperative sleep is quiet or immobile sleep and, on the other, that sleep which is quieter than the average is due to greater fatigue and hence cannot be more recuperative than the average. The inference that since enforced fatigue produces decreased motility, and since movies produce both increased and decreased motility, but mainly the former, therefore the movies produce effects equivalent to enforced fatigue is clearly unwarranted. In order to prove this, it would be necessary to show a quantitative relation between varying degrees of fatigue produced by various causes and a curve of motility which independently accounted for both increased and decreased motility. The assumption that less mobile sleep is harmful to the individual is not necessarily implied by any of the existing theories of sleep and is experimentally unsupported. The conclusion that the increased or decreased motility produced by the experimental movie situation has harmful effects upon the health or conduct of children is not supported by any evidence whatsoever obtained from the study of the children subjected to the experiment.[179]   The implication, or rather the insinuation made at several places, that average movie going at night is harmful to children is not justified by any finding of the research.[180]   The most that can be said for this piece of research, in the light of our present knowledge about fatigue and sleep, is that the movies were found to produce changes in the motility of children's sleep in the direction of more quiet and more restless sleep than usual.   What this means, the investigators should have been content to conclude, can be determined "only after more intensive research studies have been carried out," only after we have more knowledge of the physiology of sleep and fatigue in relation to each other and to health.

One more point should be mentioned.   It was found that the motility changes were relatively large in children over the age of ten, and relatively slight in younger children.   Children over the age of ten can be expected to spend their evening hours before retiring in study or other mental occupations as vigorous as those involved in viewing movies.   The experimenters explain the effects of movies in terms of the persistence of predormal impressions.   This explanation suggests that if decently intensive application to school work before retiring sets up predormal impressions — and otherwise it must be totally ineffective as study — then the doing of home-work for an hour or two before going to bed should also have an effect upon the motility of a child's sleep.   A control experiment of this sort on children over the age of ten might have yielded illuminating data.   A similar experiment might have been performed in which children read interesting fiction before retiring.   In other words, it is questionable whether the institutional schedule of the children used in this experiment provided a genuinely normal evening life, particularly in the case of the older children, with which to

179 It is at best a tenuous inference from observation of the effects of sleep deprivation.   Thus, see items 7, 8 and 10 on pp. 184–185, and note the conclusion on p. 186 : "The experimental insomnia results indicate that loss of sleep in this amount (the first third of the night) is positively detrimental to health and conduct.   An *equivalent* effect *may* be produced by seeing certain types of motion pictures."   (Italics mine.)

180 It should be noted, furthermore, that most of the experiments tested much more than average movie-going, as that average has been determined by the various attendance studies.

compare the effects of going to the movies. One would certainly not expect to find that of all the things which a child living normally at home might do in the evening, the only one which seriously changed the motility of his sleep was going to the movies.

There are two reasons for spending so much time on this study. In the first place, although it employs an elaborate instrumental technique and seems to use the concepts and theories of the respectable science of physiology, the way in which an interpretation of the data is forced bears a striking resemblance to the conjectures of Peters, Blumer and Dale. As a report of research, in which the conclusions outrun the data, it is of the same sort. Knowledge and opinion are not clearly distinguished. In the second place, the rhetorical importance of this piece of research when it is reported by Charters or Forman is peculiarly insidious. Parents are generally concerned about the health of their children and they have vague notions about the relation between long and sound sleep and juvenile health. They cannot be expected to know enough physiology or to be critical enough to question the significance of changes in motility in relation to the goodness of sleep and its effectiveness for health. Although the investigators themselves are quoted by Professor Charters to the effect that no sweeping generalization can be made about the type of film or the type of child most likely to be influenced, he concludes his summary with the statement: "Thus it appears that movies selected unwisely and indulged in intemperately will have a detrimental effect upon the health of children." [181]   This may be true, of course, but it is certainly not established by Renshaw, Miller and Marquis. So far as "scientific evidence" is concerned, it may or may not be the case.

What is much worse, however, is Mr. Forman's conclusion in a book that passed under Professor Charters' critical eye, a book

[181] *Op. cit.*, p. 35. Charters' summary is outrageously inaccurate. It omits all the controversial material and presents hypotheses as facts. Thus, he speaks of decreased motility as a symptom of fatigue, "which according to the scientific literature is equally important as a measure of fatigue" (p. 34). This is not the case. It is at best the inconclusively established position of Renshaw, Miller and Marquis. Note also: "These facts indicate the conclusion that parents who allow their children to go to a movie should do so with the knowledge that the experience is about as disturbing to sleep patterns as sitting up till midnight" (p. 34).

which had wide circulation among parents who did not examine the original research or even Professor Charters' more critical summary of it. He plays upon the questionable analogy between the effects of drugs, sleep deprivation and going to the movies. He uses big scientific words which, to the uninformed layman, have only horrifying connotations. Thus he writes: "Decreased motility after a movie or after loss of sleep is a manifestation of the same cause as increased motility, namely fatigue; partial asphyxiation; oxygen starvation; partial anaesthesia." [182] Or this: "Some movies, declare the investigators, yield as great effects in the production of immobilization as those following the experimental insomnia. Restlessness or a drugged stupor — the choice is unimportant." [183] This is vicious rhetoric, but it might not have been detected as such by the thousands of parents who naturally were upset by it. Finally I quote Mr. Forman's supreme effort: "Clearly, these investigators are not alarmists, nor does any such attitude enter in the slightest degree into their work. They give the considered and carefully calculated results of their findings. They paint no pictures. Yet every reader can so easily paint the picture for himself. Imagine the children from the age of six on, exposed to the flood of movies pouring across the screen, loaded chiefly with the well-known movie trinity of love, sex and crime; with all the violence, vulgarity and false values that so many movies have. It is a question whether this child will become so excited as to lose sleep for a week or that the other child will be so drugged and exhausted by emotional fatigue that his sleep will be a kind of stupor. Whichever of the two happens, the price we pay is exorbitant." [184] The price we pay for propagandist popularization of this sort is also enormous.

(e) The study [185] made by Dysinger and Ruckmick of the University of Iowa, on the emotional responses of children to the movies, is similar to the one we have just reviewed in that it also

[182] Forman, *Our Movie Made Children,* The Macmillan Company, Publishers, p. 87.
[183] *Op. cit.,* p. 88.
[184] *Op. cit.,* pp. 88–89, by permission of The Macmillan Company, Publishers.
[185] *The Emotional Responses of Children to the Motion Picture Situation,* The Macmillan Company, Publishers, New York, 1933. Cf. C. M. Diserens, *The Influence of Music on Behavior,* Princeton, 1926.

employs physiological techniques.   The problem here is entirely
one of measurement.   Scientific research is certainly not needed
to inform us that movies are exciting and that they arouse emotions in children.   It would be difficult to account for their
popularity with either children or adults, were this not the case.
Nor does this piece of research establish the physiological character of emotional reaction.   That has long been known by
educated laymen as well as by scientists.   The only questions
which Dysinger and Ruckmick are able to answer in terms of
their experimental procedure are first, as to the quantity of certain specific physiological changes, *supposed* to be indicators of
emotion, under the influence of motion pictures; and second,
as to the relation between the quantity of change and the age
and sex of the child being studied, and also different types of
scenes, chiefly those of danger and of love.

This formulation of the problem indicates at once the assumptions which the investigators are forced to make.   They depend
primarily upon the psychogalvanic reflex, i.e., upon changes in
the electrical resistance of the skin which can be measured by
the psychogalvanometer.   The variation in the electrical properties of living tissue has been experimentally studied in the last
fifty years, but it is not yet well established that the psychogalvanic response is a reliable index of specific emotional disturbance.   Professor Landis in reviewing the literature of the subject
reports the work of Dr. Wechsler as probably the only serious
investigation of the problem of the specificity of the reflex to
emotion.   "Much of Wechsler's work does tend to confirm the
hypothesis," he writes, "but he reports enough negative instances
and findings which do not easily fit into the hypothesis to make
one exceedingly skeptical of the fact that a thoroughgoing case
can be made for the theory of emotional specificity." [186]   He goes
on to say: "A survey of the literature shows that psychologists
have identified this electrical reaction with almost every conceivable mental process, and with only the most questionable
evidence to back their claims." [187]   Dysinger and Ruckmick
acknowledge that psychogalvanic change is responsive to many
factors, among them bodily movements.[188]   The latter factor

[186] C. Landis, *The Expressions of Emotion* in *Foundations of Experimental Psychology, Worcester,* 1928 : p. 515.   [187] *Ibid.,* p. 515.
[188] *Op. cit.,* pp. 5, 102.

they sought to control so far as possible. But they are far from being sufficiently skeptical of the psychogalvanic reflex as specifically correlated with emotional change in such a way as to be a reliable index of it. Furthermore, the neurological analysis of the psychogalvanic reflex as controlled by the autonomic nervous system raises a question about the specificity of the reaction to such different emotional changes as those involved in fear and sex, the two chiefly studied by these investigators.

The psychogalvanic records were supported by two other types of data. (1) The pneumo-cardiograph was used to register changes in pulse. But the pulse is, at present, as much an unknown variable in the physiological pattern of the emotions as the psychogalvanic reflex. The use of the electro-cardiograph, which gives a much more sensitive and accurate registration of heart reactions than the pneumo-cardiograph attached to the wrist, has not resulted in clear evidence of circulatory change as a specific index of emotion. Here, as in the case of the psychogalvanic reflex, there is undoubtedly *some* relation between any physiological process controlled by the autonomic nervous system and the bodily conditions of emotion, but these physiological processes are also related to many other factors and are therefore at the best only crude indicators of emotionality. Furthermore, the present state of our knowledge about the psychogalvanic reflex and heart reactions does not enable us to interpret unambiguously the size and the time of changes recorded by the psychogalvanometer and the pneumo-cardiograph. There are large individual differences which require that the record of physiological response under experimental conditions be carefully checked against the normal resting state of each individual, which is often extremely difficult to determine. Dysinger and Ruckmick did not employ such controls to a sufficient extent; [189] a critical interpretation of their quantitative data is almost impossible. (2) The other type of data which they used, along with the psychogalvanic reflex and heartbeat, was verbal reports by their subjects concerning the emotions experienced during motion pictures they witnessed. Without this type of data, they would have been unable to tell from their physiological registrations whether any emotion or what specific emotion had been aroused.

[189] Vd. *op. cit.*, pp. 113–114.

The procedure was as follows. They studied 89 subjects under laboratory conditions; 61 under theatre conditions. The comparability of the two sets of records is questionable. In the laboratory, a movie was viewed for only fifteen minutes at a time. The ages of the laboratory group ranged from six to fifty years; no characteristics of the subjects are mentioned, other than their normality in intelligence, to indicate whether they constitute a fair sampling of the population. The ages of the theatre group varied from 9 to 22, and roughly divided into three groups centering around the ages of 9, 16 and 22. The experimenters attempted to get reports from their subjects on the exciting parts of the movie at the end of each session. They were not always successful in eliciting reliable or otherwise satisfactory responses; they abandoned this part of their procedure entirely in the case of the theatre group.

Their findings do little more than confirm common sense and common opinion. In the first place, they discovered wide individual differences.[190] This must be remembered as qualifying all the rest of their findings. In the second place, they found age differences: in the case of adults, the psychogalvanic response is at the minimum of intensity; scenes of conflict and danger elicit larger responses from children under the age of 12; scenes of love and sex elicit the largest response from adolescents about the age of 16.[191] They concluded from this, what everybody knows, that adults should not try to estimate the probable effect of a motion picture upon a youthful audience in terms of their own experience during observation of it. With respect to sex differences, they found that the male response to danger scenes exceeded somewhat the average female reaction, but there was no clear difference in the response to scenes of love and sex. When the wide range of individual differences at all ages and for both sexes is remembered, and when the unreliability and ambiguity of the psychogalvanic reflex as an index of emotionality is considered, it becomes difficult to determine whether this study contributes anything at all in the way of knowledge.[192]

But Dysinger and Ruckmick do not confine their conclusions to the narrow field of data which can be obtained by the use of

190 *Op. cit.,* p. 110.   191 *Op. cit.,* pp. 110–112.
192 It should also be noted that the investigators found only slight emotional

the psychogalvanometer and the pneumo-cardiograph, despite the fact that in their opening paragraphs they tell us that they "offer no thesis as to whether they (children) should or should not be thus excited or within what limits a certain amount of excitement is salutary and wholesome on the one hand, or detrimental and unhealthful on the other. This is a subject which must be pursued by those who are experts in mental hygiene."[193] Nevertheless, they do draw certain practical conclusions which are curiously inconsistent with each other as well as with the limitations they imposed upon themselves. Thus, on the one hand, they say: "It is an undeniable fact, from the data of this study, that there are large individual differences in the emotional reactions to the motion pictures and differences that are traceable to a variety of contents of the plots of these pictures. . . Yet it is clear that in the last analysis attendance at the motion picture theatre is a matter of individual mental lives and must be regulated or at least judged according to the individual psychophysiological organism."[194] But, on the other hand, "we must be guided in practice by such generalizations as can be safely drawn from average scientific results. . . When, therefore, a psychoneurotic adolescent, for example, is allowed frequently to attend scenes depicting amorous and sometimes questionably romantic episodes, the resultant effect on that individual's character and development can be nothing but baneful and deplorable."[195] A few pages earlier, we find: "During the adolescent period, a considerable degree of response to amorous scenes seems to be characteristic. The desirability or undesirability of such a degree of stimulation of the sexual emotions during adolescence is a point on which public opinion, mental hygiene, and ethics may speak with authority."[196] And again, raising the question whether emotional arousal of children at all age levels by scenes of conflict and danger is detrimental to the health of the child, Dysinger and Ruckmick admit that "there is enough disagree-

---

reaction in adults according to psychogalvanic measurements. But this cannot mean that movies do not excite adults.

[193] *Op. cit.*, p. 3, by permission of The Macmillan Company, Publishers.
[194] *Op. cit.*, p. 115, by permission of The Macmillan Company, Publishers.
[195] *Op. cit.*, pp. 118–119, by permission of The Macmillan Company, Publishers.
[196] *Op. cit.*, p. 114, by permission of The Macmillan Company, Publishers.

ment among authorities on the issues that are involved to indicate that a more positive statement ought to come from the physiologist or the physician, rather than from the psychologist." [197]

From all of this it is certainly not clear whether the investigators are able to draw any conclusions, practical and otherwise, from their findings. In one place they say explicitly that "conclusions in the field of social control seem to be too far from the data of the study for the expression of an opinion." [198] But they do not hesitate to hold that their records are clear on one point, namely, that "profound mental and physiological effects of an emotional order are produced." [199] If all this means is that children of all ages are emotionally excited by the movies they see, the proposition must be granted, whether or not it is supported by the ambiguous quantitative data obtained in this investigation. As a matter of fact, in their own introductory chapter, Dysinger and Ruckmick, prior to a survey of the data, held that "there is no doubt that the motion pictures now have a strong emotional setting that induces in many instances profound bodily and mental effects." [200] It is interesting to note that this follows a statement to the effect that "as scientists we had no bias or prejudice in the matter, no particular 'axe to grind.' We were simply inquisitive and tried to get at the facts." [201] But what facts, since the investigators before investigating seem to know so well that movies "carry with them a deep emotional tone, especially in the case of children"? [202] We have examined their research to discover the singularly limited character of their actual findings. What do they mean, then, when they reiterate in their concluding sentence: "Let those moralize and standardize who will: our fundamental facts speak loudly for themselves"? [203] Even Professor Charters seems unable to make much of Dysinger and Ruckmick's findings beyond saying that their study shows that the emotional reactions of children to movies can be measured, and that it "indicates the significant social conclusion that a few children at the age of nine years react to erotic scenes in motion pictures, and that this reaction occurs in increasing numbers of children until it

[197] *Op. cit.*, p. 115.   [198] *Op. cit.*, p. 115.
[199] *Op. cit.*, p. 119. How their records support this conclusion is just what is not at all clear from an examination of the data.   [200] *Op. cit.*, p. 6.
[201] *Op. cit.*, pp. 5–6.   [202] *Op. cit.*, p. 6.   [203] *Op. cit.*, p. 119.

reaches its climax among the 16 to 18 year olds." [204]   Mr. Forman, however, has no difficulty in making the facts speak loudly. [205]

The problem of the excitement of emotions is, as we have repeatedly seen, a crucial one with respect to the influence of the arts upon moral character and social conduct.   The problem is not whether the arts arouse the emotions, or even the quantity and conditions of this arousal, but what effect the excitement of the passions has upon the moral nature and the subsequent behavior of the individual.   The question is whether the emotions aroused artificially are experienced artificially and thus purged, or whether they disturb the harmony and order of moral character and lead to vicious and antisocial conduct.   Such questions Dysinger and Ruckmick could not answer by means of their experimental techniques and procedure.   Unless it be thought that the mere fact that the movies are exciting is bad, we must turn elsewhere to discover whether the emotions they arouse in children have any moral and social consequences, either through the efficacy of purgation or through its failure.   The remaining Payne Fund studies can be considered as attempts to answer this question in some part.   They constitute the major evidence obtained by investigation relevant to the problem of the influence of the movies upon the character and conduct of children.

(f)   We shall consider, first, the work on *Movies and Conduct* [206] by Professor Blumer of the Sociology Department of the University of Chicago.   His study, Professor Blumer tells us, is "an exploration into a field of conduct which, while intriguing, has deterred investigation because of its intangible character.   The customary methods of study used in social and psychological science have not seemed to be of much promise. In this investigation the writer has dispensed with sophisticated techniques." [207]   The unsophisticated, or naïve, technique which Professor Blumer decided to use is, for the most part, the same as that employed in the Blumer and Hauser study of delinquency and crime.   It is the technique of getting people to write as carefully as possible about their experiences with motion pictures.

[204] *Op. cit.*, pp. 28–29.   [205] Vd. *Our Movie Made Children*, Chapters 6 and 7.
[206] The Macmillan Company, Publishers, New York, 1933.
[207] *Op. cit.*, p. xi, by permission of The Macmillan Company, Publishers.

In this investigation, the subjects consisted of 634 university students, 481 college students, 583 high-school students, 67 office workers, 158 factory workers, and 1200 fifth and sixth grade school children taken from areas of various degrees of delinquency. In the case of the school children, questionnaires were used. It is not necessary to repeat here the general criticisms of the questionnaire.[208] The same criticisms apply to autobiographical documents written under guidance. Although Professor Charters insists that Blumer took all known precautions against error to insure the validity of these personal reports,[209] the reliability of the data thus collected is as questionable here as in Blumer's other study. That the anonymity of the writers was preserved; that the investigators built up a *rapport* with their subjects in order to secure frank, honest and unexaggerated statements; that the stories were checked for their internal consistency and inconsistent ones discarded; that in the case of 60 students an interview held six months later, on the assumption that in this period of time the individual would forget any false or fictitious statements made in his autobiography, discovered no discrepancies; that a comparison of documents obtained from different groups of individuals revealed their substantial similarity — these are hardly sufficient precautions, when it is remembered that the autobiographies were written under the influence of guidance questions, many of which are highly suggestive if not leading.[210] "Unless there be some fault in the manner in which students were asked to write," Professor Blumer tells us, "this massing of experiences on a number of outstanding facts points to the reliability of the accounts." [211] Inspection of the schedule of guidance questions reveals one fault; but that is minor in comparison with the naïveté of this autobiographical technique.

But we need not be further concerned with the question of the reliability of the data of this research, because Professor Blumer, in a concluding remark on his method, refers to this study as "exploratory in character." [212] He further says that he is "not in a position, consequently, to make any remarks of an evaluative character concerning the role of motion pictures in

---

208 Vd. Chapter 10, fn. 20, *supra*.   209 *Op. cit.*, p. 37.
210 Vd. *op. cit.*, Appendix A.
211 *Op. cit.*, p. 7, by permission of The Macmillan Company, Publishers.
212 *Op. cit.*, p. 192.

comparison with other agencies playing upon the lives of people." [213]   He should have gone further and said that, since by his own admission this is an *exploratory* study by means of an *unsophisticated* technique, no conclusions whatsoever can be drawn from the findings. Furthermore, his procedure is obviously unable to solve the causal problem of the influence of the movies upon moral conduct, unless it be supposed that an individual's own statement of what has been responsible for his past behavior is to be taken simply as the aetiology of his actions. [214]   To make a causal interpretation of his data, Professor Blumer would have to determine, according to the canon of inference suggested by Dr. Dale, that "the peculiar type of behavior under study always has motion picture attendance and no other variable as a constant antecedent." [215]   I should certainly be unwilling to subscribe to so simple-minded a rule of causal inference, particularly in the field of voluntary human behavior, but even on this low level of "scientific logic" Professor Blumer's work is necessarily inconclusive.

What, then, can an exploration of this sort contribute, beyond being valuable as an exercise in the use of questionable techniques? Professor Blumer's answer is that "the main use of these autobiographical materials has been to show the different kinds of ways in which motion pictures touch the lives of young people." [216]   Only a portion of the huge mass of materials collected could, of course, be presented in the report. "Only that which seems most significant has been chosen." [217]   But the criteria of significance are not stated. It will be remembered that in his study of delinquency and crime, Professor Blumer reported only the positive findings; space did not permit him to record what he there told us was the much larger bulk of negative material. There is no valid statistical check on the proportion of positive and negative cases in relation to particular points. Although Professor Blumer says that he has found it possible "to tabulate statistically many of the experiences spoken of in the documents," [218] the figures are irregularly presented.

[213] *Op. cit.*, pp. 192–193.
[214] Statements of this sort, even if perfectly veracious, are merely personal, unsupported opinions of dubious probability.
[215] *Children's Attendance at Motion Pictures*, p. 8.   [216] *Op. cit.*, p. 7.
[217] *Op. cit.*, p. 11.   [218] *Op. cit.*, p. 8.

Even if they were always given in clear style, they would be of doubtful significance since "individuals were not required to write either one way or another about many forms of experience." [219] For this reason, "these counts can in no sense be thought of as conclusive" ; [220] for the same reason, they have no statistical meaning whatsoever.   Yet, although such tabulations may be thought of "as having greater value than as if they were based on material secured by a formal questionnaire", which according to Professor Blumer solicits "arbitrary answers," [221] percentage figures derived from answers obtained by formal questionnaires do appear in the course of the report.   With all this in mind, we turn now to the various chapters in which Professor Blumer presents selections from his mass of case histories, that seem significant to him.   We shall ignore, of course, the raw materials.   The accounts read like any amateur fiction. We shall confine this examination to Professor Blumer's statement of his findings and the interpretations or opinions he thinks himself entitled to offer. [222]

The general problem of the investigation is divided into the following topics : impersonation and childhood play, imitation by adolescents, day-dreaming and fantasy, emotional possession ; fear and terror, emotional possession ; sorrow and pathos, emotional possession ; love and passion, emotional possession ; thrill and excitement, emotional detachment ; and schemes of life.   It is difficult to see how this constitutes an analysis of the problem of the influence of the movies upon juvenile conduct, even as a set of categories for directing merely exploratory research.   The emphasis is obviously upon imitation and emotion.   We shall expect, therefore, to find Professor Blumer expressing opinions about the way in which the movies influence conduct through suggesting patterns for imitation and through their emotional hold upon children and youth.   In the latter connection, the problem of emotional purgation must arise.   I have used the

[219] *Op. cit.*, p. 8. Furthermore, in some instances, the same item is classified differently in two enumerations (see pp. 152 and 155). The unreliability of the classification casts further doubt on the significance of the tabulations.
[220] *Op. cit.*, p. 8.   [221] *Op. cit.*, p. 8.
[222] "The general plan of procedure followed in this report has been to let the accounts of experience speak for themselves. Consequently they are used very liberally. The remarks of the author are limited mostly to interpretation" (p. 12).

word "opinion" because it is clear that Professor Blumer cannot infer from his data that the movies are a *sufficient cause* of any type of moral conduct. The nature of their influence, whether through imitation or emotional excitement, must necessarily be subordinate, as one among many environmental circumstances under which the moral character of the growing child is formed. I must add here Professor Blumer's prefatory remark that "no treatment is given in this volume to the influence of motion pictures on sex conduct and life. Materials collected in the course of the study show this influence to be considerable, but their conclusion has been found inadvisable. The omission is not to be construed as implying the absence of the influence." [223]

In the matter of childhood play, Professor Blumer tells us that the influence of motion pictures is widespread, although "it is difficult to determine exactly the extent of this influence." [224] Some figures are given; thus, "of 200 small boys under twelve years of age who were asked if they played at things seen in the movies, 75 per cent answered in the affirmative. Of 70 ranging in age from 12 to 14 years, 60 per cent indicated that they played at what was seen in the movies. Among a group of boys between 14 and 16 years, 25 per cent admitted still engaging in play reflecting the influence of the movies. All these groups consisted of boys living in one of the slum areas in Chicago." [225] Of 1200 grade-school children interrogated by questionnaires, over 50 per cent reported that their play was patterned to greater or less extent on what they had seen in the movies. But what is the significance of this finding, assuming for the moment that it is statistically reliable? Children have always played at cops and robbers, or at keeping house, or at being doctor, or at war and soldiers. The pattern of their play has always, long before the movies, reflected the pattern of life about them or the models found in fiction. After some discussion of the great sociological concept of roles, Professor Blumer concludes that "there remains the important problem as to the effect of child-hood play on specific conduct. Thus, while it is clear that motion pictures exercise a significant influence on the pattern and content of play, and in doing so, familiarize the child with

[223] *Op. cit.*, p. xi, by permission of The Macmillan Company, Publishers.
[224] *Op. cit.*, p. 20.
[225] *Op. cit.*, p. 20, by permission of The Macmillan Company, Publishers.

certain forms of conduct, *just what this signifies in the way of subsequent behavior cannot be declared at present.*"[226]   (Italics mine.)   But this is precisely the problem of the influence of the movies on conduct.   The influence, if any, is neither simple nor direct.   Nor does Blumer seem to see the aetiological significance of his finding that "the taking of the role of the gangster or the policeman or the cowboy or the robber seems to be just as frequent among children in areas of little or no delinquency as among the children living in the areas of high rates of delinquency."[227]

In the matter of adolescent imitation of the movies, Blumer's research is similarly inconclusive.   He admits that it is extremely difficult "to ascertain the extent of this imitation with exactness";[228] yet it seems clear to him from the evidence that the degree is by no means small.   Some adolescents, according to their own collected confessions, imitate what they see in the movies with respect to such matters as beautification and dress, mannerisms of various sorts, such as good posture in standing and walking or facial expressions, and the romantic techniques of love and courtship.   Blumer makes much of the fact that boys and girls of adolescent age learn about the art of love from the movies.   He seems to forget that adolescents learned about the art of love before there were movies, from fiction of all sorts as well as from the adult life which surrounded them.   But he, nevertheless, realizes that nothing follows from his findings. "We have consciously refrained," he says, "from placing any judgment on the value or harmful consequences of what is imitated from motion pictures by youth, since the interest of this study has been merely to show that such imitation goes on and to give some idea of its character."[229]   Blumer's study, at this point at least, is certainly not relevant to the problem of the moral influence of the movies on youthful conduct.   Adolescence is the period in which romantic love is a dominant con-

[226] *Op. cit.*, p. 28, by permission of The Macmillan Company, Publishers. Charters says : "Blumer found in studying two thousand children what every parent knows about his own child — that the movies dominate the patterns of play in a wide variety of forms" (*Motion Pictures and Youth : A Summary :* p. 40).

[227] *Op. cit.*, p. 21, by permission of The Macmillan Company, Publishers.

[228] *Op. cit.*, p. 56.

[229] *Op. cit.*, p. 58, by permission of The Macmillan Company, Publishers.

cern. It cannot be said that children over the age of fourteen are too young to be interested in romance; nor does the fact that they imitate what they can learn from books, plays, movies or the adult world, have any moral significance *unless* it can be shown that such imitations lead them to transgress moral principles or prevailing customs in the matter of love. Peters' study showed that the patterns of romantic conduct in the movies — those which children could imitate — are of the same sort as the conventional practices in the community. Blumer presents no evidence to the contrary, nor does he show that sexual immorality results from the imitativeness of adolescents.

In the matter of day-dreaming and fantasy, we are again left without any conclusion as to the influence of the movies on conduct. Although in the light of his adolescent case-histories, "it can scarcely be doubted that motion pictures affect the day-dreams and fantasies of boys and girls of different ages" — as of course fiction has always done — Blumer goes on to say: "It is difficult, however, to interpret the meaning of this day-dreaming in the life of the individual. As in the case of childhood play, we are presented with a vivid picture of the touch of movies, yet are unable, in a large measure, to indicate its effect on the general conduct of the individual." [230]   Blumer reviews what he calls the various theories about day-dreaming and, finding no acceptable interpretation of the effect of day-dreams on conduct, refrains from evaluating the evidence on "motion picture fantasy." But he cannot resist conjecturing about the problem: "If it be true that the content of day-dreaming represents what people would like to do, and would do if conditions made it possible, then the study of day-dreams offers us an indication of what the movies would do in the way of overt behavior if external conditions were such as to allow for the actual expression of impulses." [231]   It should be noted here that Professor Blumer takes no account of reason in the control of voluntary behavior. A good man is not one who does whatever he can according to external conditions, but only that which he should according to prudence. Even Blumer's guess about the possible effect of day-dreaming upon conduct is unsupported by a sound analysis of the conditions of moral behavior.

[230] *Op. cit.*, p. 72, by permission of The Macmillan Company, Publishers.
[231] *Op. cit.*, p. 73, by permission of The Macmillan Company, Publishers.

The next four chapters contain the findings about emotional possession. Emotional possession is defined as referring to "experiences wherein impulses which are ordinarily restrained are strongly stimulated." [232] It is difficult to tell precisely what this pseudo-technical language of current sociology means. What it seems to amount to is that individuals during emotional excitement are likely to act differently from when they are calm; there is less control of action by reason; the passions aroused are likely to dominate. The state of emotional possession, Blumer tells us, is usually short-lived. The problem, therefore, is whether "emotional possession" due to the movies is extensive enough in quantity and duration to cause immoral conduct, conduct in which passion rather than reason rules. Whether the emotions artificially excited by motion pictures are also artificially purged and are thus prevented from disordering the soul is the other side of the same question. We should naturally expect Blumer to give us evidence that will show specifically how conduct is affected by emotional possession.

But that is not the case. Thus, with respect to fear and terror, we are given a large number of autobiographical reports in which college students, for the most part, remember how some picture or other frightened them. For the most part, the experience of terror was of short duration although, as one would expect, there were some cases in which the fear persisted. It is interesting to observe that a large number of these accounts concur in naming certain movies, all of the same type, as causing excessive fright. But it is more interesting to note that the evidence presented fails utterly to answer the question about the effects of such emotional possession upon subsequent conduct that is morally significant. Blumer again admits that "it is difficult to evaluate motion pictures in this respect. While, as we have seen, many informants declare that the witnessing of a terrifying picture has left some permanent effect on them, in the main the effect was temporary." [233] Similarly in the case of sorrow and pathos, there is no evidence whatsoever to show that the tears and grief which movies sometimes arouse, according to these autobiographies, have any effects upon subsequent conduct. The loss of self-control to which Blumer frequently

[232] *Op. cit.*, p. 74.
[233] *Op. cit.*, p. 90, by permission of The Macmillan Company, Publishers.

refers in these two chapters usually means no more than that the child or youth was moved to various expressions of fear and sorrow during the performance itself. For the most part, the emotions ceased upon being thus expressed; the effect was thus usually transient.[234]   So far, then, all that we have learned from this material is what we already well knew, namely, that children are emotionally excited by movies, usually in a volatile and transient manner and sometimes to an extent that involves overt expression at the time the emotion is experienced. To this extent, at least, it would seem that there is no purgation. But on the other hand, it does not necessarily follow from such failure of purgation that the child's subsequent acts form vicious habits and corrupt moral character. That remains to be shown.

With respect to love and passion, the story is the same. It seems that adolescents are emotionally excited by narratives of love and romance. Thus, of 458 high-school autobiographies, 55 per cent reported a mild susceptibility to the appeal of romantic love scenes; of the same group, 30 per cent "showed either admission or evidence that the writer had been made more receptive to love by love pictures."[235]   Five cases are offered of college boys who report the way in which they used the movies as part of a technique of love-making. But what does this all mean? Again Blumer points to the transiency of the emotional state. "However," he adds, "the repetition of this experience through the witnessing of a series of passionate love pictures *may* have a cumulative effect on the individual."[236]   (Italics mine.) The remainder of his comment on the evidence is mere opinion. Thus: "The individual, as a result of witnessing a particularly emotional picture, *may* come to a decision to have certain kinds of experiences and to live a kind of life different from his prior career. It is perhaps of some social significance to observe that the impulses which are brought into play in witnessing passionate love pictures or scenes are those which our conventions and standards seek in some measure to check. In this sense, *without attempting to evaluate the matter*, it seems that emotional possession induced by passionate love pictures represents an *attack* on the *mores* of our contemporary life. It is *probable* that motion pictures exercise this indirect influence upon other phases of our conventional, social, and moral

[234] *Op. cit.*, p. 102.   [235] *Op. cit.*, pp. 107–108.   [236] *Op. cit.*, p. 116.

order." [237]   (Italics mine.)   I am sure that Mr. Blumer could have held this opinion without reading a line of his own evidence.

The chapter on emotional possession with respect to thrill and excitement adds nothing. "As in the case of the other kinds of emotions which we have considered, usually the feelings of excitement in children are short-lived." [238]   No evidence is offered to show the influence of such excitement upon conduct, although Blumer does suggest that while a boy is in a mood of excitement, he *may* be ready to do things from which normally he would shrink or which he would hesitate to do. He cites here his own study on delinquency and crime to support this. This chapter contains a few concluding remarks about emotional possession. Professor Blumer realizes that "to have induced emotional possession is a mark of the effectiveness of dramatic art." [239]   He indicates that the chief ways in which emotional possession expresses itself seem to be temporary activities, such as "shouting, jumping, and excited movement occasioned by the witnessing of 'thrillers'; such as the shrinking and avoidance in the case of fright; such as the weeping in the case of sadness; such as the sighing and breathing and fondling in the case of romantic and passionate love." [240]   So much the autobiographical materials, however unreliable, seem to show. "Finally," he adds, "we should not fail to see, despite the usual transitoriness of emotional possession, that *occasionally* it *may* leave some enduring effect upon the individual." [241]   (Italics mine.)

Like the data on emotional possession, the materials on emotional detachment contribute nothing to the problem of the influence of the movies on conduct, except more that is conjectural. I turn, therefore, at once to the last chapter in which findings are presented, that dealing with "schemes of life." The problem here is the determination of the way in which motion pictures influence ideas and attitudes. Blumer confesses that "it is rather difficult to estimate the extent of this general influence and even more difficult to assess its significance." [242]   But he feels that it is easier to do so with respect to specific points. Thus, in a section devoted to "stereotyped views," he presents

[237] *Op. cit.*, p. 116, by permission of The Macmillan Company, Publishers.
[238] *Op. cit.*, p. 125.   [239] *Op. cit.*, p. 127.
[240] *Op. cit.*, p. 127, by permission of The Macmillan Company, Publishers.
[241] *Op. cit.*, p. 128.   [242] *Op. cit.*, p. 144.

case materials which seem to show the way in which the movies cultivate race prejudices of one sort or another. The excerpts quoted pile up on one side, and there is no way of telling from the evidence as given, what proportion of the cases those cited represent. We shall find, however, in the careful work of Thurstone that the effect of the movies in forming attitudes may take either direction depending on the movie; and May's research shows that the cumulative effect of the movies is practically negative with respect to race prejudice, for instance.

This indicates the distortion that results from the unsophisticated case-history technique used by Professor Blumer, and especially from the manner in which he selects the materials to report according as they seem significant to him. The rest of the chapter, reciting excerpts from students' confessions about the way in which movies affected their ideas of life and love, parental control, travel and college, their ambitions, their desire to be good, their loyalty to family, and so forth is not worth detailed review, since it is of the same sort. There is no way of assessing the extent or significance of the influence in any of these particulars. It remains to be shown that the "schemes of life" which Blumer finds formed by the movies cause conduct, in the first place, and cause conduct which is morally reprehensible, in the second. The movies are, after all, only one source among countless others of the ideas and attitudes which children form. As Blumer himself points out, it is quite possible "for people to place entirely different interpretations upon the same picture and to derive from it quite different lessons. The implication is that if one is to foretell the effects of a motion picture one must know, in general, something of the interests and experience of those to whom the picture will be shown." [243] In other words, the kind of data which Professor Blumer has collected is utterly unable to solve the problem of the influence of the movies upon conduct.[244]   One is left wondering whether

[243] *Op. cit.*, p. 191, by permission of The Macmillan Company, Publishers.
[244] But compare Charters' summary. "The Council also wanted to know 'the extent to which motion pictures influence the conduct of children and youth either in desirable or undesirable directions and particularly in regard to patterns of sex behavior.' Blumer in his conduct study, Blumer and Hauser in their delinquency study, and Cressey and Thrasher have assembled massive and significant data upon this question" (p. 2). In the light of "a mass of evidence from the studies of Blumer and his associates . . . it was possible to secure

he realizes how irrelevant his entire research is to this problem, until one remembers that it is supposed to be merely exploratory.

In a final chapter Mr. Blumer tells us what he thinks about the movies. These opinions are offered as an interpretation of his findings. He feels, for instance, that motion pictures are "a genuine educational institution," not in the restricted and conventional sense of academic instruction, but "in the true sense of introducing him (the adolescent) to and acquainting him with a type of life which has immediate, practical and momentous significance." [245] Being educational in this sense, movies *may* conflict with other educational institutions. Blumer proceeds to develop this conjectural conflict, which is to be contrasted with Professor Charters' admission that the entire Payne Fund research is unable to "rank the motion pictures in a scale of influence in relation to other agencies such as the home, the school, the church and the press." [246] As well as being an educational institution, "the forte of motion pictures is," according to Blumer, "in their emotional effect." This is to be expected, of course, since "in the last analysis they are a form of art—even though popular art—and their appeal and success reside ultimately in the emotional agitation which they induce." [247] But the tendency of commercial motion pictures is to dull discrimination and confuse judgments. Motion pictures have no definite goal of conduct. "They are not seeking to establish any definite set of values. They are not endeavoring to provide a consistent philosophy of life." [248] Their effect, therefore, is likely to be confusion. "In so far as one may seek to cover in a single proposition the more abiding effect of motion pictures upon the minds of movie-goers, it would be in the judgment of the writer, in terms of a medley of vague and variable impressions—a disconnected assemblage of ideas, feelings, vagaries, and impulses." [249] These few excerpts are offered, not because they have any status as conclusions of a piece of scientific research or as interpreta-

---

hundreds of cases in which the information and attitudes acquired in the movies were directly operative in the conduct of children" (p. 36). See also pp. 60–61. Needless to add, Forman uses Blumer's case materials to great advantage.

[245] *Op. cit.*, p. 196.   [246] *Op. cit.*, p. 4.

[247] *Op. cit.*, p. 198, by permission of The Macmillan Company, Publishers.

[248] *Op. cit.*, p. 199.

[249] *Op. cit.*, p. 199, by permission of The Macmillan Company, Publishers.

tions of significant data, but to exhibit Professor Blumer's mode of thinking.[250]

(g) Vastly superior in its plan and procedure, the research by Professors Shuttleworth and May of Yale University on *The Social Conduct and Attitudes of Movie Fans*[251] more directly bears upon the problem of the effect of the movies upon children's conduct than the work of Blumer. Shuttleworth and May recognize that their investigation is closely related to the research of Professor Thurstone and his associates on the formation of attitudes. But a clear distinction can be made. Professor Thurstone's work deals with the effect of single motion pictures upon the attitudes of children with respect to a particular matter, such as war or race prejudice; the effect, for example, of a particular movie upon children's attitudes toward the Chinese. Because his problem was thus narrowly limited, Professor Thurstone could use much more precise experimental techniques than those employed by Shuttleworth and May. The latter sought "to determine the *net effect* of the *general* run of movies on children's attitudes toward the Chinese as well as the net effect on a variety of conducts and a score of other attitudes. The complaint against the movies is not that specific movies influence specific attitudes sometimes favorably and sometimes unfavorably, but rather that the general run of movies and the total of motion picture experiences of children are unfavorable."[252] To investigate this more general problem, Shuttleworth and May had to eschew the experimental method and make a survey, by means of a variety of tests, to detect differences between children who attend the movies very frequently and children who attend them only infrequently. The investigators appreciated the limitations of their survey procedure which, leaving them without precise experimental controls, made it "difficult to say definitely what part of the observed differences can be attributed to the influences of the movies."[253]

[250] Some one should assemble a mass of case-histories to show the intellectual and moral effects of social science upon college students. The movies may not have any philosophy to teach, but the teaching of the social sciences is antiphilosophical and reinforces the sophistry that is natural to adolescents.
[251] The Macmillan Company, Publishers, New York, 1933.
[252] *Op. cit.*, pp. 1–2, by permission of The Macmillan Company, Publishers.
[253] *Op. cit.*, p. 2.

The children studied numbered 1400, selected from among about 7000 children in grades from five to nine in New York and Connecticut schools. The selection was based upon the movie-going habits of the children. The extreme cases were chosen, the 10% to 15% of the total group who reported the most frequent attendance and the 10% to 15% who reported the least frequent attendance. The movie group attended the movies on the average of 2.8 times per week; the non-movie group had an average attendance of only a few times a year. The two groups were equated for such factors as age, sex, school grade, and socio-economic status; with few exceptions, they were also equated for intelligence and the nationality of their parents.

The findings of this research are expressed in terms of the statistical reliability of the differences between the two groups of children on the various points which the test instruments could be used to study. The question arises at once as to the reliability of these tests. The investigators admit that the tests were not used, as in Thurstone's work, to construct the metrical device of an attitude scale, but rather were more in the nature of a questionnaire or survey. Used in this manner they are, of course, subject to the same criticisms: the data they elicit are only opinions. The investigators did not attempt to determine the statistical reliability of the test as a whole, but rather the reliability or steadiness in responses to particular questions. They found that the reliability of the responses was not high. The other defect which they discovered in their testing technique was that the procedure was not particularly sensitive for differentiating responses; the way in which the test questions were worded seemed to make a considerable difference in the character of the response. Even with all these limitations upon the reliability and validity of the data, the test instruments employed by Shuttleworth and May are superior to the questionnaires and guided autobiographies of Blumer because, in the first place, a statistical check can be made with respect to their reliability and, in the second place, the data collected are susceptible to statistical treatment and presentation. The character test results were supplemented by teachers' ratings on deportment, school marks, conduct and character, and by classmates' ratings of the reputations of their fellows. In short, a

large battery of different types of tests and ratings were used to
determine the differences between movie and non-movie children
with respect to a long list of items in the field of moral character
and conduct.

The results are presented according to the type of device used
to obtain the data. Thus, by means of character tests and ratings of reputation, the following "probably significant differences" were found between movie and non-movie children: the
latter are better in school deportment, are slightly superior in
scholastic marks, are rated higher in reputation by teachers and
classmates, have better reputations for co-operation and self-
control, are slightly less deceptive in school situations and
slightly more skilful in judgment, and are slightly more stable
emotionally; the movie children are mentioned more frequently
as friends; there is no reliable difference between the two groups
in honesty, persistence, suggestibility and moral knowledge.
The case of honesty indicates something about the general character of these findings. Thus, the non-movie children have a
superior *reputation* for honesty in school, whereas the tests of
out-of-school honesty reveal no difference between the groups.
The investigators comment on this by saying that "dishonesty in
a school system is not evidence of a depraved character but is
rather a symptom of conflict between the pupil and the teacher
or school requirements. These data, accordingly, must be considered in the light of the facts concerning reputation."[254] The
largest differences between the movie and non-movie children
in favor of the latter are in total reputation, teachers' deportment
record, and in co-operation as measured by a test device.

Shuttleworth and May felt that the foregoing data were insufficient because the tests and records used were not constructed
in the first instance with reference to the types of attitudes which
the movies are supposed to create. The negative results obtained
may, therefore, be accounted for in part by the fact that many
of the items were not pertinent. The investigators constructed
an entirely new battery of attitude tests and questionnaires
"especially designed for the purposes of this study."[255] But
here again the investigators report that "the findings are essentially negative"[256] with respect to moral knowledge, attitude

254 *Op. cit.*, p. 22, by permission of The Macmillan Company, Publishers.
255 *Op. cit.*, p. 27.   256 *Op. cit.*, p. 69.

and opinion, and in a very wide variety of situations "most of which carry distinctly ethical and moral implications." [257]   By means of a further attitude test, they obtained no evidence to show any significant differences between the movie and non-movie groups in attitudes for and against occupational or racial groups, except in the case of college professors, actors and dancers, the former being more admired by the non-movie children, the latter by the movie children.   But, the investigators add, "interest in a type, however, does not indicate approval" ; [258] as a matter of fact, "in the case of chorus-girls, the movie children more than the non-movie children say that few chorus girls are worthwhile members of society."   As might be expected, the movie children tend to say, for instance, that "most police-men torture and mistreat those suspected of crime" ; but, on the other hand, there is the unexpected result that "movie children say that Protestant ministers are highly intelligent" and deny that "social workers are busybodies." [259]   There is no evidence to show that movie children believe that criminals reform, or that they are militaristic.   "Five approaches to sex attitudes show no differences or inconsistent and contradictory differences." [260] On the matter of prohibition, there is no evidence of approval or disapproval, "the movie children believe that there is much drinking and much violation of the prohibition laws." [261]   No difference was found in attitudes toward crime and criminals, but "there is some evidence that movie children believe that few criminals escape their just punishment.   On the question of the criminal reforming, there is evidence showing that the movie children believe that feminine charms are more potent in reform-ing the criminal than fear of the police." [262]   The movie children "believe few teachers to be too easy and few schoolbooks to be interesting" ; [263] but, on the other hand, the movie children are "more sensitive to parental approvals and more discriminating in judging the things which they should get permission to do." [264] The movie children are less concerned about distress and famine in India and China and more concerned about losing a good friend.   "The movie children read more but the quality of their

[257] *Op. cit.,* p. 69.   [258] *Op. cit.,* p. 70.   [259] *Op. cit.,* p. 70.
[260] *Op. cit.,* p. 70.   [261] *Op. cit.,* p. 70.
[262] *Op. cit.,* pp. 70–71, by permission of The Macmillan Company, Publishers.
[263] *Op. cit.,* p. 71.   [264] *Op. cit.,* p. 71.

reading is not as high. They go to more dances. They report more recreations in which parents participate." [265] The reason why the movie children go to the movies is that "they like them or have nothing else to do. Non-movie children do not go to movies because they dislike movies or have too much else to do." [266] In general, they found that the movie children are more "socialized" and non-academic in their tastes and occupations; that is, they go out more, are more interested in clothes, read more non-academic literature and are more sophisticated and worldly; but they are also more "romantic" or non-realistic about the outcome of situations. In the matter of preferences for different types of movies, they found no significant differences between the two groups except for mysteries and comedies; on the other hand, non-movie children tend slightly to prefer vaudeville to movies.

Shuttleworth and May were reasonably perplexed as to how to interpret these findings. In the area of attitudes where they expected to find differences and where they had labored to construct special tests to detect them, "the total of the findings is more negative than positive" [267] and such differences as they found did not form a pattern of related or consistent attitudes. On the other hand, the character tests and teachers' ratings seemed to reveal a number of significant differences. They therefore undertook a further investigation to discover whether the differences in conduct and attitude could be explained in terms of home-background, whether they could be related to movie attendance and, if so, how important the influence of the movies is in comparison with other factors. They found that parental disapprovals constituted only a minor factor in influencing the attendance of both movie and non-movie children; they discovered no evidence to show that movie children are turned loose to run wild; the largest difference that they found in the home environments of the two groups was that the parents of the movie children go themselves much more frequently to the movies than the parents of the other group. On the other hand, the movie children name a larger number of activities, other than going to the movies, in which they participate with their parents. The most surprising discovery was the influence of the community in which the child lived. Thus,

[265] *Op. cit.*, p. 71.   [266] *Op. cit.*, p. 71.   [267] *Op. cit.*, p. 72.

"when *all* the children of one community are compared with all of another community, the difference between them in attitude is much greater than between movie and non-movie children of the same community." [268]   In the case of attitudes, they conclude that "the influence of the community far overshadows in importance the influence of the movie." [269]   But they also found that the more frequently a child went to the movies, the greater his difference from a non-movie child with respect to reputation and deportment in school and co-operation.   The correlation between frequency of movie attendance and these three factors is, however, extremely low.   The investigators conclude at this point that even if correlation meant causation, which it does not, "one would have to say that the movies are not a very significant causal factor." [270]   If anything, their findings favor the theory that "differences in movie habits, conduct and attitude are mutually reinforcing as opposed to the theory that one set of differences is the cause of the other." [271]   In general, "factors of age, school grade and home-background are as important and possibly more important in influencing the conduct and attitudes of children as the movies." [272]

Shuttleworth and May's research is thus predominantly negative with respect to the problem of the influence of the movies on moral character or conduct.   Without interpretation, their findings can be summarized as follows: there is no difference in about 90% of the comparisons between movie and non-movie children; of the remaining 10%, 8% favored the non-movie group and 2% the movie group.   They offer a number of interpretations of this overwhelmingly negative finding: of the 90%, "we may say (1) that the movies are exerting no influence in these areas, or (2) that differences in these areas are not such as would cause differences in movie habits, or (3) that other factors such as community differences tend to obscure real differences, or (4) that one type of movie is exerting strong influence in one direction which is canceled by an opposite influence from another movie." [273]   They urge no choice among these guesses. With respect to the slight positive finding of significant differences in 10% of the comparisons, they also suggest a number of

[268] *Op. cit.*, pp. 81–82.   [269] *Op. cit.*, p. 83.   [270] *Op. cit.*, p. 81.
[271] *Op. cit.*, p. 83.   [272] *Op. cit.*, p. 83.
[273] *Op. cit.*, p. 85, by permission of The Macmillan Company, Publishers.

interpretations: "we may say (1) that these differences are caused directly by the movies, or (2) that the movies exert a selective rather than a causal influence and that these differences are causes of attendance rather than results, or (3) that the equating process was not observed far enough and the differences were thus due in part to other unknown causes, or (4) that movie habits and these attitudes are interacting forces." [274] They discuss these alternatives at some length, but offer no demonstration that any of them is better than a guess. They conclude: "That the movies exert an influence *there can be no doubt*. But it is our *opinion* that this influence is specific for a given child and a given movie. The same picture may influence different children in distinctly opposite directions. Thus in a general survey such as we have made, the net effect appears small." [275] (Italics mine.) Even this conclusion is too definite and strong in the light of the evidence presented. No causal interpretation whatsoever can be made of the data, and this Shuttleworth and May generally realize. What makes one child a virtuous man and law-abiding citizen and makes another corrupt in character and anti-social in behavior cannot be explained in terms of the movies, so far as this piece of scientific research goes. If anything, its findings indicate that the movies are not even important as a minor factor in the development of moral character or in determining conduct.

The inconsistency of this research with the general tenor of Blumer's data and opinions is too great to be overlooked. Even if the data of the May-Shuttleworth research were as unreliable — which is not likely in view of the superiority of their procedure both in obtaining the data and treating it statistically — the fact of inconsistency would be no less significant. To some extent the two studies are not comparable, because Blumer used no control groups. But the opinions of the investigators are comparable. In both cases, supposedly, they are formed in the light of the evidence. They are clearly opposed. These two pieces of scientific research have hardly improved upon the prevailing conflict of opinions.

The work of Shuttleworth and May, furthermore, is generally corroborated by the less analytical survey made by Mrs. Mitchell

[274] *Op. cit.*, p. 85, by permission of The Macmillan Company, Publishers.
[275] *Op. cit.*, pp. 92–93, by permission of The Macmillan Company, Publishers.

of 10,000 Chicago school children and also by the much more
careful piece of experimental work done by Professor Thurstone
and Miss Peterson. It is, therefore, extraordinary indeed to
observe the way in which Professor Charters in his summary
judges the significance of the May and Shuttleworth investigation and makes little of its obvious inconsistency with the
opinions of Blumer. Thus, after a slightly distorted review of
the findings, Charters concludes: "This attitude study of May
and Shuttleworth is of peculiar interest because it is the only one
in which the influence of the motion picture is not clearly apparent either as a cause or as an aggravation of precedent conditions.
*Superficially one might claim that this study indicates that motion
pictures have no influence upon boys and girls. That position
May and Shuttleworth do not take. They say that movies do
exert an influence upon children and indicate that this influence
is greater than appears on the surface. The studies of Stoddard,
Thurstone, Blumer, Thrasher, and their associates support this
position with a huge mass of specific data.*" [276] (Italics mine.)
Charters omits all the qualifications with which May and Shuttleworth hedge their *opinion* that the movies exert *some* influence. [277] Why should the one study which is predominantly
negative in its findings be "of chief value as a caution," merely
indicating "clearly that the influence of a motion picture is only
one of several influences and the attitudes of children are a
product of many influences"? [278] Why are such other factors
as native temperament, past experience, family ideals, school instruction, community mores said to have an effect only theoretically, when May and Shuttleworth showed the influence of
the community, for instance, to be larger than that of the
movies? And how, finally, is Charters able to insinuate that
in other studies the influence of the motion picture is "clearly
apparent *either* as cause *or* effect *or* as an aggravation of pre-

[276] *Motion Pictures and Youth*, p. 16, by permission of The Macmillan Company, Publishers.
[277] The word "influence" which is used in most of these Payne Fund reports
and in Charters' summary is highly ambiguous. It means everything from a
remembered impression, as reported in an autobiographical document, to a
habit, disposition or relatively permanent attitude, as discovered by some method
other than the interrogation of the subject.   [278] Charters, *op. cit.*, p. 17.

cedent conditions?"[279]   (Italics mine to indicate that the showing, even if made, is meaningless.)

Charters also points out that the survey method of May and Shuttleworth is not as sensitive as the attitudes scale technique of Thurstone and Peterson.[280]   It will be remembered that May and Shuttleworth pointed this out themselves and, at the same time, stressed the difference between the problem of their investigation and that of Thurstone.   That Thurstone discovered positive effects upon attitude as a result of witnessing specific motion pictures is not only not inconsistent with the May-Shuttleworth findings, but the story is not completely told unless one takes account of the direction of the change of attitude in the light of prevailing moral and social standards.   It is not sufficient to say, as Charters does, that "the more exactly controlled studies of Stoddard, Thurstone and others showed specific and significant differences produced."[281]   It is not surprising, therefore, to find in Forman's book that "Thurstone has established a case for the direct and powerful influence of motion pictures upon the mental attitudes of children.   Drs. May and Shuttleworth, with technique not so sensitive, under conditions not so clear cut, have been able to discover few indications illuminating the problem."[282]   Mr. Forman never takes occasion to comment on the worth of Professor Blumer's methods or Dr. Dale's.

(h) There is no question that in its scientific technique the work of Professor L. L. Thurstone and Miss R. C. Peterson of the Department of Psychology of the University of Chicago is clearly the best of the Payne Fund researches.[283]   The experimental procedure involved the use of attitude scales and paired-comparison schedules to detect a shift in the attitude of children on some issue having affective value, as a result of their witnessing a motion picture bearing on that issue.   The attitudes of the subjects were recorded about two weeks before their exposure to the movie, and then on the day after exposure, the amount and

[279] Op. cit., p. 16.   [280] Op. cit., p. 17.   [281] Op. cit., p. 61.
[282] Op. cit., p. 133.
[283] Motion Pictures and the Social Attitudes of Children, The Macmillan Company, Publishers, New York, 1933.

direction of change was measured with fair precision by means of the scales. The pictures used were selected for their suitability from between six and eight hundred films. Many of the test instruments, though not all, were especially constructed for the purposes of the experiment. The experimental groups included children of the fourth to the eighth grade, high-school students and, in one experiment, college students, either in the city of Chicago or in smaller towns in Illinois. The statistical treatment of the data and the statistical processes involved in the construction of the scales are impeccable. These techniques are among the best available in the field of psychometrics to which Professor Thurstone is a leading contributor. In only a few instances can one criticize the verbal statements, which the scales involve, for ambiguity or unclarity; thus, such statements as "Some Chinese traits are admirable but on the whole I don't like them" or "The Negro should have freedom but should never be treated as the equal of the white man" or "In a thousand years the Negro *might* become the white man's equal; then his social position *should* be equal to the white man's" (italics mine), complicate the interpretation of the responses. The student is asked to put an x next to the statement if he disagrees with it. In cases of this sort, does the x negate both parts of the statement, or only the first? But the number of such statements is few, and hardly invalidates the results obtained from the scale.

The first series of experiments was concerned with the effect of single pictures. In the first of these, the testing of 133 children in Genoa, Illinois, a town of about 1200, discovered that the motion picture "Four Sons" resulted in a change of attitude favorable to the German people, and slightly less favorable to war. In another, conducted with 240 children in Mendota, a town of about 4000, the motion picture "Street of Chance" made the children less favorable to gambling "even though the gambler was an interesting, likeable character in the film." [284] In another, conducted with 254 children in Princeton, Illinois, a town of about 4700, the motion picture "Hide Out" had no measurable effect on the children's attitudes toward prohibition or bootlegging, although some effect had been expected in the light of the criticism of the movie as a portrayal of a college bootlegger. In similar experiments, using "Son of the Gods"

[284] *Op. cit.,* p. 15.

and "Welcome Danger" — the first a movie that had been considered friendly toward Chinese culture, and the second one which the Chinese had criticized as unfriendly — it was found that the first made the children more favorable to the Chinese, whereas the second made the children less favorable, but to a much slighter degree. The motion picture "The Valiant," which was used to test a change of attitude toward capital punishment, did not give a statistically significant result, although the change was in the expected direction toward greater disfavor. "Journey's End" similarly gave an extremely small change, of questionable statistical significance, in the direction of an unfavorable attitude toward war; whereas "All Quiet on the Western Front" gave an extremely large change in the same direction. The investigator's comment is that probably "Journey's End" is too sophisticated in its propaganda for high-school children.[285] To test change of attitude toward the punishment of criminals, "The Criminal Code" was used. This experiment was performed with both a high-school and a college group. The latter were more in favor of leniency toward criminals before seeing the picture, although their change in the direction of leniency was slightly less than the change in that direction of the high-school group. In still another experiment with the same film, no statistically significant result was obtained. Finally, "The Birth of a Nation" was used to measure shifting attitudes toward Negroes. Here the largest effect was found, the children becoming much less favorable toward Negroes. The power of Thomas Dixon as a propagandist is again confirmed.

In another series of experiments, Professor Thurstone and Miss Peterson attempted to measure the cumulative effect of a number of motion pictures. Thus, for example, using both "Journey's End" and "All Quiet on the Western Front," they found a cumulative effect on the children's attitude, the pictures tending to reinforce each other. But it should be noted that the group who saw "Journey's End" after they had seen "All Quiet on the Western Front" showed no greater absolute change in attitude than the group who saw only the latter; whereas the group who saw both in the order indicated showed the largest absolute change in attitude. And, in an experiment on attitude

[285] Op. cit., p. 26.

toward the punishment of criminals, it was found that two pictures, "The Big House" and "Numbered Men," neither of which by itself had a measurable effect, did however cause a significant change when combined.

In another series of experiments, the investigators sought to determine the persistence of these changes in attitude. Thus, after an interval of six months, the children who had been made more favorable to Germans by "Four Sons" were tested and found to be slightly more favorable after this interval. The investigators say: "We suggest as an explanation the fact that there was no theatre in Genoa regularly showing pictures and that the motion picture "Four Sons" was probably the subject of considerable comment and discussion among the children because a motion picture was a relatively rare occurrence for this group." [286] After five months, children who had seen "Son of the Gods" were slightly less favorable toward the Chinese than immediately after witnessing the film, but still distinctly more favorable than they had been before seeing it. Even after nineteen months, the favorable effect still persisted in a statistically significant quantity. Similar results were obtained in measurements of attitudes toward gambling after five months, toward the punishment of criminals after two and one half months, and toward the negro after a number of intervals. In only one case, was the effect not found to persist but rather to change in the opposite direction. Eight months after children had been made less favorable toward war by "All Quiet on the Western Front," they were found to have shifted in an even larger quantity toward an attitude of favor. The experimenters say: "We have no explanation for this effect. There was, undoubtedly, some interposed propaganda which made the children more favorable toward war. . . The change is obviously too large to be attributed to chance error in measurement." [287]

These are the findings of Thurstone and Peterson, carefully ascertained and clearly expressed. They themselves make no further comment on the significance of their study. They are content, in a final chapter, to summarize their measurements and to say in conclusion "that the experiments we conducted show that motion pictures have definite, lasting effects on the social

[286] *Op. cit.*, p. 52, by permission of The Macmillan Company, Publishers.
[287] *Op. cit.*, pp. 59–60. By permission of The Macmillan Company, Publishers.

attitudes of children and that a number of pictures pertaining to the same issue may have a cumulative effect on attitude." [288] They are so careful throughout the body of their report and in their conclusions to avoid any gratuitous interpretations of their data, any conjectures or opinions or evaluations, that the full significance of their study is insufficiently indicated. In only one place do they remark that a particular movie may "be said to have a socially approved effect, since it made the children more severe in their judgment of gambling." [289]   It may be asked whether the other changes in attitude are socially desirable or undesirable, whether, for instance, pacificism or militarism, severity or leniency toward criminals, prejudice for or against a particular racial group, is a better attitude to cultivate, on either moral or social grounds?   Thurstone and Peterson recognize that such questions are beyond the scope of their investigation as empirical science.   Nevertheless, the point should be made that the direction of the change in attitude on any given issue may be either toward a desirable or undesirable social point of view and that the amount of change varies, not only in direction, but from none in quantity to a very considerable degree.

It is clear from this summary that the Thurstone-Peterson results do not in any sense conflict with those of May and Shuttleworth. It is also clear that their results do not permit any social evaluation of motion pictures as influencing moral character and conduct. We simply know, as a result of Professor Thurstone's efforts, that movies do have an effect upon the formation of children's attitudes with respect to certain social questions. We have a limited scientific measurement of the propaganda power of the movies, the first that has probably been made of any type of art. Science here confirms what is an ancient and generally accepted opinion among men of experience that works of art, particularly literature and the stage, are potent media of propaganda. Whether for good or ill is a question that can be answered only in the particular case in terms of the merits of each side of the issue toward which the propaganda is being directed. There is no evidence whatsoever to show that the movies as a medium of propaganda are opposed to the cur-

---

[288] *Op. cit.*, p. 66. By permission of The Macmillan Company, Publishers. Cf. Forman, *Our Movie Made Children*, p. 134.
[289] *Op. cit.*, p. 14.

rently dominant attitudes and conventions of our society; in fact, the evidence of Professor Peters' research seems to point to their consistency with the prevailing practices and, for the most part, their harmony with contemporary evaluations. The communist might protest that the movies are vicious as propaganda because they tend to support the existing capitalistic-bourgeois structure of society. The Platonist and the Christian, if he is truly a philosopher or a saint, might object that the movies perpetuate the moral and social imperfections of men and societies as they now actually exist, instead of presenting a vision of the ideal and being a summons either to establish human life in a better order or at least to renounce it as it is.

The work of Thurstone and Peterson can be used as a model by which to judge all the other Payne Fund studies. It is the briefest of all the reports because it confines itself strictly to the presentation of data and a summary statement of the findings. *The findings thus stated constitute the conclusions of the research*. There are no expressions of gratuitous opinions, no evaluations unsupported by evidence, no "theoretical speculation" or offering of guesses and conjectures about what the data may — or may not — mean. In these respects, as well as in its experimental technique, the work of Holaday and Stoddard is also good. The study of May and Shuttleworth is, however, not only less exact and carefully controlled in its procedure, but there is an unnecessary last chapter in which the investigators go beyond their evidence to guess about its meaning. All the rest stand sharply in contrast to these three, and particularly to the Thurstone-Peterson report, in the extraordinary degree to which they consist of opinions, evaluations and "speculations" that are not based upon the data of research.

Our survey of opinion and scientific investigation with respect to the influence of movies upon adults and children, is now finished. It has been a laborious but a necessary task, made more laborious than it need have been because of the manner in which most of the Payne Fund studies are reported. Had all the studies been presented in the style of Professor Thurstone, rigorously confined to a statement of clearly summarized findings, the three thousand pages would have been many times reduced and the task of this review would have been considerably simplified. The importance of distinguishing between knowledge and opinion, the necessity of separating findings of fact from evaluations and conjectures, the unpleasant duty of exposing prejudice and distortion as well as incompetence in scientific method, required a kind of critical examination that could not be abbreviated.   Now that it is done, we can turn for the last time to consider the position of the practical man facing the conflict between art and prudence, which in its contemporary phase has been made so complicated by the efforts of investigative science.

CHAPTER TWELVE

The Problem in Practical Philosophy

1. A BRIEF recapitulation is necessary here. We have analyzed the nature of practical problems in general. We have applied that analysis to the formulation of the particular practical problem with which we are here concerned, the problem of the arts in the state.[1] Three basic alternatives were indicated: inaction, regulation, extirpation. In the case of each of these alternatives, a number of questions required to be answered before a prudent man would feel justified in proceeding, questions of fact about the influence of the art under consideration and questions of evaluation directed toward weighing the positive and negative values involved. At other times in the history of this problem, the issue has been formulated in terms of extirpation; but in the current instance of the problem, concerning the motion picture, the issue is between the alternatives of inaction and some type of regulation or control. That the issue is formulated in this way acknowledges that there is a balance of positive and negative values. It would be better to leave the art alone if any sort of action would substantially diminish the good without proportionally lessening the evil. A policy of regulation or control can be justified only by the assurance that action of a given sort would minimize the regrettable influences of the art without impairing or destroying its contribution to human welfare. A sound practical decision here must be guided not only by a consideration of the probable effectiveness of different courses

[1] Vd. Chapter 8 *supra*.

of action in view of all their probable consequences, but also by a consideration of the various effects of the art upon its audience.

Our review of all the questions which a prudent man must face indicated the need for knowledge and, more than that, the need for a distinction between knowledge and opinion. Since practical problems are concerned with contingent matters, and since the distinction between knowledge and opinion turns upon the criterion of necessity and contingency, it was seen to follow that the prudent man must depend upon opinion for the solution of practical problems. Though there is some knowledge of contingent matters, it is possible only by abstracting from their contingency. Though there is some knowledge that is relevant to practical problems, it is always of great generality. It provides the basic principles, but these are always insufficient for casuistry. The prudent man must deliberate about the contingent circumstances of the particular case, and in order to supplement the principles he must, therefore, take counsel from prevailing opinions. His task is easy if common or expert opinion is relatively clear and definite on one side of the issue; it is difficult in proportion as there is unclarity and conflict in the field of opinion which he must consult.

In the contemporary world, the situation is complicated by the existence of empirical or investigative science which claims to be better than opinion. We have seen that it is, that science is a mean between knowledge and opinion, sharing in some part the traits of both.[2] But we have also seen that there is a radical difference between the natural sciences and that part of empirical psychology and social research which seeks to be a science of human behavior. Whereas scientific knowledge about natural phenomena is clearly better than opinion, largely by addition rather than correction, what claims to be scientific knowledge about human affairs seldom adds to or corrects the prevailing opinion about these matters. From the practical point of view, the value of scientific research about human behavior depends upon its superiority to opinion, either through novelty, or by greater definiteness and higher probability, or in resolving oppositions by adding the weight of scientific evidence to one or another side. It is always necessary to test the claims of scientific research [3] by such criteria, as well as by the common

[2] Vd. Chapter 9 *supra*.   [3] *I.e.*, in the field of human behavior.

standards of reliability, accuracy and inference in scientific method. To make this test, we examined the attempts at scientific research about motion pictures in relation to human behavior, in the light of a survey of existing opinion on the subject. We are now prepared to summarize the results of that critical review and to state whether the position of the prudent man has been altered by the efforts of science.

2. We divided the problem into two parts by distinguishing between the mature and the immature, because we found good analytical reasons for supposing that the influence of an art, both in extent and character, is different for these two elements in its audience.[4] The analytical point is further supported by a survey of existing opinion concerning motion pictures. In the case of the mature, there is no settled common opinion. The clear fact is conflict, both in opinions commonly held and among experts. But in the case of the immature, there seems to be a predominance of common, and even of expert, opinion, on the affirmative side. i.e., that motion pictures have a somewhat undesirable influence on children and youth.[5] This predominance of opinion can, perhaps, be most accurately described as a *fear* or *concern* about the physical, intellectual and moral effects of motion pictures on the young. Even if there were no scientific research, the prevalence of this feeling might move the prudent man to consider whether action of some sort might not be desirable. He would not be similarly moved if the audience of motion pictures comprised adults only. *That he is moved to such consideration indicates nothing about the sort of action to be taken, if any.* But before we proceed further with the analysis of the practical problem, as it thus arises, let us determine whether scientific research has made any difference whatsoever.

A. *In the case of the mature.* Little of the scientific work bears directly on this problem, except the research of Professor Peters and, in part, the investigation of the movies and crime by Professors Blumer and Hauser. So far as it has any bearing, it adds little, if anything, to the prevailing affirmations, denials and doubts. The little that can be considered a contribution is the finding of Professor Peters that, with respect to a number of patterns of behavior, types of conduct depicted in the movies are

4 Vd. Chapter 6 *supra.*   5 Vd. Chapter 11 *supra.*

judged either to be like or better than common practices in the community ; and the finding of Professor Blumer that *some* criminals, or individuals having criminal propensities, actually did or possibly could learn something about the techniques of crime from the movies.   But it is highly questionable whether Peters' method and assumptions permit any significant interpretation of his data, and, similarly, whether Blumer's data are reliable enough to warrant any scientific conclusion.   That Blumer's autobiographical materials showed, furthermore, that *some* criminals and delinquents *believe* that the movies *in some part* contributed to their specific acts of criminality, adds nothing to the conflict of opinion, since there is also autobiographical material showing that *some* criminals and delinquents *believe* that the movies are totally irresponsible for their misbehavior (Blumer ; Mitchell), and other, better evidence to show that some movies form attitudes of disfavor toward crime and criminals (Thurstone-Peterson), as well as evidence of no significant difference in such attitudes between groups frequently and infrequently attending the movies (May-Shuttleworth).   The last two pieces of research mentioned deal, of course, with children.   They are mentioned here because the Blumer-Hauser investigation treated juvenile delinquency as well as adult criminality.   The evidence in the May-Shuttleworth research is ultimately of the same sort as the Blumer-Hauser materials, i.e., the opinions of individuals interrogated or tested ; but the procedure of the former is better because of the use of control groups and the susceptibility of the data to statistical treatment.

Two other findings can be mentioned, though their significance is obviously slight : (1) the finding of Dysinger-Ruckmick that adults are not emotionally excited by movies to any considerable degree ; and (2) the finding of Holaday-Stoddard that adults learn a great deal of information from the movies.   What the first of these findings means is difficult to say, both because the physiological measurements are of questionable import and because it conflicts with common sense which tells us that movies could not hold their audience unless they were exciting. The second must be qualified by the distinction between reliable and inaccurate information.   Here the investigators' criterion of reliability is of doubtful applicability to the content of narratives.

Finally, when it is remembered that the problem is about the influence of the movies on moral conduct and character, the insignificance of the scientific work is further seen. The opinions of criminals and delinquents about the causes of their behavior are certainly no better than other opinions, as providing a solution of the aetiological problem. The interpretation of the findings about attitudes is not indicated by any knowledge that we have about the causal efficacy of such attitudes in the determination of voluntary conduct. The other findings are even more remote from the problem. Apart from the unreliability of the data and the inconsistency of the findings, the results of scientific research fail to improve upon the state of opinion in this field.

Before we dismiss the case of the mature, two points remain to be considered. (1) It may be said that excessive attendance at movies is bad for adults. This must be conceded, of course, since the word "excessive" entails the judgment that it is bad. But the prudent man will recognize that this sound moral disapproval of excessive indulgence in amusement of any sort points only to a casuistical problem in the individual case. (2) It may be said that the influence of the movies is bad because they fail to cultivate, or because they degrade, the aesthetic sensibilities of their adult audience. We shall consider this point later in a discussion of the motion picture as fine art and in relation to the aesthetic sensibilities of its popular audience.[6]

B. *In the case of the immature.* It will be interesting here to begin by considering the three conclusions which Professor Charters thinks follow inevitably from the Payne Fund studies on motion pictures and youth. (1) The motion picture is "a potent medium of education."[7] The evidence of this influence, which Charters thinks is "massive and irrefutable,"[8] consists of the Holaday-Stoddard finding about the amount that children learn and remember from witnessing movies, the Thurstone-Peterson finding about the formation of attitudes, the Dysinger-Ruckmick finding that children are emotionally excited by movies, and Blumer's autobiographical materials. It is difficult to see how anything but Holaday and Stoddard's work bears upon

[6] Vd. Chapter 15 *infra.*
[7] *Motion Pictures and Youth: A Summary*, New York, 1933: p. 60.
[8] *Op. cit.,* p. 60.

intellectual education. Their conclusion was generally favorable to the movies as an informal educational device, qualified only by the finding that factual errors as well as correct information are learned. The rest of the massive and irrefutable evidence must be related to moral education, and here it is absolutely impossible to interpret the studies cited to support an evaluation of the movies as a factor in the training of character. (2) "For children the content of motion pictures is not *good*. There is too *much* sex and crime and love for a balanced diet for children." [9] (Italics mine.) Whereas the studies mentioned above indicated the power of motion pictures, here the investigations of Dale, Blumer, Thrasher, Peters and their associates "clearly indicate that the power flows *too much in dangerous directions*." [10] (Italics mine.) We have already seen that the data collected — to whatever extent they are reliable — show nothing of the sort. The work cited cannot be made the basis of the moral evaluation which Charters states as its conclusion. (3) "The motion picture situation is very complicated. It is one among many influences which mold the experience of children. How powerful this is in relation to the influence of the ideals taught in the home, in the school and in the church, by street life and companions or by community customs, *these studies have not canvassed*." [11] (Italics mine.) The negative finding of May and Shuttleworth is then cited, but Charters adds the findings of Holaday-Stoddard and Thurstone-Peterson, as if they were inconsistent with it. That is not the case. All three pieces of research indicate what Charters calls the complexity of "the motion picture situation." In any event, this third conclusion curiously undermines the significance of the other two, even if we do not question their validity independently. If the movies exert any influence upon the characters of children, they must do so in conjunction with or in opposition to other leading forces, such as home, school, church, friends, books. If the relation of these factors is not known; if, as Charters admits, a simple cause and effect relationship cannot be said to prevail, it does not follow, as Charters elsewhere tries to insist, that the lover of children should be "concerned with the question of how well the commercial motion picture [120] plays its individual part in the education of children and not with whether it is

[9] *Op. cit.*, p. 60.   [10] *Op. cit.*, p. 61.   [11] *Op. cit.*, p. 61.

more or less important than another instrument."[12]   Those interested in the welfare of children may well be concerned with this question, but that concern is not augmented or given definite direction by the results of scientific research.

For the sake of contrast and also to present a more accurate picture of the scientific findings, I offer the following summary. (1) In the matter of juvenile delinquency, as in the case of adult criminality, there is a balance of affirmative and negative opinion.   So far as there are any scientific data even remotely relevant to this point, they are extremely unreliable and plainly inconsistent: the autobiographical materials Blumer collected and supplemented by his own opinions, on the one hand, and the data and opinions of English investigators, the autobiographical materials of Mrs. Mitchell, and the findings of May and Shuttleworth, on the other.   (2) In the matter of moral influence, the relevance of the scientific data is questionable.   To whatever extent they are relevant and can be considered as reliable, the findings are inconsistent and tend to be negative. There is only, *on the one hand,* the autobiographical material of Blumer with regard to emotional experience and the formation of ideas, supported by the measurement of emotional responses by Dysinger and Ruckmick, and the finding of Holaday-Stoddard about how much children learn.   This is certainly not a showing that the movies corrupt the moral character of the immature.   Nor is it made so by Dale's survey of the major themes of motion pictures and his amazing discovery that stories of love, sex and crime predominate, because, *on the other hand,* the finding of Holaday-Stoddard, supported by the English reports, show that children learn little from the movies that they are not already prepared for by prior experience.   Furthermore, the finding of May-Shuttleworth shows that for the most part there are no significant differences in moral attitudes, etc., between children who frequent and children who abstain from the movies; the finding of Thurstone-Peterson shows that the attitudes of children may be formed by movies in opposite directions, either *or* both of which may be desirable *or* undesirable; and the finding of Peters that the movies either conform to the mores as they are practised or, for the most part, are "better" than such practices.   If all of this has any significance, after

[12] *Op. cit.,* p. 18.

unreliability of methods and data have been taken into account and inconsistencies nullify each other, it tends to cast some doubt upon the popular concern about the moral influence of motion pictures upon the immature.

(3) In the matter of health, fears rather than opinions predominate. Parents have been generally concerned about the injury that may be done by violent emotional disturbances, especially the anxieties and panics, which movies seem to produce in some children.   Their worry is not clearly supported by the physiological measurements of Dysinger and Ruckmick, since the physiological significance of the size of a psychogalvanic response is not known, nor can its bearing on general health be guessed.   The experimental evidence here, furthermore, shows marked individual differences and inconsistent emotional effects. The autobiographical materials of Blumer merely confirm what most parents already know : that *some* children are violently excited by *some* motion pictures.   But they also indicate that, for the most part, these emotional experiences are extremely short-lived.   Even when they are not transient, the autobiographical data do not show whether they are harmful or beneficial.   Finally, there is some experimental data to show that exposure to movies may disturb sleep either in the direction of increased or decreased motility, but again there are marked individual differences and there is no sound experimental or theoretical basis for the interpretation of these changes in motility as bearing on health.   (4) In the matter of intellectual education, the opinion of teachers is predominantly against the movies, as an impediment to study and school work, and this seems to be supported by the May-Shuttleworth finding that children who frequently attend the movies have lower scholastic standing than those who do not.   But neither the opinions of teachers nor the scientific data can be made the basis for a causal conclusion.   If there is a reliably determined relationship between frequency of movie attendance and school grades, the correlation does not mean that either one is the cause of the other.   On the other hand, the findings of Holaday and Stoddard, supported by the autobiographical materials of Blumer, show that the movies contribute substantially to the information and ideas of their juvenile audience. But this evidence does not indicate what evaluation should be made of the educational worth of this contribution, even though

it is discovered that in some proportion erroneous and misleading information is acquired.

In short, the scientific work that has been done is of little or no practical value to the prudent man. On the crucial point — the influence of motion pictures on moral character and conduct — science has not improved or altered the state of existing opinion. In those few instances in which the scientific work has been well done and reported with proper scientific restraint — the researches of Thurstone-Peterson and Holaday-Stoddard — the findings do not warrant any moral judgments about the effects discovered. We must proceed, therefore, without the benefit of science.

3. We proceed, not to a solution of the problem, but to a deeper understanding of it. Practical problems are solved only by those who have the obligation to act in one way or another. This practical problem is a peculiarly difficult one, and the better its peculiar intricacies are understood, the sounder the practical judgment that is made in the light of such understanding. Our task here is not to make this judgment, but to make the conditions of it as clear as possible.

We must move from the level of considering the circumstances and facts of the particular case — the role which motion pictures play in contemporary life — to the level of the abiding principles of practical thinking about the arts in relation to man. The dilemmas the practical man faces today in the case of the movies are familiar ones in the light of the history of what seems to be a perennial problem. What makes the problem perennial? The answer can be only that it arises from some essential weakness in human nature. Human defect must be the source of any practical problem which persists from generation to generation. Practical wisdom consists in going to the sources. It is knowledge of the causes of this practical problem, knowledge of human imperfection. Such knowledge, viewed in the practical order, can be formulated by a few general principles to guide deliberation. The generality of these principles makes them inconclusive in deciding upon one or another practical alternative, but they illuminate the problem in a way that will make any decision a better expression of right reason.

The problem in practical philosophy arises from the inevitable conflict of art and prudence. Each in itself is a virtue and contributes to the perfection of man, but that perfection is limited by what seems to be a disharmony in the virtues themselves, which Maritain sees as the essential human antinomy made by the conflicting claims of morality, on the one hand, and of intellectuality, art or science, on the other.[13] We must, therefore, investigate the place of art and prudence in the hierarchy of the virtues: (1) the separation and coincidence of their spheres as virtues of the practical intellect, (2) their relation to the virtues of the speculative intellect, (3) their relation to the moral virtues. In doing so we shall first consider art in its most general significance, and not in the restricted sense of fine art. The narrower problem of prudence in relation to fine art—more difficult than the problem in the case of useful art—can be treated only after subordinate distinctions are made. In the ancient and mediæval tradition the word "art" was used with the utmost generality. It is only in modern times that usage has given it the restricted meaning.[14] After we have completed this analysis we shall be able to state the few practical principles that may be of some help to the prudent man in dealing with the motion picture as a fine art.

A. We begin with the respects in which art and prudence are similar. In the first place, both share the nature of virtue, both are habits which perfect powers of operation [121]. If, in the language of Aristotle, the virtue of a thing is that which makes its activity good,[15] it is not enough to define a virtue as an operative habit. It is rather a habit of good operation. The criteria of good operation are, as we shall see, different in the case of art and prudence, according as their ends are different; but in their status as virtues each is a good of the soul in the same sense, though not of the same grade. In the second place, both are

[13] I am indebted to *Art and Scholasticism* for its penetrating analysis of this conflict, made in the tradition of Aristotle and St. Thomas Aquinas. The Aristotelian locus is *Nichomachean Ethics* (hereafter referred to as *Ethics*), Bk. VI, especially Ch. 4 and 5. The Thomistic locus is primarily the Treatise on Habit in the *Summa Theologica* (hereafter indicated by the abbreviation *S.T.*). What follows is in part an exposition of, in part a commentary on, the traditional discussion.

[14] For the purposes of this book, we have so far used the word "art" as equivalent to "fine art"; moreover, we have used it to name, not the ability by which such works are produced, but the works themselves. [15] *Ethics*, II, 6.

virtues of the practical intellect, both are habits of rational operation in the practical order, that is, the end of the operation is
something other than knowledge itself; it is not the good of
truth, but some other good.   This point entails two distinctions.
(1) Art and prudence are intellectual and not moral virtues.
The distinction between intellectual and moral virtues turns on
the distinction between two principles of human action : reason
and appetite.   "Every human virtue must needs be a perfection
of one of these principles.   Accordingly if it perfects man's
speculative or practical intellect, it will be an intellectual virtue ;
whereas if it perfects man's appetite, it will be a moral virtue." [16]
(2) Art and prudence are practical and not speculative habits.
The distinction here turns on the distinction between the practical and speculative intellects.   The differentiation can be made
in terms of the end of intellectual operation or in terms of the
matter operated upon.   *"Wisdom, knowledge* and *understanding"* — the three virtues of the speculative intellect — "are about
necessary things, whereas *art* and *prudence* are about contingent
things." [17]   That art and prudence are virtues of the practical intellect indicates further a number of things they have in common : both involve a certain conformity of the practical intellect
to right appetite, though here there is a subordinate difference
between art and prudence in the way in which they are related
to the will ; both are concerned with means and ends in the order
of goods ; both require the exercise of judgment applying knowledge in the particular case [122].

B.   The distinction between art and prudence can be made in
three ways : (1) in terms of the kind of operation which is perfected, the power of operation which is habituated ; (2) in
terms of the end or object of operation ; (3) in terms of the
manner of operation.   We shall examine these distinctions in
the order indicated.

B1.   Art and prudence are usually distinguished in terms of
the difference between making and doing, or between production and action. [18]   But these words, as they are commonly or

[16] *S.T.* I–II, Q. 58, A. 3 ; also Q. 58, A. 2.
[17] *Ethics*, VI, 1, 1139a2–15 ; *S.T.*, II–II, Q. 47, A. 5 ; also *S.T.*, I, Q. 79, A. 11.
[18] Cf. *Ethics*, VI, 4, 5 ; *S.T.*, I–II, Q. 57, A. 4 ; II–II, Q. 47, A. 5 ; Maritain,
Ch. 3.

even technically used, do not convey the distinction that is intended with sufficient precision.   The word "action" is often
used broadly to name any operation ; the word "production" is
sometimes used narrowly to name the making of a physical thing,
such as a chair or a house, and sometimes used otherwise, as when
we say that the physician produces health in the patient.[19]   Furthermore, there is a distinction between the practical and the
productive arts which relies upon a special difference between
doing and making within the sphere of art itself.   It is confusing,
therefore, to use the same words to distinguish art, whether practical or productive, from prudence.   I shall, therefore, avoid
this traditional language as far as possible in trying to express
the distinction which the tradition clearly indicates.   Once the
distinction is grasped, the problem of variant verbal usages is
simply surmounted by a schedule of translations.

The distinction between art and prudence is most exactly
made by the difference in their relation to the will.   It is this
difference which aligns prudence with the moral virtues and art
with the virtues of the speculative intellect.   It also makes prudence a cardinal or principal virtue, whereas art and the other
intellectual habits are virtues only in an imperfect sense.   The
perfect virtues are those which involve the will directly and require rectitude of appetite.   They do not merely confer the
faculty of doing well, but cause the good deed to be done.
"Those virtues which imply rectitude of the appetite are called
principal virtues.   Such are the moral virtues, and prudence alone
of the intellectual virtues, for it is also something of a moral virtue." [20]   In other words, a habit may either confer only the aptness to act, or also the habitual right use of that aptness.   Habits
of the first sort are virtues only relatively ; they do not make a
man good simply as a man, but relatively ; thus, a good grammarian or a good carpenter.   This difference depends upon whether
the habit is or is not subjected in the will.   "The subject of habit
which is called a virtue in the relative sense, can be the intellect,
and not only the practical intellect but also the speculative, without any reference to the will : for thus the Philosopher (*Ethics*,
VI, 3) holds that science, wisdom and understanding, and also

[19] Or one says he *does* something to *make* his patient healthy.
[20] *S.T.*, I–II, Q. 61, A. 1.

art, are intellectual virtues. But the subject of a habit which is called a virtue simply, can only be the will, or some power insofar as it is moved by the will." [21]

In these terms the distinction between art and prudence is clear. Rectitude of the will is essential to prudence but not to art. Prudence is something more than a merely rational habit, such as art is, since it includes application to action, which application is an act of the will. [22] Art, on the other hand, is unaffected by the direction of the appetite and confers merely the aptness for good work of a certain kind, and neither the habit of using that aptitude nor the will to use it well [123]. "In order that man may make good use of the art he has, he needs a good will, which is perfected by moral virtue." [23] It follows as a consequence of the different relation of art and prudence to the will, "that more praise is given to the craftsman who is at fault willingly, than to one who is unwilling; whereas it is more contrary to prudence to sin willingly than unwillingly, since rectitude of the will is essential to prudence, and not to art." [24]

The translation of this analysis into the one which defines prudence as the virtue of action or doing, and art as the virtue of production or making, is accomplished by distinguishing between the interior and exterior acts of the will, or between the act of the will proper and those acts of other powers which can be commanded by the will, acts of the intellect or of the passions or of the motive power. [25] The sphere of prudence is the interior act of the will. It regards the operation of all those powers which can be commanded by the will in so far as the effects of such operations abide in the agent. The sphere of art is external to the will. Not only are its operations exterior to the will, but the effects of these operations are changes in external matter, as well as in the agent. By using the word "making" to name an operation passing into outward matter, and "doing" an operation abiding exclusively in the agent, art is spoken of as the right reason of things to be made, and prudence the right reason of things to be done [124]. But the exception

[21] *S.T.*, I–II, Q. 56, A. 3.   [22] *S.T.*, II–II, Q. 47, A. 1, ad. 3.
[23] *S.T.*, I–II, Q. 57, A. 3, ad. 2.
[24] *Ethics*, VI, 5, 1140^{b}22–25; *S.T.*, I–II, Q. 57, A. 4. Cf. I–II, Q. 47, A. 8; II–II, Q. 21, A. 3, ad. 2.
[25] Vd. *S.T.*, I–II, Q. 6, A. 4; Q. 8, preamble; Q. 18, A. 6.

in the case of the liberal arts, the effects of whose operations abide in the agent, and the fact that doing as an interior act may be the efficient cause of operations which have external effects, as in the case of acts of justice or injustice, require that the criterion of externality, if it is retained to distinguish art from prudence, be defined not in terms of what is exterior to the soul but rather in terms of what is exterior to the will. This point will become clearer after we have differentiated the liberal and servile arts, the practical and productive arts. For the present, we are concerned only to identify the sphere of prudence with those interior acts proper to the will itself.

The interior act of the will is divisible according as it regards ends or means. With respect to means there is the act of choice, and choice depends upon counsel and judgment. Moreover, choice is effective only if the acts which constitute the means chosen, or are required for the use of the means, are commanded. The nature of choice, which is an interior act of the will, indicates the role of prudence. Choice can be considered either as intellect influenced by appetite or as appetite influenced by intellect.[26] In the latter consideration, prudence can be defined as the virtue whereby the intellect rightly moves the will in its act of choice. The acts of prudence are properly assigned as (1) taking counsel, (2) judging of what is thus discovered, and (3) commanding, which is applying to action the things counselled and judged.[27] It is this last act which makes prudence something more than a rational habit. Prudence is not merely knowledge of what to seek and what to avoid, but the application of such knowledge to action through the choice of means, which involves an act of will.[28] To define prudence as right reason about *means to be chosen*, rather than right reason about *things to be done*, more explicitly indicates that the sphere of its operation is the interior act of the will. Because the sphere of art is exterior to the will, the perfection of art consists in good judgment regarding the means to be employed in achieving particular ends, but does not involve command, whereas command is the chief act of prudence [125]. It also follows that an art can be lost by forgetfulness because it is simply an intellectual habit, and forgetfulness regards knowledge only. Although

---

[26] *Ethics*, VI, 2, 1139^{b}5 ; *S.T.*, I–II, Q. 13, A. 1.
[27] *S.T.*, II–II, Q. 47, AA. 8, 16.   [28] *S.T.*, II–II, Q. 47, A. 1.

prudence in so far as it depends upon knowledge can be hindered by forgetfulness, it is primarily corrupted by the passions in so far as its principal act is not judgment but command.[29]

Maritain summarizes the distinction we have so far made by the statement: "The Man of Learning is an Intellectual demonstrating, the Artist is an Intellectual operating, the Prudent Man is an intelligent Man of Will acting well." [30]   This not only emphasizes that the difference between art and prudence as intellectual virtues arises from the latter's relation to the will, but also indicates the similarity between art and the speculative virtues [126].   It is necessary, however, to expand this statement by discriminating the different ways in which men can be artists.   This will more adequately define the sphere of art as intellectual operation.

In the first place, since art is a virtue of the practical intellect, the operations of art must be distinguished from the operations of the speculative intellect by reference to an extrinsic end.   As in the case of prudence, knowledge is used by art for the sake of something else.   The artist is competent to judge of the means for certain ends.   The artistic habit is an aptness to work in such a way that the thing to be done or made will be well done or well made.[31]   The distinction of different sorts of art, therefore, depends upon the different types of result which intellectual operation can effect [127].   The result may either be a condition of the soul itself, other than the artistic habit, or it may be some kind of transformation in things external to the soul.   Thus, the operations of such liberal arts as grammar and logic result in the acquisition of knowledge by the person who possesses these arts.   The possession of such arts and the possession of the results which such arts are able to achieve must not be confused, even though they belong to the same person [128].   Knowledge and wisdom are virtues of the speculative intellect.   They are habits, the acts of which are acts of knowing.   But grammar and logic are arts, and as such are virtues of the prac-

[29] S.T., II–II, Q. 47, A. 16; see esp. ad. 3.   Cf. S.T., I–II, Q. 58, A. 5, ad. 3; and Ethics, VI, 5, 1140b28–30.
[30] Op. cit., p. 20.
[31] At this point and subsequently I use the words "doing" and "making" to make subordinate distinctions within the field of action which passes into outward matter.   St. Thomas uses the single word "making" to name all such extrinsic operation.

tical intellect. They are habits, the acts of which are well regulated operations of acquiring knowledge. They differ from their results as the process of learning differs from the possession of learning. The arts which result in the changed condition of something other than the operator himself necessarily involve bodily motions on the part of the artist. But it is not this which distinguishes the liberal from the servile arts. Rather it turns on whether what is changed in another is soul or body. Thus, teaching which is the art of making other men learned is a liberal art, whereas healing which is the art of making other men healthy is a servile art. The defining characteristic of the servile arts is that the result of the work done is an effect produced in matter [129].

It is necessary, furthermore, to distinguish between practical and productive arts, between the arts of doing and the arts of making. All art can be spoken of as productive if the intention is to indicate that the operations of art terminate in the *production* of an effect. But this is to say no more than that art is a cause of change. The effects of art can be distinguished according as the result is an accidental change in a substance, a change that could occur naturally, or according as the result is a thing that has individuality through being a unique composition of accidents or substances. In the latter case, that which results is quasi-substantial. It is like a substance in that it is a whole composed of parts, and as an individual whole it is subject to accidental determinations. Furthermore, such quasi-substantial entities are always works of art and are never the result of natural change simply. Thus, the arts of navigation and medicine can be distinguished from the arts of ship-building and shoe-making. The former are practical; the latter productive. The former effect accidental changes that might have occurred without the intervention of art. This indicates that the change is due to an active principle in the natural order. The practical arts must, therefore, work by *co-operating with nature*.[32] They are never the sufficient cause of their effects. The productive arts, on the other hand, work by operating on nature, utilizing natural potentialities to impose an artificial form that the matter is able to receive. The criteria of this distinction between the practical and the productive apply perfectly in the case of the

[32] Vd. Aristotle, *Physics*, II, 199[a]15. Cf. Maritain, p. 45.

servile arts, arts which either co-operate with or operate on formed matter. But their application is not clear in the case of such speculative liberal arts as grammar and logic. In one respect, they can be viewed as productive : they result in such entities as sentences and propositions. In another respect, they can be viewed as practical. If teaching is practical because it must co-operate with the natural principles of the intellect to cause learning in the pupil, so are the operations of grammar and logic practical when they are considered as constituting the process of self-instruction.[32a]

The fine arts are clearly productive rather than practical. Poems, sonatas, statues are like shoes and ships rather than like the health caused by the physician or the change of place caused by the navigator. The work of fine art is an individual thing. Its formal principle is compositional.[33] Though its elements, considered separately, are the accidents of a substance, its individual being is constituted as a structure of these elements, a whole organized out of these elements as its proper parts. The difficult problem with respect to the fine arts is whether they are liberal or servile. Poetry and music are like the liberal arts in that what they produce has its being in the soul rather than in matter. Words and musical notations are merely symbolic devices employed in communication. When communication is effected, the poem or musical composition exists as it is received by the imagination of the recipient. The work of fine art, which is liberal in the sense defined, is distinguished from the work of speculative art in that the latter, also communicated by words, is received by the intellect. But plastic works, such as statues, paintings and, *perhaps*, motion pictures, seem to have their primary existence in matter. The difference seems to be that the manifold printings of a poem do not multiply the individual work ; the multiple renditions are all renderings of one piece of music ; but the oneness and identity of the painting seem to be restricted to the single canvas on which it is made. Upon

[32a] The art of teaching is nothing but the liberal arts exercised on the intellect of another.

[33] The accidental forms which are the terms of changes effected by the practical arts are natural accidents, whereas the forms of arrangement and composition which terminate productive activity are not natural, though such artificial forms, as accidental, can be located in the category of posture. Vd. *Physics*, I, 188[b]20 ; *S.T.*, III, Sup., Q. 79, A. 2, ad. 3.

further consideration it will be seen that this difference is only an accidental trait of the plastic arts as they exist today. A symbolism which makes multiplication and communication possible has not been invented for painting, but there is no intrinsic obstacle to its invention. The case of the dance is instructive. A notation has been devised for separating the dance-composition from particular instances of its execution. The motion picture is similarly instructive. The multiplication of films does not multiply the motion picture as a work of art; it merely conveys the same work at once to a widely scattered audience. Because the mode of their existence is in the soul and not in matter, except accidentally through the use of matter as a medium of communication, works of fine art are essentially liberal rather than servile.

The basic distinctions in the sphere of art are (1) between liberal and servile, (2) between practical and productive. The fine arts are a special group of productive arts, liberal rather than servile, and distinguished from the speculative liberal arts in that the productions of the latter are intellectually received and the former imaginatively. More subtle distinctions can be made, but they are not necessary for our present purposes. Nor is it necessary to treat at length the modern distinction between fine and useful arts [130]. This distinction arises not from the nature of the work itself, but from the intention of the artist or the intention of the recipient. In one sense, the work of art is always the end of the artistic operation; but the artist may regard his work either as an end in itself or as a means to further ends. Independently of the artist's intentions, the recipient of his work may regard it as an end in itself, as something to be enjoyed, or as a means, as something to be used. Thus, a chair may be intended by its maker as a thing of beauty and be used by those who acquire it; or intended for use, the chair may become a museum piece in the course of time. So music may be used to lull the weary to sleep, and paintings may be used to cover walls. The distinction between beauty and utility is not a distinction in the nature of works of art any more than it is a distinction between different sorts of natural things. The same thing is capable of being intended or regarded in both ways, because any particular thing is capable of being treated as a means to be used or as an end to be enjoyed. If this were not the case, there could be no practical problem about works of fine art in relation to their effects upon men [131].

One further distinguishing characteristic of art is imitation. Man is creative, in a secondary sense, through the virtue of art. The limitation upon human creativity, which makes it a remote image of the divine, is that art imitates nature. The practical arts imitate nature in the manner of their operation. The productive arts imitate nature by making objects which are like natural things either in form or in function. The distinction, therefore, between the man of learning and the man of art is that the latter is an intellectual operating imitatively.

In passing now to other distinctions between art and prudence, all of which are necessary in order to understand their relation, it should be recognized that whatever is said of art applies without qualification to the fine arts. The conflict between art and prudence may be more intense, however, in the case of the fine arts because they are essentially liberal and work their effects in the soul itself.[33a]

B2. Art and prudence can be distinguished by their ends. The end which prudence serves is the final good of man. The end of each art is a particular good, the good of a particular work to be done [132]. There are many arts, each independent of the other, as there is a multiplicity of particular goods which man can achieve by his practical or productive operations. But, strictly, there is only one prudence as there is only one ultimate good of human life. The division of prudence into such species as private and public — the prudence whereby a man rules himself and the prudence whereby he governs others or is governed by another — does not multiply the ends to be served, but regards the same end under different aspects.[34] The unity of prudence is the unity of ethics and politics, analytically separable as directed toward the separate and the collective common good. "Reason stands in different relations to the productions of art and to moral actions." The sphere of morality is the sphere of prudence. "In matters of art, reason is directed to a particular

[33a] For a discussion of this conflict in the sphere of the useful arts,—particularly in relation to economic goods and private property,—see Maritain, *Freedom in the Modern World,* New York, 1936 : Appendix I, esp. pp. 197, 204 ff.
[34] *S.T.,* II–II, QQ. 48, 50.

end, which is something devised by reason; whereas in moral matters, it is directed toward the general end of all human life." [35] To say that the end of art is the particular good which it produces is not to forget that art is a virtue and perfects its possessor as well as the matter upon which it operates. But art makes a man good relatively, not simply. It does not make him good as a man, but rather good as a musician or a grammarian, a shoemaker or a physician. The human perfection of possessing an art is relative in the sense that it makes a man good in relation to a particular kind of work.[36] But prudence makes a man good simply in the sense that it makes him act well as a man. It follows, therefore that "the craftsman needs art, not that he may live well, but that he may produce a good work of art, and have it in good keeping; whereas prudence is necessary to man that he may lead a good life." [37] It follows, also, that prudence is indispensable to man. This cannot be said of any particular art.

This distinction is clearly related to the preceding one. The operation of prudence involves the will and depends upon its rectitude, since means can be prudently chosen only if they are chosen for the right end which in the moral order is either the final good or something which is good because ordained thereto. But a man is no less an artist if he does not look further than the particular good in which his operation terminates. His will is not involved except in the limited sense in which he exercises his art voluntarily; nor need his will be rectified even in this limited sense, since he can use his art to produce a bad as well as a good work. It is for this reason that St. Thomas says that the ends "to which the moral virtues incline are as the principles of prudence, whereas the products of art are not the principles but the matter of art." [38] If the artist be well-intentioned, however, and seek to use his art to do good work, prudence enters into his activity to the extent that a choice of means may be involved in the accomplishment of this particular good. An art is the mastery of the means for procuring a certain end, but this mastery does not preclude the possibility of alternative ways of working. A kind of artistic prudence may, therefore, be necessary. Thus, we speak of a prudent business-man or a prudent navigator. But such prudence, though it is true prudence be-

[35] *S.T.*, I–II, Q. 21, A. 2, ad. 2.   [36] *S.T.*, I–II, Q. 56, A. 3.
[37] *S.T.*, I–II, Q. 57, A. 5, ad. 1.   [38] *S.T.*, I–II, Q. 65, A. 2, ad. 4.

cause it devises fitting ways of obtaining a good end, is imperfect
"because the good which it takes for an end is not the common
end of all human life, but of some particular affair." [39]   That
artistic prudence is imperfect prudence indicates the essential
difference between prudence and art in terms of the ends toward
which their operations are directed [133].

That a sort of prudence is involved in the work of a particular
art is not inconsistent with the fact that the sphere of art is
included within the sphere of prudence.   A man need not be
an artist of a particular sort, but every artist is a man.   As a
man, the artist has other ends than those in which his operations
as an artist terminate. [40]   The subordination of art to prudence
can be seen in a number of ways.   In the first place, the exercise
of art is voluntary and as an exterior act of the will it is subject
to prudence which determines the will directly.   The work of
art, though it is the end of the worker as an artist, is never an
end in itself.   It can be a means to other ends; it may have many
practical consequences.   *As such*, whether or not it shall be
made in a particular case is subject to the judgment of prudence.
The judgment whether something should be made regards ulterior ends and is prudential.   The judgment how it should be
made regards the thing itself and is artistic.   In the second place,
art is itself a virtue and though a particular art is not indispensable, the possession of any art perfects man relatively.
Whether an art should be acquired is, therefore, also subject
to the judgment of prudence which considers all things that are
contingently desirable as means to happiness.

Though the entire sphere of art is subordinate to prudence,
because particular ends are subordinate to the general end and
because all exterior voluntary acts are subject to the will, art is
nevertheless free within its own sphere of operation.   The violation of this freedom means the end of art.   Although art cannot
decide whether a particular work should be done, whether
it is good for the artist to do or for other men to receive, once
this question is decided only art determines the means to be
used in accomplishing its relative end.   "Precisely because, given
a work of a certain kind to be done, there are strictly determined
ways of realizing it, depending upon the pure exigencies of the
work itself and brooking no liberties, the virtue of art," as Mari-

[39] *S.T.*, II–II, Q. 47, A. 13.   [40] Cf. Maritain, pp. 131–133.

tain says, "will not have the work interfered with and directly controlled by anything other than itself; it insists that it alone shall touch the work and keep contact with it to bring it into being. In short, art requires that nothing shall attain the work but *through itself as intermediary*." [41]   It is this autonomy of art within its own spheres, combined with the limitation of its sovereignty by the subjection of the sphere of art to prudence, that makes art the source of peculiar difficulties in the government of human affairs.[42]   Both art for art's sake and art for the sake of man are dangerous partial truths.   Neither can be denied, neither can be affirmed, without the qualification that is contained in the other.

B3.   Finally, there is the distinction between art and prudence in terms of the difference between reason's operation in relation to the will's act of choice and in relation to creative work.   An art is constituted by rules of operation not only reflecting knowledge of available means but also providing for the intelligent application of this knowledge to the particular contingent matter at hand.   These rules must, of course, be possessed by the artist as habits of proceeding in definite and fixed ways for the accomplishment of his work.[43]   It is for this reason that every art can also be called a science.   What is formulated prescriptively as the rules of the art can also be formulated declaratively as a body of knowledge.   In the ancient tradition the opposite of art was empiricism, as we would say the opposite of proceeding scientifically is trial and error.   The empiric in medicine was one who lacked the art of healing because, lacking the relevant sciences, he worked by trial and error rather than in the light of fixed rules.   Prudence is essentially empirical or artless, which is only to say that it is without rules.   As Maritain points out, prudence having for its matter "not something to make, some object determined in being, but the pure use to which the subject puts his liberty, has no certain definite paths or fixed rules. Its fixed point is the direct end to which the moral virtues tend and its business is to determine the right means.   But to attain this end and to apply the universal principles of moral science, its precepts and counsels, to the particular action to be produced, there are no ready-made rules. . .   In every particular case there

[41] Maritain, p. 132, by permission of Messrs. Sheed and Ward, Publishers.
[42] Cf. Maritain, Note 139.   [43] Cf. Maritain, p. 18; also Ch. VI.

will be a particular way of conforming to the end. It is for prudence to discover that way, by using paths or rules subordinate to the will (for the will to make its choice as circumstance and opportunity occur), in themselves contingent and not predetermined but determined with certainty and definitely laid down by the judgment or decision of the prudent man, and therefore by the Schoolmen termed *regulae arbitrariae.*" [44]

This distinction is further understood when the concept of "artistic prudence" is remembered. Because of the contingency of the circumstances, as in the case of such practical arts as navigation, because of the inadequacy of the relevant sciences, as in medicine, or because of the individuality of the work to be done, as in the fine arts, rules of art are insufficient fully to determine the procedure. Though the artist has some knowledge of the means, and accordingly has rules of operation, vitally efficient as habits, these are not enough. The kind of judgment which prudence makes is required. In relation to his particular end, the artist must seek counsel and make a choice of alternative means in the light of the circumstances. To prudence belongs "the application of right reason in matters of counsel, which are those wherein there is no fixed way of obtaining the end." [45] Although prudence in the simple sense [134] has nothing to do with the matter of art "because art is both directed to a particular end and has fixed means of obtaining that end, yet, by a kind of comparison, a man may be said to act prudently in matters of art. In certain arts, on account of the uncertainty of the means for obtaining the end, there is need for counsel, as for instance in the arts of medicine and navigation." [46] Elsewhere St. Thomas says that we do not take counsel in "those things which have a fixed way of being done, as in works produced by art, with the exception of those arts that admit of conjecture, such as medicine, commerce and the like." [47] In short, prudence enters the sphere of art precisely at the point at which art itself fails [135]. The nature of artistic prudence thus clearly indicates the operational difference between prudence and art. If they were not

---

[44] Maritain, pp. 16–17, by permission of Messrs. Sheed and Ward, Publishers. "Hence it is that no *science* can take the place of Prudence, for science, however casuistically complicated it may be supposed to be, never has any other than general and ascertained rules" (p. 17).   [45] *S.T.,* II–II, Q. 47, A. 3, ad. 3.
[46] *S.T.,* II–II, Q. 47, A. 5, ad. 2.   [47] *S.T.,* I–II, Q. 14, A. 5; note esp. ad. 3.

different employments of reason, the one could not supplement the other in this way. The essence of the one is intelligence disciplined to make a unique determination of rules in the individual case; the essence of the other is intelligence formed habitually by generally applicable rules [136].

As there is artistic prudence, so also in a sense there is an art of prudence. St. Thomas quotes St. Augustine's definition of virtue as *ars recte vivendi*,[48] finding it applicable to prudence essentially, and to the moral virtues by participation; though he adds the comment that "Augustine usually applies the term *art* to any form of right reason, in which sense art includes prudence."[49] But even in the more restricted sense of the word "art," there is an art of prudence. If prudence be understood simply as right reason about the means to be chosen for the ends of life, the art of prudence — the body of principles and rules which prudence supplements in casuistical application — is constituted by the practical sciences of ethics and politics. Though ethics and politics can thus be regarded as arts, it is better not to do so because they are distinguished from all other arts by the ends they serve, as perfect prudence is distinguished from artistic prudence by the fact that it is directed to the ultimate good of man and not to the good of a particular work. The uniqueness of ethics and politics is thus seen in terms of their unique relation to prudence as a cardinal virtue. If the unique status of ethics and politics is not recognized, the prudence which they require for application cannot be distinguished from artistic prudence. There is danger of confusion in these analogical uses of the words "art" and "prudence," especially if the meanings are not carefully qualified in such notions as artistic prudence and the art of prudence [137]. It is, furthermore, important not to allow these analogical uses to obscure the clear distinctions between art and prudence as separate and independent virtues.

C. In the light of these distinctions we can now discuss art and prudence in relation to the speculative virtues, on the one hand, and the moral virtues, on the other. Both art and prudence depend on the speculative virtues to some extent. The correlation of particular arts with particular sciences indicates the speculative content of the arts. Art requires some knowledge of universals as the substance of its rules. This knowledge

[48] *City of God*, IV, 2.   [49] *S.T.*, I–II, Q. 58, A. 2, ad. 1.

is of the sort we have called scientific. What corresponded to our particular empirical sciences were called practical and productive arts in the ancient world. This not only emphasized the essential contingency of such knowledge, but also the operational and creative aspects of science as technique. The close relation between investigative science and technology in the modern era indicates that the point is more than a matter of naming. Prudence, unlike the various arts, does not depend upon any body of knowledge particularized in subject-matter. Like the moral virtues, prudence can be without wisdom and science, but not without understanding. "It is by the virtue of understanding that we know self-evident principles both in speculative and practical matters. Consequently just as right reason in speculative matters, in so far as it proceeds from naturally known principles, presupposes the understanding of those principles, so also does prudence, which is right reason about matters of action." [50] Prudence does not appoint the end to the moral virtues.[51] The end is appointed by *synderesis*, the habit of first principles in the practical order.[52] To say that only such understanding of the last end is necessary for prudence does not mean that prudence is not aided by the practical sciences of ethics and politics, which supply it with particular principles. It means only that he who is untutored in these sciences can, nevertheless, be a prudent man if he is directed to his due end by the light of natural reason.

Art is not only more intellectual than prudence, which is more on the side of the will, but, as Maritain points out, art more closely approximates the speculative virtues. "Because of its matter, which is contingent, it accords with prudence more than with science; according to its formal reason and in so far as it is a virtue it accords with science and the habits of the speculative intellect more than with prudence." [53] In the sense in which the speculative virtues are superior to the moral virtues because they perfect the reason rather than the appetite, art is superior to prudence. But in the sense in which the moral virtues are better as virtues and more necessary for a good life, prudence is superior to art.[54]

[50] *S.T.*, I–II, Q. 58, A. 4.   [51] *S.T.*, II–II, Q. 47, A. 6, note esp. ad. 3.
[52] *S.T.*, I, Q. 79, A. 12.
[53] Maritain, pp. 19 20, by permission of Messrs. Sheed and Ward, Publishers. Cf. *S.T.*, I–II, Q. 57, A. 4, ad. 2.   [54] *S.T.*, I–II, Q. 66, A. 3; Q. 61, A. 1.

The crucial difference between art and prudence reveals itself in their relation to the moral virtues.   Art is independent of the moral virtues, and they in turn do not rely upon it.   The moral virtues, ordering the passions and the will in conformity to reason, are habits of the appetitive faculty.   "It does not depend on the disposition of our appetite whether we judge well or ill of the principles of art, as it does when we judge of the end which is the principle in moral matters : in the former case our judgment depends on reason alone.   Hence art does not require virtues perfecting the appetite as prudence does."[55]   It follows that a man can be good as an artist of a particular sort without being a good man ; conversely, a good man need not be an artist of any particular sort.   But to be a good man is to be a prudent man, and conversely.   Prudence is impossible without the moral virtues and they without it.[56]   "No moral virtue can be without prudence ; since it is proper to a moral virtue to make a right choice, for it is an elective habit.   Now right choice requires not only the inclination to a due end, which inclination is the direct outcome of moral virtue, but also correct choice of things conducive to the end, which choice is made by prudence, that counsels, judges and commands in those things which are directed to the end.   In like manner one cannot have prudence unless one has the moral virtues, since prudence is *right reason about things to be done*, and the starting point of reason is the end of the thing to be done, to which end man is rightly disposed by moral virtue."[57]   It is only in the exercise of art that moral virtues enter.   Thus, it is the virtue of justice, and not his technique, which inclines a craftsman to do his work faithfully.[58]   The artist is at fault as a man if he uses his art for the wrong ends ; he is at fault as an artist only if, intending to produce a good thing, he produces a bad one, or produces a bad one while intending to produce something good.[59]

D.   It would seem that the excellence of a work of art is due only to a technical mastery of materials by the artist and is unaffected by the direction of his moral character toward good or evil.   It would seem that, whatever the state of his soul in

[55] *S.T.*, I–II, Q. 58, A. 5, ad. 2.   Vd. also Q. 57, AA. 3, 4.   [56] *Ethics*, X, 8.
[57] *S.T.*, I–II, Q. 65, A. 1.   Cf. Q. 58, AA. 4, 5 ; II–II, Q. 47, A. 7.
[58] *S.T.*, I–II, Q. 57, A. 3, ad. 2.
[59] *S.T.*, I–II, Q. 21, A. 3, ad. 2.   Vd. also Q. 57, A. 4 ; II–II, Q. 47, A. 8.

the line of morality, the artist's work is a creature of his art and
is a thing apart.   These things would seem to follow from the
fact that art does not presuppose rectitude of the appetite, that
art is not a cardinal virtue and hence is not integrated in the moral
character as prudence is.   But, in the case of the fine arts, the
situation is complicated by two factors.   Of greatest importance
is the fact that for most of the fine arts, poetry and music certainly, the object of imitation is human action, the moral life.
The artist, therefore, cannot help but reveal the tenor of his
moral judgments.   The greater his technique, the clearer will
be the revelation.   The mediæval distinction between principal
and instrumental cause is relevant here.   As in the case of any
servile work, the workman's artistic intelligence is the principal
cause and the skill of his hands the instrumental cause of the
production, so in the case of the fine arts, the virtue of art itself
is only the instrumental cause, the artist's soul being the principal
cause of the work done.   The work of fine art is the image of
its maker [138].   In the field of morality, there is the maxim:
According as a man is, so does the end seem to him.[60]   In the
field of the fine arts, the maxim becomes: As a man is, so are
his works.[61]   This last must be understood in two senses because
the work, so far as its grade of technical excellence is concerned,
marks the level of his art, as well as reveals the state of his soul.
In other words, the work of fine art can be made the basis of
two judgments: an artistic or technical judgment and a moral
judgment.   The latter is strictly not a judgment of the work of
art, nor of the artist as a technician; it is a judgment of him as a
man [139].   The fine arts are unique in this respect.   One
could not judge of the moral integrity of a physician or an engineer, a geometrician or a grammarian, from knowing his work.
One could only judge thereby of the man's skill in healing or
building, in demonstrating or reading.   We shall return to this
point later in a discussion of the sorts of criticism applicable to
works of fine art.

The other factor which distinguishes the fine arts from the
servile arts in relation to morality is the intention of the artist.
To the extent that he looks upon the thing he is making as an
end in itself, to the extent that he aims at beauty rather than
utility of any sort, he is directed toward a good of the tran-

[60] *Ethics*, III, 7, 1114ᵃ32.   [61] Maritain, p. 11.

scendental order. The utility of the work of fine art, the use to which it may be put by others, is not inconsistent with the purity of the artist's intention. The work of art is always the end of the workman's effort. This is not inconsistent with the view of the work as a means to other ends. Nor is it inconsistent with the distinction among intentions on the part of the worker viewed as a man. It is the man with an art to use who uses it either for the sake of the thing to be made, as an end in itself, or for the sake of producing means to further ends. Two consequences follow from the first of these intentions in human work. (1) The will of the artist must be rectified in "the line of beauty," as the will of the prudent man must be ordained to the moral good. Or, as Maritain says, the artist aiming at beauty "must be in love with *what he is doing*, so that his virtue becomes in truth, in St. Augustine's phrase, *ordo amoris*." [62] The artist who aims to produce useful things is not in love with *what* he is doing, but rather with what he is doing it *for*. The intention of beauty is analogous to the intention of truth in the work of the speculative arts. It is only the love of truth which ultimately distinguishes the dialectician from the sophist. (2) The rectification of the will by ordination to goods of a transcendental order, such as truth and beauty, gives the fine or speculative artist who is thus devoted a justification above the ordinary standards of morality. It is this which intensifies the conflict between art and prudence in the case of the fine arts because of "the very transcendence of their object." [63] As Maritain points out, the artist and the contemplative "both perfected by an intellectual habit binding them to the transcendental order, are in a position to sympathize." [64] The artist who aims at utility can appeal to no values which are outside the scope of the prudent man, who judges of all means to be used in the moral order. The prudent man cannot tell him how to work, but he can say whether his work is worth doing or whether it should be avoided in the economy of human needs and employments. But to find fault with the work of fine art — the work and not the artist — the prudent man must treat it as if it were useful, must regard it as an instrumentality in the moral order. Only thus can he have "the certitude that he is defending against the artist, a sacred

[62] Maritain, pp. 48–49. [63] Maritain, p. 82. [64] Maritain, p. 85.

good, the good of Man." [65]   But the artist who has worked with the intention of beauty can protect his work, though not himself, from the criticism of the prudent man by noting the transgression that had to be committed in order to bring it into the sphere of morality.   Insisting upon the transcendence of the object, he, too, can be "certain of defending a good which is no less sacred, the good of Beauty." [66]

E.   The conflict between art and prudence is rooted in the separation of man's intellect and will.   This is the essential human imperfection.   It is the primal source of sin.   Were these two faculties not separate, there could be no discrepancy between knowledge and virtue — every virtue would be a kind of prudence [67] — there would be no distinction between the cardinal virtues, which perfect the will and those relative or imperfect virtues which merely confer an aptness of the mind for good operation, there would be no diremption between the spheres of morality and intellectuality.   Prudence, integrated with the moral virtues, is on the side of will.   Art, aligned with the speculative virtues, is on the side of intellect.

The proximate sources of the conflict are (1) the essential ambivalence of works of art and (2) the duality of the workman as an artist and as a man.   The work of art, whatever the intention of its maker, is never an end in itself.   Relative to the artist it may be an end, but once it leaves his hands it has the status of any other particular thing which impinges causally on human life.   It is, therefore, subject to two judgments: a technical judgment which regards it as the product of art, and a moral judgment which regards it as contributing toward or detracting from human welfare.   Similarly, the worker can be judged as an artist and as a man: as an artist in terms of the excellence of his technique, as a man in terms of his ends.   In the case of the fine arts, the work itself can be the ground for both these judgments of its maker, without need to consult his explicit intentions.   In any case the prudent man is competent to make only the second of these judgments.   It is this competence and, more than competence, the obligation which the prudent man has to be vigilant in everything that concerns man's welfare, that brings him into conflict with the artist and the work of art.   The conflict is always initiated by the prudent man.   It never originates

[65] Maritain, p. 84.   [66] Maritain, p. 85.   [67] Vd. *S.T.*, I–II, Q. 58, A. 2.

with the artist, at least so long as the latter respects the limitations of his competence. The artist *as such* cannot judge of moral matters as the prudent man quite properly judges of art. There is a fundamental asymmetry here in the relation between art and prudence. The work of art and the artist both come within the sphere of morality because the artist is also a man and the work of art a thing of benefit or harm to other men. The work of art may also transcend the moral sphere in the order of truth and beauty, but even this transcendence is only in aspect, because the true and the beautiful are also good in relation to human appetite. The reverse is not the case, except in the transcendental convertibility of the good with the true and the beautiful. In this transcendental sense, the good life is true and beautiful. It is work of divine art. Here, then, is the asymmetry: whereas there can be both an aesthetic and a moral judgment about works of art, only the prudent man is competent to judge of moral matters.

The conflict between art and prudence can occur in a number of ways which should be distinguished. (1) It may occur in the soul of the individual man as a conflict of virtues [140]. When the moral virtues conflict, when a choice must be made in the particular case between the claims of justice and mercy, for instance, it is the task of prudence to resolve the issue. But when the conflict is between art and prudence, the arbiter must be sought elsewhere because prudence can not be judge in its own case. It will rarely happen that the virtues will be of equal strength. It is more likely that the man will be first an artist and then a man, or conversely. (2) It may occur in society. Then it is a conflict between different men, men in whom different virtues predominate. (3) In its social incidence, the problem may concern only the good of the artist as a man. The prudent man as his friend may try to stimulate the conflict of virtues in the soul of the artist for his greater good. (4) Or the problem may be with respect to the good of the multitude who are the recipients of works of art. It is only in this last form that the conflict of art and prudence becomes a political problem. This is the form in which it has been traditionally discussed. The species of prudence,[68] whereby a man rules others, whether in the state or in the family, considers not the good of

68 *S.T.*, II–II, Q. 48; Q. 50, AA. 1, 2, 3.

the artist so much as the good of those who receive the products of his work, the separate moral good of those who are within his charge as well as the good of the community. Furthermore, it should be noted that in its political incidence, the problem has almost always been about works of fine art, particularly music and poetry. The current practical problem about motion pictures is the concern of political prudence, not with the moral welfare of the artists involved, but primarily with the good of the state or the family, and the well-being of every member of the cinema's vast audience.

The root and sources of the problem indicate why in any of its forms it is *almost* insoluble. To call the conflict of art and prudence an antinomy, as Maritain does,[69] is to recognize that there is reason on both sides. There is no question, on the one hand, that prudence should govern art to whatever extent the work of art or the artist comes within the sphere of morality. But, on the other hand, the government by the prudent man must be external because the artist is necessarily autonomous in his own sphere. Though the prudent man is obligated to take account of the arts because they produce goods and evils which fall within his view of the means and circumstances of human life to be ordered and controlled, he is not by virtue of prudence competent to direct the work of the arts. In the sphere of his own activity, the artist must be relatively independent. He alone has the special competence for making or doing well whatever is subject to his technique. Furthermore, the work of art which is good technically may be morally pernicious in its effects, or the reverse may be the case. Such discrepancies may occur even though the artist is a man of moral integrity and works with the best intentions, because the effect of the work depends upon the moral fibre of its recipients as well as upon its intrinsic morality, whereby it reflects the soul of its maker.

The position of prudence is, therefore, anomalous. It has a task of ruling which exceeds its competence. It is a limited sovereign charged with responsibilities disproportionate to its limited powers. The prudent man cannot ignore the artist and his work, as the artist is able to ignore the prudent man. Considering the positive values of the arts in human life, he must

[69] *Op. cit.,* p. 138. Cf. pp. 82–86. Maritain is here thinking only of fine art. The same restriction applies to the remainder of this chapter.

seek to increase their production, he must strive to preserve and enhance these values.   Considering the negative values, he would be unwise if he tried to interfere with the operations of art, but he must nevertheless try to prevent them from interfering with his own efforts for the sake of human happiness.

4.   In the light of this analysis, a few principles of practical wisdom can be formulated.   They do not solve the antinomy of art and prudence.   On the contrary, they acknowledge its insolubility except in ideal terms — the ideal of a supernatural perfection, healing the wound of intellect divided against will. They do not seek to *reconcile* art and prudence, but only to effect a *compromise* between them [141].

We have seen that the prudent man has three practical alternatives with respect to art: (1) extirpation or total exclusion, (2) various forms of regulation and control, (3) inaction, or granting the arts their freedom.   The first is a drastic remedy, justified only when the disadvantages accruing clearly outweigh the benefits.   In prohibiting an art entirely, the prudent man acts within his powers.   He is not thus involved in what for him is the impossible task of directing an art within its own sphere of operation.[70]   Extirpation lays hands on an art externally.   It does not meddle with its workings.   But when, in the case of the motion picture as always in the case of fine arts, there is a balance of positive and negative values, the prudent man must choose the remaining alternatives.   Our analysis has shown the way in which giving the arts their freedom is compatible with the regulation of them that is sometimes necessary. It depends upon the type of regulation, whether it be external to artistic activity itself, supervising only the circumstances under which works of art are received, or whether it attempt to dictate the content of art, violating the workshop itself by entering it without the credentials of technique.   Regulation of the latter sort is clearly unwise.   It engages the prudent man in matters exceeding his competence.   It is better to kill an art than to choke or mangle it.   If it is allowed to live, it should be granted the freedom indispensable to its vitality and vigor.   But to grant an art freedom in its proper domain — the process of production

70 Herein may lie the partial practical wisdom of Plato's expulsion of the dramatists.

itself, in which the artist's technique is the instrument of the artist's soul — does not mean that it should be allowed to run wild in the community. It is proper for the prudent man to supervise the ways in which works of art reach their audience, to say, not what shall be made, but what shall be received and by whom and under what conditions.[71] Here the difficulties of the prudent man are of another order. He does not go out of his proper sphere in imposing a censorship which rejects a work of art as unfit to be received. But he must be guided in such action by knowledge or opinion concerning the effects of the particular work upon moral character and conduct [142]. Knowledge, in the proper sense of this word, he cannot have. If opinion is uncertain and conflicting, and if scientific evidence is either not available or no more certain and unambiguous than opinion, the casuistical problem may be genuinely insoluble. This, of course, does not abrogate the principle that the prudent man should seek to do what he can to increase the benefits of a particular art and to minimize its undesirable consequences: *to do what he can*, within the limitations imposed upon him by the inviolable autonomy of art, on the one hand, and by his honest doubts and uncertainties concerning the relevant facts, on the other.

One other principle is clear. The proper end of the artist is to do good work according to the standards of his art. Moral instruction is not his task [143]. The artist *qua* artist seeks neither to help nor hinder the moralist and statesman. As an artist his virtue is that of making *things* as they should be made, and not of making *men* as they should be, by aiding them toward their proper end. The latter task belongs to the moralist or statesman, as well as to the parent, the priest and the teacher, through their possession of prudence. The primary sources of moral training are the home, the church and the community, including the school. If, as in the Platonic view or in certain contemporary European policies, the primary responsibility rests with the State, then the State either explicitly or surreptitiously absorbs the home, the church and the school. They cease to be independent agencies. The State is the community personified as parent, priest and teacher. The other alternative is to leave the training of the young to the home, the church and

[71] Cf. the practical proposals of the encyclical, *Vigilanti Cura*, July 2, 1936.

the school as relatively independent agencies.   The American choice between these alternatives is definite, whether or not its wisdom can be demonstrated.   In either case, however, it is clear that moral instruction is not the primary function of the artist.   The fact that works of art can be used by parent, priest and teacher to serve their ends, does not make the artist a moralist or teacher any more than it makes him a parent or a priest.

This division of responsibilities indicates another course of action for the prudent man.   Granting the arts their freedom, he can safeguard human welfare by concerning himself with what is most properly subject to his power: moral training [144]. The effect of any work of art is a product of two factors: the work itself, as that which is received, and the nature of the particular men who are its recipients.   The second of these factors is directly within the province of the prudent man.   The metaphysical maxim, *that which is received is in the recipient according to the mode of the recipient,* is applicable to the reception of works of art.   Their effect is determined by the mode of the recipient, his moral and aesthetic sensibilities.   This is not to forget that those moral and aesthetic sensibilities are capable of being formed by works of art, as well as by other sources of training.   The prudent man, seeking to cultivate moral character, is justified in using works of art in the process, or in excluding them if they threaten to interfere with his work.   We must not overlook, as Maritain points out, "the necessity for prohibitive measures.   Human frailty makes them indispensable: it must be protected.   It is none the less clear that prohibitive measures, however necessary they may be, remain by nature less effective and less important than a robust intellectual and religious training, enabling mind and heart to resist *vitally* any morbid principle." [72]

The compromise between art and prudence is accomplished by recognizing their limitations, unless they are aided by superior wisdom.   Eric Gill has said: "Look after goodness and truth, and beauty will take care of herself." [73]   The formula is

[72] Maritain, p. 224, by permission of Messrs. Sheed and Ward, Publishers. See Note 145 *infra.*
[73] *Beauty Looks After Herself,* New York, 1933 : p. 245.   See the remainder of this essay, pp. 208–245, and the essay entitled *Art and Prudence* in the same volume, pp. 11–29.

true, and also convertible: look after truth and beauty, and goodness will take care of herself. It is the human task to look after all three, but by means of different powers or virtues. Only confusion and misfortune can result from the transgression of a natural division of labor in the realization of these basic values. If the artist and the prudent man are not one — if the conflicting virtues are not perfectly reconciled by a unity of intellect and will — then each must do what is within his limited power as well as possible. On the one hand, the prudent man can best meet the opposition of the arts to his work by reinforcing his own efforts in the moral sphere. On the other, the artist can best meet the opposition of the moralist and the statesman to his work by producing what is good as art. This is by no means a solution of the conflict. But to ask for a real solution is to ask for too much. We must be satisfied with what we can achieve according to the circumstances of our time and the universal limitations of human nature. Even though a work of art which is technically good may be objectionable on moral grounds; even though it does not follow that the better a work of art is aesthetically, the more entertainment, contemplative pleasure, recreation, excitement and purgation, it will give to an audience, because this will depend so much on the character of the audience; nevertheless, if the artist asks for freedom to work, he has an obligation to do good work. He has in conscience no other reason honestly to ask for freedom. In turn, the prudent man has the obligation to look after truth and goodness, so that the artist can be free to look after beauty. He should attend to his own business first, which is to strengthen all the forces whose proper office it is to make men good. Art is not among them. The conflict of art and prudence may be inevitable in any case, but it is embittered by frustrations if it occurs before each side has striven well in its own sphere of operation.

5. One point remains. In the contemporary criticism of motion pictures, aesthetic and moral standards are frequently confused.[74] The moralist can judge a work of art in two ways: either as it reflects the moral character as well as the mentality of its maker, or as it is an influence upon the conduct and character

[74] See Notes 142, 143 *infra.*

of other men.   It is difficult to separate the first of these from
the aesthetic judgment, because the work is never merely a
technical accomplishment.   Both moral and technical criteria
inevitably enter into the intrinsic criticism of works of fine art.
They are only analytically separable, as the soul of the artist and
his art are analytically separable as principal and instrumental
causes of the work done.   The analytical separation is, nevertheless, important for the sake of clarity.   If we use the word
"aesthetic" to name the kind of criticism, combining both moral
and technical criteria, which is *intrinsic* because it regards the
work in relation to the artist, we should then use the word
"political" to name the kind of criticism, combining moral and
political criteria, which is *extrinsic* because it regards the work in
relation to its audience.   In the light of these distinctions we
can correct two confusions prevalent today, though as ancient
as Plato [146].

(1)   In the field of aesthetic criticism itself, the technical excellence and the moral quality of a work vary independently.
It is, therefore, incumbent on the moralist who indulges in
aesthetic criticism to be cognizant of technical criteria, as the
technician is also obliged to recognize that the values of workmanship are insufficient to judge a work of fine art.

(2)   The aesthetic and political values of a work also vary
independently.   Intrinsic and extrinsic criticism are not only
analytically separable; they are actually separate because they
regard the work in different relations.   A work which is good
by intrinsic standards may be judged bad extrinsically, and conversely.[75]   The moral judgment in intrinsic criticism must not
be converted into a moral judgment in extrinsic criticism.   This
illicit transposition is frequently made because moral criteria
enter into both aesthetic and political criticism.   Political prudence should be actuated only by political criticism.   As a result
of such confusions in criticism, the prudent man is often led to
violate the principles which should guide him in the consideration of art.

These distinctions in the types of criticism, and the separation

[75] That a work of art is good as such, that it has been well made by the
artist, does not mean that it will be more good than evil in its effects upon
the men who receive it; similarly, that a work of art is badly made does not
mean that it will do more evil than good.

of the various sets of criteria in terms of which works of fine art can be judged, follow from the analysis of the separate spheres of art and prudence, their independence of each other and their different relations to the moral virtues. It is not necessary, therefore, to explicate the general thesis any further. But it is necessary to apply it to the motion picture as a fine art, because of contemporary confusions in that field. If the principles of aesthetic criticism applicable to motion pictures were explicitly recognized, if in aesthetic criticism itself moral and technical criteria were separated, the prudent man would be aided in confining himself to purely political judgments as the basis for his actions. In addition, if a better understanding of the motion picture as art can be achieved, and canons of cinematic criticism can be established, these may lead not only to technical improvements in production but also to the cultivation of higher standards of popular taste.

This brings us to the last stage of our analysis. We have dealt sufficiently with the problem of the motion picture from the point of view of prudence, but we have only suggested the analysis that must be made from the point of view of art. The following points will therefore be considered in the last part of this book: (1) the specific character of the motion picture as a work of fine art, (2) the technique of the art and the principles of criticism founded upon this technique; (3) the aesthetic goodness of a good motion picture in relation to the aesthetic goodness of excellent productions in generically similar forms of art; (4) the relation of grades of technical accomplishment in motion pictures to grades of aesthetic sensibility in their tremendous and heterogeneous audience. These points will enable us to interpret to the maker of motion pictures what it means to say to him that as an artist he owes us the obligation to work well.

PART IV

Cinematics

CHAPTER THIRTEEN

Form and Matter

IN this chapter we pass from the extrinsic or political criticism of motion pictures to an intrinsic or aesthetic consideration of them. From the political point of view, we are concerned with the motion picture show as a whole, the entire programme of entertainment offered at motion-picture theatres. This whole show is hardly a single aesthetic object, even when it is discussed in terms of the standards of a balanced programme. Those standards are the standards of good entertainment and not good work in art. The aesthetic object is primarily what is called the feature picture; but the animated cartoon and some of the short films can be similarly considered as products of the art of making motion pictures. I am excluding the other elements of the programme, the news reel, the topical film — dealing with sports, animal life, nature study, distinguished by its aim to be informationally instructive — photographed vaudeville, and travel pictures. All of this group of excluded materials, except the vaudeville shorts, have the common trait of being more or less explicitly informational and educative. They are lessons in current history or geography or other aspects of the world of nature and human activity.[1] On the other hand, the materials

[1] For a discussion of such material, see P. Rotha, *Documentary Film*, London, 1936, and R. Spottiswoode, *The Grammar of the Film*, London, 1935 : Ch. VIII. These writers overemphasize the importance of the documentary. Compare the much sounder position of Professor A. Nicoll, *Film and Theatre*, New York, 1936 : pp. 44–61.

which have been selected for consideration have this in common, that they tell a story. This criterion of selection and rejection anticipates the most important point in the analysis that is to follow, but it cannot be helped. I hope that the analysis will make this criterion intelligible by defining the specific character of the motion picture as a work of fine art. For the present, the isolation of what is to be considered must be tentatively accepted.

The order of discussion is determined by the priority of the question about the specific nature of motion pictures. This consists in asking about the *sameness* and *difference* of motion pictures with respect to all other works of fine art. By finding the essential similarities and distinctions we shall be able to state the genus and difference of the motion picture or, in other words, to define it as a species of fine art. We shall be able to say what it is, to formulate its essence or nature.[1a] Once we have this definition, all other technical considerations will simply follow. Because of the relation between the thing to be made as *end* and technique as a mastery of the *means*, the analysis of the work of art must precede the discussion of the art itself, the technique. In the same way, discussion of technique must precede a formulation of the standards of taste, the criteria of aesthetic goodness and badness. Technique is formulated in terms of the rules of an art, although it always exists in the habits of the artist. From these rules are derived the principles of aesthetic criticism which enable a person to analyze his immediate judgment of taste, of liking or disliking. I do not mean to say that the judgment of taste can be demonstrated as a conclusion from such principles as premises. The judgment of taste is at once casuistical and immediate. As immediate, it precedes any analysis; it is an expression of aesthetic sensibility and not of thought. But taste has reasons, and the technical analysis of an art is able to provide taste with rational illumination. The difference between good and bad taste lies in this: the former is disciplined by analysis. Having reasons as a matter of habit, it is no less spontaneous than bad taste which lacks such cultivation. But the judgment of taste is also casuistical, which means that even in the light of the same

[1a] These words — "genus", "species", "essence", "definition" — are here being used analogically in the process of classifying the different kinds of fine art. See Chapter 2, fn. 3a *supra*.

analysis men may reasonably differ in liking or disliking the same work of art. In passing from the discussion of technique to the problems of taste, we shall first compare the goodness of a good motion picture with the goodness of other kinds of art, of the same sort generically. Then we can ask about the relation between the grades of technical accomplishment in the art of the motion pictures and the grades of aesthetic sensibility in their audience. The crucial problem of taste is always one of the relativity of aesthetic excellence to aesthetic cultivation.

I happily acknowledge that, in this analysis of motion pictures, I am doing no more than following the *Poetics* of Aristotle. Unlike those who dismiss it as a *description* of Greek literature, I find in it principles of sufficient generality to apply to all poetry and, in fact, to all works of fine art [147]. I can find such principles nowhere else. Nor am I deterred by those who will reject at once what is to follow because it rests on the authority of Aristotle. The authority of Aristotle is no greater than the soundness of his analysis. To depend upon him as I propose to is not a slavish following but, as the present instance must show, an interpretation of his insights for the sake of applying them to a form of art about which he knew nothing whatsoever. What one finds in the text of the *Poetics*, as in any other, depends upon how one reads it. Read philosophically, it contains a body of principles which can be consistently stated and completely generalized. Scholars may not be able to find all this explicitly in the text, but the text nevertheless warrants such interpretation. Whether the interpretation is faithful to Aristotle's actual thought and intentions is a question for the scholars; whether an interpretation which the text permits and suggests is sound and illuminating is the only question a philosopher considers. There may be other interpretations, also sound and illuminating. The best interpretation, from the philosophical point of view, is that which is soundest and most illuminating, not that which is most accurate as an archaeological reconstruction of Aristotle's thought.

The basic principle in the analysis of any work of art is that it is an imitation of nature.[2] We have already sufficiently ex-

---

[2] In this and the following chapters, the word "art" is used with the restricted meaning of "fine art." Vd. Chapter 12 *supra*.

amined the nature of imitation.[3]   To say that the motion picture
is a work of art is to say no more than that it is something made
by man and hence an imitation [148].   Our problem now is to
say what kind of work of art it is.   To do this we must employ
three subordinate principles: works of art can be differentiated
with respect to (1) their object of imitation, (2) their medium
of imitation, and (3) their manner of imitation.   The relation
of these three is complex.   For the present it need only be said
that the medium is that which is employed to imitate what is to
be imitated — the object — and the medium can be employed in
different manners.   In one sense, the object determines the form
of the work and the medium its matter; in another sense, the
object determines the matter and the medium and manner determine the form of the imitation.   Failure to recognize the
various meanings of form and matter has resulted in much confusion in the use of these terms by aestheticians.   Thus, the story
which a novel tells is sometimes viewed as its matter, its subject-
matter, and the way in which the novelist uses words to tell the
story becomes the subject of our consideration of its form; on
the other hand, the words and their arrangement are the matter,
in the sense of the materials, which the novelist uses to produce
a work which is called a novel because it has a certain form, the
form of a story.   Form and matter are systematically ambiguous.
This ambiguity cannot be avoided, but confusion can and should
be avoided by an explicit recognition of the various and related
senses of these words.   These various distinctions of form and
matter indicate that there is no one right order in which to consider the object, the medium and the manner of imitation [148a].
Proceeding analytically from the general to the specific, we must
ask first about the object imitated and then about the medium
and manner of the imitation.   In this way we can determine the
more inclusive kind before we attempt to introduce subordinate
distinctions.

The first question is whether all the fine arts have the same
object of imitation.   Aristotle's statement that "the object of
imitation is the action of men"[4] has been interpreted as applying
to all of the fine arts.[5]   But the only indications that it was

[3] Vd. Chapter 2 *supra* and Notes 13, 15, 19 and 148 *infra*.
[4] *Poetics*, 2, 1448a1.
[5] Vd. S. H. Butcher, *Aristotle's Theory of Poetry and Fine Art*, London, 1932 :

Aristotle's intention to include the plastic arts along with music, poetry and dancing are insufficient, in view of obvious analytical difficulties [149]. The distinction between works of art in motion and those at rest requires us to say that only the former imitate human action. An action is a change. It must be measured by time and have a beginning, a middle and an end. In a strict sense, therefore, it is impossible for works of art which do not involve motion to imitate action. This does not mean that painting and sculpture, in which human figures occur, are not suggestive of the whole action, some stage of which is represented. It is precisely this suggestiveness which accounts for the narrative quality that is often attributed to plastic works. But when Aristotle refers to human action as an object of imitation, he means a *whole* action. Imitation, furthermore, must not be confused with "suggestiveness"; the latter is a purely psychological phenomenon whereas imitation requires formal marks of similitude between the object and its imitation. It is impossible, therefore, for works of art at rest — the class of works conventionally called plastic — to imitate a changing object.[5a] Their object of imitation is visible figure: natural and geometrical shapes, light, shade and color, arrangements and configurations. The first division among works of fine art is thus made in terms of different objects of imitation: figure, on the one hand, and human action, on the other.

The next question is whether human action is *univocally* the object of imitation for all the non-plastic arts, whether they are distinguished *inter se* only by reference to the medium in which they imitate. The Aristotelian answer would at first seem to be in the affirmative. But a closer reading, here as before, leads to the contrary conclusion [150]. The clue is in the statement that "even dancing imitates character, emotion and action, by rhythmical movement."[6] This statement must be read consistently with the proposition that action is the object of imitation of all the arts in motion and with the analytical point, subsequently made in the *Poetics*, that character and emotion are

pp. 123–137; R. P. McKeon, *Literary Criticism and the Concept of Imitation in Antiquity*, in Modern Philology, August, 1936. Cf. M. Carroll, *Aristotle's Aesthetics of Painting and Sculpture*, St. Louis, 1905.

[5a] As the first division of natural things is in terms of rest and motion, so the first division in the arts which imitate natural objects must be made accordingly. [6] *Poetics*, 1, 1447^{a}27.

among the elements of poetry as an imitation of action. What is the relation of character and emotion, as objects of imitation along with action, to character and emotion, as elements of a narrative along with plot, diction, spectacle, etc? To answer this question it is necessary to define the concept of human action. This will enable us to make an important subordinate distinction among the arts which are said to share this common object of imitation.

A human action is a moral event. It may or may not involve bodily movements which are sensibly apparent. Bodily movements *as such* are not human actions. Considered merely as a series of bodily movements, human behavior is not essentially different from that of animals [151]. The essential quality of human behavior is that it is voluntary, that it is an act of the will or an act commanded by the will. It is for this reason that human behavior is properly called moral behavior: it involves reason and the passions, whether the latter be well ruled or insubordinate. That which is essentially a human act is always either good or bad as a step toward or away from the due ends of human life. We have already fully discussed the nature of human behavior.[7] There is no need for further exposition here, except to make the point that what Aristotle means by the wholeness of a human action, that which makes it a single, complete act, is the unity of the moral change involved. It is a unit of the moral life in the sense that the terms of the change are contrary moral qualities. In the performance of every voluntary act, a man necessarily becomes better or worse, though often the alteration of character is negligibly slight. It is obvious that the type of human action which the arts imitate must be clear and perspicuous: significant moral change.

We have seen that human action can be regarded either as intrinsic operation, a change abiding in the agent, or as the cause of extrinsic operations effecting changes in external things, especially other persons. This distinction is related to two other distinctions: (1) the distinction between the good of the individual and the good of the community, and (2) the distinction between justice and all the other moral virtues. Justice always involves the relation of men in a society. When the acts of any of the moral virtues, other than justice, are regarded in their

[7] Vd. Chapters 8, 9, 12 *supra*,

social consequences they are parts of justice generally considered. On the other hand, acts of particular justice, such as fairness in the exchange of external goods, can be regarded, not only in their social consequences, but also with respect to the moral character of the agent. The words "ethical" and "political" can be used here to distinguish two different considerations of human action, its ends and virtues. The ethical consideration regards all acts and virtues in relation to the separate common good of each man, his individual welfare or happiness. The political consideration regards all acts and virtues in relation to the collective common good, the good of a multitude of men associated in a community. When it is said that human action is an object of imitation, that object must be distinguished according as it is regarded from the ethical or the political point of view. If what is imitated is a moral change occurring in a single individual, considered quite apart, the object of imitation is human action in its ethical dimension. If what is imitated is a moral change occurring in one individual as related to changes in one or more other individuals, the several individuals being reciprocally related as agents and patients, the object of imitation is human action in its political dimension. Unfortunately there is no simple way of naming these two different objects of imitation. We shall have to say, therefore, that works of art in motion can be divided according as they imitate human action as an ethical object or human action as a political object. In the former group are music, lyric poetry and the dance; in the latter, narrative poetry and the motion picture.

When Aristotle mentions character, emotion, and action, he is not naming three different objects of imitation. He is naming the same object under different aspects. The unit of the moral life involves all three. (1) Character is constituted by the virtues, and among these primarily the moral virtues and prudence. Every moral change can, therefore, be regarded as a change in character. (2) Emotions, or better, the appetite and passions, are the matter of the moral virtues. The moral virtues are appetite rectified and the passions regulated in conformity to reason. The conflict of the passions with reason is the source of moral problems. Emotional changes, i.e., changes in the relation of the passions to reason, are involved in every change of character. (3) Action, when divided against character and emo-

tion, is the operation of the will, either the interior act of the will
or the exterior acts commanded by the will, having social consequences.   Since moral behavior is voluntary, every moral change
involves action in either or both of these senses.   Moral
change as an object of imitation can, therefore, be described as
a change of character, as a change in emotions, or as an action.
In the fullest sense, it is all three, although the emphasis may be
placed differently in different circumstances.   When moral
change is regarded in the ethical dimension, the emphasis is upon
change in character and emotion.   When moral change is regarded in the political dimension, the emphasis is upon action.
This explains why Aristotle, in considering the object of imitation for music and the dance mentions all three, whereas he only
names action in defining the object of imitation for narrative
poetry.   Changes in character and emotion are involved, of
course, but in the analysis of the elements of narrative poetry
the primary emphasis is upon plot as an imitation of action because in the political dimension men are related as agents and
patients — protagonists and antagonists — only through their external acts.

This account of the object of imitation of the non-plastic arts
must be supplemented by an analysis of the way in which any
work of art imitates its object.   The matter of art, i.e., the
medium in which the artist operates, is always sensuous, either
directly as in the case of tones and colors, or indirectly as in the
use of such symbols as words or notes to evoke sensory images.
We shall ignore, for the moment, the complicating fact that
notations are primarily sensuous as well as evocative of images in
their function as symbols.   The similitude which is involved in
imitation must always include a sensible similitude, although it
need not be only that.   Yet it is the first or basic similitude, the
one which carries all the others as its implications.   Moral change
is sensible only through bodily movements of one sort or another, including, of course, the movement of the passions subjectively experienced, the movements of speech, changes in
voice, in facial expression, posture, etc.   To imitate moral change
a work of art must, therefore, have a primary sensible similitude
to those movements of the human body through which human
behavior is expressed.   It is not necessary for the movements to

be externally or objectively sensible. A work of art may imitate emotional change through similitude to the private or subjective experience of such bodily changes in ourselves.

Let us consider, first, the arts which imitate human action in its ethical dimension. They are distinguished *inter se* according to their different media: (1) music, the medium of which is tone, (2) the dance, the medium of which is bodily movement, (3) lyric poetry, the medium of which is language. The nature of its medium indicates that the primary similitude of music is to natural sounds and principally, if not exclusively, the human voice. Only in the human voice can be found the similitude of *all* the formally distinguished elements of music: an ordered series of tones of varying durations and intensities. This sensible similitude is primary. It is through this primary similitude that music imitates emotional change and alteration of character. The variations of the human voice are expressive of emotional change. Furthermore, the temporal order of tones of varying quality and intensity resembles the course of emotional flux as it is subjectively experienced. In the case of the dance, there is an even greater primary similitude between the medium in which it is created and its object of imitation, moral change as expressed in external bodily movements, including facial expressions and gestures, but excluding the movements of the voice in speech or otherwise. Imitation requires difference as well as similarity. Dance movements are different from natural movements of the human body through being conventionalized and through being ordered formally. The dance does not imitate natural bodily movements for their own sake, any more than music imitates the human voice for its own sake. Rather it is through this primary sensible similitude that the dance is able to imitate moral change. In the case of lyric poetry, a twofold analysis must be made because of the sensuous and symbolic character of words. As sensuous, the language of lyric poetry imitates emotional change in the same way that music does. As symbolic, the language evokes an imaginative experience in which there are formal elements of correspondence to the subjective phases of the moral life. That music, the dance and lyric poetry have the same ultimate object of imitation, though they differ in media and therefore in the objects to which they bear a sensible similitude, can be further seen in certain perfect integrations of these arts : the dance with music, music with the words of a lyric.[8]

It may be said that the ballet, in contrast to the dancing of a single person, imitates human action in its political dimension, that it shares this object of imitation with narrative poetry and the cinema, and is particularly close to the drama [152]. The point raised cannot be discussed without distinguishing between the classical ballet and the ballet with a literary programme. The latter, it is true, *seems* to tell a story in the same sense that a play does, but the question remains whether in doing so the medium of the dance has not been misused in subordination to a programme which is conceived narratively. The dancers are employed as if they were actors. This is indicated by the fact that the dance movements in the programmatic ballet are much less formal or conventionalized, and partake much more of the expressive gestures and facial grimaces which constitute the bodily movements of pantomime. The pantomime is, in a sense, a drama without words. Viewing bodily movement as medium of artistic construction, it will be seen at once that there is the greatest difference between the classical ballet and the natural movements of men in action, and the least difference in the case of the movements of actors in a dramatic spectacle. The programmatic ballet and the pantomime are intermediate between these extremes in the degree of sensible similitude to the natural object. Formal difference is maximized by the degree to which the elements of the medium are conventionalized.[9] The marionette show should also be considered here. Its object of imitation is clearly the same as that of the drama : it differs from the drama in the medium which the latter employs, not as literature, but as spectacle. The use of mechanical puppets to obtain a sensible similitude with the bodily movements of human action increases the difference between the work of art and its natural object. This consideration of the ballet, the pantomime and the puppet show is important for our later analysis of the difference between the dramatic spectacle and the cinema. But first it is

[8] A choreography may either be devised for a piece of music or music be written for a dance score ; similarly in the case of words and music.
[9] The ballet is more *different* from its object of imitation than the pantomime. It is pantomime plus conventionalized dance movements.

necessary to discuss the group of arts which have human action in the political dimension as their common object of imitation.

It is difficult to find a single name to apply to this group. The word "literature" is both too broad and too narrow. On the one hand, literature includes whatever is made by man in the medium of words: it includes history, science and philosophy, which are clearly products of liberal and not fine art; it includes that bastard creature, the essay, which is sometimes written narratively as in the case of fables, but is usually an abbreviated and poorly conceived piece of speculative writing, popularized science or philosophy; it includes, as we have seen, the lyric poem, and the didactic poem which is usually nothing but an essay written in verse, although longer and better conceived speculative compositions were, in ancient times, written in verse [153]. On the other hand, literature excludes all imitations not exclusively in the medium of words, such as the pantomime and cinema. There are fewer difficulties with the word "narrative." It is only too broad: it includes history and biography as well as fiction and, as we have seen, includes such moralizing narratives as the fable and the parable; it also includes music, lyric poetry and the dance in the sense that these imitate change and hence can be considered as narrating in the generic meaning of "narrative" as the report of a change. The word "poetry," which in the classical tradition meant a fictitious narrative written in words but not necessarily in verse, imitating human action as a political object, is too narrow, in the same sense in which "literature" is, by excluding all imitations of that object, which are not in the medium of language.

There is no solution of these difficulties, except a restriction in the meaning of common words for the sake of carrying out an analysis. I shall use the words "fiction" and "story" to name this group of arts. These words are neutral with respect to medium. Cinema is fiction as well as a novel; a pantomime tells a story as well as a drama. I shall also use the words "narrative" and "poetry" with restricted meanings: "narrative" will be used to name only fictitious narratives which are works of fine art; "poetry," unless qualified by "lyric," will be used to name fictitious narratives in the medium of language, what the ancients regarded as epic and dramatic poetry and what we call novels and plays.

The obligation to use words univocally for analytical purposes imposes one further limitation : since "human action" is not used univocally when it names the object imitated by music, the dance and the lyric, on the one hand, and the arts of fiction, on the other, the word "story" cannot be used univocally to say that music tells a story and that a novel tells a story. If the word is used strictly to name the imitation of human action considered politically, music cannot tell a story. The same can be said for the classical ballet and lyric poetry. The supposition that music and the dance do tell stories is due to the imposition of what is foreign to their nature : a literary programme, which is genuinely a piece of fiction written in words. Destroy the programme, and the music — remaining the same as a composition of tones — becomes no more than a basis for anybody's *guess* about what story is being told, what particular instance of political action is being narrated [154]. There is a worse confusion in the field of the plastic arts. The attachment of narrative titles to paintings and sculpture is, in a highly condensed form, like the attachment of a programme to music. Most people look at pictures in which human figures occur, unless they are obviously portraits, as condensed stories. They do not recognize that it is not the picture which tells them a story, but themselves who tell the story for the picture. They invent a programme for it, which fits it even less than the programme fits music, because whereas the latter has an object of imitation that is generically the same as that of the arts of fiction, differing in aspect, works of plastic art, being at rest, cannot imitate human action or change in any sense and therefore cannot be narratives or tell stories in any sense.

The principle of this analysis has been that the *same* object of imitation determines a genus in the classification of the arts, and that the species of each genus are differentiated, first, by subordinate differences in object ; second, by differences in medium ; and third, by differences in manner of imitation. Applying this principle we have so far established three groups of arts : (1) plastic works, (2) music, the dance and the lyric, (3) the arts of fiction or story-telling. Before we proceed to distinguish the species of fiction, let us define their common object of imitation. In doing so we shall, of course, use the phrase "human action" to mean human *political* behavior : moral change in individuals related as agents and patients in a community of men. Fiction imitates a single complete action. Since the effectiveness of imitation depends in part upon its magnitude, the action imitated must be neither too large nor too small.[10] The single action is not an atomic unit, but a complex unity, a whole having parts. The fact that these parts are themselves actions does not destroy the unity of the whole if they are properly subordinated and proportioned. The completeness of the action depends upon its having a beginning, a middle and an end. Moral life is the continuum of which a single action is a segment. It is a cut out of the continuum, just as a line is, by the determination of three points, two of which are its limits and the third of which indicates whether it is straight or curved. The single action, furthermore, is a proper part of the whole. It has within its limited span all of the characteristics that can be found anywhere in the continuum. The single complete action which is a segment of moral life, viewed politically, has all of the elements of moral life: problem, conflict, choice, complication, climax, consequences, realization. It is clear at once that these parts of a single complete action must be disposed in time. They must be ordered according to the beginning, middle and end of the action. The plot, which is the essence of fictional imitation or, as Aristotle says, the soul of poetry,[11] must therefore have its parts in an order similar to their temporal ordering in the natural object being imitated. All of the structural elements which Aristotle found in poetry may not occur in all of the species of fiction, but at least three of them must: plot, character and thought. Of these plot is basic. The artist who is a maker of fiction is a maker of plots.[12]

We have assumed that the motion picture is a species of fiction. Before we attempt to distinguish the motion picture from poetry and pantomime, it is necessary to consider possible objections to this assumption, particularly the one arising from the association of the cinema with the plastic arts.

---

[10] *Poetics*, 7.

[11] *Poetics*, 6, 1450ᵃ39. "Tragedy is the imitation of an action, and of the agents mainly with a view to the action" (1450ᵇ3).

[12] *Poetics*, 9, 1451ᵇ26–27: "The poet or 'maker' should be a maker of plots rather than of verses, since he is a poet because of what he imitates, and what he imitates are actions."

The paradox of the motion picture is seen at once in the combination of the two words. A photograph is a work of plastic art, generically the same as painting and sculpture through having the same object of imitation, but differing in medium and manner. A photograph cannot be in motion. A motion picture does not consist of photographs in motion. The pictures do not move, but the succession of still pictures creates for the eye the illusion of a moving image. The illusion of motion is the same perceptual experience of motion that the eye gets from the real world. It is an illusion only because we know the way in which this perceptual experience is caused by the projected film. The technique employed in the creation of a motion picture, therefore, is not photography but cinematography. The latter is a more complicated technique; it includes all of the elements of the former. Again, it is not the motion of the successive photographs in projection which is the motion of a motion picture; rather it is the motion of things cinematographically recorded, or the motion of the camera recording them, or both. The motion is an illusion of the motion in things or in the spectator which the projection of a film creates for the eye. The problem of the specific nature of the motion picture is complicated because it has an obvious affinity with the plastic properties of a photograph, but being a changing picture the elements of which are temporally ordered, it also has affinities with music, the ballet, the puppet show, pantomime and poetry. We shall solve this problem now by showing why it is generically the same as poetry, pantomime and puppet show, differing from them in medium of imitation.

There seem to be only three possible interpretations of the nature of the motion picture. The first is that it is plastic in motion,[12a] that its object of imitation is the same as that of drawing, painting and sculpture, that it agrees with drawing and painting in being two dimensional, but differs from them in the medium of imitation, the technique of the camera being different from the technique of the pencil or the brush. One other difference remains and that is motion. The consideration of this

[12a] G. Seldes criticizes this error, but commits the equally bad one of making the analogy between the cinema and music fundamental. Vd. *The Movies and the Talkies,* Philadelphia, 1929 : pp. 16, 25–27. Cf. H. Münsterberg, *The Photoplay,* New York, 1916 : pp. 185–187.

difference leads the exponents of this interpretation to analogize the motion picture with music : as music is a temporal succession of tones and tonal groups, so the motion picture is a temporal succession of plastic patterns, groupings of visible shapes.   Thus, it is said that the motion picture is primarily a symphony in pictures, constructed out of plastic contrasts and rhythmic progressions.   If the motion picture seems to tell a story, that is only secondary and accidental, as it is in the case of the adventitious literary interpretation of paintings and sculpture.   Some writers even go as far as to say that if some miraculous power could give audiences the idea that the aim of the film was not to give them a story at all, but only a succession of pictures, the art would take a great step forward.   It would take a miraculous power, indeed, to convince anyone that the motion picture does not or cannot tell a story.   That it should not is, therefore, difficult or impossible to establish, since an art should do what it can.   The case of the color organ makes this point clear.   By means of this invention, it is possible to throw a series of changing color patterns upon a screen ; it is even possible to make the colors take the shapes of natural objects.   The technique of the color organ does not seem able to tell a story ; if its limitations are such that it cannot, then it should not try.   The productions of the color organ may be "plastic in motion" ; they are certainly not in the genus of fiction.   But the motion picture has always used words as well as pictures, as the color organ does not.   Even the silent movie employed sub-titles, both descriptive and conversational.   The words used form a part of the unity of the work, as the verbal programme of music does not, as the title of a painting does not. This indicates that the motion picture is not properly analyzed as merely plastic in motion.   It can, does and should tell a story.

The second interpretation is the other extreme.   It is that the motion picture is not only a kind of fiction, but a species of literature or poetry.   The written scenario is the primary product.   It is the story written in words, having the same object of imitation as epic and dramatic narration, the novel and the play. It differs from the novel as the play does.   The latter is written in such a manner that it can be produced upon a stage by the auxiliary techniques of the theatre and the actors.   Similarly, the scenario is written in such a manner that it can be produced upon a screen by the auxiliary techniques of the camera, the

studio and the actors.   As the first interpretation minimizes or
ignores the scenario as a story-telling device, so this second interpretation minimizes the cinematography and the art of the actor
as auxiliary to the technique of the writer.   With the invention
of sound recording, this second interpretation gained strength.
The verbal component in the motion picture increased in proportion as audible speech replaced visible sub-titles.   The exponents
of this position, among the artists as well as the critics, even went
so far as to identify the motion picture with the drama : the
screen and the stage differed only as two methods of producing
a dramatic script.   There is superficial plausibility about this
account which makes it widely acceptable.   Unfortunately it
has misled even the producers and directors of motion pictures
so that they have tried to employ their means to the accomplishment of an impossible end.   Just as the film can tell a story and
therefore should, so the film cannot project a drama upon the
screen, and therefore should not try.   The demonstration can
be simply made.   The drama as a piece of literature exists independently in writing, whether or not it is produced ; the verbal
composition is an adequate imitation of human action.   Even
those modern regisseurs who overemphasize the importance of
the auxiliary arts of the theatre must admit finally that they are
auxiliary or, in other words, that the play tells its story as read.
But there is no single piece of writing which stands to the pro
jected film as the written drama does to the produced play.   The
scenario, the most adequate shooting-script containing all the
directorial notations for the use of the camera, the construction
of the sets, the lighting, the performance of the actors, including
their dialogue, is not the finished work of art.   It is not a piece
of literature ; it would never be published and read as an adequate
rendition of a story [155].   Only the completed and projected
film is an adequate imitation of the object which is common to
the novel and the drama, the puppet show and the pantomime.

We must, therefore, take the third position, which is more
than a superficial compromise between the two extremes.   It is
that the motion picture is a species of fiction and that, in the
same genus with poetry, puppet show and pantomime, it is
distinguished from these other co-ordinate species by an essential difference in its medium of imitation.   To understand this
position fully we shall have to analyze the conditions of the

medium, the medium of cinematography, and show how it is different from the means used by the writer or puppeteer. It must be understood at once that this third position insists upon the existence of the motion picture as an independent kind of art ; it is not auxiliary to poetry as all the arts of the theatre are. The motion picture is primarily a technique of story-telling, and it is doubtful whether any defense can be made of the position that it is even secondarily the imitation of a plastic object, paradoxically in motion. In other words, the cinema is not included in the genus of fiction as pictures with a verbal programme, which is the only way in which music gains inclusion. The words and the pictures form an integral unity, whether the words be flashed upon the screen or spoken by the actors. The accompanying programme is not an integral part of the musical composition.

It may be suggested that the motion picture is like the opera, a combination of two independent works of art. But this would require the pictures to be significant independently of words, and the words to be similarly independent. This, however, is clearly not the case. Programmatic music is a mixture of arts, and opera a synthesis of separate arts, but the motion picture is a perfect fusion, an irreducible unity. Neither the verbal nor the pictorial part can be separated, as the music can be from its programme or from a libretto.

It may be objected that motion pictures are possible in the total absence of words, spoken or projected. This cannot be denied, and the best of the animated cartoons may be offered as examples. But this objection does not challenge the inclusion of the motion picture in the genus of fiction ; the animated cartoon obviously tells a story and *sometimes* does it by pictures alone. It merely insists that in these instances the art of cinematography is capable of being more closely analogized with that of pantomime than with that of the poet. It is significant that this analogy holds primarily for the animated cartoon, which does not employ human actors. But it is also significant that most puppet shows involve a ventriloquistic dialogue and that most animated cartoons, in silence or with sound, use words. The only point that can be made, therefore, is that it is not *necessary* for a narrative to use words, either as an integral part of the composition or as a programmatic accompaniment. As we shall later see, a narrative structure which does not use words is extremely limited in the scope of its imitation of human action. It must have a very simple plot and sketchily delineated characters. I shall, therefore, in proceeding with this analysis consider primarily the motion picture which uses both words and pictures, the motion picture which bears an analogy, on the one hand, to poetry and, on the other, to the puppet show and pantomime. It will be understood, I hope, that when I use the words "picture" or "pictorial," I do not mean picture in the sense of a painting, drawing or photograph. I always mean a moving picture, the moving illusion which the art of cinematography creates for the eye.

I turn now to the second step in this analysis. The genus of the motion picture being defined, we must now define the species by differentiating it from poetry and the ventriloquistic puppet show. I shall ignore the pantomime because it does not use words at all. It seems clear at once that the film, either silent or phonographic, is a different medium from that of poetry and puppets, but it is advisable to make this difference absolutely explicit in order to meet likely objections.

In the first place it is necessary to examine the nature of words as a medium of imitation. Words are to be distinguished from images. By images I do not mean visual apparitions, but any reproduction of a sensible appearance. We can imagine sounds and smells and tastes as well as sights. A word as seen or heard is not an image, but a directly sensible presentation. So is a chair a directly sensible presentation. Ordinarily we think of words as names; they signify kinds of things or designate particular things. While we do not ordinarily think of images as names, they too refer to the things of sense or the things we can understand, particular things or kinds of things. Both words and images perform a symbolic function. But there is this obvious difference between them: words have no similitude to what they signify, except the supposedly onomatopoetic sounds; whereas images are *like* the sensible appearance of the thing signified. In fact, it is the similitude of images with the things of sense which explains their power of signifying them. It is the absence of such similitude which makes the power of words mysterious and has led to their being called "symbols," although if to signify is to symbolize, images are as much symbols as words.

In ordinary usage, a symbol is a sign which is significant without similitude to that which it signifies.

The art of literature, i.e., poetry, is distinguished from all other arts by the fact that its medium of imitation is symbolic. Using words, literature creates an imaginative experience, but not merely that, since the images as well as the words signify the things of nature. Otherwise, literature could not imitate nature. It does so in two ways: by a symbolic reference and by an imaginal reference, the latter involving a primary similitude to the object imitated. But the symbolic reference is primary; a writer writes with words and not with images. Words are the matter which he manipulates, orders, changes. Words, therefore, are the medium of poetry, but the words must always be recognized as capable of having both a symbolic and an imaginative dimension. The image as such is the medium of no human art; it is not matter that an artist can directly manipulate and arrange. All the other arts employ non-symbolic matter, that is, matter which has a sensible similitude to the object imitated; thus, the tones of music and the human voice, the plastic elements of painting and the visible colored shapes of natural things.

It may be objected that the musician composes with symbols just as much as the poet. In a sense this is true, but there is also a clear difference. Musical notations are symbols whose sole function is to arouse auditory images or to direct instruments in the creation of sounds. The music does not consist of these notations but of tones, whether imagined or heard. The musical symbols have no reference whatsoever to the things of nature; they have only an imaginative reference or are directions for rendition. They are, therefore, not symbols in the same sense in which words are. Words have an imaginative reference and can be thought of as directions for rendition, but they also signify the things of nature. Furthermore, musical notations have a limited imaginative reference whereas words are unlimited in this respect: they arouse images in all sensory fields. What is here said of musical notations can be similarly said of choreographic notation or the blue-prints of architecture. These are not the media of their respective arts; they are merely short-hand devices for working in such media. Words are not short-hand but the medium itself. The plastic arts of painting and sculpture are distinguished from poetry, music, the dance and even architecture in that their medium is not only non-symbolic but that there is no short-hand, no notational system, for working in their medium. This is important for the technique of cinematography which, in part at least, works in a plastic medium [156].

The difference under consideration can be summarized as follows. The medium of every art is sensible matter, but only the medium of poetry is a sensible matter that is symbolic, that is, a matter which imitates without any primary similitude to the object imitated. But imitation depends upon similitude, and it is achieved in poetry by the way in which words arouse images and thereby create an imaginative experience that has the required similitude. All the other arts employ non-symbolic media, whether or not they are able to use notations for their elements. The other arts imitate by a similitude between their object and what they create for the senses. They do not rely upon the imagination except in so far as it is directly involved in the perceptual activity of the senses. Plastic matter is a non-symbolic medium and one for which there is no notational short-hand.

The difference, then, between the poetic and cinematic arts, as species of the same genus, is that the former works *entirely* in the symbolic medium of words, whereas the latter works *both* in the medium of words and the non-symbolic plastic medium of pictures. This is just as true of the silent movie as of the sound film. In the case of the latter, one must add still a third medium, the non-symbolic medium of sounds, musical or otherwise, which are not words. We shall postpone detailed consideration of this third medium until later; it need only be said here that it is as much an integral part of the whole as words and pictures. There are some artists who try to avoid words and create primarily in the media of pictures and sound, notably Chaplin and Disney.

The differentiation of the motion picture from the ventriloquistic puppet show can be similarly made. The latter is also a work in both verbal and plastic media, but the plastic medium of the puppet show is, like that of sculpture, three dimensional and consists of actually moving dolls, whereas that of the motion picture is both two dimensional and a cinematographic illusion of motion.

The significance of this differentiation of the motion picture from all other arts which imitate human action is more than classificatory. It grasps the essence of the art in terms of its form and matter. In one sense, it is formally fiction differing in the matter of its medium. In another sense, its matter or subject-matter is the same as that of poetry, but it differs in the formal elements of its technique.[13] In either sense, the difference is important because it defines the limitations within which motion pictures must be produced, the material limitations of their medium or the formal limitations of technique. An artist in any field should do whatever he *can* do ; he should not try to do more ; he should not be satisfied with doing less. A work of art is a masterpiece when it is produced through an acknowledgment of the limitations of its medium and by a mastery of the medium within those limitations [157]. The limitations of the motion picture are different from those of poetry, different from those of the produced play or puppet show. It is erroneous to think of the motion picture as being able to avoid the limitations of these other arts, unless one remembers at once that it does so only by having different limitations of its own. Only through an analytical understanding of these limitations can the principles of aesthetic criticism, applicable to the motion picture but not to poetry, be formulated. Otherwise we have the kind of criticism which has for the most part prevailed, a misapplication of poetic principles.

It may be objected to this analysis that the difference between the motion picture and the drama is insignificant. Both use words, but not words alone ; in addition to words, both use actors, sound effects, the plastic materials of scenery and so forth. Neither, it may be said, tells a story by words alone as the novel does. One answer to this objection has already been indicated, namely, that there are differences in dimensionality and between actuality and illusion, but it may be rejected by some as insufficient and by others as accidental. I should question such rejection as failing to recognize the essential determination of a work of art by the character of its matter. But, fortunately, there is a more striking answer to this objection, one which can-

13 Genus is to species, or difference, both as form is to matter and as matter is to form. Vd. St. Thomas Aquinas, *Summa Theologica*, I–II, Q. 18, A. 7, ad. 3.

not be brushed aside.   It is simply that the drama exists perfectly
as a work of art without the aid of production by means of actors
and spectacular effects.   In other words, the proper matter of
the drama is words alone.   It does not differ from epic poetry,
from the novel, in its medium of imitation but only in its manner.
As Aristotle said, song and spectacle are embellishments of
tragedy ; of all its parts, the spectacle is the one least connected
with the art of poetry, "for the power of tragedy, we may be
sure, is felt, even apart from representation and actors.   Besides,
the production of spectacular effects depends more on the art
of the stage machinist than on that of the poet." [14]   We can add
to this enumeration the other arts upon which the stage production depends, that of the actor, the scenist, the electrician, the
stage director and so forth.   This does not mean that the art of
the dramatic poet is unrelated to these other arts.   The manner
of writing in the medium of language, which is distinguished as
dramatic from epic, is such that the written work has the determinate potentiality for stage production.   There can be
many different stage productions of the written work, each making a somewhat different determination of this potentiality according to the insight and inventiveness of the various artists ;
just as the score of a symphony has a determinate potentiality
for orchestral rendition which different orchestras realize differently, according to their abilities to read and play the music.
To say that the written drama is an independently complete
work of art does not mean that the writer can ignore his relationship to the arts of production.   It is a poorly written drama,
if one at all, which cannot be produced because lacking in this
determinate potentiality.   The same would be said of a sym-
phonic score if the composer so disregarded the conditions of
orchestral rendition that it could never be played.   Despite the
fact that the independent completeness of the written drama is
undeniable, the European tradition has for the most part thought
of dramatic poetry in terms of the produced play.   The publication of the script is still looked upon as a by-product which is
justified only in the case of the exceptional dramatist.   In
Elizabethan times, the identification of dramatic poetry with
dramatic production was so great that the publication in book

[14] *Poetics*, 6, 1450^{b}16–20.

form of the plays of Ben Jonson as his *Works* caused derisive laughter. Despite the tradition, it nevertheless remains true that in every good produced play, the words are always primarily responsible for its goodness. Without good words the stage is lost, and with bad words even the best stage means can yield only a shabby product. The reason why the works of so few dramatists, particularly contemporary ones, are worth publishing is that they have humbled themselves to the service of the stage. The wordsman or poet should dominate the stage and not be dominated by it; he violates his art by becoming the servant of the regisseur or producer.

Whenever two or more arts combine in the production of a work, we must distinguish between them as primary and auxiliary and we must establish their positions in the order of production [158]. It is this distinction which finally clarifies the character of the motion picture. Thus, in the case of the drama, the art of the writer is primary. It must come first. There can be no production unless there is a play to be produced. Then there are all the auxiliary arts of the theatre. These may spoil or embellish the play according as they are more or less adapted to its potentialities for production. The written play, even when it has ample stage directions, which are usually at a minimum in good dramatic writing, leaves a great deal of latitude to the producer who employs all the auxiliary artists and orders their work. A musical score similarly permits the auxiliary artists who play the instruments or conduct the orchestra latitude of interpretation in rendition, but in the case of music, the composer, as primary artist, employs notations which are less equivocal directions for rendition than the words of the dramatist are for theatrical production. The relation between the composer and the instrumentalists is, however, formally the same as that between the poet and the workmen of the theatre.

The projected motion picture differs from the produced play in that its primary artist is not a writer. As we have already seen, all of the scripts involved in the making of a motion picture are incomplete taken alone or together. They could not be published and read as a play can, or even as a musical score can, for the simple reason that there is no adequate system of notations for the cinematographic materials with which a motion picture is made.[15] To the extent that there is any technical language at all, it is intelligible only to technicians and, just as most people can hear the rendered music whereas only a few can read the score, so only a few can read the various scripts of a motion picture and obtain therefrom the imaginative experience of the motion picture. The few are the directors and they can do so because they are the primary artists in the making of motion pictures. If a scenario is written by a literary artist, a person who is not also a director, a cinematographic artist, it is woefully incomplete as a set of notes for the motion picture to be made. It must be elaborated into the more adequate shooting-script or cinematographic continuity which properly orders and relates all of the formal elements of the composition, the words, the sounds, the lighting, the action of the actors, the costuming, the scenic contrivances, the manipulation of the camera, and so forth. Even then, unless this shooting-script is a perfect record of all that is to be done in the making of the film, the work of the cutting-room alters the final composition in a way not indicated in the script. In short, all the verbal records, for talking as well as silent films, are incomplete. They are not the finished work of art as the written drama or the musical score is. The motion picture comes into existence as the final product of an artist only when it is shot, cut and rolled on a film. *The camera must be used*. Even then it does not exist as a work of art for its audience. The film must be thrown upon a screen; the projector must be used.

Architecture affords the closest analogy to the organization of primary and auxiliary artists in motion-picture production. The architect is the master workman. He prescribes and orders the contributions of many subordinates, including sometimes the work of the sculptor and the painter as well as the carpenter, the electrician, the plumber, the mason, the construction engineer and the interior decorator. To do his job well he must have a sufficient grasp of all of these auxiliary techniques in order to

[15] A reading of the script of the cinematic version of *Romeo and Juliet* indicates this. Vd. *A Motion Picture Version of Romeo and Juliet*, New York, 1936 : pp. 139–230. It is not merely the inadequacy of words to convey "what the film so largely conveys in visual images." Rather the essential point is that the written work necessarily lacks the unity of the film, the integration of all its elements. This is the answer to Professor Nicoll's suggestion that cinematic scripts be published as independent works of art (*op. cit.*, p. 33).

be able to use them to his purpose as well as not to violate their peculiar limitations. Analogous to the various scripts for a motion picture, there are all the blue-prints, charts, structural specifications, floor plans and elevations. None of these, no combination of these, is the architect's final product. That is the erected building, properly placed upon its site, embellished on façade and interior, a thing to be used according to its nature, and to be seen in various perspectives under all kinds of illumination. Just as no one would confuse the work of the architect with that of his draughtsman, so no one should confuse the work of the motion-picture director with that of the writers who may be employed to make the various scripts.

A number of illuminating proportions can be formulated to add clarity to this analysis. (1) As the written play is to its production, and as the musical score is to its rendition, so the film is to its projection. (2) As the written play is to its production, and as the musical score is to its rendition, so the various verbal scripts for a motion picture are to the finished film. (3) As the architect's plans are to his building, so the various verbal scripts are to the finished film. The second of these proportions is false and misleading. This can be seen at once by comparing it to the third. But the first proportion, which is accurate, adds something in the case of the motion picture which cannot be found in architecture. There is nothing intermediary between the architect's plans and the finished building. When he has finished his work, his work is at once something to be used and seen. But when the director has finished his work in the making of a film, the technique of projection must supervene in order to give his work to its audience. The first proportion emphasizes the sameness of the film, the written drama and the musical score, but it also indicates a great difference. Only mechanical devices and conditions are imposed upon the film in projection. Projection is, therefore, almost a perfect rendition of the film-maker's work. But human artists impose their techniques upon the written drama and the musical score; their production and rendition is accordingly variable and capable of many imperfections. The first proportion indicates the element of illusion that is involved in the motion picture as received by its audience, the illusion which cannot be obtained from examining the unprojected film. The third proportion indicates that the motion picture does not exist in the medium of words alone. If it did, the second proportion would be true. The falsity of the second proportion indicates that all the elements of theatrical spectacle are *added* to the written drama, itself a complete work; whereas the cinematographic spectacle is an *integral* part of the film as a complete work. There is a partial truth, however, in the second proportion which must not be ignored. A scenario does not stand in the same relation to the film as the written play to the stage production, in the sense in which the latter can be read as an independent work of art. But as the written play possesses a determinate potentiality for *staging*, so the scenario or cinematic script possesses a determinate potentiality for *filming*. In the latter case, the potentiality is much less determinate.

These analogies and proportions make a number of instructive points about the cinema in relation to the other arts. They indicate, first, the superiority of the unprojected film as score. The mechanics of projection avoid the variability and corruptions of auxiliary artists when these are allowed to superimpose their work upon the finished product of the primary artist. The distortions and obscurities which dramatic writing suffers from over-elaborate theatrical effects, illustrate this point. The written novel, it may be thought, is also a score which like the film is free from the alterations and impositions of subordinate artists. But viewed as a score, the words of the novel are a set of directions for the productive imagination of each reader. The art of reading, in which so few readers are well cultivated, makes each of them a subordinate artist who can make something different of the novel as an imaginative experience and, for the most part, what they make is a poor rendering of the text. The projected film controls the imagination as well as the seeing and hearing of its spectator to a much greater extent. The director of motion pictures is able to obtain a reception for his work that is more faithful and responsive to his intentions than the novelist.[15a]

Comparing the various arts, we can enumerate a number of

[15a] In the novel there are many passages of words that 'want' to be made into images in order that they can have their effect. In the cinema the corresponding pictorial parts would offer the responder, not invitations to make images, but the achieved images. Thus, the cinema, to some extent, does for the responder what a novel only assists him to do.

relationships which seem to exhaust all the possibilities. (1) Either the finished work is the product of one artist or more than one. Thus, the novel and the painting are the products of a single artist. We are ignoring here, of course, the problem of the audience as a contributing artist. (2) If the work is a product of more than one artist, either there is one primary artist and all the rest are auxiliary, or the several artists are co-operators co-ordinately. It is difficult to find a clear example of the latter sort, unless it be the building of Gothic cathedrals, the accumulation of a saga or legendary epic, the production of folk-plays. Each of these is questionable as an example. It is an example only to the extent that we are ignorant of the process of creation. The opera may be suggested as a case in which there are a number of co-ordinate artists, but it may be challenged on the ground that the composer has first rank or on the ground that there is a co-ordinator who directs the co-operation of the composer, the librettist and so forth. (3) If the work is a product of a number of artists, one of whom is clearly primary, either the auxiliary artists add their work to the finished product of the master, or the primary artist is the master who directs the operations of the auxiliary artists as his aids in the production of the finished work. The former is the case of drama and music; the latter the case of architecture and motion pictures. The auxiliary artists in the former case are artists of a derived production or rendition; in the latter case, they are artists of the original creation. It makes a great difference whether the primary artist directs the work of his subordinates in the process of completing the creation, or only indirectly controls the work of the auxiliary artists who come after his creation is done. Unless the dramatist is also the producer and stage-director, he is not in a position to accept or reject the contributions of the actors, the scenery makers, the costumers, etc. But the director of motion pictures, like the architect, is *usually* able to exercise the final control over the contributions of all his co-operators. Ideally, he should *always* be. When that is not the case, it is usually because he is being interfered with by the producer who stands to him as the publisher does to an author or as the person who commissions the architect does to him.[16] For the most part such interference

16 The exploitation of directors by producers and the interference by the

is damaging, but it need not necessarily be so. One thing, finally, is clear. Unity is possible in a work of art whether it is the product of one or many artists. The notion that a motion picture cannot be a unified work of art because it is the work of many hands is absurd.[17] The work of a single man may lack unity if he be a poor workman; the work of a multitude may have a magnificent unity if, as in the case of the Gothic cathedrals, they are unified in the spirit of the creation.

This analysis further reveals the relation of the director to his subordinates. There seems to be no question among all thoughtful writers about the art of motion pictures that it is the director who is the master craftsman [159]. But the goodness of a motion picture depends upon more than his control of all the other technicians involved; it depends upon his intellectual union with the writer of the scenario. Ideally, the director should be himself the scenarist, as the architect is the maker of the plans; but practically, as the architect may use a draughtsman to make the blue-prints, so the director may use a writer to make the shooting-script as a verbal plan of the continuity. The fusion of the director and the scenarist is as desirable in the making of motion pictures as the collaboration of the author and regisseur is desirable in the production of plays. The outstanding achievements of such directors as Chaplin, Pudovkin, Pabst, Rene Clair and Murnau, to mention only a few, is to be understood in the light of this ideal identity. The work of Hollywood is frequently criticized in terms of undue prominence given the actors and actresses and the unfortunate submission of directorial technique to their whims and idiosyncrasies.[18] But the so-called star system is much less of an obstacle to the making of good motion pictures than is the failure properly to subordinate the work of the literary artist. It is an obvious mistake to suppose that because a man is a writer of good novels or plays, he is a writer for the screen. He may be good as a contributor of the verbal part, the dialogue, but if he retains the technique of literature, he is worse than a poor scenarist. He is a hindrance

latter with the director's work, for commercial reasons, is certainly no worse than the relation between authors and publishers.

[17] Cf. E. Betts, *Heraclitus, or the Future of the Films*, London, 1928: pp. 34, 94; G. Seldes, *op. cit.*, p. 90 ff.

[18] E. Dale, *How to Appreciate Motion Pictures*, New York, 1935: p. 224.

that the director must eliminate or somehow overcome. The complaints of literary artists who go to Hollywood and suffer the indignity of having their art misused, miss the point. The fault is theirs. They themselves have misused their art in failing to accommodate themselves to the conditions of cinematography which they usually do not try or, trying, fail to understand. They are seldom willing to acknowledge the director as the master whom they can serve well only by approaching his method of thinking cinematographically. They must learn to draft a scenario which, as Pudovkin says, "will provide the director not with a series of obstacles to be overcome, but with a series of impulses that can be used"; the writer who is a good scenarist must "consider, use and perhaps even discover all those specific methods that the director can later employ."[19] The trouble with most of the writers for the screen is that they hold the false view of the motion picture as a branch of literature, the film standing to the script as the theatrical production to the written play or the adapted novel. Until they are properly trained or until directors and scenarists are one, the difficulty of making good motion pictures is great [159a].

The role of the actor in the production of motion pictures is in one sense more important than in the theatre. He is an auxiliary artist in either case, but in the latter case, his work is merely an embellishment of the poet's art whereas in the former he contributes to the making of an original work rather than something derived from it. Furthermore, because of the way in which a film is made, greater perfection can be achieved in the actor's art than on the stage. The actor's performance on the stage is variable; each time it is done, it is done once for better or for worse. (One can understand Gordon Craig's desire to eliminate the actor entirely and replace him by puppets which could be manipulated in the pantomime of the stage with greater certainty and greater responsiveness to all the needs of representation. This is, in a sense, the superiority of the animated cartoon to the ordinary motion picture using human actors.) But the way in which a film is made permits a multiple repetition of the same piece of action, so that the best cinematographic rec-

[19] V. I. Pudovkin, *Film Technique*, London, 1933 : pp. 5, 24. In this book will be found the best discussion of the director's relation to the scenarist. Vd. pp. 1–47 ; 93–105.

ord of the actor's performance can be selected for its place in the film. It must be admitted that, from the actor's point of view, the conditions of acting for the screen are less gratifying than those of the stage, because they often seem to violate the canons of his art. Such complaints are like those of the writers who are unwilling to subordinate themselves through a correct understanding of their proper part. The histrionic techniques are given much greater freedom in the theatre, but a good artist is one who is willing to work within the limitations imposed upon him by the medium.[20] As in the case of the writers, the actors are technicians to be used by the director for the sake of the work being made. It is his art, not theirs, which must dominate. If it does, then the glorification of stars cannot hurt the artistry of motion pictures. Plays have always been written for famous actors; they were by Shakespeare and Molière. There is no reason why a director should not take special histrionic talent into consideration in the conception of a film. It is part of the material he must use, just as the sets and the lighting are. The only danger arises if it is not the director but some one else, the producer or the literary artist, who brings the particular actor into prominence.

I shall not consider here the other subordinate technicians in the service of the director. I have singled out the writer and the actor for discussion because of their relation to dramatic productions, in order to show the difference in their contributions to the making of motion pictures. Later in a more detailed analysis of the cinematographic technique, I shall consider the directorial use of such technicians as the camera man, the electrician, the scene constructor, etc.

The analysis so far can be summarized in the definition of the motion picture as an imitation of a complete action, having a certain magnitude, in the conjoint medium of pictures, words and sound effects, musical or otherwise. This definition holds for both silent and talking or sound films and includes, as its limiting cases, works in which one or another aspect of the medium is omitted, sometimes the words, sometimes sound or music,

---

[20] Pudovkin has recently analyzed the problems of acting in terms of film technique and the essential differences of screen and stage. The actor, like the scenarist, must understand the nature of the cinema as a work of art produced by the director. Vd. *Film Acting*, London, 1936.

but never the pictures. The chief difference between the silent
film and the talking film is not that the former lacked words,
since these were projected in the various sub-titles, but that the
former lacked sound or music as an integral part of the construction. This definition parallels Aristotle's definition of a tragedy which can be generalized as the definition of any poetic
narrative in the following manner : a poem is an imitation of an
action that is complete and of a certain magnitude, in language
embellished with each kind of artistic ornament, the several
kinds being found in its separate parts. I have omitted from
this formulation what distinguishes the dramatic from the epic
poem and what distinguishes the tragedy from the comedy.
The chief difference between the definition of a motion picture
and that of a poem is in the specification of the medium. We
must now turn to consider the three remaining points : (1) the
distinction of epic from dramatic narrative in its bearing on the
motion picture ; (2) the distinction between prose and verse ;
that is, the nature of the embellishments which are appropriate
to the various parts of cinematographic narration, not only in the
language used but by analogy the embellishments of the pictorial
parts ; (3) the distinction between tragedy and comedy.

(1) The first of these distinctions depends upon the manner
of imitation. Epic and dramatic narration, a novel and a play,
agree in the object and medium of their imitation. They differ
in their manner of working in the medium. This difference can
be simply stated : either the narration is achieved by dialogue
alone, or it is achieved by dialogue and description [160]. By
dialogue is meant the direct discourse, the speeches of the characters in conversation or soliloquy. By description is meant the
indirect discourse, that part of the narrative in which the poet
speaks in his own person of the doing and suffering of the characters, the background of their action, and so forth. Even in a
novel written in the first person, this distinction between dialogue
and description holds [161]. A play is narration by dialogue
alone ; a novel by dialogue and description. The difference in
manner is clear, but some of the consequences of the difference
may not be.

It may be objected that the difference, though clear, is not absolute. There is always some description in the writing of a
play, in the setting of time and place and in the stage directions.

This must be admitted, but the amount of description in a good play can be kept to the minimum of time and place indications, cast of characters, and indications of entrances and exits. Such description is hardly more than the frame into which the dialogue is set, which is certainly not the relation between the parts of description and dialogue in a novel.

It may further be objected that the speeches of the characters, or of the choruses in Greek tragedy, often include descriptive narrative of things and events not directly included in the action of the play. This, too, must be admitted, but it does not obscure the distinction between drama and epic. In the drama whatever description does occur must conform to the conditions of dialogue, and is therefore limited by appropriateness to the action occurring in the present. The choral interludes are not dialogue but even they must be appropriate to the adjacent action. Narrative description in a novel is not limited in this way. The relationship is reversed: in the play, description must be worked into the context of the action by means of the direct discourse of the characters, or by means of choruses commenting on the action; in a novel, the dialogue is usually worked into the context of descriptive narrative, and the comment on the action is made by the author instead of by a chorus. In short, the manner of epic narration permits the author to do himself what he must make characters or chorus do in dramatic narration.

There are a number of consequences which follow from this difference. In the first place, dramatic narration is in the present tense in the sense that the action of the characters, accompanying their speeches, is now going on. That the time of the action as otherwise indicated is in the past, or that the descriptive content of the speeches may refer to things or events in the past, does not alter this fact. Epic narration is always in the past tense, even when the time of the action is indicated to be in the present or the future. This distinction in tense must be understood in terms of the relation of the narrative to its audience. Dramatic narration presents action in the process of occurring. Epic narration always reports action as having occurred.

In the second place, it is the dramatic manner of narration by dialogue which gives the play its determinate potentiality for stage production, whereas the epic manner lacks this poten-

tiality.[20a]   The novel can be produced as a play only when it is
properly adapted for the theatre, which means that it must be
dramatized.   This means, at least, that much of the descriptive
narrative must be replaced by dialogue, but it means more than
that because the plot structure of an epic is necessarily different
from the plot structure of a drama.   In order to understand what
is involved in the dramatic adaptation of epic narratives, we must
understand this difference.   The length of a novel is to the
length of a play as the magnitude of the action which can be
imitated in epic narration is to the magnitude of the action which
can be imitated in dramatic narration.   In both cases there must
be unity of action, but as we have seen this unity is not atomic
but the unity of a complex whole having parts.   The difference
in magnitude is related to the complexity of the whole which is
a unity of the more or less numerous parts.   The difference is
not the simple-minded difference in unity of time and place
which is interpreted to mean that the action of the drama must
occur in one place geographically and at one time diurnally.
As Aristotle points out, the magnitude of action imitated dramatically is restricted for the sake of the perspicuity of the
whole; "the proper magnitude is comprised within such limits
that the sequence of events according to the law of probability
or necessity will admit of a change from bad fortune to good, or
from good fortune to bad."[21]   If too short, the drama cannot
endow the change which is central to the plot with probability;
if too long, the unity of the action will be lost because of the
incapacity of the spectator to view it as a whole.   Although epic
narrative must also conform to human capacities for beholding
a complicated action as a unified whole, it can enlarge the dimensions.   Unlike the drama, the novel can "imitate several lines of
action carried on at one and the same time."[22]   The greater
magnitude of the epic makes it possible for it to have a much
larger number of characters, both major and minor, a much
greater variety of incident and episode, and much greater freedom with respect to time and place, both in the presentation of
the simultaneous and in moving in either temporal direction.

[20a] Hardy's *The Dynasts*, Ibsen's *Peer Gynt*, and Shaw's *Back to Methuselah*,
though written dramatically, are bad as plays because defective in their potentiality for stage-production.
[21] *Poetics*, 7, 1451[a]9-15.   [22] *Poetics*, 24, 1459[b]23-27.

All of these points are related to the potentiality for stage production with which a good drama must be determinately endowed. The conditions of the theatre impose obvious limitations upon the number of characters, the number of scenes — even though all that a scene means is a change in the configuration of characters in confrontation — the amount and nature of temporal and spatial displacement, as well as upon the total time of dramatic narration. Even the kind of incident that is appropriate in dramatic narration is determined by the conditions of theatrical presentation. As Aristotle points out, the element of the wonderful or the irrational is more easily introduced into the epic; thus, the pursuit of Hector described in the *Iliad* would be ludicrous if placed upon the stage with "the Greeks standing still and not joining in the pursuit, and Achilles waving them back." [23] It is only opera which can afford to be ridiculous in this way, and the utterly undramatic character of opera is notorious for this reason.

In the third place, epic narrative is more like history than the drama is. It can encompass the movements of nations and portray the action of its characters against a background of human masses. This can be, at best, inadequately suggested in the drama. But it must be remembered that the unity of an epic is different from the unity of a history. The latter need not present a single action, but rather a single period or a single theme; its various events or episodes need not be sequentially or causally connected. A history may conform to the structure of an epic plot, but it need not. The difference and similarity between epic and historical narration is best illustrated by the *Iliad* and by *War and Peace*. In neither case is the whole war the subject of the poem, even though the war had a beginning, a middle and an end.[24] But the *Iliad* is much better as a novel because it describes a single action, projected against the background of the war, and the incidents of the war are selected or rejected for the sake of illuminating this action. *War and Peace* is more like a fragmentary history. It lacks plot and character development.

In the fourth place, the descriptive manner of epic narration permits the author greater latitude in revealing the thought, emotion and even the character of his persons, than is available to the dramatist. The latter is limited to the expressive means

23 *Poetics*, 24, 1460ª14-17.   24 *Poetics*, 23, 1459ª31-32.

of action and speech. He must work within these limitations.
The inner psychological content that cannot thus be brought to
the surface is not material for the drama. But in the novel description makes it possible for the author to expose what could
not be observed in either the speech or action of the characters.
The method of the novel is fluoroscopic and anatomical whereas
the method of the play is necessarily confined to surfaces.
Whatever position one takes about the goodness of the modern
style of psychological narrative, which is mainly concerned with
what lies below the surface, it must be admitted that the psychological novel is better than the psychological play. The limitations of the medium and manner of narration are less violated by
Dostoievski and Proust, Joyce and Virginia Woolf than by
Eugene O'Neill and Pirandello [162].

Finally, there is a basic difference in plot structure. An epic
structure is one with a multiplicity of subordinate plots properly
organized into a higher unity. Strictly, "epic imitation has less
unity ; as is shown by this, that any epic poem will furnish subjects for several tragedies." [25] The epic achieves the greatest
unity in proportion as it approaches dramatic structure. Here
again, says Aristotle, "the transcendent excellence of Homer is
manifest. He never attempts to make the whole war of Troy the
subject of his poem, though that war had a beginning and an end.
It would have been too vast a theme and not easily embraced in a
single view." [26] As a result "the *Iliad* and the *Odyssey* each furnish the subject of one tragedy or, at most, of two" ; [27] whereas
other epic narratives now lost — the *Cypria* and the *Little Iliad*
— supply the materials for many. The latter obviously are less
dramatic in structure and less unified. This indicates a distinction between types of epic narration which has recently been
made in the case of the novel : the chronicle novel and the dramatic novel.[28] In any case, the magnitude of epic narration
always exceeds that of the drama. An epic or novel cannot be
made into a play without adaptation in the direction of condensation, elimination of many subordinate lines of action, and
greater unity of plot. The dramatist "should remember what
has often been said, and not make an epic structure into a tragedy

[25] *Poetics*, 26, 1462^{b}4-6.   [26] *Poetics*, 23, 1459^{a}33-35.
[27] *Poetics*, 23, 1459^{b}2-3.
[28] E. Muir, *The Structure of the Novel*, New York, 1929.

— by an epic structure I mean one with a multiplicity of plots —
as if, for instance, you were to make a tragedy out of the entire
story of the *Iliad*. . . The poets who have dramatized the
whole story of the *Fall of Troy*, instead of selecting portions,
like Euripides; or who have taken the whole tale of *Niobe*, and
not a part of her story, like Aeschylus, either fail utterly or meet
with poor success on the stage." [29]

This is an insight too often transgressed in modern adaptations
of novels for the stage. The plot of a novel is to the plot of a
drama as many is to one. The dramatist must select one of the
many plots which the epic contains for dramatization. *Anna
Karenina* and *David Copperfield* do not make one play. They
contain many. The failure to recognize this difference in plot
structure accounts for the insignificance as well as the poetic
badness of dramatized versions of novels in modern times. In
the best Greek practice — and, as Aristotle indicates, it was not
always good — the drama which took its theme from the multiplicity of plots afforded by the epic was itself a primary work
of art. It was not merely a stage adaptation. It existed in its
own right as a piece of story-telling. But today is there any
instance of dramatic adaptation which anyone would *read* who
had read the novel? The fact that one is willing to go to the
play does not change the point, because one goes to the play not
for the work of literature but for a work of the theatre, the
spectacle and the acting. Shakespeare's plays, as were those of
most of his contemporaries, dramatized plots discovered in epic
narratives, but the play itself was the thing, poetically as well as
theatrically, because the dramatic poet had done his task of selection and reorganization well. In other respects, the plot of the
epic and the drama are the same. There are as many different
types of plot in the drama as in the epic, different according to
the ordering of the constituent parts of the action. But these
similarities must not obscure the difference between the dramatic
and the epic unity of action.

All of the differences we have discussed follow from the basic
difference between narration by dialogue alone and narration by
means of both dialogue and description. They are, as we shall
see, extremely significant for the discussion of the manner of
narration that is appropriate in the motion picture. Is the

[29] *Poetics*, 18, 1456ª10–17.

cinematic method epic or dramatic, both or neither? Novels can be dramatized because of the relation between the plot structure of the epic and the play. But can novels and plays be cinematized and, if so, what are the conditions of such adaptation if it is to be appropriate to the medium and manner of cinematographic narration? There has been much polemic recently about the relation of the play to the motion picture, but there has been no formulation of the deciding principles [163]. It is obvious that the plots of motion pictures must either be original or derived, and if derived, they must be adaptations made from plays or novels or, in some instances, short stories. Is there any difference between the motion picture which tells an original story rather than a borrowed one?

These questions will be answered presently, but here it must be pointed out that in recent years there has been a tendency to ignore or transgress the fundamental differences between epic and dramatic narration. This tendency not only accounts for many bad novels and plays, but also explains the unprincipled character of cinematic adaptations. On the one hand, at the end of the nineteenth century there arose the distinction between the old and the new drama which tried to subordinate the art of poetry to the art of stage-craft. Thus, William Archer complained of the Elizabethan drama because it did so much with words — in dialogue and without stage directions — and needed stage-craft and the supplementation of descriptive passages so little.[30] He invidiously compared Shakespeare with Ibsen and Shaw. Shakespeare did not need prefaces and did not write pages of stage directions. But a dramatist does not need prefaces and stage directions if he works properly according to the manner of dramatic narration and does not try to achieve an epic effect. The use by Eugene O'Neill of verbal asides in *Strange Interlude* is another instance of the transgression of the dramatic technique, in an attempt to get the psychological depth that is possible in a novel. And worse than all this is the way in which novels have been dramatized in an episodic fashion with a multiplicity of scenes and a tremendous diversity of places and times; the play *Dodsworth* illustrates this point. Even plays which are

[30] *The Old Drama and the New*, Boston, 1923. Cf. A. Nicoll on the way of the theatre to health and vitality by going back to its pre-19th century traditions (*op. cit.*, pp. 181–187).

not bad adaptations of novels have, because the mechanical facilities of stage-craft were available, gone in for the simultaneous presentation of scenes at different places or made rapid shifts backward and forward in time by using a partitioned stage. As Professor Münsterberg pointed out, the stage has tried to use the cinematographic manner as well as the epic manner of narration.[31] The movies have been as bad an influence upon the drama as the theatre has been upon the movies, bad because each in turn has failed to abide by the appropriate limitations of medium and manner.

On the other hand, there are twentieth century novelists who have tried to write dramatically by accomplishing the major part of their narration through dialogue. Hemingway's *Farewell to Arms* is an example.[31a] This is a less serious distortion because there is no fixed rule of proportion with respect to the amounts of dialogue and description in a novel, but it is nevertheless noteworthy that in the great novels a proper balance of the two methods is achieved and each is used for that part of the plot it is able best to serve. It is also true that a novel can be written either with no dialogue whatsoever or with dialogue at a minimum. This is significant in the light of the fact that the difference between the play and the novel is that the latter uses description as well as dialogue. If it be asked why it is necessary for dramatists to write dramatically and novelists to write epically — what is wrong about the contemporary transgressions and mixtures of the different arts of poetry — the answer is simply given in terms of a fundamental canon of art. An artist works well only if he works within the limitations of his medium and manner of imitation. He must acknowledge these limitations and master them. He must not try to avoid them by the trickery of inappropriate devices. It is not artistic wisdom to try to do through the means of one technique what is better done by means of another. "The limitations of an art are in reality its strength and to overstep its boundaries means to weaken it." [32]

One other point is involved. The different limitations of epic

<hr />

[31] *Op. cit.*, pp. 181–183.

[31a] *The 42nd Parallel* by Dos Passos is an example of a novel written cinematically.

[32] H. Münsterberg, *op. cit.*, p. 206. Goethe's maxim was : *In der Beschränkung zeigt sich erst der Meister.* Cf. G. Seldes, *op. cit.*, p. 143 ; *Poetics*, 26, 1462ᵃ13–1462ᵇ11.

and dramatic narration, the requirement that the latter be capable
of theatrical production, imposes different standards of poetic
truth upon these two kinds of poetry.   By the standard of poetic
truth I mean the law of the probable and the necessary, and not
a superficial distinction between realism and fantasy.   As we
have seen, what can be made probable in a novel cannot be made
probable on the stage and, therefore, it should not be attempted
in dramatic narration.   Hence it is necessary to define the cinematic manner in order to determine the standard of poetic truth
that is applicable to motion pictures.   The limits of what is
called "realism" and "fantasy" are different for the motion picture, the novel and the play.

(2) The two distinctions which remain to be made are subordinate to the difference between epic and dramatic poetry.   Of
these, the first is with respect to the embellishments of language.
A poem can be written either in prose or in verse and, if in verse,
in a variety of metres.   This division is independent of the previous one : we can have plays written either way and epics written either way, although it has become traditional to use the
word "epic" for the epic in verse, and the word "novel" for the
epic in prose.   There is no similar verbal distinction made in
the case of dramatic writing.   If we speak of "poetic drama"
we must at once indicate whether we mean drama-as-poetry, in
contrast to drama-as-produced, or drama in verse.   It is obvious
that the manner of imitation is unaffected by the difference in
linguistic style, a difference in the use of the medium of imitation.   The form of *War and Peace* is the same as the form of the
Iliad, just as the form of *Hamlet* is the same as the form of *The
Doll's House*, meaning by form, of course, the same type of plot
structure, the same manner of narration.

What is the significance of the difference between prose and
verse ?   The metre and melody of verse is an ornament of language.   Verse is not essential to poetry but embellishes it ; as
the theatrical spectacle is an embellishment of drama which can
be dispensed with.[33]   But there is a difference between these two
sorts of embellishment.   The one pertains to the medium of
poetry itself, language, whereas the other is completely external.
There must be some effect upon the nature of the narrative as a
whole whether it is written in prose or verse, not an effect upon

[33] *Poetics*, 1, 1447ᵃ27–1447ᵇ23 ; 6, 1450ᵇ13–15 ; 9, 1451ᵃ36–1451ᵇ2.

the development of plot but upon the way in which the verbal symbols of poetic imitation create an imaginative experience in the audience. Not only is there a difference in metre and melody, but the vocabulary and syntax of verse are different from the vocabulary and syntax of prose. There is greater concentration through ellipsis, greater ambiguity in simile and metaphor, greater elevation and intensity through the invention of phrase and idiom, all of which tends to make verse more powerful in its effect upon the emotions as well as richer in the imaginative dimension of linguistic imitation. Since poetry achieves the similitude that is essential to imitation only through the images which words arouse and since poetry, as any other art, aims to excite the passions, so to purge them [164], there is some reason for the position taken by Mr. T. S. Eliot and others that poetic drama in the sense of drama-in-verse is the ideal toward which all dramatic writing should tend.[34] The reasons will become clear to anyone who ponders why it is that lyrics are usually, if not always, written in verse rather than prose.

It may be asked, then, why no similar position has been taken with respect to epic writing. The novel as a prose epic is seldom compared invidiously with the *Iliad* or the *Aeneid* or, at least, it is not proposed that writers should cherish the ideal of a novel in verse. The question is perplexing. The text of the *Poetics* is certainly not clear on this point, in distinguishing between the song as an embellishment of tragedy in its choral parts and the versification of the whole.[35] Cervantes insisted that "an epic may be as well written in prose as in verse" and such lyric poets as Shelley and Wordsworth tried to minimize the distinction for lyric as well as for narrative poetry. One solution suggests itself. Perhaps the distinction in essence merely points to the difference between good and bad writing rather than to any fixed criteria of prosody. Good writing is poetic writing, bad writing is prosaic, regardless of metrical structure and rhyme. Bad verse is prosaic writing according to the rules of prosody just as good prose is poetic writing which ignores these rules. The solution has some insight, but it is unsatisfactory on two points: first, the difference in the music of verse and prose even

[34] T. S. Eliot, *A Dialogue on Dramatic Poetry* in *Collected Essays*, New York, 1932 : pp. 34, 38, 39, 43.
[35] *Poetics*, 6, 1449^{b}23–36. Cf. Butcher, *op. cit.*, pp. 141–147.

when both are good writing; and second, the difference in the imaginative dimension of verse and prose even when both are good writing, a difference that is somehow related to vocabulary and syntax, not to metre and rhyme.

(3) The one remaining distinction is that between tragedy and comedy. This distinction is based neither upon manner nor on medium, but upon a subordinate difference in the object of imitation. Aristotle seems to make it turn upon the character of the hero, whether he is better or worse than men are in life.[36] But this violates his own principle that poetry is "an imitation, not of men, but of an action and of life, and life consists in action, and its end is a mode of action, not a quality. Now character determines men's qualities, but it is by their actions that they are happy or reverse. Dramatic action, therefore, is not with a view to the representation of character; character comes in as subsidiary to the action."[37] The difference between tragedy and comedy must, therefore, lie in the kind of action that is being imitated, and kinds of actions are distinguished according to their termination in a mode of activity, happiness or the reverse. It is for this reason that a tragedy should not have a happy ending. Once the distinction between the tragic and the comic action is seen, the distinction between the tragic and the comic hero follows. Aristotle makes this point when he defines a tragedy as an imitation of a *serious* action.[38] The grandness, the elevation, the seriousness of the action imitated by a tragedy requires the tragic hero to be a man of elevated and noble character. But though these criteria are enough to help us discriminate comedies from tragedies, they do not explain the distinction. What makes the action being imitated "grand" or "serious"? What is the relation between these qualities and the ultimate happiness or unhappiness to which the action leads? From an analytical point of view, the *Poetics* is here least satis-

---

[36] *Poetics*, 2, 1448^{a}1–4 ; 5, 1449^{a}32–35.

[37] *Poetics*, 6, 1450^{a}16–25. He even goes so far as to say : "Without action there cannot be a tragedy ; there may be without character." Cf. 6, 1449^{b}36–39 : "An action implies personal agents, who necessarily possess certain distinctive qualities both of character and thought"; and 2, 1448^{a}1–2 : "Since the objects of imitation are men in action, and these men must be either of a higher or lower type. . ." It follows, as McKeon says, that "with the differences of agents, the actions themselves are differentiated" (*loc. cit.* fn. 5 *supra.*). Cf. Butcher, *op. cit.*, 234–236. [38] *Poetics*, 6, 1449^{b}24.

factory. We are left wondering whether we have caught the essence of tragedy and comedy, whether the distinction is an essential or accidental one.[39] I am unable to resolve these perplexities; nor am I satisfied with any resolution which has been offered. But one suggestive point can be made. The distinction between tragedy and comedy is related to the emotions which poetry can arouse and the way it effects a catharsis of them. Tragedy causes pity *and* fear and through exciting these emotions purges them. The excitement and purgation of these emotions is made part of the definition of tragedy and would therefore seem to be of its essence. Though the effect of a poem upon its audience is something extrinsic to the structure of the work the effect indicates a power or property involved in the nature of the work itself.[40] We might, therefore, define comedy in terms of its effect: it does not arouse any specific emotion, but purges the latent passions, not only pity and fear but any other emotion, notably love, through laughter. These definitions stated, one must ask whether there are any pure comedies or pure tragedies; or whether all narratives can be arranged in a series, between these ideal terms as limits, the gradations of tragedy and comedy being alloyed with the elements of undifferentiated excitement proper to melodrama.[41]

The distinction of tragedy and comedy is independent of the other two. Thus we can have a tragic epic as well as a tragic drama, a comic epic as well as a comic drama, and any of these may be written either in prose or verse. But the three distinctions we have just examined are systematically related: the distinction between tragedy and comedy is based on a difference in the *object* of imitation, although it seems to be detected in terms of the effect of the imitation upon the emotions and their purgation; the distinction between prose and verse is based on a difference in the use of the *medium* of imitation, the linguistic style; and the distinction between epic and drama is based on a difference in the *manner* of imitation. We have so far been concerned with these distinctions within the genus, fiction, and in one species,

[39] Vd. Scott Buchanan, *Poetry and Mathematics*, New York, 1929: p. 175 ff.
[40] Vd. Note 17 *infra*.
[41] Vd. T. S. Eliot, *Wilkie Collins and Dickens* in *Collected Essays*: "You cannot define Drama and Melodrama so that they shall be reciprocally exclusive; great drama has something melodramatic in it, and the best melodrama partakes of the greatness of drama" (p. 382).

poetry. They apply in other spheres. Thus, there are many works to illustrate that history and philosophy may be written either in prose or verse [165]. Historical narrative may approximate the poetic form of the epic or the drama, as for instance in the case of Herodotus and Thucydides. It is difficult to think of an illustration of comic history; but both Herodotus and Thucydides, as well as Gibbon and Spengler, write in the tragic pattern. We are here concerned, however, with a more obvious application of these distinctions. Since the motion picture is a species of fiction or story-telling, differing from poetry in its medium, these subordinate distinctions within the realm of poetry should apply to and illuminate the nature of the motion picture.

First, tragedy and comedy. This raises no problem. To whatever extent the distinction is clearly understood in the case of poetry, it holds for the motion picture. That most motion pictures are clearly neither one nor the other, and have a large melodramatic component, is not surprising, since the same thing is true of most plays and most novels. There is nothing in the nature of motion pictures to prevent them from achieving the tragic or the comic mode as fully as literature. If it be suggested, on the one hand, that because the motion picture uses language only in part it is less able than poetry to satisfy the conditions of tragic imitation, it must be offered, on the other hand, that the cinematographic medium is richer than literature in potentialities for exaggeration, incongruity and quick contrasts, the weapons of comedy. The brilliance of Chaplin, Lubitsch and René Clair comedies, the essential comic touches in the horse-play and farce of the early Mack Sennett productions, even the comic line in recent musical extravaganzas, illustrate this point. Just as the dramatic excels the epic manner in comedy, so the medium of the cinema may make it superior in this respect to poetry. The point about tragedy remains open when one thinks of such motion pictures as *The Informer* and *The Blue Angel.*

Second, prose and verse. This distinction raises two problems in connection with motion pictures. So far as language is part of their medium, the language could be either prose or verse. The brevity and character of the linguistic units in the silent film made it almost necessary for them to be prosaic as well as prose. But with the advent of talking, it is entirely possible for the dialogue part to be in verse as well as to be poetic, i.e., good writing. The proof of this point is the recent production of some of Shakespeare's plays. They indicate that a motion picture can be cinematically conceived in which the verbal part, the dialogue, has the excellence of the best writing in either verse or prose. The second question is the more important. It is whether there is any analogy between verse and prose, or between good and bad writing, and differences in cinematographic style in the use of the pictorial medium, by itself and in relation to the elements of language and sound. Considering first the distinction between verse and prose in terms of music, vocabulary and syntax, the analogy would require that there be a difference in the way in which a film is composed, both with respect to its elementary units and their arrangement in conjunction or succession. There is no question that the film can be given tempo and rhythm, that these can be varied intentionally, that the way in which the camera is used is similar to the choice of words and the way in which the sequences are ordered internally and in relation to each other by the process of *montage* is similar to syntax and phrasing. This is no more than an analogy, of course, but it is nevertheless one that yields a clear insight into a range of differences in cinematic style that are comparable to grades of literary style ⌊166⌋. If the analogy with verse and prose, distinguished according to prosody and rhyme, be too tenuous, at least the analogy in the matter of style is strong and clear. Just as there is good and bad writing, effective and inept writing, intense and dull writing — and in these senses, poetic and prosaic writing — there are the same distinctions of excellence and defect in the cinematographic technique of expression, and the same gradations from good to bad. More than that, I think I shall be able to show in a subsequent analysis of the technique that the principles of style are the same in both the literary and the cinematic medium, even though they are more difficult to state in the latter case because there is as yet no technical language of criticism established, no grammar of the elements of style.[42] It may be questioned whether there is as

---

[42] Such books as Spottiswoode's *Grammar of the Film* attempt to do this, but without clear analytical principles. The problems of style here raised are more fully discussed in Chapter 14 *infra*.

yet an adequate formulation of the principles of literary criticism with respect to style. In any event, it is clear that we have no formal grammar of the stylistic elements common to all the arts, and it is for this reason that we are continually reduced to the embarrassment of using analogies. No apology need be made for analogical discussion so long as its proportions are illuminating and give insight. That is the only test. I shall reserve further consideration of these matters for a subsequent analysis of cinematographic technique. Here it need only be said that, while but few motion pictures are stylistic masterpieces, most of the plays and novels currently produced and published are equally poor as literature, badly written, ineffective, dull, prosaic.

Third, epic and dramatic. A literary narrative must be either a novel or a play. However much it may violate the limitations of its type, however much it lacks the proper unity, it is still either one or the other. It may be bad as epic or as dramatic narration, but the distinction in manner can never be totally obscured. Does this distinction apply to the motion picture? Is the cinematic manner of narration either epic or dramatic, both or neither? This is, perhaps, the most important question that can be asked about the specific nature of the motion picture as a kind of fiction. I think it can be shown that the answer is, in one sense, neither and, in another, both. The motion picture has analogies with the play and the novel; it is never simply either one or the other. It is difficult to decide whether this means that cinematic narration is a mixture of epic and dramatic manners or whether it means that epic and dramatic do not exhaust the types of manner, the cinematic manner being an independent type, bearing certain resemblances to the other two as they do to each other. In any case, the significance of the issue is clear and, in the light of the current tendency to adapt plays and novels for motion-picture production, it is a crucial problem which the art must face.

Let us first develop the analogies by noting the similarities and differences between the motion picture and the drama, the motion picture and the novel. In the case of the drama, the comparison is more striking if we take the produced play rather than the literary work. This is proper since it is the dramatic manner of narration which makes such production possible; the production is nothing more than a determination of the written work's potentialities. Let us go to the extreme position at once and conceive a motion picture which did no more than photograph a play as it was produced in a theatre. What would the cinematographic technique of such an attempt be? If the highest fidelity to the dramatic production be the ideal, then the camera would have to be placed at some fixed focus, in the middle of the orchestra floor let us say; there should be no variation in the camera's manipulation whatsoever, or in the sound-recording devices. The microphone and the camera should be used to give us a faithful facsimile of the performance in the theatre as that might be seen and heard by someone sitting through the show. It would be a mechanical record, as a phonograph disc is in the case of a symphony played by an orchestra. This is possible, but the consideration of the possibility indicates at once what is wrong. In the first place, the camera and the microphone do not see and hear in the same way that the human eye and ear do. During a performance, the spectator's attention moves from one part of the stage to another, sometimes following one actor and sometimes another and these movements of attention are related to the tri-dimensional space of the stage, its frame and position in the interior of a theatre. The spectator does not hear with equal receptivity all that the microphone would equally record. In the second place, the total time of a play and the rhythm of its parts are obviously different from the total time and the temporal values of the sequences in the ordinary motion picture. This suggests that what would appear to be a swiftly moving narrative on the stage might become tedious and slow on the screen. In the third place, and most important of all, such a procedure would utterly deny all the technique of the camera and the microphone. The camera would have been used to do no more than transform the play from three to two dimensions in changing it from the stage to the screen. A motion picture would, in some sense, have been made, but it would not be a work of cinematographic technique. If, as we have seen, the motion picture is a work partly in a pictorial medium because it uses the camera, then its manner of narration must be in part a manner of using this medium, as the drama is a manner of using language. But to set a camera up with a fixed focus as a mere recording device is a minimum use

of the pictorial medium; it would not be a work of cinematographic art any more than the phonograph record of a symphony is a work of musical art.

It is clear, then, that the motion picture should not be, even
if it could be, the filming of a play as it is enacted on a stage.   Its
manner, therefore, is not simply dramatic.   But we must not go
to the other extreme of saying that its manner is not dramatic at
all.   The dramatist narrates by presenting the speeches and actions of men.   The dialogue of the drama, in its written form,
implies the action and the reader has an imaginative experience of
it through his understanding of the words.   In the produced
form, the actors and the stage-crafts offer a spectacle to accompany the words that makes imagination relatively unnecessary.
The motion picture also narrates by presenting the speeches and
actions of men.   To this extent it is dramatic.   But the extent is
extremely limited.   In good dramatic writing, the dialogue is
enough for the imagination.   But if the dialogue of a motion picture were read, it would hardly be sufficient to give the reader the
total imaginative experience that constitutes the reception of a
story.[43]   We understand this point as soon as we see that the
same can be said for good epic narration.   If the dialogue of a
novel were to be lifted out of the context of descriptive narrative,
the reading of it would not yield the story.   This indicates at
once that the motion picture differs from the drama in being like
the novel; but it also differs from the novel in being like the
produced drama, in making imagination unnecessary by presenting to the senses the actions as well as the speeches of the characters.   History provides an illuminating comment on this point.
In the days of the silent picture, it was the novel that seemed
most adaptable for the screen.[44]   Even with a liberal use of sub-
titles, dialogue had to be kept at a minimum, but dialogue is only
part of epic narration, and the descriptive part provided an ample
supply of narrative material for pictorial treatment.   The silent

[43] The reading of the dialogue part of any shooting script makes this point
clear.   The cinematic version of *Romeo and Juliet* affords an excellent example.   Note how much of the original dialogue the pictorial part replaces.
The left hand column, the pictorial part, is unintelligible without the right
hand column, the dialogue, and conversely.   Furthermore, the two columns
as printed do not constitute an artistic unity as the two parts do when integrated on the film and sound track for projection.
[44] G. Seldes, *op. cit.*, p. 40 ff.

movie had to depend much more upon pictures than upon words
in order to tell a story.   It discovered an affinity in the novel because it depended upon description as well as dialogue.   This
suggests the following significant proportion : description is to
dialogue in the novel as picture is to language in the cinema.
The proportion holds perfectly only for those silent motion pictures that employed sub-titles for dialogue alone ; otherwise,
language is used descriptively as it is in the novel.   With the
advent of sound and talking, the motion picture turned too im-
petuously to the drama because the new inventions made it seem
possible to include any amount of dialogue.   In discovering this
new affinity the motion picture, in the early days of sound,
either tended to forget or ignore the old one.   But the motion
picture soon learned that its fate was not so simple.   It could
not become one with the drama through the use of words any
more than it could become one with the novel because it had to
narrate, in part, by other means than dialogue.

The silent motion picture is instructive further.   In its best
productions, words were used at a minimum.   The best silent
movies tried to avoid sub-titles as far as possible, either of the
descriptive sort or dialogue.   They used the pictorial illusion of
change to tell a story.   They were essentially good as movies
because they capitalized movement.   They were pictures of action rather than of actors acting.   The Chaplin comedies and the
western melodramas are excellent examples of epic narration in
a non-linguistic medium.   The latter are, in a sense, the legendary epic of the American frontier.   *The Birth of a Nation*
is probably the best example of cinematographic technique used
in the epic manner.   But even the best of the silent movies failed
as pure pictorial epic.   In the first place, words were used even
though at a minimum.   Only the animated cartoon ever succeeded in completely eliminating all sub-titles.   In the second
place, the sub-titles usually, if not always, reported dialogue or at
least fragments of speech.   To this extent, the silent movie was
an epic that had to use both pictures and words.   The nature of
the motion picture even in its earliest days involved a dual medium.   There was a difference of opinion on this point, some
holding that it was possible for the cinema to achieve the ideal
state of being entirely wordless, others insisting that the use of
language was not only inevitable but proper, since many things

could be more effectively narrated by words than by pictures
and, hence, the attempt to be radical in the exclusion of words
would impair the speed and effectiveness of the pictorial part of
the narrative.[45] The issue was never tested during the era of
silent movies by a completely wordless production. Sound apparatus now makes the test unlikely and unnecessary. It can be
shown, I think, contrary to the opinions of many whose prejudices were formed through a devotion to the silent movie,[46]
that the use of spoken words, as well as other sounds, more nearly
realizes the essence of motion picture narration than the silent
film, with or without sub-titles.

This demonstration is made by showing the double affinity of
the motion picture for the two types of narration. We have
seen why the motion picture is not purely dramatic. We must
now see why it is not purely epic. It is not purely epic simply
because the projected film has an analogy to the dramatic spectacle. Like the drama, cinematic narration is always in the present tense whereas epic narration is always in the past. The
motion picture tells a story by presenting events as seeming to
happen now. Even when in the structure of the narrative an
earlier event is recalled, its recall presents it as if it were happening
now. Furthermore, the literary epic exists entirely in the medium of words and without any potentiality for production *as
such*. To produce an epic either as a play or as a motion picture requires the change in it we call adaptation. The written
drama is not thus adapted for production. This means that the
novel tells its story to a reader by means of the images its words
arouse. The written drama tells its story similarly. But in the
produced play the spectacle replaces much that must be imagined. This does not mean, of course, that no imagination is
required. Similarly, the projected film tells its story by means
of a spectacle that requires imagination in the same sense that the
produced play does, but not in the same sense that the written
play and novel do.

The complex character of the motion picture is best exhibited
by a number of proportions, no one of which is an adequate account of its nature. (1) The spoken dialogue is to the pictorial
illusion of a motion picture as the written dialogue is to the writ-

[45] H. Münsterberg, *op. cit.*, pp. 200–205 ; G. Buckle, *The Mind and the Film*,
London, 1926 : p. 103 ff.   [46] Vd. G. Seldes, *op. cit.*, p. 147 ff.

ten description in a novel. (2) The spoken dialogue is to the pictorial illusion of a motion picture as the speech of the actors is to the rest of the spectacle in a produced play. There is no analogy between the motion picture and the written play, because the latter consists only of dialogue. The first proportion indicates that the pictorial part of a cinema replaces the descriptive part of a novel. The superiority of the talking motion picture is seen in the way in which it exemplifies this proportion perfectly. It never uses language descriptively, whereas the silent movie used language both to report dialogue and for the sake of narrative description. The accuracy of the proportion can be tested by anyone who will witness the same motion picture first with eyes shut and then with ears closed. The narrative is spoiled in the same way that it would be if one separated the dialogue part from the descriptive part of a novel, and then read one or the other.[47] That the talking motion picture is superior to the silent movie because its parts are more nearly in the same proportion as those of a novel depends upon one further point, namely, that, of its two affinities, *the motion picture is more like the novel than the play*. The spectacle in the theatre is, as we have seen, something added to the play as poetry. It is not necessary. The distinction between drama and epic is a distinction between two manners of writing, and not between theatrical production and writing. If the dramatic manner is exhibited in the written play, then the motion picture is not dramatic. The former narrates by dialogue alone, whereas the latter narrates by dialogue and description. But the description is in the medium of pictures not of words.

We are, therefore, forced to the conclusion that because of the duality of its medium, the motion picture has a similar duality in its manner of narration. Just as it is neither a species of literature nor of plastic, so it is neither drama nor epic. Spectacle only follows as a property from the dramatic manner of narration but it is part of the essence of cinematic narration. Nor can we say that the cinematic manner is epic *plus* spectacle. With respect to its medium, the motion picture is not a combination of two separate media, as the opera is, or a confusion of them, as programmatic music is; rather it is a fusion of language and pictures. So with respect to its manner, it is not a mixture or com-

[47] Cf. R. Arnheim, *Film*, London, 1933 : p. 213 ; A. Nicoll, *op. cit.*, p. 129.

bination of the epic with spectacle; it is a fusion which, sufficiently different either from the epic poem or the dramatic spectacle, deserves a distinctive name of its own. The motion picture tells a story in the *cinematic* manner, the essence of which is more closely analogous to the epic than the dramatic manner, but differing from both in that spectacle is part of its essence.

This conclusion has a number of interesting corollaries. In the first place, we are able to understand the technique of a motion picture in terms of the proportionality of its parts. In its epic aspect, the cinema has a dialogue part and a descriptive part. In its spectacular aspect, the cinema has a dance part and a music or song part. The pantomime of the actors in a theatrical spectacle is the dance part of the drama as produced. Here lies the affinity of the dramatic spectacle and the ballet, which includes not only the pantomime but the conventional movements of the dance. The ballet usually has a music part; we need not decide whether the dance accompanies the music or the music accompanies the dance. So the theatrical spectacle has a music part in the speech of the actors. This is at a maximum in the case of dramas written in verse embellished by song, in choral interludes or otherwise. It is at a minimum, of course, in contemporary "realistic" prose drama. But the motion picture need not be and should not be realistic in this way. It has a music part, not in the lyrical quality of its dialogue, but in the union of the spectacle of action with sound effects and music. Unlike the ballet, the music part is not limited to being an accompaniment of the dance part, the movement of the actors. It can accompany the entire spectacle. The music that is part of a motion picture is bad if it is gratuitous or *incidental*;[48] it should be no more incidental than is the music in a ballet or than the musical embellishment which, though accidental to the drama as written, may be a proper part of the drama as produced. These four parts are related to the subordinate arts which co-operate in the making of a motion picture: (1) the dialogue is the work of an artist in language; (2) the pictorial description is the work of the camera-man, the scene-painter, set-constructor, costumer, electrician, etc.; (3) the dance part, in so far as it is pantomime, is the work of the

[48] Cf. R. Arnheim, *op. cit.*, p. 370; V. I. Pudovkin, *Film Technique*, pp. 155–174; D. Moore, *Music and the Movies* in Harper's Monthly Magazine, July, 1935; and L. Sabaneev, *Music for the Films*, London, 1935.

actor; (4) the sound and music part is the work of a musician and the man who controls the phonography. There are certain overlappings, of course; thus, the spoken dialogue is the combined effort of the writer, the actor and the sound-control man. Nor are all the parts co-ordinate. Because of its similarity to the epic manner of narration, the cinematic way of telling a story must place primary emphasis upon the pictorial part. The basic fabric of the epic is its descriptive narration; the dialogue is woven into it. So the pictorial sequences provide the thread of continuity which ties together all the other elements of cinematic composition. The pictorial description is thus only subordinately the work of the camera-man, the scene-painter, etc. It is primarily the means by which the director is able to compose the narrative whole out of these various parts duly proportioned. He must work to subordinate all the elements to their proper place in the composition as well as to associate them harmoniously. The plot is the soul of a narrative, said Aristotle. The cinematic continuity is the soul of a motion picture. Because it is the work of the director, both during the recording process and in the cutting room, he must be the master to bring unity of composition out of a multiplicity of parts. The baffling perfection of some of Disney's creations must have something to do with the completeness of his mastery over all of the elements he uses.

In the second place, if the motion picture has a manner of narration peculiar to itself, it must be the director who is the storyteller and not the writer, the artist in words. The scenarist is not a poet except in the accidental fact that he uses words to draft the blue-prints and plans of the cinema. As we have seen, the scenarist and the director should either be one, or their separate work should converge as much as possible. It is only with respect to the spoken dialogue that what is essentially a technique of using language is important. A writer may be needed for this. But the scenarist and director, whether the same or different, need not be writers, need not be artists in the epic or dramatic manner of telling a story in words. They must, however, be story-tellers because their art is in the genus of fiction. The difference in their medium and manner requires them to conceive a story cinematically, which means in terms of a pictorial continuity that is able to organize all of the subordinate elements.

We are thus led, in the third place, to the simple insight that the technique of the dramatist or the novelist cannot make a motion picture. We shall presently analyze the cinematographic technique that is necessary. Here the insight stresses one point. Unless stories are conceived cinematically in the first instance, they must be adaptations of novels or plays.[49] What is true of the dramatic adaptation of the novel holds for the cinematic adaptation of either the novel or the drama. The limitations, the degrees of freedom, the unity and magnitude of the plot are different in novel and play because they are different in manner of narration. It follows, similarly, from the peculiarities of the cinematic manner that the motion picture must also differ in these respects. These differences can be briefly indicated. The motion picture has some of the limitations of the produced play; thus, if Homer's *Iliad* were cinematized, the pursuit of Hector could not be shown on the screen any more than it could be presented on the stage. The psychological depth which the novelist can reveal descriptively has been contrasted with the surface quality of the drama. Here the motion picture is a mean between the freedom of the one and the restriction of the other. Not limited to dialogue or by the realistic conditions of the stage, the motion picture can delineate the inwardness of its characters by means of pictures, to an extent greater than the play and less than the novel. In other respects, the motion picture has as much, if not more, freedom than the novel. Its space and time are not actual as are those of the produced play. The narrative can move forward and backward in time with utter flexibility. Parallel actions can be represented in condensed alternations of pictorial sequences. The superimposition of pictures makes it possible for cinematic narration to aid the memory of the spectator as the novelist can, as well as to exteriorize the thoughts and emotions of the characters. Unlike the play, in which the speech and action of the characters must be spatially correlated for the spectator, the motion picture is able to dislocate the auditory and the visual elements; thus, the picture may direct attention to the person hearing rather than the person talking, while we are listening to the latter. This is quite different from the theatrical trick of off-stage speech, because the two persons involved may

[49] Professor Nicoll considers it an ultimate desideratum that film-narratives should be original rather than adaptations. Vd. *op. cit.*, p. 31.

be confronting each other. The freedom of a motion picture is, thus, that it creates its own space and time through the use of camera and microphone and the techniques of cutting the film and correlating the film and the sound-track.

What Pudovkin and others have called filmic space-time makes the observer of the film an ideal observer of the action narrated [167]. The spectator of the play sees and hears what takes place on the stage under the limitations of ordinary seeing and hearing, except for the minor illusions stage-craft is able to produce. But the spectator of the film is made to see and hear in the way in which the camera and the microphone are able to, a way which greatly extends and alters the ordinary powers of perception. The stage-director has only a few means by which he can direct the attention of the spectator to one or another point of the spectacle at any given time. The film-director is always able to control the attention of the spectator and is thus able, like the novelist, to put the accent exactly where he wishes. The film-director and the novelist both tell a story by leading attention from point to point in the narrative. They both have a freedom in the correlation and succession of such points, limited only by the rule of probability. The connexion must always be a likely one. There is this difference, however : using words only, the novelist creates his story in the imagination of the reader. He can make the reader *imagine* anything that he can endow with likelihood, whether or not it could ever be perceived. The film-director creates his story in the *perceptions* of the spectator. He, too, is not limited by what can be ordinarily perceived, but he has less freedom within the bounds of probability than the novelist. The fact, however, that the novel and the cinema share almost the same freedom from reality and have approximately the same standard of poetic truth is another indication that the affinity between them is greater than of either with the drama. Both the film and the novel can move much further into the realm of fantasy than the play, but the way in which they make the fantastic probable is different. We shall return to this point later.

It is difficult to determine the precise difference between the novel and the cinema with respect to the magnitude of the action imitated and the structure of the plot. It is clear that the cinema is not as limited as the drama in the number of its incidents, scenes, characters, its space and time. But can it achieve the magnitude of a novel? It would seem that it cannot, that here as before it is a mean between the drama and the novel, though here it is somewhat nearer to the drama.[50] Words are more able than pictures to make a large and complicated whole perspicuous. The multiplicity of plots which is possible in a long novel such as *David Copperfield* or *Anna Karenina* cannot be handled in the cinematic adaptation. The rule which Aristotle stated for the extraction of a drama from an epic seems to apply to the cinema. Condensation and selection are required, though not to as great an extent in cinematic adaptation. It is here that the peculiar character of cinematic narration is most clearly seen as neither epic nor dramatic, but like both in different respects. If a play be adapted for the screen, it must be expanded in the direction of epic magnitude, but contracted with respect to dramatic detail. If a novel be adapted for the screen, it must be contracted in the direction of dramatic magnitude, but expanded with respect to dramatic detail. It is interesting to note, in this connection, that the actual time of film narrative is usually less than that of a produced play and less than the ordinary reading-time of a fairly long novel. The actual time, therefore, does not measure the magnitude of the narrative, but the complexity of the plot structure, the internal time and space of the story, and the number of its constituent elements. If in the shorter actual time of cinematic narration, an action of greater magnitude is imitated, it must mean that the speed of narration is greater, but it may also mean, as we shall later see, that the cinema has less intensive development of the intrinsic details of the story than either drama or novel. It may also be significant that the direction of adaptation is usually one-way. Just as novels are dramatized, but plays are seldom if ever expanded into epics — Lamb's *Tales from Shakespeare* is hardly an exception — so both plays and novels are cinematized, but there is no case in which a motion picture has been transformed into a play or a novel. This may be because most cinemas are adaptations of previously existing literary works, or it may indicate that adaptation is usually in the direction of contraction rather than expansion. The latter could

---

[50] See Nicoll's criticism of the cinematic version of *The Tale of Two Cities* (*op. cit.*, p. 160). He agrees however that "the freedom of the film brings it nearer in structure to the novel than the drama."

only be the case with respect to something other than the magnitude of the action, since plays are adapted for the screen. It may thus be connected with the point made above, the fact that there is less detail in cinematic narration than in either drama or epic. We shall later see the significance of this point in a discussion of the relative goodness of the three types of narrative manner.

This analysis does not enable us to decide whether it is better for motion pictures to be stories originally conceived in the cinematic manner or to be adaptations of novels and plays [168]. If the adaptation is properly done, the transformation will be made in terms of cinematic conditions and there will be no difference between productions of either sort. But one thing is absolutely clear. A motion picture can be good in its own way only if it is a product of the cinematographic technique. We have now sufficiently analyzed the medium and manner of the motion picture to be able to discuss the technique of the director. In all its phases it is determined, as any art is, by the conditions imposed upon the artist by the medium and manner in which he imitates an object.

CHAPTER FOURTEEN

Technique

THE technique of an art exists in the artist who has the habit of making a particular kind of thing. We can discuss the technique only to the extent that we can abstract from the actual practice of artists the rules which state the generality of their habits. It should be clear that such rules are not imposed from without upon the artist. It is not as if someone other than the artist made up rules for an art which the artist must adopt and follow. Rules of art are posterior to the habits of the artist. For the training of a novice, the explicit formulation of the rules which express the technique of a master may be helpful; but the novice becomes in turn a technically accomplished worker, not through learning the rules, but through forming similar habits. It is in the sense in which the work of the artist precedes the analysis of his technique that Aristotle's *Poetics,* and any similar discussion, is *a posteriori.* The analysis of the nature of an art and the formulation of its rules are inductive. They are based upon the work done by artists. But it is natural for the artist to be inventive, to seek novelty. There is always, therefore, in the history of an art, a rebellion going on against the academician, against the classical canons which are, after all, nothing but the work of predecessors stated in explicit rules. Sometimes the revolt leads to a genuine advance, to the opening of a new field of artistic accomplishment. Sometimes the revolt is nothing but a futile attempt to break with tradition, just for the sake of novelty itself, and then the result is usually an unjustifiable transgression of the forms and a misuse of technique [169]. The recent history of what is called "modernism" in painting and music provide illustrations of the point. In the former case, the revolt against a dead classicism has culminated in the achievement of new plastic techniques which are good in the same way that the classical work itself was good before it became stultified academicism. In the latter case, the revolt for the most part has taken the path of trying to do with the elements of music what cannot be done properly in that medium. In either case, the fruits of rebellion are to be judged on their own merits. There is nothing good or bad intrinsically in novelty itself.

Aristotle recognized this by including a history of poetry in his account of that art. The introduction of two or more actors upon the stage, the use of scene-painters, changes in diction and in the part assigned to the chorus, are incidents in the development of tragedy from Aeschylus to Euripides. As *The Frogs* indicates, the antithesis of the old and the new in tragic imitation was well known and much debated at the time. "Whether Tragedy has as yet perfected its proper types or not; and whether it is to be judged in itself, or in relation also to its audience"[1] — these questions Aristotle does not answer. Yet in noting that "tragedy advanced by slow degrees" and that "each new element that showed itself was in turn developed,"[2] Aristotle remarks that tragedy found its natural form and stopped. There is an apparent inconsistency here which disappears when it is understood that in the development of any art, its specific form is realized at a certain point and thereafter innovations must either be the invention of new species or radical departures from the genus itself. Such departures would, of course, not be part of the history of work in that form. They would institute a new field of art which would have its own subsequent history. Aristotle's praise of Homer views him as the great original innovator of poetry, of the form which is common to the drama and the epic, the comedy and the tragedy. That Aristotle, at the time he is writing, is able to say that tragedy has found its natural form means that its genus, at least, can be inductively defined. It does not mean that tragedy can have no subsequent history in which new species are added by the invention of later artists. It does not mean that within the larger genus of dra-

[1] *Poetics*, 4, 1449^{a}7–9.   [2] *Poetics*, 4, 1449^{a}12–15.

matic writing there *cannot be* other forms co-ordinate as species with the type of tragedy or comedy Aristotle defines.   Much of the modern protest against adherence to the canons of the *Poetics* is dissipated by this insight.   The rules of poetry which Aristotle formulates are not meant to bind all later artists, to keep them from invention [170].   The rules have a double use critically.   They enable us to judge whether an artist who intends to work within a given form works well within its limitations.   They also enable us to judge whether an artist who tries to create a new form has done so, or has merely gratified a rebellious desire for novelty for its own sake.   If a writer of plays violates the rules of that art, his innovations must have an artistic integrity in order to escape condemnation as mere violations. They must exhibit a genuine departure in form.   A later analyst should be able to add the definition of this form to the categories of Aristotle's *Poetics* without any transgression of its fundamental principles, since these are the principles of all poetry.[2a]

It may be objected that the innovation is justified if its novelty pleases the jaded taste of an audience.   This has been the apology for much of the experimentalism in all fields of modern art. Aristotle recognized this objection in the second of the two questions he did not fully answer.   One thing, at least, is clear.   The evaluation of works of art in relation to their audience is extrinsic criticism.   It is not part of aesthetics.   To the extent that we are here concerned with aesthetic analysis as a basis for criticism, the objection is not relevant.   We shall return to it later in discussing the relation between the intrinsic goodness of a work of art and the pleasure it gives an audience.

In writing of the technique of motion pictures, it would be folly to ignore the fact that they have a history and a future. The few books which have been written on this subject have indulged too easily in prophecy, only to have the rapidly chang-

[2a] There is no inconsistency between my emphasis upon the generality of the *Poetics* and the restrictions which Aristotle seems to impose upon his own discussion.   In one sense, the *Poetics* was not about poetry in general, but only about the two species of poetry which had achieved sufficient stability and definition, sufficient maturity in form, to be analyzed, namely, tragedy and epic.   But a generality is attained in the analysis of tragedy and epic which yields principles applicable to any other species of fiction, whenever such species come into being and mature.

ing art belie them within a few years. Thus, Münsterberg in
1916 was certain that the perfection of sound apparatus could
never make the talking motion picture a work of art within the
limitations of cinematic technique.[3]   It would be as gratuitous
now to prophesy that color is impossible, or that the illusion
of tridimensionality through stereoscopy is impossible, impossible in the sense that the development of these devices will
necessarily destroy the nature of the motion picture [171].

Compared to other arts, the motion picture is extremely young.
In its short career, it has undergone an amazingly large number
of transformations, most of them the result of mechanical inventions or perfections.[4]   The dependence of the technique of
motion pictures upon the machines available at a given time is
not peculiar to it.   This is true of all arts.   The dramatic art, as
a way of writing that is capable of theatrical production, has
been influenced by the invention of theatrical devices.   Art is
operative.   Like the experimental or investigative sciences, the
arts are, therefore, dependent upon the physical conditions of
operation, upon the instruments, the machines, the mastery of
the physical conditions.   The history of music and plastic, like
the history of experimental science, is an account of a changing
technique following the invention of instruments and apparatus.
The importance of this insight is that it places the present discussion of the cinematographic technique in its proper perspective.
The present stage of the art of motion pictures is the result of an
inventive past.   It will undoubtedly be altered by an inventive
future.   The perfection of radio television may utterly destroy
the motion picture by absorbing its audience or the future may
hold the answer to this challenge as well as the threat of it.

The task of the analyst and the critic does not require him to
be a prophet.   He must avoid prophecy even though in so doing
he cannot speak with the finality which all analysts secretly

[3] *The Photoplay*, pp. 202–203. Even Arnheim as late as 1933 was a poor
prophet. Vd. *Film*, pp. 201–206, 239–250. Cf. Seldes, *The Movies and the Talkies*, Philadelphia, 1929 ; p. 124 ff. Note his astonishment at the Russian insight
into the future of sound film (p. 149 ff.). As early as 1929, Pudovkin had
seen its essential principles and knew that it was a development and not a
denial of the cinematic art. Vd. *Film Technique* : pp. 143–144.
[4] The most important transformation was not mechanical. It came with the
realization that the motion picture was an art of story-telling. Vd. Seldes,
op. cit., pp. 18–19, 22–23.

cherish.   Yet there is a proper sense in which the account of a
changing art can have finality, the sense in which Aristotle felt
that the poets of his day had revealed the generic forms of their
art in such a way that definitions could be made and essential
distinctions reached.   The nature of the motion picture can be
defined and the elements of its technique formulated because the
art has developed to a point where its form is exhibited and the
limitations within which work must be done are clear.   If new
machines annihilate these limitations, they will also set up new
limits.   We can say with finality that the future holds only three
alternatives: (1) the motion picture will cease to be a living,
growing art, as Gothic architecture ceased with the invention of
structural steel; (2) the art of the motion picture will grow by
the addition of new species, as in a sense silent and talking pictures are species of the same art, differing in medium; (3) the
art of the motion picture will continue in its own line, while inventions create the conditions of a new art, different from the
motion picture as the motion picture is from the produced play
or the published novel.   In any of these alternatives, the present
analysis based upon contemporary work in the art may hold for
its entire future if it holds right now.   It can hold in such a way
that future changes will do no more than require an harmonious
extension of its principles.

We can abbreviate our discussion of the technique of motion
pictures by considering only that part of their technique which
is peculiar to them.   The motion picture is in the same genus as
narrative poetry.   Therefore, those elements of technique which
have to do with the object imitated by fiction must be common
to the motion picture, the epic and the drama.   They are primarily plot, and secondarily character and thought.   In other
words, plot, character and thought are common elements of
story-telling.[5]   But the motion picture differs from epic and

[5] *Poetics*, 6, 1449^{b}36–1450^{a}14 ; 1450^{a}37–1450^{b}12.   The elements of fiction can be
classified according as they are related to the medium of imitation, the manner
or the object.   Plot, character and thought relate to the object of imitation
and, hence, are common to all fiction.   Diction and song belong to the
medium of imitation ; spectacle to the manner of imitation.   Aristotle provides us with an analysis of diction, but unfortunately for the application of
the *Poetics* to the cinema there is no analysis of spectacle.   The analysis of
diction will be different for epic, dramatic and cinematic narration because
they differ in medium or manner of imitation, or both.

dramatic poetry both in the medium of its narration and the manner. The elements of its technique which have to do with medium and manner will, therefore, be peculiar to it, as the element of spectacle in dramatic poetry is peculiar to it and need not be considered in an analysis of epic poetry. The elements which are peculiar to the art of the motion picture are thus, first, the pictures and, second, the relation of the pictures to spoken words and other sounds. The first of these is due to the difference in medium, the second to the difference in manner of narration. We shall consider the problems of technique with respect to these elements in the order indicated. But it will be seen at once that the difference in narrative manner cannot be entirely separated from the problems of plot, character and thought. Thus, although both an epic and a dramatic poem must have a plot, their difference in manner requires a difference in plot structure, a difference in the way character is delineated and thought is expressed or indicated. We shall, therefore, return to the technical problems of the motion picture with respect to plot, character and thought after we have considered the elements arising from medium and manner.

We are aided in this analysis of the technique of narrating in pictures by an analogous discussion of the element of diction in Aristotle's *Poetics*.[6] Under the head of diction Aristotle considers the poet's technical problems in the use of language, his medium of imitation. He first classifies the parts of language: (1) the letter, which is an indivisible and non-significant sound; (2) the syllable, which is also a non-significant sound but one which is divisible into its component vowels and consonants; (3) the word, which is a significant sound, like the syllable, divisible, but its parts not significant; (4) the phrase or sentence, which like the word is a significant, divisible sound, but unlike the word, the parts into which it is primarily divided, words, are also significant. Aristotle does not add a fifth part, the paragraph, which is significant as whole and divisible into significant parts, sentences. He divides words into (a) connectives, (b) nouns and (c) verbs. Connectives are not significant by themselves, but only as parts of sentences. Nouns and verbs are significant by themselves, the latter differing from the former in that their significance includes a reference to time. He does

6 *Poetics*, 20.

not go further in the division of the parts of speech to mention adjectives and adverbs as modifiers of nouns and verbs. The distinction between the phrase and the sentence is made in terms of their different kinds of unity : the unity of the phrase depends upon the primary unity of the thing signified thereby ; the unity of the sentence depends upon a secondary unity of composition, the unity of a whole made up of *related* parts. If we ignore for the moment the distinction between prose and verse, the poet's problem in the use of language as a means of imitation has to do with words, phrases and sentences, with significant sounds, in short. It is only when he is concerned with the sound-values of words, their tone and quantity, that he need be concerned with letters and syllables. From the point of view of significance — and it is through the significance of language that poets are able to imitate their object — the word is the basic unit of composition. The problems of literary style, therefore, reduce to two, (1) *vocabulary*, the choice of words, and (2) *syntax*, the various modes of combining words into significant phrases and sentences.

In making an analogous division of the parts of the pictorial medium, we are not merely appealing to an analogy. Independently of any particular division of the parts of language, it must be recognized that the pictorial medium is necessarily divisible into parts, that some of these parts are not significant units of narration, and that the basic parts must be capable of composition into significant wholes. The analytical task, therefore, is to discover the atomic significant parts and the modes in which they can be combined. The analogy is merely helpful in illuminating distinctions made in a new medium. More people understand the parts of speech than of any other medium of imitation. It is not surprising, therefore, to find analysts of music speaking of the language of tone and finding parallels between words, phrases and sentences, and the tonal units and combinations of musical composition. A good analysis of the vocabulary and syntax of music exists and we might just as easily use it as an illuminating analogy for the pictorial medium. But there is good reason for preferring the analogy of language. It is a medium for imitating an object which the cinema shares with poetry. The few writers who have attempted to discuss the technique of the pictorial medium of narration have naturally resorted to this analogy, notably Pudovkin and those who have

followed him.   I can add little to their discussion except analytical clarity.   I shall attempt to formulate the principles they
indicate.   For the concrete details and the illustrations one
must go to their work [172].

What is called *montage,* or editing, in the process of making a
film gives us a clue to the basic parts of pictorial narration.   The
word *montage* is better to use than editing, because the latter has
a literary connotation which is inapplicable in the case of the
film.   An author's work is completed *before* it is edited; a film
is not completed *until* it is edited.   The English word "cutting"
is, perhaps, the best name for the process which consists in dividing and combining the matter of the film.[7]   In language, a
sentence is divisible into its words and compounded out of its
words.   The word is further divisible but not into significant
parts.   The word, therefore, is the atomic or indivisible unit of
significance.   The atomic or indivisible unit in the pictorial
medium must similarly be the smallest significant unit of narration, the unit out of which significant sequences are compounded
and into which they can be divided.   If we take a film we can
discover at once two units: (1) the single frame, that is, a single
photographic impression on the negative; if this were cut from
the film and printed, it would be an ordinary photograph; (2) a
series of such frames made by a single setting of the camera,
whether in position or in motion, rotary or translatory, that is,
a series of photographs all of which are made under a single
condition of the camera.   It is clear that the single frame[8]
cannot be the atomic unit we are seeking, because it has no
projective existence.   What is seen upon the screen depends
upon the succession of such frames in the projector.   In order
to give the content of the single frame a projective existence, it
would be necessary to duplicate it enough times so that a series

[7] Pudovkin defines *montage* as "constructive editing" (*op. cit.,* pp. 141, 147).
But editing, or cutting and joining, is necessary in all film-making because the
order of actual shooting is not the order of narrative continuity.   It seems
inadvisable to use "*montage*" to name only the type of editing which does not
follow a simple time-space order, i.e., the order of a chronicle.   I shall, therefore, use the words "*montage*," "editing" and "cutting" as synonyms to name
the process of making a continuous film out of the discontinuous materials
produced by the camera, operated according to locations and not narrative
continuity.   *Montage* is the process of returning to, and in most cases improving upon, the plan of the scenario.   [8] The single frame is also called a "still."

of such frames, having identical photographic content, would in projection throw a single motionless picture on the screen.[9] This indicates that in the cutting process a single frame cannot be cut and moved about in the ordering of filmic material. The smallest part which is cuttable for purposes of composition is a series of frames. This series may be constituted by frames all identical in photographic content or by frames differing in photographic content; if the latter, the difference may be due to a change in the setting of the camera or to a change in the things being photographed, or to both. We can conclude, therefore, that the single frame is like the letter; both are absolute units in their respective media because they are indivisible, and both are non-significant parts. A series of single frames which is too short to be cut for the purposes of narrative composition is like a syllable. It is divisible into the individual frames, as the syllable is into its letters; but like the syllable, neither it nor its parts are significant. In the case of the film, unlike language, it is the number of frames which determines the cuttability of the series because upon the number of frames in succession depends the projective unity upon the screen. It should be added, at once, that it is not merely the number but the relation of the photographic contents of the frames; they must either have the same content in duplication or be a continuous photographic record of a change. The atomic unit of pictorial significance is thus determined by the conditions of photographing and projecting the film. The filmic analogue of a word is thus a series of frames which has an inner continuity because of the photographic condition and satisfies the projective condition of being cuttable as a whole, the whole series being a unit which, when cut, can be moved about at will in the process of *montage*.[9a]

A sentence cannot be composed of the same words in succes-

[9] This should be called a "cinematographic still" because it has projective existence.

[9a] By "cuttability" is meant the property of being a significant projective unit. What is thus cuttable is not indivisible, but its parts are not cuttable because they are not projectible. This basic unit is defined by Nicoll as "the picture of any piece of action taken in one complete whole by the camera" (*Film and Theatre*, p. 42); and by Spottiswoode as "a portion of film portraying physical objects without visible or temporal discontinuity" (*The Grammar of the Film*, p. 44). These definitions fail because what they describe *may* be further divisible into genuinely cuttable parts.

sion.   At least two of the words in a sentence must be different
in order to give it its characteristic unity as a relation of different
parts.   A phrase must also contain at least two different words,
although its unity is different from the unity of a sentence.
The difference between a sentence and a phrase is that a phrase,
though composed of two or more different words, has the same
kind of unity of reference that a single word has, that is, a phrase
which is complete in itself has the same kind of significance that
a single noun or verb has.   Just as a connective word has no
significance standing by itself but only in a sentence, so there are
incomplete phrases which are merely connective, that is, only
have significance when joined with other words to make a complete phrase or a sentence.   The cuttable units of the film can
be joined together as words are in phrases or sentences, and the
same condition must be satisfied, namely, that different units be
joined together.   The construction of a sentence or a phrase
sometimes requires the use of connective words as well as the
nouns and verbs, adjectives and adverbs, they connect; sometimes, however, the sentence is organized without explicit connectives.   In order, therefore, to discover the modes of syntax
in the pictorial medium, we must discover the types of connection that can be used in joining its units together.   One series of
frames may succeed another without any sign of division or connection other than the obvious shift in the setting of the camera.[10]
This shift in the photographic condition is like a mark of punctuation; it is like the space which is left in either writing or
printing between the separate words, the letters of which are not
similarly separated.   Or one series of frames may be connected
with another by means of such devices as the fade-in and the
fade-out, the wipe or overlap, the mix and the dissolve.[11]   These
devices are transitional; they both connect and separate.   They

[10] This type of succession is called a "cut."   A cut divides two cuttable units
in the absence of any explicit mark of division and transition.   Spottiswoode
defines a cut as "the instantaneous transference from any shot to its successor"
(op. cit., p. 44).
[11] The cut differs from these devices in that it merely *divides* whereas they
not only divide but *connect*, making the transition from one shot to another
explicit.   For definitions of these devices, see Spottiswoode, op. cit., p. 45.
The cut is fundamental and most frequently used.   Vd. p. 127.   Cf. Nicoll's
discussion of linkage : op. cit., pp. 80–85.

are achieved either by the control of light and focus in photography, or by methods of developing the film.

It is difficult, if not impossible, to find a perfect analogy between linguistic and pictorial syntax. We shall use "piece" or "shot" to name the succession of single frames which constitute the unit series, the least cuttable part of the film. This series may be long or short, as a word may be long or short because of the number of its letters and syllables. What is like a monosyllabic word is called a flash ; a flash is, thus, the shortest possible series that can be cut. We shall now use the word "scene" to name a sequence of different shots which are punctuated only by camera shifts. The photographic content of these different pieces must have a certain continuity which is obtained by the identity of the objective scene being photographed. In other words, it is the identity of locale that makes a scene. Pudovkin's analysis of the scene of an automobile accident illustrates the point.[12] It contains (1) a shot showing the street with cars in movement, against which background a pedestrian is seen crossing with his back to the camera, (2) a very short flash of the face of the startled chauffeur as he steps on the brake, (3) an equally short flash of the face of the victim, his mouth open in a scream, (4) a longer shot of legs near the revolving wheels taken from above as if from the chauffeur's seat, (5) a shot showing the sliding braked wheels of the car, (6) a shot showing the corpse by the stationary car, a piece in which there may or may not be any motion. This is a sequence of six units, each of which is a filmic whole. The sequence itself is a filmic whole. Its unity, like the unity of a complete phrase, depends upon the singleness of its objective reference, which is here the scene, a unit of action which can be verbally called an automobile accident. This sequence is thus like a phrase having six words, the whole of which refers to one thing.[13] As in the case of the phrase for which it is usually possible to find or invent a single

---

[12] *Op. cit.*, pp. 67–72.

[13] If constructed by cuts, it is like a phrase without explicit connective words such as "college professors annually forgetting last year's students." But phrases usually have connective words, such as "professors *in* college." Scenes, on the other hand, usually have their parts connected only by the altered setting of the camera in shooting the same locale.

substitutable word, it is possible to substitute a single piece for
this scene by photographing the automobile accident as seen
from the window of an adjacent building.

A sequence of scenes is like a sentence.   We shall use the word
"sequence" without qualification to name the basic narrative unit
of the film.   Sequence does not mean simply a series.   The shot
is a series of single frames or stills; the scene is a series of shots;
the sequence is a series of scenes.   It not only contains different
shots (different words), but these different pieces are themselves
grouped into different scenes (different phrases), and the unity of
the whole is a narrative unity and not a unity of reference to a
single objective locale.   Thus, to expand the above illustration,
the succession of scenes showing the person leaving his house,
going to work, being run over, in an ambulance and then in a
hospital bed would be a sequence of this sort.   The analogy of
the sequence with the sentence makes another point clear.   A
sentence may be made up of a number of different words not
organized in phrases.   So, too, a sequence may be composed out
of different shots, without the subordinate organization of these
shots into scenes.   Just as a single word can be substituted for a
phrase which refers to the same object, so a single shot can be
used instead of a scene.   Sequences, therefore, are of three sorts:
(1) composed of different shots; (2) composed of different
scenes; (3) composed of different shots and different scenes.
The sequence which is composed only of shots differs from a
scene, which is also composed of different shots, in that the latter
is unified by identity of locale.   The sequence always involves
a change of locale.   It is interesting to note here that the three
fundamental series of single frames are distinguished by different
principles of unification: (1) the shot is the simplest series, unified by the identity of the camera condition; (2) the scene is a
more complicated series, unified by the identity of the locale
which can be explored photographically from countless different
angles and in many different ways; (3) the sequence is the most
complicated series, unified by the narrative content, by the connection of its parts in time, or causally, or in terms of the thought
and feeling of the characters.   It should also be noted that there
are subordinate differences in scenes and sequences according
to the type of transitional device employed, or the lack of such
devices in simple cutting.

The analogy with language fails at a number of points. Phrases usually employ connective words; but scenes as frequently employ no transitional devices to connect their parts. They may simply have punctuation of the sort that spacing is, i.e., the cut.   Sentences must either employ the copula as a connective or have the distinction of noun and verb; but sequences, like scenes, may employ no explicit transitional devices.   They may be punctuated in the same way that scenes are.   There is nothing clearly analogous to the distinction between noun and verb.

There is at present no settled rule of cinematic technique which prescribes the use or non-use of such transitional devices as the fade-in and fade-out, the wipe or the dissolve.   They can be used in putting together the constituent parts of a single scene, or the scenes of a sequence; but they can also be used in putting together the sequences out of which the whole film is composed. In other words, there is nothing like the period which divides the sentences of a paragraph, or the method of paragraphing which separates different groups of sentences.   On the other hand, a sentence may be more or less complex.   It is possible for a single sentence to become a whole paragraph through complexity of structure.   The film as a whole is an organization of sequences into something vaguely analogous to paragraphs and chapters.   A single sequence may be like a single complex sentence and in this sense be like a paragraph, or it may be one of a number of sequences joined together to make a higher unit of action than any of these narrative parts taken alone.   The division of a novel into chapters or of a play into acts and scenes usually is determined by some break in the action, some significant change of time and place.   The largest units of filmic composition are separated in the same way.   The chief difference is that the parts of a film are not joined together or separated from each other in any way that uniformly indicates the same type of division.   Thus, if the dissolve were always used to connect sequences together into paragraphic unity, if a fade-in and fade-out were always used to separate the sequence groups which constituted different paragraphs, if a blank screen were always used to make the chapter kind of separation, and if the simple cut were used to separate the parts of a scene or a sequence, then such uniform marks of connection and separation would explicitly indicate the various units of filmic composition. This is at present not the case.[14]

We can best summarize the analysis so far by presenting the analogy between the parts of language and the parts of a film in the following table [173].

Language		*Film*	
(1)	letter	(1)	single frame (still).
(2)	syllable	(2)	uncuttable series of frames.
(3)	word	(3)	a cuttable series of frames, a single piece or shot.
	(a) noun		(a) *possibly*, a motionless piece (a cinematographic still).
	(b) verb		(b) *possibly*, a piece showing motion.
	(c) connective		(c) fade-in, fade-out, wipe, dissolve.
(4)	phrase	(4)	scene (a series of shots).
(5)	sentence	(5)	sequence (a series of shots, or scenes, or scenes and shots).
(6)	paragraph	(6)	a series of sequences having narrative unity.
(7)	chapter	(7)	the largest divisions of the filmic continuity into the main parts of the total action.

It will be remembered, of course, that at every level there is not only similarity but difference. The latter is just as important as the former in understanding cinematographic technique.

This analysis now enables us to discover what makes for *style* in the use of the pictorial medium. Language not only contains many words, but many different words for saying the same thing. There could be no problem of a choice of words unless there were synonyms, words which have both similarity and difference in meaning. In writing we choose one word rather than another because it says the same thing but in a slightly different way, and it is this different emphasis of connotation or suggestion that we wish to achieve. The filmic analogy here is clear. The same piece of action, the same things either changing or at rest, can be photographed in many different ways. All of the different ways of photographing the same thing are like so many synonymous words for saying the same thing. We have already seen that the basic cuttable unit is determined by a single setting of the camera for photographing whatever is to be photographed. This unit is like the word. It is, therefore, proper

[14] Cf. Spottiswoode, *op. cit.*, pp. 118–121.

that synonyms should be determined by differences in the manipulation of the camera. The following is merely an exemplary
list of such differences: [15] (1) the camera can either be at rest
or in motion; (2) if at rest, it can be focused at various angles
and from various distances, that is, the shot may be from above
or below, it can be close-up or at middle range or a long distance
shot; (3) if in motion, either (a) the camera is rotated on its own
axis, panoramically from left to right or right to left, or by
tilting from up to down, or down to up; or (b) it is moved
toward or away from the things being photographed and the
line of this motion may be at any angle and may achieve any
distance within the limits of visibility; (4) for any of these different shots, the illumination may be dull, moderate or intense
and, by different lenses, the focus may be softened or sharp-
ened; (5) in some cases, the eye of the camera may be masked
in such a way as to give the picture something other than the
ordinary rectangular frame; (6) the speed of the camera may
be slow or fast.[15a] Each of these different ways of photographing the same thing is like a different way of saying the same
thing. In the case of words, there is the distinction between
the ordinary words of common usage, strange or newly coined
words, ornamental words, and words that are the condensations
of metaphors.[16] In the camera's setting there are similar distinctions. Thus, the use of the camera at middle range at the customary visual angle is like an ordinary word, the use of the
camera at an unusual distance or from an unusual angle is like a
strange word, the masking of the camera's eye is like a condensed
metaphor, and so on. Furthermore, a word may be chosen
because it is shorter or longer; or the same root may be used in
a lengthened or contracted form. So we have the distinction
between the quick flash which is an extremely short series of
frames, just long enough to cut, and series of greater length.

It may be suggested at this point that there are other variables
which we have ignored, such as the pantomime of the actors, the
construction of the interior sets or the selection of the exterior

[15] For a more detailed enumeration, as well as a description, of such devices,
see Spottiswoode, *op. cit.*, pp. 47–49, 131–140, 146–153. Cf. Arnheim, *op. cit.*,
pp. 47–94, 115–136.
[15a] Changes in camera-speed, i.e., slow motion and fast motion, make the
temporal close-up possible. Vd. Pudovkin, *op. cit.*, pp. 146–154.
[16] *Poetics,* 21.

backgrounds, and so forth. These, too, it may be offered, are like different ways of saying the same thing. It will be seen at once, however, that these factors determine the plastic properties of the individual frame as a photograph.[17] We are here concerned with the plastic arrangement of all the things being photographed, including the posture and facial expressions of the actors. Two positions are possible: (1) these variables, like the camera variables, increase the number of synonymous units in the pictorial medium; or (2) the plastic variables are like the musical variables in language. We may choose one word rather than another because of its tone or its quantity, particularly in writing verse. The way we arrange the things to be photographed gives us the plastic dimension of the pictorial medium, as the sound of words gives us the musical dimension of the linguistic medium. Style must, of course, take both sorts of factors into account. In writing, we not only choose words for their significance but for their music; so in cinematic narration, we must consider both the camera and the plastic variables. In fact, they are inseparable except analytically.

Vocabulary is only one of the two sources of difference in linguistic style. The other is syntax, the way in which words are grouped, combined and separated. Furthermore, words can be used in place of phrases, or conversely. Sentences can be made longer or shorter, simpler or more complex, and the order of their parts can be direct or inverted. Upon these syntactical differences depend the tempo and the rhythm of the style. Here the analogy between music and language is great. There is phrasing in music. Tones have either shorter or longer duration. There are differences in rhythm and tempo. In the pictorial medium, the analogy is found in the way in which scenes are composed of shorter or longer shots, in the substitution of a single shot for a whole scene or conversely, in the way in which sequences are composed of scenes or shots or both, in the length or brevity of the sequences, and so forth. Thus, to return to the example of Pudovkin, the stylistic effect would have been very different if each of the pieces in the scene of an automobile accident had been equally long, or if they had been arranged in a different order. I am ignoring here an absurd or senseless

---

[17] For an analysis of the plastic properties of the individual frame, see Nicoll, *op. cit.*, pp. 39–40; Spottiswoode, *op. cit.*, pp. 141–157.

order, such as beginning with the shot of the motor car, cutting into the middle of it with the legs of the man run over, then the man crossing the street, and finally the face of the chauffeur. This would be like a nonsensical scrambling of words. If a phrase or a sentence is a significant unit, then such word-scramblings are not phrases or sentences. Similarly, it is not any arrangement of pieces that can constitute the significant unity of a scene or of a sequence. But there are, nevertheless, many different arrangements which can be significant. The choice among these is a stylistic matter, as the choice of camera setting is. Depending upon such choice, there will be a difference in the tempo and rhythm of the pictorial materials of the film.[18] Furthermore, just as the choice among synonyms is for the purpose of saying the same thing in a different way, so differences in phrasing and sentence structure accomplish the same effect but with different emphasis, suggestion or connotation. From the point of view of the narrative content, the different possible ways of arranging the shots, i.e., the unit series, in scenes or sequences similarly constitute ways of saying the same thing but achieving different effects. Finally, as in language there can be parentheses and words or phrases which echo earlier passages, so in filmic construction an explanatory or contrasting piece can be cut into a sequence, or a piece from an earlier scene can be cut-back to by including it as a part of a later sequence. There are in addition such devices as the temporal close-up, double exposure, the superimposition of one series of frames upon another, the piecing together of different strips of film, which are syntactical procedures achieving effects analogous to those obtained by unusual combinations of words.

A number of points follow from this technical consideration of the pictorial medium. In the first place, we saw earlier that the distinction between prose and verse is only one of the basic differences in linguistic style. There is also a distinction between prosaic and poetical writing which turns upon gradations of excellence in the handling of language. While there is no clear analogy in the pictorial medium to the distinction between prose and verse,[19] there are criteria of excellence which distinguish the

[18] Cf. Spottiswoode, *op. cit.*, pp. 207–223 ; Nicoll, *op. cit.*, pp. 112–119.
[19] Professor Nicoll thinks there is. "The short shots correspond to the numerically short syllables, the long shots to the syllables numerically long" (*op.*

gradations of cinematographic style. These criteria are analogous to the standards of good and bad writing. We shall return to this point later in a discussion of the principles of criticism.

In the second place, the way in which a film is put together out of its pieces, scenes and sequences explains what is meant by filmic form, filmic space and time. A produced drama exists for its audience perceptually. A novel exists for its readers both perceptually and imaginatively, since what is perceived in the reading are merely symbols, the significance of which involves the imagination. This difference between the produced play and the novel is, as we have seen, related to a basic difference between the time and space conditions of these two kinds of narrative. The epic writer can control the imaginative time and space of his narrative as the dramatist cannot. He can move freely within its dimensions, lengthening and shortening the time, ignoring distance, transcending the order of past, present and future, achieving simultaneities that are not physically possible. The film-director has the same freedom, even though the projected film exists for its audience perceptually. The perceptual dimensions of a motion picture are like the imaginative dimensions of a novel. Because of the way in which the parts of a film can be made, cut and composed, both in the process of shooting and in the process of *montage*, the film can be given a continuity like that of a novel, which lengthens and shortens time, makes distant things seem spatially contiguous and contemporaneous, and revives the past as easily as it projects the future. It is not remarkable that the imagination can be made to transcend the limitations of actual space and time, but the remarkable thing about the film is that it can make a perceptual experience like an imaginative one. This is what is meant by saying that the spectator of the film is like an ideal observer of the action narrated.[20] And it is the director who, in controlling

cit., p. 116). But while this may be thought to establish an analogy between rhythm in the pictorial medium and cadence in language, it does not enable anyone to discriminate among filmic rhythms the regular measures of prosody and the irregular cadences of prose.

[20] This explains why Pudovkin speaks of *montage* as "an instrument of impression." It is not "merely a method of the junction of separate scenes or pieces, but a method that controls the 'psychological guidance' of the spectator" (*op. cit.*, p. 47).

the shooting and the cutting, creates these ideal conditions of observation.

In the third place, this analysis of cinematographic technique indicates the relation of the scenarist to the director [173a]. A scenario is a verbal plan of the film. It is not an imitation in language of the action which the completed film imitates. Starting with the outline of plot and character, the scenarist must transform this outline into a filmic continuity by reducing it to its scenes and sequences. To do this, the scenarist must think pictorially and not linguistically because he is preparing a narrative to be received perceptually rather than to exist imaginatively [174]. He must determine the narrative content of each scene by writing directions for the actors, the set-constructors, the costumers, the manipulation of the camera and the lights, but more than all this he must analyze the scene into its ultimate pieces, the basic series of frames taken by a single stance of the camera and which are cuttable and transposable. As Pudovkin expresses it, this part of the work is like differentiation in calculus. Its necessary correlative is integration. The latter is achieved in the process of *montage*, in the cutting and piecing room. This means that a good scenario is usually a rough draft of the completed film. The work of the scenarist is to expand a simple narrative outline into a detailed shooting script. This gives the director, before the shooting begins, a notion of the ultimate parts of the film. It also indicates a possible ordering of these parts into a complete continuity. The scenario is good to the extent that its analysis of the whole into its atomic parts is adequate and to the extent that it has properly ordered these parts. A perfect scenario would leave the director no freedom either in the shooting or the cutting, since nothing could be added or subtracted from its directions for making the various parts and putting them together. The director would merely have to execute these orders in his control of all the subordinate artists. But a perfect scenario rarely, if ever, exists. A good shooting script usually forecasts but does not completely prescribe the work of the director. In the course of shooting, the analysis of the story into its filmic parts continues; and in the course of cutting, the synthesis of the parts into a filmic continuity is completed. The relation between the shooting and the cutting is thus clear. The former is the analytical side of the work. During this stage, the film-maker is progressively reducing the whole to its elementary constituents. The latter is the synthetic or constructive side of the work. During this stage, the film-maker is organizing the whole out of its constituents. Since the shooting precedes the cutting in time, the former must anticipate the latter. The cutting cannot be well done unless all of the pieces are provided out of which scenes and sequences can be built. Usually more pieces than are ultimately used must be made. The business of cutting involves selection and elimination as well as joining and transposing. Sometimes an insight which occurs during the cutting process requires a return to the business of shooting.

The technique of making a film is thus, in one sense, more complicated than the work of writing a novel. The novelist seldom creates the words he uses. There is nothing closely analogous to the related phases of shooting and cutting. The novelist may start from a rough outline of plot and character, progressively sketch in the details and write drafts of various parts until he is able finally to compose the whole. The work of the dramatist is similar. But in neither case is there a sharp separation both in time and work of the making of the atomic parts and the organization of them into a whole. There is a similarity, however, in all of these arts between the vision of the completed work and the technical steps involved in realizing the vision. The novelist must at all stages of his work be guided by his conception of the whole, even though that conception necessarily changes somewhat as the work proceeds because unforeseen details alter the original plan. The film-director must, from the beginning, have a conception of the continuity of the projected film. However much this conception is altered during the shooting and cutting, it is always the guiding insight which must control the analytical and constructive processes. It is for this reason that the director and the scenarist must either be one man or have a sympathetic understanding of each other's work. If they are two, they must share a vision of the completed film. If the director is not his own editor, it is furthermore necessary for the work of *montage* to be controlled by the insight of the scenarist and the director. That the director should either be the scenarist or be closely allied to him is clear, but it is even clearer that the director should himself do the cutting or control it. A director who is neither scenarist nor editor is little more than a supervisor of the various technicians involved in the process of shooting.

Finally, the rules of *montage* can be formulated. They follow from the simple point that the continuity of the film must make its spectator an ideal observer of the action. Each of the ultimate pieces out of which the finished film is composed is a way of seeing the action. The lens of the camera is the eye of the spectator. According to the various camera conditions, the spectator sees each of the phases of the action from a certain angle, a certain distance, himself at rest or in motion, and with a certain degree of attention to detail. In other words, the technique of the shooting process concentrates the attention of the spectator in a special way upon the parts of the action. Each cuttable piece of film is a unit of observation. The cutting and joining, then, is nothing more than a connection of these units in such a way as to make the spectator a continuous observer of the action. The psychological principle involved is the natural shifting of attention during ordinary observation and thought. In looking at something, our eyes move from one part of the situation to another, focus more sharply on some detail or more vaguely take in the whole. As we look, our attention may shift from the visible situation to the memory of a past experience or to the imagination of a possible one, related in some way to what is now being seen. There is no distinction in the making of the film between what, in projection, is something seen and what is something remembered or imagined. A memory or an imagination is also a unit of observation for the spectator. Only the locale of the action will make the distinction for him between what is present in the narrative time and what refers to past or future. The actual tense of each unit is present. The process of *montage* must so put the unit pieces together that their sequence constitutes a significant shifting of attention both in the perceptual field and in the field of related memories and imaginations. There is, of course, no one ordering of the pieces which is the only right way. The natural shifting of attention is controlled by the degree of interest, the relevant past experience, and the state of the emotions. We look more intently and in greater detail at the things in which we are interested. We observe with greater precision what our past experience has prepared us for. If we are excited, our attention shifts more rapidly from one thing to another ; and according to the state of our emotions, what we observe evokes different memories and imaginations. Through the process of cutting and joining, the director is thus able to make the spectator of the projected film an observer of one sort or another. The position of each piece in a sequence and the order of sequences is determined by the director's wish to control attention in a certain way. Each shot must contain within itself an impulse toward the transference of attention to the next. The series of shots composing a single scene makes the spectator an observer who has first looked at this, then at that, then remembered or imagined something, returning again to the field of perception. According as the shifts are rapid and each piece is longer or shorter, the spectator is a more or less excited observer. According to the content of what he remembers or imagines, his emotions are determined. According to the details his attention is concentrated upon through repetition of the same unit, the high points of the narrative are accented and he becomes both an expectant and an analytical observer, prepared for what is to follow as well as isolating the more important aspects of what has already happened.

The same rules hold for the construction of a sequence out of separate scenes and shots, as well as for the construction of a single scene out of the unit pieces. There is only this difference. In the latter case, the spectator is an ideal observer of a single situation. In the former, the spectator traverses space and time. The shifts of attention are, therefore, more radical. In the ordinary process of natural observation, the observer must be attending to something during all the intervals of space and time ; but in filmic observation, all of the irrelevant content of these intervals can be eliminated. Transgressing the limitations of space and time, the attention is made to shift from a scene at one place and time to a scene at another, with or without intervening perceptions, memories or imaginations. The ordering of the scenes into sequences, and the ordering of these sequences into even more inclusive sequences, determines these shifts of attention and, through doing so in various ways and at various speeds, makes the spectator a more or less excited observer, endows him with the determinations of emotion and interest, develops his expectancy and alters the accent of his concentration. A simple example of constructive *montage* is Griffith's great invention of the rapid alternation of parallel sequences showing the progressive preparation of a man for the electric chair and the progressive effort of his wife to obtain a pardon from the governor. The spectator is made an observer whose attention shifts more and more rapidly from an action going on at one series of places to a related action going on at another series of places. He is, therefore, more and more excited. The particular shots in the prison scenes concentrate his attention upon details which an observer moved by pity and fear would see. The memories which are cut into these sequences accentuate these emotions sympathetically; and so on. This continuity could not have been made if the particular pieces had not been shot in specific ways determined by a definite foresight of how they were to be used. But it is not made in the process of shooting. It is the creation of *montage*.

The process of *montage* has three phases. A scene must be created by the ordering of its atomic pieces. A sequence must be created by the ordering of scenes, or shots, or scenes and separate shots. The continuity of the whole must be created by the ordering of all the sequences. The film as a work of art is thus made by the cutting and joining of all its constituent pieces in more or less comprehensive series. Two errors of emphasis must be avoided. On the one hand, the importance of the cutting process may be over-emphasized. It is obvious from this analysis of the cinematographic technique that the work of cutting must be definitely anticipated in the shooting; otherwise, the cutter has inadequate materials to operate upon. On the other hand, the importance of *montage* may be under-emphasized. The cutting process cannot, of course, be avoided since the time order in which the various pieces of film are shot has no relation to the narrative order of the film's final continuity. But the cutting may be done in a perfunctory manner, consisting in nothing more than an organization of the pieces according to the plan of the original scenario. This would neglect the great opportunities for filmic construction which the cutting process makes possible. A mastery of the technique of the pictorial medium of narration requires that a proper correlation be achieved between the shooting and the cutting and that the possibilities of each process be temperately exploited for the sake of the whole. Either over-emphasis or under-emphasis upon the shooting or the cutting will destroy the balance of factors which enables pictures to tell a story clearly and effectively. The shooting process must make pieces of film which contain the entire narrative potentially — more, perhaps, but never less. *Montage* must select from these potentialities and organize them coherently for projection, which is their actualization. The relation between the dramatic script and the produced play is the analogue of the relation between the pieces of film made in the shooting and the final continuity effected by the cutting. The only difference is that the theatrical spectacle, for which the script has determinate potentialities, is not essential to the drama as a work of art, whereas the projectible filmic continuity is the essence of the completed work in the pictorial medium.

This completes our discussion of one aspect of film technique, the aspect concerned entirely with the pictures. If the motion picture were a work in this medium alone, our task would be largely done. But the medium of the motion picture includes words and sounds, and the manner of cinematic narration employs words for dialogue and pictures and sounds for description. I shall ignore the silent film in which words were used both for dialogue and description. The phonographic film requires us, therefore, to complete our task of analysis by discussing the technique of combining the pictorial parts with words and other sounds.

First, the relation of pictures and words. Among the writers on this subject, two extreme points of view have been expressed. On the one hand, the position is taken that the pictures should predominate and that the spoken dialogue should be reduced to a minimum ; on the other, it is held that the pictures should no more than provide the background or context for the dialogue. These extreme positions result from viewing the motion picture either as predominantly epic or predominantly dramatic in its manner of narration. Of the two, the second is less tenable than the first. Cinematic narration is nearer to the epic than the dramatic manner. The obvious solution of the dilemma is found in the principle which governs the novelist's use of dialogue and description. He uses each for that part of the total narrative in which it is most effective. A novel achieves dramatic intensity by the use of dialogue; it achieves epic scope through descriptive narration. In the case of motion pictures the principle is the same. Pictures should be used to do what pictures can do best, and words for what words can do best.[21] No simple rule of the proportion of these two parts can be formulated. The proportion must be determined by the nature of the individual story which, because of its plot structure and the magnitude of the action being imitated, may either be more like an epic or a drama. It must also be determined differently in the several parts of the same story : now the one and now the other may predominate, pictures as the narrative moves rapidly from incident to incident, dialogue as it reaches a situation of great dramatic intensity. One thing is clear. The cinematic narrative must never be capable of expression through the medium of words alone. The pictures would then become a dispensable accessory as the stage spectacle is for the well written drama. This explains the difficulty of making cinematic versions of Shakespeare. Whether good cinematic adaptations of Shakespeare can be made is not the question. They cannot be made if all or most of the dialogue is preserved, or if the pictorial medium is employed to do what Shakespeare's words do better.

The only other problem involved in the relation of pictures and words is that of synchronization.[22] During the years of experimentation with sound, it was natural for the aim to be perfect synchronization of the audible speech with the vision of the movements of speech. Synchronization is still desirable whenever the speech is heard at the same time that the speaker's face is seen. But it has been learned that the simultaneity of the heard speech and the seen speaker is not always desirable. The hearer of the speech may be witnessed by the spectator of the film

[21] Cf. Arnheim, *op. cit.*, pp. 211–214 ; 227–234. "The verbal part alone of a sound film is quite meaningless and is, indeed, without artistic value. Sound film — at any rate real sound film — is not a verbal masterpiece supplemented by pictures, but a homogeneous creation of word and picture which cannot be split up into parts that have any meaning separately" (p. 213). Also vd. Nicoll, *op. cit.*, p. 129 ff. ; Seldes, *op. cit.*, pp. 139–147.

[22] We shall not discuss the art of dialogue writing because it is not part of the director's art. It is the technique of an auxiliary artist, as is the art of the actor, the costume-maker, the scene-painter, etc. The problem for the director is how to use the dialogue furnished him by his literary subordinate.

while he hears the speech of an unseen speaker. This dislocation of speech is another device by which the director can control
the attention of the spectator, combining the things which he
wishes him to observe at the same time through sight and hearing.
Furthermore, the development of this technique adapts the
spoken word to the cinematic medium, avoiding the necessity
of photographing dialogue as it occurs upon the stage. The
tempo of the early talking films was distorted by the elongation
of pieces in which conversation took place. The camera was
forced to remain too long in a single setting in order to obtain a
simultaneity that is more often better avoided. As a result,
the rhythmic alternation of units of attention of varying durations
could not be achieved. The dislocation of speech also makes
it possible for the heard words to convey memories and imaginations. The words are not synchronized with speech movements
but with other actions and, by means of this correlation of actions
with words heard by the spectator but not spoken by the actor,
thought is revealed. The introduction of sound thus extended
the director's power of exhibiting what is hidden from ordinary
observation. The spectator of the film is not only an ideal observer in the sense in which he transcends the limitations of space
and time ; he also transcends the limits of objectivity : he can see
what the actor is remembering or imagining ; he can hear what
he is thinking in an introspective soliloquy.[23]

Second, the relation of pictures to sounds other than words.
Such sounds are either musical or natural. The latter are usually
spoken of as "sound effects." The difference between sound
effects and music is that the former are an essential part of the
narration whereas the latter is an embellishment which can be
dispensed with, as the entire spectacle can be in the case of the
drama. The rule governing the use of sound is like the rule
governing the use of words in relation to pictures. Sound effects should be used *whenever* and *only when* they play a part
in the narrative that they can play better than either words or
pictures. Furthermore, the microphone must be used selectively
in the same way that the camera is. Not all the sounds which
are involved in the action are recorded, just as not all the visual
angles or parts of the action are photographed. The director

[23] Cf. Pudovkin, *op. cit.*, pp. 155–165 ; Arnheim, *op. cit.*, pp. 239–251 ; Spottiswoode, *op. cit.*, pp. 173–189 ; Seldes, *op. cit.*, pp. 150–152.

uses the microphone to determine what the spectator of the film shall hear and how he shall hear it, from what direction, at what distance and with what intensity. As the shifting focus of the camera may direct the attention of the spectator to what is being seen by one of the actors, so the microphone may direct his attention to what is being heard and the way in which it is heard by an actor. The reverse is also possible in both fields: the spectator may have his attention called to what one of the actors fails to see or hear. In either case, the sound effects are part of the total pattern of observation which the director creates [175]. They are units which must be worked into the continuity, just as the separate pieces of film are.[24] The sound variables of direction, distance and intensity enable the director to employ sound as an indication of unseen movement or as an accompaniment of seen movement. Things can be heard approaching or receding; their spatial location can be signified by the direction of sound. The crescendo and diminuendo of natural sounds offers still another potentiality for narration. Just as the speed of alternation of the pieces in a scene or of the scenes in a sequence determines the excited or lethargic character of attention, so the gradual increase or decrease in the volume and intensity of sound determines an increase or decrease in the clarity of attention upon whatever it is focused. This variation in attention can also be achieved by change in illumination, but not so effectively because the limits of visibility do not permit as great a range of intensities.

The music that is included may either be part of the action or an accompaniment of the action [176]. In the former case, it plays the same role as non-musical sounds and words, for which it can be substituted mimetically. In the latter case, it is an embellishment. The propriety of the music used as an embellishment depends primarily upon the correlation between the tempo and rhythm of the music and the tempo and rhythm of the pictorial sequences. Music used in this way is not being used programmatically but because of the fitness of its temporal structure. Like a certain use of sound effects, it may accentuate the rhythm of attention. But music may also be used because it imitates change of character and the course of the emotions. It thus becomes an integral part of the total narrative.

[24] As Nicoll points out, there is also linkage by sound; that is, sound effects may be used as transitional devices (*op. cit.*, p. 142 ff.).

This discussion can be summarized in terms of the correlation of the film with the sound track, i.e., the record of the audible words, sound effects and music.   Pudovkin states the basic insight as the principle of asynchronism and counterpoint.[25]   The process of cutting and joining must be applied to the sound track as much as to the film itself.   *Montage* enabled the film to escape from a simple-minded naturalism which restricted it to the inappropriate conventions of the stage.   *Montage* is similarly applicable to all of the elements of the sound track and similarly necessary in order to achieve all that can be done in the medium of phonocinematography.   The scenarist and the director must plan the separate units of sound, whether of speech or sound effects or music, as they plan the separate pieces of film.   These units must be cuttable as such and projectible.   The continuity of the sound track can then be composed from them, as the sequences of film are.   But the two continuities cannot be created separately.   They must be determined in relation to each other. The principle of asynchronism insists upon a degree of freedom in this relationship.   Both non-coincidence of sound and sight and correlation of sound and sight are possible, and one or the other must be used in the process of *montage* according to the effect desired.

The principle of counterpoint is based upon the analogy of musical composition.   The asynchronization of film and the sound track is like the harmonization of the different voices in polyphonic music.   Absolute synchronism is, in contrast, like unisonal music.   Just as in the polyphonic structure, the different voices are harmonized, one carrying the melodic line and others the accompaniment, the contrapuntal effect being achieved through the transition of the melodic line from one voice to another; so in the process of *montage*, the film and the sound track can be related in such a way that one of them carries the narrative theme forward at any given time while the other is a harmonized accompaniment, and the carrying of the narrative may shift contrapuntally from the film to the sound track and conversely.   The brilliance of this insight justifies Pudovkin in his enthusiastic view of the future possibilities of sound film.[26] But it has an even greater analytical virtue.   It explains why the

[25] *Op. cit.*, pp. 155–174. Cf. Arnheim, *op. cit.*, pp. 251–269.
[26] *Op. cit.*, pp. 173–174.

multiple media in which the motion picture is made do not destroy its unity. Pictures, words, sounds and music can be organized into a single narrative continuity by the process of *montage* which not only selects and arranges the materials provided in each of the media but, at every point, *either* gives to one or another the narrative dominance and harmoniously subordinates all the rest, *or* by synchronization, carries the narrative forward in several media at the same time. The effect of the latter is like the introduction of unisonal passages in polyphonic music. It is difficult to say which of various media is more important, whether for instance the narrative is for the most part carried by the pictures or the words. It can, however, be said that just as the description in a novel provides the context for the dialogue, so in cinematic narration the pictorial sequences usually constitute the basic continuity into which all the other elements are worked. This does not prevent the narrative from passing at various points into the verbal dialogue or into the sound effects.

This leads us, finally, to a consideration of the elements of plot, character and thought which are common to all forms of fiction, since these elements are determined by a common object of imitation. Of these, plot is primary. It is the imitation of action.[27] Character and thought are imitated only to the extent that they are conditions, correlatives or consequences of action [177]. By character is meant the determinate habits of choice of any person involved in the action: the moral virtues.[28] By thought is meant the intellectual or emotional processes which precede action that is deliberative or impulsive, which accompany action of any sort, or which occur in the aftermath as reflection upon actions done.[29] I shall not stop here to discuss modern "psychological" narratives, plays or novels, which attempt to imitate character or thought primarily, and therefore subordinate the plot. We are here concerned with the problems of technique and not the principles of criticism. Only in the latter connection is it necessary to question whether the psychological narrative violates the proper object of fictional imitation. It may be argued then that there are two species of novels: those which imitate action and those which imitate thought and character.

[27] *Poetics*, 6, 1449[b]36. [28] *Poetics*, 6, 1450[b]9.
[29] *Poetics*, 6, 1450[b]4–8; 19, 1456[a]33–1456[b]8.

Our problem here is to analyze the technique of treating plot, character and thought in the cinematic media and manner.

With respect to plot structure enough has already been said about the magnitude of the action, the multiplicity of incidents, and so forth, which are appropriate in cinematic imitation. The technique of the director or scenarist must include an ability either to create a plot of the right structure and dimensions, or to adapt other types of fiction for the cinema. The most important thing here is to know how to combine the epic scope with a dramatic development of plot, the union of which is made possible because the cinema unites words and spectacle in a way that is not possible upon the stage. The director who has a thorough grasp of the technique of working in the compound media of the motion picture could not possibly make the error of trying to photograph a stage play, on the one hand; or of failing to realize that a motion picture has greater potentialities for dramatic concentration than a novel, on the other. In all arts the basic technique is the skill of the artist with respect to the elements of his medium. If he has an intelligent mastery of these, it is unlikely that he will fail in the manner in which he imitates the proper object of his art, unlikely but not impossible, as the history of the arts makes clear.

With respect to the treatment of character and thought, the technique of the cinema is much more like that of the produced play than that of the novel. Aristotle, considering Greek dramatic and epic poetry, insisted upon the primacy of plot because action could be imitated directly, while character and thought could be imitated only *through* action, including speech, and therefore indirectly. Character and thought must somehow be revealed. They must be made known through the ways in which they naturally externalize themselves. In dramatic writing, character is best exhibited through actions other than speech and thought through speech, although the reverse is possible in both cases. The addition of the theatrical spectacle increases the efficacy of action to reveal both character and thought. But in any case, only one mode of expression should be employed. Speech should not be used to reveal any aspect of thought or character that is exhibited by the dramatic incidents, that is, in the non-verbal actions of the *dramatis personae*, for as Aristotle asks, "what were the business of the speaker, if the thought were revealed quite apart from what he says?"[30]   In epic writing, the author has a choice which Aristotle did not consider. He can, on the one hand, reveal both character and thought in the dialogue or by means of the descriptively narrated incidents of the plot. This is the manner of the best Greek epics. They have the dramatic type of objectivity. But the novelist can, on the other hand, use words to characterize directly. He can describe the characters of his persons quite apart from the incidents of the plot. He can report their intellectual and emotional processes directly. The direct revelation of character and thought is possible in epic writing because words are used in two ways: in dialogue and description. The modern novel is a development of this possibility. To speak of it as subjective or psychological is merely to indicate that it does not have dramatic objectivity. Plot does not have primacy because character and thought are imitated as directly as action and independently of its incidents.

We have already seen that the medium and manner of the cinema permit the director to exploit the private realm of introspection, in the sense that pictures and dislocated speech can be used to indicate psychological processes, mainly memory and imagination. But closer examination of these devices shows that the director is working within the limitations of the dramatist. The pictures are pictures of action. The words are used in the direct discourse of speech. Unlike the novelist, the film-director and the dramatist cannot use words to describe character. It may be said that the director can *characterize* by his choice of the actor to play the part, the costuming, the make-up of the actor, and so forth, but these means are the same ones which the stage-producer employs in creating a spectacle to emphasize the intentions of the dramatist. In short, whether or not there can be two kinds of novels, the objective and the subjective, it is clear that the manner of dramatic imitation requires an indirect revelation of character and thought by means of dialogue and incidents. Because the film uses pictures to describe and words only for dialogue, cinematic imitation has the same limitations. It must have dramatic objectivity. The film-director, like the dramatist, must indicate character and thought either through incident or speech, in dialogue or soliloquy, choosing the more

[30] *Poetics*, 19, 1456b7-8.

effective means at any point and avoiding duplication. A paradox remains. The cinema does have some power to explore the introspective realm which the drama lacks, even with the aid of spectacle. Pictures can be used to show what a person is thinking and, to a lesser extent, feeling. Words in direct discourse can be used to express an inner soliloquy or the memory of a conversation. The paradox is that the cinema, moving in the psychological dimension, does so by dramatic rather than epic means.

Once again the double affinity of the cinema with the drama and the novel is shown. On the one hand, in plot structure the cinema is more like the novel than the play. On the other hand, in its revelation of character and thought the cinema operates, *for the most part*, within the narrower restrictions of dramatic narration, because it uses words exclusively in dialogue. In his treatment of plot, character and thought, the director must possess, therefore, the technical accomplishments of the novelist and the dramatist.

This completes our analysis of the technique of motion-picture production. We have examined it with respect to all the elements of a motion picture: plot, character, thought, pictures, words, sound effects and music. Of these, only music is an accessory, a dispensable embellishment. The analytical method of this discussion may give the false impression that because there are these six separable elements, the director must possess an equal number of separate techniques. The technique of motion-picture production is one, just as the motion picture produced is one. The separations we have made are entirely analytical. The technique of the director is the art of telling a story in the combined media of pictures, words and sounds and in a manner that is peculiar to the union of these media. The history of the motion picture records the interesting fact that its pioneers did not recognize that cinematography was an art of story-telling. But from the day that the cinema was acknowledged to be a kind of fiction, its technique grew organically with every new mechanical contrivance or perfection, as well as with the discovery and development of the tricks of shooting and cutting by such original masters as Griffith, Chaplin, Murnau, Pabst, Pudovkin and René Clair.

CHAPTER FIFTEEN

Criticism and Taste

Two general questions remain for discussion : (1) what is a *good* motion picture ? and (2) what is a *likable* motion picture ? The first states the problem of criticism ; the second the problem of taste. A critical judgment differs from an expression of taste in that it considers a work of art in terms of its nature and technique ; it says whether the work is well done. The judgment of taste says merely that we do or do not like the work, that we do or do not prefer it to some other. It refers the work to our capacity for enjoyment. Criticism is evaluative in terms of standards of technical accomplishment. Taste is appreciative in terms of the quantity of aesthetic pleasure. The two judgments are capable of being made independently, yet they are obviously related [177a]. What we mean by good taste is taste critically culti-vated. A person has good taste if he gets pleasure in proportion to the objective goodness of the work. The discussion of taste properly follows, therefore, an analysis of the principles of criticism. In the case of a popular art, such as the motion picture, there is the problem of popular taste, which may or may not be the same as good taste. To the extent that these two are not the same, the problem of the relation of an art to considerations of taste is independent of aesthetic criticism.

The principles of criticism are, however, not independent of the preceding analysis of the specific nature and technique of the motion picture. Our prior discussion has, for the most part, been analytical rather than evaluative, but there have been unavoidable anticipations of the critical problem, indications that the analysis inevitably leads to the discrimination of good from bad workmanship. Thus, in the discussion of pictorial technique, the elements of the medium were isolated in such a way that it is now possible for us to distinguish good from bad style. Similarly, in the discussion of cinematic narration, what is proper in the handling of plot, character and thought was suggested. The task now is to make such indications and suggestions explicit in an effort to formulate systematically the canons of criticism applicable to motion pictures.

One general insight explains the implications which the prior analysis has for criticism, the insight that an artist should not try to do more than he can with the elements of his medium, and should not be willing to do less. This is a critical insight. It is the most general principle of technical criticism. It marks the goal of workmanship in any field of art. And it explains why it is necessary to understand the specific nature and technique of a particular art in order to formulate critical standards specifically applicable to it. The rules of an art express the mature artist's discipline and are prescriptive for the novice, forming his habits. These rules can become norms and it is through this transformation of requirements into standards that we pass from technique to criticism.

We are first concerned with the type of criticism which we have called technical, to distinguish it from (1) extrinsic or political criticism, and (2) the sort of intrinsic moral criticism which is the other part of aesthetic criticism.[1] Here as before we are considering the work of the primary artist, the director, and perhaps also the work of one of his subordinates, the scenarist, with whom he must be closely united. If they are not the same person, it is the motion picture as their collaborative work which is to be criticized. To the extent that the director should control the contributions of all the other auxiliary artists, their work is indirectly criticized through holding him responsible for it.

The critical problem is divisible into two subordinate questions of style. "Style" is probably the best word to name all of the technical accomplishments of an artist. The work of any artist has style, but the style is not always good. When we say that work lacks style, we do so because we have identified style

[1] Vd. Chapter 12 *supra*.

and good style. I shall make this distinction between two separable questions of style in terms of the arts of fiction. Analogous distinctions can probably be made for arts having other objects of imitation. And I shall consider, first, the literary arts of fiction, which imitate action in the medium of language, because in this field the distinction is generally recognized between (1) narrative style and (2) linguistic style. The poet as a story-teller is both a maker *of* plots and a maker *in* language. If there is any priority of the former to the latter sense in which he is a maker, it is because the object of imitation is prior to the medium. In any case, relative to these two respects in which he is a maker, he may be more or less technically accomplished. Whether these two styles are independent, whether the poet who has great narrative gifts may nevertheless write badly, is a difficult question. But the criteria of good style are, at least, analytically separable into these two dimensions. The elements of narrative style are those elements of *any art* of fiction determined by the object of imitation: plot, character, thought. The elements of linguistic style are those elements of the *literary* arts of fiction determined by the medium of imitation: the elements of language. All of these elements are referred to by Aristotle's single word "diction." Diction is common to all literature. The elements of spectacle and song are peculiar to dramatic literature, not as literature but as produced theatrically. It may be asked whether there is any dimension of style determined by the manner of imitation. The answer is that the manner of imitation is involved in both narrative and linguistic style. The difference between the dramatic and the epic manner is not only a difference in the use of language but a difference in the treatment of plot and character.

If there is anyone for whom this analytical separation of narrative and linguistic style is not clear, he can be aided by the following consideration. Let us suppose a bilingual writer, a writer who has equal mastery of English and French. Such a writer must first decide whether he is going to write a novel or a play, after which he can conceive his narrative in terms of plot, character and thought, starting with a rough sketch of these elements and gradually increasing the detail. His conception may be relatively complete before he starts writing, and to this extent his narrative style is determined. But he cannot start

writing without choosing his language. It is this choice which
determines the appropriate problems of linguistic style, just as
his decision to write a novel or a play previously determined the
appropriate problems of narrative style. To whatever extent
the choice of language and the actual writing alters the precon-
ceived narrative, the two dimensions of style are not independent.
It may even be that the preconception of the narrative influences
to some extent his choice of the language in which to write. It
is not being maintained that these two sorts of style are absolutely
independent, but only that they are actually somewhat independent, as well as analytically separable.

The distinction made in terms of the literary arts of fiction
holds perfectly for the motion picture as a non-literary member
of this group of arts. The director is subject to criticism on two
separate counts of style. Like any other worker in the field
of fiction, he has a narrative style, good or bad. He must handle
plot, character and thought in the cinematic manner. But he is
not only a maker *of* plots, but a maker *in* the complex medium of
pictures, words and sounds. Treating this manifold medium as
integrated, we shall speak of filmic style as the analogue of linguistic style. Film is here understood as including both the
photographic record and the sound track. The analysis of
filmic style is more complicated than that of linguistic style because of the complexity of the medium. We must distinguish
pictorial style from the style of the sound track; each has its
elements and its *montage*. Furthermore, filmic style involves
the problem of *total montage*, the organization of the different
components of the complex medium into the single continuity
which is the motion picture. There is nothing analogous to this
complexity in linguistic style. We do not, for instance, consider the dramatist's linguistic style and the producer's theatrical
style as integrated parts of the same effort.

It is necessary to repeat once more the warning already given,
that all of these separations are analytical only. The work of
art is a unity of all its constituent elements, both those determined
by the object of imitation and those determined by the medium.
The writer, who is not our supposititious master of different
tongues, does not actually separate his making of plot and his
making in language. The director must think of the problems
of story-telling and the problems of film-making at the same

time. The minimum condition of good style in all the arts of fiction is, therefore, to make good narrative sense, and this means a proper handling *together* of all of the elements which now, for the purposes of analysis, we shall separate. It is only the critic who is an analyst and therefore makes such separations. The artist is a creator, not an analyst. Nor is the audience, excepting the critic, analytical. The judgment of taste is an appreciation of the work of art as a whole because it is as a whole that it is enjoyed. But a critic must pay attention to the parts and the elements. It is for this reason that an over-developed critical faculty often hampers an artist or spoils enjoyment.

1. We shall deal first with the standards of good narrative style. For the most part, these are the same for all of the arts of fiction. In briefly summarizing them, our aim, therefore, must be to emphasize those aspects which are peculiar to cinematic narration.

(1) *Primacy of plot.* To understand this principle, we must first distinguish between the theme of the plot and the developed plot. The theme of the plot is the matter of the story : the particular action being imitated [178]. Only two points are needed to determine the theme : a beginning and end, the beginning stated by the problem of the action and the choice, the end by the ultimate consequences of this choice. What lies between these two points is, as we shall see, the body of the story. The theme of a plot can be stated in a sentence or two. The fully developed plot cannot be stated except by the whole narrative. Thus, Aristotle states the theme of the *Odyssey* as follows : "A certain man is absent from home for many years ; he is jealously watched by Poseidon and left desolate. Meanwhile his home is in a wretched plight — suitors are wasting his substance and plotting against his son. At length tempest-tost, he himself arrives ; he makes certain persons acquainted with him ; he attacks the suitors with his own hand, and is himself preserved while he destroys them." [2] The theme of *Crime and Punishment* can be even more briefly stated : A man commits a crime and, after a period during which there is a growing suspicion of his guilt, is apprehended and punished. It is clear that many dif-

[2] *Poetics*, 17, 1455[b]18–22. Aristotle adds : "This is the essence of the plot ; the rest is episode."

ferent narratives may have the same theme. When it is said that there is only a small finite number of original plots, themes are meant. An enumeration of the themes of fiction could probably be made. It would be a classification of the particular types of action which fiction can imitate. The number of themes would be small because the number of moral problems is small and the variety of consequences following upon moral choices is limited. A story-teller's originality depends upon the way in which he develops the theme he has taken. When Aristotle says that the poet is a maker of plots, he does not mean that he is a maker of the themes of fiction, but of their development. The themes are not made. They are discovered or selected. The poet makes a plot by taking a theme and adding to it all the particulars of narration : the incidents and episodes of the action, the delineation of character, the expression of thought. The best illustration of this point can be found in the Greek tragedies, many of which have the same theme. The three Electra-Orestes plays reveal that the work of Aeschylus, Sophocles and Euripides as plot-makers consisted in the development of the same theme : a son and daughter facing the problem of knowing or suspecting that their mother, aided by her lover, murdered their father, choosing revenge and reaping the consequences of matricide. This is the theme of *Hamlet* also, and of countless other plays, notably in recent years O'Neill's *Mourning Becomes Electra*. These dramatic narratives differ in their treatment of the same theme : they all have differently developed plots.

This distinction between theme and development is important, negatively, in showing that the criticism of fiction should not be concerned with the theme. It is not a relevant point in criticism to say of a story that its plot is not original, if what is meant is its theme. Since an artist is a maker, originality is relevant to the criticism of his work, but the originality we must look for in fiction is in the plot-development. It should be noted in passing that ethical criticism is similarly misdirected if it judges a story in terms of its theme. On the positive side, this distinction is important as showing that although theme is separable from character and thought, as well as from the incidents of the action, the developed plot involves not only the addition of all the incidents, but also of character and thought. The incidents of the action cannot be detailed without revealing character and thought. Aristotle at one point makes the extreme statement that a tragedy is possible without character, but not without action.[3] This must be interpreted to mean that a plot cannot be developed without detailed incidents of action, but that the character of the agents or their thought need not be similarly detailed. Illustrations of such plot development can be found in most melodramatic narratives, in detective and mystery stories. The Russian film *Potemkin* is an extraordinary example of a well developed plot without character or thought or, at least, with a minimum development of these elements. The extremity of Aristotle's statement is, however, merely a way of insisting upon the primacy of plot. It should not be interpreted to mean that character and thought are not integrally related to the development of the plot through its constituent incidents.

That the plot is the primary element in narration depends upon the object of imitation. If a story were not the imitation of action in the political dimension, and of character and thought only as they are involved in such action, plot would not be primary.[4] As we have seen, action necessarily includes character and thought as its causes and effects. Character and thought are habits or intrinsic operations which express themselves in the extrinsic behavior. The primacy of plot means, therefore, that character and thought should be revealed by means of external action, and not directly and apart from action. But it may be objected that the primacy of plot depends not merely on the object of imitation, but also upon the manner of imitation; that it must be primary in the drama, but need not be so in the epic. We have previously considered the psychological novel as an exception, or better as a paradoxical species of fiction in which character and thought become the primary objects of imitation because the epic manner affords the writer direct means of describing the introspective realm. A psychological novel is possible without action, or with the incidents of action given in a minimum of detail. But whatever be the solution of the question whether such novels constitute a proper species of epic narration or whether they are violations of the art of fiction,[5] it is

[3] *Poetics*, 6, 1450ª24. [4] Vd. Note 176 *infra*.
[5] Vd. *Poetics*, 23, 1459ª17-20. Cf. Lubbock, *The Craft of Fiction*, New York, 1929 ; Forster, *Aspects of the Novel*, New York, 1927 ; Muir, *The Structure of the Novel*, New York, 1929 : p. 146 ff. For an analysis of the relation of

at least clear that the dramatic manner of narration makes the psychological play either impossible or undesirable. The critical problem in the case of motion pictures is thereby solved. The cinematic manner of narration is more like the dramatic in that it cannot, without great difficulty, reveal thought and character directly. It should do so by means of the incidents of action, including, of course, the speeches.[6] It follows, therefore, that the first criterion of good narrative style in motion pictures is the primacy of plot: it is an imitation of action through the incidents of action, and of character and thought subordinately by indirect means of revelation.

(2) *Unity of plot.* Since we are concerned with the motion picture, we shall henceforth ignore narratives, such as the psychological novel, in which plot is not primary. The unity of the plot depends upon the unity of the action. This can be understood negatively. A plot is not properly unified if it depends upon the unity of its hero or the unity of a problem or the unity of a period. In all of these cases, the plot development is bad because episodic. If its unity depends upon the singleness of its hero, any incidents are admitted into its structure so long as they are incidents in which the hero is an agent and whether or not they are causally related as the parts of a single action. Such narratives are like biographies, the unity of which is the life of a single person. The psychological novel may be like a biography, but the drama and the cinema should not be.[7] The same can be said for the other types of inappropriate unity, illustrated by stories in which a number of different individuals and actions are put together because they are parallel instances of the same human problem, such as intolerance or ingratitude, or by stories in which the only unity is that all the events and persons occur at a certain

plot and character in fiction, see Buchanan, *Poetry and Mathematics*, New York, 1929: pp. 69–73, 122–128, 132–133.

[6] Direct discourse is, for the novelist, an indirect way of revealing thought and character. He can describe them directly by indirect discourse. Many commentators on the film disagree with this judgment about the restriction of the cinema to dramatic surfaces. They think that the cinema has much greater power than the stage for psychological penetration. Vd. Nicoll, *op. cit.*, 174 ff.; Arnheim, *op. cit.*, p. 151 ff.

[7] This does not mean that the film cannot be used as a medium for biography. Recently it has been well used in this way. But biography and fiction in the medium of language must be guided by different principles and subject to different standards of judgment. Similarly in the case of the film.

time or at a certain place or somehow cross each other's paths in space and time.

Positively, unity of plot can be understood in terms of the way in which the parts of a single action are organized into a whole. Unity of plot involves a unity in time, but not a unity of time: the action need not occur at one time, but the parts of it must be ordered sequentially in time. The principle of this ordering defines the unity of plot. The plot is divisible in two ways. First, it can be divided into a beginning, a middle and an end. The beginning is constituted by the problem of the action, and by the choice among alternative courses of action which is made by the protagonist. The middle is constituted by the complications which follow upon this choice: the further choices which the protagonist makes because of the consequences of his first choice, and the consequences in turn of each of these choices. It is in this part that most of the incidents and episodes of the action occur, that character is gradually revealed in greater detail and thought is more fully expressed. The inner complications of the action become interwoven with extraneous events in the outer world, which can be summarized as the good or bad fortune attending the career of the protagonist. This is what Aristotle means by saying that "incidents extraneous to the action are frequently combined with a portion of the action proper to form the complication." [8] The progressive complication finally reaches a climax, a turning point in the story. After this point is the end, constituted by the dénouement, a catastrophe or a benign resolution according as the story is tragic, comic or melodramatic, and an aftermath. This division of the parts of a single action indicates that the unity of the plot depends upon causality in the ordering of the incidents — not all the incidents because the extraneous ones happen as if by chance or fortune, but those incidents which proceed from the character and thought of the protagonist. Furthermore, the unity is emphasized by the fact that the dénouement is the ultimate consequence of the original choice made with respect to the initial problem. It is this which binds the beginning, middle and end of a story together into a single whole.

The other division of the plot is into two parts: the complication and the unraveling, the former including everything from

[8] *Poetics*, 18, 1455ᵇ22–25.

the beginning to the turning point of the action, the latter being
what happens thereafter.   This division shows the unity in terms
of the crucial turning point, which must be the consequence of
what precedes and the cause of what follows.   The significance
of this second division will be seen later in the point about the
magnitude of the plot: it must be large enough to include a turning point that is intelligible in the light of what has gone before
and is illuminated by what follows.   The first division indicates
another necessary feature of the plot structure: the middle part
should always be the largest part.   A story cannot be well told
if too large a part of it is involved in getting the problem stated
and the first choice made.   The beginning is *too large* if it is
larger than the middle.   The same is true of the end.

(3)   *The probability of the plot.*   This point follows in part
from the rule that the incidents of the action must be causally
related.   A causal consequence is that which either happens
necessarily as the result of some prior happening or that which
happens for the most part.   The incidents are probable, therefore, if they occur as normally they would in terms of human
nature and the nature of the physical world.   In other words,
the sequence and conjunction of events which constitute the
unified action of the plot must be such that the story is a likely or
probable one.   The rule of probability thus applies not only to
the action of the protagonist, but to the portraiture of character
and the expression of thought.   Even if the character is inconsistent or the thought irrational, it must be consistently inconsistent and irrational.   "A person of a given character should speak
or act in a given way, by the rule of necessity or probability, just
as this event should follow that by necessary or probable sequence." [9]   The rule further applies even to the extraneous
events that enter into the complication.   Though they appear
to the protagonist to happen as if by chance and as signs of good
or bad fortune because they are not foreseen or ordained by him,
they must nevertheless be probable incidents.   It is the violation
of this rule of probability which makes episodic plot development
bad, and similarly plots in which character and thought are inconsistent.[10]

While it is generally recognized in criticism that a good story
must be a likely story, the rule of probability to be followed in

[9] *Poetics*, 15, 1454ª32–37.   [10] Vd. *Poetics*, 9, 1451ᵇ32–38 ; 15, 1454ª26–27.

good plot construction is misunderstood whenever it is supposed that the criteria of probability in a poem are the same as in science. Poetic truth is not logical truth. What Aristotle says of tragedy, that "the element of the wonderful is required," applies to all fiction. The good story-teller is always one like Homer, gifted in telling lies skilfully. "Accordingly, the poet should prefer probable impossibilities to improbable possibilities."[11] This indicates that the rule of probability is not the same in fiction as in science. For knowledge, the impossible can never be probable. The probability of a story does not depend on the nature of things alone as does the probability of knowledge. It depends upon the art of the story-teller. The rule of probability is, therefore, the requirement that he make his story *appear to be a likely one*, whether or not its separate elements, viewed from the standpoint of science, are impossible or absurd or slightly probable. The impossible and the absurd are intolerable in fiction only if the narrator fails to veil them with poetic charm, which is another way of saying that he fails to make them seem probable. "Once the irrational has been introduced and an air of likelihood has been imparted to it, we must accept it in spite of its absurdity."[12] Aristotle goes so far as to approve of Agathon's dictum that in story-telling even an improbable event can be made to appear probable because, as he says, "it is probable that many things should happen contrary to probability."[13]

The importance of this insight into the nature of probability in fiction cannot be overemphasized in the light of the tendency of current criticism to misunderstand the point. Much of the criticism of motion pictures uses the canon of probability as if the likelihood of a story depended upon its being life-like in the simple-minded sense of conforming to reality as it is.[14] There is probably no greater error which the artist or critic can make than this simple-minded realism or naturalism. If the rule of probability be interpreted as a requirement that art be realistic or naturalistic, it falsifies the nature of art as imitation involving both similitude and difference. Far from being better because

[11] *Poetics*, 24, 1460ª26–28. [12] *Poetics*, 24, 1460ª32–36.
[13] *Poetics*, 18, 1456ª24–25. Cf. 25, 1461ᵇ9–15.
[14] Cf. Dale, *How to Appreciate Motion Pictures*, New York, 1935 : "One of the most important things the motion picture can do is to show truthfully the consequences that come from making certain choices in life" (p. 96). See also pp. 206–208.

it is highly probable — in the sense of realistic — such a story is bad as a work of art. A highly fanciful tale, a tale that the realists would despise, is much better fiction if it satisfies the sole condition of being invested with poetic likelihood by narrative skill. In short, the principle of probability in artistic imitation, differing from the principle of probability in science, determines two extremes which are bad: improbable fantasy, on the one hand, and "scientific" realism, on the other. The story must be probable, but it must also be a story, and not a piece of faithful reporting. In other words, fiction is *like* history, but it is *not* history. The difference resides in the different conditions of probability that apply in each case. The *Odyssey* with all its impossible adventures on sea and land is a good story because of Homer's great gift in telling lies, a much better story as a work of art than an accurate historical narrative of just what actually did take place in the voyage of Odysseus from Troy to Ithaca. There is, of course, one further paradox involved. Even the historian or the realistic novelist at his worst extreme cannot avoid being an artist in fiction. He is always telling a story whether or not he is willing to acknowledge that the conditions of good story-telling are not the conditions of science. In a sense, realism and fantasy are impossible extremes. They are never really reached. There is no story which is totally devoid of probability, nor one which is not a work of the imagination. The limits, therefore, merely indicate that a good story combines in proper proportion the factors of the wonderful and the probable. The artist who tries to be realistic never succeeds, but in trying so hard to go in one direction, he may fail to achieve a good proportion of these factors.

It is evidence of the essential rightness of Pudovkin's understanding of the technique of the cinema that he always recognizes the pitfalls of naturalism.[15] The tendency toward simple-minded naturalism is more insidious in film-making than in writing, because of the superficially realistic character of photographs. It is this which makes *montage* crucially important, for it is by *montage* that naturalism can be most effectively avoided. But the basic principle of *montage* requires that film sequences be composed in a probable order, not the kind of probability which

[15] He is joined in this by other competent writers about the cinema : Seldes, Arnheim, Spottiswoode, Nicoll.

consists in fidelity to the way things actually appear, but the imaginative probability of the way in which things might appear to an ideal observer. We shall return to this point later in a discussion of filmic style. Here it is important only to note the way in which the rule of probability relates narrative and filmic style in the making of a motion picture. To be good, a motion picture, like any other work of fiction, must avoid the extremes of reportorial realism and the improbably fantastic. Criticism which fails to understand this principle is as bad as art which futilely seeks to reach either extreme.

(4) *The structure of the plot.* This locus of criticism has a number of subordinate topics. *First,* the simplicity or complexity of the plot. In one sense of complexity, the more complex plot is better; it not only contains a great number of incidents, both internal to the action and extraneous, but requires greater subtlety on the part of the narrator in ordering the incidents to bring about a progressive complication and a more striking climax. The aesthetic principle here applies to all arts and not only to fiction: the artist must achieve a unity, and his skill is greater according as there is a greater multiplicity of parts out of which he makes the whole. But in another sense of complexity, the less complex plot is sometimes better and sometimes worse. Here we are concerned with the problem of subordinate plots of the sort which occur in Shakespearean tragedy, or with the double thread of plot which issues in a double dénouement: prosperity or success for one person, and defeat or misfortune for another. The critical standard must be differently applied to works that seek tragic effects, on the one hand, or comic and melodramatic effects, on the other. Simplicity of plot heightens the tragic effect. It concentrates all attention upon one protagonist; it makes his ultimate fate the single consequence of the action. It is questionable, therefore, whether the subordinate and often parallel plots in Shakespearean tragedy are not blemishes on their plot structure, despite the position of certain modern critics that the tragedy is thereby enriched. But in comedy and melodrama in which a happy ending is appropriate, it is no less appropriate to have the villain defeated or end ignominiously. Here happiness of the ending is increased by the inclusion of misfortune for the antagonist along with prosperity for the protagonist. Aristotle's comment on the story which has a

double thread of plot is worth noting here. "It is accounted the best," he says, "because of the weakness of the spectators, for the poet is guided in what he writes by the wishes of his audience. The pleasure, however, thence derived is not the true tragic pleasure. It is proper rather to comedy" [16] and, I would add, melodrama. That most motion pictures are either comedies or melodramas may be due to the wishes of the audience, their preference for the double thread of plot. We shall return to this point later in a discussion of the problem of taste. It has no significance for criticism.

There is another distinction which Aristotle makes between simple and complex plots in tragedy; [17] in the former the change of fortune takes place without reversal of situation and without recognition or realization. Reversal of situation occurs when an event suddenly produces the opposite effect to that which it at first portends; recognition or realization is a change from ignorance to knowledge about some matter that is crucially relevant to the motives and passions of the person involved. Both reversal and recognition involve the factor of surprise. It is clear, therefore, why the more skilful narrative, whether tragedy, comedy or melodrama, will have a complex plot in this last sense.

Second, the magnitude of the plot. This point is closely related to the preceding one. It differs in that the critical problem turns not upon whether the story seeks a tragic, a comic, or a melodramatic effect, but upon the manner of narration. Thus, the plot of any story must imitate an action having sufficient magnitude to permit a turn of fortune, which means that it must be large enough to have a beginning, a middle and an end as separate parts, but not so large that these parts cannot be viewed as a single continuity. But, as we have seen, the magnitude of an epic can be greater than that of a drama. It can involve more persons, more incidents, each of these parts having its proper magnitude. In other words, a novel can, and should, have a more complex unity than a play, more complex in the first two senses: having more parts, and having subordinate and parallel plots. The cinematic manner of narration combines the features of both the novel and the play. The rule of magnitude for the motion picture must, therefore, be stated as follows. The mag-

---

[16] *Poetics*, 13, 1453ª32–37.   [17] *Poetics*, 10, 11.

nitude of the plot must be thought of in two dimensions: (1) extensity, or the number of persons, incidents, parallel actions, etc., involved, and (2) intensity, or the amount of detail in the development of a single incident. The epic magnitude is primarily in the dimension of extensity, although it may develop some of its more important incidents with dramatic intensity. The dramatic magnitude is primarily in the dimension of intensity. A motion picture must combine epic extensity with dramatic intensity. To do this, it cannot achieve the magnitude of either in its primary dimension. Its proper magnitude, therefore, is a proportion between something less than the largeness of the epic in extensity and something less than the definiteness of the drama in detail. The narrative style of a motion picture is obviously bad if it transgresses this rule. It either becomes diluted as a succession of episodes which are thin because they lack dramatic definiteness, or it becomes cramped and motionless because it has overindulged the dramatic depiction of a few of its incidents. In short, just as Aristotle said that the plot of a poem must either be epic or dramatic in structure and not both at once,[18] so we must say that the plot of a motion picture must be *both* epic and dramatic in structure, and *not either exclusively*. In other words, it must be cinematic. A motion picture is bad in narrative style if its plot is taken either from a play or a novel without the transforming work of adaptation.

All of these points of criticism can now be summarized in the single principle that good narrative style has unity, clarity and coherence. A story is a whole made up of parts. It must be sufficiently complex and subtle to engage attention, achieve suspense and surprise, and excite emotion, but not so complex and subtle that the unity, clarity and coherence of its parts are lost. If anything, most motion pictures are too simple and obvious in their narrative style. The achievement of unity, clarity and coherence is not a mark of skill unless it is accomplished by a mastery of complexity and subtlety. This general principle of criticism applies to all works of fiction. Anyone who can judge good narrative in a novel, can do so also in a drama and a motion picture, provided only that he is sensitive to their essential differences as well as their essential sameness.[19]

---

[18] *Poetics*, 18, 1456ᵃ10–14. [19] Cf. *Poetics*, 5, 1449ᵇ16–17.

2. We now turn to the criteria of goodness in filmic style. Because of the analogy between the elements of linguistic and filmic style, we can profit by a brief review of Aristotle's standards of good writing. His first principle has a generality which has never been surpassed in later criticism. Good writing must have clarity without meanness or, in other words, it must be intelligible without being ordinary.[20] A style is ordinary or mean which lacks elevation and distinction, which is not unusual in its use of words. In order to achieve such elevation, a writer must employ unusual and strange words, invent new idioms and constructions.[21] But with elevation also comes subtlety, and subtlety is in a sense the opposite of clarity. Subtlety at the expense of clarity is bad, as is clarity without subtlety, resulting in meanness. This basic principle can, therefore, be stated as the requirement that language be so used as to preserve a balance between clarity and subtlety, the latter for the sake of sublimity and elevation, the former for the sake of intelligibility. This principle of linguistic style neatly parallels the principle of narrative style which requires a similar balance between unity and complexity.

The principle applies both to vocabulary and to syntax: to the choice of words, and to phrasing, the invention of idioms, sentence and paragraph structure. It is most easily seen in the case of vocabulary. As previously pointed out, there could be no problem of style in the field of vocabulary did not language have the richness of synonyms. Otherwise there could be no choice of words. In any group of synonyms, two kinds of words can be distinguished: (1) the ordinary words of current popular usage, and (2) unusual, strange words, invented words, or ordinary words somewhat altered by lengthening or shortening.[22] If words of the first sort predominate, the style is to that extent mean and commonplace; if words of the second sort predominate, the style is to that extent lofty and distinguished. But there is the danger in using too many words of the second sort, that the writing will become an unintelligible jargon.[23] There must, therefore, be a proportional use of words of both sorts to achieve both clarity and elevation. The same analysis can be

[20] *Poetics*, 22, 1458[a]19.
[21] *Poetics*, 22, 1458[b]1–3 : "Nothing contributes more to produce a clearness of diction that is remote from commonness than the lengthening, contraction and alteration of words." [22] *Poetics*, 21, 1457[b]1–6. [23] *Poetics*, 22, 1458[a]24–26.

made in the field of syntax. There would be no problem of style here were it not possible to say the same thing in many different ways, that is, if many phrases and sentences were not related in the same way as synonymous words. On the one hand, a writer may use the ordinary constructions and idioms of common speech; on the other hand, a writer may invent new idioms, depart from the usual constructions in the direction of greater brevity or greater explicitness, or employ other sorts of strange and unfamiliar phrasing. If he writes exclusively in the first way, he writes clearly but in a commonplace manner. If he writes exclusively in the second, he is likely to become unintelligible. He must avoid both extremes: the commonplace and jargon too difficult to understand. Only in this way can he write with clarity and distinction.

To this first principle, Aristotle adds a second concerning the use of metaphor, either metaphorical words or metaphorical phrases.[24] He says it is of paramount importance to have command of metaphor: "it is a mark of genius, for to make good metaphors implies an eye for resemblances."[25] The reason why the use of metaphor is so important is not far to seek. Language is here being considered as a medium of imitation. Imitation depends upon similitude and difference. The metaphor is the condensation of an analogy or, perhaps, a whole series of analogies, involving many likenesses and differences. Metaphors are therefore compact units of imitation. In them language is best adapted to the task of imitation. But there is a danger of excess here as before. A liberal use of metaphor is desirable for enriching the imitative symbolism of language, but a style too metaphorical becomes a riddle, as too many strange words and unusual constructions produce a jargon.[26]

A third principle might be added: the appropriateness of the language to the nature and magnitude of the part of the plot being narrated. Good linguistic style, in other words, must be adapted harmoniously and in a different way to different phases of the narrative. Thus, to give one illustration of such correlation, certain parts of the narrative must move more rapidly, others

[24] *Poetics*, 21, 1457ᵇ7–9: "Metaphor is the application of an alien name by transference either from genus to species, or from species to genus, or from species to species, or by analogy, that is, proportion."
[25] *Poetics*, 22, 1459ᵃ5–6. [26] *Poetics*, 22, 1458ᵃ24–26.

more slowly. The writing must correspondingly have the same tempo, gaining speed by concentration, the use of suggestion and ellipsis, contrast, and so forth. An earlier question about the relation of narrative and linguistic style is thus in part answered. They should be correlated; the needs of the narrative usually determine the devices employed in language.

It should be noted above all that in this discussion of linguistic style, Aristotle is nowhere concerned with the distinction between verse and prose. Rather he is thinking of good writing, the perfection to be achieved in using the medium of language. The distinction between good and bad writing is a distinction between poetical and prosaic writing. The former is elevated and clear. The latter is clear but commonplace, or may even be commonplace without being clear. For the most part, the trait of elevation is most frequently achieved in verse, the trait of clarity most frequently achieved in prose. This is probably the reason why good writing which is both elevated and clear is called poetical, and writing which is merely clear is called prosaic. There is, of course, nothing analogous to the distinction between prose and verse in filmic style, but as we shall now see there is a clear analogy of good and bad filmic style with poetical and prosaic writing.

The analogy is most easily grasped if we consider, first, the pictorial medium by itself. The further problems of filmic style which involve the combination of the pictorial sequences with the sound track are more complex than anything in the use of language. Furthermore, the pictorial style of a motion picture is, in a sense, its basic style, first because the pictures usually carry the narrative continuity into which sound and verbal elements are set, and second because it is by means of the pictures that metaphor, suggestion, ellipsis, contrast, condensation are best achieved in the film. It is through its pictures and not through its words that the cinema wins distinction in style.

The analogue of synonyms in vocabulary is the variety of ways in which the camera can be set and operated for shooting the same piece of action or the same object. As we have seen there is as much, if not more, variety in camera settings than there are synonyms for most words. All the possible camera settings fall into two groups: (1) the usual position, distance, angle and speed of ordinary vision and (2) the unusual, strange, and almost impossible position, distance, angle and speed — impossible in the sense that the eye could not see in the way the camera is able to. Shots from above or below, moving shots, certain types of close-ups and telescopic shots, slow motion, special focus, are examples of the latter group; the middle distance, motionless, horizontal shot is the best example of the former.

There is similarly in *montage* the analogue of the different types of verbal syntax. Ordinary idiom and construction are like that cutting and joining of pieces of film which provide a customary sequence. The invented idiom and variant construction, the new metaphorical expression, are like the unusual filmic orderings produced by inventiveness in *montage*. The first criterion of good linguistic style, therefore, applies perfectly to work in the pictorial medium: the pictorial material must maintain a proper balance of clarity and elevation or subtlety, both in vocabulary and syntax. Some of the better German and Russian films, particularly the early inventive ones, went too far in the direction of the unusual and strange in camera setting and *montage*, with a resultant loss of clarity.[27] They were aiming in one right direction, but failed to preserve their balance. Most of the American films which are produced are clear enough, but lack any distinction, subtlety or elevation. They, too, are aiming in one right direction, but unfortunately not in the other. The danger of trying to be poetical without safeguarding clarity is that one becomes "arty"; the converse danger is that one becomes dull and commonplace. Of the two evils, the latter is worse because the former is a sign of invention and originality that needs only to be moderated in order to achieve the proper perfection of pictorial style.

We can also discover an analogy between the use of metaphor in language and the condensation of similitudes that can be obtained in the pictorial medium by the use of the camera and by *montage* [179]. Thus, to take a simple example, the use of a blurred focus is the pictorial metaphor of something as if seen through a haze. The use of a certain camera mask is the obvious metaphor of something as if seen through a keyhole, and so forth. By cutting and joining two pieces of film that have certain parallel elements, the filmic analogue of metaphorical phrasing is achieved. There are countless other ways in which by a

[27] Vd. Seldes, *op. cit.*, pp. 102–108, 131–134.

skilful use of pictures, likenesses can be suggested. But here, as in language, metaphorical excess is destructive of clarity. The filmic pieces or sequences can be made unintelligible in the effort to make them too compact of similitudes.

Finally, the third principle of pictorial style is the appropriateness of the pictorial devices to the part of the narrative which they are made to convey. Just as language can be used in such a way that its speed, its gravity, its definiteness or indefiniteness are fitting to the given part of a narrative, so the pictorial elements can be and should be adapted to different narrative purposes.

The criteria of good pictorial style are thus seen to be generally the same as the criteria of good linguistic style. But pictorial style is only one part of filmic style. We must now consider the other parts, the dialogue and the sound effects, and the ultimate problem of the organization of all of these parts into a filmic unity, which is the last problem of filmic style. With respect to dialogue by itself, there is nothing to add to the criteria of good linguistic style, though, perhaps, the criterion of appropriateness should here be stressed. With respect to the sound effects by themselves, there is little if anything to say. They only present a problem in style when they are considered in relation to the pictures. This is the problem of the total *montage* of the film: the cutting and joining of the sound track, on the one hand, the pictorial pieces, on the other, and the composition out of these of the finished film. In terms of the task of total *montage*, it may be asked of particular units of dialogue or particular sound effects whether they are suitable. It is important that they be good in themselves, but this is not enough: they must also be good as parts of a whole. These two requirements sometimes conflict. When they do, the second should dominate the choice.

The final principle of good filmic style is that the total *montage* preserve a balance between clarity and variety. Variety is achieved by shifting the basic narrative thread from the pictures to the words and sounds, or from the latter to the pictures. The technique of total *montage* is still too young to permit an explicit formulation of the rules of parallelism, harmony and counterpoint, governing the correlation of the pictures and the sound track. Yet Pudovkin's insight that there is in this correlation something analogous to the melody and the accompaniment in polyphonic music is at present sufficient to enable us to discriminate distinctive filmic style from what is ordinary and commonplace. His insight can be stated in another way. Simple clarity is achieved to the extent that the *montage* is realistic or naturalistic. Elevation and variety are achieved to the extent that the *montage* is imaginative and inventive. This final criterion of good filmic style is, therefore, a proper balance between realism and fantasy.[27a] It is not easy to accomplish. If most American films are, on the one hand, lethargically naturalistic in their style, the outstanding foreign films, particularly those of Germany and Russia, are often too radically fanciful. The former try to appear as if they did not employ the technique of *montage* at all and thereby lose distinction; the latter try to carry the technique of *montage* too far, and thereby lose clarity.

This concludes our formulation of the standards of criticism applicable to the cinema. Three related points remain to be discussed. Though not directly concerned with style, they are relevant to the critical problem. The first has to do with the role of embellishments and the effect of an art upon emotions; the second has to do with the comparative goodness of excellent work in three fields of fiction, the novel, the play, and the motion picture; the third has to do with the *non-technical* criteria in intrinsic criticism.

1. An embellishment is a part of a work of art which can be dispensed with and which, when employed, has no function other than to heighten the emotional effect. This is the role of song and spectacle in the production of Greek tragedy. It is the role of all the theatrical effects in contemporary dramatic productions. These are not essential parts of the dramatist's work. They are embellishments he may employ through the aid of a producer. As Aristotle says of the tragedy, "fear and pity may be aroused by spectacular means; but they may also result from the inner structure of the piece, which is a better way, and indicates a superior poet." [28] It is proper that a narrative should excite emo-

27a I am here using the words "realistic" and "fantastic" to convey, first, the distinction between the probable and the wonderful, and second, the factors of similitude and difference in imitation. Either of the two words becomes a term of reproach when it signifies an overemphasis upon one of these related opposites to the exclusion of the other.

28 *Poetics*, 14, 1453^{b}1–2.

tions; the pleasure of such excitement through imitation is the kind of pleasure art should afford. The only point here is the inferiority of a work in which that pleasure is given by extraneous devices rather than by the inner structure of the work itself. Thus, in literature the excitement should be caused by the poet's skill as a maker of plots and a maker in language. When a drama is produced, the embellishments are justifiable if they merely intensify the excitement otherwise caused. They are a mark of weakness in the poet if they are the primary source of excitement. In motion pictures, music is the only embellishment. Music is properly used to heighten emotional effects caused by the narrative and filmic skill of the director, by the goodness of his plot development, his pictorial style, his total *montage*. If it is used to arouse emotions that would otherwise be untouched, it indicates a weakness in the film. If it is not used either to intensify or create emotions, it is an inartistic accessory and should be completely eliminated. I am here referring, of course, only to music which is not an integral part of the plot development, as speech is. The music which is heard during a scene at a dance-hall or which is heard when a person is seen singing is hardly an embellishment of the cinema in which it occurs, and even less so is the music of a musical comedy.

2. It is important to compare the goodness of a good motion picture with the goodness of a good novel or a good play. In the first place, it enables us to discuss the merits of different media for imitating the same object. In the second place, it places a negative limitation upon the criticism of motion pictures. They must be criticized in terms of their own possible perfection and not in terms of a greater perfection, if that is possible, in the co-ordinate arts of the drama or the novel. In other words, criticism must measure a motion picture by standards of specific goodness, and not the generic goodness that is possible in the art of fiction.

Let us first consider the comparative excellence of good dramatic and good epic narration. Can it be said that either one is superior to the other? Aristotle tried to argue that a good tragedy was better than a good tragic epic.[29] He made the following points. That art is higher which appeals to a better audience. The epic is addressed to a more cultivated audience,

29 *Poetics*, 26.

who do not need the spectacle. But, on the other hand, the goodness of a tragedy is independent of the spectacle, which is only an embellishment. If the only superiority of the epic is that its effect is produced without spectacular means, the good tragedy at once eliminates that point of superiority. And the good tragedy is superior to the good epic because "it attains its end within narrower limits; for the concentrated effect is more pleasurable than one which is spread over a long time and so diluted." [30] The dramatic unity is more difficult to achieve than the epic unity. Finally, the tragedy has all the epic elements "with music and spectacular effects as important accessories; and these produce the most vivid pleasures." [31] This last point must not be misunderstood. If the embellishments are properly used as accessories, they enhance rather than detract from the perfection of the art in which they occur. Even though tragedy should not depend upon spectacular means to produce its proper effects, the use of such means are an advantage when they heighten these effects. It is, therefore, a point of superiority that "all of the elements of an epic poem are found in tragedy, but the elements of a tragedy are not all found in the epic poem." [32]

Aristotle's argument can be reversed if one of his basic principles be denied, namely, that the plot of an epic ought to be constructed on dramatic principles. [33] This means that Aristotle would praise an epic the nearer it approached dramatic unity and dramatic manner of narration, differing only, perhaps, in its greater magnitude in the dimension of extensity. It was by this criterion that Aristotle praised the *Iliad* as an almost perfect epic poem. This means, furthermore, that in epic narration, thought and character should be indirectly revealed through the incidents of action and the speeches rather than directly described. If one takes the position that the epic manner of narration properly permits the writer to describe thought and character apart from the incidents of action and the dialogue, then it follows that the novel is able to do narratively what a play cannot. Furthermore, the comparison must not be made solely for tragic narratives. In comedies and melodramas which effectively employ double threads of plot and subordinate plots, the novel is better able to handle the greater complexity than the drama. The fact that

[30] *Poetics*, 26, 1462^b 1–3.   [31] *Poetics*, 26, 1462^a 14–17.   [32] *Poetics*, 5, 1449^b 18–19.
[33] *Poetics*, 23, 1459^a 17.

the drama is a work produced under greater limitations is not a mark of superiority if it does less within those limits than a novel can do within its proper scope. The only point, then, that remains in favor of the drama is the virtue of the embellishments which are not an essential part of its literary existence. It seems a better conclusion, therefore, to say that each of these two manners of narration in the medium of language has compensating and peculiar virtues. The one has greater magnitude in the dimension of extensity, and this, as Aristotle admits, is an advantage for "it conduces to grandeur of effect, to diverting the mind of the hearer, and relieving the story with varying episodes." [34] The other has greater magnitude in the dimension of intensity and this is correlated with its potentiality for theatrical production and enhancement by spectacular effects.

To extend this comparison to the motion pictures, we must consider first the difference in medium, which does not exist in the case of the drama and the novel. There are a number of obvious defects in the pictorial medium. The symbolic power of words to control the imagination in all fields of sensitivity is greater than the representative power of pictures, which is limited to the field of vision. What is called "pictorial symbolism" — the metaphorical use of pictures — is vastly inferior to the range and modes of metaphor in language. Furthermore, words are peculiarly suited to convey abstractions and complicated relations. Pictures are not. Even though sound effects be added, and the words of dialogue, these limitations remain to some extent. It is questionable whether film can ever achieve the complexity and subtlety of narrative by words alone, whether dramatic or epic. This can be tested by considering the plot development of a good motion picture, a good novel and a good play. I think it will be found that the plot of the best cinema is simpler, that character is less definitely delineated, that thought is less fully expressed, that the constituent incidents are less fully described or represented than in a correspondingly excellent novel or play [180].

This can be said in another way. Because of its manifold medium, the cinema partakes of both the epic and the dramatic manner of narration. But in doing this, it has less magnitude in the dimension of extensity than a novel, and less magnitude in

[34] *Poetics*, 24, $1459^{b}28-31$.

the dimension of intensity than a play. The motion picture thus compares unfavorably with the novel and the play if it be held that greater magnitude in these two dimensions entails a unification of greater complexity and is, therefore, a point of superiority. It is not merely that the average motion picture is shorter in length of performance than a play, or quicker to see than the average novel is to read. This shortness is, however, a sign of slighter achievement with respect to either of the dimensions of magnitude. This may account for the fact that novels and plays can be cinematically adapted, but a motion picture is seldom if ever enlarged to make a novel or intensified to make a play. By the same argument it can be said, of course, that a novel is better than a play because the direction of adaptation is usually from the former to the latter. If this argument is rejected in the case of the novel and play, by recourse to the principle that each has its own compensating virtues, then it must be rejected, too, in the case of the motion picture.

This amounts to denying the possibility of comparing the perfections of different species of art in the same genus. Each is good in its own way if it work well within its own proper limits and, by mastering its peculiar limitations, each has special virtues that the others do not have. What, then, are the peculiar virtues of cinematic narration? The motion picture has, in the first place, a greater degree of narrative condensation than either the novel or the play. This follows from its combining epic extensity with dramatic intensity. A motion picture is able to tell a story more effectively, in one sense, than either of the other two types of fiction. If a more concentrated effect is more pleasurable, the motion picture is superior to the drama as that, in turn, is to the novel. This greater narrative condensation has another aspect. The different arts can be compared with respect to what they require in the way of imaginative participation on the part of their audience. In one sense, the novel requires most since it reaches its audience through the medium of symbols alone. In another sense, the drama requires most since its limited extensity requires the audience to supply imaginatively the background of the action. They must imagine what is going on concurrently or what happened before the action that the play narrates. In still a third sense, the motion picture requires most since what is actually given to the senses of its audience or conveyed symbol-ically is only a small part of the story that is told. The audience must supply the rest by a running interpretation of the little it sees and hears. If speed, ellipsis and suggestion are traits of good narration, the good cinema possesses them to a high degree because of its medium and manner.

In the second place, the point may be made that imitation should achieve a maximum of similitude along with a maximum of difference. This is another way of saying that in fiction both realism and fantasy must be maximized to achieve its characteristic kind of truth. The motion picture can achieve this double maximization better than either the produced drama or the novel. The former working within the actuality of the stage has much less difference from the reality it imitates than a motion picture. The latter working entirely within the medium of language and depending upon the imagination can seldom achieve the realism of the cinema. In other words, the motion picture can be *at once* more realistic and more fantastic than other types of narration, even though it cannot be as realistic as the stage or as fantastic as a novel. The peculiar excellence of a good motion picture is best comprehended by this point. It may be objected that the ballet and the puppet show have this same excellence, but both of these attain the double maximization of similitude and difference by means of conventionalization. It is the latter fact which is their special virtue, one which leads some to the opinion that the ballet and puppet show are the highest forms of imitation having action as its object. Be that as it may, the point remains that motion pictures have this peculiar merit, and it is one of great importance in the field of art. This is the perfection of Mickey Mouse, of Charlie Chaplin, of *Potemkin, The Deserter, Tabu* and *Blue Light*, of *Fury, The Scoundrel* and *The Informer*, which either cannot be achieved upon the stage or in a novel at all or, if the motion picture is the adaptation of a literary work, is more fully realized upon the screen.[35] One other point follows. The purgation which a work of art causes depends upon its difference

[35] The list of motion pictures, each of which has the kind of perfection proper to the cinema, can be greatly extended : *The Birth of a Nation* (in its day), *The Last Laugh, Storm Over Asia, Kameradschaft, The Deserter, M, Le Million, A Nous La Liberté, Zoo in Budapest, Maedchen in Uniform, La Maternelle, The 39 Steps, Mr. Deeds Goes to Town*, the *Maltese Falcon, It Happened One Night, Ruggles of Red Gap, Thunder in the East, A Night at the Opera, Front Page, Viva Villa, Night Flight* — to name only some.

from reality, as the excitement of emotions depends upon its realism. The peculiar excellence of a good motion picture, therefore, in maximizing the similitude and difference is extraordinarily effective in doing what art should do. In proportion as a motion picture is poor because it is too realistic or too fantastic, it fails not only intrinsically by the applicable standards of criticism, but it fails also in relation to its audience.

The superiority of the novel and the drama may, however, still be argued. Because of their greater use of words, they can be more "philosophical." Words not only arouse images; they convey abstractions, ideas, propositions, as well. It has been said that "poetry is not written with ideas, it is written with words"; but it can just as rightly be said that philosophy is written with ideas and not with words. Both statements are wrong, because words seldom fail to express ideas, and ideas are usually expressed in words. Pictures are not the conventional symbols by which we express abstractions; their intention is much more the intention of proper names or of words used concretely to denote particular things. It seems to follow, therefore, that literature is more "philosophical" than the cinema. It is more richly endowed with intellectual significance because of its medium of imitation. I have quoted the word "philosophical" because, whatever be the merits of the argument in terms of the limited intentionality of pictures as compared with words, it is at least questionable whether it is a proper virtue of fiction to be philosophical in this sense. The greater universality which makes poetry more philosophical than history is not dependent upon the power of words to express abstractions.[36] The cinema does not lack the universality that properly belongs to fiction. The expression of philosophical doctrine is not a proper function of fiction.

3. So far we have been concerned only with style. But good style is not enough to make a work of art great. This is commonly recognized whenever we speak of a good story poorly told or a poor story well told. The grades of aesthetic excellence, in short, are not determined exclusively by technical standards, by criteria for judging the artist's mastery of the means he must

[36] "One relates what has happened, the other what may happen." Therefore, "poetry tends to express the universal, history the particular" (*Poetics*, 9, 1451^{b}4–7).

employ.   Aesthetic criticism is more inclusive than technical criticism.   It can remain intrinsic, in the sense that it regards the goodness of the work of art, and not its effects upon those who receive it, without being limited to considerations of technique. Aesthetic criticism turns upon two other criteria: (1) the magnitude of the conception, and (2) the worth of the subject-matter or content.   The relation of the various criteria in aesthetic criticism can be stated in terms of the causes of the work of art.   It is said that art — the virtue of making in the artist — is the formal cause of the work done.   But this fails to distinguish between means and end in the artistic operation.   The conception of the work to be done determines the end of the process of making.   It is the intention of the final cause of artistic activity. The virtue of art is both the formal cause and the efficient cause of the work, because art as technique is concerned with the means to be used in actualizing the conception, in realizing the end foreseen.   As Maritain says, the conception of the work, "bearing on the *end* of the activity may be described in relation to Art, as the intention of the ends of the moral virtues in relation to Prudence.   It belongs to a different order from the *means*, the *ways* of realization, which are the peculiar province of the virtue of Art, as the means of attaining the ends of the moral virtues are the peculiar province of the virtue of Prudence." [37]   The material cause of the work of art can be regarded in two ways: (1) the physical matter operated upon, and (2) the subject-matter as determined by the object of imitation.   Finally, there is the distinction between the principal and the instrumental cause: the rational soul of the artist is the principal cause, and his virtue of art the instrumental cause. [38]

The parts of aesthetic criticism can, therefore, be distinguished as follows.   Technical criticism regards the work in terms of the virtue of art as the instrumental efficient cause.   The criticism of the work in terms of the artist's conception — there is no conventionally accepted name for this part — is closely related to technical criticism because it judges the means in relation to the end, the final cause.   Ethical criticism regards the work in terms of its material cause — its subject-matter.   Both the criterion of conception and the criterion of subject-matter refer to the soul of the artist as principal cause of his work.   The judgment of his tech-

[37] *Art and Scholasticism*, pp. 182–183. Cf. p. 203.   [38] Vd. Chapter 12 *supra*.

nique as an instrumentality is subordinate to the judgment of the man who uses the instrument. In order to understand more fully the relation of the several parts of intrinsic criticism, it is necessary to discuss briefly each of the non-technical criteria.

(1) The conception of a work of art must not be confused with the choice of subject-matter; nor is it, as Maritain says, "the plan of the work or its scheme of construction (which is already a realization — in the mind)." [39] Since the work of art is an individual thing, the conception of it is not an idea, i.e., an abstraction, a universal intention. It is best described as the artist's *vision*, his intuitive apprehension of the individual thing he is able to make.

The conception of the work to be done is prior to the process of production, as in the moral order the intention of the end is prior to the choice of means, and in the biological order conception is prior to birth. Conception is independent of what follows. Good intentions are not sufficient, but the goodness of the intention is not lessened by a wrong choice of means. On the other hand, what follows is not entirely independent of conception. The means chosen cannot be better than the end for which they are intended.

It follows, therefore, that technical criticism must always involve a reference to the artist's conception, as the means must always be judged in relation to the end. Thus, we can distinguish between a slight conception executed with great technique and a great conception poorly executed. In neither case can the work be truly great. Greatness in a work of art requires not only that the means be adequate to the conception which they are employed to realize, but also that the conception justify the use of the means. It is difficult to say which is the more grievous source of defect in a work of art. On the one hand, the artist is vainglorious who conceives a work that exceeds his powers. On the other hand, a display of technique disproportionate to a meagre end is meaningless virtuosity. "Clearly the more exalted the conception, the more the means run the risk of proving inadequate." [40] It is equally clear that a mastery of the means is likely to elevate the artist's vision of attainable ends.

It does not follow, however, that technical criticism is not independent of, and analytically separable from, the measure of

[39] *Op. cit.*, pp. 181–182. [40] Maritain, *op. cit.*, p. 183.

the conception.   Although the goodness of the work as a whole
must be judged both in terms of the end striven for and in terms
of the means employed, it is nevertheless possible to discriminate
between more and less adequate means to the same end.   This is
the locus of the purely technical judgment which can always be
made separately from the evaluation of the work as a whole.   We
can always ask two questions : *How much* had the artist to say ?
And *how well* has he said it ?   These two questions can be
answered separately, even though the question, *How great* is his
work ? depends upon the answer to both.   Neither alone suffices.

(2)   In all the arts which imitate human action, the content or
subject-matter is necessarily moral.   Human action is, as we have
seen, moral behavior, whether viewed politically or in the life
of an individual man.   The same word *praxis* which is used to
distinguish the sphere of morality from the sphere of art (*poiesis*),
is also used to define the object imitated by poetry and music.
The matter of these arts is thus seen to be the sphere of moral
problems.   The components of plot in fiction include problem
and choice, complication and resolution.   The problems in fiction are moral problems.   The choices made are the expressions
of moral character.   The complications following thereupon, and
the dénouement, describe the course of moral life, its directions
and vicissitudes, its strivings, achievements, failures.

It is impossible, therefore, for a work of art, particularly in the
genus of fiction, to avoid being a commentary on moral matters.
It does not have to be spuriously didactic or homiletical, it does
not have to be "philosophical" in the sense of asserting and arguing fundamental propositions, it need not contain a single explicit
proposition, in order to stand as a commentary.   It is that because
of its subject-matter and because the work of art cannot help reflecting the moral character of its maker.   As he is, so will his
work be.   We have already seen that the judgment of the work
of art in terms of its maker's handling of subject-matter is really a
judgment of the artist.   Strictly, a work of art cannot be called
"moral" or "immoral."   But in the sense in which the work of
art is the image of its maker's soul, a work of art cannot be good
unless it is made by a good man.   When a work of art is criticized
as immoral — quite apart from its effects upon men — what can be
meant is that it is not good materially, whatever be its formal and

technical excellence. Viewing it in terms of its subject-matter, we can say that it is morally sound or unsound. It can be unsound in two ways: (1) by reflecting a soul which is insensitive to moral distinctions or which seeks to escape them entirely; (2) by reflecting a soul which is morally disordered or deformed [181]. A work of art which is unsound in either way cannot be great. To suppose that it can be is to ignore the subordination of technique as an instrumental cause in its production.

Here, again, the point of independence and analytical separability must be stressed. As technical competence can vary independently of conceptual power, so can it vary independently of moral character. A work that is morally unsound can be well conceived and well done. We can always separate the questions: *What* has the artist to say? *How well* does he say it? The answer to the first is a judgment of the worth of the work of art as a commentary on morals. Here, as before, the answer to the question, *How great* is the work? depends upon the answer to the question about content as well as the question about technique. But that certainly does not make these two questions indistinguishable or incapable of independent answers.

In the field of intrinsic criticism, the technical criteria are always most fully discussed. This can be accounted for in a number of ways. In the first place, the technical approach most vigorously regards the work as a thing in itself, and in relation to the artist, not as a man, but as a specially disciplined maker. The other approaches go outside the narrow sphere of art. In the second place, it is impossible to formulate any standards for measuring the worth of an artistic conception. The principles of technical criticism follow from the rules of art. But there are no rules of conception. It is the creative act, as unregulated as induction is in science, as spontaneous and capricious as inspiration. We are able to measure the magnitude of the artist's vision in terms of the degree of complexity unified and intricacy made clear. But this is at best a rough judgment, and one that is relative to our own powers of discrimination and understanding. In the third place, there is no need to formulate the standards of intrinsic ethical criticism because these are, after all, based upon the principles of morality itself. To whatever degree the cultivation of moral sensibilities makes us competent to judge human character, it makes us competent to pass on the soundness or unsoundness of a work of art. But in so far as the work is to be technically judged, what is usually called aesthetic cultivation — sensibilities instructed by a knowledge of technique — is necessary.

It is only the technical criteria, furthermore, which are different for each particular art. The moral criteria are the same for all the arts, certainly for all the arts which imitate human action. The same is true of the judgment in terms of conception. In attempting to formulate the principles of aesthetic criticism applicable to the cinema, our specialized task is completed when we have fully considered the technical criteria. It is necessary, however, to call attention to a number of errors prevalent today in cinematic criticism, as well as in judgments of literature, arising from misconceptions of the parts of intrinsic criticism or their relation. Some of these have already been discussed and need not be further analyzed here.[41]

(1) It is erroneous to suppose that the judgment of a work of art as morally sound or unsound, in the sense above indicated, is praise or condemnation of it as a vehicle of moral instruction. The latter judgment regards the work, not in itself, but as it is used or received by men. It passes at once into the field of extrinsic criticism.

(2) It is erroneous generally to convert an intrinsic into an extrinsic judgment; that is, to convert any judgment of the goodness of a work of art, based on ethical or technical criteria, into a judgment of the goodness of its effects. Intrinsic and extrinsic values are independently variable because the latter is dependent not only upon the character of the work of art but upon the mode of its recipients.

(3) It is erroneous to deny that ethical criteria enter into the complete aesthetic judgment, along with technical criteria; but it is equally erroneous to deny that these two sorts of intrinsic criticism are analytically separable, or to deny that the values they judge are independently variable. Failure to preserve these distinctions leads to a confusion of different sorts of criticism rather than an orderly combination of them.[42]

[41] Vd. Chapter 12 *supra*.
[42] T. S. Eliot in vigorously attacking the first of these errors is often driven by his impetus into the second. Vd. *Religion and Literature* in *Essays Ancient and Modern*, London, 1936; and *Collected Essays*, New York, 1932 : p. 42.

(4) Intrinsic ethical criticism which is not fully sensitive to the considerations of technique is as bad as technical criticism which disregards entirely the conception and the subject-matter of the work of art.

(5) In so far as the subject-matter of a work of art is considered, only ethical standards are applicable. Much of contemporary discussion of the subject-matter of fiction is irrelevantly sociological. It turns upon the critic's estimate of the importance of problems in terms of contemporary issues. Novels and plays which deal with the vital social and economic questions of the day are praised. Motion pictures are frequently condemned for not facing these issues, which are only locally serious in the hubbub of current affairs. The error here is twofold: in the first place, the sociological critic fails to realize that the problems proper to an art imitating human action must be universal. The problems of Greek tragedy are the problems of all tragedy. Changing social and economic conditions do not alter basic moral problems. In the second place, he fails to distinguish between art and propaganda.[43] The outstanding Russian films are good, not because but in spite of their devotion to the communistic programme. In a sense it is a mark of their excellence that they have been able to carry the alien burden of propaganda and sociology. The Hollywood productions which are bad are not bad because of their disinterest in so-called serious social problems. Those which are good as works of art are not handicapped by being fiction-coated sociology, tracts for the times, comments on the burning issues of the moment. Whatever their technical excellence or defect, whether morally sound or unsound, most American films are at least free from the incubus of propaganda and reform. The same cannot be said, unfortunately, for the work of our outstanding playwrights and novelists [182]. Aristotle introduces his discussion of literary criticism by a remark which serves well here as a conclusion: "The standard of correctness is not the same in poetry and politics, any more than in poetry and any other art."[44]

[43] Cf. Eliseo Vivas, *Art, Morals and Propaganda* in The International Journal of Ethics, October, 1935. Also Spottiswoode's discussion of the relation of cinematic technique and subject-matter, with reference to the Marxist position in these matters: *op. cit.*, pp. 262–274. Cf. Seldes, *op. cit.*, pp. 125–127.
[44] *Poetics*, 25, 1460[b]13–15. Vd. all of Ch. 25.

These errors must be avoided if the cinema is to be properly criticized. The cinema should not be criticized in terms of technical standards applicable to plays and novels, except to the extent that all the arts of fiction have generic similarity. The goodness of a motion picture must be judged in terms of the specific perfection that is possible in its own field.

In the light of the standards I have formulated as applicable criteria of criticism, it is possible to review the productions of the cinematic art. There have been few excellent and many mediocre motion pictures.[44a] But by similar standards, one is forced to say that there have been few good and many poor novels, few good and many poor plays. If, as Mr. Seldes wrote, the few good motion pictures are a small accomplishment "when placed against the vast bulk of silly and commonplace movies," if one feels that "centuries of producing cheap novels, tawdry plays, vapid songs and formless paintings have not equalled the mass of twaddle which the moving picture has accumulated in its three decades," one must also go on with him to "wonder whether any medium of expression arrived, within thirty years of its beginning at such a high point as the handful of few good movies have reached."[45] But one can go further. If one considers the productions of all the arts of fiction in contemporary society, it can be maintained, I think, that the proportion of good and bad work is about the same in the fields of the novel, the play and the motion picture. If there is any difference, it is in favor of the motion picture. I doubt if, in proportion to the number of plays produced or novels published each year, there are as many good works as there are good motion pictures in proportion to their total number. I can express this judgment in a more strik-

[44a] Considered absolutely, rather than proportionately. The number of excellent cinematic works — memorable for their outstanding perfection — is extraordinarily large. A partial list is given in fn. 35 *supra*.

[45] *Op. cit.*, pp. 7–8. This was written in 1929. Seven years have made a great difference. What of the next ten? "In the case of an art that is only twenty-five years old it is of very little importance how many masterpieces have been produced, but it is indispensable to make certain that the first steps have definitely been taken in the right direction, and to have enough imagination to realize the marvellous potentialities of film as an artistic medium" (Arnheim, *op. cit.*, p. 8). In any case, the judgment of an art is not made in terms of numbers and proportions, but in terms of its great works, whatever their number,

ing way.   Consider the poor novel and the poor play.   They are insufferable.   One cannot sit or read through them, and there are many of this sort.   Why is it, then, that there are few movies which are as intolerably poor as bad plays and novels.   Although the poor motion picture is as simple-minded in its narrative style and as commonplace in its filmic style as the narrative construction and the literary level of most of the fiction that is published or theatrically produced, the worst cinema is rescued from the lowest level by marks of technical accomplishment that give it something of the wonderful that is essential to the enjoyability of art.   It may be that all literate persons are also able to write and, therefore, the technical mastery of both medium and manner, evidenced in even the poorest piece of literature, has ceased to move them to wonder, whereas the cinematic technique is still so special a thing that the poorest motion picture bears the marks of art, as similarly the least competent painting or the least successful musical composition.

I return to Mr. Seldes' point that what the cinema has achieved in its short career is a benign portent of its future.   The prophecy is not important as such, but it does raise the question whether it is not the past of the novel and the play which have established them in the judgment of most critics as serious and respectable forms of art.   It is certainly not their future.   The motion picture has little in the way of past, but it certainly does have a future.   The promise of it warrants dignified critical attention as much as the glorious tradition of literature enables critics to pass upon contemporary works as if they merited the same serious consideration as the great masters.   However bad current criticism is in the fields of literature — and it would be difficult to exaggerate its lack of principles and its confusions — it is not nearly as bad as the kind of criticism which motion pictures receive.   The technique of the motion picture is vastly superior to the critical acumen of its commentators.   If men like Pudovkin were engaged in writing the criticisms as well as producing the pictures, insight such as his into the basic rules of the art might become articulated into sound canons of criticism.   The development of the motion picture might be considerably aided by such penetrating and relevant criticism [183].   At present, the cinema suffers in comparison with literature by having an even less significant body of critical commentary upon its work.

I am aware that there are many who do not share this critical estimate of the range and proportion of excellence in the productions of the cinematic art. I think this is partly due to the lack of relevant critical standards and consequent errors of critical judgment. I am not moved by the misguided sociological critics who find so few motion pictures that treat of the serious economic and political problems of the day. Nor am I moved by the critics who, failing to distinguish the theme of the plot and the style of its development, in both manner and medium of narration, complain of the lack of originality. Then there are the "aesthetes" who accept too readily what is offered as serious and worthy work because the auspices under which it may be produced are socially respectable or because only the "élite" enjoy such works. I am certainly not moved by the contempt for the movies which such critics have never been able to overcome, because movies belong, not to the élite, but to the people. The prejudice of the professional aesthete is too patent. After a period of long contempt for the movie, he passed, as Mr. Seldes points out, to fulsome praise for "whatever was not popular; later the worship of all foreign films and the denigration of all American films."[46] His original contempt merely changed its coat. It was still the same prejudice against any art that succeeds in being popular.

Mr. Seldes' classification of the great, the bogus and the lively arts is worth mentioning at this point.[47] The average Broadway play or the one that wins a Pulitzer prize, the average novel or the one that is widely discussed, is usually an example of bogus art. It is a work that parades its respectability by claiming through external marks to belong to an artistic tradition in which there have been great works of art. There are few if any bogus motion pictures because the cinema is still a lively art nourished by wide popular approval rather than by the applause of the self-elected élite. This does not mean that motion pictures often attain the level of great art, but only that they seldom counterfeit greatness.

[46] *Op. cit.*, pp. 95–96. Cf. Spottiswoode's criticism of the extremists in denunciation and praise : *op. cit.*, pp. 308–312. The cinema is not the supreme art ; but it is no less an art than literature and music. In one sense it may be "premature to assess today the place of the cinema among the arts" ; but its great works can be judged now by standards as rigorous as those applicable to any of the fine arts.
[47] *The Seven Lively Arts*, New York, 1924 : pp. 309–320, 349–357.

Out of a lively art, such as was the theatre in the days of Shakespeare, real greatness is more likely to arise than out of a field of art that glories in its tradition and deceives itself by its bogus respectability.   Great and lively art have this in common : they are able to please the multitude.   There are two external marks which taken *together* are fairly reliable indices of great art : (1) gross popularity at any one time or over a period of time, and (2) the range of the levels of taste it is able to satisfy.   The lively arts possess the first mark.   Great works emerge when they reach sufficient complexity to please the discriminating as well as the multitude.   Bogus art, on the contrary, despises the first mark of greatness in art.   It is intended only for the academician, the cultivated, the "aesthetes."   I offer in contrast the work of Walt Disney as lively art that also reaches greatness, a degree of perfection in its field which surpasses our best critical capacity to analyze and which succeeds at the same time in pleasing children and simple folk.

These distinctions, employing as they do the criteria of enjoyment and popularity, lead us to our last problem, the problem of taste.   This problem must be generally formulated in terms of the relation of excellence in art to the pleasure it affords audiences of different degrees of aesthetic cultivation [184].

There is the position of Plato in the *Republic* [48] that the enjoyment of the multitude is, if anything, an evil which the artist should avoid.   Aiming at their pleasure the artist is likely to produce whatever the people praise, for which their reasons are utterly ludicrous.   And in the *Laws* he remarks that "by the ancient and general Hellenic rule, there was none of the freedom of the present custom of Sicily and Italy which leaves things to the majority of the audience and decides the victory by their votes, a practice which has corrupted the poets themselves (since their standard in composition is the debased taste of their judges, with the result that it is actually the audience who educates them), and equally corrupted the tastes of the audience." [49]   Plato is right in saying that the standard by which a work of art can be judged is the same standard as that which gives pleasure to the best man, the properly cultivated ; but only if the judgment referred to is a critical judgment and not a judgment of taste.

[48] 493 D–E.   [49] 659 A.

There is no difference between good taste and critical judgment, except that the former is immediate and habitual and the latter is analytical and discursive. The question, however, is whether the same work of art can satisfy good taste — the taste of the educated — and popular taste; whether, as Plato says, the necessity or willingness to please the multitude inevitably corrupts the artist as well as his audience. It is on this question that Aristotle takes an opposite stand. He does not fail to distinguish the more refined audience from the vulgar who need spectacles or a double thread of plot or surprising reversals of situation to excite and please them.[50] But making this distinction does not lead him to condemn the poet who is able at the same time to please the few and the many. There is, in other words, no intrinsic incompatibility between the goodness and the popularity of art.

The issue can be approached from another angle by asking what the responsibility of an artist is to any audience whatsoever and to different levels of audience. He cannot honestly shirk the basic obligation to give pleasure to someone. If it is his intention to produce good work, it must be his intention to give delight. But to whom? To persons of good taste certainly, since the goodness of their taste is determined by the same criteria as the goodness of his work. He cannot stop here, however, without incurring the danger of counterfeiting greatness by satisfying the taste of the few. Who knows whether they are the genuinely elect or the self-appointed élite? The intention to do good work obliges the artist to seek the largest possible audience, a universal audience, man generally. This is not the same as merely pleasing popular taste, because the multitude does not include the cultivated. The choice is not one of pleasing the few rather than the many, but between pleasing the few or all: *the cultivated and the undisciplined at the same time but not in the same way.*

I return here to the principle of commensurate enjoyment.

[50] *Poetics,* 14, 1453^{a}30–35 ; 18, 1456^{a}18–21 ; 26, 1461^{b}26–29. Cf. *Politics,* VIII, 5, 1340^{a}1–2 ; VIII, 7, 1342^{a}18–28 ; III, 11, 1282^{a}1–21. As in ethics, the judgment of the prudent man is a measure of good acts, so in aesthetics, the judgment of the artist is the measure of good work. Aesthetic cultivation consists in learning to take pleasure in the things the competent artist enjoys. The approval of the vulgar — those lacking such cultivation — does not signify artistic excellence ; but neither does it necessarily signify the contrary.

An artist has every man to please, but each type of man according to his capacities. Good work is complex. But its complexity is unified. It is at once subtle and clear. Therefore, it is able to reach many levels of audience. In the lowest range of taste, only the simple outlines and surfaces are appreciated. In the highest range, the intricate structure and the manifold detail. The artist may not have any social duty to cultivate the taste of men. That may be the task of the critic and the teacher. But the critic and teacher cannot succeed without the aid of works of art, the goodness of which consists in their power to appeal to all ranges of existing taste. The cultivation of taste is a gradual development of aesthetic capacity. It must begin wherever it finds the individual's sensitivity according to natural endowment. The judgment of taste is an appreciation of relative beauty : the work found beautiful is always proportional in complexity to the grade of the spectator's sensibility. Good taste is not cultivated by a transition from the enjoyment of poor work to the discovery of beauty in good work, but rather by the gradual appreciation of the excellence of work that was at first appreciated for much less than its full perfection [185].

The motion picture, being the most popular of the arts, has the greatest responsibility to cultivate good taste because it already has accomplished the first part of this task by its success in pleasing the uncritical. They are already on the lowest rung of the ladder. They can be elevated if the art provides them with motion pictures complex enough, subtle enough and yet clear enough, to afford them easy steps upward. Motion pictures face this responsibility in another way. They must be simple enough for children and complex enough for adults. The level of the adult multitude may, of course, be little better than that of the child, but in any case the task remains the same. It is certainly questionable whether the level of taste of the readers of popular novels or the spectators of popular plays is different. The audience which the three arts of fiction have in common probably enjoy only what is common to the three arts : the narrative surface. There is no discrimination of the qualities of style that are appropriate in each of the three arts. At the lowest level, what the movie-goer enjoys is the story and that only in its general outline. To cultivate his taste he must be made sensitive to the elements of style, both narrative and filmic, which distinguish a motion picture from other forms of story-telling [186]. This cannot be done by the "art film," the bogus production for little theatre groups. It can only be done by the film, which like a play by Shakespeare, tells a story plainly for the simple folk as well as reaches the heights of poetical style.[51]

It may be objected that an art has no educational responsibility to provide aesthetic cultivation. But by its nature it must please by giving the delight of contemplation, the satisfaction of rest and recreation, the relief of purged excitement. All of these are aspects of aesthetic pleasure derived from imitations. The judgment of taste is merely the approval of a work that gives such pleasure. Art, therefore, cannot divorce itself from the task of pleasing or of winning approval. The only choice it faces is whether to please all men or only good men. This depends upon whether the artist, if he is himself a good man, must not try to make men good [187]. If so, he must seek to please all men in the hope that by so doing he will gradually assimilate the weak and the strong. In the case of the cinema, there is a selfish as well as an altruistic motive for such an effort. It is only by cultivating a critical audience that the motion picture will ever be able to reach the maturity of its own possible perfection.

One word remains to be said. The distinction between good and bad — in morals, in art, in taste — which has run through the many pages of this book carries with it an air of righteousness that is the unfortunate semblance of those who insist upon talking about what is right. In closing I would like to efface the priggishness that may be the impression which such discussion gives, whether intended or not. I return, therefore, to the Christian insight about the two ways of looking at any human thing. On the one hand, the differences among men or among the works of their art can be viewed in the light of proximate human standards. On the other hand, they can be viewed from

[51] Thus, in a play of Shakespeare, as T. S. Eliot points out, "you get several levels of significance. For the simplest auditors there is the plot, for the more thoughtful the character and the conflict of character, for the more literary the words and phrasing, for the more musically sensitive the rhythm, and for the auditors of greater sensitiveness and understanding a meaning which reveals itself gradually" (*The Use of Poetry and the Use of Criticism*, Cambridge, 1933 : p. 146).

the distance of Divinity. The sinner and the saint are widely separated in quality as men, according to the first view; their difference is absorbed in the weak humanity they share, according to the second. Similarly the poorest work of art is an extraordinary human achievement — than which the greatest perfection of man's art seems not much better — if one views their difference from a distance which emphasizes only their common origin, the power with which all men are gifted to make things. Yet looked at more closely and in terms of merely human standards, the relative perfection which man achieves is an excellence which far surpasses his poorest efforts. Again, the same can be said for the difference between the man of exquisite taste and the man of simple pleasures. Before God they are both sensitive animals able, because endowed with intellect as well as senses, to enjoy what they can contemplate as well as what they can devour. But men make much of this difference of taste as they view it in its human setting, separating as if in different worlds and almost as if different creatures, the learned and the lewd, the sensitive and the dull, the refined and the vulgar. Because man is able to grasp analogically the vision of things in divine knowledge, he should not be content with the limited truth of his human discriminations; but neither should he surrender these discriminations which are, after all, right in their own terms, for an insight about human affairs that cannot be genuinely his. In short, he must be true to his humanity and be humble in it. To do this, he must always look at human things from both points of view. If he obliterate human distinctions by wholly embracing the divine vision, he arrogates a perfection that he cannot rightly possess. If he exaggerate human distinctions by wholly relying upon human standards, he fails to qualify those standards by the imperfection of his nature. One error leads to sentimentalism; and the other to pomposity. In either case he commits the sin of pride.

Notes

1. That the philosopher has recourse to myths indicates that he must use the method of the poet at times, either because the inadequacy of knowledge about the topic in question or because the difficulty of making the point intelligible to a given audience requires him to move in the realm of opinion and on the level of imagination. The poetic technique is not in itself bad, but it should be used as the philosopher uses it. This explains the rivalry between poetry and philosophy: the philosopher cannot leave poetry alone, any more than the poet can get along without philosophy, without ideas. Both use words, and words cannot be used exclusively either to evoke images or to signify ideas; they always do both. This accounts also for the special treatment which Plato gives to poetry among the arts. He recommends the regulation of music, but he exiles the poets. In doing so, he is not eschewing poetry but rather banishing all those who try to be poets without trying to be philosophers at the same time. And he directs his attack primarily against the dramatists because they treat of themes that belong to moral philosophy. As he says in the *Laws*, the lawgiver must be the only dramatist for the people (Book VII, 817). The *Republic* is the tragedy that should be presented to them. Cf. O. de Selincourt, *Art and Morals*, London, 1935: pp. 95–96.

2. It may be objected that Plato does not admit a distinction between aesthetic and political standards for judging the arts. Works of art are good in proportion as they please the good man, and since the good man cannot take pleasure in what is morally

bad, there can be no diremption between the moral and aesthetic standards for judging works of art. It is not clear to me that Plato takes this position without reservation. Although he certainly takes it in the ideal or limiting case of the best work, best both technically and in its moral qualities and effects, he seems to recognize the distinction between these criteria in other cases. Certainly in contrast to Aristotle, Plato tends to oppose the separation of intrinsic (aesthetic and technical) and extrinsic (moral and political) criteria in the judgment or criticism of works of art. (Cf. Note 16, *infra*.)   As Ritter points out, Platonic criticism is never merely formal, but considers the content — the moral content — of the work of art (*The Essence of Plato's Philosophy*, New York, 1933 : pp. 368–369).

2a.   Plato gives other reasons in Book III of the *Republic* for his different treatment of dramatic and non-dramatic narration. The epic poet can tell a story without speaking in the person of his characters ; moreover even if he employs dialogue, no one is called upon to act the part mimetically, as in the case of dramatic presentations. Thus, such poets may be saved from impersonating vicious characters, and mimicry is entirely avoided. (Vd. 392 D– 398 B.)   But the unfortunate effects upon the poet of his use of dialogue, and of his own pantomime upon the actor, is not the whole point. Only the poet who eschews the dramatic manner can be the severer story-teller "who will imitate the style of the virtuous only, and will follow those models which we prescribed at first when we began the education of our soldiers" (398 B). Though the greater effectiveness upon the audience of dramatic spectacles, as compared with the recitations of the dithyrambist, is not here considered, it is certainly crucial to the final expulsion of the dramatists in *Republic* X and in the *Laws*.

3.   There are many ways of explaining why Plato treated the dramatic poets differently from all other artists. They are all based upon the fact that the dramatist like the philosopher uses words and deals with moral problems. And on the further assumption that the only value of poetry is didactic, the philosopher solves the conflict between himself as a teacher and the dramatist by banishing the latter. The total exclusion of an art from the state is a much more drastic measure than any proposal of censorship or regulation. It is this which makes the Platonic position so difficult to justify practically. It may even be true that as teaching, moral or speculative, all poetry which is not written by philosophers is bad. But the exclusion of mere poets is not fully

justified by this truth unless teaching is the only function of poetry. Poetry may serve other useful ends and, therefore, poets may have a function to perform as well as artisans and soldiers. The Aristotelian answer to Plato is directed against the too narrow conception of the utility of poetry as exclusively didactic; it is not directed against Plato's disapproval of poetry as bad teaching or as a source of possible corruption in the life of children.

4. The recognition that the arts are a form of recreation or entertainment, that art is the most distinguished form of play, is not inconsistent with Plato's emphasis upon the utility of the arts as exclusively didactic. In both the *Republic* and the *Laws*, Plato proposes detailed regulations of children's games because he considers play as educative; *a fortiori* so are the arts and all other amusements. But to see that the *means* of recreation may have an educational influence should not prevent one from seeing that they are means of *recreation*. The utility of recreation is not the same as that of education, though the same means may serve both ends and though both recreation and education are necessary for a good life. Cf. Ritter, *The Essence of Plato's Philosophy*, pp. 346–348, 369.

5. Plato's theory of the arts as imitations must not be confused with Aristotle's definition of art as imitation (see Note 15 *infra*). For Plato all human productions, history, science and philosophy as well as the fine and useful arts, are imitations, differing in their degree of proximity to reality. As Plato uses the term imitation, it signifies a cognitive relation between the imitation and its object. Knowledge is distinguished from opinion by the same criterion which distinguishes philosophy from poetry as good from bad imitation. The conception of art as cognitive in character — because all knowledge is imitation and conversely — includes the conception of its chief function as didactic. Aristotle disagrees with the latter point because he disagrees with the former. The work of art is not a medium of knowledge but an object of knowledge. "Music perhaps more than any other art gives us an enjoyment of being, but does not give us *knowledge* of being; and it would be absurd to make music a substitute for metaphysics" (J. Maritain, *Art and Scholasticism*, New York, 1930: Note 55). Maritain summarizes the Aristotelian criticism: "Plato, with his theory of the various degrees of imitation and poetry as an illusion, misconceives, like all extravagant intellectualists, the peculiar nature of art; hence his contempt for poetry: it is clear that if art were a *means of knowledge*, it would be

wildly inferior to geometry" (*Op. cit.*, p. 56).   Cf. R. P. McKeon, *Literary Criticism and the Concept of Imitation in Antiquity*, in Modern Philology, August, 1936: pp. 3–16.

6.   There are two aspects to Plato's question whether there is a use in poetry as well as a delight.   On the one hand, Plato seems sharply to distinguish pleasure and utility.   But unless pleasures as such are intrinsically and absolutely evil, they must be good in some sense; and unless they are finally and absolutely good, they must be good as means and, hence, have a kind of utility.   Plato does not take either of the extreme positions about pleasure, and therefore must have a narrow conception of utility when he opposes pleasure to it.   On the other hand, his conception of education is so broad that it seems to include all other utilities: whatever is useful in man's life is educative.   Thus, as we have seen, Plato regards even the games of children primarily, if not exclusively, as educational.   If anything which is for the ultimate good of man is educational, then of course the arts cannot be useful except didactically.   Since Plato has already charged the poets with teaching lies and corrupting moral character by exciting the base passions, his challenge to them to prove their utility, i.e. as educative, is either merely rhetorical or an admission that they can defend themselves against his charges.   So interpreted, the question Plato raises at this late point in the discussion is not new.   But if the poets are not precluded from answering first, that pleasure is itself a utility and second, that there are utilities, such as recreation, which are not educational, or at least not exclusively so, then the question is a crucial turn in the argument.   That it occurs so late, that Plato does not wait for the poets to answer it, suggests that he did not mean it as anything more than a rhetorical summary of an argument which he feels satisfied has shown poetry to be worse than useless.   If so, the question only becomes crucial when Aristotle re-opens it in the light of quite different conceptions of pleasure, utility and education.

7.   Plato and Hegel — both reactionaries as judged in terms of the political issues of their own day!   The Periclean party favored individualism and the free federation of city-states; Periclean policies resemble the liberalism and democracy of the nineteenth century.   As Plato was the opponent of the Periclean trend, so Hegel is the philosopher of contemporary fascism.   Yet the differences between Plato and Hegel are as striking as the similarities. M. B. Foster has recently analyzed these differences in terms of Christianity (*Political Philosophies of Plato and Hegel*, Oxford,

1935). Hegel's philosophy, he says, "is enabled to surpass Plato's by its absorption of the truths of Christian revelation, but at the same time this absorption is insufficient and incomplete" (p. 140). Hegel failed to assimilate the doctrine of Creation, failed to understand the relation of Divine and human law. "It is an old story that Plato contains anticipations of Christian doctrine, and it is precisely these implications which are further developed in the philosophy of Hegel. The Christian revelation is not a body of doctrine alien to truth; it contains truths which, when elicited from it by the work of thought, can be perceived in some cases to be the proper conclusion of the development begun in Greek speculation" (p. 141). Foster's concluding chapter on the notions of ruler and sovereign summarizes his insight concerning the bearing of Creation upon the political philosophies of Plato and Hegel. His neglect of the philosophy of St. Thomas, the most adequate fulfillment of Greek wisdom in the light of Christian revelation, is inexplicable except by ignorance or prejudice. The prejudice is indicated: he admits that "no modern philosophy has absorbed the entirety of Christian doctrine"; a footnote adds, "still less any mediæval one" (p. 192).

8. "It is worth noting that Plato commits himself to no opinion on the merits of these Egyptian conventions in art. He merely appeals to the example of Egypt as proof that the permanent maintenance of artistic canons is possible, and commends the serious attention which that people have given to the problem" (A. E. Taylor, Introduction to his translation of *The Laws of Plato*, London, 1934: p. xxvi). Cf. J. E. Harrison, *Ancient Art and Ritual*, New York, 1913: Ch. 1. The close relation between Egyptian art and religious ritual has a bearing on the stability of the artistic conventions.

9. On the subject of the position of pleasure in the order of the goods, the *Philebus* should be consulted. In the *Gorgias*, Plato associates the pleasures derived from poetry with those produced by the art of personal adornment and the art of the pastry-cook — all of them pleasures of the moment.

10. The conflict between poetry and politics is a special case of the antinomy of art and prudence. It may be suggested that Plato solves this antinomy by his conception in the *Laws* of a Minister of Education who is at once the curator of public morals and censor of the arts. He must be a prudent man who understands art, and an artist who possesses the special art of prudence in addition to all others. This would be the reconciliation between

art and prudence which, as Maritain says, only "Wisdom, being endowed with the outlook of God and ranging over Action and Making alike," can achieve (*Art and Scholasticism*, New York, 1930: p. 86). But the art of prudence, involved in all the moral virtues, is one which the Saints alone fully possess. Maritain quotes Gardeil as asking : "If you must have works of art, are not those who model in human clay the likeness of God's own features to be preferred to Phidias?" (Note 17). Is it in this sense that the philosopher-king or his minister of education, making good men, is to be the only artist in the state? But God alone makes works of that kind. "The Saints are truly and literally His masterpiece" (Maritain, *op. cit.*, p. 15). The philosopher-king, modeling in human clay and having only an imperfect wisdom, is merely an imitation of the Ideal. In proportion as human philosophy at best is only a remote participation in Divine Wisdom, the conflict between art and prudence remains unreconciled. It should be remembered, however, that Plato describes the philosopher-king as the artificer of every civic virtue. (*Republic*, 500 D). Can the theological interpretation be avoided? Book VI seems clearly to say No.

11. The discussion in the *Republic* (492–493) is illuminating on the point of the plurality and the circularity of the factors responsible for moral character or its corruption. Plato condemned public opinion, the sophists, and the arts, as corrupters of youth, and in so doing recognized that the sophists and the poets reflect public opinion as well as influence it. Such reciprocity complicates the problem of the causes of excellence or defect in moral character. The problem is the same today. "For the cinemas, jazz-bands and cheap novels to which a modern Plato or Tolstoy would rightly point as having pernicious moral effects — more rightly indeed than Plato and Tolstoy pointed to the great works of art which specially irritated them — can be regarded as the effect of the current moral atmosphere no less than its cause" (O. de Selincourt, *Art and Morality*, London, 1935 : pp. 112–113). But this contemporary Platonist is here only voicing an ancient opinion. We have not solved the problem of the causes of virtue and vice in particular men. The comment which Aristophanes makes on the point in his comedy, *The Tagenistae*, still holds. He ascribes the ruin of a young man to "a book, or to Prodicus the sophist, or to bad company." The enumeration of external factors might have been indefinitely extended, but no enumeration, however complete, of such accidental circumstances reaches the heart of the problem of right conduct.

12. The difference between Plato and Aristotle with regard to speculative and practical questions is striking. In the realm of speculative philosophy, Plato is resolutely dialectical, unwilling to rest in any position as if it were clearly knowledge rather than opinion; but in practical matters, especially in political philosophy, he achieves an extraordinary definiteness and proposes policies as if they were firmly grounded not only on clear principles but also on knowledge of contingent facts. Aristotle, on the other hand, uses dialectic in the approach to speculative problems only to clarify and order the opinions of his predecessors, but he presents his own solutions as knowledge, resting on self-evident principles and demonstratively developed therefrom; whereas in the practical realm he moves with a circumspection born of his fundamental insight that action involves contingent singulars of which our knowledge is inadequate. If the Platonist can always ask embarrassing dialectical questions about Aristotelian science, the Aristotelian in turn can always challenge the practicality of Platonic proposals in practical philosophy.

13. When matter is said to be the principle of the difference between the work of art and its object of imitation, what is meant is the matter of the medium in which the artist works and not his subject-matter. The medium consists of the materials out of which the artist composes, and these materials not only individualize the work of art, as matter in the natural composite is the principle of individuality, but also differentiate it from the object imitated which, being natural, must be constituted by prime and not prejacent matter. But if matter is understood as subject-matter, then the matter does not differentiate the work of art, because its subject-matter is the same as its object of imitation from which it differs formally. Thus, the matter of life, human action, is the same as the subject-matter of poetry. The difference between poetry and life would then be formal. These distinctions are more fully discussed in Chapter 13.

"Aristotle says relatively little concerning the process of imitation, and that little has been subject to great differences of interpretation; yet what he says of natural objects and their production and of artificial objects and their making affords sound basis for reconstruction of his theory of imitation. The natural object, composite of form and matter, acts according to the natural principle of its being; in imitation the artist separates some form from the matter with which it is joined in nature — not, however, the 'substantial' form, but some form perceptible by sensation — and joins it anew to the matter of his art, the medium which he uses. . . For Aristotle, consequently, imitation may be said to be, in the fine arts, the presentation of an aspect of things in a matter other than its natural matter, rendered inevitable by reasons other than its natural reasons; in the useful arts it is the realization of a function in another matter or under other circumstances than those which are natural" (R. P. McKeon, *Literary Criticism and the Concept of Imitation in Antiquity*, in Modern Philology, August 1936: pp. 18–19; by permission of the University of Chicago Press).

14. Art imitates nature (1) in the sense that the process of art imitates natural operations and (2) in the sense that the products of art imitate natural things. The first sense applies primarily to such practical arts as medicine; the second sense applies primarily to the productive arts, fine or useful. It is in the second sense that poetry is defined as an imitation of action.

15. The issue turns on the difference between the Platonic and Aristotelian conceptions of imitation. For Plato works of fine art, scientific treatises and philosophical discourses are all imitations because they all involve some similitude to reality. They differ only in their proximity and fidelity to the common object of imitation. In what sense are science and philosophy imitations? The Platonic answer is that knowledge depends upon the similitude between the knower and the known. Hence whatever is knowledge is an imitation and whatever is an imitation is knowledge. It must follow from these identifications that natural things which are said to be imitations of the ideas are also knowledge. Aristotle insists upon making distinctions in kind rather than degree. Poetry is not merely bad philosophy or science or history; it is not knowledge in the same sense at all. We must distinguish the knower, the knowledge whereby he knows and the object of his knowledge. While it is true that there is a kind of similitude between knowledge and its object, the similitude is not sensible nor is it known. Our knowledge is in a relation of similitude to reality but it is not knowledge *of* this relation. It is knowledge of reality. An imitation involves a sensible similitude to its object and this similitude is known; in fact, it is only when this similitude is known that we recognize one thing as an imitation of another. Therefore, works of fine art are imitations and not knowledge; history, science and philosophy are knowledge and not imitations. In short, works of art are objects of knowledge, and they are objects which are known as imitations because other objects are also known to which they stand in a known

relation of similitude. This means, of course, that to imitate, on the part of the artist, or to appreciate imitations, on the part of his audience, requires knowledge as an indispensable condition. But a necessary condition of a thing's being is not an essential part of its nature. It does not follow, therefore, that artistic imitation *is* knowledge. (Imitations are *like* knowledge in that both require the priority of their objects and both involve an intentional direction of the mind to these objects. But knowledge aims at the *maximum* formal similitude with the object, whereas imitation does not; and imitation is the transposition of a form to an alien matter, whereas knowledge is the form of the thing known in the intellect, entirely apart from matter.) The distinction can be summarized in terms of the difference between the fine and liberal arts. Both are productive. But the fine arts are disciplined powers of operation which *use* knowledge in the production of imitations, whereas the liberal arts are disciplined powers of operation productive of knowledge itself.

The Aristotelian answer to Plato's criticism of poetry is not met, therefore, by pointing out that Plato's criticism is based upon his thesis that knowledge is imitation, which makes poetry an inferior kind of knowledge. The Aristotelian answer attacks that theory of knowledge, and makes distinctions which indicate a genuine difference between the proper functions of poetry and philosophy. Cf. Maritain, *Art and Scholasticism*, New York, 1930: pp. 56–64; and McKeon, *Literary Criticism and the Concept of Imitation in Antiquity*, in Modern Philology, August 1936.

16. No Greek would have understood the modern conflict between art for art's sake and art for man's sake, but he would have understood an issue stated in terms of the separability or inseparability of intrinsic and extrinsic criticism. Intrinsic criticism regards the work of art as the end of the artist's activity and judges it as a thing well or poorly made. The aesthetic criterion of beauty is thus closely related to standards of technical excellence. Extrinsic criticism regards the work of art as something having an audience, something which is received by men in a certain way because it is a product of art, and judges it in terms of its effects upon its public. It does not matter whether the artist intended to address this public or desired that they be moved in any fashion whatsoever. When the work of art has left his hands, it becomes a thing in its own right and has a career of influences for which he is responsible as a cause, and therefore he can be criticized as a man who has done this, and not only as a man who has tried to make this thing a good thing of a certain sort. In short, a man

cannot be an artist without being a public figure, unless he refuses
to communicate what he has made; and a work of art has two
relations, one to the man as an artist and the other to the man who
through making it has an influence upon other men. These two
relations are, of course, not actually separable. The same man is
at once both an artist and a public figure; the thing made may be
at once both a work of art and a public benefaction or nuisance.
But the question remains whether a clear analytical separation can
be made between aesthetic and technical criticism of the work of
art and the artist, on the one hand, and moral and political criticism,
on the other. The difference between Plato and Aristotle is not
that Plato ignores the intrinsic criteria of judgment and Aristotle,
on his part, neglects the extrinsic. The difference is that Plato
seems to deny, though nowhere explicit, that a man can be good
as an artist without being good as a man or that a work of art can
be technically excellent unless it is also ethically sound and beneficial in its moral and political effects; whereas Aristotle quite
explicitly separates the two criteria of judgment and acknowledges
the independent variability of technical and moral goodness in a
work of art; that is, the work can be technically good without
being morally sound and even though its influence upon an audience is politically bad. The *Poetics* is a work in technical
criticism, even though purgation and the pleasure men derive from
imitation are mentioned. Purgation is more appropriately discussed in the *Politics*, and the pleasure of contemplation is more
fully discussed in the *Ethics*. A tragedy may be technically bad
if it fail to effect a proper purgation of pity and fear, but this
failure, so far as the *Poetics* is concerned, is merely an external
mark of an intrinsic disorder or defect in the parts of the drama.
(This basic issue in criticism is discussed in Chapters 12 and 15.
Cf. Note 2 *supra*.)

Mr. T. S. Eliot is the ablest contemporary exponent of the
Platonic position. In his *Dialogue on Dramatic Poetry* (*Collected
Essays*, New York, 1932, by permission of Harcourt, Brace and
Company, Inc.) one of the participants says: "You can never
draw the line between aesthetic criticism and moral and social
criticism; you cannot draw the line between criticism and metaphysics; you start with literary criticism, and however rigorous
an aesthete you may be, you are over the frontier into something
else sooner or later. . . I may begin by moral criticism of
Shakespeare and pass over into aesthetic criticism, or vice versa."
And he is answered by an Aristotelian who says: "And all you
do is to lead the discussion astray" (p. 42). See also, in the same
collection, Mr. Eliot's essay on Arnold and Pater which deals with

the nineteenth century's difficulties about art for art's sake or for the sake of something else. Cf. L. Callahan, *A Theory of Esthetic, According to the Principles of St. Thomas Aquinas*, Washington, 1927: Chapter IX on art and morality.

17. If purgation be considered part of the definition of a tragedy, or any work of art, then intrinsic and extrinsic criticism are not analytically separable because the purgation effected is not in the work but in its audience, although there is something in the work which causes this effect. (The "power" of a work of art consists in its appropriate effects upon an audience, these effects being determined, of course, by something in the nature of the work. Thus, catharsis, viewed psychologically, is part of the power of art in relation to men. So also are the pleasures proper to each sort of art. It is in this sense that catharsis is a property.) Thus, the relief of fatigue which chairs provide is not part of the definition of a chair; it follows from the essence of a chair as a thing which can be sat upon that chairs can rest men who sit upon them. What follows from the essence but is not part of the essence is a property and not an element in the definition. The essence of poetry is imitation of human action in the medium of language; its power to effect the catharsis of emotion is a property following from this essence. If it be objected that the definition of tragedy includes the specification of the emotions as pity and fear, the objection raises the question whether Aristotle has *properly* defined tragedy if his only way of doing so is to mention "pity and fear." If in the genus poetry, tragedy is to be differentiated from comedy, the specific difference must be something intrinsic to the structure of that type of poem; thus, that the action imitated be *serious*. A poem's power to purge pity and fear stands to its form *somewhat* as man's ability to become a scientist is to his essence as a rational animal. Even if because of accidental circumstances a man does not become a scientist he is no less essentially a man; so even if because of accidents a tragedy fails to effect the catharsis of pity and fear, it must be no less essentially a tragedy — on the supposition, of course, that there is an essential difference between tragedy and comedy.

18. Works of fine art can be sensual as well as aesthetic objects because they are known by sensitive intuition. Strictly speaking, they are not received as works of art when they are degraded into sensual objects. The pleasure of titillated senses is not the pleasure of knowing proper to a work of art as an imitation and as beautiful. (Aristotle points out that the pleasure may be due to the imi-

tation itself or to the execution, i.e., the technique, or to the coloring or some such other cause. Vd. *Poetics*, 4, 1448ᵇ15–20. The first two are proper pleasures. The third is sensual.) The danger of such degradation is greatest in the case of plastic and music, although it is also possible in poetry, not only because of the appeal to the ear but because the imagination moves the sensitive appetite. In the aesthetic reception of art, the senses serve the intellect as its instrument of apprehension because the thing to be known is a sensible individual thing, but the knowing is nevertheless an operation of "intellectualized sense," to use Maritain's phrase. In the sensual reception of art, the sensitive faculty is involved, not as an instrument of reason, but as causing the passions. The possibility of these two modes of reception for any work of fine art — though for some much more than for others — indicates the problem of obscenity, of impurity and carnality, which concerns the moralist when he judges art in relation to man. Cf. Maritain, *Art and Scholasticism*, New York, 1930: Notes 54 and 55; and L. Callahan, *A Theory of Esthetic*, Washington, 1927: pp. 109–110, 114–117.

19.   That works of fine art, through being imitations, give men the pleasure of learning is not inconsistent with the point that such works of art are not knowledge in the sense in which science and philosophy are. (See note 15, *supra*.) The work of art is an object of knowledge and not a medium of knowledge; it is something to be known and not that whereby something is known, although in knowing it as an imitation, the spectator knows not only it but its relation of similitude to the already known object of imitation. The mediæval distinction between the *id quod* and the *id quo* of knowledge is relevant here. (Vd. St. Thomas Aquinas, *Summa Theologica*, I, Q. 85, A. 2.) A science is not that which is known but that whereby what is known of that which is known is known. That which is known is that which is. Secondarily, however, because the intellect is reflexive, knowledge can itself be known as if it were an object. (Secondarily, therefore, *a* science or philosophy can be an aesthetic object.) The work of fine art is primarily a thing which is and hence primarily an object to be known. To treat it as a means of knowledge — which men do when they look at a picture as if it were a chart or map, or read a novel as if it were a biography — is possible because to produce it the artist had to have knowledge of the object imitated, and this knowledge is incorporated in the thing as an imitation. Hence this knowledge can be extracted by one who uses the work of art as a means for knowing the object imitated. It is possible,

therefore, for works of art to be the *id quo* of knowledge secondarily, as science and philosophy can be the *id quod* of knowledge secondarily; but not as properly because the latter usage depends upon the essential reflexivity of the intellect, whereas the former depends upon something more extrinsic, namely, that knowledge is a necessary condition of imitative art. (The same work, e.g., an anatomical drawing, can be regarded as a piece of fine art or as scientific; it can be received as an imitation or as communicating knowledge. But the mode of reception is different and this is a difference in human products *quoad nos* and not *secundum se*.)

When, therefore, Aristotle describes the pleasure which art affords as the pleasure of cognition, he is not identifying art and knowledge. Science and philosophy give knowledge to the man who is able to learn them, knowledge of reality. Works of art, because they are imitations, give the man who already has some knowledge — in this case, of the object imitated — the pleasure of learning because in knowing the work of art as an imitation, he not only knows the thing itself but also perceives its similitude to other things he knows. As Maritain says, the joy produced by a work of art "does not proceed from the truth of *imitation as a reproduction of things*, it proceeds from the perfection with which the work expresses or manifests form, in the metaphysical sense of the word, it proceeds from the truth of *imitation as manifestation of a form*" (*Art and Scholasticism*, New York, 1930: p. 59). It is imitation which makes the thing intelligible to us, and this accounts for the pleasure of learning which all men, even philosophers, experience in knowing works of art. Aristotle must not be interpreted to mean that works of art give this pleasure *only* to men whose capacities for learning are limited. Art gives this pleasure to all men alike, though only some are able to enjoy the delight of learning through philosophical discourse.

Because works of fine art are primarily objects of knowledge they have a speculative character which distinguishes them from works of useful art which are primarily instruments of operation and not things to be contemplated. The recognition of this speculative character in works of fine art must not, however, lead to the Platonic confusion of them with works of liberal art which are primarily media and not objects of knowledge.

20. The speculative character of works of art, like that of games, must not be understood as identifying them with science and philosophy as means of knowledge; it is rather to be found in the impracticality which characterizes participation in them. The

comparison drawn by St. Thomas between wisdom and games is enlightening: "The contemplation of wisdom is rightly compared with games for two things to be found in games. The first is that games give pleasure and the contemplation of wisdom gives the very greatest pleasure, according to what Wisdom says of itself in Ecclesiasticus: *My spirit is sweet above honey*. The second is that the movements in games are not contrived to serve another end but are pursued for their own sake. It is the same with the delights of wisdom" (quoted by Maritain, *Art and Scholasticism*, New York, 1930: pp. 34–35). Works of art are even more like wisdom in that they give pleasure through being objects of contemplation, known for their own sake.

21. As indicated in Note 18 *supra*, there are different kinds of pleasure. We do not call a work of art or any other spectacle amusing because it arouses the pleasures of the senses as such; quite the contrary, the movements of sensuality are often far from being amusing. It amuses us by engaging us as spectators, and it can do this only by offering us something to know. Each art, says Aristotle, ought to produce, not any chance pleasure, but the pleasure proper to it (*Poetics*, 1462^{b}14). In like vein it can be said that the fine arts, as a class, ought according to their nature to produce a proper pleasure. To yield the pleasure of contemplation follows as a property from the nature of fine art in the same way as purgation does. Cf. Butcher, *Aristotle's Theory of Poetry and Fine Art*, London, 1932: pp. 198–205.

21a. In the *Metaphysics* Aristotle seems to suggest that the original distinction of the fine arts from the useful was the recreational service of the former, i.e., a special type of utility. "At first he who invented any art that when beyond the common perceptions of man was naturally admired by men, not only because there was something useful in the invention, but because he was thought wise and superior to the rest. But as more arts were invented, and some were directed to the necessities of life, others to its recreation, the inventors of the latter were naturally always regarded as wiser than the inventors of the former, because their branches of knowledge did not aim at utility" (981^{b}12-20). He adds that last in order came the speculative sciences which aimed neither at pleasure nor at the necessities of life. They partook, more than the fine arts, of the nature of Wisdom.

22. Vd. Aristotle, *Nichomachean Ethics*, Book VI; St. Thomas Aquinas, *Summa Theologica*, I–II, Q. 57; Q. 58.

23. It should be readily admitted that there is a correlation between the goodness of a work of art and the goodness of the mind it pleases. In his discussion of the relative merits of dramatic and epic poetry, Aristotle appeals to the criterion of the more refined, the more cultivated audience. "The more refined in every case is that which appeals to the better sort of audience" (*Poetics*, 26, 1461^b27). But Aristotle is not here thinking of a good audience in terms of standards of moral excellence. He speaks of the patrons of the theatre as being "too dull to comprehend" the narrative without the accessories of the stage. In other words, the test of art is not made by the response of the good man in every sense, but only the man who is good intellectually, whose aesthetic sensitivity is technically trained. In sharp contrast is Plato's remark that "the finest music is that which delights the best men, the properly educated, that, above all, which pleases the one man who is supreme in *goodness* and *education*" (*Laws*, 695, italics mine). If "education" means only aesthetic or intellectual cultivation, that is not enough; moral goodness is also required. The difference between the Platonic and the Aristotelian tests naturally follows from their difference with regard to the separability and independence of intrinsic and extrinsic criteria in the judgment of works of art. See Note 16 *supra*. Cf. Butcher, *Aristotle's Theory of Poetry and Fine Art*, London, 1932 : pp. 211–213. "To the ideal spectator or listener, who is a man of educated taste and represents an instructed public, every fine art addresses itself; he may be called the 'rule and standard' of that art, as the man of moral insight is of morals."

24. Ethics and politics are not inexact on the level of their principles because these are truths of the speculative sciences imported into the practical order by being directed to the ends of action. But action is with respect to contingent singulars always; action is always particular, here and now in this case. Therefore, in the practical order principles are insufficient to determine action, since knowledge of the particular circumstances is also required. It is this knowledge which is intrinsically inadequate and which makes ethics and politics uncertain as practical sciences, that is, as knowledge devoted to directing action. This uncertainty on the casuistical level must not be permitted, however, to obscure the clear practical wisdom of the principles. Cf. Aristotle, *Ethics*, I, 1, 7 ; also St. Thomas Aquinas, *Summa Theologica*, I–II, QQ. 1–5 ; Q. 10, A.2 ; Q. 13, A.6.

The correlation of ethics and politics is primarily made in terms of justice as a moral virtue and as the proximate principle of human law, and in terms of education, both moral and intellectual, as a political instrument. Vd. Aristotle, *Ethics*, I, 1; V; X, 10.

25. The Platonist may object that Aristotle's general principle of relativity in ethics and politics is practically insidious because the mere suggestion to man that perfection is relative to capacity and other circumstances makes him, weak as he is, acquiesce in his weakness. Plato's refusal to consider anything except the ideal may, therefore, be a wiser recognition of human frailty than Aristotle's perpetual concern with the limitations of human nature and the extenuating circumstances under which men act. But when human frailty is understood in the light of the Christian doctrine of original sin, the difference between Plato and Aristotle becomes clearer. Aristotle is considering the type of happiness which St. Thomas distinguishes from beatitude as imperfect (*Summa Theologica*, I–II, QQ. 1–5). It is the only kind of happiness which man can achieve without Grace, and this different men achieve in different degrees according to their capacities. Plato is considering the happiness of the saints, the happiness of Man specifically. Beatitude is the last end of the human species, though not all men achieve it and no man achieves it without supernatural aid. Aristotle's position is obviously better in practical *philosophy* — merely human, concerned with an imperfect end and proceeding in terms of natural knowledge. Plato's position is better *only* as an anticipation of moral *theology* having sacred sources, concerned with a perfect end, and proceeding in terms of the revelation of Providence and Divine Law. The philosopher-king is, after all, only a man and not God. Cf. Note 10 *supra*.

26. Bishop Bossuet makes a significant comment on this passage in Book VII of the *Politics*: "I do not know why he (Aristotle) was not willing to extend further this precaution. Youth and even infancy remain for a long time with men; or rather they are never entirely *défait*" (*Maximes et Réflexions Sur La Comédie*, Paris, 1694; edition of 1881 by Eugene Belin: p. 57).

27. Making a clear distinction between the recreative and didactic functions of art, Aristotle makes different political provisions for the arts viewed as performing these different functions. He does not disagree with Plato about the supervision of music and poetry as occurring in early education. Even though his analysis of the nature of art shows that works of fine art are not essentially didactic, he recognizes that they can be used didactically and that

the immature mind, not receiving them aesthetically, is likely to use them in that manner, gathering instruction where none was intended. Therefore, it is necessary to prescribe the kind of music for educational purposes and to be careful in the selection of the tales told to children. Even here Aristotle is not as definite as Plato in the decision that this supervision of the arts shall be performed by an official of the State. But with respect to the service which the arts perform for the mature population, Aristotle nowhere considers any need for regulation. As amusements, pleasing, purging, giving rest and recreation, they are of many kinds and levels of refinement and so are suited to the different kinds of men, the rude as well as the cultivated. Is the sharp difference that here appears between Plato and Aristotle due to the fact that Plato considers most men as children for whom the arts are always primarily didactic and therefore dangerous unless supervised? Or is it due to the fact that Plato fails to consider the recreative as well as the didactic function? The difference is made even sharper by Plato's total exclusion of the dramatists, a measure that seems extremely imprudent in the context of the Aristotelian analysis.

The relation of the distinction between the recreative and didactic functions of works of art to the distinction between the mature and the immature in their audience, raises the question whether children have a need for the arts as sources of rest and relaxation. The question is a difficult one. Childhood is the period of play; children do not need to be rested from work. But it may be said that as the games which children play are to the exercise and development of their bodies, so the arts which they enjoy, especially the fiction, the music and the pictures, are to the exercise and development of their imaginations. This, however, while not a didactic use of the arts, is essentially educational and not recreative. Plato is right, therefore, if he thinks of the arts as primarily educational in the life of children.

Cf. Butcher, *Aristotle's Theory of Poetry and Fine Art*, London, 1932: pp. 220–221 and 238–239. The Aristotelian doctrine has seldom been expounded; even those who claim him as their master are half-hearted because they are Platonists at heart. "Sir Philip Sidney, for example, who in his *Apologie for Poetrie* repeatedly states that the end of poetry is 'delightful teaching' or 'to teach and to delight' has no suspicion that he is following the *Ars Poetica* of Horace rather than that of Aristotle." This is the case generally in the Elizabethan period and the Renaissance. There are notable exceptions: in the Renaissance, Castelvetro; and much later, Dryden. Dryden's *Essay of Dramatic Poetry* should be compared with Mr. T. S. Eliot's *Dialogue on Dramatic Poetry* as re-phrasing the issue between Aristotle and Plato.

28. Cf. Jane Harrison, *Ancient Art and Ritual*, New York, 1913 : pp. 25–26, 135. "The spectators are a new and different element, the dance is not only danced but it is watched from a distance, it is a spectacle ; whereas in old days all or nearly all were worshippers acting, now many, indeed most, are spectators, watching, feeling, thinking, not doing. It is in this new attitude of the spectator that we touch on the difference between ritual and art ; the *dromenon*, the thing actually done by yourself, has become a *drama*, a thing also done but abstracted from your doing" (p. 127).

29. Vd. Butcher, *Aristotle's Theory of Poetry and Fine Art*, London, 1932 : pp. 243–255. "In the medical language of the school of Hippocrates it (the word 'purgation') strictly denotes the removal of a painful or disturbing element from the organism, and hence the purifying of what remains, by the elimination of alien matter" (p. 253). The purification of what remains should be emphasized as much as the eliminative aspect. This purification, in the case of the emotions, is the clarification of them which comes from understanding. This the arts achieve by being spectacles which somehow include the emotions they elicit. The emotions aroused are projected and as projected become objects of contemplation : to be known and understood as well as experienced.

In accepting this interpretation of purgation "we do not ascribe to tragedy a direct moral purpose and influence. Tragedy, according to the definition, acts on the feelings, not on the will. It does not make men better, though it removes certain hindrances to virtue. The refining of passion under temporary and artificial excitement is still far distant from moral improvement" (Butcher, *op cit.*, p. 269).

30. The good man, the virtuous man, is one in whom the soul is the principal cause and the body the instrumental cause of his actions, or in other words one in whom reason rules and the passions are governed. When the body uses the soul, when the passions use reason, the proper order is inverted. In the language of St. Thomas, the problem is the relation of the intellectual appetite or will to the sensitive appetite whose motions are the passions. The passions are not in themselves evil ; they are evil only when they are not controlled by reason, only if "by passions we understand none but the inordinate movements of the sensitive

appetite, considered as disturbances or ailments. But if we give the name of passions to all the movements of the sensitive appetite, then it belongs to the perfection of man's good that his passions be moderated by reason" (*Summa Theologica*, I–II, Q. 24, A. 3). Cf. *Summa Contra Gentiles*, IV, 70.

Reason controls the passions in two ways: first, by understanding their objects which, as particular goods or evils, are understood by being seen as instances of universal goods and evils; secondly, by understanding the passions themselves as motions of the sensitive appetite, their causes in the soul and in outward circumstances. It is through understanding them that reason is able to moderate the passions and assimilate them to the life of the soul rather than to oppose them as entirely evil. This moderation and assimilation of the passions constitute the moral virtues. To the extent that artificial purgation involves an understanding of particular passions in the context of a spectacle which reveals their nature, the arts working purgation are an aid to reason in the moral life. Cf. Spinoza's doctrine that through knowledge of the passions we are freed from bondage to them (*Ethics*, V, Scholium to Prop. 4); also Aquinas, *Summa Contra Gentiles*, IV, 22.

31. Mr. Selincourt criticizes Aristotle's doctrine by supposing that he conceived purgation only as dispelling the surplus quantity of emotion, adding that the expression of emotions "is as likely to stimulate as to dispel them, and more likely to increase than to diminish their surplus, making us hungry where most it satisfies and exciting rather than cloying the appetites which it feeds" (*Art and Morality*, London, 1935: p. 68). Mr. Selincourt makes the Aristotelian theory of purgation mechanical and then triumphantly finds obvious faults in the mechanism. The questions he raises (p. 64) about the completeness of purgation as *elimination* and about its permanence are fair; but he quite arbitrarily attributes to Aristotle the position that "the mind achieved its freedom through the banishment, rather than the control and purification or anything else, of what was disturbing its peace." Several pages later (69 ff.) he develops the notion that the arts give liberation from the passions through purification by understanding, as if this were entirely a modern notion which we owe to Spinoza and principally to Hegel. Cf. Butcher's interpretation of Aristotle, *op. cit.*, pp. 253–255; and Notes 29 and 30 *supra*.

32. The Platonic question, coming at the end of an extended discourse which prescribes the method for achieving a well ordered state, is impossible because it requires the poets to demonstrate

their utility in a society which is *already* and *otherwise* well ordered. *If* a society can be well ordered without the aid of the arts and *if* a society to be well ordered requires that the arts be strictly regulated or banished, how is any possibility left open? A fairer question would be: Can a society be well ordered without the services which the arts perform? This question would at least permit the poets to attempt to show their utility. Plato has answered this latter question before he reaches the tenth book of the *Republic*. A society can be well ordered through the rule of a philosopher, and we have seen what the philosopher thinks about the place of the arts. The poets must, therefore, meet Plato's challenge by denying his premise. A society cannot be well ordered by the rule of a philosopher because men who can be so ruled are able to rule themselves well and there is no political problem of how to achieve a well ordered state. The ideal state dissolves into an ideal anarchy. The political problem is rather how to rule men who are unable to rule themselves. When the problem is thus stated practically in the light of human weakness, the ruler, even though he be a philosopher, recognizes the need for force and persuasion, admits the relativity of the laws to particular circumstances, and willingly accepts whatever aid the arts can render in their function as amusements. Cf. *Republic*, I, 347 D

33. The dialectical victory rests on the distinction between those effects of art which *properly* follow from its nature and those which are *accidental*. Thus, that works of art *can* be objects of contemplation is a property; that they *can* be among the causes of vice is an accident. What effects a work of art *actually has*, however, is always a question of fact.

34. "All truth belongs of right to Christian thought, as the spoils of the Egyptians to the Hebrews. *Quaecumque igitur apud omnes praeclara dicta sunt, nostra Christianorum sunt*, because according to that saying of St. Ambrose, which St. Thomas delighted to quote, *every truth whoever said it, comes from the Holy Spirit*" (Maritain, *Introduction to Philosophy*, London, 1930: p. 97). Cf. E. Gilson, *The Spirit of Mediæval Philosophy*, New York, 1936.

34a. Book VI of the *Republic*, which delineates the character of the philosopher-king and discusses the manner of his coming, his acceptance by the people, his mediation of the human and the divine, can certainly be read as a prophecy of Christ incarnate. There is the insight that "in the present evil state of governments, whatever is saved and comes to good is saved by the power of God" (492 E).

Vd. also 501 A, B which describes the new dispensation as an absolutely fresh start in human affairs; and 502 B which asserts that the coming of one such ruler will "bring into existence the ideal polity about which the world is so incredulous." Thus interpreted, the *Republic* identifies the ideal state with the City of God, which must await the coming of His Son. It is, indeed, no earthly city. Of course, such interpretation removes the *Republic* from the field of ordinary political philosophy, and dissolves, — perhaps resolves, — the issue between Plato and Aristotle. See Notes 25 *supra* and 35 *infra*.

35. I am indebted to my friend Mr. William Gorman for this analogy. It deserves an essay from his pen, in which he would develop the *differences:* Christ, as teacher, was not a philosopher; His imitation was not a piece of philosophic writing, nor does the imitation of Him depend on the possession of any kind of philosophic knowledge. One does not *need* to know, in the Greek sense of 'know,' to be a saint. Through the coming of Christ the Greek problem of how man can become virtuous is radically altered, as radically as Grace perfects Nature. Cf. Note 25 *supra*. (On the relation of natural to infused virtues, see St. Thomas Aquinas, *Summa Theologica*, I–II, Q.63, AA.3,4; QQ.65, 68.)

36. "Now, since several acts are seen to belong to the will, such as desire, delight, hate, and so forth, we find that the one principle and root of all is love. . . Now to be attracted towards a thing, as such, is to love it. Wherefore every inclination of the will, as well as of the sensitive appetite, has its origin in love" (St. Thomas Aquinas, *Summa Contra Gentiles*, IV, 19). Cf. *Summa Theologica*, II–II, Q.53, A.6: "As the Philosopher states (*Ethics*, VI), *pleasure above all corrupts the estimate of prudence*, and chiefly sexual pleasure which absorbs the mind, and draws it to sensible delight." On the vices of lust, see II–II, QQ.153, 154.

37. It may be objected that there are profound anticipations of the doctrine of original sin in the *Dialogues*. Thus, in the *Phaedrus* the myth of the charioteer describes the conflict between man's higher and lower nature in terms of reason and the passions; and in the *Phaedo* the essential evil of this life is the subjection of the soul to the body. Cf. Note 38 *infra*. Admitting this, it must nevertheless be said, first, that Plato's account of the soul makes its subjection to the body inexplicable, and, second, that in his approach to moral and political problems, especially the latter,

Plato does not seem to be guided by his own psychological insights. In contrast, Aristotle's *Ethics* and *Politics* are practical
applications of his psychology.

38. "According to the teaching of faith, we affirm that man was,
from the beginning, so fashioned that as long as his reason was
subject to God, not only would his lower powers serve him without hindrance, but there would be nothing in his body to lessen
its subjection; since whatever was lacking in nature to bring this
about God by His grace would supply. Whereas no sooner did
his reason turn away from God than his lower powers rebelled
against his reason, and his body became subject to sufferings that
counteract the life it receives from the soul" (St. Thomas
Aquinas, *Summa Contra Gentiles*, IV, 52). "Many obstacles prevent man from reaching his end. For he is hindered by the weakness of his reason, which is easily drawn into error, which bars
him from the straight road that leads to his end. He is also
hindered by the passions of the sensitive faculty, and by the affec-
tions whereby he is drawn to sensible and inferior things, since
the more he adheres to them, the further is he removed from his
last end" (*Ibid.*, III, 147).

39. See Note 35 *supra*.

40. Vd. St. Augustine, *The City of God*, II, 14: "Must we not
licac award the palm to a Greek, Plato, who in framing his ideal
republic, conceived that poets should be banished from the city
as enemies of the state? He could not brook that the gods be
brought into disrepute, nor that the minds of the citizens be depraved and besotted, by the fictions of the poets. Compare now
human nature as you see it in Plato, expelling poets from the city
that the citizens be uninjured, with the divine nature as you see
it in these gods exacting plays in their own honor. Plato strove,
though unsuccessfully, to persuade the light-minded and lascivious
Greeks to abstain from so much as writing such plays; the gods
used their authority to extort the acting of the same from the
dignified and sober-minded Romans. And not content with
having them acted, they had them dedicated to themselves, con-
secrated to themselves, solemnly celebrated in their own honor.
To which, then, would it be more becoming in a state to decree
divine honors — to Plato, who prohibited these wicked and
licentious plays, or to the demons who delighted in blinding men
to the truth of what Plato unsuccessfully sought to inculcate?"
See also Book II, Ch. 13.

40a.   In sharp contrast to Jeremy Collier's opinion is the position
taken by "B" who is the Platonist in Mr. Eliot's *Dialogue on
Dramatic Poetry:* "B. The morality of our Restoration drama
cannot be impugned.   It assumes orthodox Christian morality and
laughs (in its comedy) at human nature for not living up to it.
It retains its respect for the Divine by showing the failure of the
Human.   The attitude of the Restoration drama towards morality
is like the attitude of the Blasphemer towards Religion.   It is only
the irreligious who are shocked by blasphemy.   Blasphemy is a
sign of faith.   Imagine Mr. Shaw blaspheming!   He could not.
Our Restoration drama is all virtue.   It depends upon virtue for
its existence" (*op. cit.*, p. 33, by permission of Harcourt, Brace and
Company, Inc.).

41.   "Plato, therefore, whose authority I had much rather justly
construe than unjustly resist, meant not in general of poets, in those
words of which Julius Scaliger saith, *Qua authoritate barbari qui-
dam atque hispidi abuti velint ad poteas e republica exigendos;*
but only meant to drive out those wrong opinions of the Deity,
whereof now, without further law, Christianity hath taken away
all hurtful belief, perchance, as he thought, nourished by the then
esteemed poets" (*Apology for Poetry*, ed. by A. S. Cook, New
York, 1890: pp. 42–43).

42.   Elizabethan criticism, even when it pretends to follow the
Poetics, is influenced by the writers of the Italian Renaissance who
also make much of their indebtedness to Aristotle but are primarily
reviving the neo-Platonic critical theories of the Hellenistic period.   Thus, Minturno (*De Poeta*, 1559) makes a Horatian defense of poetry against Plato by showing its value as a kind of
learning.   "The Renaissance," says Spingarn, "was in closer accord
with Horace than with Aristotle, in requiring for the most part
the *utile* as well as the *dolce* in poetry" (*Literary Criticism in the
Renaissance*, New York, 1899: p. 48).   Castelvetro (*Poetica*,
1570) is a rare exception in asserting that the end of poetry is
delight and delight alone.   "If utility is to be conceded to poetry
at all, it is merely as an accident, as in the tragic purgation of terror
and compassion" (*Ibid.*, p. 55).   And Spingarn in summarizing
the various conceptions of poetry held by the Italian critics
admits "that at bottom the conception was an ethical one, for,
with the exception of such a revolutionary spirit as Castelvetro,
by most theorists it was as an effective guide to life that poetry
was chiefly valued.   Even when delight was admitted as an end, it
was simply because of its usefulness in effecting the ethical aim"

(*Ibid.*, p. 58). This holds for Elizabethan criticism as well. Webbe (*Discourse of English Poetrie*, 1586) considers poetry to be a delightful form of instruction. Sidney follows Scaliger and Minturno. Bacon defines poetry as "feigned history" and treats it, therefore, as a kind of knowledge. Ben Jonson holds that poetry "contains all that is best in philosophy, divinity and the science of politics, and leads and persuades men to virtue with a ravishing delight, while the others but threaten and compel. It therefore offers to mankind a certain rule and pattern of living well and happily in human society. This conception of poetry Jonson finds in Aristotle; but it is to the Italians of the Renaissance, and not the Stagyrite, that these doctrines really belong" (*Ibid.*, p. 279).

The Renaissance answer to Plato given in Aristotle's name is not only one which Aristotle would disown but one which Plato himself would as readily reject. Neoplatonism is certainly a bastard in the history of thought.

43. Dryden is being radical here only about Comedy. He has just conceded in the immediately preceding sentence that "Tragedy fulfills one great part of its institution, which is, by example, to instruct" (Hudson's edition of *Dryden's Dramatic Essays*, London, 1912 : p. 83). Yet in his *Defense of an Essay of Dramatic Poetry*, Dryden makes the more general statement : "Delight is the chief, if not the only, end of poetry ; instruction can be admitted but in the second place ; for poetry only instructs as it delights" (*Ibid.*, p. 62).

44. What Spingarn shows to be the case in the literary criticism of the Renaissance holds for the seventeenth century. Dryden and Rapin are no better Aristotelians than Castelvetro and Ben Jonson ; nor, of course, are they good Platonists, which can be seen by comparing them with Bishop Bossuet. Cf. Note 42 *supra*.

45. Cf. Butcher, *Aristotle's Theory of Poetry and Fine Art*, London, 1932 : p. 224. But Butcher wrongly attributes the doctrine of poetic justice to Plato by misreading the passage in the *Laws* (660) as a direction to the poets to exhibit the perfect requital of vice and virtue. In the same vein Mr. Krutch says : "Though the doctrine of poetic justice seems palpably absurd, it must be admitted in frankness that the whole question is bound up with, and receives support from, Plato" (*Comedy and Conscience*, New York, 1924 : p. 81). The seventeenth century

doctrine of poetic justice is an unfortunate confusion of moral
and aesthetic principles.   That it is neither Platonic nor Aristotelian is clear from the *Laws* and the *Poetics*.   That it is not
Christian can be seen in the following passage from St. Thomas:
"In the estimation of such men the order of punishments is apparently the reverse to that given above.   For to those, injuries
to the body and loss of external goods seem the greatest punishment; while they think little of the disorder of the soul, the
decay of virtue, and the loss of divine fruition, wherein man's
ultimate beatitude consists.   Hence it is that they think that God
punishes not the sins of man : because they see that sinners for
the most part are sound of body, and outwardly prosperous,
while virtuous men are sometimes none of these things. . .   Now
God the disposer of things knows the measure of human power.
Wherefore at times he apportions bodily and external goods to
a virtuous man as a help to virtue, and in this he bestows a favor
on him.   But sometimes he withdraws those things from him, because he sees them to be a hindrance to his enjoyment of God. . .
It will be no punishment for a virtuous man if he be deprived of
external goods to the profit of virtue.   On the other hand, for
the wicked it will be a punishment if they be granted external
goods whereby they are incited to evil-doing" (*Summa Contra
Gentiles*, III, 141).

46. Thus, on the one hand, poetry is defended by the opinions
that it teaches and delights — teaches morally by example and
through poetic justice, delights the senses, either directly or
through exciting the passions — and, on the other hand, it is attacked by the opinions that delight is no justification and that
poetry either teaches poorly or falsely.   What a picture of modern thought this is!   A discussion which misconceives the issue,
which either lacks entirely or grasps only superficially the ethical
and political principles in terms of which a sound dialectic must
proceed, and which even fails to define the few concepts it employs.   This history of English criticism from the sixteenth to
the nineteenth century is typical of other modern efforts to regain Greek wisdom, vapid and misleading because at best an
unacknowledged borrowing from, or an explicit commentary on,
Greek sources by writers who had either never read the texts
or read them incompletely.   The history of literary criticism
shows how little the modern world has added to Plato and Aristotle except through misunderstanding them.

47. Bossuet differs from Plato in one important respect.   Plato

condemned the arts because of their effects. Bossuet, as a Christian, condemns them as intrinsically evil.

48. Cf. William Whewell, *Elements of Morality*, London, 1848: Part V, Ch. 15. "As we have seen the State is necessarily driven to aim at the Moral Education of its members, and yet has no prospect of effectually promoting this object by its ordinary means of action, Law and Punishment. For Law deals with external acts; Morality, and therefore Moral Education, with internal motives and intentions; and how is the State to penetrate and to mould these? . . . It is plain that the State cannot do these things of itself; and cannot do them at all, except it can for that purpose obtain the aid of the Religious Teachers of its people. Using the term Church in a general sense, as implying the Teaching Body in every Religion, the State can educate the people by the aid of the Church, and in no other way." Having established that "the State, as a State, cannot educate the people; and can do this only by calling in the Church to its assistance," Whewell then raises the question of the relation of the Church to the State. Vd. Ch. 16. Cf. Maritain, *The Things That Are Not Caesar's*, New York, 1931.

49. The collective common good, which is the good of the multitude of men as associated, is ordered to the separate common good, which is the good common to the multitude of men considered as individuals of the human species. Cf. Maritain, *Art and Scholasticism*, New York, 1930: p. 76; *Three Reformers*, New York, 1932: pp. 21–24, and especially Notes 27, 28, 29 and 32; and *Freedom in the Modern World*, New York, 1936.

50. Vd. Father Gerald Phelan's discussion of *Beauty in Nature and Art*, Proceedings of the American Catholic Philosophical Association, 1935: pp. 175–179. "Sense knowledge, appetition and intellectual apprehension converge in the aesthetic experience and give rise to a relation which is neither purely intentional (cognitional) nor purely tendential (appetitive). We do not tend towards the beautiful as we tend towards the good, *i.e.*, in order to possess it."

51. Cf. L. Callahan, *A Theory of Esthetic According to the Principles of St. Thomas Aquinas*, Washington, 1927: pp. 43, 65.

52. Recreation is indispensable as a means, of course, and not as an

end. "Nor can we find any action in connexion with man, that is not directed to some other end, with the exception of speculative consideration. For even playful actions, which would seem to be done without any purpose, have some end due to them, namely, that the mind may be relaxed, and that thereby we may afterwards become more fit for studious occupations: else we should always have to be playing, if play were desirable for its own sake, and this is unreasonable" (St. Thomas Aquinas, *Summa Contra Gentiles*, III, 25).

53. Speculatively and in general, Bossuet said, St. Thomas has put the art of the comedian in the class of the innocent arts. But when he regards ordinary usage, he considers it among the infamous arts, and gain derived from it is illicit gain. Bossuet here quotes a passage which must be reconciled with the text of II-II, Q.168, AA.2, 3: "On the other hand, certain things are said to be ill-gotten because they are gotten of a shameful cause, for instance, of whoredom or stage-playing or the like" (*Summa Theologica*, II-II, Q.87, A.2, ad.2). Whereas in Q.168, A.3,ad.3, St. Thomas says that the occupation of play-actors is not unlawful in itself and those who reward them for their services act justly in doing so. Bossuet asks how these two passages can be conciliated except by saying that when St. Thomas excuses the art of the comedian or when he approves of it, he regards it according to its idea in general and metaphysically; but when he considers it naturally as it is practised, there is no opprobrium which he will not heap upon it.

54. In the last chapter of the *De Regimine Principum* (Part II), St. Thomas considers the duty of a Prince with regard to the place of pleasures in the institution of civil life. The first principle is that "since an excess of enjoyment unduly draws man to indulge in pleasures — a thing most harmful to a city — it is necessary to be moderate in its use." He then enumerates the ways in which excessive indulgence in pleasure leads from the path of virtue, finally pointing out that "men who have become dissolute through pleasures usually grow lazy and, neglecting necessary matters and all the pursuits that duty lays upon them, devote themselves wholly to the quest of pleasure." It is, therefore, harmful for a city to superabound in delightful things. But there is a second principle, that enjoyment is evil only in excess and is beneficial in due proportion; wherefore he concludes: "It is proper to have a moderate share of pleasure, as a 'spice of

life,' so to speak, wherein man's mind may find some recreation."
(Translation by Father Gerald Phelan, Toronto, 1935 : pp. 125–
127.)

55. "Playful actions themselves considered in their species are not
directed to an end ; but the pleasure derived from such actions is
directed to the recreation and rest of the soul, and accordingly
if this be done with moderation it is lawful to make use of fun.
Hence Tully says : *It is indeed lawful to make use of play and
fun, but in the same way as we have recourse to sleep and other
kinds of rest, only when we have done our duty by grave and
serious matters*" (*Summa Theologica*, II–II, Q.168, A.2, ad.3).
Cf. Notes 20 and 52 *supra*.

56. Paraphrase of the remark of Leon Bloy (quoted by Maritain
from *La Femme Pauvre*) : "There is only one sorrow, the sorrow of not being a saint" ; to which Judith Érèbe added : "There
is another still, not even to be sorrowful at not wishing to be a
saint" (quoted by Maritain from *Roseau d'Or*, Fourth Series,
1929). Vd. *Art and Scholasticism*, p. 113 and Note 184.

57. Vd. *History of Feudalism* by Gukorsky and Trachtenberg,
and *History : Pre-Class Society* by Nikolsky, published in Moscow
by the State Text Book Publishing House, 1935. These are good
examples of the influence of the dominant political philosophy
of the State upon the texts used in the education of its future
citizens. One could find similar, though less obvious, examples
in the history books chosen by the Board of Education in any
large American city.

58. Cf. R. H. Tawney, *The Acquisitive Society*, Harcourt, Brace
and Company, Inc., New York, 1920 by permission. As Tawney
points out, by separating property from creative ability, we
"divide society into two classes, of which one has its primary
interest in passive ownership, while the other is mainly dependent
upon active work" (pp. 68–69). "The real economic cleavage is
not, as is often said, between employers and employed, but between all who do constructive work, from scientist to laborer,
on the one hand, and all whose main interest is the preservation
of existing proprietary rights, upon the other, irrespective of
whether they contribute to constructive work or not" (p. 79).
"The truth is that at present it is idle to seek to resist the demands
of any group of workers by appeals to the 'interests of society,'
because today, as long as the economic plane alone is considered,

there is not one society but two, which dwell together in an uneasy juxtaposition, like Sinbad and the Old Man of the Sea, but which in spirit, in ideals, and in economic interest, are worlds asunder.   There is the society of those who live by labor, whatever their craft or profession, and the society of those who live on it" (p. 135).   Cf. Mr. Tawney's Halley Stewart Lectures on *Equality*, New York, 1929, especially Chapters 3 and 6.

59.   "These people evidently think that socialism calls for equality, for levelling the requirements and the personal lives of the members of society.   Needless to say, such an assumption has nothing in common with Marxism, with Leninism.   By equality Marxism means, not equality in personal requirements and personal life, but the abolition of classes, i.e., (a) the equal emancipation of all toilers from exploitation after the capitalists have been overthrown and expropriated; (b) the equal abolition for all of private property in the means of production after they have been transformed into the property of the whole society; (c) the equal duty of all to work according to their ability and the equal right of all toilers to receive according to the amount of work they have done (*socialist* society); (d) the equal duty of all to work according to their ability and the equal right of all toilers to receive according to their requirements (*communist* society).   And Marxism starts out with the assumption that people's tastes and requirements are not, and cannot be equal in quality or in quantity, either in the period of socialism or in the period of communism.   This is the Marxian conception of equality.   Marxism has not recognized, nor does it recognize, any other equality."   This is taken from a speech by Stalin at the Seventeenth Congress of the Communist Party of the Soviet Union in 1934.   A little later Stalin quotes from a speech by Lenin on *Deceiving the People with Slogans about Liberty and Equality* in which Lenin said: "But the claim that we want to make all men equal to each other is an empty phrase and a stupid invention of the intellectuals."

60.   Tolstoy is a primitive Democrat, as well as a primitive Christain.   He is so primitive a Christian that he denies the role of Christ's Church in the life of man.   He is so primitive a Democrat that he is really an anarchist who believes in the brotherhood of man.   These paradoxes would almost shame Rousseau.   In fact, *What is Art?* is the Russian answer to the question propounded by the Academy of Dijon.   Like Rousseau, Tolstoy is sound neither in morals nor in politics.   But unlike Rousseau,

Tolstoy is sincere. He has the integrity of a truly great artist. He has the virtues of magnanimity and friendliness. And there is genuine religious perception in his insistence upon the bonds of human community. The essence of Christianity, he writes, is "the recognition by every man of his sonship to God and of the consequent union of men with God and with one another" (*What is Art*, Ch. 16). He uses the communication of men as the criterion by which to judge art, as all other phases of human life. He saw, before John Dewey did and for different reasons, that it follows properly from the nature of art to unite people. "Art, all art, has this characteristic, that it unites people. Every art causes those to whom the artist's feeling is transmitted to unite in soul with the artist, and also with all who receive the same impression." The difference between Christian and non-Christian art — that is, between good and bad art — is the manner and nature of this union. Non-Christian art "while uniting some people, makes that very union a cause of separation between these united people and others; so that union of this kind is often a source not merely of division but even of enmity toward others. Such is all patriotic art, with its anthems, poems and monuments; such is all Church art, that is, the art of certain cults, with their images, statues, processions and other local ceremonies." But Christian art unites all men and destroys the barriers of sect and nationality. The Christian art of our time, says Tolstoy, can be and is of two kinds: "first, art transmitting feelings flowing from a religious perception of man's position in the world in relation to God and to his neighbor — religious art in the limited meaning of the term; and secondly, art transmitting the simplest feelings of common life, but such always as are accessible to all men in the whole world, the art of common life — the art of the people, universal art. Only these two kinds of art can be considered good art in our time."

Tolstoy denounces the art of the aesthete, the art of the élite, the art which belongs to special classes in society. As a Christian or as a Democrat — which of course are the same for him — he enumerates the perversions of art: the art of the galleries and concert-halls, amusement-art, upper-class art (*Op. cit.*, Ch. 17). "Art is not a pleasure, a solace, an amusement" (*Op. cit.*, Ch. 18). How much like Rousseau are his denunciations, how much like Dewey his feeling for the common touch of art!

61. In his *Discourse on the Arts and Sciences*, Rousseau uses the word "art" primarily to refer to the practical arts, as we do when we speak of the arts and crafts; but his denunciation ap-

plies generally, nevertheless, to all the arts, the fine and liberal as well as the useful, since these are among the factors which have civilized, and hence corrupted, mankind. The opening sentences of the *Discourse* are worth quoting here: "The question before me is, 'Whether the Restoration of the arts and sciences has had the effect of purifying or corrupting morals.' Which side am I to take? That, gentlemen, which becomes an honest man, who is sensible of his own ignorance, and thinks himself none the worse for it. I feel the difficulty of treating this subject fittingly, before the tribunal which is to judge of what I advance. How can I presume to belittle the sciences before one of the most learned assemblies in Europe, to commend ignorance in a famous Academy, and reconcile my contempt for study with the respect due to the truly learned? I was aware of these inconsistencies, but not discouraged by them. It is not science, I said to myself, that I am attacking; it is virtue that I am defending, and that before virtuous men — and goodness is even dearer to the good than learning to the learned." Precious rhetoric — and but a mild foretaste of the argument which follows!

62. "The problem is to find a form of association which will defend and protect with the whole common force the person and goods of each associate, and in which each, while uniting himself with all, may still obey himself alone, and remain as free as before. This is the fundamental problem of which the Social Contract provides the solution" (*Social Contract*, I, 6). As Maritain says, this way of stating the political problem "simply amounts to establishing an organic whole without its parts being subordinate to one another. This is absurd; but Jean-Jacques is happy. The more difficult the problem, the more merit he will have for devising the solution" (*Three Reformers*, Messrs. Sheed and Ward, Publishers, New York, 1932, p. 132). As for the social contract which solves the riddle, it is a myth which places the origin of society "in the deliberate will of man, not in nature, and it gives birth to a product of human art, not to a work proceeding from nature; it presupposes that 'the individual alone is the work of nature.' . . . In the state of nature we only existed as persons, in no way as parts; in the state of society, we no longer exist except as parts. Thus does pure individualism, precisely by misconceiving the reality which belongs to the social bonds added to individuals by natural need, end inevitably in pure bureaucracy as soon as it undertakes to construct a society" (Maritain, *ibid.*, pp. 133–134 by permission).

63. Rousseau, like Bossuet, claims not to understand the doctrine
    of purgation. Thus, he says: "I remain to know if passions too
    much irritated do not degenerate into vices. I know that the
    poetics of the theatre pretends to do quite the contrary and to
    purge the passions while exciting them, but I have trouble in
    well conceiving this rule" (*Lettre à D'Alembert*, ed. Hachette,
    Paris, 1916, p. 31). Cf. Bossuet, *Maximes et Réflexions*, ed. by
    Belin, Paris, 1881 : p. 57.

64. My friend, Mr. Gorman, quite properly mistrusts Milton as a
    Christian and doubts his understanding of original sin and the
    problem of evil. He is affronted by the picture Milton gives
    of the rugged individual sallying forth into the arena of good
    and evil to win the good fight — the picture of a Renaissance
    humanist, and not of a Christian who knows that the devil is no
    foe to seek out for combat. My only defense for including
    Milton in this discussion is that he is an excellent example of the
    distortions which arise in the modern confluence of Christianity
    and democracy, or at least of that aspect of democracy which
    is libertarian and individualistic. Milton is better than Rousseau
    as a Christian democrat. Rousseau is really sound as neither.
    Tolstoy is better than Milton, being more truly a Christian at
    heart and more essentially a democrat. (Cf. Note 60 *supra*.)
    Yet in his discussion of the arts, Tolstoy's democracy is subordi-
    nated to his Christianity. We are forced, therefore, to turn to
    John Dewey as the purest expression of democracy — purest in
    two senses, both in its analytical refinement of the notion of
    democracy and in its freedom from any admixture of Christian-
    ity.

65. In a chapter on the nature of the battle over censorship, Mr.
    Walter Lippmann points out that the censor himself may be cited
    as proof of this assertion that the danger is believed to be not in
    the ideal itself but in the peculiar corruptibility of a certain part
    of the community. The censor exposes himself daily to every
    corrupting influence. No one has ever been known to decline to
    serve on a committee to investigate radicals on the ground that
    so much exposure to their doctrines would weaken his patriot-
    ism, or on a vice commission on the ground that it would im-
    pair his morals. Apart from certain residual tabus which have
    the power to cause irrational fear, the essence of censorship has
    always been, not to suppress subversive ideas as such, but to
    withhold them from those who are young or unprivileged or
    otherwise undependable. . . When you look at censorship as

a whole it is plain that it is actually applied in proportion to the vividness, the directness and the intelligibility of the medium which circulates the subversive idea. The moving picture is perhaps the most popular medium of expression there is; it speaks clearly to the lowest and the most immature intelligence. It is therefore forbidden to present many scenes which the theatre is free to present. (*Men of Destiny*, New York, 1928.)

66. Dewey's point about the arts as educative through being instruments of *communication* in society, establishes a *social* meaning of education, which must be clearly distinguished from the *didactic* sense in which the arts are viewed by Plato as instruments of moral and intellectual *instruction,* and from the *aesthetic* sense in which Aristotle views the arts as satisfying man's desire to learn by providing him with objects of *contemplation.* The value of communication follows properly from the nature of art as imitation, or, as Dewey says, "representation," in the same way that the values of contemplation, purgation, and recreation do. Dewey's analysis here is in the Aristotelian manner. It should be clear, furthermore, that this *social education* concerns the whole population, children and adults alike. When a democrat talks about the educational value of the arts he is not thinking exclusively about the training of the young but rather about the effects of the arts in binding all members of the community more closely together through the sharing, actual or vicarious, of experiences.

67. That democracy in its primary meaning is a social condition and not a set of political institutions can be seen in the fact that Soviet Russia, while not yet liberal in its government policy nor given to representative legislation, is deeply concerned with increasing the extent of popular education. This can be seen also in Moscow's policy toward the arts. Thus Lenin, as reported in the *Moscow News* for January 24, 1935, speaks of the arts not only as giving pleasure and recreation to the masses, but as indispensable in augmenting social education (i.e., communication) and in welding a vast population into an actual social unity. In Russia the problem of transforming a feudal into a democratic order is most urgent, and this can be done, Lenin realized, more effectively by the arts than by any other agency. Because of the extent of illiteracy, the radio as an avenue of communication and the motion picture as an art are the primary means by which Russia hopes to democratize its society.

This does not mean that art is *degraded* into propaganda. If

what Dewey and Lenin understand as social education or communication is propaganda, then propaganda is an essential function of the fine arts in a democracy. It is not only Marxists who
use the arts in this way. Cf. Éliseo Vivas, *Art, Morals and
Propaganda*, 46 International Journal of Ethics, 82–95.

68. In an address on *Art and the People* delivered in Manchester
in 1932, Mr. Eric Gill concluded: "'Art and the people,' then,
means two things: it means, first, the art *of* the people—the
art they actually produce; and, second, it means that which is
produced for their entertainment or 'uplift.' As to the first: we
know that under Industrialism the art of the people is the art of
making things by machinery. . . The art of the people in an
industrial civilization should be plain art—the application of
skill and obedience to the making of what is necessary in the way
that machines necessitate and utility demands. But all bread and
no jam is too dull—the people won't stand it. That brings us
to the second thing, the art of Entertainment. To enjoy plain
necessities demands a highbrow mind. The people are not high-
brow—'the People,' not only the working class but their employers as well. Therefore, as a set-off, the people must be
entertained. But we must remember it must be entertainment
suitable to the people whose work demands nothing from them
but skilful obedience and often obedience without skill—people
whose work is no longer their means to culture—people whose
tastes will necessarily be purely animal. And I mean 'animal' in
quite a good sense—healthy animal—football and games, including golf, lovemaking, and simple and sweet and rather noisy
music with simple and exciting rhythms, plentiful and almost in-
nocuous beer, cheap tours in charabancs. None of these things
need be bad things. I'm not saying that they need be anything
but first class in their kind. I am only saying that it is absurd to
attempt to foist high aesthetics on people whose working life
does not develop in them any intellectual responsibility. . . . Art
is not just a few pictures in museums and picture galleries—any
more than architecture is just a few buildings built by Fellows
and Associates of the Royal Institute of British Architects"
(*Beauty Looks After Herself*, Sheed and Ward, Inc., New York,
1933, pp. 149–150, by permission). See also *Art and Industrialism* in the same collection of essays.

69. Jeremy Collier was not unmindful of the potency of the
music which regaled the audience at the play-house. "This
sort of music," he said, "warms the passions, and unlocks the

fancy, and makes it open to pleasure like a flower to the sun. . .
Now why should it be in the power of a few mercenary hands
to play people out of their senses, to run away with their under-
standings, and wind their passions about their fingers as they
list? Music is almost as dangerous as gunpowder; and, it may
be, requires looking after no less than the press or the mint. 'Tis
possible a public regulation might not be amiss. No less a philosopher than Plato seems to be of this opinion" (*A Short View
of the English Stage*, 4th ed., London, 1699: pp. 278–279). But
although his diatribe against the comedy did much to provoke
and even formulate the policy of William and Mary toward the
theatre, there was no censorship of music.

69a. It is only in its extrinsic or political significance that the
drama has suffered. Its devotees, who usually pretend to be
interested in art for its own sake, have no cause for weeping.
Their pretense is open to suspicion if they complain that the
theatre is no longer a national amusement, but a local and comparatively unimportant one. Chamber music has not suffered as
an art from social indifference to its existence, although lack of
patronage does cause economic suffering. The arts cannot be
protected against the lack or loss of popular favor except by museums and endowments, which always have about them the air
of mausoleum and the preciosity of the élite. One might just
as well deplore the fact that illuminated manuscripts are now
kept in glass cases, while printed books circulate in the millions,
or that more people hear music over the radio than in the nave
of a cathedral, or that the use of steel has made Greek columns
and Gothic arches unnecessary and inappropriate, as regret the
gradual passing of the stage because inventions have made another and competing art more popular. One should even save
some of these tears for the movies against the possible day in
which television may make it unnecessary to leave one's home
for the entertainment which fiction can provide.

70. The full title page of the *Histrio-Mastix* runs as follows: "The
Player's Scourge, or Actor's Tragedie, divided into two parts.
Wherein it is largely evidenced, by diverse arguments, by the
concurring Authorities and Resolutions of sundry tests of Scriptures; of the whole Primitive Church, both under the law and
gospell; of 55 Synodes and Councels; of 71 Fathers and Christian writers, before the year of our Lord 1200; of above 150
foraigne and domestique protestant and popish authors, since;
of 40 Heathen philosophers, historians, etc. That popular stage-

plays (the very Pompes of the Diviell which we renounce in Baptisme, if we believe the Fathers) are sinfull, heathenish, lewde, ungodly spectacles, and most pernicious corruptions; condemned in all ages, as intolerable Mischefes to Churches, to Republickes, to the manners, mindes and soules of men." And so on.

71. In his recent encyclical, *Vigilanti Cura*, Pope Pius XI said: "Recreation in its manifold variety has become a necessity of people who labor under the fatiguing conditions of modern industry, but it must be worthy of the rational nature of man and, therefore, must be morally healthy. . . It admits of no discussion that the motion picture has achieved in these last years a position of universal importance among modern means of diversion." It is this fact which increases the concern of the moralist. On the other hand, the person interested in the cinema as fine art is similarly aroused. "Nor must films be degraded to the level of entertainment. Entertainment is an ambiguous term; those who deplore it are accused of a kill-joy puritanism, or an inaccessible and 'highbrow' critical standard; those who commend it certainly refer it to opiates, rather than stimulants. If this be so, it must be tolerated only on sufferance. The tired business man might be thought to have sufficient means of relaxation without the cinema; but if he must be further catered to, it should be made perfectly clear that the films which satisfy him are of an inferior nature" (Spottiswoode, *The Grammar of the Film*, Faber and Faber, Ltd., Publishers, London, 1935: p. 313 by permission).

72. The movies, having an international audience, face this problem in a more acute form than any other art. Thus, in 1927 English critics represented the popular sensibilities of their country as being offended by American movies; whereas in 1935 England invited instruction from America as to how to avoid giving offense to American audiences whose sensibilities had been quickened by various campaigns against indecency. And in a recent English Parliamentary debate about the cinema, it was maintained that western films, both American and English, are in many scenes revolting to their eastern audiences. A careful study of the matter by the Indian Cinematograph Committee resulted in precisely the opposite conclusion. Western films were not offensive to Indian audiences, not did they bring western manners into contempt, as Mr. Aldous Huxley and the Members of Parliament had so loudly claimed. England, with the burden of empire, may have been justifiably worried about

the effects of movies upon the Indian estimate of their western masters; but whether Indian audiences are offended by western films is a question of fact that must be answered by consulting Indian audiences.

73. The self-imposed code of regulations governing the production of motion pictures contains the following provision: "The treatment of low, disgusting, unpleasant, though not necessarily evil, subjects should be subject always to the dictate of good taste and a regard for the sensibilities of the audience." Also: "Obscenity in word, gesture, reference, song, joke, or by suggestion (even when likely to be understood only by part of the audience) is forbidden." It enumerates repellent subjects which, if treated at all, must be treated within the careful limits of good taste; and has specific restrictions with respect to such matters as costumes and nudity, dances, references to religion, etc. In general this code, adopted in 1930, goes further in specific censorship and prohibition than many critics of the cinema have thought of proposing.

74. The motion picture code already referred to contains these general principles: "1. No picture shall be produced which will lower the moral standards of those who see it. Hence the sympathy of the audience shall never be thrown to the side of crime, wrong-doing, evil or sin. . . . 3. Law, natural or human, shall not be ridiculed, nor shall sympathy be created for its violation." In a subsequent section devoted to the statement of reasons supporting these general principles, it is said with respect to the first of them: "Sympathy with a person who sins is not the same as sympathy with the sin or crime of which he is guilty. We may feel sorry for the plight of the murderer or even understand the circumstances which led him to his crime. We may not feel sympathy with the wrong which he has done. The presentation of evil is often essential for art or fiction or drama. This in itself is not wrong provided: (a) That evil is not presented alluringly. Even if later in the film the evil is condemned or punished, it must not be allowed to appear so attractive that the audience's emotions are drawn to desire or approve so strongly that later the condemnation is forgotten and only the apparent joy of the sin remembered; (b) that throughout, the audience feels sure that evil is wrong and good is right." With regard to the third general principle, the following explanation is offered: "By natural law is understood the law which is written in the hearts of all mankind, the great underlying principles of right

and justice dictated by conscience.   By human law is understood
the law written by civilized nations.   The presentation of crimes
against the law is often necessary for the carrying out of the
plot.   But the presentation must not throw sympathy with the
crime as against the law nor with the criminal as against those
who punish him.   The courts of the law should not be presented
as unjust.   This does not mean that a single court may not be
represented as unjust, much less that a single court official must
not be presented this way.   But the court system of the country
must not suffer as a result of this."

75.   Thus, with respect to nudity, the section of the code explaining its particular provisions says: "The effect of nudity or semi-
nudity upon the normal man or woman, and much more upon
the young and upon immature persons, has been honestly recognized by all law-makers and moralists.   Hence the fact that the
nude or semi-nude body may be beautiful does not make its use
in the films moral.   For, in addition to its beauty, the effect of
the nude or semi-nude body on the normal individual must be
taken into consideration. . .   Nudity can never be permitted as
being necessary for the plot.   Semi-nudity must not result in
undue or indecent exposure.   Transparent or translucent materials and silhouette are frequently more suggestive than actual
exposure."   With respect to dances, it is said: "Dancing in general is recognized as an art and as a beautiful form of expressing
human emotions.   But dances which suggest or represent sexual
actions, whether performed solo or with two or more, dances
intended to excite the emotional reaction of an audience, dances
with movement of the breasts, excessive body movements while
the feet are stationary, violate decency and are wrong."   The
provisions with regard to sexual matters are as follows: "The
sanctity of the institution of marriage and the home shall be upheld.   Pictures shall not infer that low forms of sexual relationship are the accepted or common thing.   Adultery, sometimes
necessary plot material, must not be explicitly treated, or justified
or presented attractively.   Scenes of passion should not be introduced when not essential to the plot.   Excessive and lustful kissing, lustful embraces, suggestive postures and gestures, are not
to be shown.   In general, passion should be so treated that these
scenes do not stimulate the lower and baser elements.   Seduction or
rape should never be more than suggested, and only when essential
for the plot, and even then never shown by explicit method.
They are never the proper subject for comedy.   Sex perversion
or any inference to it is forbidden.   White slavery shall not be

treated. Miscegenation is forbidden. Sex hygiene and venereal diseases are not subjects for motion pictures. Scenes of actual childbirth, in fact or in silhouette, are never to be presented. Children's sex organs are never to be exposed." And in the explanatory section, the following is added: "Scenes of passion must be treated with an honest acknowledgment of human nature and its normal reactions. Many scenes cannot be presented without arousing dangerous emotions on the part of the immature, the young or the criminal classes. Even within the limits of pure love, certain facts have been universally regarded by lawmakers as outside the limits of safe presentation. In the case of impure love, the love which society has always regarded as wrong and which has been banned by divine law, the following are important: Impure love must not be presented as attractive or beautiful. It must not be the subject of comedy or farce or treated as material for laughter. It must not be presented in such a way as to arouse passion or morbid curiosity on the part of the audience. It must not be made to seem right and permissible. In general it must not be detailed in method and manner."

76. In his Encyclical on the *Christian Education of Youth* (December 31, 1929), Pope Pius XI writes: "More than ever nowadays an extended and careful vigilance is necessary, inasmuch as the dangers of moral and religious shipwreck are greater for inexperienced youth. Especially is this true of impious and immoral books, often diabolically circulated at low prices; of the cinema, which multiplies every kind of exhibition; and now also of the radio, which facilitates every kind of communication. These powerful means of publicity, which can be great utility for instruction and education when directed by sound principles, are only too often used as an incentive to evil passions and greed for gain. St. Augustine deplored the passion for the shows of the circus which possessed even some Christians of his time, and he dramatically narrates the infatuation for them, fortunately only temporary, of his disciple and friend Alipius. How often today must parents and educators bewail the corruption of youth brought about by the modern theatre and the vile book!

"Worthy of all praise and encouragement therefore are those educational associations which have for their object to point out to parents and educators, by means of suitable books and periodicals, the dangers to morals and religion that are often cunningly disguised in books and theatrical representations. In their spirit of zeal for the souls of the young, they endeavor at the same time to circulate good literature and to promote plays that are

really instructive, going so far as to put up at the cost of great
sacrifices, theatres and cinemas, in which virtue will have nothing
to suffer, and much to gain."

It is worth adding here the comment made on much of contemporary secular schooling: "Every form of pedagogic naturalism which in any way excludes or weakens supernatural Christian
formation in the teaching of youth, is false. Every method of
education, founded wholly or in part, on the denial of original
sin and of grace, and relying on the sole powers of human nature,
is unsound. Such, generally speaking, are those modern systems
bearing various names which appeal to a pretended self-government and unrestrained freedom on the part of the child, and
which diminish or even suppress the teacher's authority and
action, attributing to the child an exclusive primacy of initiative,
and an activity independent of any higher law, natural or divine,
in the work of his education."

Not only the arts, then — books, plays, cinemas — but the home
and the school can fail in its duty to youth!

77. This has been recognized by the producers of motion pictures
in their code of self-regulation. It says: "Most arts appeal to
the mature. This art appeals at once to every class, mature, immature, developed, undeveloped, law abiding, criminal. Music
has its grades for different classes; so have literature and drama.
This art of the motion picture, combining as it does the two
fundamental appeals of looking at a picture and listening to a
story, at once reaches every class of society. By reason of the
mobility of a film and the ease of picture distribution, and because
of the possibility of duplicating positives in large quantities, this
art reaches places unpenetrated by other forms of art. Because
of these two facts, it is difficult to produce films intended for only
certain classes of people. The exhibitors' theatres are built for
the masses, for the cultivated and the rude, the mature and the
immature, the self-respecting and the criminal. Films, unlike
books and music, can with difficulty be confined to certain selected groups. The latitude given to film material cannot, in
consequence, be as wide as the latitude given to book material. . . Everything possible in a play is not possible in a film,
because of the larger audience of the film, and its consequential
mixed character. Psychologically, the larger the audience, the
lower the moral mass resistance to suggestion. . . Small communities, remote from sophistication and from the hardening
process which often takes place in the ethical and moral standards of groups in larger cities, are easily and readily reached by

any sort of film. The grandeur of mass settings, large action, spectacular features, etc., affects and arouses more intensely the emotional side of the audience. . . Hence the larger moral responsibilities of the motion pictures."

78. Such policies have their own difficulties. Laws regulating the attendance of minors at motion-picture theatres at certain hours or during the showing of films marked for adults only, have been evaded by parents and exhibitors. When the matter has not been regulated by statute but left to the wisdom and discretion of parents, their negligence and malfeasance has been enormous, and indefensible on the ground that they were, or could not help being, ignorant of what pictures were suitable. The production of movies for exclusively juvenile audiences and the preparation of special children's programmes is expensive and has been attended by financial failures which indicate the weakness of public sentiment and co-operation. The economic factors in motion-picture production, distribution and exhibition cannot be disregarded unless the state takes over and subsidizes the industry, which would entail another set of difficulties and disadvantages. The motion-picture code claims that "a careful distinction can be made between films intended for general distribution, and films intended for use in theatres restricted to a limited audience," but adds that "in general the practice of using a general theatre and limiting its patronage during the showing of a certain film to 'Adults Only' is not completely satisfactory and is only partially effective."

79. In his chapter devoted to moral education, Whewell says: "But though the Laws, with their Sanctions, and the public currency of moral sentiments and opinions in harmony with the Laws, form an important part of the moral education of the citizens, the moral judgments of each person are, for the most part, formed, in a still greater degree, by the influence of Parents, and other Friends, among whom childhood and youth are spent. This Domestic Training is the most effective portion of everyone's moral education." Whewell also recognizes the role of the arts in moral education: "There is a National Morality, which is of wider extent, and more deeply seated in men's minds, than the written Law. The expressions of moral judgments respecting actions and characters, which are put forth in speeches upon public occasions, in the poetry and literature of the nation, and the like, take for granted a general agreement of men on points of Morality: and such expressions of moral judgments also produce

their impression on individuals; they diffuse and perpetuate the judgment which they express, and form a part of the Moral Education of the citizens" (*Elements of Morality*, III, 26). Cf. the Encyclical Letter of Pope Pius XI on *The Christian Education of Youth* (December 31, 1929).

80. "How can people be so blind as to call fables the child's system of morals, without considering that the child is not only amused by the epilogue but misled by it? He is attracted by what is false and he misses the truth, and the means adopted to make the teaching pleasant prevent him profiting by it. Men may be taught by fables; children require the naked truth" (*Émile*, Translated by W. H. Payne, New York, 1907: p. 80).

81. The difference between philosophical and scientific knowledge — scientific in the modern sense of empirically investigative — is that the former deals with the essences and properties of things, and the latter with their accidents. It is, therefore, impossible to demonstrate philosophically what effects a particular work of art actually has upon particular individuals. This can be known — as all accidents are known — only by some type of empirical inquiry.

82. It is interesting to note here a paragraph in the code governing the production of motion pictures: "It has often been argued that art in itself is unmoral, neither good nor bad. This is perhaps true of the *thing* which is music, painting, poetry, etc. But the thing is the *product* of some person's mind, and the intention of that mind was either good or bad morally when it produced the thing. Besides, the thing has its *effect* upon those who come into contact with it. In both these ways, that is, as a product of a mind and as the cause of definite effects, it has a deep moral significance and an unmistakable moral quality."

83. The value of the motion picture as communicative seems to be social rather than moral. But this is only a matter of emphasis. In a democracy, social education is an obvious necessity. This is true to some extent of all societies. Man is a social as well as a rational animal. The fulfillment of his social nature is as much a moral value as the perfection of his reason and the extension of its dominion. To be good as a man is to be socialized. The negative aspects of socialization are usually emphasized: obedience to law and conformity to custom. These are products of the moral virtues viewed as habits of public conduct. The positive aspect

of socialization is communication. Whatever increases communication is, therefore, morally valuable as making men more human.

84. This is a condensation of a number of Thomistic texts: on the distinction of the speculative and practical intellects, *Summa Theologica*, I, Q.79, A.11 ; on the distinction of the sensitive and intellectual appetites, *ibid.*, I, Q.80, A.2 ; on the will as moving the intellect, *ibid.*, I, Q.82, A.4 ; on the intellect as moving the will, *ibid.*, I–II, Q.9, A.1 ; and on the object of the will as the intelligible good, *ibid.*, I–II, Q.8, A.1.

85. Cf. the preamble to Q.8, *Summa Theologica* I–II.

86. Cf. *Summa Theologica*, I–II, QQ.8, 12. For the purposes of the present discussion I omitted reference to enjoyment or fruition as an act of the will with regard to the end. Vd. *Summa Theologica*, I–II, Q.11.

87. Vd. on choice, *Summa Theologica*, I–II, Q.13 ; on consent, *ibid.*, Q.15. and on use, *ibid.*, Q.16.

88. Cf. *Summa Theologica*, I, Q.82, A.2 ; Q.83, A.1 ; and *ibid.*, I–II, Q.10, A.2.

89. "The will is moved in two ways: first, as to the exercise of its act ; secondly, as to the specification of its act, derived from the object. As to the first way, no object moves the will necessarily, for no matter what the object be, it is in man's power not to think of it, and consequently not to will it actually. But as to the second manner of motion, the will is moved by one object necessarily, by another not. . . If the will be offered an object which is good universally and from every point of view, the will tends to it of necessity, if it wills anything at all ; since it cannot will the opposite. If on the other hand, the will is offered an object that is not good from every point of view, it will not tend to it of necessity" (*Summa Theologica*, I–II, Q.10, A.2). Cf. *ibid.*, Q.9, A.3, ad.3.

90. "The last end moves the will necessarily, because it is the perfect good. In like manner, whatever is ordained to that end, and without which the end cannot be attained, such as *to be* and *to live* and the like. But other things without which the end can be gained, are not necessarily willed by one who wills the end ;

just as he who assents to the principle, does not necessarily assent to the conclusion, without which the principles can still be true" (*Summa Theologica*, I–II, Q.10, A.3, ad.3). Cf. the following: "Now there are some things intelligible which have not a necessary connection with first principles; such as contingent propositions, the denial of which does not involve a denial of the first principles. And to such the intellect does not assent of necessity. But there are some propositions which have a necessary connection with the first principles: such as demonstrable conclusions, a denial of which involves a denial of first principles. And to these the intellect assents of necessity, when once it is aware of the necessary connection of these conclusions with the principles; but it does not assent of necessity until through the demonstration it recognizes the necessity of such connection. It is the same with the will. For there are certain individual goods which have not a necessary connection with happiness, because without them a man can be happy: and to such the will does not adhere of necessity. But there are some things which have a necessary connection with happiness, by means of which things man adheres to God, in whom alone true happiness consists. Nevertheless until through the certitude of the Divine Vision the necessity of such connection be shown, the will does not adhere to God of necessity, nor to those things which are of God. . . It is therefore clear that the will does not desire of necessity whatever it desires" (*Summa Theologica*, I, Q.82, A.2).

91. "Reason in contingent matters may follow opposite courses, as we see in dialectic syllogisms and rhetorical arguments. Now particular operations are contingent, and therefore in such matters the judgment of reason may follow opposite courses, and is not determinate to one. And forasmuch as man is rational it is necessary that man have free-will" (*Summa Theologica*, I, Q.83, A.1). Cf. *ibid.*, I–II, Q.13, A.6: "Man does not choose of necessity. And this is because that which is possible not to be, is not of necessity. Now the reason why it is possible not to choose or to choose, may be gathered from a twofold power in man. For man can will and not will, act and not act; again, he can will this or that, and do this or that. The reason of this is seated in the very power of reason. For the will can tend to whatever the reason can apprehend as good. Now the reason can apprehend as good, not only this, viz., *to will* or *to act*, but also this, viz., *not to will* or *not to act*. Again, in all particular goods, the reason can consider an aspect of some good, and the lack of some good, which has the aspect of evil: and in this respect, it can apprehend any

single one of such goods as to be chosen or to be avoided. The perfect good alone, which is Happiness, cannot be apprehended by the reason as an evil, or as lacking in any way. Consequently man wills Happiness of necessity, nor can he will not to be happy or to be unhappy. Now since choice is not of the end, but of the means, it is not of the perfect good, but of particular goods. Therefore man chooses not of necessity, but freely." Cf. also: *ibid.*, Q.17, A.2, ad.2.

92. Vd. *Summa Theologica*, I–II, Q.57, A.4; also AA.3, 5; and Q.58, AA.2, 3. Cf. *Nichomachean Ethics*, VI, 4, 5.

93. "Command is an act of the reason, presupposing, however, an act of the will. In proof of this, we must take note that, since the acts of the reason and of the will can be brought to bear on one another, in so far as the reason reasons about willing, and the will wills to reason, the result is that the act of reason precedes the act of the will, and conversely. And since the power of the preceding act continues in the act that follows, it happens sometimes that there is an act of the will in so far as it retains in itself something of an act of reason, as we have stated in reference to use and choice; and conversely, that there is an act of the reason in so far as it retains in itself something of an act of the will" (*Summa Theologica*, I–II, Q.17, A.1). Cf. also: "Prudence is *something more than a merely rational habit, such as art is*, since it includes application to action, which application is an act of the will" (*Ibid.*, II–II, Q.47, A.1, ad.3).

94. "Choice follows the judgment of reason about what is to be done. Now there is so much uncertainty in things that have to be done; because actions are concerned with contingent singulars, which by reason of their vicissitude, are uncertain. Now in things doubtful and uncertain, the reason does not pronounce judgment, without previous inquiry: wherefore the reason must of necessity institute an inquiry before deciding on the objects of choice; and this inquiry is called counsel" (*Summa Theologica*, I–II, Q.14, A.1).

95. "Prudence is the *right reason of conduct*. Hence that which is the chief act of reason in regard to conduct must needs be the chief act of prudence. Now there are three such acts. The first is *to take counsel*, which belongs to discovery, for counsel is an act of inquiry. The second act is *to judge of what one has discovered*, and this is an act of the speculative reason. But the prac-

tical reason, which is directed to action, goes further, and its third act is *to command*, which act consists in applying to action the things counselled and judged. And since this act approaches nearer to the end of the practical reason, it follows that it is the chief act of the practical reason, and consequently of prudence" (*Summa Theologica*, II–II, Q.47, A.8). Cf. *Nichomachean Ethics*, VI, 5, 10.

96.   "The end is the principle in practical matters : because the reason of the means is to be found in the end. Now the principle cannot be called in question, but must be presupposed in every inquiry. Since therefore counsel is an inquiry, it is not of the end, but only of the means. Nevertheless, it may happen that what is the end in regard to some things, is ordained to something else ; just as also what is the principle of one demonstration, is the conclusion of another ; and consequently that which is looked upon as the end in one inquiry, may be looked upon as the means in another ; and thus it will become an object of counsel" (*Summa Theologica*, I–II, Q.14, A.2). Cf. *ibid.*, II–II, Q.47, A.7 : "It does not belong to prudence to appoint the end to the moral virtues, but only to regulate the means." Cf. *Nichomachean Ethics*, VI, 10.

97.   Cf. *Summa Theologica*, II–II, Q.47, A.13 ; I–II, Q.57, A.4, ad.3.

98.   "Prudence is indissolubly linked to moral virtue, and moral virtue to prudence, since the principles of prudence are determined by the moral virtues, and moral rectitude is determined by prudence" (*Nichomachean Ethics*, X,8, 1178ª15–19). Cf. *Summa Theologica*, I–II, Q.58, AA.4, 5.

99.   Cf. *Summa Theologica*, II–II, Q.47, A.11 ; Q.50, A.1 ; and *Nichomachean Ethics*, VI, 8.

100.   "If, however, prudence be taken in a wide sense, as including also speculative knowledge, as stated above (Q.47, A.2. ad.2), then its parts include *physics*, *dialectics* and *rhetoric*, according to the three methods of prudence in the sciences. The first of these is the attaining of science by demonstration, which belongs to physics (if physics be understood to comprise all demonstrative sciences). The second method is to arrive at an opinion through probable premises, and this belongs to dialectics. The third method is to employ conjectures in order to induce a certain suspicion or to persuade somewhat, and this belongs to rhetoric.

It may be said, however, that these three belong to prudence properly so called, since it argues sometimes from necessary premises, sometimes from probabilities, and sometimes from conjectures" (*Summa Theologica*, II–II, Q.48).

101. "It will only be, to use a scholastic distinction, *quoad creaturas*, not *simpliciter*, that there is a realm of *credibilia* which are not *scibilia*, though it might possibly be said that this account requires to be modified in the light of the principle that the identity of knowledge in God and in the creatures is only one of analogy" (A. E. Taylor, *Philosophical Studies*, The Macmillan Company, Publishers, London, 1934: p. 369, by permission). "The ideal of knowledge is that it should be at once immediate and articulated. In actual life, the immediacy is most manifest in perceptional knowledge, where articulation is at a minimum. The articulation is clearly manifest in scientific knowledge, as conceived by Aristotle, where conclusions are known along with and through premises which are, in the last resort, themselves immediately apprehended. But, even in the case where such scientific knowledge is best exemplified, that of pure mathematics, the whole of the premises relevant to the conclusion are not consciously envisaged in the act of 'knowing the conclusion through its premises.' Hence the ideal of knowledge is not actually attained even here, since the apprehension is not full and complete 'vision'" (*Ibid.*, p. 397).

102. A proposition can be assumed as highly probable if it "is probable to all or to most men, or to the wise, and of the wise, either to all or to most or the most famous, provided it is not contrary to common opinion; for anyone would admit easily what is held by the wise so long as it is not contrary to the opinions of most men" (Aristotle, *Topics*, I, 1, 100ᵃ25–100ᵇ15).

103. Elsewhere St. Thomas distinguishes opinion from doubt and suspicion. "Some acts of the intellect have unformed thought devoid of firm assent, whether they incline to neither side, as in one who *doubts*, or incline to one side rather than the other, but on account of some slight motive, as in one who *suspects*; or incline to one side yet with fear of the other, as in one who *opines* (*Summa Theologica*, II–II, Q.2, A.1). Cf. *Summa Theologica*, I, Q.79, A.9. Opinion is there defined as "an act of the intellect which leans to one side of a contradiction, whilst in fear of the other." Opinion is not distinguished from science as lower from higher reason. The higher reason deals with eternal things,

whereas the lower reason is the scientific part of the soul, "for necessary truths are found even among temporal things, of which natural science and mathematics treat. And the opinionative and ratiocinative part is more limited than the lower reason; for it regards only things contingent" (*Ibid.*, Ad. 3). Both science and opinion are habits of the possible intellect, but not in the same way. "One self evident proposition convinces the intellect, so that it gives firm assent to the conclusion, but a probable proposition cannot do this. Wherefore a habit of opinion needs to be caused by many acts of the reason, even on the part of the *possible* intellect: whereas a habit of science can be caused by a single act of the reason, so far as the *possible* intellect is concerned" (*Summa Theologica*, I–II, Q.51, A.3).

104. "It is, of course, to be remembered that the recognition of a real difference between knowing and believing does not carry with it the consequence that I am never mistaken when I think I know. That I sometimes suppose myself to know when I do not really know is a fact having the same sort of signification as the equally familiar facts that I sometimes suppose a demonstration which really involves a fallacy to be cogent, that I sometimes suffer from hallucinations of the senses, and that my memory is sometimes at fault. What the fact really shows is merely that there is no psychological criterion by which we can infallibly discriminate knowledge from belief, any more than there is such a criterion for the discrimination of sense or memory from imagination" (A. A. Taylor, *op. cit.*, p. 385, by permission). "The nature of the distinction between knowing and believing, like that of the distinction between seeing and remembering, may be clear and intelligible enough, but it furnishes no infallible criterion for application to the specific instance, just as, in the realm of moral practice, the doctrine of the Categorical Imperative, accepted without reserve, would furnish no infallible criterion for the rightness of the individual act" (*Ibid.*, p. 396, by permission). The distinction between what is actually true and what is actually false cannot be used to distinguish knowing from believing or opining, since "the difference between the true and the false will be a difference of some kind in what is apprehended, not the manner of its apprehension" (*Ibid.*, p. 370).

104a. To say that science is investigative and that philosophy is not does not mean that there is no sense to the phrase "philosophical research." Mathematicians do research, but it is entirely in the reflective dimension. Mathematical research does not require the mathematician to undertake specially planned observations. Scientific research, on the other hand, is always primarily in the observational dimension. We have used the word "investigation" to denote research of this sort exclusively.

If it be admitted that mathematics is knowledge, then it must be admitted that knowledge is possible without investigation. If investigation is an essential mark of science, then mathematics is not scientific knowledge. Yet mathematics has greater precision and certainty than the natural sciences. Hence a type of knowledge exists which is better than science. This type of knowledge we have called philosophy. But it is important to add a Platonic caution here. Vd. *Republic*, 533 C, D. Mathematics is truly a branch of philosophy only to the extent that it does not rest on hypotheses (postulates, assumptions). To the extent that it does, it is more like science, or what Plato would have called opinion. It is not surprising to find that in the modern world mathematics is praised because it is postulational, because its truths are conventional and have the same kind of hypothetical necessity possessed by the contingent truths of investigative science. The modern world dispraises philosophy.

Despite the modern tendency to assimilate mathematics to science, mathematics is essentially philosophical knowledge, and is only properly developed when it rests upon principles. In this respect it is like metaphysics, differing in that the principles of metaphysics are primitive, whereas those of mathematics are derived. Metaphysics, not mathematics, is the type of all philosophical knowledge. The only reason for using mathematics to typify philosophy is that, for contemporary discussion, only mathematics can be used to exemplify non-investigative knowledge.

The analysis of the nature of "scientific knowledge" in the *Posterior Analytics* indicates why Aristotle, like Plato, would not have considered either modern investigative science or modern mathematics essentially scientific, but rather a mean between knowledge and opinion. The kind of cognition Aristotle there calls "science," we must call "philosophy," to preserve the distinctions needed in the modern world. The essential traits of philosophical knowledge are summarized in *Posterior Analytics*, II, 18, 19.

105. The essential contingency of scientific knowledge is the contingency of its data. Science changes as the result of further investigation. The general proposition established inductively from *old* data is replaced by an induction from *new* data. As the probability of a proposition is relative to the relevant knowledge

at a given time, so the inductions of science are relative to the data at a given time. The contingent truths of scientific knowledge have a kind of hypothetical necessity: they predicate certain consequences as necessarily following from a supposed state of affairs, but science is unable to establish the supposed conditions as necessary and universal. Philosophical truths, in contrast, have categorical necessity. They are not conditional. Cf. the doctrine of the pragmatic *a priori* in C. I. Lewis, *Mind and the World Order*, New York, 1929. The distinction between natural and social science is that the conclusions of the latter are not even hypothetically necessary.

106. Vd. St. Thomas Aquinas, *Summa Theologica*, I–II, Q.18, A.5: "Certain acts are called *human* or *moral* inasmuch as they proceed from reason" (Italics mine). And Q.18, A.6: "Certain actions are called *human* inasmuch as they are *voluntary*" (Italics mine). "If any other actions are found in man, they can be called actions *of a man*, but not properly *human* actions, since they are not proper to man as man" (*Ibid.*, Q.1, A.1). If an action "does not proceed from deliberate reason, but from some act of the imagination, as when a man strokes his beard, or moves his hand or foot, such action properly speaking is not moral or human, since this depends on the reason" (*Ibid.*, Q.18, A.9).

The distinction of acts as moral or *un*moral turns on whether the act is voluntary. Within the genus of moral acts there is the further distinction between moral and *im*moral acts, according to the relation of reason to the passions in the movement of the will. These two meanings of moral, (1) as divided against unmoral and (2) as divided against immoral, must not be confused.

107. "The apprehension of the imagination, being a particular apprehension, is regulated by the apprehension of reason, which is universal; just as a particular active power is regulated by a universal active power. Consequently in this respect the act of the sensitive appetite is subject to the command of reason. On the other hand, the condition or disposition of the body is not subject to the command of reason: and consequently in this respect, the movement of the sensitive appetite is hindered from being wholly subject to the command of reason. Moreover it happens sometimes that the movement of the sensitive appetite is aroused suddenly in consequence of an apprehension of the imagination or sense. And then such movement occurs without the command of reason: although reason could have prevented it, had it foreseen. Hence the Philosopher says (*Politics*, I, 2) that the reason governs

the irascible and concupiscible not by a *despotic supremacy*, which is that of a master over his slave ; but by a *politic and royal supremacy*, whereby the free are governed, who are not wholly subject to command" (*Summa Theologica*, I–II, Q.17, A.7).   See also the eighth article of this question in which it is shown that the vegetative functions are not subject to the command of reason.

Though the passions cannot cause involuntariness simply (*Ibid.*, Q.6, A.6, A.7), but only in a certain respect, they may make a man for the time being non-rational and hence non-voluntary : "This influence of a passion on man occurs in two ways.   First, so that his reason is wholly bound, so that he has not the use of reason : as happens in those who through a violent access of anger or concupiscence become furious or insane, just as they may from some other bodily disorder ; since suchlike passions do not take place without some change in the body.   And of such the same is to be said of irrational animals, which follow, of necessity, the impulse of their passions : for in them there is neither movement of reason nor, consequently, of will.   Sometimes, however, the reason is not entirely engrossed by the passion, so that the judgment of reason retains, to a certain extent, its freedom, and thus the movement of the will remains in a certain degree.   Accordingly in so far as the reason remains free and not subject to the passion, the will's movement, which also remains, does not tend of necessity to that whereto the passion inclines it.   Consequently, either there is no movement of the will in that man, and the passion alone holds its sway ; or if there be a movement of the will, it does not necessarily follow the passion" (*Ibid.*, Q.10, A.3).

108.   To the question what makes one man more virtuous than another, St. Thomas answers that it may be due to "greater habituation, or a better natural disposition, or a more discerning judgment of reason, or again a greater gift of Grace" (*Summa Theologica*, I–II, Q.66, A.1).   Compare the discussion of the causes of sin in Questions 75–81 of the same Treatise.

109.   "The internal cause of sin is both the will, as completing the sinful act, and the reason, as lacking the due rule, and the appetite as inclining to sin.   Accordingly, something external might be the cause of sin in three ways, either by moving the will itself immediately, or by moving the reason, or by moving the sensitive appetite.   Now, as stated above (Q.9, A.6 ; Q.10, A.4), none can move the will inwardly save God alone, Who cannot be the cause of sin, as we shall prove further on (Q.79, A.1).   Hence it follows that nothing external can be a cause of sin, except by

moving the reason, as a man or devil by enticing to sin; or by moving the sensitive appetite, as certain external sensibles move it. Yet neither does external enticement move the reason of necessity, in matters of action, nor do things proposed externally, of necessity move the sensitive appetite, except perhaps it be disposed thereto in a certain way; and even the sensitive appetite does not, of necessity, move the reason and will. Therefore something external can be a cause moving to sin, but not so as to be a sufficient cause thereof: and the will alone is the sufficient completive cause of sin being accomplished" (*Summa Theologica*, I–II, Q.75, A.3).

110. "Nothing prevents a man who has a habit from acting either in accordance with it, or against it: thus a grammarian may speak either grammatically or ungrammatically. It is the same with the habits of moral virtue: thus a man who has the habit of justice may perform just actions, and may act unjustly. The reason is because the use of habits is subject to our will: and will may be borne to either of two opposite alternatives". (*Summa Contra Gentiles*, IV, 70).

111. Those who seek instruction and are not immune to demonstration can be referred to Aristotle's *De Anima*, Book III, and St. Thomas's Treatise on Man in the *Summa Theologica*, I, especially QQ.75, 76, 79–83; also the discussion of the nature of voluntary and natural motions in the *Summa*, I–II, QQ.6, 9, 10.

111a. When it is understood that the fine arts cannot be an essential cause of moral behavior or moral character, it must also be seen that they cannot be essentially didactic in the moral sphere, since this would require them to be causative of the virtues. The demonstration turns on the following propositions: that moral character is constituted by virtues and vices; that virtues and vices are habits caused by voluntary acts; that voluntary acts are caused by the will freely choosing; and that reason is the first cause of free choice. The objects which specify voluntary acts do not cause them; the circumstances of voluntary acts are necessary but not sufficient conditions; the knowledge applied in choice is incapable of determining it. Works of fine art must (1) be the objects of voluntary action, or (2) be among the circumstances of such action, or (3) provide some of the knowledge relevant to choice. In any of these three alternatives, works of fine arts must be causally insufficient and accidental with respect to the determination of action.

112. It is not only in the service of prudence that a critical survey of this sort should be made. It should be done, and even more thoroughly, for the sake of our universities, from which most of this work emanates. They harbor and support such research. Can their good name, and even more their intellectual integrity, survive if they permit empirical psychology and the social sciences, as well as the kind of 'philosophy' with which these are associated, to continue in their present temper; if they do not recognize and fight the appalling intellectual confusions which spread from these fields into all the educational and scholarly efforts of the academic community; if they do not require their professors to be educated men, cultivated by sound philosophy whatever be their field of teaching or research? Investigations of the Payne Fund variety, which are examined in Chapters 10 and 11, are probably the worst example of the kind of work that is done today in psychology and the social sciences, but they are a true example nevertheless. The existence of such research in our universities, and of ever so much more that is essentially similar, calls upon anyone who has the impulse to reform things for man's greater good to direct such efforts to the improvement of universities, as much as, if not more so than, to the regulation of the arts.

113. I have devoted much time to the analysis of the process of judicial proof and the rules of evidence and procedure which govern the trial of issues of fact in English and American courts. The kind of evidence which Blumer and Hauser present would not be admissible even as a basis for expert opinion in legal proceedings, and the standards of scientific research are supposed to be so much higher than those of litigation. The impartiality of the scientist is so often contrasted with the partisanship and rhetorical trickery of the advocate. Yet what must one think when one finds Blumer and Hauser obviously making a case against the movies, despite the utter unreliability and obvious inconclusiveness of their data? There is a familiar rhetorical trick which lawyers who prefer victory to truth and justice often employ. They somehow manage to get the evidence before the jury even though they know that, upon objection from opposing counsel, it will unquestionably be ordered stricken from the record as inadmissible because irrelevant or prejudicial or improbable. Is not the fact that Blumer and Hauser pile up huge masses of lurid and prejudicial case-histories for the reader to be impressed by, despite the fact that they admit this material to be unreliable and inconclusive and despite the fact that they suppress a much larger num-

ber of case-histories having an opposite tenor, an instance of an analogous rhetorical trick? Bad enough in a law court, it is abhorrent in a scientific report.

114. Would that it were possible today to say, as St. Thomas does of the spurious *De Spiritu et Anima*: "That book has no authority, and so what is there written can be despised with the same facility as it was said" (*Summa Theologica*, I, Q.77, A.8. ad.1).

114a. It may be objected that biased interpretations are unavoidable in social science research because the social sciences are so much more like opinion, — so much nearer to history and journalism, — than the natural sciences. It is not unusual to find a historian criticized for his bias, nor is the historian surprised or shocked to receive such criticism, that is, if he does not pretend to be a "scientific historian." Bias does not impute lack of integrity, but merely that in writing about human affairs, in dealing with matters deeply imbued with moral significance, evaluation is difficult to repress. It is only reprehensible when concealed, or when there is a confusion between the historian as a reporter and as a commentator. So in the field of social science, it may be difficult or impossible to avoid passing moral judgment on the facts discovered, or to resist interpreting these facts from a point of view. It is only fair to ask, perhaps, that whenever this is done, it be explicitly acknowledged. If the social scientist cannot succeed in imitating the objectivity of the natural scientist, — and it seems clear that he cannot, in so far as he is a student of human behavior, — he should accept the responsibilities of his dual role as investigator and moralist. He might then be less surprised or chagrined when bias and prejudice were discovered in his work.

115. Vd. Note 112 *supra*. Something should be done to make our universities, our research foundations and our social scientists ashamed of work of this sort, if they pretend to have any regard for truth, the good name of science and scholarship, and high standards of intellectual integrity. Some of the Payne Fund investigations were done in universities accredited with leading departments of social science and psychology. If this is the kind of work which can be produced under such auspices, what must be the level of teaching and research in less fortunate institutions?

116. It may be objected that there is nothing unseemly in a Christian or a moralist seeking the aid of a heretic or a sophist in answering a question of fact, if the heretic or sophist happens to be a

skilled investigator and if the investigation, which the Christian or moralist is unable to make, is needed to answer the question of fact.   But this objection is not tenable if the interpretation of the data of research, as well as the way in which its problem is formulated and its method conceived, rests upon assumptions which are inadmissible in the light of Christianity or sound moral philosophy. The research of Professor Peters is a good illustration of this point.   Because of his assumptions, involving as they do a denial of morality and religion, his findings cannot possibly answer the questions of fact which a Christian or a moralist would formulate about the influence of motion pictures on standards of conduct. The misalliance of the religious with social scientists is much more evident in certain quarters than others.   Thus, we find the Detroit (Mich.) *Christian Advocate* saying, in an editorial on August 8, 1935 : "People have been suspicious of the movies for years.   But nobody had any authoritative information to show whether in the long run the movies were actually good or bad. We now have, thanks to the Payne Foundation, a scholarly and thoroughly scientific mass of information which proves beyond the shadow of a doubt that the movies are positively vicious and demoralizing."   The appeal to science is, however, notably absent from the writings of Pope Pius XI on the problem of motion pictures.   Vd. the Encyclical *Vigilanti Cura*, issued July 2, 1936.

117.   "At the time when I was Research Adviser for the New York State Crime Commission, one of the sub-committees made a great many of these studies.   When we came to the end of all the case studies, one of the members of the Commission said, 'Obviously, what is needed is more boys' club,' and that was put down as a recommendation.   I am for boys' clubs.   I think it is a good idea. The trouble was it did not necessarily have anything to do with the research.   We did not need case studies to demonstrate the need for boys' clubs.   On such a basis — and here is the important thing ; and this is why I feel rather deeply about it — studies are made of the motion pictures, in which children are asked where they got this idea or that.   Then these answers are compiled, and an indictment of the motion pictures is made.   In other words, someone has asked a boy in the Juvenile Court : 'Do you go to the motion pictures ?' this boy having been caught stealing or something.   'Yes,' he replies.   'Did you ever commit a crime after you had seen a movie ?'   'Yes.'   Down in the investigator's note-book that goes.   'What kind of pictures do you like to see ?' and so forth and so on.

"I am sorry that other obligations and duties have prevented me from writing what I conceive might be a piece of satirical literature. One could go to any Sunday School and ask the boys whether they had ever been to Sunday School after having been to a movie, and the answer would be the same, because presumably they have been to a lot of movies in their lives, and in the one case they have gone to Sunday School and in the other case they committed crimes. It just does not mean anything. The thing can be reduced to the greatest absurdity" (Professor Raymond Moley in an address on "Do the Movies Teach Crime?" delivered before the Motion Picture Club of New York, March 11, 1935).

118. The analysis of the problem of causation, given in Chapter 9 *supra*, indicates that it cannot be said that motion pictures are *the* cause, or even *a sufficient* cause of crime. The most that can be said is that the movies are one among many factors in the total set of external circumstances under which human beings act. That they, whether mature or immature, act criminally or obey the law is not *caused* by any of these circumstances, singly or in combination. To think otherwise is to deny that human behavior is voluntary and proceeds in the light of knowledge and after deliberation. That the conflict between reason and the passions is resolved in some cases in favor of reason, and in others by the dominance of the passions, could only be explained if we knew what made some men morally weak and others strong. This we do not know well enough to state the sufficient causes of crime. But the recognition of our inadequate knowledge entails the further acknowledgment that no factor or combination of factors in the environment can explain moral behavior, either virtuous or vicious. We do not know, in short, whether, if there were no movies, or if fewer children attended movies, or attended them less frequently, or if motion pictures were altered in specific respects, there would be more or less juvenile delinquency and crime. Even if it be granted that there is some evidence that in an indefinite number of cases — the proportion of which to the total we do not know — juvenile misbehavior has *appeared* to imitate conduct shown in the movies, or has *seemed* to employ techniques which could have been learned from movies, it does not follow that these same instances of juvenile misconduct would have failed to occur, but only that particular details of the conduct *might* have been different. They *might not* have been, however, since the same details could have been learned elsewhere.

119. One comment, which Mrs. Mitchell makes as the result of her study, must be mentioned. Much effort and time, she says, are

spent in recommending the proper books for children. Not only public libraries but intelligent parents everywhere make this effort. "But there is no widespread effort to guide children to the appropriate movies as there is in the case of books" (*Children and Movies*, p. 65). Despite the fact that most children prefer the movies to books — the same can be said, of course, for most adults — only 1.6% of 10,000 children were found to have their movies selected for them by their parents. Furthermore, in modern times there has been an increasing production of specifically juvenile literature, whereas it is true that most films are made for adult entertainment. Mrs. Mitchell says in conclusion: "The movie is the world's greatest story-book. Filled with life's tales, it is for all. But the juvenile edition is not yet off the press" (*Ibid.*, p. 148).

120. The moral critics of motion pictures, among them many of the Payne Fund investigators, use the word "commercial." Is it to insinuate that Hollywood is a manufacturer and not an artist? If so, the slur should be challenged. Motion pictures are commercially produced and distributed, but so are books and plays, and even paintings and music. We do not refer to the "commercial novel" or "commercial music." The implication that the profit motive — from what part of our civilization is it absent? — necessarily implies badness or even absence of art is obviously nonsense. Elizabethan drama is an outstanding case in point. On the contrary, art which supports itself economically by public patronage is motivated to be good at least as amusement, and such goodness is not unrelated to the achievement of aesthetic excellence. Commercial movies, like commercial books, plays, paintings and music, may therefore have a brighter future as art than movies produced, let us say, by communist Russia or fascist Germany as a political enterprise. The political motivation of art is more inimical to the autonomy it needs than the economic condition under which it works for a living by trying to please a public seeking pleasure at its hands. The alternatives at present are clear. Because of the expense involved in motion-picture production, they must either be made by private individuals for a profit or made by the state as a political undertaking. For a profit! That is the unfortunate condition imposed upon all activities in an acquisitive society. There is a third alternative, but it requires the complete reconstruction of our social order: the abolition of profit, on the one hand, and an avoidance of collectivism, on the other. How different education might be, and medicine and law, as well as the fine arts, in a truly distributive society!

But, granted the existing political economy, how short-sighted is Professor Charters' recommendation that "producers of motion pictures who have a love for children and an interest in their development address themselves to the problems of children's movies as the publishers of books have attacked the problem of providing a children's literature" (*Motion Pictures and Youth*, New York, 1933 : p. 62). Writers and publishers do this because it is profitable to do so, whether or not this is the only reason ; at least, they do not do so philanthropically. The complicating fact is that books can be published for children as a separate enterprise, but the audience of motion pictures is at once adult and juvenile, in the rough proportion of two to one. Adults do not usually read and enjoy children's books. They could not be expected to attend and enjoy children's movies, if the criteria of appropriateness were the same in the two cases. Unless it can be shown that the production and exhibition of motion pictures specifically intended for children and not for adults can be made a profitable enterprise, it does not clearly follow, as Professor Charters thinks, that "the simple obligation rests upon those producers who love children to find a way of making the motion picture a beautiful, fascinating and kindly servant of childhood" (*Ibid.*, p. 63). Their failure to do so is not evidence that they do not love children, but that the love of children, as all other things in the present society, is circumscribed by economy.

It is highly questionable whether, under these circumstances, the responsibility is primarily on the producers rather than the parents. There is a great deal of evidence that parents are extremely lax with regard to the movie-going of their children. The movies have become for many of them a refuge from the burden of taking care of their children. This hardly creates a moral obligation on the part of the producers or a political obligation for those who would control the arts for the public welfare. If children are too young to go to certain movies, which is a better way of saying if certain movies are too old for children, why do parents allow them to go ?

121. It is necessary to reconcile what appear to be conflicting texts on this point. On the one hand, Aristotle says : "In making the end is other than the making itself ; but the end of doing cannot be other than the doing itself, for doing well is itself the end" (*Ethics*, VI, 5, 1140^{b}7). And St. Thomas expands this to mean that "the good of an art is to be found, not in the craftsman, but in the product of the art, since art is right reason about things to be made ; for since the making of a thing passes into external matter, it is a perfection not of the maker but of the thing made"

(*Summa Theologica*, I–II, Q.57, A.5, ad.1). Prudence, in contrast, as right reason of things to be done, is said to perfect the agent. On the other hand, St. Thomas defines virtue as *"that which makes its subject good, and its work good also"* (*Ibid.*, II–II, Q.47, A.4). Since art is a virtue, it would seem to follow that it must be a perfection of the maker as well as the thing made ; and of prudence it must also be said that it perfects what is done as well as the doer. The texts are reconciled by the distinction between perfect and imperfect virtue. The imperfect virtues — the speculative habits and art — "rectify the operation of reason without regarding the rectitude of the appetite," and thus confer only an aptness for good work, but not the habit of will to use that aptness. The perfect virtues — prudence and the moral virtues — regard the appetite and, therefore, confer a habit of action and not merely an aptitude. "From having habits of the latter sort, man is said simply to do good and to be good. . . But habits of the first kind are not called virtues simply, because they do not make the work good except in regard to a certain aptness, nor do they make their possessor good simply" (*Ibid.*, I–II, Q.56, A.3). Possession of the art makes a man good as a grammarian or a physician, but not as a man ; whereas prudence and the moral virtues constitute a good man. When it is said, therefore, that art perfects the thing made and not the maker, what is meant is that the perfection in the maker is *relative* to the goodness of what is made, as the perfection in the thing made is *relative* to the aptness of the maker. The analogy with justice is instructive. Justice perfects a man in relation to the good of other men ; but unlike art, just actions make the agent good simply as a man. The end of justice, as of all the moral virtues and prudence, is the general well-being of man ; whereas the end of art is the good of a particular work ; it aims at the good of the worker *only* in relation to his work.

The end of art is the perfection of some thing ; art confers actuality and goodness upon it. The end of prudence — and the moral virtues — is the fullness in actuality of man himself, and hence his goodness. But the virtues themselves — whether art and the speculative virtues or prudence and the moral virtues — do not *as such* perfect man because they are only habits ; i.e., potencies and not acts.

122. "The truth of the practical intellect depends on conformity with a right appetite. This conformity has no place in necessary matters, which are not affected by the human will ; but only in contingent matters which can be effected by use, whether they

be matters of interior action, or the products of external work. Hence it is only about contingent matters that an intellectual virtue is assigned to the practical intellect, viz., art as regards things to be made and prudence as regards things to be done" (*Summa Theologica*, I–II, Q.57, A.5, ad.3). But in the case of art the appetite need be rectified only with regard to a particular good, whereas in the case of prudence, the will must be directed to the general good of man. Cf. Maritain, *Art and Scholasticism*, pp. 47–48 and Note 94.

123. Art does not consider how the human appetite may be affected generally. "As long as the geometrician demonstrates the truth, it matters not how his appetitive faculty may be affected, whether he be joyful or angry; even as neither does this matter in a craftsman" (*Summa Theologica*, I–II, Q.57, A.3). For this reason art is, paradoxically, a *dangerous* virtue. Unless it is supported and disciplined by the moral virtues, craft can become cunning in the service of evil. The sophist is one who can take pleasure in making the worse appear the better reason, and is fiendishly skilled in the art of doing so. It is moral defect which causes, not a corruption of the liberal arts he possesses, but malice in their use.

124. Aristotle says: "Making and doing are two different things. We are safe in believing ordinary people's views on this subject. . . So different indeed, that neither is a part of the other: for doing is not making, and making is not doing" (*Ethics*, VI, 4, $1140^a 1$–5). Whatever clarity attached to the Greek words *praxis* and *poiesis*, and to the mediæval *agibile* and *factibile*, is not retained by their English equivalents. When St. Thomas says that making is an action passing into outward matter whereas doing is an action abiding in the agent (*Summa Theologica*, I–II, Q.57, A.4; II–II, Q.47, A.5), the distinction between operations as intrinsic and extrinsic must be understood in terms of the difference in their ends. Art is an operation terminating in an extrinsic good; prudence is an operation terminating in the good of the agent. Instead of saying that the sphere of art is making and the sphere of prudence is doing, it is better in English to say that prudence is reason applied in the moral sphere and that art is reason applied in all other operations. In distinguishing the practical from the productive arts, both of which involve extrinsic operations, the English words "doing" and "making" can be given meanings that conform more closely to popular usage. Cf. Maritain, *Art and Scholasticism*, pp. 5–7.

125. "The perfection of art consists in judging and not in commanding: wherefore he who sins voluntarily against his craft is reputed a better craftsman than he who does so involuntarily, because the former seems to do so from right judgment, and the latter from a defective judgment. On the other hand it is the reverse in prudence, as stated in *Ethics*, VI, for it is more imprudent to sin voluntarily, since this is lacking in the chief act of prudence, viz., command, than to sin involuntarily" (*Summa Theologica*, II–II, Q.47, A.8).

126. It is necessary to qualify Maritain's statement here, because there are speculative arts dealing with such operations as "demonstrating." The similarity between art, including the speculative arts, and such speculative virtues as understanding, knowledge and wisdom (vd. *Art and Scholasticism*, pp. 19, 84, 38) must be qualified by some difference between the man of learning and the artist. The difference between the necessary and the contingent is satisfactory except for the speculative arts. The difference is better found either in the ends of operation or in the manner thereof. In terms of the first, the end of the liberal artist is the acquisition of knowledge, the end of the man of learning is its possession. In terms of the second, the operations of art are imitative; those of cognition are not.

127. The distinction of different types of art — liberal and servile, practical and productive, fine and useful — depends upon a metaphysical analysis of the status in being of the work done, upon a physical analysis of the process of artistic change, and upon a psychological analysis of the artist as a voluntary agent. These analyses are too complicated to be given here. They can be found in a paper of mine, *Creation and Imitation: An Analysis of Poiesis*, published in the *Proceedings of the American Catholic Philosophical Association*, 1935: pp. 153–174. The locus of the principles in Aristotelian and Thomistic texts is indicated throughout.

128. The speculative arts perfect the soul relatively even when they are not in act, because they confer an aptness for good operation. When they are exercised properly, the speculative possessions in which they result perfect the intellect simply.

129. "Even in speculative matters there is something by way of work: e.g., the making of a syllogism or of a fitting speech, or the work of counting and measuring. Hence whatever habits are

ordained to suchlike works of the speculative reason are, by a kind of comparison, called arts indeed, but *liberal* arts, in order to distinguish them from those arts that are ordained to works done by the body, which arts are, in a fashion, servile, inasmuch as the body is in servile subjection to the soul, and man, as regards his soul is free (*liber*).   On the other hand, those sciences which are not ordained to any suchlike work, are called sciences simply and not arts.   Nor, if the liberal arts be more excellent, does it follow that the notion of art is more applicable to them" (*Summa Theologica*, I–II, Q.57, A.4, ad.3).   This definition of liberal art requires that it include all works in the soul and not only those in the speculative reason.   The liberal arts thus properly embrace both the speculative arts, such as grammar, logic, geometry, and the fine arts.   Cf. *Art and Scholasticism*, p. 21.   It should also be noted that it is the servile arts which conform to the essential notion of *making* as extrinsic operation.   The others are called arts only "by a kind of comparison."

130.   "The truth is that the division of the arts into the arts of the beautiful (the Fine Arts) and the useful, however important it may be in other respects, is not what Logicians term an 'essential' division; it derives from the end pursued, and the same art can quite well pursue usefulness and beauty at the same time.   Such, *par excellence*, is the case with architecture" (*Art and Scholasticism*, Note 39, by permission of Sheed and Ward).   Can it be said, therefore, that "certain arts tend to make a work of *beauty*, and thereby differ essentially from all the rest" (*op. cit.*, p 33) ?   The fine arts are *essentially* distinguished in the manner in which they, as liberal arts, are distinguished from all the servile arts.   Within the field of liberal arts, fine are distinguished from speculative works by the mode of their being.   Vd. *Creation and Imitation: An Analysis of Poiesis*, (*loc. cit.*, Note 127 *supra*): pp. 163–169.

I owe to my friend Herbert Schwartz the further insight that the fine arts can be distinguished from the speculative and the useful arts in that imitation itself is their end.   Works of fine art are, therefore, properly spoken of as imitations, whereas useful products and speculative works are not.

131.   "What is required is the perfect practical discrimination between the end pursued by the workman (*finis operantis*, said the Schoolmen) and the end to be served by the work (*finis operis*), so that the workman may work for his wages, but the work be controlled and set in being only in relation to its own proper good and nowise in relation to the wages earned; so that the

artist may work for any and every human intention he likes, but the work taken by itself be performed and constructed for its own proper beauty alone" (*Art and Scholasticism*, pp. 77–78). But the end of the workman *as a workman* is the work done, whatever be his intentions *as a man*, whether he work for wages or for the sake of the work to be done itself, or for the sake of ends which the work can serve when produced. And the work produced can be regarded as an end in itself only when considered in relation to the workman. If *operis* in the phrase *finis operis* and the phrase *bonum operis* (vd. Maritain, p. 14) is univocal, then, in a strict sense, *finis operantis est bonum operis*, and *finis operis est bonum hominis*.

132. To say, as Maritain does, "prudence operates for the good of the worker, *ad bonum operantis*, art operates for the good of the work done, *ad bonum operis*" (*Art and Scholasticism*, p. 14), is not inconsistent with the point made in Note 131 *supra*. This can be seen in terms of the distinction between man operating, either prudentially or artistically, and the operation itself; and between the operation and its result, the work done considered in itself.

133. "Prudence is threefold. There is a false prudence, which takes its name from its likeness to true prudence. For since a prudent man is one who disposes well of the things that have to be done for a good end, whoever disposes well of such things as are fitting for an evil end, has false prudence in so far as that which he takes for an end is good, not in truth but in appearance. Thus, a man is called *a good robber*, and in this way we may speak of *a prudent robber*, by way of similarity, because he devises fitting ways of committing robbery. . . The second prudence is indeed true prudence because it devises fitting ways of obtaining a good end; and yet it is imperfect from a twofold source. First, because the good which it takes for an end, is not the common end of all human life, but of some particular affair; thus when a man devises fitting ways of conducting commerce or of sailing a ship, he is called a prudent business-man or a prudent sailor; secondly, because he fails in the chief act of prudence, as when a man takes counsel aright, and forms a good judgment, even about things concerning life as a whole, but fails to make an effective command. The third is both true and perfect prudence, for it takes counsel, judges and commands aright in respect of the good end of man's whole life; and this alone is prudence simply so-called, and cannot be in sinners, whereas the first prudence is in sinners alone, while

imperfect prudence is common to good and wicked men, especially that which is imperfect through being directed to a particular end" (*Summa Theologica*, II–II, Q.47, A.13). Artistic
prudence is the type of true but imperfect prudence which can
be in good and wicked men alike. Note ad. 2 of the same article :
Perfect prudence "implies a relation to right appetite, because its
principles are the ends in matters of action ; and of such ends one
forms a right estimate through the habits of moral virtue which
rectify the appetite."

134. "In some arts there is counsel about matters concerning the
ends proper to those arts. Hence some men, in so far as they are
good counsellors in matters of warfare or seamanship are said to
be prudent officers or pilots, but not simply prudent : only those
are simply prudent who give good counsel about matters regarding
man's entire life" (*Summa Theologica*, I–II, Q.57, A.5, ad.3).

135. There is a difference among the arts in respect to the degree
to which a sort of prudence is needed to supplement the regulated
habits of operation in which the art consists. Thus, among the
servile arts, the crafts of the plumber, the automotive mechanic,
the mason, etc., are at one extreme in being, for the most part,
adequate to the task to be performed, requiring little in the way
of counsel or prudential judgment ; at the other extreme are the
arts of the strategist, the physician, the business man, etc. Among
the liberal arts, the separation is sharper. The speculative arts are
perfectly adequate. The grammarian and the logician operate
well only as they operate according to rules. There are no contingencies that require counsel. But in the case of the fine arts
"the work to be done is, so far as it is beautiful, an end in itself,
and because such an end is something absolutely individual, utterly unique, the artist has every time a fresh and unique way of
conforming to the end, and so regulating the matter" (*Art and
Scholasticism*, p. 49). In other words, the speculative arts, viewed
as sciences in the second intention, are superior as knowledge to
the fine arts which, if viewed as sciences, are in the first intention
and have an admixture of opinion.

136. Hence the difference in teachability of the different sorts of
virtue. The speculative virtues are, of course, eminently and
essentially teachable. The arts are teachable in proportion as
good operation is according to rule and does not require much
supplementation by artistic prudence. Among the arts, the
speculative liberal arts and the mechanical servile arts are the most

teachable. Prudence is essentially unteachable, if teaching be understood univocally in the sense in which knowledge or the art of logic can be taught. The moral virtues, in so far as prudence constitutes them by appointing the mean in matters of appetite and conduct, are as unteachable as prudence. The distinctions between prudence and art and between prudence and knowledge thus help to answer the questions which Plato raised in the *Meno* and the *Protagoras*.

137. The failure to distinguish between prudence and knowledge and between prudence and art is the source of the Socratic error of identifying knowledge and virtue. Vd. *Summa Theologica*, I–II, Q.58, A.2. The ultimate root of this error in ethics is a defective psychological analysis, failing to separate intellect and will.

138. "The soul of the artist with all its human fullness, with every object of its love and worship, all the intentions, human, moral and religious, outside the artistic order which it can pursue, is the principal cause, using the virtue of art as an instrument; and so the work is wholly of the soul and the will of the artist as principal cause, and wholly of his art as instrument, without the artist losing a tittle of his mastery over matter and his integrity, his purity and ingenuousness — just as our good acts are wholly ours secondarily and wholly God's primarily, without on that account being any the less free" (*Art and Scholasticism*, p. 134, Sheed and Ward. See also pp. 132–133). For a discussion of principal and instrumental causes, see *Summa Theologica*, I, Q.105, A.5., ad.2; Q.118, A.2; Q.88, A.1; and *Summa Contra Gentiles*, III, 70, 103, 147. For a discussion of the technical meaning of "image," according to which meaning it can be said that the work of fine art is the image of its maker's soul, see *Summa Theologica*, I, Q.93, AA.2, 6, 9; Q.4, A.3. Cf. E. Gilson, *The Spirit of Mediaeval Philosophy*, New York, 1936: p. 98.

139. Hence, as Maritain says, what thanksgivings the artist would "offer to morality, if he knew his own good. By protecting his humanity it indirectly protects his art as well. For however beautiful it may be in other respects, the work of art always ends by betraying, with infallible cunning, the vices of the workman. . . And because the artist as such expresses himself and ought to express himself in his work as he is, then, if he is morally deformed, his art also, the intellectual virtue which is perhaps what is most sincere in him, runs the risk of receiving and deserving

the birchings of morality. The conflict is inevitable. Man extri-
cates himself as best he can, rather badly than well" (*Art and
Scholasticism*, pp. 118–119, Sheed and Ward). But, it may be
objected, that it is the man as a man, and not as an artist, and it is
certainly not the work of art, which deserves the birchings of
morality when the work reflects the deformed soul of its maker.
In another sense, however, the greatness of a work of art is never
merely a matter of workmanship. It is never merely *how* the
artist speaks in his work, but *what* he has to say. The judgment
of the content, always ultimately based on moral criteria, coalesces
with the judgment of technique in the aesthetic evaluation of
works of art. Despite the presence of moral criteria, the criticism
is *aesthetic* if it regards the work of art in itself. It is in this
sense that Maritain is right when he says: "Diminish the man in
the artist, you necessarily diminish the art itself, which is of the
man." . . . Unless the artist is convinced that "his contribution,
while including pleasure, is nourishment and not intoxication only,
his work will always remain in some aspects defective and mean.
The greatest poets, and the most disinterested, the most 'gratuitous,' had some message for mankind" (*op. cit.*, pp. 134–135,
Sheed and Ward).

140. "As the artist is first a man and then an artist, it is easy to see
what conflicts will rage in his heart between Art and Prudence,
his character as a Maker and his character as a Man" (*Art and
Scholasticism*, p. 15, Sheed and Ward). "Only the artist who
consents to be a man, who is not afraid of morality, who is not
at every moment terrified of losing the flower of his ingenuousness, enjoys the real gratuitousness of art. He is what he is,
careless of what he may appear to be; he affirms, if he wants to
affirm, he believes, loves, chooses, gives himself, follows his inclination and fancy, recreates and amuses himself, enjoys himself
playing" (*op. cit.*, p. 138, Sheed and Ward).

141. A compromise is effected when conflicting parties are kept
apart by courtesies reciprocally extended. It is a practical expedient and superficial with respect to the basis of the issue. Art
and prudence are reconciled only when they are *united* by a
harmony of intellect and will. This can be accomplished, as
Maritain points out, only by Wisdom "endowed with the outlook
of God" (*Art and Scholasticism*, p. 86, Sheed and Ward). Human
wisdom is not enough. The gifts of a supernatural religion are
needed. "Truth to tell, I believe it to be impossible outside
Catholicism to reconcile in man, without diminishing or forcing

them, the rights of morality and the claims of intellectuality, art or science. Morality as such aims only at the good of the human being, the supreme interests of the acting Subject; Intellectuality as such aims only at the Object, its nature, if it is to be known, what it ought to be, if it is to be made. . . A superhuman virtue is necessary to secure the free play of art and science among men under the supremacy of the divine law and the primacy of Charity, and so to realize the higher reconciliation of the *moral* and the *intellectual*" (*op. cit.*, pp. 138–139).

In an essay devoted to this subject and acknowledging its discipleship to Maritain, Eric Gill describes the opposition of art and prudence as a lover's quarrel. Each is devoted in part to the interests of the other, yet each claims a precedence and a dominion over the other, each is jealous of its rights in human life. He concludes that, although the prudent man should have no quarrel with good art, the conflict goes on and will "never be settled until most men of prudence are also artists and most artists have become men of prudence. This pleasing state of affairs will not come about until the present civilization has passed away" (*Beauty Looks After Herself*, Sheed and Ward, New York, 1933 : p. 29).

The makers of motion pictures are not the only artists in our day about whom it can be asked whether they are also prudent men. If the unity of Christian wisdom, the existence of a truly Christian civilization, is needed to prevent "the ungodly divorce between Art and Prudence," the deficiency of it will exhibit itself in all fields of human endeavor, in science and philosophy as well as in the fine arts, in music and painting as well as in the novel, the play and the motion picture. For this, as for other modern evils, the only remedy may be the re-establishment of Christendom. Those who do not share this faith and hope must move to a solution on a lower level.

142. In his recent encyclical *Vigilanti Cura* (July 2, 1936), Pope Pius XI said: "Everyone knows what damage is done to the soul by bad motion pictures. They are occasions of sin; they seduce young people along the ways of evil by glorifying the passions; they show life under a false light; they cloud ideals; they destroy pure love, respect for marriage and affection for the family. They are capable also of creating prejudices among individuals, misunderstanding among nations, among social classes and among entire races. On the other hand, good motion pictures are capable of exercising a profound and moral influence upon those who see them. In addition to affording recreation, they are able to arouse noble ideals of life, to communicate valuable conceptions," etc.

The question must be asked whether the judgment of motion pictures here made is in terms of their content or in terms of their effects. If the former, the judgment is an aesthetic one; and indirectly it involves moral condemnation of the makers of motion pictures in so far as "bad" motion pictures betray the souls of their makers. But if the latter, the judgment must rely upon knowledge or become tautological. If a "bad" motion picture is one which has certain deleterious effects, then the difficult question is which motion pictures are bad, i.e. which have these effects? By definition every one *knows* that a motion picture is bad if it has these effects; but everyone does not *know* the answer to the question of fact indicated. Nor can it be answered by a judgment of the morality or immorality of the content of motion pictures, because the intrinsic and extrinsic values of works of fine art are independently variable.

143. It is interesting to note that the encyclical *Vigilanti Cura* takes the Platonic position with respect to the function of art: "We call to mind that it is necessary to apply to the cinema a supreme rule which must direct and regulate the greatest of arts in order that it may not find itself in continual conflict with Christian morality or even simply with human morality based upon natural law. The essential purpose of art, its *raison d'être*, is to assist in the perfection of moral personality, which is man, and for this reason must itself be moral." . . . We therefore recommend "the necessity of making the motion picture 'moral, an influence for good morals, an educator.'" In another place, Pope Pius asks: "Why, indeed, should there be a question of merely avoiding evil? Why should the motion picture simply be a means of diversion and light relaxation to occupy an idle hour? With its magnificent power it can and must be a light and a positive guide to what is good." This conception of art as essentially didactic confirms the Platonism of the encyclical, elsewhere revealed in the identification of intrinsic and extrinsic criticism. See Note 142 *supra*.

144. If the home, the church and the school, or the State, succeeded in the task of training youth, there would be little to fear from the arts. If human character, formed as well as possible, is still corruptible by works of art, then nothing can be done to safeguard men from corruption because it is the weakness of their souls that no human effort can remedy. This was Milton's insight when he praised Plato for his positive programme of good institutions. The arts can interfere in moral affairs only to the extent that men

are susceptible to such interference. The wise course for the prudent man is, therefore, to make them less susceptible by the efficiency of his positive efforts. In following this programme it may be necessary, of course, for the Church or the State or the individual parent to prevent the arts from interfering with these efforts. Preventive measures should seek, not to regulate the arts directly, but only to regulate the conditions of their reception: what shall be seen and what rejected. This is the policy recommended in the recent papal encyclical. It is the policy ever pursued by vigilant parents.

There is no question that protection from misleading influences is justified during the course of moral training and even for adults to the extent that they must be treated as children. But fears about the effects of external factors is often more a confession of the weakness of home, church and school as positive moral forces than an indication of the existence of the menace feared. That school teachers should be so concerned about what children learn from the movies is a terrifying admission of doubt about the influence of their own teaching. A good teacher so instructs the mind that it is incapable of being hurt by the multifarious errors received from all other sources. In fact, assured of his power and of the strength of his discipline, he is happy to assume the role of antagonist to all other teachers, in school or out, who seem to oppose him. The same is true of the home and the church in the matter of moral training. The agitation about the movies, resulting in extensive scientific research, has not resulted in any findings that are nearly as much cause for alarm as the terrible confession of inadequacy which the agitation itself so plainly bespeaks.

145. "Prudence is right in being apprehensive of the effect on the masses of many works of art. And Catholicism, knowing that evil is to be encountered *ut in pluribus* in the human race, and yet obliged to concern itself with the good of the multitude, must in certain cases deny to art, in the name of the essential interests of the human being, liberties which art would jealously assert. The 'essential interests of the human being' here in question must be understood not only in relation to the passions of the flesh, but also in relation to the subject-matter of all the virtues, the integrity of the mind first of all — not to mention the interests of art itself, and the need it has of being protected by the disciplines of religion against the dissolution of everything there is in man. It is difficult no doubt in such a case to preserve the balance. At all events to be frightened of art, to flee from it or to put it to flight, is

certainly no solution. There is a superior wisdom in trusting as much as possible to the powers of the mind" (Maritain, *Art and Scholasticism*, Note 154, Sheed and Ward).

146. In a recent essay on *Literary Criticism and the Concept of Imitation in Antiquity* (in Modern Philology, The University of Chicago Press, August 1936: p. 24ff.), Professor McKeon summarizes the Platonic position by saying that art is "always subject to moral, political, educational and scientific criticism, for there can be no other, no purely aesthetic, criticism of art." The Aristotelian position is described, in contrast, as separating different types of criticism according to the sciences from which they derive their principles: poetics or politics or rhetoric. But Professor McKeon denies that there is a genuine philosophical issue between Plato and Aristotle on this point. He regards the difference between them, which at first appears to be doctrinal, as a difference of method. He writes: "The Platonic and the Aristotelian approaches to the consideration of art differ, therefore, not in the manner of two doctrines which contradict each other, but rather in the manner of two approaches to a subject which are mutually incommensurable. Even more, the differences between the two approaches and the peculiarities of the two methods indicate no superiority of the one over the other, nor are there problems soluble by the one which are impervious to the analysis of the other." It should be clear that a contrary position is taken in this book. Plato and Aristotle are treated as contradicting each other on crucial points. Their points of difference about art and about ethical matters depend upon fundamental doctrinal disagreements in metaphysics and psychology. The Platonic position can be upheld only by demonstrating the error of the analysis, made according to Aristotelian principles, of the relation of art and prudence, to each other and to the moral virtues. Either intrinsic and extrinsic criticism are separable or they are not. Either moral and technical criteria are separable or they are not. Either the will and the intellect are one or they are not. If such dilemmas can be avoided, then the issue Professor McKeon raises is a deeper one than the question about Plato and Aristotle. It can be stated as follows: either there are right and wrong answers to philosophical questions, apart from all methodological considerations, or there are not. The solution of this dilemma turns upon the answer to the question whether propositions in isolation can be judged true or false or whether they are merely to be accepted or rejected as elements in a system, an approach. The answer to this question, it seems to me, must be affirmative.

The negative answer can be shown to be self-contradictory. The erroneous position is taken in my book, *Dialectic* (New York, 1927). The errors therein are easily detected.

147. Three recent books on the novel are vaguely discursive rather than clearly analytical because they are not guided by principles their authors could have found in the *Poetics*: Percy Lubbock's *The Craft of Fiction* (New York, 1929), E. M. Forster's *Aspects of the Novel* (New York, 1927) and Edwin Muir's *The Structure of the Novel* (New York, 1929). The same is true of the best treatises on the cinema: V. I. Pudovkin's *Film Technique* (London, 1933), Gilbert Seldes' *The Movies and the Talkies* (Philadelphia, 1929), R. Arnheim's *Film* (London, 1933), R. Spottiswoode's *Grammar of the Film* (London, 1935) and Allardyce Nicoll's *Film and Theatre* (New York, 1936). The general applicability of Aristotle's analysis of art is exemplified by a treatise by Dr. Herbert Schwartz: *An Aristotelian Analysis of the Elements, Principles and Causes of the Art of Music*, Cleveland, 1936.

148. I have demonstrated this proposition elsewhere. See *Creation and Imitation: An Analysis of Poiesis* (*loc. cit.*, Note 127 *supra*). It is not only that man makes imitatively, but that the work made imitates a natural object through being both formally *similar* and materially *different*. It is interesting to observe that both Arnheim and Spottiswoode, while failing to analyze the cinema as an imitation of nature — misconceiving imitation as copying — take great pains to emphasize the *differences* between nature seen and nature filmed. Quite properly they make the artificiality of the film depend on these differences, which Arnheim calls 'formative media' and Spottiswoode 'differentiating factors.' Vd. *Film*, p. 17 ff. and *The Grammar of the Film*, pp. 117, 127 ff.

148a. The individual work of art is a unique composition of the elements of a given medium. Its individuality is, in this sense, formal rather than material, because it is due to the singularity of the artificial form — a form of composition or arrangement — which has been imposed upon the matter of the medium. But the individual work is a work of a given sort. Its kind is determined, first, by its object of imitation and, second, by its medium and manner. The object of imitation is the source of its generic form, and the medium and manner of its specific differences. Viewed in relation to kinds of art, both object and medium are formal determinations. But object and medium can be viewed in relation to the individual work of art.   Then it will be seen that what in the individual work is related to the *object* of imitation, namely, its particular content, stands to its structure, i.e., the organization of the elements of its *medium*, as *matter* stands to *form*.   This explains why the attempt to ignore or even to deny the imitative character of fine art, — the effort to "abstract" a bare structure from all content, to make artistic activity the mastery of a medium without any object of imitation, — is properly regarded as the error of "formalism".   The opposite error is "copyism", which makes the content of art reportorial and forgets that art is necessarily constructive.   It might be called the error of "materialism".   Vd. *Art and Scholasticism* : pp. 90ff.

149.   In *Poetics*, 1, 1447ª19–20, the "medium of color and form" is mentioned, but the statement speaks of imitation as representing "various objects."   This passage certainly does not require the plastic arts to have the *same* object as poetry and music.   In *Poetics*, 2, 1448ª5–6, Aristotle discusses good and bad men as objects of imitation and adds : "It is the same in painting.   Polygnotus depicted men as nobler than they are, Pauson as less noble, Dionysius drew them true to life."   This passage, like others which mention painting, merely points to a similarity between the plastic arts and other arts which represent men *somehow*.   It certainly does not define the plastic object.   Cf. *Poetics* 6, 1450ª25–27 ; 25, 1460ᵇ7–11.   Furthermore, it must be remembered that the human form is not exclusively the subject-matter of painting and sculpture.   Finally, there is the passage in the *Politics*, VIII, 5, 1340ª28–1340ᵇ : "In the other senses there is no imitation of manners ; that is to say, in the touch and taste ; in the objects of sight, a very little ; for these are merely representations of things, and the perceptions which they excite are in a manner common to all.   Besides, statues and paintings are not properly imitations of character, but rather signs and marks which show the body is affected by some passion.   However, the difference is not great, yet young men ought not to view the paintings of Pauson but of Polygnotus, or any other painter or statuary who expressed character.   But in poetry and music there are imitations of character ; and this is evident, for different harmonies differ from each other so much by nature, that those who hear them are differently affected, and are not in the same disposition of mind when one is performed as when another is."   The plastic arts, in so far as they imitate human figures, can at best indicate the *results* of passions ; they cannot *properly* imitate change of character or

the movement of the passions which is the object imitated by music and lyric poetry.

150. In *Poetics*, 1, it is said that "rhythm, language, or harmony, either singly or combined" produce imitation (1447^a23). But this cannot be interpreted to mean that rhythm, language and harmony are the sole media of the arts. Color and form, the voice, bodily movement are also mentioned as media of imitation. And later rhythm, tune and metre are spoken of as means which the arts employ (1447^b25). The text in grouping all the arts which use rhythm, language or harmony, singly or combined, certainly does not indicate that all the members of this group imitate the *same* object and differ *inter se* only in medium. But that all the arts of this group have rhythm in common can be taken to indicate their temporal character. They are arts in motion and able, therefore, to imitate human action. They imitate change by means of a rhythmic ordering of their elements, the elements differing according to the different media in which they imitate.

151. When stories are told about animals, the animals are personified. In other words, animals must be humanized, must be made voluntary and thoughtful, in order for their behavior to become an object of artistic imitation.

152. "If there is a future for drama, and particularly for poetic drama, will it not be in the same direction indicated by the ballet?" (T. S. Eliot, *A Dialogue on Dramatic Poetry* in *Collected Essays*, New York, 1932 : p. 34).

153. The essay is usually not narrative but expository or argumentative. Even when it approaches narrative form, it does so in the same sense that a philosophical dialogue is narrative. It is a soliloquy, a narrative of the soul's conversation with itself. Most essays are a hybrid of fiction and philosophy, or science, or history. At its worst, the essay is popular journalism, filling the current periodicals with remote reflections of knowledge or ideas. At its best, the essay is a monograph, cutting a small piece out of a large subject. The best essays are expanded footnotes, and the reader must supply the text.

154. Opera may be excepted from the condemnation of programme music. It is not a confusion of the arts but a combination of them. The parts combined can have independent and significant exist-

ence. The libretto can be read as poetry without hearing the music. The music can be heard without reading the libretto or the lyrics. The music, apart from the libretto, does not tell a story. The opera is well contrasted with the cinema : the former is merely a combination of separable works in different media ; the latter is a thoroughly integrated fusion of work done in a pictorial and a linguistic medium.

155. The recent publication of the shooting-script of *Romeo and Juliet,* along with Shakespeare's text, supports rather than refutes the point that the scenario is not a piece of literature. Professor Nicoll appears to think the general practice of "printing screen plays no doubt will come immediately the cinema starts to build up its independent stock of plots" (*op. cit.,* p. 33). He does not mean that they will be published for the use of technicians, as architect's plans are recorded. He means that they will be generally read. This, it seems to me, is unlikely. The scenario does not have the unity of a work of art, in the sense in which that is possessed by the novel or the play as literature. It is nothing more than the plan for a work not yet finished.

156. I have used the word "symbol" for signs which signify without sensible similitude to that which they signify. In this sense, words are symbols, and pictures, in their primary reference, are not. But pictures, like anything else in the world, may symbolize what they do not sensibly resemble. But this is always a secondary reference and depends upon the primary non-symbolic reference of the picture to that which it sensibly represents. This can be understood in terms of St. Thomas's distinction between the literal and the metaphorical interpretation of words. The literal is always primary ; all of the metaphorical meanings depend upon it. Thus, the word "arm" in the phrase "the arm of God" must first be read literally as signifying a bodily member ; then, and only then, can "arm" be interpreted as meaning operative power, because the arm as literally signified can stand for a power of operation of which it is the instrument. So a picture's first significance is literal : it refers primarily to what it resembles. Thereafter, it can become symbolic, referring secondarily to whatever is signified by the thing it resembles, the object of the literal reference. This explains what Pudovkin means by the symbolic use of pictures (*Film Technique,* p. 49), and what such writers as Spottiswoode mean by secondary *montage,* implicational and ideological (*op. cit.,* pp. 231–233). Good examples are provided by Arnheim (*op. cit.,* pp. 185–194), and by Professor Nicoll in the discussion of what

he calls "pictorial symbolism." The test always seems to be that the pictures signify "what would have taken many hundreds of words fully to express" (*op. cit.*, pp. 108–112). The test is right. The metaphorical in language is always a condensation of what would take many more words to state literally. The discussion of the pictorial medium would be clarified, however, if the distinction was made in terms of the literal and metaphorical dimensions of pictorial meaning, instead of talking about "symbolism."

157. "No doubt, if there is next to no matter, the work of the artist will the more easily succeed. But art, as has been sufficiently dinned into our ears, ought not to be on the lookout for what is easy. It must have opposition and constraint, the constraint of rules and the opposition of matter. The more obstinate and rebellious the matter, the better will art, by its success in mastering it, realise its own end, which is to make matter resplendent with a dominating intelligibility" (Maritain, *op. cit.*, p. 130, Sheed and Ward).

158. "In all ordered powers, that one is directive of another, which has the better knowledge about the plan to be followed : thus we may observe in the arts, that the art which is concerned with the end, whence is taken the entire scheme of the work to be produced, directs and governs the art that is immediately productive of the work" (St. Thomas Aquinas, *Summa Contra Gentiles*, III, 78). "A power directed to a principal effect naturally has lesser powers administering to it. This may be clearly seen in the arts : the arts which dispose the material are subservient to the art which introduces the art-form ; and the art that introduces the art-form is subservient to the art which is concerned with the end of the art-product ; and again the art that is concerned with an anterior end is subservient to the art that is concerned with the ultimate end" (*Ibid.*, IV, 75). In these passages St. Thomas is thinking primarily of useful arts, but the analysis applies as well to the fine arts, particularly the point that the arts which dispose the material are subservient to the art which introduces the art-form. The latter, in the case of the cinema, is the art of the director ; the arts of the actor, the camera-man, the electrician, the dialogue-writer, etc., merely dispose the materials which he must use. Cf. Pudovkin, *op. cit.*, pp. 138–139.

159. Professor Münsterberg recognized this point many years ago (*The Photoplay*, New York, 1916 : pp. 192–193). The chief problem raised by the supremacy of the director is his relation to

his closest subordinate, the scenarist. Pudovkin states the basic
principle: "Naturally one might postulate as the ideal arrangement the incarnation of scenarist and director in one person. But
I have already spoken of the unusual scope and complexity of
film creation, that prevents any possibility of its mastery by one
person. Collectivism is indispensable in the film, but the collaborators must be blended with one another to an exceptionally close
degree" (*op. cit.*, p. 103). In art, as in economics, collectivism
does not mean the absence of government. Close collaboration
with auxiliary artists leaves the director still supreme. Thus, in
his relation to the scenarist, the director must have the final word:
"either the director must be directly associated with the work of
the scenarist from the beginning, or, if this is impossible for some
reason or other, he must inevitably go through the scenario, removing anything foreign to him, maybe altering separate parts
and sequences, maybe the entire subject-construction" (*ibid.*, p.
94). Later writers have followed Pudovkin in this, as in other
matters. Cf. Seldes, *op. cit.*, pp. 90–95, 98 ff.; Spottiswoode, *op.
cit.*, pp. 195–196; Arnheim, *op. cit.*, pp. 196–197.

159a. "Anyone capable of writing a good scenario cannot be unfitted save in purely superficial ways to direct the production —
as, for example, if he does not know studio routine. For he is
not a man of pen and paper but of the camera and celluloid. He
is not a writer, and a film script is not literature. Hence the appeal to authors by which film producers every now and then try
to curry favor with the intelligentsia is utterly absurd. Especially since sound films came on the scene is the cry heard: 'Now
film is talking; now we need the co-operation of the novelists!'
It is greatly to be hoped that authors, for their own sakes and for
that of film art, will resist this temptation, which promises wide
renown and an ample income. For they would not cut a good
figure. Eisenstein and Pudovkin are not expected to write novels;
Galsworthy and Dreiser should not be expected to write films.
Even in the sound-film era the simple yet so often ignored words
are true: 'Film art needs film artists and nothing more'" (Arnheim,
op. cit., pp. 196–197, Faber and Faber, Ltd.).

160. "The poet may imitate by narration — in which case he can
either take another personality as Homer does, or speak in his
own person, unchanged — or he may present all his characters as
living and moving before us" (*Poetics*, 3, 1448^{a}21–23). Aristotle's language is open to criticism, first, because of the unfortunate restriction on the word "narration," and second, because

it shows him to be thinking about the difference between the *written* epic and the *produced* drama, rather than about both as works of literature.

Plato makes the same distinctions in different language. He speaks of the styles of poetry as (1) wholly imitative (tragedy and comedy) or (2) wholly narrative (dithyramb) or (3) a union of the two (epic). Vd. *Republic*, 392 D–393 C. Verbal translation is easily made. I have used the word "dialogue" to denote what Plato means by the imitative style of story-telling and what Aristotle means by the method of presenting the characters as living and moving before us ; and the word "description" to denote what both Plato and Aristotle mean by the pure narrative style.

161. A novel is better written in the third than in the first person. "Homer, admirable in all respects, has the special merit of being the only poet who rightly appreciates the part he should take himself. The poet should speak as little as possible in his own person, for it is not this that makes him an imitator. Other poets appear themselves upon the scene throughout, and imitate but little and rarely. Homer, after a few prefatory words, at once brings in a man, or woman, or other personage ; none of them wanting in characteristic qualities, but each with a character of his own" (*Poetics*, 24, 1460^{a}5–12).

162. The "psychological novel" does not have unity of action. Its unity is historical or biographical rather than fictional, the unity of a man, a life, a period. "Unity of plot does not, as some persons think, consist in the unity of the hero. For infinitely various are the incidents in one man's life which cannot be reduced to unity ; and so, too, there are many actions of one man out of which we cannot make one action" (*Poetics*, 8, 1451^{a}17–19). The novel should differ "in structure from historical compositions, which of necessity present not a single action, but a single period, and all that happened within that period to one person or many, little connected together as the events may be" (*Poetics*, 23, 1459^{a}22–24). Furthermore, the psychological novel tends to imitate the same object as music and lyric poetry : change of character, the alteration of emotions. It would be better written as a sonnet sequence.

163. There have been many excellent discussions of the differences between film and drama-as-produced, but all of these have been on the level of differences in technique rather than in terms of fictional form. Vd. Pudovkin, *op. cit.*, pp. 51–58 ; Seldes, *op. cit.*,

54–55 ; Spottiswoode, *op. cit.*, pp. 104–109. Professor Nicoll has
made an extensive enumeration of the technical facilities possessed
by the screen, in contrast to the limitations of the stage in the production of spectacle : *op. cit.*, 62–119. His comparison of *The
Barretts of Wimpole Street* as a theatrical and as a filmic work is
instructive.

164. "Fear and pity may be aroused by spectacular means ; but
they may also result from the inner structure of the piece, which
is the better way, and indicates a superior poet. For the plot
ought to be so constructed that, even without the aid of the eye,
he who hears the tale told will thrill with horror and melt to pity
at what takes place. This is the impression we should receive
from hearing the story of Oedipus. But to produce this effect
by mere spectacle is a less artistic method, and dependent on extraneous aids" (*Poetics*, 14, 1453^{b}1–8). The use of verse instead
of prose because of its emotional effect is, similarly, resorting to
an extraneous aid for doing what the plot itself should accomplish ;
but it is not as dispensable a device as the spectacle because the
medium of the drama is language.

165. "Even when a treatise on medicine or natural science is brought
out in verse, the name of poet is by custom given to the author ;
and yet Homer and Empedocles have nothing in common but
the metre, so that it would be right to call the one poet, the other
physicist rather than poet" (*Poetics*, 1, 1447^{b}16–21). "The poet
and the historian differ not by writing in verse or in prose. The
work of Herodotus might be put into verse, and it would still be a
species of history, with metre no less than without it. The true
difference is that one relates what has happened, the other what
may happen" (*ibid.*, 9, 1451^{b}1–6). "It clearly follows that the
poet or 'maker' should be the maker of plots rather than of
verses. . . And even if he chances to take an historical subject,
he is none the less a poet ; for there is no reason why some events
that have actually happened should not conform to the law of the
probable and the possible, and in virtue of that quality in them he is
their poet or maker" (*ibid.*, 9, 1451^{b}27–31).

166. Professor Nicoll uses the words "cutting" and "montage" to
distinguish the prosaic and the poetic in cinematic style. "Cutting
or assembling implies merely the gathering together of the filmic
material and its arrangement in logical order. Montage, on the
contrary, implies an emotional, creative and imaginative approach,
and its aim is, not to lead a story forward by intellectually appre-

ciable stages, but to stimulate and arouse the minds of the spectators into feeling and hence into emotionally accepting the purport
of a particular scene. . . If cutting is prose, montage is poetry.
The simplest possible example would be, say, that of a shot showing
the head of a ferocious panther dissolving into that of a villain's
head. Rather obvious, perhaps, but still montage. A more complex example occurs in the long walk from London to Dover in
David Copperfield; there, instead of showing merely the tramping
figure of the boy, use was made of a series of exceedingly short
shots each with a symbolic and imaginative coloring, punctuated
by shots of milestones recording the stages of the lonely journey"
(*Film and Theatre*, pp. 52–54, by permission of Thomas Y. Crowell Company). In making the distinction in this way, Professor
Nicoll has overemphasized one criterion. He makes the distinction between cutting and montage analogous to the distinction
between a literal and a metaphorical use of words. But this is
only one variable in linguistic style. The distinction between
the prosaic and the poetic is more complex, both in the linguistic
and the pictorial medium. Furthermore, *montage is cutting, cutting is montage*. The principles of syntax are the same in prose
and verse. These matters are more fully discussed in Chapter 14
supra.

167. There is a partial anticipation of Pudovkin's insight in Münsterberg's earlier work (*op. cit.*, pp. 183–185). But Pudovkin makes
the clearest formulation of the time and space conditions of filmic
construction. Vd. *Film Technique*, pp. 55–64. He conceives the
art of film-construction as able to create an ideal spectator of events.
The attention of the spectator is entirely in the hands of the director. "The lens of the camera is the eye of the spectator. He
sees and remarks only that which the director desires to show
him, or, more correctly put, that which the director himself sees
in the action concerned." The others follow Pudovkin. Cf.
Seldes, *op. cit.*, p. 131 ff.; Arnheim, *op. cit.*, pp. 27–34; Spottiswoode, *op. cit.*, p. 156 ff.; Nicoll, *op. cit.*, pp. 85–91; 95–100.
"The director simply looks with his camera at what he chooses
and the audience is compelled to do the same" (Nicoll, *op. cit.*,
p. 88). "The presence of these attributes — the power to alter
size at will and to concentrate on just those elements which are
regarded as significant — alters the entire scope of the cinema
from that of the theatre, both in directional method and in that
of scenario composition" (*ibid.*, p. 89, Thomas Y. Crowell Company).

168. It is significant that the Greek tragedies were usually adaptations of epic material, as later the plays of Shakespeare were converted plots found in non-dramatic literature, historical or fictional. There is no reason why the drama having an original plot should be regarded as intrinsically superior to the dramatic adaptation of epic narratives. The same holds for the cinema. But one thing is clear : the better the original is in its own form, the more difficult the adaptation. This is an obstacle to be surmounted in cinematic versions of Shakespeare. It is not that Shakespeare's plays are intrinsically non-cinematic, but rather that — because they are so good as plays in the medium of language — they are extremely difficult to adapt to the medium and form of another art.

169. "When artists devote themselves merely to exploiting what has once been discovered it almost necessarily follows that talent, cleverness, sheer technique, the merely operative activity peculiar to the *genus* art should gradually gain the upper hand ; rules which were once living and spiritual will then become material, and that form of art end by exhausting itself. A renewal will be necessary. Heaven grant that a genius may be found to achieve it ! Even so the change will perhaps lower the general level of art ; it is nevertheless the very condition of its life and of the production of great works. We may believe that from Bach to Beethoven and from Beethoven to Wagner art has suffered a decline in quality, spirituality and purity. But would anyone be bold enough to say that any one of these men was less necessary than the other ? . . . It is perfectly true that there is no necessary progress in art, that tradition and discipline are the true nurses of originality ; and that the feverish acceleration which modern individualism, with its frenzy for revolution in the mediocre, imposes upon the succession of art forms, abortive schools, and puerile fashions is the symptom of a far-spread intellectual and social poverty. Novelty nevertheless is fundamentally necessary to art which, like nature, goes in seasons" (Maritain, *Art and Scholasticism*, pp. 46–47, Sheed and Ward). Cf. *Theonas*, Chapters VII, VIII and IX, for a fuller discussion of the idea of progress — and the myth of necessary progress — in the intellectual spheres, philosophy, science, art.

170. The rules of an art should govern all workers except the genius. The ordinary dramatist or novelist produces a monstrosity — or, what is worse, a triviality — if he transgresses the canons of the *Poetics*. Lacking the genius of Cervantes or Tolstoy, the writer of a novel who disregards the primacy of plot, not only tells a poor

story, but fails to achieve the first condition of artistry : unity. *Don Quixote* and *War and Peace* are great *books*, but not great *novels*. They are great in spite of, not because of, their *apparent* violation of the simplest rules of the art of story-telling. The master, as Maritain says, is not the slave of rules even when he is governed by them. He makes use of them. "He possesses and is not possessed by them : he is not *held* by them, it is he who *holds*, through them, matter and reality ; and sometimes, in the high moments when the working of genius in art resembles the miracles of God in nature, he will not act against the rules, but outside and above them, in conformity with a higher rule and a hidden order" (*Art and Scholasticism,* p. 40, Sheed and Ward). Moreover, when genius operates to create a new art-form, the work produced will be of a new kind and will therefore require new rules for those who, lacking genius, seek to follow the master. "For the modern artist the problem is absurdly situated between the senility of academic rules and the primitiveness of the natural gift : in the former art has ceased to exist, in the latter it has not yet come into being, except potentially. Art exists only in the living intellectuality of the *habit*" (*ibid.,* p. 42, Sheed and Ward. Cf. Notes 77, 78).

171. Thus, Spottiswoode objects to both color and stereoscopy on the ground that they would add complicating elements, increasing the tendency toward naturalism rather than the differentiation of the cinema as an imitation. They would interfere, he says, with the requisite freedom in *montage.* Vd. *The Grammar of the Film,* pp. 146–156. And yet Spottiswoode admits that, despite gloomy prophecies, sound and speech have not been impediments. Arnheim raises the same objections. He supposes that the impulse toward color and stereoscopy is due only to the false ideal of exact imitation, by which he means, not imitation at all, but faithful copying of nature. Vd. *Film,* pp. 69–76, 234–239. He fails to understand that artistic problems are not fundamentally altered by mechanical inventions of any sort. A colored stereoscopic film will be as much an imitation as a black-white, flat one. His sarcasm about the "faultless film" (*ibid.,* pp. 283–290) as one "which contains a maximum of likeness to nature," entirely misses the point. The history of the development following the invention of sound-film indicates this. Seldes grasps the essential principle. The limitations of its medium constitute the technical problems of an art. If particular limitations are overcome mechanically, that does not mean that the medium is without *any* limitations. "The colored-stereoscopic-talkie will have to discover new limitations

and perfect itself within them" (*The Movies and the Talkies*, p. 143). The technique of the motion picture will certainly be complicated by further inventions, as it was complicated by the invention of sound, but its essential problems will remain the same, because it is an art of story-telling in a medium which fuses language and pictures. It is a minor point whether the language be read or heard, whether the pictures are black-white or colored, flat or tri-dimensional.

172. An examination of the literature shows Pudovkin's book *Film Technique*, first published in English in 1929, though containing papers of earlier date, to be the great original work in the field. This does not mean that he is the great original artist. He gratefully acknowledges his indebtedness to the Americans who "were the first to discover in the film-play the presence of peculiar possibilities of its own" (*op. cit.*, p. 53). The work of D. W. Griffith, for instance, and, perhaps also, Mack Sennett and Chaplin, contributed the fundamental inventions in the use of the camera and even in the process of *montage*. Pudovkin is not being considered here as a director, but as an analyst. He was the first to recognize the relation of director and scenarist, the first to enumerate the various devices in shooting and cutting which are the elements of cinematic technique, the first to formulate, however unsystematically, the principles and rules of motion-picture making, the first to recognize that "the foundation of film-art is *montage*." But, as Ivor Montagu points out in his Preface, "Pudovkin is no Aristotle. He is not even, like Kuleshov, an instructor" (*op. cit.*, p. viii). He is an artist writing analytically about his art, which is clearly not the art of analysis itself. Unfortunately those who have followed Pudovkin — Arnheim, Seldes, Spottiswoode — are not Aristotles either. They, too, lack the principles of aesthetic analysis, although they improve upon Pudovkin in the orderly enumeration of details. Their books are, in a sense, commentaries on *Film Technique*, marred by unnecessary divergences in technical vocabulary.

Pudovkin records his debt to Kuleshov, a young painter and theoretician of the film. "It was from him that I first learned of the meaning of the word '*montage*,' a word which played such an important part in the development of our film-art. From our contemporary point of view, Kuleshov's ideas were extremely simple. All he said was this: 'In every art there must be firstly a material, and secondly a method of composing this material specially adapted to this art.' The musician has sounds as material and composes them in time. The painter's materials are colour, and he combines them in space on the surface of the canvas.   What then is the material which the film director possesses, and what are the methods of composition of his material ?   Kuleshov maintained that the material in film-work consists of pieces of film, and that the composition method is their joining together in a particular, creatively discovered order.   He maintained that film-art does not begin when the artists act and the various scenes are shot — this is only the preparation of the material.   Film-art begins from the moment when the director begins to combine and join together the various pieces of film.   By joining them in various combinations, in different orders, he obtains differing results" (*op. cit.*, pp. 138–139, George Newnes Limited).

173. The original insight into the analogy between the units and their combination in the pictorial medium and those of language, is Pudovkin's (*op. cit.*, p. 72).   But he fails to develop it, or even to use it in his account of *montage* and cinematic style.   The analogy is referred to by Seldes (*op. cit.*, pp. 133–134), and by Nicoll (*op. cit.*, p. 42).   But neither grasps its principles because neither sees that the isomorphism of the pictorial and linguistic media depends upon *formal grammar*, an analysis of the elements of significant utterance and their syntax, applicable to *any* language, and more than that, to *all media* of art, of which language is only one. Seldes, for instance, says without apparent justification that the phrase and not the word is the unit of prose.   Nicoll criticizes Pudovkin for likening the basic cuttable, the shot or piece, to a word, maintaining that "it always expresses an action with subject and predicate" and therefore should be "likened to a complete sentence or at least to a clause."   Nicoll's error is in supposing, first, that the grammar of an artistic medium is a *logical* grammar ; and second, that the analogy should provide a scheme for translating pictures into language and conversely.   To say that the shot is like a word or that the sequence is like a sentence does not mean that the narrative content of a shot, if expressed linguistically, could be stated by a single word or that it would take a sequence to express pictorially what can be said by a sentence. A narrative sentence involves a change of time.   It is not merely the report of an action.   While every shot, except a cinematographic still, records an action, only a sequence involves a change of time.   The shot and the scene are constituted by identity of filmic time.   The *same time* does not mean, of course, the *same instant*.   The scene is the unit event ; shots are its component parts.   The sequence involves a transition from one event to another and is therefore the narrative unit.   In short, it is neces-

sary to make a grammatical analysis of language as used narratively
— in history or fiction — in order to perfect the analogy between
linguistic and cinematic media of narration. The basis of the
analogy is, however, syntax : the discovery of the unit and different
orders of complexity in the combination of units. (In terms of
narrative structure, the analogy can be stated as follows : *shot :* a
movement or any part of a movement ; *scene :* an event or incident ; *sequence :* an episode. Sequences may be contained in
sequences, as larger episodes may include others. An episode is
constituted by its incidents, an event by a number of related
movements.)

173a. "The scenarist may conceive in his mind every detail of
every shot and precisely determine its length, write every necessary word, lay down every natural sound or piece of music ; and
in that event, the director is a mere mechanical executive, a manipu-
lator of actors and properties to a given formula. Or, on the
other hand, the director may dispense with a written scenario,
shooting a whole film with a clear conception of it in his mind,
and cutting it with the same guide. Neither of these extremes
is likely to be realized in practice. The complexity of the film
medium . . . demands a programme in words of the action which
the director makes the basis of his work. But the film and not
the scenario is the ultimate work of art ; the scenarist, if necessary,
is necessary only as an assistant ; and even where the director disappears except as an automaton, the process of montage survives
intact. Someone must do the creation ; it must be filmic and not
literary creation ; and if it is done by the scenarist his montage can
at the worst be bad ; it cannot be non-existent. The use of montage may reside in one person or another, or it may be divided
between them ; but it is always present" (Spottiswoode, *op. cit.*,
pp. 195–196, Faber and Faber, Ltd.).

174. "In constructing the plot and working it out with the proper
diction, the poet should place the scene, as far as possible, before
his eyes. In this way, seeing everything with the utmost vividness, as if he were a spectator of the action, he will discover what
is in keeping with it, and be most unlikely to overlook inconsistencies" (*Poetics*, 17, 1455^{a}22–26). "As for the story whether
the poet takes it ready made or constructs it for himself, he should
first sketch its general outline, and then fill in the episodes and
amplify in detail" (*ibid.*, 17, 1455^{a}34 — 1455^{b}2). It is interesting to
compare these two remarks with Pudovkin's rules of scenario construction (*op. cit.*, pp. 3–16). Thus : "The novelist expresses his

keystones in written descriptions, the dramatist by rough dialogue, but the scenarist must think in plastic (externally expressive) images. He must train his imagination, he must develop the habit of representing to himself whatever comes into his head in the form of a sequence of images upon the screen" (p. 14, George Newnes Limited). And: "If we try to divide the work of the scenarist into, as it were, a succession of stages, passing from the general to the particular, we get the following rough scheme: (1) the theme; (2) the action (the treatment); (3) the cinematographic working-out of the action (filmic representation)" (pp. 5–6, George Newnes Limited).

175. "A primitive example of the use of sound to reveal an inner content can be cited in the expression of the stranding of a town-bred man in the midst of a desert. In silent film we should have had to cut in a shot of the town; now in sound film we can carry town-associated sounds into the desert and edit them there in place of the natural desert sounds" (Pudovkin, *op. cit.*, pp. 156–157, George Newnes Limited; for other examples, see pp. 157–161).

176. "Music," Pudovkin maintains, "must in sound film *never be the accompaniment*. It must retain its own line. . . Just as the image is an objective perception of events, so the music expresses the subjective appreciation of this objectivity" (*op. cit.*, pp. 162–165). Arnheim differs from Pudovkin on this point, holding that "music may have one of two functions in film. It may either be an integral part of the production or an accompaniment" (*op. cit.*, p. 270). And Spottiswoode enumerates three uses of music: an imitative, an evocative and a dynamic use. Vd. *op. cit.*, pp. 190–192. The first is a substitution of music for language through onomatopoeia. The second is the employment of music to imitate the emotional change which is part of the narrative, and hence to evoke the emotions of the spectator sympathetically. This is what Pudovkin means by music retaining its own line, and what Arnheim means by music as an accompaniment. The third is the use of music as a parallel to the tempo and rhythm of the pictorial *montage*. Here, as Spottiswoode says, "the score should have no independent purpose." It is this use of music which Pudovkin denies, calling it an accompaniment. Cf. Nicoll, *op. cit.*, pp. 125–128; L. Sabaneau, *Music for the Films*, London, 1935: pp. 15–31, 108–118.

177. A double use of the word "action" must be noted. The object

of imitation for fiction is political action, as the object of imitation for music, the dance and lyric poetry is ethical action, i.e., change in character and emotion. Here action is divided against character as different objects of imitation. But the object of fictional imitation — action in the sense indicated — can be analyzed into its objective aspect, which is also called action, and its subjective aspects, character and thought or feeling. There are, therefore, three elements of fiction related to the object of imitation, and these are called plot, character and thought. The plot is an imitation of action in the second sense, i.e., divided against character and thought as *aspects* of the same object of imitation. Since that is action in the political dimension, its objective aspect is primary. Fiction is, therefore, said to imitate action (in the second sense) primarily, and character and thought only as they are involved in the action.

177a. Both the critical judgment and the judgment of taste are casuistical; hence uncertain, disputable and never conclusively established by any appeal to norms and principles. Criticism, "though it can always derive its inspiration from philosophical principles, — always a good thing, but risky, — remains on the same plane as the work and the particular" (Maritain, *op. cit.*, p. 226).

178. The theme stands to the episodic details and the incidents as the form of the plot to its matter. It is in this sense that the theme is said to be the essence of the plot. Many plots may be identical in theme, differing individually in their accidents.

The universality of the theme, in contrast to the singularity of the thematic development, indicates that the object of imitation is, as Aristotle says, a sort of universal. It is not, in the case of poetry, a particular action but a kind of action. The same theme is common to many plots. This means that many stories imitate the same type of action. A type of action is a uniformity *experienced*, a universal in the imagination resulting from many perceptions and memories. It is not an explicit universal, fully *abstracted* and intellectually grasped. Each of the many stories sharing the same theme is individuated by the accidental details of plot development, an individuation due, not to the object of imitation, but to the artist's unique composition of the elements of his medium. The object of imitation is never individual. If, in the case of the narrative arts, it were individual, there would be no distinction between fiction and history. The *possible*, which fiction *imitates*, must be *universal*. The *actual*, which history *reports*, must be *individual*.

179. Spottiswoode discusses the pictorial simile in terms of cinematic devices for expressing relations, for saying "like." Vd.
The Grammar of the Film, pp. 248–254. Filmic metaphors and
similes are usually referred to by the unhappy phrase 'pictorial
symbolism.' Excellent examples, however, are given by Nicoll,
Film and Theatre, pp. 108–112 and Arnheim, *Film*, pp. 185–194.

180. "Most good films are characterized by very simple themes and
relatively uncomplicated action. Bèla Balàzs, in his book *Der
Sichtbare Mensch*, quite correctly remarks that the failure of the
majority of film adaptations of literary works is to be ascribed
mainly to the fact that the scenarists concerned strove to compress
a superabundance of material into the narrow confines of the picture" (Pudovkin, *Film Technique*, p. 8, George Newnes Limited).

181. T. S. Eliot's use of heresy as a critical criterion emphasizes
the immorality of works which deny morality or which set up
personal and private standards. "When morals cease to be a
matter of tradition and orthodoxy, — that is, of the habits of the
community formulated, corrected and elevated by the continuous
thought and direction of the Church, — and when each man is to
elaborate his own, then *personality* becomes a thing of alarming
importance" (*After Strange Gods*, New York, 1934: p. 58).
The application of this criterion is excellently illustrated by Eliot's
criticism of three stories, by Katherine Mansfield, D. H. Lawrence and James Joyce. Vd. *op. cit.*, pp. 37–40. For him Joyce
is the most ethically orthodox and Lawrence the almost perfect
example of a heretic. Cf. Maritain's criticism of Proust, Gide
and Dostoievski in *Art and Scholasticism*, pp. 135, 224–226.

182. What I have called "sociological criticism" makes two errors.
First, it judges a fictional work according to its choice of theme
and not according to the detailed treatment of the chosen subject-
matter. In this it is guilty of being superficial. Second, in so far
as it considers the subject-matter in detail it applies the standards
of scientific rather than of poetic probability. In addition to
these two errors, the sociological critic supposes that it is a function of art to influence mass movements or, at least, to play some
part in the social currents of the day. That art should be social
or political propaganda is the current form of the Platonic supposition that art should be didactic. The Marxists are, of course,
sociological critics, but this approach is not exclusively theirs, as
witness the reasons currently given for praising the plays of Odets
and Rice, the novels of Dreiser and Sinclair Lewis.

This is the type of criticism which Dale applies to motion pictures. It runs all through his report on *The Content of Motion Pictures* and his chapter, answering the question what are motion pictures for, in *How to Appreciate Motion Pictures*. The latter book says in conclusion: "The motion picture as a medium of art must get into closer touch with the times. There is little hint in the current motion pictures of the tremendous changes which are occurring in modern civilization. The motion pictures, as developed today, are far from being the social mirror which reveals the mind and manners of our time. The motion picture must rise to a higher level of interpretation and express modern purposes and needs" (*op. cit.*, pp. 228–229). It should be added that this book is a manual of motion picture criticism prepared for high-school students.

It is, of course, possible to treat a work of fiction as if it were didactic and to criticize it accordingly. But those who do so should be cognizant of the different senses in which literature can be didactic: (1) the logical sense, in which it is construed as containing syllogisms and as aiming to establish conclusions by evidence or premises; (2) the rhetorical sense, in which it is construed as aiming, not to prove, but to persuade by quasi-arguments and emotional appeals; (3) the analogical sense, in which it is construed as "teaching" in the same way in which life or experience is said to teach. Everything that is knowable is didactic in this last sense. But certainly fiction (imaginative literature) is not didactic logically; only intellectual literature is that. The sociological approach treats fiction as didactic rhetorically, by reducing it to a form of propaganda in which the chief device is rhetorical induction, the argument from example, especially an example that stirs the emotions sympathetically. But the sociological critic must recognize that a novel, for instance, can be good as fiction and bad as propaganda, or conversely. He must also be made to see that the didactic intention, — whether logical or rhetorical, — violates the medium of fine art as a means of imitation, and not of proof or persuasion. Oratory is as much out of place in poetry as it is in science.

183. As Spottiswoode points out, criticism cannot cause but it can aid the improvement of an art. "A demand for better films will doubtless promote their supply" (*op. cit.*, 314). But more important than criticism of the sort that comments on individual works is the development of a critical tradition. Professor Nicoll quotes Will Hays as saying: "Recognition of the motion picture as an art by the great universities (will mark) the beginning of a

new day in motion picture work. It (will pave) the way for
the motion picture's Shakespeares." Nicoll adds : "This is no
strained and fantastic statement. It means simply that through
the aid of the detailed analysis and critical evaluation similar to
that which the drama has been accorded, the ground will be prepared for a surer mastery of effect ; from the principles thus established the cinematic form of expression will be provided with
that sense of purpose already attained by other arts of more extended ancestry. Shakespeare could not have been without the
preparation made for him by the humanistic work of the acad-
emies ; the 'University wits,' trained in the study of literature,
were his immediate predecessors and masters" (*op. cit.*, p. 163,
Thomas Y. Crowell Company).

184. "To every taste the sweet is pleasant ; but to some the sweetness of wine is most pleasant, to others, the sweetness of honey, or
of something similar. Yet that sweet is absolutely the best of all
pleasant things, in which he who has the best taste takes most
pleasure" (*Summa Theologica*, I-II, Q.1, A.8).

185. When the commensuration of levels of art with levels of audience is considered, it cannot be said that poor quality in art de-
grades taste or that art is degraded by having to meet the weak
sensibilities of an audience. As Ivor Brown has pointed out, this
argument about supply and demand in the arts is endless. Vd.
Art and Everyman, London, 1929. Given individuals may be
capable of more subtle appreciations than they achieve in their
first contact with a particular field of art. They are not degraded
because they start with simple appreciations which are vulgar
only in the sense that they are so universally shared ; nor can they
be permanently degraded so long as they have a capacity for
progress as their appetite is satisfied on each level. The arts, on
the other hand, must exist on all levels to enable individuals who
have the power to develop, to begin where lack of cultivation
necessarily makes them start. One might as well say that education is degraded and vulgar because it must begin in the elementary grades or that people who have not had the capacity for more
than elementary education have been degraded or vulgarized by
what they have received.

186. "I would add that if the act of perception of the beautiful
takes place without speech or any effort of abstraction, conceptual discourse can nevertheless play an immense part in the *preparation* for that act. Indeed, like the virtue of art itself, taste, or

the capacity to perceive beauty and pronounce a judgment on it, presupposes an innate gift, but can be developed by education and instruction, chiefly by the study and rational explanation of works of art. All things being equal, the better informed the mind is of the rules, the methods and the difficulties of art, and above all of the end pursued by the artist and his intentions, the better it is *prepared* to receive by means of the intuition of the senses the intelligible splendour emanating from the work and so spontaneously to perceive and *relish* its beauty" (Maritain, *Art and Scholasticism*, pp. 163–164, Sheed and Ward). The cultivation of critical discriminations with regard to the cinema — necessarily in the light of analysis and a knowledge of its rules — is a condition of good taste here as anywhere in the field of art. Spottiswoode describes the course of such cultivation in terms of a gradual appreciation of the elements of filmic style. (Vd. *op. cit.*, pp. 257–262.) The first obstacle to be overcome is the interest in the story which the motion picture tells. The spectator must be trained to see *how* the story is told as, in the field of literature, he must be taught to see *how* it is written. But the printed book is open to inspection, for repeated readings, in part and whole, and in different ways. Music can be studied in the same way. The cinema, because of the manner of its presentation, is more easily enjoyed than studied. This second obstacle may be insuperable for most people. The motion picture may be doomed to having the smallest, technically sensitive audience for the same reason that it has been able to achieve the largest popular audience.

187. The same alternatives occur in the field of oratory. Should a good orator be able to persuade all men or only good men? Should an orator who is a good man desire to persuade all men or only good men? The problem changes according as one puts the emphasis upon the virtue of art, which makes a man good in a specific respect, or upon the moral virtues and prudence which make him good *simply* as a man. To the extent that ethical criteria enter into the aesthetic goodness of a work of art, the artist should seek to please only good men. But in so far as he is a good man himself, must he not wish to make other men good? He can do this, *as an artist*, only by providing all men with the right objects in which to take pleasure. It is for the prudent man to pursue the same end by didactic and legislative measures.

Index of Notes

ACCORDING TO THEIR ORIGIN IN TEXT

Index of Topics

The numbers preceded by the sign # refer to the Notes which follow the text.

ACTION : meaning of word, ethics, 213 ff. ; meaning of word, aesthetics, 546 ff., # 177 ; and inaction, 217-8, 222-3.

ACTOR : and the cinema, 485-6.

AMUSEMENT : art as, 7, 30-1, 39-40, 44 ff., 78.
Vd. *Recreation.*

ART : practical and productive, liberal and servile, fine and useful, 432-6, # 17, # 127, # 129, # 130, # 131, # 135 ; principal and instrumental causes of, 444, 572 ff., # 117 ; two judgments of, 444, 452-4 ; vd. *Criticism;* two intentions of 444-5 ; finality of analysis of, 516-7 ; and nature, 25 ff., # 14 ; vd. *Imitation;* good and bad, 584-5 ; as commercial, 131 ff., # 120.
    Vd. *Amusement ; Form ; Matter ; Contemplative ; Recreation ; Communicative ; Rules ; Criticism.*

ART AND PRUDENCE :
1. Difference between : in kinds of operation perfected, 428-36, # 121, # 123, # 132 ; in ends, 436-9 ; in manner of operation, 439-41 ; in relation to other virtues, 441-3.
2. Conflict between : 90-1, 220-8, 446 ff., # 110 ; sources of, 436-7 ; occurrences of, 447-8 ; solubility

of, 448-9, # 141 ; practical wisdom about, 449-454.
3. Cinema as heir to problem of : 6, 117-20, 144-6, 182.
4. Research on problem of : criteria for examination of, 261-3 ; examination of, 264-417 ; summary of, 420-6.
5. History of political action on problem of : 120 ff.

ASCETICISM : 85 ff.

ASSERTION : proper and improper, 239-40.

ASYNCHRONISM : and counterpoint, 540-1.

AUDIENCE : art and the, 35-6, 63, 581-4.
    Vd. *Taste ; Popularity ; Commensuracy.*

AUXILIARY : and primary arts, 479 ff., # 158.

CENSORSHIP : kinds of, 213 ff., 141 ; paradox of, 106, # 68 ; history of actions of, in Greece, 121-2 ; in Rome, 122-4 ; in Renaissance, 124 ff. ; in modern times, 138-41.
    Vd. *Motion Picture.*

CHARACTER : cinematic treatment of, 542 ff.

CHILDREN : literature for, 183-9 ; motion picture as influence on, 171-7,

679

ART AND PRUDENCE

Index of Names

Addison : 68, 75.
Aeschylus : 492, 514, 556.
Agathon : 32, 555.
Alain : 45, 48, 50, 85.
Allen : 289, 316, 330.
Ambrose, St. : 606.
Aquinas, St. Thomas : 59, 73, 77, 79,
  80–92, 97, 102, 120, 124, 142, 147,
  159, 182, 194, 195, 222, 228, 241, 249,
  253, 261, 301, 440–1, 591, 598–602,
  606–8, 611, 613–4, 629–34, 636–8,
  644–55, 661.
Aristophanes : 72, 104, 121, 592.
Aristotle : 10, 14–5, 19–20, 21–53, 56–8,
  67–70, 73, 76–8, 80, 83, 90, 110–3,
  120, 122, 126–7, 147, 177, 179, 191,
  193, 196, 202, 221, 226, 228, 298, 301,
  361, 429, 459–64, 478, 491, 497, 511,
  514–5, 518, 542, 549–50, 553, 555,
  557–8, 565–8, 588–90, 593–4, 596–7,
  599–603, 605, 608–11, 619, 633, 635,
  638, 644, 646, 658, 662–3.
Arnheim : 657, 662, 667–8, 671, 673.
Ascham : 64, 185.
Astor : 323.
Augustine, St. : 58, 59, 61, 91, 165, 301,
  608.

Babson : 264–6, 269.
Bacon : 610.
Bates : 317.
Beard : 19.
Bedford : 70.

Bell : 26.
Bellows : 142–3.
Blanchard : 319, 320, 322.
Bloy : 614.
Blumer : 270, 272–85, 312, 319, 324,
  420–5, 639.
Bossuet : 59, 62, 73, 77–80, 82, 86–7, 90,
  91, 104, 120, 124, 147, 162, 179, 182,
  203, 221, 228, 261, 301, 602, 610–1,
  613, 618.
Bowdler : 133.
Bridges : 133, 156.
Brill : 268.
Bronner : 319.
Brown : 675.
Bulwer : 140.
Bunyan : 185.
Burgess : 326–7, 337.
Burt : 316, 320.
Butcher : 600–1, 603–5, 610.
Byrne : 130.

Caffaro : 59, 71, 73, 77–9.
Callahan : 597–8, 612.
Castelvetro : 603, 610.
Cato : 104, 122.
Cervantes : 496.
Chandler : 325.
Chaplin : 484, 476, 499, 544, 570, 668.
Chapman : 128.
Charters : 283, 284, 286–7, 312, 345–8,
  364–5, 369, 390, 402, 410–11, 422–3,
  644.

683